D1132213

Black Identity and Black Protest
in the Antebellum North

**The John Hope Franklin Series
in African American History and Culture**

Waldo E. Martin Jr. and Patricia Sullivan, editors

Black Identity & Black Protest in the Antebellum North

Patrick Rael

The University of North Carolina Press
Chapel Hill & London

© 2002 The University of North Carolina Press
All rights reserved
Manufactured in the United States of America

This book was set in New Baskerville
by Tseng Information Systems, Inc.
Book design by Jacquline Johnson

The paper in this book meets the guidelines for permanence
and durability of the Committee on Production Guidelines
for Book Longevity of the Council on Library Resources.

Publication of this work was aided by a generous
grant from the Z. Smith Reynolds Foundation.

Portions of this book appeared earlier in an online article,
"Black Theodicity: African Americans and Nationalism
in the Antebellum North," *The North Star* 3, no. 2 (Spring 2000).
Available at http://cedar.barnard.columbia.edu/
~north/volume3/rael.html.

Library of Congress Cataloging-in-Publication Data
Rael, Patrick.
Black identity and Black protest in the antebellum North / by
Patrick Rael.
p. cm. — (The John Hope Franklin series in African American
history and culture)
Includes bibliographical references (p.) and index.
ISBN 0-8078-2638-3 (cloth: alk. paper)
ISBN 0-8078-4967-7 (pbk.: alk. paper)
1. African Americans—Northeastern States—Race identity.
2. African Americans—Northeastern States—Intellectual life—
19th century. 3. African Americans—History—To 1863.
4. Free African Americans—Northeastern States—History—19th
century. 5. African American leadership—Northeastern
States—History—19th century. 6. Protest movements—
Northeastern States—History—20th century. 7. Northeastern
States—Race relations. I. Title. II. Series.
E185.9 .R34 2001
974'.00496073—dc21
20010027124

cloth 06 05 04 03 02   5 4 3 2 1
paper 06 05 04 03 02   5 4 3 2 1

*To the memory of
my grandfathers*

Contents

List of Tables and Illustrations

Tables

Figures

Plates

Acknowledgments

I am happy to at last publicly thank those who have generously contributed their faith, knowledge, and financial support to this long endeavor. I am grateful to the University of California, Berkeley, for funding early stages of the project through a Mellon Summer Dissertation Prospectus Development Fellowship, a Eugene McCormack Graduate Scholarship from the History Department, and a Humanities Graduate Research Grant. Fellowships from the Smithsonian Institution and the Library Company of Philadelphia allowed me to conduct much of the research for the dissertation, and a Ford Foundation Dissertation Fellowship from the National Research Council allowed me to complete it. A generous junior sabbatical program at Bowdoin College, postdoctoral fellowships from the Center for the Study of American Religion at Princeton University, and a J. Franklin Jameson Fellowship from the American Historical Association and Library of Congress gave me the time and resources necessary to turn the dissertation into a book.

It is warming to finally assemble in one place the names of the many students, friends, colleagues, and mentors whose care has been indispensable. The inevitable failings of and errors in this book appear in spite of their best efforts to steer me right, and are mine alone. At the University of Maryland, Marvin Breslow, Leslie Rowland, and Ira Berlin helped me begin to understand the nature of history; I continue to learn from all three. This project began as a dissertation at the University of California at Berkeley, where Jim Gregory listened to my first questions on the topic. The comments made by Waldo Martin Jr. and Michael Rogin on my dissertation were invaluable. The more I learn about historical writing and the African American past, the more my admiration grows for Leon F. Litwack, who supervised the dissertation. UC Berkeley proved a great asset in introducing me to James Cook, Betty Dessants, Samuel Weinstein, and Tom Wellock, all of whom helped this project (and me) grow in important ways.

For their collegiality, I am indebted to those at several institutions: at the Library Company, Phillip Lapsansky; at the Smithsonian's Afro-American Communities Project, Shannon Barker and James O. Horton; at Princeton, Marie Griffith, William Hart, Melani McAlister, Albert Raboteau, Brad Verter, and Robert Wuthnow; and at the Library of Congress, Les Vogel and David Wigdor. Bowdoin has also provided me with remarkable colleagues who helped me think through various problems: Lisa Collins, Tom Conlan, Nancy Edwards and Arthur McKee, Paul Franco, Seth Garfield, Eddie

Glaude, Peter Laipson, Matt Lassiter, Daniel Levine, Charlotte Magnuson, Mridu Rai, Warren Rosenblum, Randy Stakeman, and Susan Tananbaum.

For comments on the manuscript, portions of it, or papers based upon it, I am grateful to David Brion Davis, Paul Harvey, Evelyn Brooks Higginbotham, Jim and Lois Horton, Dan Littlefield, Michael O'Malley, Wilson Moses, Lewis Perry, Peter Ripley, Brenda Stevenson, Jim Stewart, Patricia Sullivan, and Shane White. Richard Newman signed on to the idea of this book early on; his encouragement, fellowship, and support merit special thanks. Laura Comay, Leslie Harris, and Peter Hinks offered advice or insight at crucial junctures. For research assistance, I am grateful to the tireless efforts of Joy Cushman, Jennie Kneedler, Scott Logan, Rich Mrazik, Tina Nadeau, and Sif Thorgiersson.

Finally, a book in itself could be written in praise of the special people whose friendship I have enjoyed. I owe diverse, special debts of gratitude to Jennifer Johns, Marilyn Reizbaum, and Elizabeth Hutchison. John McKirgan and Sonvy Waidler offered me not just their house but their home. The longstanding friendship of Todd and Tanya Dehart likewise transcended the academic. I hope that in reading these pages those in my family may understand just how much of them is in this book and how deeply I appreciate their unfailing love and support. To Nicola Denzey I am thankful beyond words. Companion, guide, colleague, and compatriot, she has given me travels of every variety and a home to return to when they are done.

Black Identity and Black Protest
in the Antebellum North

Only when lions have historians
will hunters cease being heroes.
African proverb

I am glad the time has come when the
"lions write history."
Wendell Phillips to Frederick Douglass, 1845

We must begin to tell our own story, write our own
lecture, paint our own picture, chisel our own bust, . . .
acknowledge and love our own peculiarities.
*William J. Wilson, African American journalist
and educator, 1853*

Of Men, Lions, and History

On a warm August afternoon in Newcastle, England, in 1863, the British Association for the Advancement of Science met to hear papers presented by scholars in its Ethnological Section. Before a rapt audience, one of its distinguished members, Dr. James Hunt, lectured lengthily on the superiority of the white race over its darker cousins. In the middle of the lecture, from the midst of the audience, a lone black man rose to challenge Hunt. Arguing for the innate ability for African-descended people to "rise," the man engaged the learned racial theorist on none of the grounds of the new racial science. Instead, he told a tale from Aesop, of a man and a lion, both walking down the street, arguing over which represented the superior species. According to the story, hard pressed to prove his case, the man was delighted to spy a public house, the sign for which depicted a man wrestling a lion to the ground. Considering his argument won, the man pointed to the picture as evidence of men's superiority over lions. The lion, however, simply asked, "Ah, but who painted the picture?"[1] The meeting erupted. Defenders and challengers of black capacities descended into verbal melee, and the session adjourned prematurely.

The fable of the man and the lion has potent ideological significance, for both the antebellum context of racial thought and modern-day appraisals of that context. First, it suggests that interpretations—whether of current events, history, or ideas—often are subject to the prejudices and presuppositions of the person who constructs those interpretations. In this case, the man was predisposed to see evidence of human superiority in the sign. Second, it implies that the ability to construct interpretations is an expression and vehicle of power, which may be used to sustain or subvert iniquitous social relations. In the story, the painting reinforced the superiority of humans over lions. Third, it demonstrates that the evidence used as authority to support interpretations often is not as objective as it is assumed to be. The lion in the story, for example, challenges the authority the man invokes on the basis that its source renders it biased. Finally, the fable reveals the process of interpretation itself as contested ground. Regardless of the intent of the man who painted it, once in public the sign's meaning could be endlessly controverted—in this case in the service of the political struggle between the man and lion.

The man who stood at the Newcastle meeting to relate the fable had been held as human chattel in the American South for the first twenty-four years of his life. William Craft had escaped perpetual servitude through a daring flight to the free states with his wife, Ellen. She, lightly complected, had posed as a young white master traveling north with his slave, William. The ingenuity, courage, and tenacity of the Crafts was typical of the thousands of enslaved African Americans who risked all to demonstrate to themselves and the world that they were the property of none but themselves. The Crafts had lived through a remarkable range of experiences that the western world had to offer. They had risen from the utter depths of slavery, a category of legal personlessness that had built the modern world, to champion the natural rights and fundamental humanity alleged to buttress the best governments of that world. They were in a unique position to appreciate the ironies contained in Aesop's fable. They were, like a great many other African American activists in the period, remarkably aware of the ideological forces surrounding the struggle for freedom in a country devoted to white supremacy.

Throughout the antebellum period, black northerners—like the lion in the fable—painted their own paintings. They championed the values of antebellum society in ways that argued for their own freedom and equality, and they constructed interpretations of current and historical events that served their distinct needs. In painting their own paintings, they added yet another layer of irony to the fable by relying primarily on the canvases and colors provided by an America bent on repressing them. Black people con-

using oppressor material

tested nearly every notion employed in their degradation. From national history to personal morality, they resisted ideological conceptions intended to justify their iniquitous treatment. In developing a distinct body of protest thought from the ideological material of antebellum America, the lion in fact painted its own painting, overtop that of the man. In instance after instance, African Americans in public appropriated the ideas of antebellum society, only to reformulate hostile notions into potent sources of empowerment and uplift.

Craft's telling of the story of the lion's painting suggests a level of ideological sophistication not usually attributed to this early stage of black protest thought. Nearly every tenet of twentieth-century black protest thought, however—from Martin Luther King Jr.'s concern with the "content of our characters" to Stokely Carmichael's call for "Black Power"—can trace its roots to the body of thought developed by black spokespersons in the context of a dynamic, changing antebellum North. That thought, in turn, grew out of a complex, often one-sided dialogue with a society committed to white supremacy and black repression, which structured their thought in important ways. Rather than withdraw from public discussions regarding the nature and destiny of the nation, they believed the best hope for the amelioration of their people's benighted plight lay in an appeal to the hearts and minds of their oppressors. They saw themselves and America as between revolutions: the American one, which had free the nation from British tyranny and most northern blacks from servitude; and the one they awaited, which would complete the purification of the republican experiment and fulfill the mandate of God.

This book examines the foundations of black identity and protest thought in the northern United States. It reaches back to the American Revolution but focuses primarily on the period from the 1820s to the Civil War. It presents a history not of institutions or the movement for black equality and the abolition of slavery but of African American identity and social structure in the North, and of its implications for black leaders' construction of a body of protest thought. It seeks to understand the processes through which African American spokespersons (newspaper editors, clergy, leaders of community institutions, black abolitionists, and others) constructed a public racial identity and to examine how this identity in turn informed African American critiques of a democratic nation predicated on the principle of white supremacy.

Only a relatively small number of African Americans were able to consistently set forth their ideas in the public sphere. By definition, this capacity rendered them distinct from the mass of northern blacks—an elite among a marginalized and underprivileged people. The very fact that these men and women possessed the means to leave their thoughts in the historical record suggests their elevated status. Any examination of their body of thought must first question whether that thought was in any way typical of the thought of black northerners as a whole. The first task, then, is to understand these people, their milieu, and their relationship to those they purported to lead. Where did leaders come from? Were they distant from the black rank and file by virtue of their class or other status? Or were they deeply integrated into the communities from whence they came? How did their protest thought reflect their relationships with their communities? In short, how representative were these "representative" colored men and women? These questions pervade the first half of the book, which addresses questions of leadership, social structure, and identity formation. Chapter 1 sets the context for the emergence of black protest in the antebellum period. It briefly considers the place of the black North in the African diaspora, with an eye toward the factors that rendered it a particularly fruitful seedbed for the style of protest and notions of identity that emerged there. Then, through a group biography of those who attended black state and national conventions, it moves on to examine the place of black leaders in their communities and the nature of the protest thought they constructed. Chapter 2 considers the public performance of black identity in the antislavery celebration. After the northern emancipations, these events emerged as the domain of a new black leadership; they revealed the class tensions that beset northern black communities as well as leaders' efforts to combat the disunity this entailed. Chapter 3 concludes this discussion of identity formation by analyzing the antebellum controversy among black spokespersons over appropriate names for the race. This debate embodied deep tensions between an effort to mold a universal black identity and a desire to appear "respectable" before the eyes of a hostile white public.

Having fleshed out the sources of black leadership and identity, this study turns to black protest ideology itself. The driving questions here are ones that black intellectual history has long confronted but which most recent historical work on northern black communities has tended to elide: where exactly did the black protest tradition come from, and what was its relationship to the social context of an expanding, urbanizing America? In framing their protest ideology, did black thinkers draw upon the ideological currency of the antebellum North? If so, how? What were the parameters and implications of such appropriations and exchanges? Did "assimilated" black thinkers draw upon the ideas and values of the antebellum social context to fashion their arguments? Did such a position aid their causes, which were to abolish slavery and achieve a meaningful equality for free African Americans? Or did black elites formulate their protest thought by relying on ideas from outside the American intellectual context, drawing ideas from ideological traditions rooted in relatively autonomous black communities, or perhaps from African antecedents? If so, did this render their cause revolutionary, and more likely to succeed? What do the answers to these questions tell us about the ideological context of antebellum America, and about the relationship between protest ideologies and the process of social change in U.S. history?

By exploring two dominant "idea sets" into which African American thought can, for purely heuristic purposes, be placed—elevation and uplift, and ideas of nation and race—I argue that black protest thought drew upon the values and fundamental social presuppositions of a northern culture, which African American elites actively participated in constructing. Through a complex process of appropriation, refashioning, and reconstruction of ideas extant in the antebellum North, black elites crafted challenges to racial inequality that appealed to cherished American values rather than stepped outside the bounds of the American ideological landscape. Constrained like all contemporary Americans by existing language and systems of explanation, black elites found themselves challenged to develop rhetorical strategies rooted in the American tradition. They sought not to revolutionize existing discourse but instead to appeal to its core values in changing the "public mind" on racial matters.

Their first strategy addressed contemporary concerns with moral character and the virtues touted by an emerging class society. As market expansion and liberal ideology enmeshed an urbanizing North, the civic virtues thought to be required of citizens in a self-governing republic steadily became the moral virtues required of middle-class urban denizens. As cofabricators of America, black elites in the North shared these concerns, though they refracted them through the lens of their plight. The cornerstone of their efforts to uplift the race, they believed, lay in demonstrating to a corrupt public mind that African Americans were capable of the virtues required of those who would be considered equals. Chapters 4 and 5 examine black spokespersons' use of the vocabularies of elevation and respectability, first by placing African American thought within the broader American context, then by exploring the distinct uses to which black leaders put that rhetoric.

The second strategy of black public figures, invoking the discourse of nationalism in their behalf, occupies the final chapters. The counterpoint to liberalism and Enlightenment universalism, romantic ethnic nationalism posed a threat to blacks' inclusion by positing America as a white republic. Black thinkers answered this challenge by positing the race as a national entity in its own right, with a unique genius and destiny. In short, they claimed the discourse of nationalism for their own, appropriating and refashioning it in distinct ways. Chapter 6 explores the origins of black nationalism as a discourse of nationalism, locating it not so much among an enslaved "folk" but as the product of a northern intelligentsia deeply familiar with the international discourse of nation and appreciative of its growing currency in public debate at home. The final chapter explores black thinkers' use of specific nationalist tropes. It examines the ways black thinkers did this in response to the racialism rampant in American nationalism, as well as the ways in which they imbued their nationalism with a distinct sense of religious mission.

Several caveats are necessary before continuing. First, I must acknowledge the vagaries of my geographic and temporal boundaries. My "North" occasionally stretches south into places such as Baltimore and west into California. Similarly, my "antebellum" occasionally reaches back into the 1820s, if not before. I plead here only that I am interested in ideas primarily, and these often refuse to conform to the boundaries scholars find so useful. I have employed both regional and chronological boundaries in the loosest possible conceptual sense and make no implicit argument about a worldview that stopped at the Mason-Dixon Line or at the Mississippi or changed radically at any given point.

Second, because this book takes as its source base primarily statements made in public, it unavoidably follows antebellum contemporaries in slighting the participation of African American women in the freedom struggle. I do not presume that the general (but by no means complete) absence of black women's voices from the realm of public speech requires no examination. The masculinized public sphere did not constitute something normative that requires no investigation. The general absence of black women in the sources I examine here suggests a countervailing presence—the presence of important forces that tended to silence women and that deeply conditioned the shape of black public protest. The dearth of women's voices in the movement permitted the emergence of a mutually reinforcing process whereby a heavily masculinized style of public protest marginalized women's roles, thereby minimizing the possibilities that African American women might exert greater influence over the gender components of black public protest. I have surely not treated gender issues with the care they deserve. I can plead only that the relative lack of documentation on black women's roles makes it difficult to study them in the same way that male activist leaders may be studied. My subject first and foremost here is the black public protest tradition. Properly incorporating issues of gender—women's general absence and the masculinized culture that filled the vacuum—requires methods so different from those necessary for the rest of the study that they threatened to throw all other issues into shadow. This is, of course, not an argument for diminishing the importance of gender, but for privileging it in a subsequent study.

Third, it may seem that in presenting the words of antebellum black northerners I have too often removed those words from their contexts or have neglected questions of audience. Whatever the failings of such a course may be, I have chosen it consciously, in the firm belief that black leaders' words were shaped by more than their immediate contexts and reveal more than mere rhetorical exigence. If read properly, they illumine a coherent structure of values and ideological presuppositions that framed black responses to a wide variety of claims, both hostile and benign. It is in fact from purposefully removing ideas from their immediate rhetorical contexts that otherwise obscure patterns may become clear. A close reading of thousands of documents prepared for a wide variety of audiences and occasions reveals consistent patterns in black spokespersons' use of a range of speech and ideas, covering a broad spectrum from the specific to the general: from particular figures of speech (e.g., apostrophe), to specific phrases (e.g., "he who would be free must himself strike the first blow"[2]), to common tropes (e.g., the yeoman farmer), to arguments (e.g., environmentalism), to larger ideological vocabularies (e.g., the language of nationalism). These patterns manifested themselves in a variety of circumstances, suggesting that rather than adhering rigidly to doctrine, black leaders drew upon an evolving storehouse of words, values, and ideas to craft their public statements. Some of their arguments surely tended to respond to specific charges; for example, blacks frequently responded to the claim that they ought to be expatriated to Africa by claiming their right to American identity based upon nativity, civic contribution, and military participation. Such statements also revealed, however, the more fundamental ideological terrain upon which elite African Americans operated: for instance, the idea that military prowess offered a measure of civilization or even conceptions of a world divided into groupings of national peoples (complicated though allegiances among them might have been). My copious presentation of blacks' own words intends not simply to counter their historical voicelessness but to buttress my claims for the integrity of their thought. That context in many instances failed to determine the use of language suggests that blacks' ideas did, in fact, have lives that transcended immediate rhetorical exigency.

Finally, I must acknowledge my own historiographical agenda in preparing this book, which is meant in part to respond to three strands in the literature. The first strand embraces scholarship that has relied on *structures* (such as nationalism or elevation) and *dichotomies* (integration vs. separation, assimilation vs. nationalism, or accommodation vs. resistance) to understand black thought. Black northerners wove their thoughts and words out of the disparate strands of the ideological fabric surrounding them. They resolutely declined to understand their ideas as falling into the rigid abstractions scholars later erected for them. Their failure to conform to such categories represents not their incapacity for consistency and logic, however, but a failure on the part of scholars to understand what made their ideas consistent and logical. Admittedly, like much of the historiography itself, my use of ideas of uplift and nation to organize the second section of the book provides a false coherence to a fluid and dynamic set of ideas. I have preserved these categories here not simply as convenient heuristics but also as foils— to demonstrate that just as uplift was not a strategy of integration, neither was nationalism exclusively a strategy of separation. If readers are left with anything, I hope it will be a desire to reexamine the rubrics with which we approach complex notions such as acculturation, resistance, and identity formation.[3]

The second strand of historiography that I am responding to may be termed the *community-studies/culturalist* paradigm. Following on the new social history of the 1960s, this culturalist turn originally sought and increasingly has found agency among the marginalized. This generally has been all to the good, especially given the hostility with which prior historians approached women, workers, the poor, and people of color—and the neglect or contempt with which otherwise sympathetic Marxians treated folk culture. Scholars operating under the rubrics of community and culture have found among the marginalized not victims but resilient individuals, responding to oppression and crisis and giving voice to a self-authored spirit of resistance—a spirit often claimed to generate from an autonomous folk culture. In the process they have undertaken a necessary, salutary retelling of our nation's "master narrative," so that it is more accurate, inclusive, and relevant.[4]

There is little to disagree with in this work. But there is also a tendency to focus so much on stories of success that larger, potent, and malevolent contexts of power relations have all but disappeared. Whether they regard the use of urban space, the rhetoric of the public sphere, or the resources of the garden plot, recent studies of struggles between the oppressed and their oppressors seem increasingly to find victory in the ways women, workers, the poor, and people of color eke out some degree of agency and meaningful resistance in an oppressive world. The best of these highlight the notion of *contest* between the marginalized and the dominant. Yet many have tended to do so in ways that still find the marginalized "winning," though without ever achieving the fundamental structural changes necessary to reorder power relations and relieve the oppressed of their burdens. There is something easy and unsatisfactorily compensatory about this approach—an anxious attempt to declare victory in the face of frequent defeat and to find meaningful resistance in the midst of psychic maelstrom.[5]

Since its inception, however, the edifice of the community studies/culturalist paradigm has been challenged by sporadic critiques. A few critics have suggested that in their desire to salvage agency for the oppressed, scholars championing the community-studies/culturalist paradigm tend to romanticize the plight of the oppressed and neglect broader contexts of power relations. Once recontextualized, critics imply, the terms of contestation between oppressed and oppressor hardly seem equal—in fact, whatever space accrued to the marginalized as an exercise of their power appears to have been meager reward for their experience of deeply brutalizing oppression. While enslaved African Americans must be salvaged from the victim model posited by those such as Stanley Elkins, cultural autonomy seems poor compensation for the dehumanization that enslavement entailed.[6]

The stakes here are high: a desire to find agency among the subaltern may lead to a neglect of the nature of the obstacles they faced and, in the process, may fail to serve the broader emancipatory goals that underlay the original and noblest goals of the "new" histories. An approach willing to recontextualize the struggles of the oppressed may hazard reaching conclusions that are anathema to many. The risk is worth it. Important lessons—perhaps the most important—may be taught more through failure than through victory. If one is to fight the beast, one must know its nature, and this means looking it squarely in the eye.

Reconsidering black intellectual autonomy may thus require some courage, for no easy picture of the efficacy of African American protest emerges in its wake. Black historical actors lacking agency cannot be seen as active creators of their own experience, but those with it may not be exempted from their complicity in creating a world that modern readers may in many ways find objectionable. By the standards of the late twentieth century, the body of public protest speech crafted in the antebellum North tended to be elitist. On balance, it may have done more to reinforce the gender subjugation of black women and the class subjugation of working-class blacks than it did to liberate them from their respective yokes. Overwhelmingly, black elites rarely even considered such forms of liberation in terms that modern activists would understand, and never did they place these goals higher than the emancipation of the race. The price of black agency, then, may indeed have been their cofabrication of a world that we rightfully find lacking.

The third school of historical study that is relevant to this book may be termed the *black nationalist* school of thought on antebellum black protest. Scholars approaching black history from a perspective rooted in the freedom struggle of the late 1960s and 1970s have frequently implied that antebellum black protest did, or at times should have but failed to, operate from outside an American system of values. Under this logic, antebellum black protest, in embracing ideas of uplift and moral elevation, failed to achieve the ideological autonomy necessary for effectively waging a freedom struggle.[7]

I argue that black leaders before the Civil War did not "sell out" the black working class, nor did they become unwitting or co-opted dupes of a white middle class. They did not succumb to an ideologically hegemonic process whereby they assimilated the hostile values of a world bent on their oppression. They could not have done so, because the thought they built originally belonged no more to whites than it did to blacks. Formulated to consider evidence taken from folk tradition, the analytical paradigms that have been used to evaluate questions of cultural transmission—with their reductionist tensions between integration and separation, assimilation and nationalism—are not useful guides for understanding black public speech. For better or worse, black northerners cofabricated with other Americans the political and racial discourse of the antebellum public sphere. They sought not to revolutionize American political values, but to fulfill them. They thus cannot be said to have fallen victim to a process of ideological victimization.

Unforeseen consequences attended the participation of black northerners in the discourse of the public sphere. In the very act of using cherished American values to resist oppression and discrimination, they unwittingly endorsed core premises so deeply ingrained in them—the natural primacy of men over women, the virtues of bourgeois culture, and the sanctity of Western "civilization"—that alternatives were literally unthinkable. While the resistance that antebellum black thinkers carved from their intellectual milieu ultimately helped precipitate the Civil War that abolished slavery in America, their protest thought left them largely bereft when coping with the difficult realities of postwar life, such as the persistence of prejudice despite the death of slavery. These challenges—along with those posed by gender, class, and nation—continue to confront those who would be free.

" co fabricated / co fabricator

❖

In the Northern states, we are not slaves to individuals,
not personal slaves, yet in many respects we are the
slaves of the community.
Black national convention, 1848

There must be common oppression to produce
common resistance.
James McCune Smith, 1854

❖

CHAPTER 1

A Different Measure of Oppression

Leadership and Identity in the Black North

lack of (truly) shared experience

In 1854, James McCune Smith, a black abolitionist and one of the most
highly educated African Americans in the free states, corresponded with
Frederick Douglass, who was then editing a black and abolitionist newspaper. Smith lamented the difficulties facing the struggle to keep alive a
vibrant movement to end slavery and attain equality for free blacks.[1] "We
are not united as a people," he wrote, "and the main reason why we are not
united is that we are not equally oppressed. This is the grand secret of our
lack of union. You cannot pick out five hundred free colored men in the
free States who equally labor under the same species of oppression. In each
one of the free States, and often in different parts of the same State, the
laws, or public opinion, mete out to the colored man a different measure of
oppression." Smith noted differences in political rights such as suffrage: in
Maine and Massachusetts all blacks enjoyed the right to vote, but in states
like Illinois they lacked it. In others, like New York, property qualifications
pertained. In some, a man of light skin color could vote, while in others the
same man might not. In some states, blacks and whites could intermarry;
in others, they could not. In some, newly arrived African Americans had to
post a bond upon entering the state; in others they were excluded entirely;

and in still others no obstacles intervened. "The result is," Smith said, "that each man feels his peculiar wrong, but no hundred men together feel precisely the same oppression; and, while each would do fair work to remove his own, he feels differently in regard to his neighbor's oppression." Smith understood that regional variations in the proscriptions so cruelly imposed on people of African descent often mandated varied responses. In Ohio, lightly complected "quadroons" like William Howard Day and John Mercer Langston might rightly exercise the vote "because they believe it their duty as *men* to avail themselves of all privileges within their reach." Yet darker-skinned leaders like Martin Delany, who were denied the vote in states like Pennsylvania and New York, could rightly condemn such men for participating in a system that degraded all blacks.[2] The relative personal success of those who claimed to represent the mass might instill in them interests that drew them away from the very ones they championed. "When earnest men are thus rent apart by impulses they cannot control," Smith worried, how might they "in good and hearty faith earnestly unite in a common resistance to their diverse oppressions?"[3]

Smith had made an insightful point. Differing social experiences constantly threatened to rend asunder black political unity. African Americans' solidarity, and in fact their identity as black people, had to be forged through an awareness of their shared liabilities. Experience throughout the African diaspora attested to the veracity of Smith's claim. Lacking a relatively uniform "species of oppression" to bind black people into a unified whole, a great many New World societies developed complex racial hierarchies, with degrees of liberty to match, predicated on racial heritage. Complex taxonomies that separated African-descended people into negroes, mulattoes, quadroons, octoroons, and other base references to phenotype frequently settled into a three-tiered racial "caste" system, with African-born blacks usually enslaved, creole mulattoes nominally "free," and whites in command at the top of the social pyramid. In Smith's own day, echoes of the social patterns that produced these multitiered racial caste systems could be heard in American cities such as New Orleans, Charleston, and Savannah. Common to such systems were fractured notions of black identity. Quite alien to modern-day readers steeped in America's "one-drop" rule (which purports that any trace of African descent identifies one as black), common sentiment in the Caribbean and parts of Latin America understood these groups to have distinct identities—to, in effect, comprise distinct races.[4]

Despite Smith's concerns, such a pattern did not emerge in the United States. Instead, all people of African descent generally were considered "black," regardless of their apparent degree of European heritage. Confronted with the immediacy of his own oppressions, Smith could not appreciate the startling degree of uniformity in African American identity relative to the rest of the diaspora. The rare degree of uniformity that black northerners did achieve depended in large measure on the agency of blacks there. Of course, throughout the diaspora white oppressors' categorization of people of African descent also determined the fate of black identities, but black people themselves, in how they reacted to their situations, conditioned the emergence of black identities. Both, in fact, depended on a complex set of historical circumstances that patterned the growth of black racial self-conception throughout the New World. In the case of the antebellum North, African American spokespersons set forth an understanding of black identity unique up to that point of any place in the world: they asserted that all people of African descent—the slave and the free, the light and the dark, the African and the creole—shared a common oppression that mandated the need for unified political action and hence a unified social identity. Black spokespersons built a concept of blackness constructed for the very purpose of arguing for their universal freedom before a hostile white public. Of all free African-descended people in the diaspora, they were among the first and most ardent champions of the rights of the enslaved.

SLAVES OF THE COMMUNITY: THE BLACK NORTH IN THE AFRICAN DIASPORA

At first glance the nineteenth-century North would hardly seem an auspicious birthplace for the emergence of this notion of blackness. Perched on the very frontier of the diaspora, black northerners lacked the proximity to the enslaved that we might think necessary to forge an all-encompassing black racial identity. Indeed, we might expect from them just the opposite: overwhelmingly free and separated spatially from their closest enslaved brethren by the Mason-Dixon line, they might have shunned alliance with the enslaved. This is, in fact, what happened among free colored elites in nearly every other part of the diaspora where they possessed the luxury. It was certainly a threat to black racial unity in the North. In 1828, Philadelphia activist William Whipper expressed concern over the social differences that sundered the free from the enslaved. Of black participation in the antislavery cause he wrote: "those who enjoy liberty, and have accumulated considerable property are satisfied with their situation, and will not meddle with the cause; while the middle class are too busy in procuring the necessaries of life to alter their course." Evidencing considerable classism,

Whipper explained that "the lower class remain regardless of themselves or their brethren. . . . Their only object is to become votaries to the cup of intemperance, and reflect disgrace on those who enjoy a more retired life and civil society."[5]

Yet it was no accident that a unified black political identity that championed the cause of the slave emerged first in the North, during the half century before the Civil War. In fact, the North's very position on the edge of the diaspora enabled free blacks to embrace all people of African descent without the troubling implications such a move presented in, for example, the Caribbean. All the factors that led to the emergence of three-tiered racial caste systems in the western hemisphere, and which consequently splintered the racial unity of African-descended people, pertained on mainland North America to lesser degrees. Within the United States, the North conspicuously lacked the conditions necessary to form the distinct middling caste of free colored elites that characterized these systems.

The presence, size, and coherence of free black elites depended on the passage of slave societies through what may be considered three general stages. The first may be termed, after Ira Berlin, the *charter* phase, which witnessed the settlement of areas that would later develop into plantation societies. During this phase, population ratios between whites and blacks tended to favor white settlers; blacks—as slaves or free people—tended to comprise small minorities. Frontier rigors imposed a sort of rough racial equality on these settlers. Because blacks often were needed to supplement the defense provided by the scanty white population, slaves might find themselves in local militias, receiving limited freedom in exchange for service. A huge gender imbalance favoring males loosened cultural strictures against racial mixing, thus producing an early generation of light-complected folk, the children of white settlers and black. Given the fluidity of frontier race relations, white masters occasionally manumitted the enslaved offspring of these relationships, sometimes providing them with the resources and skills necessary to serve in the middling ranks of society, often as artisans and mechanics.[6]

The second phase, which may be termed *maturation*, witnessed the emergence of full-blown plantation economies based on cash-crop production for international export. The growth of plantation economies radically skewed the ratio of blacks to whites in the populations of these colonies, as planters imported Africans by the tens and hundreds of thousands to supply the forced labor necessary to grow crops such as sugar, rice, tobacco, and indigo. As the slave population increased, the nascent free colored population tended to marry among its own, thus producing a distinct class, free from enslavement yet subordinate to the small number of Europeans who dominated the political life of the colonies. As African-descended people grew as a proportion of the population, free people of color increasingly assumed control over middling economic roles as artisans and mechanics, filling the spaces whites might have occupied in societies with more Europeans and fewer Africans. The position of free people of color in these societies was always tenuous at best. For many, freedom depended on the patronage of wealthy whites; those lacking it might find themselves sinking back into the ranks of the totally unfree. Such conditions did little to enhance solidarity between free colored and black slave. On the contrary, in most New World slave societies, free people of color assiduously distanced themselves from their enslaved brethren. Evidence of their privileged heritage, their generally light skin color, demarcated them as a distinct group. In the service of their own tenuous status, free people often themselves policed the line between slave and free, sometimes owning slaves themselves, sometimes functioning as custodians of the slave system by serving as slave catchers. Adding insult to injury, the slave regime, just as it made race the preeminent ordering principle of society, by defining blackness as the principle justification of slavery, imposed conditions that in most places denied all people of African descent the opportunity to unite under a single banner. This is what James McCune Smith called "the depth and bitterness of our oppression."[7]

The final phase that must be considered in the evolution of free populations of color in New World slave societies is the relative *decline of plantation economies* in the nineteenth century. Throughout the Atlantic basin, the very success of plantation capitalism helped foster its successor, industrial capitalism. As the new economy emerged, cash crops like sugar remained significant, and output steadily increased. But plantation production itself occupied an increasingly small proportion of the entire Atlantic economy. As a result, planters faced increasing difficulties in sustaining their interests against emerging bourgeois capital and its novel ideas of free labor. Such ideas intertwined with the ideology of the age of democratic revolution to threaten and eventually destroy slavery, though this process took place slowly and unevenly over a long century. The decline of the relative significance of the plantation economy also meant that alternatives to slave labor systems did not require the degree of efficiency possible under slave labor to maintain their marginal productivity. (They approached it anyway, by using other forms of semifree bound labor, such as indentured Asian labor or apprenticeship systems, which were sufficiently dissimilar to slavery to be permitted by antislavery ideology.) The steady dismantling of slave societies meant fresh infusions of black people into the ranks of the unenslaved, in patterns that disrupted the conditions that bred and sustained free colored elites. In the Brazilian Northeast, for example, the increasing marginalization of sugar in the international economy combined with undercapitalization and technological backwardness to cause the gradual, effective end of slavery before its legal abolition in 1888. In such instances, local economic decline sundered slaves from their masters, sometimes through sale to more profitable regions but sometimes through a series of complex master-slave negotiations that secured the eventual freedom of slaves or their offspring. As a result, large numbers of African-descended people, usually much poorer than their long-free brethren, joined the ranks of those who were at least nominally free.[8]

This three-phase scheme is meant as nothing more than a convenient heuristic. Huge variations in place, timing, and preconditions enormously affected the evolution of black society throughout the New World. The phases are helpful primarily in identifying the complex set of historical factors that combined to dictate the existence and shape of free black society throughout the diaspora. In particular, they help set forth the circumstances that led to the stratification of African-descended society into two distinct groups, one free and light-complected and the other black and enslaved, with disparate senses of racial identity.

While free black communities appeared in every slave society, black identity was most likely to fracture in those with the largest gulfs between the free and the enslaved. In such societies, "free people of color," as they termed themselves, were likely to be light-complected, as a result of their mixed racial heritage; skilled, as a consequence of their favored status; and propertied, as the outgrowth of generations of relative greater economic opportunity. They were usually found in societies with very large slave populations, where they accounted for a relatively small and disproportionately urban percentage of the entire African-descended population. They were likely to boast of being several generations removed in their descent from slavery, and certainly in their descent from Africa. As a result, their cultural outlooks can best be described as creole: they descended from Africa, yet were generated primarily through the native-born and were tinged heavily with the European outlooks of white ancestors and the island elites to whose status they might dare aspire. This group tended to see itself as entirely distinct from the great mass of the enslaved, which in such societies tended to greatly outnumber whites and be employed primarily in the back-breaking labor required to grow the most profitable crop: sugar. Worked hard under unimaginably harsh conditions, this slave population could almost never reproduce itself, and so was constantly supplemented by incessant infusions of Africans from the Atlantic slave trade. As a result, the enslaved developed traditions rooted deeply in continuously imported African cultural heritage, boasting cultural outlooks quite distinct from those of native-born free people of color. The large-scale plantation societies that produced highly stratified black populations also reified the boundary between free people of color and the enslaved through stringent safeguards against slaves entering the population of the free. In such societies, where the well-being of the plantation economy dictated nearly every facet of racial policy, there were few incentives to manumit slaves and many reasons not to. Not the least of these were motives of social control; it was commonly thought that slaves who could not hope to become free would be less likely to try to become free. Consequently, the line between the slave and free possessed none of the fluidity that characterized it in places where plantation agriculture did not dominate the economy. Ira Berlin has contrasted such non-plantation "societies with slaves" with the "slave societies" produced by plantation economies.[9]

These patterns played out more or less predictably throughout the Atlantic basin. Sugar cane, the prize commodity of the plantation complex, grew best in hot, wet climates and demanded the greatest concentration of capital and labor. In places where the climate and geography most favored the growing of cane, like wet portions of the Caribbean and the Brazilian Northeast, slave populations were largest, and elite free colored communities most likely to emerge. In mainland North America, the limited sugar economy of the Gulf Coast and the labor-intensive rice economy of the low-country Carolinas each produced weaker versions of Caribbean-style free populations of color. Living within state structures that paid little heed to the unique social conditions of these limited areas, however, free people in the United States fared relatively poorly in protecting their elite status. Farther north and inland, secondary crops like tobacco and indigo required successively smaller workforces and more temperate climates. In such places, like the Chesapeake, where the decline of the tobacco economy slowed the growth of slavery in the nineteenth century, free blacks were more numerous than in the wealthiest plantation economies, yet free colored elites were less likely to emerge. As climate and geography reduced agricultural possibilities to cereal grains and staples, slavery ceased to offer clear economic benefits to planters. In northern colonies, slaves took a role in the provisioning trade, which supplied meat and foodstuffs to Caribbean colonies otherwise engaged; worked crops like wheat in small numbers (often cheek-by-jowl with white masters and free blacks); or performed domestic service in the burgeoning cities.[10]

The North of the United States occupied a conspicuous position in the complex set of circumstances that bred free black communities. Enslaved black people had been present in the North since the seventeenth century, and they continued to enter the population as northern cities engaged in the international slave trade. Yet the North never developed widespread, large-scale plantation agriculture and therefore had no need for slave labor. Thus, in the North, the percentages of black people in the population never reached the levels they did in the South, the Caribbean, or Northeastern Brazil. The most immediate consequence of this was that there simply were not that many African-descended people in the North. Only in New York and Pennsylvania did blacks number more than 10 percent of the total population for any sustained length of time. In most northern locales and for most of the time, the number of blacks in the population hovered below 5 percent. In contrast, the black population in the southern states seldom fell below 30 percent, and often topped 40 or even 60 percent (Table 1.1).

As a consequence of their marginality in the northern population, free African Americans in the region rarely became collectively associated with distinct economic roles as artisans and mechanics. White workers tended to occupy those niches and guard them zealously; when they did not, the largely urban and domestic character of northern slavery did little to prefer free over enslaved blacks. In terms of status distinctions, the difference between slave and free did not matter nearly so much as it did in the West Indies or northeastern Brazil. With freedpeople being so marginalized in an economy dominated by whites, black community leaders tended to be drawn from the ranks of prominent slaves. Accounts of Negro Election Day and Pinkster celebrations attest to the prominence of favored slaves among northern black elites. Only with freedom did a new generation of community leaders—many of them, like Philadelphia's Richard Allen, formerly enslaved by wealthy white men—emerge from the ranks of the free. Neither did many distinctions in black society emerge along color lines. The factors that created such differences, frontier conditions of gender imbalance evolving into thriving plantation economies, did not exist. New England, and to lesser degrees the mid-Atlantic states, had been settled by colonizing families rather than by enterprising men. More equitable gender ratios in such settlements meant that white men could afford to shun relations with black women. Confusing distinctions between "negros" and "mulattoes" never clouded the North's incipient racism, which came to define all people of African descent as sharing a common degradation. Finally, the black population in the North was, relative to others in the New World, able to reproduce itself quickly. The largely urban or pastoral character of the

Table 1.1. African-descended and White Populations in Selected Regions, as Percentage of Total Population, 1720–1860

A. The Caribbean

	Barbados			Cuba			Martinique		
	Whites	Slave	Free Black	Whites	Slave	Free Black	Whites	Slave	Free Black
1720s	—	—	—	—	—	—	20.8	76.7	2.5
1740s	24.4	75.5	0.2	—	—	—	—	—	—
1760s	19.5	80.0	0.5	—	—	—	14.2	83.5	2.3
1770s	—	—	—	56.2	22.7	21.2	—	—	—
1780s	—	—	—	—	—	—	10.9	85.3	3.7
1800s	19.3	78.0	2.7	—	—	—	10.7	82.2	7.2
1820s	15.0	80.3	4.7	44.2	40.7	15.1	9.8	79.7	10.6
1830s	12.8	80.7	6.6	—	—	—	7.7	66.7	25.6
1840s	—	—	—	—	—	—	8.4	59.5	32.1
1860s	—	—	—	56.5	26.9	16.5	—	—	—

B. United States

	Lower South			Upper South			North		
	Whites	Slave	Free Black	Whites	Slave	Free Black	Whites	Slave	Free Black
1790s	58.2	41.1	0.7	66.0	32.1	1.9	96.6	2.0	1.4
1800s	58.7	40.5	0.8	66.5	30.8	2.7	97.0	1.3	1.7
1820s	52.8	45.6	1.7	67.0	29.5	3.5	97.7	0.5	1.9
1840s	55.3	43.2	1.6	69.7	26.6	3.7	96.8	<0.1	3.2
1860s	54.5	44.8	0.7	74.6	22.1	3.3	95.9	<0.1	4.1

Sources: Derived from David W. Cohen and Jack P. Greene, eds., *Neither Slave Nor Free* (Baltimore: Johns Hopkins University Press, 1972), 335–39; U.S. Department of Commerce (Bureau of the Census), *Negro Population, 1790–1915* (Washington, D.C.: Government Printing Office, 1918), 45, 57.

slave regime there combined with temperate climes to minimize the major sources of slave mortality that existed farther south. Whereas most slave societies were not able to reproduce their own populations until freedom eased their burdens, northern blacks did so in their first generation. With the exception of importations of African slaves into New York in the middle of the eighteenth century, the black North was either creole or native-born. Nothing like the cultural distinctions among black people in the Caribbean existed in the North to exacerbate rifts between the free and enslaved.[11]

In time, the economic marginality of slavery in the North combined with the expansion of bourgeois capitalism and revolutionary ideology to doom the institution there. North of the Mason-Dixon line, slavery fell gradually, primarily between 1776 and 1827, depending on the degree to which it had served the economic interests of the states.[12] Freedom in the North thrust together two black populations (one enslaved and one nominally free) that, relative to the rest of the diaspora, had shared to a remarkable degree culture and economic status. Now, deprived of the distinctions wrought by legalized bondage, they shared even more. Free blacks in the North lived tenuous lives undeserving of the adjective "free," but their legal claim to liberty was far more solid than that of free blacks in any slave society. An entire category of legal destitution, and the threat that it imposed on the free who might descend into it, had been removed. Free black northerners continued to hold considerable grounds for fear, but their championing of the rights of the enslaved need no longer pose the same threats it did elsewhere, where the free could conceivably be legally reenslaved. Before the northern emancipations, free blacks had constituted one of the least elite of all free colored communities in the diaspora, and abolition did nothing to elevate this group; but by pushing tens of thousands of the formerly enslaved up into it, freedom did expand it. In short, relative to the slave societies of the South or the rest of the diaspora, the highs of black society in the post-emancipation North were not as high as they might have been in other places, but neither were the lows so low.[13]

The factors that characterized free black populations in other parts of the diaspora, and which were mirrored to a lesser degree in the American South, did not pertain to nearly the same degrees in the post-emancipation North. The pattern that produced a highly stratified black social structure featured marked differences between those commonly described as "black" and those commonly described as "mulatto," with the mixed-race population tending toward the urban and prosperous. This pattern prevailed in the Caribbean and in parts of the Lower South in the United States. Moving northward, away from the wealthiest portions of the plantation economy, it

Table 1.2. Mean Value of Property Claimed, by Region and Racial Group, 1860

| | Racial Group | | | | | |
| Region | White | Mulatto | | Black | | |
	Mean Value	Mean Value	% of White Value	Mean Value	% of White Value
New England	$538.37	$31.11	5.8	$130.39	24.2
Mid-Atlantic	$710.71	$88.68	12.5	$87.33	12.3
Midwest	$470.14	$166.78	35.5	$72.02	15.3
Upper South	$849.11	$46.67	5.5	$27.23	3.2
Lower South	$1,437.69	$314.25	21.9	$46.67	3.2

Source: "1860 Free Population with Black Oversample—Preliminary," in Steven Ruggles, Matthew Sobek, et al., eds. *Integrated Public Use Microdata Series: Version 2.0* (Minneapolis: Historical Census Projects, University of Minnesota, 1997).

Note: Sampled data, for comparison purposes only.

lessened appreciably. Free African Americans in the Upper South tended to be less well off than those in the Lower South, and skin complexion served less as a marker of status. By the time one reached the North, only echoes— dim but significant—of these patterns persisted.

By nearly every measure free black social structure in the antebellum North manifested the most attenuated versions of social distinctions that divided black society elsewhere. Sampled data from the federal census of 1860 reveal that there was virtually no difference in the urban-rural distribution of black and mixed-race African Americans in New England. Farther south, as the economy depended increasingly on agricultural and plantation labor, the balance skewed noticeably, until folk considered of mixed racial descent comprised only 20 percent of the rural free African American population of the Lower South states and 65 percent of the urban free African American population. The North also lacked evidence, common in the Caribbean and Lower South, that light-complected African Americans gained the social and economic benefits of their mixed racial heritage. Free black and mulatto African Americans in the mid-Atlantic states of Pennsylvania, New York, and New Jersey differed little in the amount of property they claimed to own. In New England, black Americans actually outclassed their lighter complected counterparts. In contrast, light-complected free African Americans in the Lower South on average claimed almost seven times as much property as did free blacks (Table 1.2).

Table 1.3. Property Holding in Free Population, 1860

	Percentage of Property Holders in Population		
Region	White	Free Black	Difference
North	18.1	11.7	−6.4
Upper South	19.4	9.8	−9.5
Lower South	18.8	17.9	−0.9

Source: "1860 Free Population with Black Oversample — Preliminary," in Steven Ruggles, Matthew Sobek, et al., eds., *Integrated Public Use Microdata Series: Version 2.0* (Minneapolis: Historical Census Projects, University of Minnesota, 1997).

Note: Sampled data, for comparison purposes only.

Free African Americans in the North generally lacked the opportunity for social mobility that was available in the more highly stratified Lower South. In 1860, African American northerners claimed between 10 and 12 percent of the property claimed by whites in the region; free African Americans in the Lower South claimed over 14 percent of the property claimed by whites in that region. And while the percentage of free African American northerners who claimed property lagged behind whites by over 6 percentage points, the difference in property holding between free African Americans and all whites in the Lower South was negligible (Table 1.3). Ranking by decile those who claimed property underscores the compressed nature of black social structure in the North. Free African Americans in the Lower South exhibited their stratification into wealthy and poorer classes by spreading relatively evenly across the spectrum. Northern free blacks, on the other hand, clustered clearly toward the lower deciles, with over 45 percent massed in the first decile (Figure 1.1).

Data on occupational status reinforce findings regarding the compressed social structure of the black North. Free black men in the North enjoyed little of the occupational status that accrued to free African Americans in the Lower South. Leonard Curry's analysis of occupational skill levels of blacks in antebellum cities demonstrates the great disparities between the North and South. Whereas in Boston nearly 80 percent of employed free blacks occupied jobs that required no or few skills, less than 20 percent of Charleston's free male black workforce was so employed. In contrast, almost 60 percent of free black workers in Charleston were skilled mechanics, artisans, or professionals (such as teachers or clergymen). These cities represented extremes: intermediate cities like Providence, Rhode Island, or

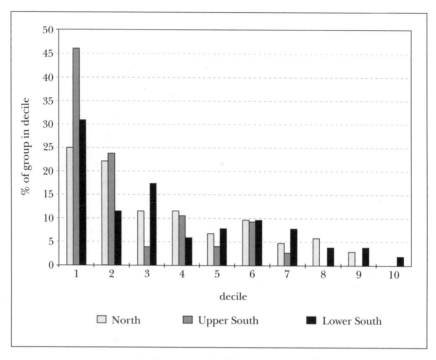

FIGURE 1.1. *Free Black Property Holders, Ranked by Decile, 1860*

Louisville, Kentucky, conformed in lesser degrees to these regionally defined patterns.[14] In every case, however, there was a marked difference between employment patterns in the Lower South, where the plantation fostered the socioeconomic conditions necessary to form highly stratified free
African American populations, and those in more northerly climes. African
Americans in these latter regions suffered under the apparent paradox of
economies that were likely to countenance the abandonment of a marginal
labor institution like slavery, yet were just as likely to fail to provide those
freed with the skills necessary to compete when liberated.

By all accounts, the North offered a minimally opulent freedom to many,
while the Lower South offered much greater economic opportunity to those
few fortunate enough to be free. Northern white newspapers frequently
ran pieces, sometimes reprinted in the black press, attesting to these differences, as well as to imperfect understandings of the socioeconomic forces
that produced them. One such article spoke of the "distinct class" formed
by the "free colored population" of Louisiana. Lauding these free elites for
their "commendable spirit of emulation," the author noted their services
as "masons, brick-layers, builders, carpenters, tailors, shoe-makers, &c.," as

well as "musicians, jewelers, goldsmiths, tradesmen, and merchants." This "sober, industrious, and moral class" was reported to be "far advanced in education and civilization," apparently in contradistinction to free blacks found elsewhere in the nation.[15] In contrast, many in the North had difficulty even defining the qualities that might render one elite in black communities above the Mason-Dixon line. Joseph Willson, a black southerner who wrote an extended commentary on Philadelphia's black elite in 1841, noted a general uniformity of social experience that made it nearly impossible to identify social distinctions among Philadelphia's black high and low. In trying to define this elite, he confessed "that the difficulty of establishing, successfully, a distinguishing line of separation is very great." Neither wealth, education, nor "moral worth" alone could serve to distinguish elite black Philadelphians from their popular brethren. Instead, Willson could offer only a vague prescription: the elite were those blacks whose income "enables them to maintain the position of householders, and their families in comparative ease and comfort."[16]

Economic forces thus helped compress African American social structure in the North, so that relative to other places in the African diaspora, the range of experience available to free black northerners was simply not that broad. Whites tended to see black people in the North as racially uniform: as Joseph Willson reported, "the great body of the public have been accustomed to consider [blacks] so closely allied to each other, as to render it very improbable, if not impossible, that any social differences could be held in recognition among them."[17] Throughout the North, policy and informal practice often subjected blacks in toto to degradations shared by elite and popular alike. Elite blacks never ceased excoriating white northerners for practicing a brand of racial prejudice that effaced important class distinctions among them. "Why," asked the editors of the *Colored American*, "should a colored man, who is equal in wealth, in education, in refinement and in taste, be subjected to legal disabilities—debarred the institutions of the country—crowded into negro pews in the church, and into dog-cars on the Railroad, or pantries on board the Steam-boats?"[18] Charged black abolitionist Charles L. Remond, "[T]he most vicious is treated as well as the most respectable."[19]

Understandably, blacks were far more sensitive to their intracommunity differences than were whites. But the relative uniformity of their social experience led them, too, toward a more highly integrated notion of black identity. As a consequence, free black elites in the northern states were more likely to align themselves with other African-descended people across a broad range of differences that in other places fractured black identity.

Other factors peculiar to the United States helped foster this process. Alone among New World slave societies, the United States abolished slavery disparately across regional lines. Nowhere else in the western hemisphere did a society exist half slave and half free for anything like the nine decades the United States endured. Unlike those emancipated by European powers in the Caribbean colonies in the nineteenth century, emancipated black northerners could not simply turn their energies to a future of liberty; a great many had family and friends who still struggled under the slaver's lash.

Furthermore, this peculiar state of affairs pertained not in a mere colonial dependency, subject to varying degrees of legal restrictions that tended to render it less free than its mother country, but in a sovereign nation that, like all nations, guaranteed minimum rights for all who properly belonged within its fold. To make matters worse, this sovereign nation justified its bloody nascence upon the principle of universal human liberty—the proposition that "all men are created equal, that they are endowed by their Creator with certain unalienable rights." In contrast to Latin American slave societies, which could envision degrees of legal semifreedom, the colonies (and later states) of British mainland North America predicated their very identities on the stark contrast between freedom and slavery.[20] Resulting regional differences over matters as weighty as the definition of freedom, citizenship, and slavery introduced legal and logical inconsistencies that the antebellum generation contained with only the greatest difficulty, and which eventually precipitated civil war.

These political commitments also had great consequence for the meaning of free black life in the United States. A society that theoretically envisioned a sharp division between slave and free wrestled incessantly with the reality of racial semifreedom within its borders. The market revolution in the North inculcated an ideology that excoriated slaveholding but stood mute on the rights of those freed. This left free blacks huddling under the weak shelter of humanitarian sentiment and revolutionary logic against the maelstrom of economic imperative, centuries-long prejudice, and an emerging racial science that found it increasingly easy to write blacks out of the brotherhood of man. The newly emancipated understood their precarious place in the civic community; they were being steadily excised from the American social contract. With biting sarcasm, one black editor noted how quickly "the democratic principle is adopted" in America, where "the rich and poor, the high and the low" could "all come together as equals . . . to hate the colored man."[21] In this *herrenvolk* democracy, it was not difficult for the nominally free to find common cause with their brethren in chains.[22] Black Ohioan Peter Humphries Clark believed that "in a country where the laws bear equally on all, we would combine more readily in action for our enslaved brethren." He warned, "[I]f we do not unite now, when almost forced to by the pressure of prejudice, we will not when that pressure is removed."[23]

Add to this the actual physical connections between North and South—a great many black northerners had actually been born in the South—and the consequences for northern black identity become clear: such factors made it all the more likely, all the easier, for northern free blacks to embrace all people of African descent as a single large group. Free of a slave category into which their activism might hurtle them, they had the freedom to champion the cause of the slave. Moreover, more than any others in the diaspora, they had undergone social experiences that made them likely to do it. Not so high that they saw their interests as distinct from those of the enslaved, neither were they so low (that is, enslaved) that they lacked the freedom to act on their vision. Thus, in 1848 free African Americans gathered in a national convention and declared, "We are not slaves to individuals, not personal slaves, yet in many respects we are the slaves of the community. We are, however, far enough removed from the actual condition of the slaves to make us largely responsible for their continued enslavement, or their speedy deliverance from chains." Many, in fact, had known the dreaded institution firsthand: "Our backs are yet scarred by the lash, and our souls are yet dark under the pall of slavery." This was the solution to James McCune Smith's dilemma. Though different in important ways, the social experience of blacks slave and free was *close enough* to posit a unanimity of interest. The convention continued: "We are as a people, chained together. We are one people—one in general complexion, one in a common degradation, one in popular estimation.—As one rises, all must rise, and as one falls all must fall."[24]

DREGS FROM THE BITTER CHALICE: BLACK LEADERS IN THE CONVENTION MOVEMENT

Despite the North's singular place in the diaspora, patterns of plantation society did echo there, at least to the extent that they helped define the elites in its free black communities. In general, the qualities that identified free African American elites in the Lower South demarcated them in the North, though in much diminished fashion. This trend varied intraregionally: border cities like Cincinnati and Philadelphia were more likely to follow it than were cities farther to the north, like Boston or Buffalo. But in all cases it suggested cleavages that, in places where they were more exacerbated, rent African American identity into free colored and enslaved black castes. Consider, for example, the skill level of northern free blacks' occupations.

Table 1.4. Occupational Skill Level, by Complexion and Region of Birth, 1850–1860

Occupational Level	North				South			
	Black		Mulatto		Black		Mulatto	
	N	%	N	%	N	%	N	%
Skilled	203	24	198	36	404	24	416	41
Unskilled	654	76	353	64	1,285	76	599	59
Total	857	100	551	100	1,689	100	1,015	100

Source: 1850 and 1860 U.S. Federal Census manuscripts, Afro-American Communities Project, Museum of American History, Smithsonian Institution, Washington, D.C.

An analysis of census data from five northern cities in 1850 and 1860 suggests that a strong predictor of highly skilled or professional workers was a combination of southern birth and light skin color.[25] Over three-quarters of northern-born black men found themselves relegated to unskilled employment. In contrast, southern-born "mulattoes" residing in the North were the African Americans most likely to occupy positions as mechanics, artisans, and professionals: 41 percent of those studied did (Table 1.4). Analysis of another measure of status, total property claimed on the census, also favored southern-born African Americans with mixed racial origins. In the five cities studied, southern-born mulattoes on average claimed total property amounting to $470—almost twice as much as the next highest group, northern-born mulattoes, who claimed $245; northern- and southern-born blacks trailed, at $192 and $166, respectively (Table 1.5). These patterns reflect the same characteristics that created mulatto elites in the South: light-complected northerners born in the South, where higher ratios of blacks to whites left them occupying the middling ranks of society, were more likely to have been trained in an employable skill. Upon moving to the North, where blacks had been denied training in such occupations and hence lacked the capacity to fill them, these black southerners found themselves occasionally able to short-circuit the vicious cycle of poverty and fill rare niches in the labor market. A black Philadelphian commented in 1855 that "most of the colored mechanics in Philadelphia had received their [mechanical] education in the South," but "the colored people of the city of Philadelphia could not obtain opportunity to learn mechanical trades." The same was true as far north as New Bedford, Massachusetts, where it was reported that "colored mechanics are principally from the South."[26]

Table 1.5. Mean Total Property Claimed, by Complexion and Region of Birth, 1850–1860

Complexion and Region	Mean
Mulatto	
South	$469.94
North	$244.91
Black	
North	$191.89
South	$165.95

Source: 1850 and 1860 U.S. Federal Census manuscripts, Afro-American Communities Project, Museum of American History, Smithsonian Institution, Washington, D.C.

How did the self-proclaimed black leaders who crafted the black public protest tradition fit into this relatively compressed range of opportunities? One attempt to determine this may begin with a study of those who pretended to positions of leadership: participants in the black convention movement. From 1830 through the Civil War and into Reconstruction and beyond, African American northerners convened periodically to discuss their common plight, ponder solutions, and craft statements of their sentiments to the black masses and to white America. The proceedings of these conventions are commonly considered a central source of information on the protest thought developed by free black elites in the antebellum era.

Convention proceedings indicate that the elites who spearheaded the movement did not lack confidence in their own capacity to represent the black rank and file. Their statements, addressed generally to "our brethren and fellow citizens" or "the free people of colour of these United States," went to so little trouble to justify their claims to speak for all that their negligence can only be considered evidence of their founders' self-assurance in their roles. These were conventions "of the colored people," with no qualification apparently required. Still, black conventioneers may have had no claim whatsoever to their self-appointed stations. In what ways did they constitute a leadership? The conspicuous dearth of women among their ranks suggests at least one important realm in which they were not directly representative of the black non-elite. And there is scant evidence that those they purported to lead either supported or challenged their roles.

Though obscure, the details of the representative process at these conventions offer some important clues. The ubiquitous published "calls," or notices requesting black people to attend upcoming conventions, offer the clearest starting point for discerning methods of representation in the conventions. Modeled on a long American tradition of calls for public meetings, even their earliest incarnations invoked a set of established conventions. Often, they appeared to have offered little more than rhetorical flourish. In a typical case, the planning board for a meeting of blacks in Canada exclaimed: "Call Meetings! Send up your Delegates! Let there be a full attendance of the people." [27] The call for the national convention in 1864 urged blacks to "come from the cities, towns, hamlets and districts of every section of the country." [28] While such statements seem to offer little concrete evidence about the mechanics of representation, neither should they be dismissed as meaningless. They reflect one of the great imperatives confronting convention organizers: attracting high attendance. When black leaders in Ohio called for "at least five hundred delegates," [29] they understood that their ability to muster large numbers of participants constituted a basic requirement for the legitimacy of both their organizations and their own claims to leadership. In a democracy, who would concede the authority of representatives who could not show that they represented anyone?

Calls sometimes revealed a sincere desire for mass participation by reaching across lines of class and region. Ohio blacks catalogued a list of disparate professions they wished to unite in 1858: "Let the farmer leave his plow, the blacksmith his anvil, the painter his brush, the shoemaker his last, the carpenter his plan, the barber his razor, the servant his waiter, the school teacher his occupation, the minister his desk." [30] A "North American Convention" organized by African Americans who had fled to Canada issued a call that conflated typical rhetorical adornments with an important message of cross-regional unity: "Come from the Atlantic shores and the west of the Rocky Mountains. Come from the New England hilltops and valleys to the Convention. The slave, too, from the rice-swamps and cotton fields of the south shall have a hearty welcome on the Queen's free soil." [31] Gestures such as these signaled the democratic motives underlying much of the convention movement.

Black convention organizers knew that mass attendance alone did not sufficiently guarantee the legitimacy of their meetings. Quality of representation concerned them as much as sheer numbers. Many calls tempered a desire for mass attendance with requirements that delegates emerge from a more orderly process of selection. Calls frequently limited participation to "appropriate and chosen representatives" and "regularly appointed delegates." [32] Convention organizers justified these limitations on the basis that

the legitimacy of their meetings demanded that representation be appor-
tioned fairly—in order, for example, "that no community shall be represented beyond its due proportion."[33] Early in the national convention movement organizers envisioned the solution to the dilemma of ensuring proper
representation in a network of local societies, all created or endorsed by a
national "conventional board" which would attest to their legitimacy.[34] They
developed a constitution to govern this structure, which required that delegates be adult men from the places they represented. Representation in the
national convention was to be proportionate to the size of the community
represented—a notion similar to what prevailed in the lower, more egalitarian body of Congress, the House of Representatives. Two weeks prior
to each convention, properly elected delegates were to submit documents
from their local organizations confirming their status as representatives.[35]
Understanding that many blacks lived in areas too poorly organized to hold
regular meetings, framers left a loophole, permitting those lacking local
established organizations to arrange impromptu public meetings to select
delegates.[36] Provisions covering such exceptions contradicted the need for
representation predicated on consistent principles, but they were necessary
concessions to the realities of a sparsely settled black North. Although they
threatened the legitimacy of conventions by exposing the delegate selection
process to abuse, they seemed necessary in light of the need to demonstrate
the conventions' widespread support among black northerners.

In time it became apparent that black northerners could not sustain the
grandiose organization they initially envisioned. They had difficulty simply
holding the movement together, and after 1835 they held national conventions only sporadically. It was unlikely that their numbers would ever
grow large enough to sustain the size of organization, and the legitimating
restrictions such numbers could support, that they had first imagined. In
the meantime, small controversies within the conventions constantly challenged leaders to grapple with the tension between demonstrating their
democratic proclivities and protecting the integrity and reputation of the
movement. Requests from those without regular delegations to participate
in conventions sparked considerable contention among convention delegates. Should such members be seated as regular delegates despite not
having been elected? Lacking clear election guidelines, members might
challenge each other's legitimacy, as happened during the national convention of 1834. In that case, Philadelphia leaders charged a rival New York
faction of packing the convention against it.[37] In the future, what principles
would resolve such disputes? All agreed on the necessity of rules to check
the arbitrary or wanton exercise of power in the conventions. The question

was whether conventioneers should favor what they termed the "largest liberty," and thus open the convention to well-wishers denied the chance to become legitimate delegates, or, as those in favor of a narrower liberty contended, should restrict membership in order to maintain the integrity of the elective process. Beset with these dilemmas, the national convention of 1833 exasperatedly resolved to develop "some more efficient plan of representation."[38]

Proponents of more restrictive admission requirements tended toward a Federalist-style elitism that betrayed clear class prejudices. Lewis Woodson, often touted as the father of a black nationalism rooted in the experience of the masses, expressed more than a little snobbery in discussing proper representation at black conventions. Given, he said, that "the great body of us are not, at present, sufficiently enlightened to see or appreciate our own best interest," it fell upon the worthy few to take on leadership roles. Woodson feared that representational politics would never secure for African Americans the necessary leadership. Being degraded, the black masses could not be expected to "elect men the most eminent for their wisdom, integrity and patriotism." The black masses, "whose ignorance has made them vicious," would never be likely to favor "the wise and good." Voicing a belief that few other black leaders would have dared to state aloud, Woodson claimed "that men need qualification for self government."[39] Such statements rang close to the words of Whiggish white abolitionists, who likewise looked with suspicion upon an unfettered franchise. Most voters, complained a Pennsylvania abolitionist to black friends, "have no correct knowledge of the science of government." Voters were more easily drawn by "a 'racoon skin,' a barrel of 'hard cider,' a filthy or blackguard speech, or vulgar expression" than by "matters of consequence to the nation."[40]

The more egalitarian majority challenged such notions as contrary to the ethos of the entire movement. In arguing for the seating of irregular delegates as full members of the convention, prominent activists like Frederick Douglass and Henry Highland Garnet claimed that the objects of the conventions were "a common cause" to which all people of African descent belonged. They had assembled "to assert principles embracing the largest liberty for all, and to take broad ground in favor of the free expression of opinion." To exclude anyone with a stake in their cause "would be subversive of the very spirit which has brought us together."[41] Prominent convention figures offered similar arguments in virtually the same language at national conventions in 1835, 1847, 1848, and 1853.[42] In general, this "largest liberty" position prevailed. With important qualifications, loose provisions for delegate selection became the rule rather than the exception. In lieu of a sanctioned hierarchy of local societies, the conventional board of the 1830s asked blacks "to form Societies in every city, town or village, wherever it may be practicable, and send their full complement of delegates to the ensuing Convention."[43] Later convention organizers forgot entirely the early, unworkable plans for a sustained national organization. Despite inevitable inconsistencies in representation, they relied instead on a less formal network of existing community institutions. When the American Moral Reform Society, a Philadelphia-based organization with a sizable black leadership, called for its annual meeting in 1837, it announced that "Auxiliary Societies, religious bodies, as well as Temperance and Education Societies, are hereby invited to send delegates."[44] The call for a national convention in 1853 urged "the people in various neighborhoods, church organizations, Benevolent or Literary societies" to meet and elect delegates.[45]

Yet neither did conventioneers abandon measures designed to retain the integrity of their gatherings. The need for delegates might mandate lax selection provisions, but even those who most championed democracy in the conventions understood the need for clear and consistent principles of representation. The ideal was to rectify transient necessary evils at the first opportunity: one leader argued that "delegates elected by the people should, as soon as practicable, entirely supersede the voluntarily associated."[46] The early gatherings debated restricting participation by requiring from delegates "proper credentials from their respective societies or meetings held for the purpose of electing them as such," and demanding that delegates be adult males who had resided for at least six months in the localities they represented.[47] Conventions in the 1840s and 1850s continued to require credentials from local organizations, sometimes restricting those lacking institutional sanction to purely honorary roles.[48]

Convention organizers never entirely abandoned strictures on representation, because doing so posed clear risks. First, it rendered the convention movement vulnerable to those hostile to its very interests. Lax participation requirements inconsistently applied threatened to bring enemies into conventioneers' very midst. Thus most provisions permitting noninstitutional delegates to attend did so on the basis that "they contribute to the furthering of the objects of the Convention."[49] Conventions with special agendas especially saw the need to protect their integrity, such as the controversial one held by black nationalists in 1854 to plan the establishment of a separate colony in Africa, the Caribbean, or Central America. Knowing that theirs was a position under siege in the mainstream black press and fearing disruptions by opponents and rival emigrationists, they refused to recognize those who disagreed with their objectives and required delegates to bring creden-

PLATE 1. *"Grand Celebration ob de Bobalition ob African Slabery."* Lithographs such as this one from Edward Clay's popular Life in Philadelphia *series lampooned blacks' efforts to rise through institution building, implying that African Americans naturally lacked the capacity to adhere to rules of order and decorum. Lithograph by Edward Clay,* Life in Philadelphia *(Philadelphia: S. Hart, 1829); courtesy of The Library Company of Philadelphia.*

tials authenticating their commitment to emigration.[50] Second, in addition to risking the convention's very objectives, loose qualifications for representation also opened the door to disputes, which damaged the credibility of the entire movement. It was one thing to argue inside the convention hall; it was quite another to arm an already hostile public with the idea that blacks could not manage even minimal organizational endeavors. The dangers here were palpable. Whites had long parodied blacks' efforts to organize, using what passed for "negro dialect" to lampoon their organizations as "bobalition" (abolition) societies, their meetings as irredeemable displays of buffoonery and vice (Plate 1). Long the butt of whites' ridicule, black public figures could hardly afford displays of disunity.[51]

Regardless of how it was settled, the debate between those favoring larger or smaller liberty at the convention pointed to leaders' inclinations or disinclinations toward power sharing, presumably with the non-elite. No consensus was ever achieved on the issue, though in general the trend increasingly favored inclusion. Few conventioneers spouted anything close to the rhetoric of a Lewis Woodson; many championed restrictions for reasons that had more to do with a sensitivity to public image than a commitment to Federalist-style politics. Of course, these two impulses were not completely distinct: concern with presenting a respectable image clearly reflected social aspirations. While perhaps they cannot be considered the nation's most ardent champions of mass participatory politics, many leaders seemed inclined to broaden convention participation, providing of course that the newcomers were supportive, respectable, and respectful of existing convention authorities. (In a great many other arenas, including convention addresses themselves, African American spokespersons indefatigably championed the radical egalitarianism of the American Revolution.) Rather than suggesting the hegemony of a small class of black elites, then, the convention movement illustrated themes of conflict and contention. While cadres of prominent national figures dominated the movement, they hardly suppressed debate. Instead, movement stalwarts exerted what authority they had in less direct ways, largely through their steadfast presence, and through the control of the movement's larger agenda, which their ubiquity conferred.

Consider the sensitive issue of labor politics. The national convention of 1848 hotly debated a resolution declaring that, just as white workers would be elevated through "respectable industrial occupations"—by which was meant farming, skilled craft, mercantile, and professional occupations—so too would blacks. In effect yet another call for blacks to flee menial trades for the skilled crafts, the resolution was challenged by lesser lights in the convention, who likely understood all too well the difficulties entailed in following such advice. Such resolutions were commonly offered at conventions; what was new here were the challenges mounted against them. One J. D. Patterson attacked the resolution as elitist, complaining that "those who were in the editorial chair and others, not in places of servants, must not cast slurs upon those, who were in such places from necessity." Patterson had felt compelled to speak when he heard Martin R. Delany, Douglass's co-editor, say "that he would rather receive a telegraphic dispatch that his wife and two children had fallen victims to a loathsome disease, than to hear that they had become the servants of any man." A John L. Watson of Cleveland supported Patterson. He too lambasted Delany, this time for having said the previous day that "if we became the boot-blacks, the white mechanics would look down on us, but if we became mechanics, etc., they would respect us."[52]

Another resolution regarding labor also unsettled the proceedings. This one declared, "The occupation of domestics and servants among our people is degrading to us as a class, and we deem it our bounded duty to discountenance such pursuits, except where necessity compels the person to resort therein as a means of livelihood."[53] Abner H. Francis, a delegate from Buffalo, "heartily supported" the resolution. Painting a picture of his own rise from menial occupations to the head of a mercantile business that brought in $20,000 to $30,000 a year, he agreed with others who had also lifted themselves up out of what they termed "degrading occupations." Frederick Douglass defended the resolution by softening its implications. While he did not agree with the claim "that any useful labor was degrading," he wished to end the division of skilled and unskilled occupations by racial caste. He advocated that the convention declare that "what is necessary to be done, is honorable to do" and advise its people to "leave situations in which we are considered degraded, as soon as necessity ceases."[54]

The resolution's opponents lost both issues. With the exception of these few dissenting voices, the convention passed both resolutions by wide margins. In addition, language to their effect appeared in the convention's "Address to the Colored People of the United States." Penned by the resolutions' chief defenders, the address declared that menial occupations had been filled by blacks for so long that they had "become a badge of degradation" that suggested that "colored men are only fit for such employments." While they conceded that "any kind of needful toil" was honorable, they advised blacks "to cease from such employments . . . by pressing into others" — namely, the skilled trades.[55]

The issue flared again in the 1853 national convention, when Dr. James McCune Smith challenged the report of the Committee on Social Relations and Polity. Smith, whose education and professional status as a physician hardly made him a representative of the worker, nonetheless challenged the committee's report "because of the statement in it that the colored people of this country are not producers."[56] A floor debate erupted, during which elites like Smith and James Mercer Langston, an Ohio attorney, argued that blacks had made considerable headway in taking up "useful" and "respectable" occupations; others argued that blacks were "mainly consumers," something widely considered troublesome in antebellum political economy. The conflict ended in a draw: an amendment to the report congenial to Smith's position failed, but so too did passage of the unamended report. While hardly victories for the everyday black worker, these conventions illustrate tensions that never would have made it into the cryptic minutes of meetings in the early 1830s. In highlighting the divide between the black rich and poor, they revealed not so much a widening gulf between the monied and the impoverished, but a new accessibility to the convention movement, which, though limited, nonetheless permitted the voices of the struggling to be heard for the first time. Surely those voices were weak, but their arguments were at least debated on the convention floor, and they caused a considerable softening in the language of the conventions. The 1853 convention resolved that menial employment taken "from necessity" did not "of itself bring reproach upon a people." Instead, it cautioned parents against permitting their children to become accustomed to such work, for such would "give them rather the downward, than the upward tendency."[57]

For every gesture conventioneers made that revealed an elite, exclusionary social perspective, they set forth another in the opposite direction. When New York blacks met in 1831 to oppose the American Colonization Society's efforts to return blacks to Africa, they claimed that the society's members made poor spokesmen for blacks. Society men did not know blacks, they claimed: "Their patrician principles prevent an intercourse with men in the middle walks of life, among whom a large portion of our people may be classified." Similarly middling blacks spoke out against wealthy African Americans who pursued their own self-interest at the expense of racial activism. "Shame on our rich men, with their *two, three, four* and *five thousand dollars* annual income, besides a prosperous business!" In refusing "to educate their children *liberally*, FOR THE PUBLIC GOOD," they pursued their own class interests at the expense of a larger racial struggle, one black newspaper complained. "We never can be a people until we maintain our own cause and support our own institutions. We must give more liberally, and act more efficiently, or *never claim to be freemen, nor expect to be elevated*."[58] Poet Francis Ellen Watkins raised the same grievance: "We have money among us, but how much of it is spent to bring deliverance to our captive brethren? Are our wealthiest men the most liberal sustainers of the Anti-slavery enterprise?"[59] And as often as they seemed to foster their own roles as leaders, they lamented the necessities that placed the responsibilities for the entire movement on their shoulders. "Is a public meeting called? One class of men have to officiate," a black leader complained. "Is a society formed for literary purposes? The same men are engaged in it. Is a public committee sent out for any important object? You will find the same names enrolled on that committee."[60] Such statements were not mere efforts at self-aggrandizement but legitimate worries about the health and direction of the movement. Leaders' omnipresent calls for black racial unity may temper considerably valid reservations about their middle-class biases.

It is not clear, then, that the convention movement yielded a truly representative class of black leaders. The objective of this review of convention leaders is not to treat them as a representative sample of leaders so much as to test the degree to which self-proclaimed leaders deserved the title. This requires an understanding not only of the social forces that produced elites in black communities but also of the material foundations that helped determine the shape of black identity in any given place—that is, the ways in which economic opportunity and demographic realities combined to lead blacks toward certain options in crafting their identities and away from others. This is of vital importance in understanding the position in their communities of those who crafted the black public protest tradition, for it related directly to their capacity to represent the non-elite. One black writer argued that the race's grievances could be laid before the public by "none other than those conscious of suffering." Because they had "drank the dregs of the embittered chalice" of prejudice and slavery, he wrote, "the oppressed are ever their own best representatives."[61] But, as a relative elite, had black leaders partaken of the same dregs as their popular brethren? Had they even drunk from the same chalice?

Of the several hundred men (and a very few women) who attended black state and national conventions in the North between 1830 and 1865, the names of sixty-five were correlated with federal census manuscripts of 1850 and 1860 for five cities spread geographically throughout the North: Boston, Buffalo, Chicago, Cincinnati, and Detroit. The resulting information offers a prosopography, or group biography—a cross-section of black conventioneers that may be considered suggestive of broader trends.[62] In some ways, this sample group may be considered more elite than many who might have been considered black community leaders. Several thousand likely played key community roles during this period yet never attended a convention. For example, owners of grogshops, dance and gaming halls, and oyster bars, who were particularly likely to function as important working-class black community figures, had cultural styles that would have been considered anathema to the middle-class ethos of the conventions. And conventions excluded women leaders almost entirely. In other ways, though, the sample group is skewed toward the bottom end of the black leadership pyramid. Many of the names on the rolls of black conventions represent most of what is known of the individuals' activism. A great many made it to the conventions, participated in them fully, signed the petitions, and returned to their homes having uttered not a word that survives in the convention records. The sample group is clearly imperfectly representative, but it is close enough to provide a basis for drawing general conclusions and designing further research. To set this group in context, one may compare it to both the mass of African Americans in the five cities examined as well as to another sample group easily identified as an elite. One of the surest ways to identify such an elite is to rely on claims to property ownership. Almost 22 percent (1,104) of African Americans in the five cities examined claimed to own real or personal property on the federal census. This privileged one-fifth stood apart from the mass in distinct ways and provides a comparison group by which the leaders (convention participants) may be measured.

The sixty-five leaders identified in the sample group resembled the property-holding elite in several important measures of economic and social status. Following patterns that created African American elites throughout the New World, markers of nativity and skin complexion helped identify this elite. Despite a northern context that flattened socioeconomic possibilities for blacks, being southern-born and light-complected still parlayed into enhanced economic possibilities for northern blacks. The majority of black northerners in the five-city sample group (58 percent) were in fact southern-born. Of these, 37 percent were classified on the census as "mulatto."[63] This group of southern-born mulattoes was overrepresented among the elite of property holders; representing 24 percent of the mass sample population, southern-born mulattoes constituted 34 percent of the propertied. The leader group was also spearheaded by southern-born mulattoes: 45 percent were classified as mixed-race and had been born south of the Mason-Dixon line. In fact, the leader group was more heavily skewed away from northerners and blacks than was the property-holding group (Table 1.6, panel a).

Other status markers place the leader group among a community elite (Table 1.6, panels b–f). Leaders were more likely to be literate than were the property holders (93 percent vs. 74 percent), and far more likely to be so than the mass of their peers in the five cities (65 percent). They were very likely to earn their livings in skilled or professional occupations; 79 percent of them did so, compared to only 60 percent of the property holders and 29 percent of the mass. The average amount of property they accumulated ($1,446) exceeded that of the propertied ($1,157) and the mass ($256), despite the fact that thirty-two leaders (almost half) claimed no property at all. When ranked by decile according to the total wealth they claimed on the census, leaders occupied either the lowest rank (the unpropertied) or its highest reaches (Figure 1.2). These property-holding patterns suggest a bifurcated leader class—some whose positions stemmed from their wealth and others who considered themselves leaders by virtue of their community status, professional training, or commitment to activism.[64] Regardless of

Table 1.6. Measures of Status among Black Northerners, 1850–1860

A. Region of Birth and Skin Color

Region and Skin Color	Leaders		Five Cities		Economic Elite	
	N	%	N	%	N	%
North						
Black	6	9	990	22	157	15
Mulatto	11	17	606	13	138	13
South						
Black	18	28	1,837	41	386	37
Mulatto	29	45	1,095	24	358	34
Total	64	100	4,528	100	1,039	100

B. Literacy Status

Literacy Status	Leaders		Five Cities		Economic Elite	
	N	%	N	%	N	%
Illiterate	4	7	1,242	35	244	26
Literate	53	93	2,311	65	699	74
Total	57	100	3,553	100	943	100

C. Occupational Skill Level

Occupational Level	Leaders		Five Cities		Economic Elite	
	N	%	N	%	N	%
Skilled/professional	50	79	1,301	29	644	60
Semi-/unskilled	13	21	3,236	71	437	40
Total	63	100	4,537	100	1,081	100

wealth, leaders tended to live lives that at least superficially would have rendered them representatives of middle-class ideals. The great majority were, like the propertied elite, married (84 percent, compared to 86 percent for the propertied and 52 percent for the mass of adult males). Like members of the propertied group, the overwhelming majority were the heads of their household (92 percent for leaders, compared with 95 percent for the propertied and 60 percent for all adult black men).

Finally, the men in these households tended to be married to light-

Table 1.6. Continued

D. Value of Real and Personal Property

Property Value	Leaders[a]		Five Cities[a]		Economic Elite[a]	
	N	%	N	%	N	%
$0	32	49	3,925	78	0	0
$1–$999	14	22	800	16	800	72
$1,000–$4,999	15	23	249	5	249	23
$5,000+	4	6	55	1	55	5
Total	65	100	5,029	100	1,104	100

E. Marital Status

Marital Status	Leaders		Five Cities		Economic Elite	
	N	%	N	%	N	%
Single	10	16	2,379	48	159	14
Married	54	84	2,592	52	939	86
Total	64	100	4,971	100	1,098	100

F. Status in Household

Household Status	Leaders		Five Cities		Economic Elite	
	N	%	N	%	N	%
Head of household	60	92	2,938	60	1,049	95
Family boarder, dependent, or servant	5	8	1,993	40	55	5
Total	65	100	4,931	100	1,104	100

[a]The mean property value declared by each group was as follows: Leaders, $1,446.15; Five Cities, $255.70; Economic Elite, $1,157.25.

Continued on next page

complected wives: 70 percent of the leader group, as opposed to 50 percent for the propertied group and 44 percent for the mass (Table 1.6g). In nineteenth-century America, this was no trivial matter. Light-complected spouses were widely viewed by status-conscious African Americans as preferable, not for the clichéd reason that whites set standards of beauty for blacks who were too unenlightened to set their own, but because light complex-

Table 1.6. Continued

G. Complexion of Wife

	Leaders		Five Cities		Economic Elite	
Wife's Complexion	N	%	N	%	N	%
Black	15	28	1,328	52	416	45
Mulatto	38	70	1,120	44	466	50
White	1	2	113	4	52	6
Total	54	100	2,561	100	934	100

Source: 1850 and 1860 U.S. Federal Census manuscripts, Afro-American Communities Project, Museum of American History, Smithsonian Institution, Washington, D.C.

Note: "Leaders" group defined as adult male participants in black state and national conventions identified in federal census manuscripts, 1850 and 1860; "Five Cities" group defined as adult men in federal census manuscripts for Boston, Buffalo, Chicago, Cincinnati, and Detroit, 1850 and 1860; "Economic Elite" group defined as adult men who claimed property in federal census manuscripts for Boston, Buffalo, Chicago, Cincinnati, and Detroit, 1850 and 1860. "Adult" in all categories defined as 18 years or older.

ion was a marker of class status among African-descended people throughout the diaspora. Such patterns were prevalent in the Lower South and Caribbean, where the three-tiered racial caste systems predominated. In New Orleans, a reporter for Frederick Douglass's *North Star* noted the resulting prejudices of members of the city's light-complected creole elite. Socialized with a diminished northern sensitivity to complexional distinctions, he was appalled when one woman remarked that "she would prefer to see her daughter in concubinage to a white, than respectably married to a colored man!"[65] Upwardly mobile men who lacked light skin complexion as a birthright could assert their newfound status by marrying into the ranks of the light-complected free elites. Even in the North, their wives' complexions proved significant: in the five-cities sample group, this trait—more than literacy, regional nativity, or their own skin color—predicted a man's occupational skill and wealth. Fully 72 percent of men with dark-complected wives earned their livings in jobs requiring no or few skills. In contrast, the average property claimed by those married to light-complected wives ($519) exceeded that of any other group defined by a single characteristic. Not even a combination of regional nativity and the man's own skin complexion yielded

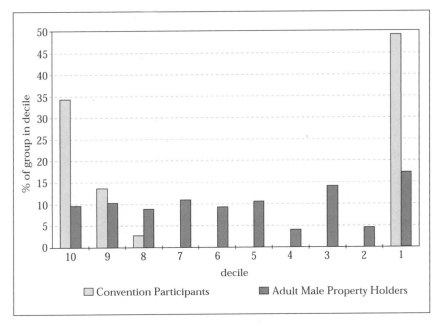

FIGURE 1.2. *Distibution of Property Holding among Adult Male Property Holders and Convention Participants*

figures so high (southern-born men of mixed racial heritage claimed an average of $460 in total property).

As measured by those who participated in the convention movement, leaders represented the cream of free black society. For all its limitations, however, this black leadership represented a considerable advance over its predecessors. "For too long others have spoken for us," read the inaugural issue of *Freedom's Journal,* the first black newspaper published in the North. So commonplace did such utterances become in later years that it is difficult to appreciate them in their context.[66] In the 1820s, the notion of an independent black leadership may have struck blacks as welcome and whites as threatening, but it struck everyone as novel; it represented the first sustained effort by black leaders to speak for their people. It must be remembered that the middle-class black leaders who arose after the northern emancipations offered an alternative to less egalitarian forms of leadership—the black "kings" and "governors" of master-sanctioned slave festivals like Election Day or Pinkster—and to paternalistic white benefactors in the gradual antislavery movement, who posed obvious limitations as defenders of black interests. The former group owed their positions of leadership in part to popularity among fellow African Americans, but the sine qua non of this form of leadership was the patronage of wealthy masters. Just as the festivals themselves had manifested deep tensions between black agency and white hegemony, so too did the leadership it produced. The new generation that emerged out of independent black institutions and the antislavery movement left conspicuously little room for these older figures.

A quite different source of leadership in black communities came from the benevolent whites who championed the cause of the slaves in their name. Literally speaking *for* blacks in legal proceedings, leaders of the manumission societies tended to assume a patronizing attitude toward their charges, which revealed considerable racial insensitivity.[67] The thinking of Revolutionary-era abolitionists like Benjamin Rush reveals the need for distinguishing the issue of slavery from that of race: Rush considered blackness a disease that demanded not only pity and humanity from whites but also blacks' physical separation from them.[68] Many post-Revolutionary black northerners endorsed the Federalists, among whom the bulk of white gradual abolitionists numbered, but the honeymoon did not last long. New Yorker Joseph Sydney's 1809 oration commemorating the abolition of the slave trade in the previous year constituted one of the latest black endorsements of Federalism in print. Sydney urged fellow blacks to "unite with our Federal friends" against that "great hotbed of democracy," the slaveholding South.[69] African American elites' alliance with their northern white counterparts waned steadily in ensuing years, eroded by the implosion of the Federalist Party, the channeling of Federalist sympathies into the moderate racism of the American Colonization Society, and the rise of a new mass party system, which appealed to burgeoning white supremacy across class and regional lines, always at the expense of black rights. The middle-class black leaders who emerged in the decades after the northern emancipations may not have shared every facet of class life with popular African America, but they represented a considerable advance over what had come before.

It would be easy to overstate the case for this new generation of independent black leaders. Even the earliest black institutions, like the Mother Bethel African Methodist Episcopal Church in Philadelphia, retained smothering ties with white parent institutions. And black abolitionists' struggle to maintain their independence from white immediatists occasioned some of the bitterest conflicts to beset the movement.[70] In contrast to previous generations, however, the new black leaders who emerged with freedom spoke with rare independence and from a position far more representative of their constituents than had any others up to that point.

MOST NEEDED BLESSINGS: POLITICAL IDENTITY AND
THE PRACTICAL BASES OF RESISTANCE

Black leaders relied overwhelmingly on the power of public speech to sway their audiences. The body of thought they thus crafted represents an important yet neglected source of information on the formation of black protest thought and black identity. Scholars have long sought the sources of black identity in the culture of the slave community. When turning their eyes northward to the nominally free states, they have applied essentially the same framework to their search for black identity. In many ways, this transition works: like enslaved African Americans, or working-class white Americans, most free African Americans built their sense of themselves through shared daily experiences and participation in a cultural milieu of words and rituals that united them and gave meaning to their lives. At the workplace, in the church pew, before the domestic hearth, in boardinghouse common rooms, on the city streets, and in theaters and grog shops, free African Americans built community through behaviors that few elite contemporaries may even have seen and that fewer still have recorded for posterity.

Yet there was another realm of identity construction, which is too often conflated with the community ethos of African Americans. In addition to defining themselves through the practice of folk or popular culture, northern free blacks also constructed black identity through self-conscious acts of public political speech. They thus built a notion, prepared specifically for the public sphere, of their shared interests as an oppressed race. We know of this largely rhetorical instance of black identity formation through the huge body of newspapers, convention proceedings, reprinted speeches and sermons, and published pamphlets that represents the richest historical record of northern black life in the decades before the Civil War. Because it required both the medium of the press and the freedom to pursue public careers, setting forth this public voice took place primarily under the aegis of a black elite, sufficiently resourced to render it distinct from the popular African America it claimed to represent. The construction of this rhetorical form of black identity, then, may be considered primarily an elite process, while the folk construction of black identity occurred at the level of popular black society. The two were not mutually exclusive: non-elite African Americans frequently voiced their opinions in the black press, for instance, and elite African Americans frequently participated in the activities through which popular African America created itself. The important distinction lay in the mode of construction the media used to accomplish the task.

Scholars have tended to note little difference between sources document-ing each of these distinct processes of identity construction. Consequently, they have employed both kinds of sources to answer pressing questions of cultural identity. For example, some have taken the language of elite black public culture as evidence of the degree to which African Americans did or did not assimilate to American cultural norms. Setting aside the issue of whether such a question obscures more than it illuminates, it is not clear that the texts produced by northern black elites offer much of a definitive nature about processes usually considered under the rubric of the cultural-ist paradigm. Issues of cultural transmission, which question how "African" the northern black public protest tradition was, are not easily approached through a body of public speech intended for mass consumption by both whites and blacks. In the murky waters of the public sphere, the search for "survivals" and the culturally distinct becomes quite perilous. Could simple invocations of "Africa" have constituted an expression of cultural African-ness? White speakers also invoked "Africa," obviously for reasons other than their own cultural dependence on that continent. Mere professions of loy-alty to or affinity with Africa cannot be taken alone as evidence of a shared cultural heritage with West Africans, much less as retentions of that cul-ture; black public expression was too complex to be reduced to such one-dimensional readings. The rhetorical exigencies of operating within public sphere discourse often circumvented the operations of "culture" as defined by the community-studies/culturalist paradigm. Consequently, nothing says that those who claimed affinity with Africa were especially African, nor that those who denied such affinities were not. "African," like "white" or "Ameri-can," was a construction.

Consider, for example, the typical case of William Hamilton, an early and well-to-do leader of New York African Americans. At an 1815 gathering celebrating the abolition of the Atlantic slave trade, he lectured his Afri-can American audience, beginning and ending with a lengthy discussion of Africa, its characteristics, and its troubled history. Everything in his rhetori-cal style suggested his close identification with that continent. He frequently invoked the collective "we" when speaking of Africans and used "our" when speaking of their history. At many points, he turned to apostrophe in sym-pathetic, possessive lamentations, as in: "O! Africa, what carnage hast thou witnessed." Yet when he told his African American audience that "our par-ents" had been brought from Africa to labor for white men, he could not literally have meant his own. Although he termed himself "a descendant of Africa," Hamilton's own genealogy suggested different roots: he was reputed to be the illegitimate son of Federalist Alexander Hamilton.[71]

Hamilton's oration reveals not so much patterns of African cultural transmission as it does the discursive process through which African Americans created, as did other Americans, a fictive national family. The purpose of this process had everything to do with racial politics: in an age increasingly dedicating itself to the belief that only those belonging in legitimate nations could contend for liberty, such professions of national affiliation seemed paramount. Hamilton's oration thus says much more about the ways African Americans crafted their identity in public than it does about what of Africa actually remained in them. Shortly after Hamilton's address, when the American Colonization Society began arguing for the deportation of African-descended people from America, such direct declarations of identity with Africa became scarce. In a later address from 1827, Hamilton chose to ignore altogether discussion of an African past, focusing instead on white Americans' failure to live up to the noble ideals set forth in the Declaration of Independence and Constitution.[72] For several decades African Americans eschewed professions of identity with Africa not because they had "assimilated" American values or had lost their true or original identity. They did so because those associations had become dangerous. Regardless of their actual cultural relationship to Africa, African American spokespersons subordinated the use of the continent as a trope to the demands of an increasingly hostile realm of public speech. The black national convention of 1847 understood the primacy of public sphere discourse in their oppression and hence saw its need in their activism: "We struggle against opinions. Our warfare lies in the field of thought," it declared.[73] Black political identity was concerned with nothing if not crafting an identity with efficacy on that battle plain.

None of this is to argue that there were no African cultural elements in the North. To the contrary, and despite white Americans' persistent denials of the fact, the behavior of African-descended people infused into American popular culture deep strands of an African cultural heritage, albeit in increasingly diminished form after the turn of the nineteenth century. But care must be taken in looking for such strands. Searching for them in public speech undermines the case for African culture in the North by drawing incredible inferences from sources that cannot bear their weight and, in so doing, obscures an important yet distinct process of identity formation.

If conclusions from such texts regarding the cultural identity of northern free blacks must remain suspect, much can be learned from such sources about the nature and significance of the public identity that black spokespersons constructed in the service of racial politics. The political discourse of the public sphere provided a touchstone for African Americans' understanding of themselves as an oppressed people. Nothing intrinsic to their natures united the millions of Africans who had been brutally torn from their cultures and their descendants into a solidified political whole, yet somehow Americans both black and white came to understand reality and predicate policy on just this basis.

One source of such a unified identity came from white Americans themselves, who declared African-descended people uniformly unfit for self-rule and irrevocably degraded. Paradoxically, the abolition of slavery in the North intensified rather than diminished the uniformity of black people in white minds. The removal of slavery as a point of distinction between whites and blacks placed a premium upon racial demarcation. Thus Tocqueville observed that "in the North the white no longer distinctly perceives the barrier that separates him from the degraded race, and he shuns the Negro with the more pertinacity since he fears lest they should some day be confounded together."[74]

Of course, this source of a unified black identity could never serve as a source of group pride and power for blacks themselves. Another source was far more potent. The folk culture and community ethos of enslaved and free African Americans proffered perhaps the strongest basis for a unified black identity. Built in response to their common experience of oppression from cultural material brought from Africa and synthesized in America, this sense of shared communal identity in some way shaped the contours of the lives of every African-descended person in America. Indeed, it shaped the lives of European-descended Americans as well, though few whites acknowledged it. However, potent as such a source of identity was, it found little support in the public sphere. There, the distinct folk culture of African Americans, which white Americans defined as defective perversions of civilized culture, proved unfit for the task before it. There, the voice of everyday African Americans was effectively silenced. Public sphere discussions demanded an appreciation for and understanding of the ways public sphere debates operated, something that black folk culture was not primarily disposed to do.

A third source of communal black identity—African American public protest thought—offered a solution to this dilemma. Championed by elite free black northerners who commanded access to public sphere debates, this notion of blackness was rooted not in the culture of the slave cabin but in the discourse of urban America, and especially that of the North. The notion of black identity crafted by self-proclaimed black leaders responded to the essentializing racial rhetoric brewing out of the racial Thermidor of the early nineteenth century and the unjust policies and practices it spawned. In places where powerful white enemies might be converted and powerful white allies might be enlisted, such protest launched a barrage of attacks on a prejudiced public mind. Furthermore, it countered the centrifugal forces of class and status that might have pulled apart black identity, as indeed happened in nearly every other site in the diaspora. The result was a truly political basis for black resistance, a positive notion that all people of African descent belonged under the banner of a single political category—in contemporary parlance, a black nation.[75]

Such a nation existed primarily as a rhetorical gesture, largely confined to a public sphere to which the enslaved had limited access, not as a lived experience of cultural blackness that was shared much more widely. Yet while its appeal among popular African Americans never proved complete, and hence limited its efficacy as a uniting force, its ability to speak to a public sphere dominated by white people fostered its power tremendously. It was here that black folk culture was weakest, and it was here that white Americans were most likely to acknowledge the legitimacy of black political demands.

In the antebellum period, the factors that united all African-descended people in the minds of northern black elites were not claims of organic ties and deep cultural linkages. Black resistance grew more from leaders' pragmatic assessment of their situation rather than from their assertion of a distinct cultural "genius" of African-descended people.[76] In fact, black spokespersons took great pains to demonstrate that they acted in unison not because they sought to function as a "class," "monopoly," or "combination"—entities considered distinctly illegitimate in the antebellum ideological context of classical liberal economics and republican political ideology—but because they had been singled out for maltreatment despite the humanity and culture they shared with whites.

They laid out their positions most clearly in a debate conducted in the press in 1837. On the one hand, William Whipper, a Philadelphia activist and founder of the biracial American Moral Reform Society (AMRS), and Robert Purvis, another leading light in Philadelphia's black abolitionist circles, argued against "complexional distinctions," or the principle that blacks ought to act alone to further their interests. Squared off against the Philadelphians were editor Samuel Cornish of New York, Henry Highland Garnet, another outspoken black New Yorker, and William J. Watkins, a free black teacher from Baltimore. Watkins initiated the fracas when he publicly denounced Whipper's AMRS for its position on black-only institutions. Whipper had pledged to keep the doors of the AMRS open to whites sympathetic with the cause and denounced those who failed to follow suit in their own institu-

question of vacred composition
of groups — cf. debate in 1960s

tions. To exclude whites from their midsts, Whipper argued, was to commit the very crime against which black activists contended. It was "to be governed by the most invidious of all creeds that ever regulated human duty, viz. the complexion of the human body."[77] To limit participation in their movements to blacks alone smacked of a chauvinism that violated core precepts of the nation. That whites violated those principles as a matter of course excused nothing; their hypocrisy, he argued, could not rationalize blacks' adoption of racialism. Whipper had a point: black leaders built a powerful case on exposing the hypocrisy of white Americans who endorsed the Declaration of Independence while simultaneously crediting it to the unique genius of the Anglo-Saxon race. Committed first and foremost to democratic principles that seemed to hold all they needed, black leaders could ill afford to risk hypocrisy themselves.

Whipper's opponents argued that the object was never to build institutions that sought to cultivate black unity for its own sake. Watkins advocated racially distinct institutions for his people "not because they are *colored*— but because, being colored, they are, for the most part, despised, neglected, and denied the facilities enjoyed by others."[78] Cornish agreed: "We say that our *condition* in the community is a *peculiar* one, and that we need SPECIAL EFFORTS and special organization, to meet our wants and to obtain and maintain our rights." The editor insisted that he did not "love one class of men more than another" and was as much opposed to "complexional distinctions" as anyone. "Yet we are one of an oppressed people," he wrote, "and we deem it alike our privilege and duty, to labor *especially* for that people, until *all their disabilities are removed*."[79] Garnet agreed with Cornish, saying it should not be assumed that "by watering and preserving the plant that perfumes our room, that therefore we dislike all other plants in the world."[80] Watkins illustrated the position through a story: on a ship at sea, two men, one white and one black, fall overboard. Five passengers, four white and one black, rush to help. The four white passengers, being prejudiced, all reach for the white man. The black passenger runs to the rescue, stretching out not one hand to the white victim and one to the black, but both to the black man—the one who, "under the circumstances, most needs help." None of this required "the least want of compassion for the white man."[81] Garnet concurred. Refusing to submit to a logic that whites manipulated to their own advantage, he highlighted the ways white Americans benefited by selectively invoking liberalism's guarantee of equal treatment before the law while simultaneously claiming a race-national loyalty that elevated them above all others. "We have no sympathy with that cosmopoliting disposition which tramples upon all nationality, which encircles the universe, but at the same time theorizes away the most needed blessings, and blights the dearest hopes of a people." [82] If whites could invoke the rules selectively for their own benefit, blacks had no choice but to do the same.

As frustrations with the pace of change mounted, later black activism predicated itself increasingly on the principles established in the Whipper-Cornish debate. The national convention of 1848 told African Americans to "get up societies among yourselves, but without exclusiveness." The convention endorsed the notion of race-specific action only as a necessary stopgap. But it conceded the pragmatic need for distinct action, noting the paradox that "we shall undoubtedly for many years be compelled to have institutions of a complexional character, in order to attain this very idea of human brotherhood." [83] The national convention of 1853 urged the establishment of schools solely for the black youth—"not that he himself is so widely different from the white youth," but because he was *treated* differently. "Force of circumstance compels the regulation of schools by us to supply a deficiency produced by our condition." During the same convention, a committee considering the establishment of a manual labor school for blacks argued similarly, stating that a distinct school would be unnecessary if blacks could get the same advantages from existing schools as did whites. [84] The black nationalism of the antebellum period may be considered primarily a result of blacks' resignation to the reality of the rampant racialism of their day more than to an internal sense of widely shared Africanness. "Endeavor to shun it as we may," Martin Delany sighed, "we cannot ignore the fact, that the world is at present . . . enquiring into the condition of the colored races, as a distinct people from the white races." [85] As did Garnet, Delany was saying that, given that racialism could not be eradicated from the American scene, blacks needed to employ it on their own behalf.

This was resistance: deadly serious, overtly political, and potentially militant. Yet it hardly constituted an expression of cultural nationalism that would be familiar to late-twentieth-century audiences. Resistance built on claims of cultural identity offers a source of cohesion that it hopes transcends, and hence is stronger than, that built on political identity. Pragmatically built political identities based on the recognition of shared oppression, it says, are rather easily broken: ruling classes may easily co-opt elite elements of the oppressed or, as James McCune Smith understood, rend the unity of the oppressed by inflicting different measures of oppression on different groups among the oppressed. In contrast, resistance based on cultural identity claims affinities that can never be sundered by otherwise divisive fractures like class, skin color, or regional origin. Purportedly rooted in culture rather than condition, they are immune to co-optation.

But the ideological milieu of antebellum black activists offered poor soil on which such a transcendent cultural identity might flourish. Antebellum black activists were committed above all to the race-blind promises of the Enlightenment and the liberal marketplace; their primary method was to expose the rampant hypocrisy of those who professed faith in liberty and equality but practiced slavery and racial discrimination nonetheless. Black leaders called for racial separation only as a temporary expedient, one predicated on the practical distinctions in the treatment of white and black Americans rather than on inherent cultural or biological differences between the races. They avoided pursuing a strategy that claimed inherent differences between the races because it undermined the twin pillars of their protest thought: the ideology of the American Revolution, which stressed the universal humanity of mankind, and the ideology of environmentalism, which claimed that mutable nurture rather than fixed nature had dictated blacks' lowly fate.

Read through the lens of the culturalist paradigm, calls for separate black institutions are often taken as evidence that black leaders pursued a strategy of cultural separation. In noting that their calls for separate institutions were qualified by their universalism, it would be easy to suggest the opposite—that spokespersons ultimately pursued a strategy of integration and cultural assimilation, even if they used separation as an intermediate stop-gap. Yet neither claim will suffice. Spokespersons' statements are virtually moot on the crucial issue of acculturation, the modern sense of which was not even thinkable to antebellum Americans. To argue that black leaders sought separation only as a temporary and pragmatic response to oppression is not to argue that black thought was ultimately integrationist or as-similationist, for to do so would be to remain bound by modern-day terms of debate, which fail to appreciate the mental world of the antebellum North. Black leaders viewed their efforts, and hence constructed their identity as a race, as the public struggle for their political liberty and rights in a republic. Issues of culture were subordinated utterly to this larger endeavor. The public nature of their quest added an opaque layer of rhetorical exigency to black protest thought, which leaves it largely impenetrable to questions of acculturation. In searching for evidence of cultural autonomy or dependence where it cannot be found, preoccupation with determining the cultural content of black public protest can yield only a misreading of the evidence, regardless whether it ultimately finds or negates cultural autonomy.

This does not mean that the pragmatic political identity forged by black leaders was free of the conundrums and inconsistencies that have plagued later black identities built on cultural claims. By asserting the distinct interests of black people, it effaced the important reality that many of African descent were also of European descent, for example. Yet despite that, they appropriated the premises of racialism in the service of their own empowerment; contra Whipper, black northerners generally veered away from the dangers of biological and cultural essentialism inherent in many whites' use of it. In fact, their reticence to consciously embrace the essentialism of emerging racial science likely inhibited their development of a black identity predicated on organic cultural links. Even the most ardent advocates of united and exclusive black action premised their arguments not on innate cultural or biological rationales, but on the absolute need to respond communally to group maltreatment. Garnet believed it was oppression's "*mode of operation*—the *how* of the matter" that required attention.[86] James McCune Smith understood that "there must be common oppression to produce common resistance."[87] Resistance based on claims of a distinct and organic cultural genius emerged only around the turn of the twentieth century, the result of ten decades' worth of frustrated struggle combined with new intellectual constructions of culture.[88] Though black leaders became terribly disillusioned as the 1860s loomed, painful experience had not yet led them to alternatives to resistance based on the claims of pragmatic political identities.[89]

Instead, antebellum black nationalism envisioned no race-specific action beyond the time when it was necessary to remedy existing imbalances, and it played only a minor part in nurturing rhetoric of a distinct black culture that might linger on beyond the present time of need. Few black elites in this period even acknowledged the existence of a distinct black culture that they could embrace without harming the movement. Fewer still expressed anything close to an understanding that racism was not simply an aberration in an otherwise perfect political system, but was instead paradoxically intertwined with it—tied to its very core. Far more often they echoed the words of Elizabeth Wicks, a leader in a black women's antislavery society. When African Americans had successfully redeemed the nation, she declared, "all the families and nations of the earth shall be of one mind," and "all nations shall adore one God."[90]

Each belongs here or anywhere, just as much
as the well-off—just as much as you;
Each has his or her place in the procession.
Walt Whitman, "I Sing the Body Electric"

CHAPTER 2

Besieged by Freedom's Army

Antislavery Celebrations and Black Activism

Since the time when they first compelled Africans to work and live in their midst, white Americans manifested an ambivalent fascination with their bondsmen. In the North as well as the South, the bodies of African Americans often served as blank screens upon which white Americans might project their own desires and insecurities. Their perceptions of slave folkways tended to reflect their own secret fears and longings rather than the realities of African culture. When in the summer of 1831 an anonymous white resident of Lynn, Massachusetts, attended for the last time the discontinued African American festival known as Negro Election Day, his feelings of loss for an opportunity to experience black culture moved him to poetry:

> And is Election Day no more? . . .
> No more shall "the Governor"
> Sit in his great arm-chair,
> To encounter the stare
> Of the idle mixed multitude,
> Black spirits and white.[1]

Negro Election Day, a distinctly black manipulation of white election-day celebrations, offered the Lynn poet opportunities to observe and, more importantly, vicariously participate in, black folk culture. Moving from images of distanced observation to those of inclusion, the poet's lyrical recollection of Election Day destroys the space between the white observer and the black festival-goer, inserting the writer directly into the proceedings. Election Day permits him at first merely to watch Old Willis play the fiddle, Gid "hustle coppers," or "the niggers play 'paw-.'" As the poem continues, his participation deepens, becoming more intimate: he would eat "'Lection cake," "drink muddy beer," and finally dance with "Suke."

The Lynn poet celebrated dwindling opportunities to experience safely what seemed to him the freedom of the vulgar and alien culture of African slaves, lamenting that whites would no longer casually share public spaces with blacks as an "idle mixed multitude." As blacks in the North became free, whites excluded them in new ways from the realms of public culture. Even in entertainments designed for whites that depicted blacks, such as blackface minstrelsy, African Americans were excluded. Instead, white people themselves appropriated the mantle of blackness, smearing burnt cork on their faces in a gesture of control over a black culture newly harnessed for the expression of antebellum America's expanding anxieties.[2] Freed from bondage and the controls of white masters, and subject now to the dangerous tutelage of radical white abolitionists, black people exhibiting their solidarity and expressing their culture in public no longer seemed at all safe to most northern whites. The success of black slaves against European armies in the Haitian Revolution and the southern slave conspiracies of Gabriel Prosser, Denmark Vesey, and Nat Turner offered uncomfortable reminders that black people were neither pets nor children whose culture was to be enjoyed at whim. In the decades following the turn of the nineteenth century, African American folk festivals like Election Day ceased to function as quaint releases from the rigors of daily life, as events to be relished with security. Instead, they became expressions of an uncivilized presence in the midst of a society as increasingly concerned with its propriety as with its safety. In language laced with concern over the lower orders of all colors "gambling and dancing" and drinking and parading together, northern cities and states passed ordinances restricting or banning public celebrations catering to black people.[3]

If the passing of Negro Election Day helped signal a fundamental transformation in the racial perceptions and practices of white people, it also marked a transition in the ways African Americans in the North inserted themselves into the public life of America. Black public celebrations did not die, they merely transformed. In the wake of slavery's demise in the North, and in the face of hostile new measures designed to uphold slavery in the South by fostering racial inequality in the North, a new generation of black leaders employed the public celebration in the freedom struggle. While black public gatherings continued to offer opportunities for the expression of northern African American culture, freedom transformed them in significant ways. The absence of master paternalism sharply reduced the social controls that had made the festivals safe for men like the Lynn poet, rendering them considerably more threatening to whites. The presence at celebrations of outspoken new black leaders and their white abolitionist allies enhanced such fears. The primary figures of authority hovering over African American celebrations shifted from white masters, who formerly had been conspicuous if only through their absence, to new generations of black community activists, who concerned themselves with the most intimate details of the celebrations.

Under the guidance of this new class of leaders, black public celebrations took on new forms and functions. The design, preparation, and execution of the antislavery celebrations themselves illustrated the process through which black activist elites employed celebrations to fold black public expression into the antislavery movement, creating a culture of abolitionist agitation. In the process, these elites sought to reinforce their authority as leaders by exerting their capacity for staging mass gatherings that could attract the attention of their constituency. Evident in their plans and discussions were their ambivalent attitudes toward those they purported to lead. African American elites, though they felt socially distinct from many black people in their communities, understood the need to forge bonds with their non-elite brethren, which would advance both the freedom struggle and their own authority as leaders.

In shaping post-1830 celebrations, the social outlooks and concerns of these new leaders replaced the begrudging compliance of patronizing and relatively disinterested masters. Whereas Pinkster and Election Day had been occasions for displaying the culture of non-elite African Americans, the new festivities took on the social perspectives of their new orchestrators, who tended to be drawn from the elites of their communities. The forms that these gatherings took provide examples of the social tensions that beset antebellum black communities in the North as well as the limited bonding between elite and non-elite that also occurred. While elite African Americans remained sundered from their non-elite brethren, they tried to use public celebrations as a way of incorporating the non-elite into a culture of activism, one that promised new fruits in the struggle to free the enslaved and elevate the emancipated.[4]

GLITTERING FOLLIES OF ARTIFICIAL DISPLAY

From the middle of the eighteenth century through the 1820s, scattered records of black public festivities such as Election Day, Pinkster, and Militia or Training Day offer rare glimpses of insight into African American folk culture and its expression in the urban North. These celebrations permitted black people to express themselves with the qualified sanction of the slave regime and its successors. Opportunities to congregate, gamble, drink, eat, sing, dance, and wear fine clothing all provided cathartic release from pent-up frustration, as well as respite from daily toil. Cultural fusion engineered by black people lay at the center of such festivals and revealed the propensity of enslaved African Americans to appropriate the culture of Anglo-Americans, layering on it forms and meanings derived from an African cultural heritage. Pinkster, for example, began as a Dutch celebration of Pentecost observed throughout the eighteenth century in the Hudson River valley. By the last quarter of the eighteenth century, the importation of slaves into New York directly from Africa and the weakening of Dutch cultural observances in the wake of the American Revolution had transformed the holiday into a distinctly African American event. Negro Election Day served as African Americans' take on white election day gatherings in New England. Early summer in the North also witnessed Militia or Training Days, during which slaves and freemen gathered to watch black men train with arms. These events, all descended from the social practices of European Americans, became in slave practice opportunities to express African culture as embodied in song, dance, and a host of other communal activities.

Black people employed the festivals to signify upon the cultural forms of whites, parodying and satirizing the society of their masters and former masters. Election Day manifested protopolitical features, as when local blacks elected "Governors" or "Kings" who dictated black and even white behavior for the limited time they were granted total authority. While whites ridiculed the fierce electioneering for these positions that occurred among leading African Americans in the weeks before the festival, such activities partially lampooned white election behavior. Negro Militia Days, during which laughter and rum were reportedly present in ample quantities, were clear attempts to mock white training days. They offered liberal opportunities to illustrate the ironies of governments that called upon their disfranchised inhabitants for protection in time of need.[5] The festivals of the

North provided unique social spaces in which conventional social hierarchies could be explored and even overturned, if only temporarily.[6]

These celebrations died out by 1830, leaving a vacuum in our knowledge of black popular expression in the critical decades before the Civil War. Yet it was no coincidence that Pinkster festivals, Election Days, and Training Days ended in the very period following slavery's death knell in the North. These celebrations had all been associated with the peculiar institution. Masters could rarely exert total control over them: black people shaped them into expressions of a distinct African American folk culture, using them to subvert oppressive authority in a carnivalesque fashion, if only temporarily, and to eke out space within an oppressive system of bondage. However, such events also functioned for white masters as mechanisms of social control, carefully channeling slave resentment through periodic celebrations that only partially undermined masters' authority. In some ways, the act of permitting such limited subversions actually reinforced masters' paternalistic control; their very ability to voluntarily concede their power for limited times signaled their security in their status and constituted an expression of their power. The enslaved and the slaveholders thus understood the usefulness of the slave celebrations differently. The festivals encapsulated a delicate, unspoken balance between slaves, who sought in them the most freedom possible within the confines of bondage, and masters who attempted to reinforce their authority through their concession of limited freedom.[7]

Few whites understood the covert subversion embodied in the black folk expression of the master-sanctioned celebrations. As with the Lynn poet, northern whites had widely viewed Pinkster, Election Day, Training Day, and other celebrations associated with the religious calender as manifestations of blacks' general incapacity to comport themselves publicly in civilized and respectable ways. At one Pinkster celebration, James Fenimore Cooper had observed with a mixture of fascination and revulsion thousands of black people "beating banjoes, singing African songs, drinking, and worst of all, laughing in a way that seemed to see their very hearts with in their ribs." White accounts of black celebrations had enthusiastically embraced racial stereotypes of non-elite African Americans. According to white observers, dancing black people at Pinkster celebrations presented the image of "twisting, wriggling histerical slaves who, for the time, were thousands of miles away in the heart of superstitious Africa." These slaves and former slaves had employed a "hoggish sort of grunting, a bawling and mumbling" as they sang to "barbarous ill-composed" music. Election Day had demonstrated for whites the "spirit of emulation and imitation which is peculiar to their race, and the monkey tribe." The remarks of one observer typified the general attitude of whites toward the slave festivals, in the process enumerating the fears that would make the postslavery celebrations so threatening: "The whole of their vacation was marked by excesses such as might be expected from a class so ignorant and so excitable when freed from restraint."[8]

It was little surprise, then, that the generation of black community figures who emerged from the slave era to lead a new spate of institutions sought to distance themselves from the old festivals, criticizing whatever holdovers remained from the old celebrations. In part, black leaders rejected the exhibitions of African American folk culture in public festivals as painful reminders of black northerners' former servility. The new celebrations struck many leaders as holdovers from a time when whites could afford to permit expressions of black culture in public because of their domination of black bodies. In truth, such expressions had not been merely reflections of masters' power. Black elites, however, by virtue of their freeborn status, time out of slavery, or relative prosperity, were themselves often removed from first-hand experience of the empowering possibilities of such festivities. Steeped deeply in the values of European and American "civilization," they generally failed to appreciate the emancipating potential offered by the public expression of black folk culture.

Sundered from the culture of popular African America, many elite community figures associated expressions of black folk culture with what they took to be ingratiating displays that only fostered the racial prejudice that so inhibited black elevation. Frederick Douglass criticized the alleged preference of non-elite black northerners' for flamboyant public celebrations: "The enemies of our people see this tendency in us, and encourage it. The same persons who would puff such demonstrations in the newspapers, would mob us if we met to adopt measures for obtaining our just rights."[9] The problem, as white abolitionist Gerrit Smith pointed out, was that, hampered by prejudice, blacks suffered under the need to uphold higher standards than whites. "They can join secret societies, and yet be respected," he told a black audience, "but if you indulge in the puerilities and fooleries of the Regalia and Processions of secret societies, you are laughed at for the nonsense, and are denounced for such wicked waste of your wages."[10] Black temperance advocates in Canada echoed the need to demonstrate greater self-control than did whites. "This is our fourth of July," it said of its anniversary celebration. "Though white men get drunk on their's, let us keep sober on ours."[11] Consequently, black national conventions in 1832 and 1834 recommended that African Americans discontinue parades: they were said to be "highly prejudicial to our interests as a people" and to "increase the prejudice and contempt of the whites."[12] These statements all reflected a principle, commonly asserted throughout the period by black leaders in a variety of contexts: "Let us remember," admonished Douglass, "that every impropriety committed by one of us, is charged to the account of our whole people."[13]

Black leaders also believed that working-class African Americans were too ready to forego the serious interests of the race in favor of the immediate gratification of public celebrations. Frederick Douglass complained that black people happily attended such "popular demonstrations" in droves and that these activities were "swallowing up the best energies of many of our best men, contenting them with the glittering follies of artificial display, and indisposing them to seek for solid and important realities."[14] Likewise, Samuel Ringgold Ward believed that Emancipation Day celebrations could not, "from their very nature," lead blacks to larger goals—the "very highest possible attainments in moral eminence."[15]

Often, though, popular black celebrations seemed to conflict with the moral values of black spokespersons. One black Philadelphian decried those who "indulge in the love of show and extravagance, in anniversary processions and entertainments."[16] As editor of *Freedom's Journal*, the nation's first black newspaper, Samuel Cornish launched continual harangues against these offenses to bourgeois sensibilities. Denouncing a black parade in Brooklyn in 1828, he declared, "Nothing serves more to keep us in our present degraded condition, than these foolish exhibitions of ourselves." Public displays of the "debasing excesses" of black people wearing festive clothing and marching together on urban streets made them "laughing stocks" among the city's whites. "Nothing is more disgusting to the eyes of a reflecting man of colour than *one of these grand processions*, followed by the lower orders of society."[17] The New York *Colored American*, under the editorship of Cornish and later Charles B. Ray and Philip Bell, also voiced consistent disapproval of large public antislavery celebrations. In 1837, when a black society in New York City protested the trial of a fugitive slave by holding a raucous "anniversary" parade, the paper defended the group. But it also took the opportunity to "ENTER OUR PROTEST against street processions."[18] In 1840, Newark held a "quite revolting" celebration, according to the paper: "A number came in from the country, with a drum and fife, formed a procession, which was falled in with by a few of the more thoughtless of the place, all of whom conducted themselves in a manner deeply mortifying."[19] James McCune Smith concurred, deploring as antirepublican blacks' "popinjay martial shows[,] in which citizen soldiers show how nearly they can imitate in dress, in step and in music, and standing armies which tyrants alone require." [20]

LARGE AND RESPECTABLE

Despite their concern with the presentation of vernacular black culture, black leaders did not abandon public celebrations. To do so would have been to abandon an important vehicle for effecting change. Celebrations did, after all, occur in public—a public now accessible to freedpeople in ways it never had been before and one that black leaders had no intention of abandoning. For all its dangers, public expression did offer a means of altering white perceptions of blacks. If directed properly, it might even remedy an inequitable racial status quo. Organizers of a women's antislavery fair declared that the funds raised from the public event would be spent "informing and influencing the individuals whose aggregate makes up the public mind" on the horrors of slavery.[21] Even Frederick Douglass conceded that an upcoming August First celebration (the anniversary of British emancipation in the West Indies) would "doubtless be an admirable demonstration, well calculated to impress the public mind with ideas and principles which must save the nation, if it be ever saved, from the crime and curse of slavery." [22] According to Douglass, antislavery celebrations allowed leaders "to bring our people together, and enable us to see and commune with each other to mutual profit." [23] In his report of Rochester's Emancipation Day celebration for 1848, William C. Nell explained the educational role of banners at public celebrations: "Flags were displayed at prominent stations on Main street, and as they waived in the streets, the uninitiated learned the *why* and *wherefore* of this gathering of freemen." [24]

The problem confronting black activists was thus to pursue the freedom struggle by presenting blacks as a powerful public force. The answer lay in orchestrating public festivities that balanced the concern for presenting black behavior with the need to attract large crowds of participants. This is what black critics of public celebrations had missed—that new events could be formulated that might bypass the dangers of the master-sanctioned festivals. Nothing better illustrated the competing imperatives of the new generation than a stock phrase that appeared in nearly every black-authored account of antislavery celebrations. Reporters referred so frequently to black public gatherings as "large and respectable" that the phrase became a genre convention. Its ubiquity suggested not its meaninglessness, however, but its centrality to black leaders' goals.

Large numbers being the first requirement of successful mass celebrations, organizers consciously engineered their events to appeal to a popular black audience. George Weir, a black leader in Buffalo, invited the black community throughout the state "to marshal her sons and daughters to innumerable hosts, throughout the entire length and breadth of her borders; and at the appointed time crowd every avenue and thoroughfare that shall lead safely to the Queen city."[25] The public processionals and parades often incorporated into Emancipation Day celebrations enhanced the populist nature of these events. A New York City gathering that protested a fugitive slave's trial in 1837 marched along Broadway, bearing banners, wearing hats labeled with antislavery mottoes, and playing music.[26] In 1838, those attending a Cincinnati celebration of Emancipation Day "assembled to a large number" along with their school children, and "went in procession through a portion of the city, to the church," where they heard addresses and prayers.[27] In Boston in 1843, a procession of African Americans celebrating Emancipation Day was so large that "multitudes" were unable to enter the church where it ended.[28]

Martial displays and music further underscored the pageantry of celebrations, designed to attract mass crowds. Such was the case with an Emancipation Day gathering of former slaves in 1842 in Chatham, Canada, where on the free soil of Great Britain African American men could bear arms without incurring the wrath of proslavery mobs. The festivities began at daybreak, with cannons firing a twenty-one-gun salute, and continued on throughout the day and evening, when black soldiers in the Queen's pay hosted a feast with dancing.[29] In 1848 in Rochester cannon also were fired, "in imitation of the great American Fourth of July demonstrations."[30] Plans included not one but three mounted marshals, who led a procession while "Adams's famed Bugle Band filled the air with the most witching music."[31] New Bedford African Americans in 1858 put on an impressive military display for Emancipation Day, which must have been typical of many:

> At about 10 o'clock, the New Bedford Blues, Capt. Robert Gibson, numbering some twenty guns, and accompanied by the North Bridgewater Brass Band, Geo. E. Kingley, leader, eighteen pieces, marched to the New Bedford and Taunton depot to receive the Liberty Guards, of Boston, Capt. Lewis Gaul. The Guards turned out twenty-five muskets, and were accompanied by the Malden Brass Band, Thomas H. Perkins, leader. Both companies then proceeded to Concert Hall, where a collation was furnished by the Blues to their visitors. Subsequently, the companies reformed, and after marching through several of the principal streets,

halted at the residence of Mr. Richard Johnson, on elm street, where re-freshments were amply provided.

The parade also featured a "procession of colored seamen" and "a company of colored boys, numbering some twenty or more, who were very neatly dressed, and looked well."[32]

Military themes often combined with displays of flags and banners to enhance the mass appeal of black public celebrations. A Philadelphia gathering in 1836 to celebrate West Indian emancipation began when "a number of Ladies" presented "a splendid, appropriate, and chaste *Silken Banner*, emblematic of British W.I. Emancipation." Similar banners flew over many other antebellum gatherings and celebrations. Blacks in Newark protesting a fugitive slave trial in 1837 marched in front of a band, "their hats ornamented with mottoes, such as 'No Slavery,' 'Down the Kidnapping,' &c."[33] To celebrate Emancipation Day in Boston in 1846, "a procession was formed, accompanied by the Union Brass Band, displaying several Banners telling the story of Liberty and Slavery." It paraded through the city to the chapel, where it heard prayers and speeches. At the same time, "another company appeared in Cavalcade, attended by Holcroft's Brass Band," and proceeded to Watertown to hear speeches and make toasts.[34] Buffalo's celebration for 1849 combined musical and visual elements with a martial theme. A grand marshal, accompanied by his "Staff," led a procession of carriages "from which were displayed beautiful and appropriate Banners, presenting a grand and imposing spectacle." Accompanied by a brass band, the procession moved to a local park, where orations were heard and prayers offered.[35]

As did the Buffalo event, the processions generally ended at either a meeting house where speeches were heard or at large outdoor gatherings where food was served. At some celebrations, dancing and socializing supplied key ingredients to the evening festivities. After an Emancipation Day dinner in Cincinnati in 1838, organizers held an "intellectual fair," which looked suspiciously like a good old-fashioned party: "The tables were removed, a platform erected, and seats sufficient to accommodate a numerous concourse of people were prepared, and at 5 o'clock the crowd reassembled, filling every part of the premises."[36] A white observer of black revelers at a Chatham, Ontario, celebration in 1842 noted that "after dark they returned to a room provided them by the kindness of the officers, where having procured some good fiddlers," they danced late into the night.[37] In 1848, Rochester's African American leaders staged two parties. One was "a Fair, commemorative of the Jubilee," for adults. According to a reporter, "parties availed themselves of this medium of interchanging civilities, promenading, &c., an excellent Band tendering its notes to enliven the scene." Meanwhile, "Irving Hall was tastefully decorated for a 'Liberty Festival,' where many of the more youthful class repaired to wind up the day in a manner gratifying to themselves."[38] Given many black reporters' concern with putting a sober and respectable face on accounts of black celebrations, it is likely that dancing was a common though unreported feature of many Emancipation Day gatherings. Organizers intended spaces for dancing and socializing to offer opportunities for a commingling of diverse people, meant to impress upon whites the vision of unified black communities.

The dinners associated with antislavery celebrations offered another highlight that might attract large numbers. Celebrations designed as mass gatherings often offered food for all comers, frequently in a convenient outdoor locale. On August 1, 1832, in Chillicothe, Massachusetts, celebrants "partook of an excellent dinner prepared by the committee in a beautiful grove: after which, several appropriate toasts were drunk."[39] Five years later in New York City, the day ended in a giant dinner, at which "more than three thousand souls partook of this 'feast of fat things,' and mingled their hearts and their voices in songs of PRAISE!"[40] Philadelphia Emancipation Day organizers in 1841 promised an open-air meeting at Wilson's Garden for "dining[,] reading regular and spontaneous sentiments, and various speaking exercises."[41] A "goodly number" of Bostonians in 1843 were treated to a large dinner after Emancipation Day festivities, their children retiring "to an adjoining room where their friends had provided a *Pic Nic.*"[42] In 1848 in New Bedford, Massachusetts, organizers planned an outdoor dinner in a suburban grove, with a committee of women "furnishing the tables with refreshments, for all who may attend freely to partake."[43] Ten years later, organizers offered both "a grand chowder" and "an old-fashioned clam bake."[44] In 1848 in Niles, Michigan, Henry Bibb recorded details of a typical feast:

> A general invitation was given by the marshall of the day, to partake of a fine dinner which had been prepared for this occasion; all were invited without regard to color, to partake of the cheer in commemoration of the day that gave 300,000 slaves their liberty. A regular and well formed procession moved from the grove appointed for the meeting to the table, where we found a sumptuous entertainment consisting of all the luxuries of the season awaiting us. A well ordered or better repast is seldom got up.[45]

Reporters often attested to the success of these devices at attracting large crowds. The audience for a Philadelphia celebration of British West Indies Emancipation in 1836 consisted of "several hundred persons—all of whom appeared to be gratified with the proceedings."[46] In 1837, New York leaders staged an Emancipation Day celebration that witnessed the gathering of 3,500 black and white citizens in the Broadway Tabernacle to listen to Lewis Tappan, the white abolitionist, and Theodore S. Wright, a local black leader.[47] A Cincinnati celebration of Emancipation Day in 1838 attracted so many that "the church was filled to overflowing."[48] In the relatively small town of Niles, Michigan, Henry Bibb participated in an Emancipation Day celebration in 1848, reporting that "several hundred persons were in attendance."[49] Capturing best the mass appeal of the black public celebration, William C. Nell remarked that an August First celebration in Rochester in 1848 was so well attended that the city "seemed besieged by Freedom's army."[50] A hostile white press sometimes confirmed large numbers. In 1837, a society of black abolitionists in New York City decided to celebrate its anniversary in the midst of a trial of a fugitive slave. "A party of negroes amounting to several hundreds" gathered, causing local whites some alarm.[51]

THE MOST PERFECT QUIETNESS AND GOOD ORDER

Numbers alone, however, were never sufficient to guarantee the success of antislavery celebrations. Just as important as evidence of popular support were demonstrations of the respectable character of the commemorations. Occasionally event planners heeded calls to refrain from processions; as *Freedom's Journal* reported, "no public parade added to the confusion of the day" of New York City's 1827 celebration of abolition in that state.[52] Even when processions were staged, leaders often took special care to forestall potential disorder. When announcing celebration plans, New York organizers regularly assured the public that blacks "shall do no act that may have the least tendency to disorder," promising, "we will therefore abstain from all processions in the public streets on that day."[53] Others lent a flavor of domestic tranquility to their processions by incorporating large contingents of schoolchildren.[54] Newspaper reports of celebrations delighted in remarking upon the sobriety and orderliness with which black participants had conducted themselves. Celebrants in Philadelphia in 1836 were reported to have "separated at an early hour, and retired to their homes in the most perfect quietness and good order—nothing having occurred to mar the pleasure of which all partook in the festivities of the day."[55] At the Cincinnati Emancipation Day celebration in 1838, "nothing occurred to disturb in the slightest degree, that good feeling and enthusiastic rapture which obviously pervaded every bosom."[56] Clearly, the objective of organizers was to yield the type of reports that followed the August First gathering of several thousand in Rochester, New York, to celebrate British West Indies emancipation: "The day passed harmoniously, soberly, and pleasantly, without any of those riotous manifestations which are too apt to disgrace the rejoicing days both of the blacks and the whites."[57] Others who witnessed the event remarked, "The conduct of the active participants [was] such as to draw out approbatory remarks from those who have before ridiculed like celebrations."[58]

Beyond scaling back plans for public processions, organizers employed a variety of measures to temper the popular spirit of their events. While some Emancipation Day celebrations included all comers free of charge, others restricted the offerings to ticket holders, often termed "subscribers." In Philadelphia in 1836, for instance, planners organized a "sumptuous dinner" reserved for "subscribers and invited guests."[59] Ticket requirements were more than simply a means of restricting participation, however. Often, organizers intended earnings from ticket sales to assist with fund-raising efforts. Large celebrations taxed considerably the wealth and energies of organizers; tickets offered a way to partially recoup expenses. Some organizers hoped to do more than break even, using ticket sales to raise funds for their organization or for special projects. The *Colored American* benefited from the philanthropy of at least two Emancipation Day celebrations. One held in Cincinnati in 1838 garnered five dollars for the organ, while a Detroit Emancipation Day gathering the following year collected twenty dollars for it.[60] In 1846, the Torrey Monument Association of Boston, which was dedicated to erecting a statue to imprisoned Underground Railroad conductor Reverend Charles T. Torrey, apparently sought to employ Emancipation Day as a means of raising funds.[61] Efforts to stage events with mass appeal were often rewarded. Parades, bands, military displays, and free food attracted so many to New Bedford's 1858 observance of Emancipation Day that leaders collected $29.70 in voluntary contributions.[62] A "small, though very respectable and intelligent audience" attended the anniversary of Philadelphia's Banneker Institute in 1858, netting $4.47 for the society's coffers. Based on this success, the Institute resolved to parlay the celebration's public appeal into increased membership, which it hoped would support its efforts to elevate the minds of black Philadelphians. It embarked upon a course of public lectures at a cost of twenty-five cents each, but, perhaps lacking the populistic appeal of Emancipation Day gatherings, they were so poorly attended they had to be suspended.[63]

Ticket purchases often restricted popular participation in antislavery celebrations, though to varying degrees, depending on the costs. At the exorbitant rate of $1.25, the tickets for an Emancipation Day dinner in Boston in 1839 likely permitted—by intent—only the city's most elite African

Americans to attend.[64] While fifty enjoyed the dinner, a rival temperance meal the same night, also requiring tickets, attracted a slightly larger crowd of eighty.[65] On the other extreme, the Banneker Institute planned a July Fourth celebration for 1855 at which the popular musician Frank Johnson was to play. Tickets were set at ten cents apiece, and a thousand handbills were printed.[66] Similarly, at its August First celebration the next month, the Institute charged only twenty-five cents.[67] Ticketed antislavery celebrations occupied the broad middle ground in a range of inclusive possibilities. At the most restrictive extreme were the "sumptuous dinners" held as close celebrations of black elites; at the other was the truly mass gathering, de signed to be free for all. Ticketed alternatives acknowledged the expens involved in organizing celebrations while confining participation, as tic prices rose to ever-higher strata of black society. They balanced the bene of mass participation against the great expense their orchestration incur

In addition to using tickets to restrict participation in events, org ers also signaled degrees of respectability and exclusivity through dining plans. Many events included both mass and elite components. Restricted dinners might be held in the evening after large public parades, perhaps while open "fairs" or parties were underway. Organizers designed antislavery celebrations expressly to appeal to a broad and socially heterogeneous audience by offering a range of experiences for a variety of social strata. William C. Nell likely had this goal in mind when he wrote of Rochester's celebration in 1848 that the event had "been enjoyed in various ways by the vast concourse."[68] Frederick Douglass hinted at the broad and populistic appeal of celebration days as times "when every man may seek his happiness in his own way, and without any very marked concern for the ordinary rules of decorum."[69]

At smaller gatherings, food might be confined to dinners offered for a smaller number of leaders, ticket holders, and invited guests. After an Emancipation Day parade in Philadelphia in 1836, "the company proceeded to an adjoining lot, where a sumptuous dinner, on the Temperance plan— prepared under the direction of the committee—was spread."[70] After an Emancipation Day address in Boston in 1839, organizers planned that "the friends of union, the orator, the President of the day, invited guests, and the committee [of arrangements] will proceed to the Union Dinner, to be served up at Mr. Taft's, Chelsea, at 3 o'clock."[71] Others in Boston organized a rival dinner the same year, inviting a select few to "partake of a fine *Temperance Dinner*" at a local hotel.[72] Organizers of a Philadelphia celebration in 1841 preceded the public festivities with "an elegant temperance dinner" the night before.[73]

Such restricted meals signaled that in many respects two celebrations were under way on celebration days—one for an elite leadership, and one for black working people. Leaders' efforts to regulate behavior at public celebrations further highlighted the social divisions apparent at them. The need for sobriety figured particularly prominently among organizers. As reports suggested, organizers intended more than a few festive gatherings to be dry. A Philadelphia Emancipation Day celebration in 1836 concluded with a "Temperance Festival," or dry party, open to all.[74] After an August First parade in 1838, several hundred residents of Cincinnati gathered at the house of a local patron where, "by previous arrangement, a plain, economical, total abstinence dinner had been prepared."[75] Temperate gatherings reflected the reform roots of many leaders, and the concern for respectable public behavior they implied.

Often, however, temperance at antislavery celebrations was honored only in the breach, as some gatherings advertised as "temperance" observances apparently offered at least ale and wine. A patronizing white witness lauded the sobriety of black celebrants in Chatham, Ontario, in 1842, observing that "although liquors of all kinds were in abundance, not one man of the company did we notice intoxicated." The reporter attributed this respectable behavior to the fact that many black attendees were members of the local Temperance Society and hence drank only in moderation.[76] Other reports sometimes noted a distinction between "total-abstinence" drinkers and the mere "temperance drinker."[77] That black observers often took special pains to report that at some dinners the routine toasts were made with something other than alcohol suggests that some alcohol, if not hard spirits, was often present at other gatherings.[78] Accounts of a celebratory dinner in Buffalo in 1840, for example, took pains to note that toasts were drunk with lemonade and cold water.[79] Elite black leaders may have considered true temperance quite appropriate for unelevated black urbanites with suspect self-control. Especially at their elite dinners, they likely considered themselves capable of thwarting alcohol's ill effects if they imbibed with moderation.[80] Given the centrality of temperance reform to many of the black leaders who reported on celebration proceedings, the lack of clear reference to dry meals during many celebrations suggests alcohol's presence at more than a few gatherings, some of them designed for large audiences. Though most leaders regarded working people's use of liquor with deep wariness, they may have considered the availability of alcohol an important concession to popular feeling, and necessary to attract a mass audience of non-elite black people.

OF WHAT PROFIT?

Local organizers often used antislavery celebrations as opportunities to function in their capacity as antislavery activists and to enforce their hegemony as community leaders. Those who staged antislavery celebrations stood to gain benefits that apparently outweighed the financial and even physical risks implicit in their activity. Organizers were most often community leaders and antislavery activists. As their concern with attracting a mass audience of non-elite African Americans indicated, they derived not a little of their authority directly from their communities. Planning and staging antislavery celebrations played a key role in conferring this authority.

The practice of holding smaller, restricted dinners alongside mass "pic nics" suggested a pattern of social bifurcation that was characteristic of other elements of the antislavery celebration. Meetings of local and regional leaders were far more serious than restricted "sumptuous dinner" entertainments. Emancipation Day in New Bedford in 1858 consisted of both open-air events (including a parade, military display, and picnic), and closed-door happenings capped by a regional convention of black leaders. While both spaces were "public," the convention pretended not to mass appeal but to the serious consideration of a black aristocracy of talent and education. The convention's tone contrasted sharply with the festive atmosphere of the mass gathering. Bela Perry, a delegate from New Bedford, opened the convention by hoping "that this day would be devoted to no glittering bauble of parade and show, nor to social pleasures," but to freedom, "the great principle, which was connected with the day." Charles L. Remond, a black leader from Boston, also wanted to use the occasion for meaningful antislavery activity, calling for "something more than display, something more than music, something more than prayers." Coming from celebration organizers, these statements did not reject efforts at mass appeal, they signaled a transition in the proceedings—from the gaiety of the mass parade or picnic to the contemplation of serious matters by a select group.[81] At more than a few celebrations, organizers split the proceedings into mass gatherings and more elite convention-oriented activities.[82] The conventions held at some antislavery celebrations illustrated the dual nature of black leadership. On the one hand, black leaders were community figures, active at the local level; on the other, they participated in an activist culture with networks spread across the nation and linked by a black press. National leadership had meaning only so far as leaders could count on the support of their communities.

Black elites dominated celebration domains other than the sumptuous dinners and conventions. Successful celebrations were never spontaneous, and planning them was a far from trivial matter, one that could be accomplished only by elites with resources and personal connections. The meetings to organize the celebrations themselves tended to be the province of community leaders; organized into committees of arrangements, they met often with other leaders to plan the event.[83] These men were nearly always black activists who were energetic locally in conventions, the press, or the pulpit: in Boston, Charles L. Remond and James G. Barbados; in Buffalo, George Weir Jr.; in Cincinnati, John I. Gaines; in Detroit, H. Ford Douglass; in New York, Theodore S. Wright; in Philadelphia, James McCrummell and Jacob C. White; and in Rochester, William C. Nell. Notably absent from this group were the names of national figures such as Frederick Douglass or Henry Highland Garnet. Usually committed to speak at these gatherings rather than plan them, the true celebrities of the black antislavery movement represented a yet higher strata of leadership. The very success of these national leaders as antislavery lecturers and their links to the white abolitionist movement were more likely to render them distant from the communities in which they lived.

Local leaders met in committee for months beforehand to make preparations and publicize an event.[84] In his report on a Rochester Emancipation Day celebration in 1848, William C. Nell detailed the lengths to which organizers often went: "Extensive notice had been circulated in the various counties, a majority of which responded in large delegations by cars, stage, canal, packet, and private conveyances. The railroad company reduced their fare, in accommodation to the times, and on the evening preceding the First, the sub-committees were busy securing those facilities in the public houses which the proprietors generally tendered."[85] Given the complexity of organizing such large occasions, potential problems were virtually numberless. In Buffalo in 1849, disasters both natural and manmade conspired against success. After a cholera epidemic reduced the number of participants drastically, the featured speaker, Henry Highland Garnet, failed to appear because of a dispute over the terms on which he would come. Organizers claimed he had agreed to speak for his expenses; he said he would work only for the considerable sum of forty dollars.[86] Mass celebrations confronted organizers with a host of logistical problems. Though "between three and four hundred persons" attended the Banneker Institute's open-air August First celebration in Philadelphia in 1858, "quite a number succeeded in getting upon the grounds without paying." According to one member, this problem, combined with the low cost of the tickets sold, prevented the event "from being any profit to us, in a pecuniary sense."[87] This report's qualification of its losses was significant: even if events did not go off exactly as planned, leaders nonetheless appreciated the benefits they accrued in status and community solidarity.

In some years the task of orchestrating mass events simply proved too great for local black leaders. Toward the end of July 1839, the *Colored American* reported that none of the various groups that had organized previous Emancipation Day celebrations had yet made preparations for the upcoming August First, likely because of the considerable expense involved.[88] Elites strapped for resources could always fall back on a restricted "sumptuous dinner." This was by far the cheaper route, and could be rationalized by a perceived need to limit white exposure to displays of black non-elite behavior, especially that sanctioned by black leaders.

Leaders took on the considerable burdens of organizing antislavery celebrations for two primary reasons. First, staging antislavery celebrations was crucial in establishing and maintaining their authority as community leaders. The great efforts required to organize these events constituted an expression of wealth and power within the community, manifest in the quantity of food served, the quality of the music offered, and the complexity of the web of personal relationships necessary to orchestrate the occasion. In this sense, antislavery celebrations echoed elements of the older slave festivals, which had conferred authority upon the well-off slaves of the white elites who funded them. As a concomitant of his community-conferred social status, the "King" of Pinkster or "Governor" of Election Day bore responsibility for serving up a fete for local slaves. Favored bondsmen had relied upon their wealthy masters to enhance their status, and masters themselves competed for status among each other by providing their elected charges with special clothing and the resources to host the requisite feasts. One white contemporary claimed that "it was degrading to the reputation of the owner if his slave appeared in inferior apparel" at such festivities. E. R. Potter, a Rhode Island state legislator whose slave John frequently took part in Election Day campaigning, joked to his friends that "one or the other must give up politics, or the expense would ruin them both."[89]

So too the freemen who staged antislavery celebrations used their relative wealth to position themselves as important figures willing and capable of serving the community. But if the governors and kings of black celebrations had served as a kind of community leadership deeply intertwined with the institution of slavery, the free leadership that staged antislavery celebrations sought to nullify such associations. In freedom, the governors and kings of the old celebrations receded into vestigial roles, such as grand marshal of the antislavery parade. As in Pinkster or Election Day, marshals like Buffalo's Benjamin F. Goury or Boston's James Leach were popular community figures. Yet with the exception of a select few, like New York City's Samuel Hardenburg, their names routinely failed to appear among those associated with community activism and antislavery activity.[90] Black leaders likely intended the position of grand marshal as a gesture to the popular feeling of the community, designed to create goodwill between celebration organizers and the community rank and file. The real power behind the antislavery celebrations rested with those who organized and paid for them, and these were a class of community elites who sought to remove the traces of slavery from the gatherings while simultaneously appealing to former slaves.[91]

The older festivals also had conferred authority on the masters who permitted the events. In the figure of the black community leader, the antislavery celebration melded the elected black "king" with the silent white master who had permitted and funded the older celebrations. Omnipresent in the slave festivals but notably absent from the antislavery celebrations were instances of "toasting" and other forms of social inversion behavior, which would have undermined the authority of the community leaders who organized the new gatherings. Yet while black leaders did not countenance satire directed from non-elite African Americans at themselves, neither did the black elite mock black commoners. To do either would have violated the principle of racial unity that was becoming so central to black leaders' understanding of their role in the community and nation.

THE CALL FOR COMBINATION

Beyond their role in enforcing black elites' status as community leaders, antislavery celebrations' second function was to help define a new era of aggressive and confrontational racial politics. The new stress that organizers placed on the conduct of black celebration-goers by no means guaranteed whites' favorable reception. In nearly every respect, antislavery celebrations nurtured the fears and raised the ire of an oppressive society.

In a series of "Bobalition" broadsides that appeared in the North in the 1810s and early 1820s, prejudiced whites employed the emerging language of blackface minstrelsy to parody black public celebrations. The stereotyped versions of African Americans presented in these broadsides depicted black public celebrations as the domain of leaders who went to extreme lengths but uniformly failed to impose the discipline demanded of participants. The broadsides' stereotyped versions of black speech were littered with the sort of malapropisms that gave the broadsides their titles, further suggesting black leaders' futile and ludicrous incapacity to live up to white standards (see Plate 2). A parody of a Boston antislavery celebration from 1821, in which the members of a black abolition society instruct the parade's grand marshal on protocol, revealed African Americans' alleged propensity for disorder, violence, and foppery:

> If any out of order, and he no get in agin when you tell um, you hab de authority of de shochietee [society] for hit him rap on de head. But you must on no count trike him on de shin, else you make he nose bleed, and so stain he ruffle shirt and he nice white trowsaloon. But from de well known lub of order and good principle which hab always been de character of de members of de Shocietee I think you will hab no need to exhort to such displeasant method of dissumpline.[92]

The bobalition broadsides appeared on the cusp of the transition from old to new black celebrations; they bridged the gap between master-sanctioned slave celebrations and the new era of conflicted ethnic, class, and racial politics. By putting vulgar dialect and manners into the mouths of black leaders, they conflated the preindustrial frivolity of the enslaved and the aggressive new activism of the free. They thus sought to undermine blacks' new claims to participate legitimately in public sphere discourse by pulling those claims against the stream of progress, back into the realm of a passing age of patron-client relations.

Stereotypes of African Americans that arose from antislavery celebrations reflected white fears of free black people seeking to "rise" to higher social stations through community and antislavery activism. These fears were compounded by the sheer novelty of the appearance of large groups of African Americans in public places, earnestly asserting the worthiness of their demands for equality and abolition. Pinkster and Election Days had often been confined to marginal spaces on the urban periphery; antislavery parades intruded directly onto the thoroughfares of the growing metropolis. In the first half of the nineteenth century, these streets became stages for the public presentation of conflicting class, ethnic, and racial interests. Through their organization and composition, public parades could present conceptions of labor hierarchy, class antagonism, or immigrant demands. Similarly, black northerners employed them to assert their right to public spaces and hence an equal role in the civic community. Presentation of the demands of labor radicals presented images that were troubling enough for antebellum urbanites; black parades that threatened the racial hierarchies that Americans increasingly relied upon to understand the organization of their society seemed radically subversive.[93]

The new celebrations intensified and modified old patterns of urban and

PLATE 2. *"Grand Bobalition, or 'Great Annibersary Fussible.'"* *Employing emerging racial stereotypes to mock blacks' alleged inability to replicate America's civic celebrations, "bobalition" broadsides such as these parodied a new generation of black leaders' efforts to fold older forms of public celebration into antislavery activism. Woodcut with letterpress (Boston, 1821), Broadside Collection, portfolio 53, no. 11, Rare Book and Special Collections Division, Library of Congress, Washington, D.C.*

racial violence. In the days of Pinkster and Negro Election, African Americans in public had often come under physical attack from whites. As a young white artisan in late eighteenth-century Philadelphia, William Otter and his friends had assaulted black churchgoers during services.[94] As a youth in Boston, Sol Smith, a nineteenth-century theater manager, had roamed the streets with his fellow "Republican boys" enforcing a thuggish racial order. Smith recalled an instance in 1814 in which, "as was usually done on all occasions of gathering," he and his fellows "chased all the niggers off the Common." Smith also noted, however, that Negro Election was the one day when "the colored people were permitted to remain unmolested on Boston Common."[95] Thus, while African Americans clearly had been targeted in the riots and public violence of the early national period, their public gatherings had been sanctioned within prescribed, marginalized social spaces. Up through the early nineteenth century, they had frequently participated in public violence as well. Black faces were seen amidst the pre-Revolutionary mobs of colonial New York, and African American women helped riot against New York City officials charged with collecting poor peoples' unpenned hogs in 1821. African Americans also participated in labor unrest in the city in 1825.[96]

The limited and highly qualified acceptance of black people in American public culture ended as labor competition developed along with the rising market economy. As public concern over the racial mixing of working people grew in the 1820s and 1830s, demands for segregated work and leisure spaces intensified. White northerners withdrew the exemptions they had provided on Election Days and Pinkster. Mob activity shifted from racially indiscriminate actions intended to remedy violations of public morals to overt attempts to impose racial order.[97] The early 1830s witnessed a spate of race riots in major cities such as Philadelphia, New York, and Cincinnati. In attacking churches and temperance halls, mobs targeted symbols of black social and economic "elevation."[98] At the same time, whites directed their hostility at the labor competition of non-elite African Americans. An investigatory committee attributed a Philadelphia riot in 1834 in part to the opinion of local white workers that employers preferred to hire blacks for lower wages. "In consequence of this preference, many whites, who are able and willing to work, are left without employment."[99]

Often, the local authorities investigating these events referred to the unelevated natures of black workers. The citizens' committee that investigated a Philadelphia riot in 1834 spoke directly to the issue of black behavior, urging African American leaders to impress upon the city's blacks "the necessity, as well as the propriety, of behaving themselves inoffensively and with civility at all times."[100] In the same year, whites in Columbia, Pennsylvania, laid the responsibility for a bloody race riot at the feet of African Americans: "Must the poor honest [white] citizens that so long have maintained their families by their labor, fly from their native place that a band of disorderly Negroes may revel with the money that ought to support the white man and his family, comit the most lascivious and degrading actions with impunity, and wanton in riot and debauchery. Who in this town does not know in what manner many Negroes spend their leisure hours."[101]

White workers found black celebrations especially provocative statements of blacks' new demand to be included in public life. In Philadelphia in 1842, the resentment of unemployed white workers toward an Emancipation Day parade touched off a brutal race riot. Rioters alleged that a banner carried in the parade by the Young Men's Vigilant Society depicted a town in flames, and constituted an incitement to slave revolt. They responded with a two-day campaign of violence in which a church and two meeting halls were destroyed. A white grand jury blamed the riot on the provocative nature of the black parade.[102] Reports consistently documented the provocative nature of black processions, such as the black Masons who "moved in force" down New York City streets on St. John's Day (June 25) in 1827.[103] The militant implications of Buffalo's 1860 commemoration of John Brown's death seemed to require special attention to orderliness; one black reporter made special note that "peace and quietness reigned throughout the day."[104] Rochester's celebration in 1848 recalled the radical specter of the French Revolution: the band played "the ever animating and welcome *Marseillaise*, [and] the procession came to order around the platform dedicated to 'Liberty, Fraternity, and Equality.'"[105]

The new celebrations signaled not simply the emergence of a new generation of leaders, but of a new style of protest. The antislavery celebrations of the antebellum years are often considered logical extensions of the protopolitical slave festivals, especially Negro Election Day.[106] Yet the shift from master-sanctioned slave festivals to activist-led antislavery celebrations spoke to important discontinuities in the evolution of black protest—discontinuities that mirrored changes in the tenor of America's racial politics. Whereas the slave festivals had provided opportunities for African Americans to protest an oppressive regime, the mechanism of social inversion could deflect protest by safely channeling it away from structural change. Though enacted in public, the protest involved in the slave festivals occurred largely within the confines of the master-slave relationship and its paternalistic style of politics. For these reasons, the slave celebrations may have registered dissatisfaction but generally failed to encounter the public sphere—to engage its arguments, counter its charges, or challenge its terms of debate. In contrast, the new celebrations were suited to an emerging era of conflicted mass politics, in which the realm of the public increasingly became a venue for mediating social contests that may or may not have found their way into formal politics. Far more conscious than the slave festivals of their role in public sphere discussions of race and slavery, the new celebrations had a greater claim to being overtly political, in the sense that they directly addressed the destruction of the slave system itself.

Black leaders transformed their celebrations into heightened forms of political protest by altering the moments they commemorated. The slave festivals had appropriated religious celebrations and the traditional celebrations and rituals of American social life. Antislavery celebrations created new moments, modeled instead on the civic commemorations of a much more recent American nationalism. In short, through antislavery celebrations black leaders constructed a counternarrative to America's master narrative of racial nationalism.[107] The content and details of the narrative are the subject of later chapters; for now it is sufficient to note that the form and subjects of the new commemorations—counter–July Fourth celebrations, the Haitian Revolution, the abolition of the international slave trade, the final stage of gradual emancipation in New York state, West Indian emancipation, and even John Brown's raid on Harper's Ferry—provided new opportunities to put before the white public the desires and demands of black Americans. The Banneker Institute, a Philadelphia literary and gentlemen's society, noted that such celebrations kept "before the minds of the American people *their* duty to the millions of slaves upon the Southern plantations." That August First followed soon after the Fourth of July helped, for, as one group of event organizers remarked, it "gives abolitionists a fine opportunity to expose the holl[ow]-heartedness of American liberty and christianity, and to offset the buncombe speeches made upon our national anniversary."[108] Jeremiah Sanderson accepted an invitation to speak at an Emancipation Day celebration in Boston in 1842, declaring that such celebrations had great effect on the American people. "It seems to me they must at length be convinced of the perfect expediency, and safety, as well as duty, of obeying God, 'breaking every yoke, and letting the oppressed go free.'"[109]

Organizers frequently incorporated important gestures of racial politics into the form of their events. Some Emancipation Day celebrations made important statements by providing refreshments in the form of "Free Labor produce," or goods ensured to have been grown by unenslaved workers.[110] Many events incorporated contemporary racial politics, as when Buffalo commemorated John Brown's death in 1860 with a spate of indoor sermons and speeches.[111] Even the old festivals could take on new functions in the new atmosphere of racial politics. Decades after the demise of Negro Training Day, Thomas Van Rennselaer, an African American, mistakenly received an order to attend militia training, which was open to whites only. As a form of satire, Van Rennselaer showed up for the training, where he was informed that blacks were not permitted to participate. A reporter noted sardonically that "in cases of actual necessity the State will permit them to enjoy the privilege of being shot, but can in nowise put them to the inconvenience of any previous preparation."[112]

Celebrations of Independence Day proved most malleable to the political needs of black activists. The Fourth of July provided prime opportunities to expose the hypocrisies of the slaveholding republic. Many years African Americans held Independence Day protest celebrations, usually on July 5. Black Philadelphians reportedly avoided festivities on the Fourth of July, for, in the words of the *Weekly Anglo-African*, "The people generally do not understand why one should celebrate a day that . . . brought freedom to the whites and slavery to the colored people."[113] Frederick Douglass converted an invitation to speak at Rochester's Independence Day celebration in 1852 into an opportunity to express the same convictions. "This Fourth of July is *yours*, not *mine*," he told a white audience. "*You* may rejoice, *I* must mourn. To drag a man in fetters into the grand illuminated temple of liberty, and call upon him to join you in joyous anthems, were inhuman mockery and sacrilegious irony."[114] In 1854, Boston African Americans requested Massachusetts towns to mark Independence Day in 1854 not with festivities but "by the tolling of bells, and other appropriate means." They intended this display to express "their sense of the disgrace and humiliation of the North" for passing the recent Kansas-Nebraska Bill, and for permitting the recent kidnapping of Anthony Burns, a fugitive slave.[115]

Public celebrations could also literally stage racial politics on urban streets, as illustrated by an incident that occurred in Philadelphia in 1849. When Frank Johnson, the celebrated African American musician, was invited to play in a temperance parade, several white bands refused to participate. In the midst of the turmoil, a group of sympathetic white participants agreed to march with the Johnson band, following the procession "at a sufficient distance to make the cause obvious." Shamed by the gesture, some of the dissenting white bands agreed to reform with the Johnson band among them; others threatened to bolt at such a move. In the end, the Johnson band was permitted to march in the procession as usual, with one dissenting white band distinguishing itself by marching ahead of the procession. Just as much as the content, the form and organization of public celebrations could reflect the *Sturm und Drang* of the freedom struggle.

Finally, the antislavery celebration promised to transform northern black communities from groups of former slaves into a community of racial activists. Black leaders sought to use the gatherings as a way of inculcating in non-elite African Americans a new conception of identity based on the struggle for racial equality in the North and the abolition of slavery in the South. The antislavery celebration provided a way to engage non-elites in what leaders saw as concerns that went beyond the parochial interests of the immediate community. This task was rarely simple, for the lives of most urban African Americans were dominated by daily struggles for survival. Nonetheless, through the addresses of the speakers enlisted for the occasions, black leaders set forth their vision of the race's role in history for their non-elite attendees and kept the tasks before it in the community mind year after year. Amos G. Beman noted that other nations set apart days to "recount the glory of their ancestors"; the antislavery celebration provided black people their time for such commemoration.[116] Public addresses thus served as a vehicle for incubating the collective memory and for passing it on in public spaces in the most popular way possible. It also fostered a sense of collective identity built upon leaders' understanding of the freedom struggle. Through the celebration addresses, black leaders attempted to impart moral lessons to their charges, admonishing them to embrace the virtues they viewed as the means of the race's elevation. It was no accident that black schoolchildren constituted a ubiquitous presence at the celebrations or that banners and displays depicted speakers' themes in easily digestible form. In addition to instilling moral and historical lessons, leaders evinced their faith in progress, God's predestined role for them, and the Enlightenment principle of the universal brotherhood of man, which had animated the Founding Fathers.[117]

There is little doubt that the messages event organizers sent to their non-elite audiences were laden with a didacticism born of the relative luxury of middle-class life. Yet, overriding clear differences in class and social status between elite and popular blacks, leaders shared an affinity with non-elite African Americans that they hoped to nurture through antislavery celebrations. A common identity as an oppressed people fostered close ties that might never have appeared in other contexts. The abolition of slavery in the North in the late eighteenth and nineteenth century undermined a central source of potential social distinction within black communities, ironically and quite unintentionally fostering the concept of racial unity. The idea of race developed in response to slavery's demise as a category of social definition that lumped together all people of African ancestry. Deprived of enslavement as a principle of social division, the white North increasingly employed race as a way to resurrect the alienation not just of formerly enslaved black people, but of all black people, regardless of skin shade, wealth, occupation, or former status of servitude. These pressures countered the social distinctions that bondage had bred, compressing black social structure and creating strong incentives for the establishment of a group identity. While African Americans continued to recognize important distinctions in black society, many leaders sought to transform the degrading unity that white people ascribed to the race, manipulating it into a potent source of black unity and strength.

The leaders who staged antislavery celebrations envisioned a new identity for African Americans of all social strata, predicated upon a rejection of the folk behaviors associated with slavery, such as those appearing at master-sanctioned Pinkster festivals, Election Day celebrations, and Militia Day gatherings. They embraced the opportunity to forge a common identity on the model of their own social values, though they conceded through their design of mass antislavery celebrations the necessity of some accommodation for African Americans not yet elevated. For most leaders, the mass antislavery celebration represented a new space in which black folk expression could occur under the proper oversight of an elite leadership. It offered the possibility of salvaging black folk culture from association with a disgraced, unelevated slave past and endowing it instead with progressive and emancipating associations. This process was never complete and always embodied conflict, but in the early nineteenth century it constituted America's foremost example of a cross-class protest movement.[118]

Despite the evident paternalism of black elites, African American workers still attended the fairs, celebrations, and commemorations. Participation in public festivals provided black workers with moments of respite from continual labor, times when they could relax in the comfort of others who shared their cultural styles and could enjoy themselves relatively unencumbered by the pressures of white and elite black expectations. Through such activities, black non-elites fostered the sense of community critical for maintaining the authority of black leaders as representatives of a "people." To varying degrees, black leaders understood this, even if they did not relish it. Their efforts to organize antislavery celebrations conceded the necessity of attracting audiences of non-elite African Americans, even at the risk of presenting white America with what it viewed as images of black impropriety.

To some non-elite African Americans, it may have mattered not *who* offered the picnic, so long as they had a place at the table. More likely, however, non-elite black people understood the new celebrations in the context of an increasingly hostile white America. Working-class African Americans could not help but feel the impacts of racialization in the North. They sensed it in the loss of the franchise in states where previously they had held it, in the imposition of new laws demanding that they post bond for "good behavior" when entering states like Ohio for the first time, in the clear transition of mob activity from a moral to a racial nature, in the appearance of racist stereotypes in the cheap almanacs they bought or saw, in the vitriol spewing increasingly from the proslavery press, in the labor competition introduced by European immigrants, and in the workingmen's political parties that excluded them. Some likely rejected the new black leaders, secretly or openly mocking the new paternalism just as they had surreptitiously mocked the authority of masters on Election Day. Others, however, found under freedom new possibilities for achieving community status through local activities in the church, lodge, or literary society, or even through their occupations in barbershops and boardinghouses. Such opportunities to participate in the work of community uplift permitted them to occupy the lowest rungs of the black leadership pyramid. These men and women would have peered over the divide between non-elites and elites. They would have sought and often received connection with community leaders, connections they never would have had under slavery or in a society unconcerned with labeling all African-descended people uniformly as an inferior branch of humanity.[119]

Given the broad range of social experiences from which black Americans hailed, the surprise was not that social differences existed among them but that black northerners generally managed to shelter these differences under the umbrella of racial identity and black community activism. Enjoying far greater resources than their non-elite brethren and the benefits of their unique access to both white and black worlds, black leaders who emerged from community elites proved adept at appropriating the language of freedom that emerged in the revolutionary age, fashioning it into an argument for racial equality, and offering it to the race as a tool to ease its suffering. The antislavery celebration was a key component in the process through which black leaders submerged difference and presented to white America a unified racial front.

❖

It is proper to call things by their right names.
William Lloyd Garrison

For it is through our names that we first place
ourselves in the world. Our names, being the gift of
others, must be made our own. They must become our
masks and our shields and the containers of all those
values and traditions which we learn and/or imagine as
being the meaning of our familial past.
Ralph Ellison

❖

See Dexter's
brief discussion
p. 108

CHAPTER 3

The Sign of Things

The "Names Controversy" and Black Identity

In March 1928 a young man wrote to *The Crisis*, troubled that the magazine
had referred to black people as "Negroes" instead of simply "Americans."
The letter's author, high school sophomore Roland A. Barton, considered
the term "a white man's word to make us feel inferior." The editor of *The
Crisis*, W. E. B. Du Bois, responded with a lengthy discourse on the subject of
racial names, in which he enlightened the misinformed youth and justified
his use of the term. Du Bois first explained that, while no name was historically accurate, "Negro" served well, for "wide and continued usage" had rendered it accurate enough. Responding to Barton's thought that "American"
ought to suffice, Du Bois would not hide the distinct cultural heritage—the
"spiritual ideals," "inner bonds," and "group ideals"—of the race under the
generic "American." Any shame black people felt in adopting "Negro," he
claimed, was solely the product of racism. "Exorcize the hateful complex,"
he wrote, "and no name can ever make you hang your head." Finally, Du
Bois added a pan-African tint by proudly embracing "Negro" as inclusive
of all people of African descent, regardless of national origin or degree of
white heritage.[1]

Du Bois was not the first black intellectual to make such arguments. In the first half o[...] African American thinkers in the North discusse[...] n racial names and the public identity of African-[...] period between the Revolution and the Civil War, [...] of Du Bois's arguments. Yet there was a vital dist[...] African American leaders resolved the issue in the two periods. Though [...]ey shared little else, both Du Bois and Booker T. Washington embraced the capitalized "Negro" as the preferred term for the race. While consensus was never achieved on the issue of names, "Negro" enjoyed widespread endorsement among many prominent African Americans in the late nineteenth and early twentieth centuries. The word was, however, relatively new as a moniker considered appropriate for the race by black leaders. For most of the nineteenth century, African Americans in national life had preferred "people of color," "colored people," or (more tellingly) "Colored American." And even this latter term was not original. Before that, in the eighteenth and early nineteenth centuries, black leaders deemed yet another term the best label for the race: "African." Why was it that African Americans in the first half of the nineteenth century came to reject "African"? Why did they adopt "colored," and why did they reject the option that would be preferred later: "Negro"? Contention over the appropriate name for the race has always catalyzed important debates among African Americans about their complex relationship to America. How did the antebellum "names controversy" reflect black leaders' understanding of that relationship during the first half of the nineteenth century?

The movement from "African" to "colored" signified black leaders' growing participation in the public life of the nation, and their increasing awareness of the role of words and ideas in fostering both black oppression and black liberation. Throughout the course of the debate over names, black public spokespersons steadily came to understand the power of public speech to influence the "public mind" on matters of race. The rhetorical strategies black thinkers developed to combat white supremacy depended upon these understandings. To appreciate the "names controversy," then, is to explore the principles at the core of the antebellum black protest tradition. The transition from "African" to "Colored American" and the debates that attended it signaled the crucial process by which African American spokespersons set forth the meaning of their blackness before a hostile public. They hoped this identity would help them achieve the dual goals of the abolition of slavery and the "elevation" of free African Americans to a level of equality with white Americans. African American identity was thus not quite the organic entity that Du Bois and later commentators envisioned; it was not something for black people to *discover* so much as it was something for them to *build*. The very notion that a single term could or ought to encompass all people of African descent demonstrated the constructed quality of black identity: the "names controversy" invoked a novel argument for a concept of racial unity, an argument that, unlike late-twentieth-century observers, few contemporaries could have taken for granted.

The spokespersons who crafted "Colored American" as the preferred term for the race were numbered among a small elite in black communities. In consciously promoting a racial label that could embrace all people of African descent, they hoped to cement up the disparate factors that might otherwise have sundered black unity and hampered the battles for freedom and equality. Deep tensions beset this process, as their rejection of "Negro" would attest. In the very act of sublimating their own elitist predilections under an all-encompassing term, they made sure they chose a "respectable" alternative to "African." In the first half of the century, for a variety of reasons, "negro" emphatically was not respectable. Because respectability entailed appropriating the petit bourgeois values of the urbanizing North, at the same time that black leaders gestured inclusively toward all of African descent, their navigation of the troubled waters of black identity through the "names controversy" expressed attitudes toward the black rank and file that exposed the limits of their egalitarianism.

AFRICAN IDENTITY IN THE NINETEENTH-CENTURY NORTH

The earliest free black institutions in the North had unashamedly adopted names that included the word "African." Black churches, among the earliest institutions that free African Americans established in the North, took special pains to identify themselves with Africa. In 1794, Philadelphia free blacks under the leadership of Richard Allen and Absalom Jones founded the African Methodist Episcopal Church. Reverend Thomas Paul of Boston started the African Baptist Church in 1805, while William Miller, a New York cleric, launched the African Methodist Episcopal Zion denomination when he founded the African Asbury Church in 1814. In addition to churches, secular community institutions adopted names containing the word "African." Black children attended the African Free School in New York from 1787, while in 1796 black people in Boston began a benevolent organization known as the African Society. In Philadelphia, James Forten, a wealthy free African American, helped found the Free African Society in 1787, the African Masonic Lodge in 1797, and St. Thomas's African Episcopal Church in 1794. Black New Yorkers founded the African Society for Mutual Relief in 1810 and the African Dorcas Association in 1828, while African Americans in Pittsburgh began the African Education and Benevolent Society in the late 1820s and the Pittsburgh African Educational Society in 1832.[2] Throughout the last few decades of the eighteenth century and the early decades of the nineteenth, free African Americans proudly displayed their heritage by embracing "African" as an appropriate term to describe the race.

As some scholars have suggested, the presence of "African" in the names of these institutions may have reflected a positive identification with Africa among black northerners, based on deep-rooted cultural predilections.[3] It expressed the cultural unity of African-descended people who had been stripped of the national and tribal identities of the Old World and who had synthesized from shared elements of their cultures a new African American culture.[4] Occasionally, black northerners attested to this affinity. The framers of the Laws of the African Society of Boston labeled themselves "African Members," while the constitution of the African Marine Fund, which had been founded in New York in 1810, provided for a committee "to visit our African brethren, and the descendants of our mother country, to give information of their several distresses and wants."[5] *Freedom's Journal*, the first black newspaper in the nation, promised to present "useful knowledge of every kind, and everything that relates to Africa," for it trusted that increasing knowledge of the continent would prove "that the natives of it are neither so ignorant nor stupid as they have generally been supposed to be."[6]

Yet the case for black Americans' cultural kinship with Africa based on institutional naming practices should not be overstated. Several factors mitigated severely the continued retention of African cultural elements among black people in the nineteenth-century North and, by extension, possibilities for their unmediated identity with Africa. By the turn of the nineteenth century, two generations had passed since Africans had been imported into the region in large numbers. The outlawing of the international slave trade to the United States in 1808 effectively ended the importation of African slaves into the North and hence ended fresh infusions of African culture. Even before this time, opportunities for introducing unacculturated Africans into the North had diminished. In the second half of the eighteenth century, the importation of enslaved Africans into the northern colonies from Africa declined steadily. By the last quarter of the eighteenth century it plummeted, starved by the growing demand for labor in the southern colonies and eventually the distractions of the Revolution.[7]

As a result of the de-evolution of the slave trade, the black population in most of the North—both slave and free—either leveled off or fell throughout the latter half of the eighteenth century (see Table 3.1). In the northern

Table 3.1. Black Population in Northern Colonies and States, 1630–1840

	Maine	New Hampshire	Vermont	Massachusetts	Rhode Island	Connecticut	New York	New Jersey	Pennsylvania
1630	—	—	—	0	—	—	10	—	—
1640	—	30	—	150	0	15	232	—	—
1650	—	40	—	295	0	20	500	—	—
1660	—	50	—	422	25	25	600	—	—
1670	—	65	—	160	65	35	690	60	—
1680	—	75	—	170	115	50	1,200	200	25
1690	—	100	—	400	175	200	1,670	450	270
1700	—	130	—	800	250	450	2,256	840	430
1710	—	150	—	1,310	300	750	2,811	1,332	1,575
1720	—	170	—	2,150	375	1,093	5,740	2,385	2,000
1730	—	200	—	2,780	543	1,490	6,956	3,008	1,241
1740	—	500	—	3,035	1,648	2,598	8,996	4,366	2,055
1750	—	550	—	4,075	3,347	3,010	11,014	5,354	2,872
1760	—	600	—	4,754	3,468	3,783	16,340	6,567	4,409
1770	—	654	25	5,229	3,761	5,698	19,112	8,220	5,761
1780	—	541	50	4,822	2,671	5,885	21,054	10,460	7,855
1790	538	788	271	5,463	4,355	5,572	25,978	14,185	10,274
1800	818	860	557	6,452	3,684	6,281	31,320	16,824	16,270
1810	969	970	750	6,737	3,717	6,763	40,350	18,694	23,287
1820	929	786	903	6,740	3,602	7,967	39,367	20,017	30,413
1830	1,129	607	881	7,049	3,578	8,072	44,945	20,557	38,333
1840	1,355	538	730	8,669	3,243	8,122	50,031	21,718	47,918

Sources: Jessie Carney Smith and Carrel Peterson Horton, comps. and eds., *Historical Statistics of Black America* (New York: Gale Research, 1995), 2:1539–41; U.S. Department of Commerce (Bureau of the Census), *Negro Population, 1790–1915* (Washington, D.C.: Government Printing Office, 1918), 44–45.

colonies, the proportion of African-descended people in the population fell along with their absolute numbers; in every instance, growing white populations increasingly rendered blacks a minority (Table 3.2). In the eighteenth century in southern colonies like Virginia and South Carolina, the number of blacks and whites were closely matched, comprising roughly 40 percent and 60 percent of the total population, respectively; in the Caribbean blacks often comprised 70 percent or more of the population, far surpassing the number of white colonists. In the North, however, only in New York and Rhode Island did blacks ever account for more than 10 percent of the total population. From the birth of the nation to the eve of the Civil War, blacks never amounted to more than 10 percent of the population in the North; their representation in the population declined steadily in the face of increasing European immigration. In contrast, southern blacks often constituted between 40 and 60 percent of the total population, and their proportions increased continually in the Lower South (Table 3.3). Even in places like New York City, where blacks accounted for 14 percent of the population on the eve of the Revolution,[8] living conditions minimized their retention of African cultural values. The absence of large-scale plantation agriculture obviated the need for the high densities of enslaved workers, which incubated African cultural retentions in, for example, the South Carolina Sea Islands. Instead, many enslaved African Americans lived in close proximity to white people; in the domestic servitude that characterized many parts of the North, blacks might literally have slept at the feet of their masters.

Those who served as spokespersons for black communities and who played key roles in the formation and naming of their institutions were particularly unlikely purveyors of an untrammeled African identity. Overwhelmingly native-born, many were descended from families that had been present in America for several generations and had used the benefits of their creole status to grow into positions of relative prominence in the slave, and later free black, community. While they often called themselves Africans, such creolized black leaders sometimes expressed considerable disdain for newly arrived Africans with distinct cultural styles. In short, black leaders' acculturation, which was a result of a sometimes generations-long process, deeply qualified their identification with Africa. Finally, while black naming practices illustrated a self-conscious identification with Africa, they also depended upon a broader context of Anglo-American thought, which fostered the use of the term "African." It must not be forgotten that white patrons, sometimes benevolent but always controlling, played large roles in the founding of institutions like the African Methodist Episcopal Church (in Philadelphia) or the African Free School (in New York). Indeed, the very

Table 3.2. Blacks as Percentage of Northern Populations, 1750–1840

	Maine	New Hampshire	Vermont	Massachusetts	Rhode Island	Connecticut	New York	New Jersey	Pennsylvania
1750	—	2.0	—	2.2	10.1	2.7	14.4	7.5	2.4
1760	1.5	1.5	—	2.3	7.6	2.7	13.9	7.0	2.4
1770	1.5	1.0	0.3	2.0	6.5	3.1	11.7	7.0	2.4
1780	0.9	0.6	0.1	1.8	5.0	2.8	10.0	7.5	2.4
1790	0.6	0.6	0.3	1.4	6.3	2.3	7.6	7.7	2.4
1800	0.5	0.5	0.4	1.5	5.3	2.5	5.3	8.0	2.7
1810	0.4	0.5	0.3	1.4	4.8	2.6	4.2	7.6	2.9
1820	0.3	0.3	0.4	1.3	4.3	2.9	2.9	7.2	2.9
1830	0.3	0.2	0.3	1.2	3.7	2.7	2.3	6.4	2.8
1840	0.3	0.2	0.3	1.2	3.0	2.6	2.1	5.8	2.8

Sources: Jessie Carney Smith and Carrel Peterson Horton, comps. and eds., *Historical Statistics of Black America* (New York: Gale Research, 1995), 2:1539–41; U.S. Department of Commerce (Bureau of the Census), *Negro Population, 1790–1915* (Washington, D.C.: Government Printing Office, 1918), 51–52.

Table 3.3. Blacks as Percentage of Population in Selected Northern and Southern States, 1790–1860

Region and State	1790	1800	1810	1820	1830	1840	1850	1860
North
Massachusetts	1.4	1.5	1.4	1.3	1.2	1.2	0.9	0.8
New York	7.6	5.3	4.2	2.9	2.3	2.1	1.6	1.3
Connecticut	2.3	2.5	2.6	2.9	2.7	2.6	2.1	1.9
Pennsylvania	2.4	2.7	2.9	2.9	2.8	2.8	2.3	2.0
Rhode Island	6.3	5.3	4.8	4.3	3.7	3.0	2.5	2.3
New Jersey	7.7	8.0	7.6	7.2	6.4	5.8	4.9	3.8
South
Maryland	34.7	36.7	38.2	36.1	34.9	23.2	28.3	24.9
Virginia	40.9	41.6	43.4	43.4	42.7	40.2	37.1	34.3
Georgia	35.9	37.1	42.4	44.4	42.6	41.0	42.4	44.0
South Carolina	43.7	43.2	48.4	52.8	55.6	56.4	58.9	58.6

Source: U.S. Department of Commerce (Bureau of the Census), *Negro Population, 1790–1915* (Washington, D.C.: Government Printing Office, 1918), 51–52.

notion of a monolithic entity called Africa was born not simply in the synthesis of disparate African cultures in America but also in Europeans' views of the continent as uniformly stateless, uncivilized, and degraded.[9] While black leaders softened the less charitable aspects of Euro-America's Africa, they nonetheless embraced the notion of the continent as a unified whole, often trailing the United States and Europe in important measures of civilization.

Such factors deeply mitigated the possibility that the black elites who named their institutions "African" reflected fundamental cultural affinities with the continent of their ancestors. If institutional naming practices did not necessarily reflect unchanged "African" mind-sets, what did they reflect? Rather than primarily documenting black northerners' changing relationship with Africa, naming practices revealed black Americans' awareness of the sphere of public speech as an agent that could aid or hinder their search for freedom. Already deeply conversant with American public life by the turn of the nineteenth century, many of the African Americans who served as self-appointed spokespersons for the race relied consciously on the forms and ideas of a public culture largely dominated by white people. Eking out space within this culture to set forth the race's distinct interests proved their primary task and greatest challenge. It was through public speech that African American spokespersons created—rhetorically, yet powerfully—a public identity built on blackness. Newly freed black leaders invoked Africa not as a reflection of their cultural proclivities but as a claim to participate equally in the civic life of the nation. They identified the race with Africa not because they had retained the cultural qualities of the people of that continent but because they sought the public acknowledgment and recognition accorded to those who could claim a legitimate national affiliation.[10]

Until the mid-1810s, the word "African" had served well to accomplish this task. It had functioned as an ethnic identifier, akin to those later employed by European immigrant groups, serving to define a public identity in an increasingly anonymous urban America. The black use of terms of ethnic identification in the names of their institutions around the turn of the nineteenth century may actually have fostered similar practices by other immigrant groups in the antebellum North. Starting in the 1830s, European immigrants in Boston would found institutions such as the Hibernian Relief Society, the Boston Scottish Society, and the Hebrew Literary Society.[11] In this context, "African" seemed to pose no threat beyond the omnipresent claims of inferiority leveled on all of African descent.

The opening salvo in the names controversy, and the beginning of the decline of "African," appeared in response to debates in the public sphere over the relationship between black people, America, and Africa. In 1816, a group of prominent white Americans, including such figures as Francis Scott Key and Henry Clay, established the American Colonization Society (ACS) for the purpose of repatriating black people to a country in Africa. The Society sought to appeal to both free blacks and apprehensive whites: for the latter it offered a solution to the "problem" of non-enslaved black people existing in and thus undermining a society predicated on the principle of black racial inferiority; for the former, it promised deliverance from the allegedly ineradicable mistreatment and hostility of these very white supremacist constituents.[12] While it succeeded in luring some African Americans, like New York newspaper editor John Russwurm,[13] to relocate to Liberia, most black northerners feared forced removal from the land of their birth, quickly detecting the Society's specious concern with the welfare of the race. Regardless how they interpreted and used the word "African," many black northerners grew concerned that any professions of African affinities might supply fuel to colonizationists and others who argued that black people had no true place in the nation.[14]

Given the threat represented by the American Colonization Society, most black northerners abandoned use of their standard term of self-reference.

"African" suddenly seemed to make a provocative and dangerous statement that black people were not entitled to the rights and freedoms of
other Americans—that they were not even a part of America. A letter to
William Lloyd Garrison's *Liberator* typified the argument, made countless
times throughout the antebellum period, that black people had just as much
a claim to the nation as whites. "Meeting-houses, school-houses, and all associations" of black people, its author claimed, "are daubed with the titles of
African schools, [and] African churches, [yet] WE ARE AMERICANS!" Charging that skin color alone rendered black people aliens in the eyes of whites,
the writer asked, "Are the whites, born in America, called European? Will
the Europeans own them as *their* countrymen? No!"[15] The African Baptist
Church of Boston, so named at its founding in 1806, sensed the same danger in its nomenclature, and changed its title in the 1830s. "For the very
good reason that the name African is ill applied to a church composed of
American citizens," it became the First Independent Church of the People
of Color.[16]

AN ALTERNATIVE REJECTED

It was not immediately clear that "colored" would replace "African" as the
racial adjective of choice among antebellum black northerners. One possibility was to fall back on terms already used to describe black people in
the North. A likely alternative to "African"—"Negro"—was free of troubling
associations with Africa, but it posed a different and more potent problem, which militated against adopting it as a widespread racial moniker. It
sounded perilously close to a related word that was becoming nothing but a
term of extreme disparagement: "nigger." The history of that troubled word
reveals much about not simply the names controversy but also the underlying social contexts that fed it.

"Negro" not only sounded like "nigger," it was not at all clear to antebellum Americans that the two words were very different. The process by
which the words derived their unique spellings and connotations was still
under way in the early nineteenth century, the distinctions between them
still settling. Both words descended from common ancestors, sprung from
Latinate terms for sub-Saharan Africans, whom Spanish and Portuguese
colonizers considered "black" (the Latin *niger*). English use of the terms
coincided with Great Britain's entrance into colonial ventures in the New
World in the forms of the international slave trade and piracy against Spain.
In his 1555 translation of Peter Martyr's *Decades of the New World or West India,*
Richard Eden used the word "negros," while English travel accounts report

the condition of "Nigers of Aethiop" in 1574. By 1584 the phrase was common enough to be used as a simile — "skin like a Niger" — while by 1611 to attempt the impossible was to "wash a Negro."[17] A wide variety of alternatives appeared before the turn of the nineteenth century: "negroe," "niggar," "nigger," "neger," "nagar," "negur," and "neager." The spellings of these words remained largely fluid and their connotations (whether intended to be derisive or ostensibly neutral) unfixed.

Amidst the welter of usages and spellings, it is difficult to determine any clear and consistent distinction between "negro" and "nigger" as used in America before the turn of the nineteenth century. Were the "twenty Negars" John Rolphe reported arriving in Virginia in 1619 potentially respectable "negroes" or perpetually despised "niggers"? What of the "niggor Boy" who appeared on a Gravesend, New York, inventory in 1679? African Americans themselves still failed to make the distinction in 1766, when one "Governor Cuff of the Niegro's," a black "king" in Connecticut, bequeathed his title to "John Anderson Niegor man to Governor Skene."[18] By 1786, when Robert Burns used "niger" in his poem "The Ordination," the word was an acceptable term in English letters.[19] It makes sense, then, to think not of two distinct words that were merely unclear in this period, but instead of a fluid and historically contingent complex of spellings, meanings, and significations.

This complex changed in the North in the decades before the Civil War, evolving into the words we know today. While the use of these words is often associated with plantation culture, the historical locus for the clear and permanent division of "negro" and "nigger" was not the expanding slave society of the post-Revolutionary South but the expanding market society of the urbanizing North. The primary context for the development of "nigger" was not simply the transformation of race culture in the North but the emergence of stratified class culture as well. The transformation in what might be termed the "N-word complex" embodied and illustrated broader processes of social change that had great implications — not simply for the controversy over racial names but for the class identities of its participants as well.

The process began in the decades after the turn of the nineteenth century, just as general emancipations were creating a purportedly free society. The first transformation occurred when "nigger" and words close to it (usually identified by a soft "i" sound in the first syllable and endings of "-er" or "-or") began to appear as words purportedly peculiar to American English, and most often with a solely derisive connotation. The establishment of "nigger" as such a term attended, and indeed required, the emergence of a word free from its belittling associations. As "nigger" increasingly became a term of contempt, and only contempt, "negro"—which until then had been obscured by the predominance of "er"- and "ar"-suffixed versions of the complex—emerged as an ostensibly neutral alternative. "Negro" (and versions of it) had long been used alongside versions of "nigger," but now its spelling became by and large standardized (though not capitalized), and its connotations narrowed into largely nonvulgar usages. As "nigger" became less reputable, "negro" came to be extolled as the polite alternative to a word increasingly deemed offensive in refined society.

The dialectical transformation in the complex is clear from contemporary accounts. Though wrong in their conclusions, foreign reporters in the second decade of the century began documenting the emergence of "nigger" as a distinctly American term that denoted solely contempt for African-descended people.[20] In 1818, when traveler H. B. Fearon noted to his British readers "the inferior nature of niggars (negroes)" in America, his parenthetical reference to a more appropriate term subtly signaled that "niggars" was considered an American particularism; "negroes" he invoked as its standard, clarifying referent.[21] A French visitor to the states reported in 1819 that "contempt of the poor blacks, or niggers, as they are there called, seems the national sin of America," thus illustrating that "niggers" had became not merely a word peculiar to America (or at least with peculiar connotations *in* America) but also one dedicated to maligning African-descended people.[22] It was not just foreign travelers with external frames of reference who constructed this new meaning for "nigger." Authors of dictionaries— the very mechanisms through which language was being made formal, standard, and national—participated in the process as well. When an 1819 dictionary falsely, though tellingly, offered "nigger" as a word found only in the United States,[23] the error suggested a priority higher than accuracy. The fabrication of "nigger" as a word specific to American speech helped codify its spelling and connotations. It grew distinct from "negro," which became the nonderogatory referent by which those supposedly unfamiliar with the novel regionalism "nigger" were to decipher its subject.

At the same time "nigger" was being downgraded, the status of "negro" rose. In 1818, the same year foreign travelers were marking "nigger" as a peculiarity of the Americans, an etiquette book's list of phrases to avoid advised respectable folk to eschew "Neeger" in favor of "negro."[24] New York's popular *Knickerbocker Magazine* lampooned the speech of its state's lower orders by quipping: "Although *mighty smart*, and *a mighty smart chance, mighty big*, and *mighty little* was excellent 'nigger' dialect, yet it was not so refined, as an orator might use."[25] By the end of the Civil War, authors in respectable publications like *Atlantic Monthly* had apparently become sufficiently secure

in their own class hegemony to risk using the word, albeit in the highly circumscribed context of denoting vulgar things, vulgar classes, and vulgar
speech. Wrote one such author: "When I say 'colored,' I mean one thing,
respectfully; and when I say 'niggerish,' I mean another, disgustedly."[26]

This division—of the vague and diffuse "N-word" complex into standardized forms with clearly polite and impolite alternatives—lay at the heart of
its fugitive class politics. "Nigger," whether actually used by the supposedly
ill-bred or merely placed in their mouths by bourgeois northerners who constructed their vulgarity for them, was becoming a marker of incivility and a
lack of refinement—not simply for people of African descent but for those
who *spoke* the word as well. The transformation of the "N-word" complex entailed the bifurcation of the concept into forms signifying the class status of
the *speaker* as well as the object of the term. While "negro" became a term of
neutrality or respect, and its use was acceptable in polite society, "nigger"
not only served as a term to denigrate people of African descent, but increasingly to mark in polite circles *those who uttered it* as lacking in refinement.

Evidence abounds that in both the practice and the minds of the northern middle class "nigger" was used by those considered unrefined. In the
literature and reportage of northeasterners, the phrase increasingly became associated with the speech of the low, the poor, the uneducated, the
rough, the uncivilized, the unrefined, and the backward. Appearance of the
word among working-class white urbanites comported easily with bourgeois
visions of dangerous urban "others."[27] In 1834, a riotous mob of working-
class Philadelphians went "hunting the nigs" through city streets.[28] As early
as 1828 this shortened "nig" appeared in the white representations of black
speech presented in working-class minstrel shows, where it became an en-
during staple.[29] The use of the word among the black dwellers of northern
cities would have buttressed blackface minstrelsy's pretense of authentically
replicating African American speech, for northern whites and foreign travelers noted with some surprise African American use of the term. One foreign visitor remarked on its usage by a street boy in 1816, while in 1834
Francis Lieber noted "a negro boy" under his window calling another, "by
way of reproach, '*nigger.*'"[30] The use of a term of disparagement among
those it intended to disparage, these writers intimated, surely denoted a
want of civility.[31] In northern white minds, such talk offered yet more evidence of the alien, unassimilable nature of black people, especially when
experienced in a burgeoning print culture that depicted white imaginings
of black speech. Broadsides, comic almanacs, and popular etchings presented black people as ones who bore distinct and inferior racial identities,
which, despite best attempts to appear respectable, would always out. Such

images were so powerful in invoking the low that the allegedly vulgar speech of African Americans could stand in for vulgar speech in general. As early as 1825 middle-class observers conflated black and vulgar English, arguing that terms such as "cotch" (for "catch") and "I reckon" were "clear nigger."[32] "Nigger talk" became not merely the perverse ways black people were said to speak, but an insulting term for the degraded English of ill-mannered white people as well. In his *Dictionary of Americanisms* (1859), John Russell Bartlett counted "Negroisms" among the "Americanisms" he derided as "perversions."[33]

Middle-class northerners grew to understand "nigger" as a signifier of class identities intertwined with regional affiliations. Antebellum representations of the speech of rural folk, and especially frontiersmen, invoked it as a surefire means of communicating the identity of those on the margins of civilization. Eastern representations of frontiersmen used the term frequently and indiscriminately, to speak not just of blacks, but also of Indians, Polynesians, Arabs, the Roma (or "Gypsies"), and even black animals.[34] Such folk uncouthly employed the word as a simile and metaphor: hard-laboring rural whites "worked like niggers," while suspicious ones sought them in woodpiles or fences.[35] Worked-up men on the frontier redefined the word as a synonym for aggressive passion, sometimes venting their spleen when they harmlessly "let off a little nigger" on a Saturday night.[36] They even turned the noun into verbs, one of which described a process by which logs were divided into shorter lengths by burning them in the middle.[37] When unlettered frontier card players accused each other of misplays by shortening the French *renege* to "nig," they added a racial significance that layered considerable insult onto its original meaning. What marked vulgar usages of the word for bourgeois white northerners was its promiscuous and indiscriminate employment. Unlike themselves, the ill-mannered and the countrified apparently had yet to learn that the phrase was impolite. The way they saw it, as such markers of "civilization" spread from the cities, folk who casually used such indecorous speech clearly trailed in the quest for progress, civility, and refinement.

Notably, the word appeared frequently in the speech of characters devised by a wide range of middle-class satirists. Take, for example, parodies of frontier dialect, such as "Ye great niggerish lookin', wap-sided yaw," which laced the speech of "Brother Jonathan," an English term for the prototypical Yankee and forerunner of Uncle Sam.[38] Frequently, rural characters — such as Charles Brown's Artemis Ward, David Ross Locke's Petroleum V. Nasby, or George William Bagby's Mozis Addums[39] — mouthed the epithet not first in the service of denigrating blacks but in highlighting contemporary political or social follies. Editorial cartoonists felt little compunction against placing it even in the mouths of characters averse to the South and the Democratic Party.[40] While clearly associated with claims of black inferiority, "nigger" clearly had a life of its own, at least in the minds of middle-class urban whites, among the lowly.

Of particular note was the way northerners perceived white southerners' usage of the word. Long after the "N-word" complex had bifurcated in the North, white southerners reportedly used a version loose in terms of both spelling and connotation. The southern migration of monikers for the race deemed respectable in the North apparently proceeded with considerable tardiness. In 1867, one northern traveler to the South noted that "niggers" were "not 'coloured persons' yet in the South."[41] As late as 1904, a dictionary defined "nigger" as follows: "Negro. The universal word in Arkansas, whether respect is intended or not."[42] The delay in the southern spread of "nigger" solely as an epithet strongly suggests that the North ought to be credited with the dubious distinction of generating what may be considered the nation's most potent secular blasphemy. Yet even here use of the word gradually came to denote status in class hierarchies. This might be expected in a society so highly stratified and among an upper class so anxious to secure its own hegemony. A travel account from 1860 noted that "a Southern gentleman rarely, if ever, says *nigger*." In 1863, J. Dooley reported that he had "never heard this epithet applied to slaves in the South by any person of refinement and education."[43]

The transformation of "nigger" from one among many indistinct terms with a wide variety of connotations into an irretrievably sullied term for both African-descended people and its utterers mirrored the emergence of a northern bourgeois social order concerned first and foremost with establishing its predominance by fixing cultural hierarchy—by defining the boundaries of high and low culture.[44] The switch from "nigger" to "negro" as the polite term of reference was not accomplished first by blacks, but by middle-class whites—most not by any means friendly to black interests—who sought to avoid not its disparaging connotations toward African Americans but the lack of civility it now imputed to those who spoke it. The transformation manifested merely one aspect of a much broader process whereby social elites struggled to distinguish themselves by policing American English from the encroachments of vulgar neologisms. As early as 1781, John Witherspoon, the Scottish-born president of Princeton, fussed over well-bred Americans who employed "improprieties and vulgarisms which hardly any person in the same class in point of rank and literature would have fallen into in Great Britain."[45] It was thus no accident that the bifurcation of the "N-word" complex happened where and when it did. The extraordinary antebellum expansion of print media in the urban North offered unparalleled opportunities for a status-anxious bourgeoisie to fix word spellings as well as to define some as "standard." For those aspiring to respectability but unsure of appropriate diction, a spate of etiquette manuals and advice literature reinforced appropriate daily usage of a great many words. As we have seen, these books, as well as some dictionaries, advised readers on use of the "N-word" as well.

The case against "nigger" as an appropriate term for standard English worsened as the word gained the power to undermine emerging class hierarchies. The champions of middle-class respectability, having successfully associated "nigger" in the public mind with lower-class status, had unwittingly endowed it with a new power to challenge class elites. The dialectical construction of class identities fostered both bourgeois hegemony *and* provided new opportunities for the expression of working-class resistance through cultural styles; popular use of the word "nigger" constituted merely one small instance of the ways in which white non-elites could challenge new class hierarchies through speech.[46] Middle-class identity attributed the speech of the non-elite, and particularly the word "nigger," to the vulgar, as part of a larger project of achieving political, social, and moral ascendancy over them. When they did that, they paradoxically invested the word with subversive potential. It was not simply that "nigger" happened to mark the speech of lower orders, from which the bourgeoisie was desperately trying to distance itself. It was that the word could easily be invoked as a metaphor to call forth class humiliation upon its target. Speaking of well-to-do whites who had fallen on hard times, one observer in 1857 noted the joy with which working-class folk employed the term to bring low those who thought their stations placed them above manual labor: "Many of the people express satisfaction in seeing these 'better-dressed fellers' obliged to 'nigger it,'" he commented.[47]

Significantly, the word's ability to explode class pretenses could apply to African-descended people as well. In her famous *Appeal in Favor of Americans Called Africans* (1836), Lydia Maria Child noted a double crime committed in white Americans' use of the term. Not only did it disparage a people solely on the basis of their color, but in so doing it effaced important class distinctions between high and low, regardless of skin color. When "a person of refinement from Hayti, or Brazil . . . should visit us," she charged, "the very boys in the street would dog his footsteps with the vulgar outcry of 'Nigger! Nigger!'" What was particularly reproachful about this was that the visitors had not earned their treatment through their behavior, which had been scrupulously respectable. The boys had acted "from no other provocation than the sight of a colored man with the dress and deportment of a gentleman."[48] The new use of "nigger" in the North not merely neglected to acknowledge the class status of well-to-do African Americans, it singled out such persons for particular disparagement. In the process, like the Zip Coon stereotype increasingly featured in the popular press, it fostered a category of social being undefined by the proper markers of middle-class status: refined behavior and civilized manners. In identifying all people of African descent as "niggers," it attacked the very notion of gentility, whether black or white, and thus undermined distinctions authored by an emerging bourgeoisie anxious to cement its status as "respectable."

Of course the word also found a ready home in the language of an increasingly vicious and racialized cultural politics. It appeared regularly on both the minstrel stage and in the popular media images that spewed out of the antebellum penny press. These latter were uniform in juxtaposing African Americans' use of the word with images of their ludicrous pretensions to social standing and civic equality. Distributed via broadsides, inexpensive etchings, and cheap almanacs from the 1830s on, the word followed the issue of black freedom and civil rights onto the stage of national politics. Critics of African Americans used the term to deride things beneficial to black life, including the suffrage, rights, the vote, and teachers (Yankee women). A Connecticut mob ran Prudence Crandall's "nigger school" out of operation in 1834.[49] Before and during the Civil War, Yankees suspected of abolitionism were "nigger-thieves," and before and after the war those whites who broke caste to champion black rights were vilified as "nigger-worshippers" and "nigger-lovers." Many who advocated black rights in the streets likely shared the experience of one man who, during a riot, "was struck a severe blow by a man who rebuked him for upholding Abolitionists and 'niggers.'"[50] Such abolitionists practiced what some westerners called "niggerology,"[51] while Democratic newspapers in the East declared the tentative emergence of abolitionism on the Whig political agenda "niggerism."[52] When the Whig Party went asunder, its successor, the Republican Party, was termed by some "the Nigger party" and accused by others of "niggerheadism."[53] More than once, Abraham Lincoln was called "nothing but a goddam Black nigger," and during the Civil War Confederates frequently leveled the sobriquet at their enemies, as when a Union soldier during the Civil War reported being labeled a "white nigger."[54] After the war victorious Unionists controlled what the New York Herald termed a "nigger-head Congress." In the postwar hysteria brought on by general emancipation, many white southerners feared—as might those who found the increasing use of the word offensive—the rampant spread of "niggerdom."[55] Such phrases stung the ears of respectable white northern urbanites, not because they contained a racial offense, but because they inflicted vulgarity on well-mannered ears. This meant not that the word was to be avoided in public—for surely it was used, constantly, and by respectable editors and other public figures at that—merely that its employment carried important connotations of the popular and vicious. Carrying this significance, it become a marvelous bludgeon, useful for a variety of purposes, all of which somehow were intended to degrade.

It was little wonder, then, that black elites eschewed "nigger" assiduously. In his incendiary *Appeal*, the fiery David Walker derided "niger" as a Latin word applied to blacks by white Americans "by way of reproach for our colour, to aggravate and heighten our miseries, because they have their feet on our throats."[56] Melville's narrator in *White Jacket* (1849) reported that the word "among some blacks, is held as a term of great reproach." Fugitive slaves entering the circles of black abolitionists learned new rules regarding acceptable terms for the race. Upon finding a home in Philadelphia in 1857, Harriet Jacobs encountered African American friends who "say dey was not niggers, but colored pussons."[57]

While "nigger" steadily acquired its rhetorical potency as a vulgar term for both blacks and whites, its respectable alternative—"negro"—was not so clearly distinct in usage. Nearly every noun modified by "nigger" could also be found modified by "negro." Those sympathetic with—and, of these, certainly those talking *to*—African Americans eschewed "nigger" in favor of "negro." (Though it should be noted that white abolitionists were far from lapsing into their own use of "nigger" as an epithet.)[58] Among non-sympathetic northerners, and despite the fact that few misunderstood the insult implied, popular usage was determined primarily by social setting rather than derogatory intent. "Nigger," it was claimed, was used primarily among the working class and the rural. When used at all, "negro" connoted more respectable settings where polite dialogue was favored. Speakers employed this alternative not necessarily because it lessened the racial insult of "nigger," but because it lessened the degrading class implications "nigger" wrought on those who uttered it.

For a self-styled respectable northern black elite, the shady history of the N-word complex rendered even "negro" a poor candidate for what black activists needed: a term for the race that was both common yet unsullied by degrading imputations and which expressed their universalism, their pan-Africanism, and their class aspirations. "Negro" was as yet too ambiguous, neither sufficiently distinct nor sufficiently respectable for this purpose.

First published in 1829, David Walker's *Appeal* went through three editions, each of which featured a different spelling of the still ambiguous "nigger."[59] One black northerner reflected the confusion in a letter to *Freedom's Journal*: "I have been for years endeavoring to ascertain the propriety of applying this term to us, but without effect. . . . I should like to ascertain whether we are negroes, or if those who are truly ignorant, or actuated by the principles of prejudice, call us negroes."[60] New York clergyman Hosea Easton failed to make a clear distinction in 1837, stating that "negro or nigger, is an opprobrious term, employed to impose contempt upon them [blacks] as an inferior race."[61] A white reporter echoed the sentiment of many northern blacks in 1857: "they do not like the word Negro, because of the resemblance of the word to 'Nigger.'"[62]

African American northerners correctly sensed that its story was far too complicated to serve their needs. In a series of writings by James Forten published in 1813, the Philadelphia leader used "African" and "black" as terms of self-reference but identified "negro" as a word used by hostile whites. Most black activists believed the term to have negative connotations. "Why do our friends, as well as our enemies, call us 'negroes'?" asked one black correspondent of the *Liberator* in 1831. "We feel it a term of reproach, and could wish our friends would call us by some other name."[63] In a protracted essay on the word published in 1844, racial theorist R. B. Lewis addressed the matter. Considering the word's origins, he concluded that despite its use by white abolitionists, it was a term of derision. The author, who called himself "a colored man" on the title page of his work, noted that among the Moors of northern Africa, "the word *negro* is considered insulting, and is used as an epithet of contempt to the colored people." Likewise, he added, "It has been long used by our common enemies in America. It is not only insulting, but very improper for any one to make use of it." Because of its sullied history, Lewis argued, "negro" was a term that blacks' "friends" would do well to avoid and certainly not present "to the world."[64]

Black spokespersons avoided the word not simply because of the dangerous consonance it shared with the insulting "nigger," but because it denied the very respectable, bourgeois-seeming values black leaders were forging, situating its utterers instead among the racially hostile white working classes, or their own degraded brethren. Black activists deftly intuited the great significance of properly locating an appropriate term for the race on the North's solidifying class hierarchy. The respectability that might accrue to blacks through use of a proper term was not a mere luxury that might benefit the living standards of a black elite. Respectability in antebellum terms entailed far more: it signified a source of social power, without which none could hope for the regard of the public or the protection of the state.

As an aid to achieving this status, antebellum black activists almost uniformly found "negro" wanting. By the Civil War, the word had gained deep significance in northern society. To utter it was to call up a library of degrading images, all of which suggested blacks' inability to function as proper Americans. Yet they also shunned it for the derogatory class imputations it carried for those who spoke it. African American public figures who wrestled over the proper name for the race correctly divined the significance of their enterprise. If their use of words like "nigger" suggested to whites their inherent depravity and vulgarity, the surest counterattack was for blacks to speak publicly in ways that were the opposite of low: that is, respectably. Black elites' incessant calls for the masses to comport themselves properly extended to speech as well. Editors urged their readers to inculcate in their children a litany of "respectable" habits, among which "correctness of language should be regarded as a cardinal point." Children were never to be permitted to use "provincialisms, coarse expressions, vulgarisms, nor bad pronunciation."[65] Spokespersons fully understood the implications of distinctions in pronunciation and diction. The N-word complex simply constituted another forum for them to demonstrate their respectability or their vulgarity.

As in legal documents, runaway slave advertisements, emerging racial science, and popular speech indicate, the "N-word" complex was, at best, the language of physical description.[66] Like "black," it cataloged the bodies of African-descended people, organizing them into legal, moral, and scientific taxonomies, and objectifying them to the point that they eventually disappeared altogether from public acknowledgment. This rhetorical eclipsing of the black presence was evident in the casualness with which a Union officer during the Civil War could recall that "nobody was there, save a lot of nigs,"[67] as well as in the ease with which authors put in the mouths of their southern white characters words that calmly negated the humanity—and, indeed, the very existence—of black people. In one early twentieth-century novel, when a character is asked if an important man has entered a train, he replies: "Well, wasn't nobody answerin' to that description got on. Only a couple of nigs, far as I know." Mark Twain lampooned this effacing of the black presence late in the century in *The Adventures of Huckleberry Finn*:

"Anybody hurt?"
"No'm. Killed a nigger."
"Well, it's lucky; because sometimes people do get hurt."[68]

In speaking for their humanity, it was clear to black activists even early in the nineteenth century that the word "negro" would not serve. The transition to "negro" would take at least half a century, during which the modern implications of the terms, newly established in the North, would become well worn with popular use. During the early decades of the century, however, its form and meanings were simply too fuzzy.

A RESPECTABLE ALTERNATIVE

In lieu of "negro," a majority of antebellum black spokespersons chose a different title for the race, one already in common usage by the 1830s. The foremost advocate of the new phrase was Samuel Cornish, a newspaper editor and Presbyterian clergyman from New York City. Upon assuming the editor's desk of the *Weekly Advocate* in 1837, Cornish renamed the paper the *Colored American* and began alternately using the phrases "people of color," "colored people," or merely "colored" in his columns.

Cornish was neither first nor alone in advocating "colored" as a term of reference for the race, and his selection was not arbitrary. By 1830, versions of "colored" had become the de facto terms of choice for many black northerners and sympathetic whites. By the time the first national black convention enshrined the term "free persons of colour" in the title of its proceedings and those of every national black convention that followed, the term was already in wide use.[69] Despite the fact that ultimately it proved no more immune to the process by which whites had debased earlier names for the race, in countless documents and speeches black northerners regularly fell back upon phrases containing "colored" to describe themselves and their brethren.

The title offered several benefits. Unlike other terms, "people of color" was comparatively new, and relatively unsullied by the effects of racial prejudice. Better yet, it had a respectable history and offered pleasant associations with African-descended social elites throughout the western hemisphere. As used by black northerners, the phrase derived from the French term *gens de couleur,* used in St. Domingue and other places in the Caribbean to denote a class of free and skilled mulattoes, usually artisans and merchants. In Caribbean practice, "people of color" denoted a racial "caste" between the ranks of generally darker-complected slaves and white colonizers. Every New World slave society underwent a pattern of development that proffered the possibility of such a class: distinctions among African-descended peoples created multitiered racial caste structures composed of darker-skinned slaves and marginalized free blacks on the one hand and skilled and wealthy free mulatto elites on the other. The southern colonies on mainland North America, like other slave societies, had passed through an early period of flexible race relations that permitted the emergence of a middling caste of free people of African descent. There, however, the demands of the plantation economy combined with relatively high ratios of whites to blacks to ensure that such a caste would never develop to the extent that it did elsewhere in the New World. By the early nineteenth century, only dim echoes of the Caribbean pattern remained: in cities like Charleston and New Orleans, tightly knit cliques of light-skinned mulatto elites maintained social customs designed to maintain their precarious status.

The phrase "people of color" thus originally bespoke social distinctions among African-descended people throughout the slave societies of the New World. It was the label for the free, creole, usually light-complected, African-descended social and economic elites who served as urban artisans and merchants, and who frequently distinguished themselves as a racial caste entirely distinct from black slaves. At times, this middling caste aided their enslaved brothers, as when free coloreds in St. Domingue enlisted the slaves in their revolt against French rule. At others, however, free people of color proved hostile to the interests of the enslaved. In parts of Brazil free mulattoes served as slave catchers, and many free people of color in the Caribbean held slaves themselves.[70] In the United States, free colored elites in Charleston distinguished themselves from their darker, enslaved brethren by founding institutions like the Brown Fellowship Society, which admitted only those with light skin color and the social privileges that skin color entailed. The government of Louisiana considered New Orleans free coloreds loyal enough to grant them the singular right to carry weapons in defense of the state.[71]

In the late eighteenth century, the term for this middling caste traveled to the United States, and thus reentered the one nation exceptional in the diaspora for not featuring a fully developed caste of free colored people. In the 1790s, mulatto refugees from the revolution then plaguing strife-torn St. Domingue began finding shelter in southern port cities like Charleston, bringing with them the respectable term they used to describe themselves.[72] Reinforced by infusions of refugees from the French Revolution, free black elites in the United States dragged the term out of the dustbin of its early history and began referring to themselves as "free people of color."[73] Petitions from free blacks to the South Carolina state legislature in the ensuing years witnessed the emergence of the phrase "free people of color" alongside the older, and more cumbersome, "free Negroes, Musteez and Mulatoes." Legally undefined, the new term occasioned enough confusion to create loopholes in the fabric of slavery which demanded remedy.[74] In 1848, a judge in South Carolina sought to clarify trouble created by the novel phrase. Were these "people of color" entitled to all the rights of those African-descended people traditionally defined as free? State lawmakers, he said, should use the actual words "'free negroes, mulattoes and mestizoes,' and then every one would have a certain guide to understand the words used."[75] Nonetheless, the phrase "people of color" steadily moved northward. In 1815 a free black man in Virginia petitioned for the right to buy his family from bondage as "a free man of Colour," as did one eleven years later in a petition requesting that he not be forcibly removed from the state.[76]

The phrase crossed the Mason-Dixon line shortly after the turn of the nineteenth century, coming eventually to encompass all people of African descent. Well-meaning whites in the New York Manumission Society termed newly freed blacks "Persons of Colour," though only to comment on a rising "looseness of manners & depravity of conduct" among them.[77] In 1813, James Forten Sr., a prominent black Philadelphian, published his *Letters of a Man of Color*, though within the document he often used the adjectives "African" or "black." The need to oppose the claims of the American Colonization Society only helped spread the term. Blacks meeting in Richmond in 1817 to protest the Society chose "free people of color" as a label for themselves, reflecting increasingly common usage while eschewing troubling references to Africa. In 1818, black Philadelphians, led by Forten, employed the term in the constitution of an educational society.[78]

The phrase also found a home in northern law. Prior to 1830, laws in most states above the Mason-Dixon line referred to African Americans in general under the rubric of "negro, mulatto, or mustee" (the last term describing one of black and Indian descent). "Person of colour" occasionally appeared after 1800, most often alongside "negro" and "mulatto," as if to denote a distinct racial category.[79] After 1830, this general trend began to erode. Following popular parlance, even the slow-changing realm of legal terminology had begun to break down the old distinctions in favor of the more generic "colored." An Illinois statute from 1833 referred indiscriminately to "all free negroes" and "every negro or mulatto" in the same sentence, suggesting that lawmakers had begun to recognize the distinction only intermittently.[80] The final break came when laws began substituting "person of color" as a convenient replacement for "negroes and mulattoes," as when an 1830 New York statute referred simply to "any person of colour" and made a distinction only between those who were "white, or coloured."[81]

Throughout the 1810s and 1820s, the phrase filtered into the writings of elite black spokesmen, finally entering the world of print media, which uni-

Table 3.4. Naming Preferences in Antebellum Black Conventions

	Afric or Afro	Black	Negro	Colored	Total
1830s	2	5	0	76	83
1840s	0	16	1	160	177
1850s	0	19	9	283	311
Total	2	40	10	519	571
(%)	(0.35)	(7.00)	(1.80)	(90.90)	(100.00)

Source: Robert J. Young, "The Political Culture of Northern African-American Activists, 1830–1859" (Ph.D. diss., Syracuse University, 1992), 279–80.

versalized it. By the time Samuel Cornish and John Russwurm published the first issue of *Freedom's Journal* in 1827, the term was current in New York, for the paper announced that it devoted itself exclusively to the interests of "free persons of colour." Two years later Bostonian David Walker could refer to "the Coloured Citizens of the World" in his militant *Appeal*.[82] The phrase "people of color" emerged as a term of choice among African Americans as black activism melded with white abolitionism in the 1830s. Blacks used the term in meetings held in 1830 and 1831 to oppose the American Colonization Society, lending credence to the idea that the new name arose partly in response to Society efforts to expatriate blacks to Africa.[83] From 1830 to 1860, the phrases containing "colored" dominated terms of self-reference employed in black state and national conventions.[84] While it is impossible to document exhaustively the preferences of black northerners in the incidental use of self-referential terms, it is clear that "colored" found favor in formal institutional settings, especially those wherein black spokesmen presented the race to a larger public. In a suggestive content analysis of black convention resolutions, R. J. Young found that of 571 instances in which self-referential terms were used, 519 (91 percent) featured "colored" or "people of color" (Table 3.4). The frequency with which these terms were employed remained remarkably stable from the 1830s through the 1850s. The term "black" was used 7 percent of the time, "negro" nearly 2 percent, and terms with "Afro" or "Afric" less than 1 percent. Interestingly, the rare use of the latter two terms occurred not in the 1850s, when black nationalism was in its antebellum heyday, but in the 1830s, while the abandonment of "African" was still under way. While far from comprehensive, such findings suggest the strong preference for "colored" that had developed by 1830.[85] These conclusions are reinforced by even a cursory scan of the titles of important writings by black leaders in the antebellum years: Frederick Douglass's "What Are the Colored People Doing for Themselves"; Martin R. Delany's *The Condition, Elevation, Emigration, and Destiny of the Colored People of the United States*; and Alexander Crummell's *The Relations and Duties of Free Colored Men in America to Africa*.

Black northerners' adoption of the label "people of color" indicated not merely an awareness of racial matters in other parts of the hemisphere, but some social pretension. In its original setting the term referred to free mulatto elites who considered themselves as distinct from black slaves as from white planters.[86] In the southern states, "free people of color" continued to refer not to all blacks but only to the small number of the legally free. Elite members of this free black population—who tended to be urban, light-complected, and skilled—followed the Caribbean pattern of racial and social stratification by distinguishing themselves from slaves. In adopting "free people of color," black northerners thus adopted a respectable alternative to monikers that whites associated with a race they considered slavish and a homeland they thought of as barbaric. Black spokesmen then applied this name not simply to themselves as a northern free elite, but to all people of African descent. In an egalitarian gesture, black spokesmen dropped the "free," and began referring simply to "people of color" or "colored people." By 1827, slavery had been all but abolished in every northern state, thus rendering "free" redundant and unnecessary as a term of self-reference anyway. By that time, all that remained of the original *gens de couleur* was the phrase's attractive associations with respectability and social status. The transformation of the label as it spread from the Caribbean to the northern United States represented the democratization of a term originally intended for a small class of social and economic elites. In the hands of black northerners, "colored people" came to represent all people of African descent: the slave and the free, the dark-skinned and the light, the poor and the well-off.

Far from abandoning a self-conscious affinity with Africa, the choice of "people of color" constituted an impulse toward racial unity throughout the diaspora, which offset the particularist American identity apparent in phrases like "colored American." The transition from "African" to "colored" did not sacrifice racial unity on the altar of national loyalty. To the contrary, advocates of a singular name for the race responded to the perceived need for racial solidarity throughout the diaspora, across the nation, and within northern black communities themselves. The use of a single name for the race would undermine forces that elsewhere had pulled apart a single identity for African-descended people. In other slave societies of the New World, black identity had been divided by differences based on class, occupational skill, relationship to servitude, and relationship to Africa. By subsuming under the mantle of a single term distinctions that had divided black identity in other places in the New World, black leaders hoped to advance their goal of uniting a people often unified only by their shared experiences of racial proscription.

To its advocates in the antebellum North, the word "colored" grouped under one banner everyone from the most "debased" enslaved field hands to the "colored aristocracies" of the seaboard cities. A term that South Carolina's legislature had once used as an economical alternative to "free Negroes, Musteez and Mulatoes"[87] came for black northerners to embrace all black people, regardless of status of servitude, skin color, occupational skill, or cultural outlook. Thus a meeting of black people in Trenton, New Jersey, in November 1831 could refer to "the free and slave man of color."[88] David Walker directed his incendiary appeal to "the Coloured Citizens of the World," while Henry Highland Garnet, also an advocate of militant resistance, celebrated the African past in a pamphlet titled *The Past and Present Condition and the Destiny of the Colored Race.*[89] From a label for a small group of free mixed-race artisans and light-skinned social elites from the Caribbean, black spokesmen in the antebellum North forged a term that encompassed the broadest possible range of black social experience. Relative to "African" or "negro," "people of color" offered a term free of derision; it boasted a history of use by respectable black people and was amenable to the petit bourgeois social outlooks of northern leaders. It allowed northern black spokesmen to address their dual concerns of reconstructing the public reputation of the race and retaining their own status as social elites within black communities. It was under the banner of this new term that black leaders sought to focus the energies of their people against racial oppression.

RESPECTABILITY BY FIAT

The consensus on the term "colored people" was never total. While relatively pristine, even "colored" had a history—one bound to be as troublesome as the history of African-descended people themselves. The task of developing a name both useful and unsullied was not easy, and contenders abounded. Acknowledging the ways in which prejudice had degraded terms used to describe the race, some advocated eschewing altogether phrases that identified black people as anything but American. Responding to whites' practice of tainting all words used to denote the race, William Whipper, the Philadelphia leader who helped found the American Moral Reform Society, championed the view that any appellation specific to black people threatened to reinforce in the minds of whites their already rampant prejudice. This position accorded fully with Whipper's stand against "complexional" institutions, or groups open only to blacks. Just as he repudiated organizations that acknowledged differences between blacks and whites in their membership policies, even those designed to aid African Americans, he urged his brethren to shun completely any terms that set them apart from other Americans. At the national black convention of 1835, he orchestrated the passage of a resolution admonishing black people to "abandon the use of the word 'colored,' when either speaking or writing concerning themselves; and especially to remove the title African from their institutions, the marbles of churches, etc."[90] He later explained his position: "We have too long witnessed the baneful effects of distinctions founded in hatred and prejudice, to advocate the insertion of either the word 'white' or 'colored.'"[91] Whipper argued that, because whites had twisted racial names and used racial separation to ostracize blacks, any black use of those tactics must derive from the same malevolent motives and lead to the same invidious results. By labeling themselves as distinct, whites promoted an "odious distinction" between white and black that benefited whites at the expense of blacks. "If we practice the same," Whipper warned, "these distinctions will never cease." Furthermore, thus promoting rather than destroying distinction would conflict "with the first principles of the moral government."[92]

Others agreed. Uriah Boston, a barber and activist from Poughkeepsie, New York, likewise rejected the idea that blacks should reinforce their distinct identity. He believed that "the true policy . . . for the colored people to pursue is, lessen the distinction between whites and colored citizens of the United States."[93] In 1859, an anonymous writer for the *Anglo-African Magazine* published a light-hearted attack on those who sought to retain a distinct racial identity within the nation. Specifically, he chided those attempting to enhance black solidarity by invoking the African past through racial monikers, as embodied in the title of the very magazine that published his article. "When we do marshal out our energies under a national name, we have no higher one, poor as it is to us, than 'American,'" he wrote. He went on to expose what he believed to be the poverty of seeking a pure and eternal African identity, rejecting it as a buttress for racial solidarity: "If we would individually exalt . . . our simple humanity, and feel less concern that an *African* humanity, made up of skins more or less dark, and of hair more or less frizzled, should be perpetuated to the end of time, we might rely confidently on our manhood alone, and trust it to overcome for us difficulties however appalling."[94] This author, like Whipper and his supporters, rejected any racial name that might call attention to the distinctions whites used to justify their treatment of black people. As a result, many African American newspapers chose to shun racially distinct names in favor of the simple "American." Junius C. Morel, Whipper's fellow Philadelphian, attempted to found a black newspaper entitled simply *The American*. In Ohio in 1853, William Howard Day began a newspaper with a title that, while complexion-free, still spoke to African Americans' marginalized social status, namely, the *Aliened American*. Three years later a convention of Ohio black men charged that "the appellation of Americans" was "the only title we desire."[95] In addition to its apparent racial neutrality, the name also promised to refute the American Colonization Society's dangerous suggestion that blacks in America rightfully belonged only in the land of their ancestry.

Yet while many leaders supported it, others rejected the racially neutral option propounded by Whipper and his ilk. These spokespersons opted to challenge the "public mind" by employing a name they hoped to control more successfully than "African" or "negro." Cornish, for one, attacked Whipper's suggestion that black people ought to be called "oppressed Americans." Cornish acknowledged the problem posed by all possible names for the race, which was that they were riddled with the degrading implications layered on them by hostile whites. He agreed with Whipper that a sullied history rendered most existing names for the race inappropriate. "We are written about, preached to, and prayed for, as Negroes, Africans, and blacks, all of which have been stereotyped, as names of reproach, and on that account, if no other, are unacceptable," he wrote. Unlike Whipper, he sought a label as yet unburdened with the denigrating weight of extant terms. Cornish chose "colored American" as "the true term, and one which is above reproach."[96]

To the New York editor, it was important to acknowledge the unique experience of black people as a marginalized class. This was something that names free of complexional references, even those denoting the precarious status of blacks, failed to do. "Oppressed Americans! Who are they?" he asked. "Nonsense, brethren! You are COLORED AMERICANS. The Indians are RED AMERICANS and the white people are WHITE AMERICANS, and you are as good as they and they no better than you."[97] A sympathetic correspondent supported Cornish, arguing that "oppressed American" and "disfranchised American" were "too vague and indefinite to present a proper idea of us as a people." Challenging Whipper, he wondered what the public would make of a black church or school named with such terms. "Would they understand it as relating to us exclusively?"[98] The mere invocation of marginality was insufficient if it neglected the unique history and experience of African-descended people in America. Whipper, Cornish implied, failed to understand that in the hands of black people specific racial names served not to practice the same prejudice that had victimized blacks but to remedy the imbalance of opportunity and rights created by that prejudice and visited singularly upon black people. Phrases like "aliened" seemed to neglect blacks' special sense of peopleness—a unity based not simply on shared persecution but on shared history and identity. Cornish feared that Whipper's position, in minimizing the complexional differences that made the black experience distinct, would "rob us of our nationality"—by which he meant a sense of communal identity born of shared historical experiences.[99]

Others besides Cornish maintained hope that they could reclaim racial pride from words used to describe the race. Frederick A. Hinton, a Philadelphia Garrisonian, quarreled with Whipper's American Moral Reform Society over the use of the term "colored." Writing to Cornish, he related his attempts to suggest that the Society refer specifically to colored people in their resolutions. Whipper had firmly rejected his overtures. Hinton responded indignantly that his detractors argued that "the term 'colored,' implied degradation!" and that one detractor "went so far . . . as to ask—'Why should we glory in retaining the *badge of our degradation*!!!!'" Hinton owed his feigned shock to his own belief in the absolute necessity of reclaiming pride for whatever terms were used to describe the race. "We are fully aware," he wrote, "that the degree of respectability that we enjoy, has been wrested from the hands of oppressors by the presentation of facts exhibiting [the] worth" of people of color.[100] For Hinton, a key to this process of demonstrating the equality of the race lay in imparting new and empowering meanings to the terms used to name it.

William Watkins, a Baltimore educator and frequent correspondent to northern black newspapers, also supported Cornish in the debate. Black leaders could bring to bear but minimal control over the words used to describe the race, he contended; they had little governance over the meanings words contained and the ways that they were used. Realizing this, Watkins considered the selection of an entirely new term for the race to be a mistake. "Words are used as the signs of our ideas," he wrote. Because impervious custom and common consent "established the relation between the sign or word, and the thing signified," it was nearly impossible to controvert successfully the meanings of racial labels. In Watkins's view, it ultimately mattered little what term was used to describe the race, for popular practice imparted meanings to words more effectively than did leaders. He preferred "colored" precisely because of its common usage throughout American society. "In vain do we carp at some supposed inapplicability of a term as applied to a certain object," he concluded. In the case of "colored," "custom has fixed its meaning in reference to a particular people in this country, and from this decision, however arbitrary, there is, I am sure, no successful appeal."[101]

Other commentators made the inverse point. Entirely new words could be proposed, yet the fate of alternatives like "Negro-Saxon,"[102] which never caught on, suggested that novelty itself presented problems. Some attempted to institute other names, often containing references to Africa. The term "Afric-American" was used in anticolonization meetings in New Haven, Connecticut, and Columbia, Pennsylvania, in 1831.[103] In 1859 Thomas Hamilton challenged naming practices by titling his newspaper the *Weekly Anglo-African*.[104] These alternatives, however, were never adopted by many Americans, black or white. Blacks failed to embrace them not only because of their negative associations in the minds of whites, but also because they were esoteric phrases rarely invoked in daily use. Most participants in the names controversy understood that few Americans would employ new terms on a daily basis. As one black writer stated publicly, "Language . . . is, as we all know, but the sign of things, and should be always used and understood agreeable to its general acceptation among men."[105] Leaders found themselves torn between the need to rely upon popular usage on the one hand and the clear liabilities of relying on the words of a society absolutely pervaded by racial prejudice on the other.

In wrestling with the names controversy and the principles underlying it, black thinkers had stumbled upon a debate with far-reaching consequences for the freedom struggle they waged. On the one hand, those such as William Whipper claimed that the word (or, generically, the sign) bore a very close relationship to what that word meant (that is, what the sign signified). For Whipper, invoking the sign (in his case, speaking or writing the word) invoked the thing it signified. He thus argued that by speaking the words that reflected racial distinctions he actually reified racial distinctions. As a corollary, to avoid invoking the sign (or speaking the word) was to avoid invoking the prejudice he sought to eradicate. The only way to eradicate the signified was to avoid invoking the sign. William J. Watkins had supported Cornish's endorsement of "colored," though—and none of his contemporaries noted this—his logic was actually closer to Whipper's. The "imperious dictates of custom" had fixed the relation between signs and what they signified, effectively removing the possibility for changing that relationship beyond human agency. In this respect, Watkins's interpretation of the problem was even more pessimistic than Whipper's, for while Whipper hoped that mere avoidance of the sign could eradicate what it signified, Watkins considered this an impossibility. For him, "colored" was to be embraced not as an act of self-empowerment but as the best of many bad options. It was "too convenient in practice to dispense with."[106] This position was echoed by "Sydney," another of Cornish's defenders, who claimed sardonically that Whipper should have known enough to understand that prejudice could not be conquered by a mere word.[107]

Cornish stood at the other pole, though his pessimistic defenders never understood his true position. Like Whipper, he believed that names mattered, that the sign itself bore a meaningful relationship to what it signified. Yet he differed from Whipper and Watkins and "Sydney," who all believed that relationship to be fixed and inviolate. Rather, Cornish believed that by exerting control over public discourse blacks might alter the relationship between words and what they meant. They might over the course of time change the significance of words, realigning their meanings in ways that might prove emancipatory.

Disparate understandings of the malleability of the sign separated Cornish, Whipper, and Cornish's defenders. All agreed implicitly that popular prejudice endowed racial labels with denigrating stereotypes that inhibited black freedom by enhancing distinction and prejudice. The similarities ended there. Cornish's defenders supported "colored" because they believed reclamation or even removal of the term to be beyond possibility. Given that sad reality, there was no alternative but to accept "colored" as a necessary fact of life. Whipper, on the other hand, believed it possible to help eradicate prejudice through the minimal endeavor of avoiding the terms which invoked it. Relative to Cornish's defenders, Whipper actually imagined a rather rare degree of black agency. Cornish, however, granted blacks much more. For him, everything depended on language's currency. Because "colored" was in common use, unlike new and exotic alternatives, it afforded ready access to the "public mind," and therefore promised an unprecedented opportunity to shape white opinion on matters of race. It could do this precisely because it offered the best available blend of novelty and currency—it was new enough to be as yet free from the taint of prejudice, yet common enough to actually be accepted in daily parlance.

Cornish did not intend merely to parrot an extant phrase. His call for the use of "colored" as a new label for the race suggested not that the term was newly invented, which it clearly was not, but that its relative novelty in the North had thus far saved it from the stigma already imparted to "African" and "negro." He wished to "baptize" it, to allow it to be born again so that it might bear new and improved meaning. In "colored American," which he used to title his newspaper, he synthesized a new label from the American "colored" and the Caribbean "people of color." Reborn, the new term would be both an American term free of white reproach, as well as a term embracing all people of African descent—and especially those loyal to the "America" that sought to alienate them.[108]

Insofar as it emblematized the relationship between black protest thought and a broader context of American values, the debate and its significance cannot be understated. The entire thread of black protest can be understood as analogous to the names controversy. The approaches black thinkers took to crafting a distinct protest tradition from the ideological materials surrounding them raised questions clearly addressed in those debates. Some would echo the thinking of Watkins and "Sydney," believing that white control over crucial values and tropes could never be contested, merely worked within. Others, like Whipper, sought to undermine the injurious results of what they saw as white control over hostile values and tropes by avoiding them altogether and seeking to use only those elements of northern public discourse that seemed overtly to coincide with their interests. But others, like Cornish, pioneered a different path. On a wider scale, Whipper could not envision black empowerment proceeding through the auspices of white supremacy's tactics. He could not imagine subordinating the values of an oppressive America to the cause of black freedom, nor could he foresee manipulating the tropes and founding mythology of American history in emancipatory ways. He could not consider the possibility of refashioning signs, especially those most deeply implicated in blacks' degradation, so that they might serve black freedom. In contrast, Cornish could. He considered the best opportunity for altering popular attitudes to be through the counter-manipulation of commonplace tropes and values. He sought to empower blacks by manipulating the very stratagems of white supremacy. Nothing less than public perceptions of the race were at stake. A new ability to have its interests "presented in community," Cornish hoped, would no longer permit whites to "reproach us as exoticks"—unassimilable aliens in the midst of white Americans. As so many black spokespersons understood at least implicitly, control of language thus served as a measure of control over ideas themselves, and some saw both as important components in the struggle for freedom and equality.

In the form of the next generation's black nationalists, Cornish's disciples took his position even further. As frustrations mounted in an increasingly hostile racial environment, northern black spokespersons worked continually to advance the abolition of slavery and the equality of free blacks in the midst of an increasingly hostile racial environment. Freedom in the North, always tenuous and qualified, seemed increasingly threatened in the 1840s and 1850s. This was evident to black northerners in the South's efforts to reopen the slave trade and expand the peculiar institution into the West, a pattern of steady disfranchisement in the North, the imposition of strictures in the new western states that limited black rights, and increasing instances of mob violence directed at blacks and abolitionists. Following the failure of the Liberty Party and political abolitionism in the 1840s, the 1850s proved especially arduous. The Compromise of 1850, which admitted California to the union as a free state and permitted slavery in some newly organized western territories, also implemented a harsh new fugitive slave law, which struck at the rights of free black and white northerners as well as the humanity of the slaves. The struggle over the fate of "bleeding Kansas" following the Kansas-Nebraska Act of 1854 demonstrated the violent lengths to which slavery's defenders were willing to resort to uphold the expansion of the institution. Three years later, the Supreme Court enshrined in law the principle of black inferiority when it denied Dred Scott's rights to freedom and citizenship. Frustrated by thirty years of almost fruitless activism, some black spokesmen in the North began advocating radical new strategies for black liberation and elevation.

A product of disillusionment, the National Emigration Convention of Colored People met in 1854 to consider the possibility of emigration to Africa or elsewhere. Engineered largely by Martin R. Delany, the convention took Cornish's position in the names controversy to the next logical step. The Convention resolved "that the relative terms Negro, African, Black, Colored and Mulatto, when applied to us, shall ever be held with the same respect and pride; and synonymous with the terms, Caucasian, White, Anglo-Saxon and European, when applied to that class of people." [109] Unlike Cornish, who sought the term least imbued with racial prejudice, Delany and his colleagues proclaimed by fiat all racial monikers to be inherently free from denigrating white stereotypes.

In doing so, the convention applied the same logic to the names controversy that it did to the issue of emigration and colonization. In embracing the possibility of black migration to Africa or elsewhere, the Convention considered an option that black leaders had long suppressed, because it seemed to sanction the designs of the malevolent American Colonization Society and its supporters. The Convention's great accomplishment was to find a way to advocate colonization without endorsing the American Colonization Society. In discovering this autonomy, the Convention declared itself free from the power of white colonizationists to shape black options for freedom. It tacitly acknowledged that black strategists had limited their options, if only by rejecting the emigration advocated by the Colonization Society, and hence by conceding the power of whites to shape the black search for elevation. In advocating emigration but uncoupling it from the Colonization Society, the Convention declared its intention to no longer permit any whites to dictate or limit black options. Similarly, the Convention sought to free itself, and by extension black people as a whole, from bondage to meanings dictated by a prejudiced public mind. It simply declared itself free from the debilitating effects of white use of racial labels and proclaimed all names for the race to be terms of pride.

By the late antebellum period, some black spokespersons were noting the success of the rhetorical strategy of reclaiming racial labels (and, by implication, American values) from popular prejudice. In 1859, James McCune Smith used black success in the names issue to note the qualified progress African Americans had made in the search for their own freedom. Whereas in Jefferson's day whites had referred to members of the race as "black" and "negro," they now used the term "colored people." In the minds of whites, Smith noted, his people were "no longer blacks, bordering on bestiality; they are 'colored,' and they are a 'people.'" He concluded optimistically that "the public voice has already softened the terms" used to talk of the race.[110]

CONCLUSION

Antebellum black spokesmen would have agreed with Ralph Ellison that "it is through our names that we first place ourselves in the world." They well understood the import of the name of the race in crafting its public identity. Yet they also considered most names for the race given by whites "gifts" far too dangerous to accept. Many, like William Whipper, feared drawing great attention to distinctions between the races, which seemed to justify slavery and racial proscription. Consequently, some urged African Americans to avoid altogether any references to the distinct qualities of black bodies and, by extension, of the black social experience. Other leaders claimed that to bury somatic distinctions in complexion-free names was to bury the existence of racial inequality, not to mention the distinct identities of black people. The challenge was to acknowledge the distinct treatment and identity of the race in a way that argued for its right of inclusion in the civil community. Those who championed a distinct name for the race, like Samuel Cornish, argued on just these grounds.

In all cases, participants subordinated the controversy over names to the larger goals of equal participation in American life. Black spokespersons understood their challenge to be the reformation and reconstruction of the public reputation of a people whom whites had sullied as alien, vulgar, and inferior. They sensed that their best option was simply to argue harder and louder than their critics—to rely wholeheartedly on public discussion to convince the nation of the race's right to equal inclusion in the national community. "Colored American" was less about claiming a cultural affinity with Africa and Africans than it was about asserting a political identity that could yield practical gains from intransigent enemies.

That that name became "people of color" or "colored American" illuminates tensions in black leadership styles that have persisted into the twentieth century. On the one hand, "colored American" embraced all people of African descent: the slave and the free, the African and the American, the elite and the popular, the dark and the light. At the same time, it denoted a respectability that signaled elite social pretension and offset its egalitarianism. Understanding the issue as one of developing strategies to sway the public mind, African American elites often found themselves arguing on the terrain of their enemies. Their concern with respectability, or the class values of an emerging urban middle class, often placed them in the position of endorsing measures of progress and civilization established in part by enemies. That they sought to retain their respectability did not, however, demonstrate their simple capitulation to the lures of middle-class values. They claimed respectability as their own, not as a desire to live up to the standards of others. And in this they were right, at least insofar as the values they claimed were not "white." The notion that any part of American culture or any right due to American citizens lay beyond their claim would have been totally alien to African American leaders. Having built both, they claimed both, as Colored Americans.

However, ultimately "Colored American" failed to serve the purpose Samuel Cornish had intended for it. In the antebellum era it may have been less accreted with negative meaning than other terms, but it was no less susceptible to negative imputation. By the end of the nineteenth century, it—like "African"—had become sullied by time and the malevolent intentions of hostile whites. It remained a polite term of reference, especially in the South, where whites used far worse alternatives on a daily basis well into the Civil Rights era of the mid-twentieth century. But by the turn of the twentieth century, members of a new generation of black leaders had come to consider "colored" outdated, old-fashioned, and possibly even dangerous. "Negro," now capitalized, and relatively free of the crippling class associations that had made it disreputable—became the name of choice among many African American spokesmen, endorsed by W. E. B. Du Bois and Booker T. Washington alike. By that time, African Americans had passed through decades that had witnessed the victory of the Civil War, the defeat of Reconstruction, and the nadir of Jim Crow. The consensus over names crumbled and reformed once again, as it has to the present day. Yet from its earliest incarnations to the present, the constant undercurrent in the debate over names has always been the demand for freedom, liberty, and equality.

Not only could you travel upward toward success
but you could travel downward as well; up *and* down,
in retreat as well as in advance, crabways and
crossways and around in a circle,
meeting your old selves coming and going
and perhaps all at the same time.
Ralph Ellison, Invisible Man

CHAPTER 4

Discipline of the Heart, Discipline of the Mind

The Sources of Black Social Thought

Few feelings are as painful as those accompanying the abjuration of faith. One of the most devastating events in Ralph Ellison's novel *Invisible Man* occurs when the protagonist first realizes that racial progress through self-improvement—a notion imbued in him since his earliest childhood—is false. Thus begins for him a mental journey that leaves him without faith and hence without identity, a man as veiled to himself as to white America. Ellison's protagonist decries "that spiral business, that progress goo! . . . And that lie that success was a rising *upward.* What a crummy lie they kept us dominated by. . . . How could I have missed it for so long?"[1] The story of Ellison's protagonist is the story of a young man betrayed by a precept that had demanded sacrifice in the pursuit of personal moral virtue but had failed to deliver the promised "rise" of the race. Writing in the middle of the twentieth century, Ellison captured for his own and surrounding generations the feelings of many African Americans that their faith in the notion of progress through self-improvement had been largely fruitless.[2] The passing of the self-improvement ideology as the primary basis for black protest thought in the twentieth century heralded the rise of new critiques of the

American racial system, none of which pretended to the dominance that self-improvement had enjoyed for well over a century.

The self-improvement that many African Americans abandoned in the course of the twentieth century was old even in 1900. It harkened as far back as the early-nineteenth-century North, as part of the effort of black spokespersons to explain the position of African-descended people in America and to proffer hope for the betterment of their condition. In the decades before the Civil War, black leaders set forth their understandings of self-improvement in pamphlets, speeches, newspapers, convention proceedings, and private letters. The doctrine they espoused expressed faith in the notion that the attainment of personal moral and mental "elevation" would bring about the success of the individual. Such personal successes would redound to the interests of the race by presenting white America with examples of black people on equal footing with whites. Through such examples, self-improvement would refute the contention of many whites that blacks were inherently and irrevocably degraded, arguing instead that "condition" rather than "color"—"nurture" rather than "nature"—had determined the race's admittedly lowly status. Through elevation, blacks would demonstrate to whites their worthiness for the rights and liberties withheld from them.

For many concerned with the freedom struggle, this uplift ideology has posed serious dilemmas. Rooted so deeply in the values of middle-class America, could black leaders have evinced the intellectual independence apparently necessary to develop a truly radical black nationalism, or the cultural autonomy necessary to forge healthy communities? Could black leaders have been steeped in bourgeois values without sacrificing their agency to resist? Did, as so many posit, effective resistance largely depend on cultural autonomy and intellectual independence? What limitations on their resistance might black thinkers' ideological reliance on the values of America have imposed? What, ultimately, *was* the relationship between black protest thought and the ideological context of antebellum America?

As we shall see, the languages of elevation and respectability *were* integral to the thought of African Americans living in a society of hostile European-descended Americans who outnumbered blacks and dominated the nation's political economy. Yet that did not necessarily render the use of these languages by African Americans evidence of an unhealthy assimilation into American life or of their internalization of values antithetical to their interests. Black leaders' pervasive calls for black uplift were not a capitulation to existing values nor were they symptoms of their internalization of the mores of middle-class society. Black elites *did* internalize those values, yet their faith in them must be considered distinct from black spokespersons' use of them as a strategy for racial activism. Activist men and women sought to use uplift and respectability very distinctly to resist. Through these rhetorical devices, they hoped to create the circumstances in which whites would be compelled to alter their racial attitudes so as to yield rights to blacks. A deep appreciation of the worldviews of black elites permits the possibility of a new, more nuanced view of the role of class in the formation of black protest thought.

This chapter explores the myriad points of congruence between black thought and its social, intellectual, and cultural milieu in an effort to flesh out the foundations of African American protest thought. The role of race in the formation of that thought is the subject of the next chapter, which details the ways in which the fundamentals of black social thought provided the lens through which black spokespersons analyzed the special problems imposed on them by racist ideology and practice and suggested ways to formulate solutions to the problems posed by white supremacy.

INTERLUDE: THE AFRICAN AMERICAN CONFIDENCE MAN

In Cincinnati, Ohio, on August 16, 1829, several hundred white citizens began attacking the west end of the city, where most of its African Americans resided. According to a newspaper account, for the next week local thugs could be found nightly "throwing stones, demolishing houses, [and] doing every other act of violence" to the part of town known as "Little Africa." In the end, one African American was murdered and several more injured; numerous houses in "Bucktown" had been burned to the ground, their contents pillaged. The immediate trigger of the riots was obscure, but racial tensions in the city had been mounting steadily for several years. Faced with an influx of black immigrants throughout the 1820s, white residents of the "Queen City of the West" had called for the enforcement of laws—passed in 1804 and 1807 but hitherto rarely enforced—requiring that black immigrants prove their free status, secure two white patrons who would vouch for their character, and deposit $500 with the state to guarantee their good behavior. Such measures were intended to halt a black immigration that whites found "wretched in its character and destructive in its consequences."[3]

In the wake of new calls to enforce the laws of 1804 and 1807, the riot confirmed white residents' increasing hostility toward the city's black residents. In response, many of Cincinnati's African Americans chose to leave the city altogether. The city's best and brightest numbered among them. A local white editor contemptuously lamented that the riots had "driven away the sober, honest, industrious, and useful portion of the colored population"; in his opinion, the presence of these "respectable persons of their colour" had acted as a restraint on "the idle and indolent."[4] Of the estimated one to two thousand African Americans who fled the city, several hundred migrated under the guidance of local black leaders Israel Lewis and James C. Brown. With the financial aid of Quaker abolitionists, they founded the Wilberforce colony in free country, on land purchased between Lakes Huron and Erie in Canada West.[5]

The colony did not flourish. Chronically underfunded and underpopulated, it also suffered from internal division. Israel Lewis quickly fell out with Austin Steward, a former slave and prosperous grocer from Rochester, New York, who had agreed to chair the board that oversaw the colony. After a short honeymoon, Lewis's dealings among the board went awry. Steward gave him the task of soliciting funds for the settlement from philanthropic benefactors back in the states, a delicate mission requiring tact and diplomacy. Lewis seems to have accomplished the first part of his mission well and did indeed raise some of the much needed funding. He failed, however, to submit the money he had raised to Wilberforce's governing board. According to Steward, Lewis had squandered the money on himself instead of giving it to the colony. Lewis responded by calling the charges false, and launched his own attack on Steward.

It is this controversy that concerns us here. Issues of character rapidly suffused the entire affair. Once it became public, the dispute quickly devolved into an exchange of ad hominem attacks in which the character and credibility of each man became suspect. When charged with defrauding the Wilberforce colony, Lewis acted to protect something he deemed "dearer than life"—his "public and moral character." Steward had, in Lewis's words, "brought me before the public as a base imposter, unworthy of confidence."[6] Claiming that Steward had stolen a twenty-dollar banknote from his house, Lewis filed charges against Steward and eventually brought him before a court, which found Steward innocent.[7] Testimonials offered Lewis a potent outside source to confirm his personal integrity. For nearly a decade following the dispute, Lewis continued to solicit funds for a rival colony near Wilberforce. He carried with him a statement by three citizens of the Wilberforce colony attesting to his credibility, asserting that he had paid the settlement over a thousand dollars, and charging Steward with setting forth a "foul calumny . . . for some evil and designing purpose." To this document was attached a notarized statement that the three men who had signed it were "men of respectable standing in society" to whom "all due faith and credence can be given."[8]

Steward in turn charged his opponent with sullying his reputation. According to him, the enraged Lewis had "resolved to destroy my character" and "blast my reputation."[9] Steward followed Lewis in going to considerable pains to demonstrate the questionable moral standing of his adversary. Upon arriving in Wilberforce, Steward related later, he had resided with Lewis but quickly understood that he had come into "bad company." Lewis lived with "a woman I then supposed to be his wife," intimating that Lewis had cohabited with a mistress. Despite his suspicions, Steward had been willing to "overlook the imperfections" in Lewis's character and appointed him agent for the colony. True to Steward's instincts, however, Lewis had denied Wilberforce the funds he had raised so that he might "live in a princely style"; he had spent the money "in the most prodigal manner at the taverns and other public houses." When confronted with these crimes, Lewis reputedly threatened to "cut the throats" of Wilberforce's board of managers. Steward, like Lewis, sought to enlist the authority of others with unquestioned credibility. He requested an investigation into the matter by a veritable Who's Who of respected black abolitionists, including Samuel Cornish, Charles B. Ray, David Ruggles, William Hamilton, and Theodore S. Wright. After affirming their objectivity (they were motivated only by their "duty to God, to society, and to themselves"), the members of the committee denounced Lewis as "one of the most heartless, swindling imposters which ever cursed any country," and admonished that "no confidence should be placed in him or any of his documents."[10]

Much was at stake in the controversy. Of course, the fate of the two men hung in the balance. Lewis was not alone in prizing above all his reputation for integrity; qualities of individual character took on extraordinary importance in the four decades before the Civil War, as popular moralizers both black and white attested. Also on the line was the reputation of the Wilberforce colony itself. Beyond his own respectability, Steward's primary concern was that the credibility of the settlement with which Lewis had become associated might become suspect in the public mind. Steward initially sought to keep the dispute out of the public eye, "knowing that a controversy among ourselves would go to retard our progress." But when Lewis defended himself in the black and abolitionist press, Steward had to react. Lewis, he feared, would "prejudice the public" against the Wilberforce colony, and its "purest motives" would be sullied.[11]

In addition to these relatively parochial concerns, the incident raised broader issues that had implications for nearly every American in the period. One man was guilty and the other innocent. While both might have appeared equally credible, one had to be prevaricating. Should the public choose the wrong one, the guilty man—now a liar and slanderer as well as a fraud—would escape detection, retain his reputation, and continue to operate in society unknown and unchecked. At the same time, an innocent man would lose his reputation. Vice would have subverted virtue. Hypocrisy rather than sincerity would have enjoyed the rewards of social standing and the public's respect.

The problem was that the truth was difficult to determine, for appearances could be deceiving. When one of Wilberforce's benefactors defended Lewis as a man with impressive "deportment and manner," Steward wondered what else one might assume of a true confidence man: "Is it not expected that he would appear well . . . while collecting money with the eye of the public on him?" Anyone who saw the "true character" under Lewis's "borrowed plumage," Steward continued, would find the heart of an "*arch hypocrite*." Lewis had brought "false charges" against "our most respectable citizens" in order to divert the public from the "true facts in the case." He was a man with morals so low that he would sell a lie as the truth. To Steward, that Lewis packaged himself in the guise of a credible and respectable man in fact defined him as a hypocrite and swindler.[12]

Up to this point, these concerns—the reputations of the individuals involved, the credibility of the institutions and enterprises they represented, and larger issues of determining public credibility—would have been shared by a wide range of white Americans in the antebellum North. Because the dispute took place in the context of African America, however, it held special implications that few whites could understand and fewer still could empathize with. It had started, of course, with a bloody race riot, the backdrop for which was a policy of racist exclusion that assumed the inherent depravity of all people of African descent. In terms of the controversy itself, Wilberforce's white allies lamented the public nature of the quarrel, not simply because it damaged the settlement, but because it threatened the great projects of universal emancipation and black equality. Lyman Spalding, a white abolitionist who befriended Steward, urged Steward not to allow "any difference of opinion to become public," for, he warned, "your enemies will seize upon this, and injure your prospects." Steward clearly understood the problem, concluding that Lewis's conduct "must be mortifying to *every colored man*." He continued: "It is at all times painful to us as a people, poor and despised as we are, and struggling for existence, to be called upon to record acts of unfaithfulness in those of our own color." Lewis's actions had hurt the race. By driving Wilberforce into debt and associating blacks in the public mind with fraud, he had "brought a reproach upon us as a people." Lewis, wrote Steward, "ought to be the guardian and protector of his colored brethren," but instead cheated them "in order that he may live in idleness." While Lewis "would be glad to make the public believe that he is doing every thing in his power for the benefit of his colored brethren," charged Steward, his record was "disgraceful in the extreme." Lewis responded in kind. When William Lloyd Garrison printed Steward's charges in the pages of *The Liberator*, Lewis was aggrieved; he could expect such treatment from those "not professedly engaged in pleading the cause of the colored man," he said, but was astonished that Garrison, a staunch ally of blacks, had so brought discredit to the race.[13]

Race thus complicated an already tangled set of moral imperatives. For many antebellum northerners, and especially those seeking middle-class status, character was everything. Evident in the moralizing of urban reformers, the didactic literature issuing from new presses, and the self-help mythologies of burgeoning entrepreneurs, northern Americans in the decades before the Civil War embraced a host of values that were finely attuned to an expanding market economy. Black public figures were part and parcel of this society, and the protest thought they forged drew deeply upon its emerging bourgeois ethos. At the same time, however, they were decidedly removed from that society—not by choice, but by the public manifestations of white supremacy. What did it mean for African Americans to craft a body of protest thought in an emerging class society—especially one predicating itself on reconfigured conceptions of race that denied people of African descent their basic humanity? What roles did class creation and the changing face of racism play in that process?

As the words of both Austin Steward and Israel Lewis suggest, time and again—both in statements specifically addressed to racial matters and ones not primarily concerned with race—northern black elites in the antebellum era reflected their deep participation in the construction of a northern worldview. They embraced and cofabricated many of its core premises: understandings of human character and development; the public manifestations of virtue in the forms of "respectability" and the ethic of the self-made man; and concerns with identifying the virtue and integrity of others in a new, largely anonymous marketplace of goods and ideas.

"OF TRIPLE NATURE": THE STRUCTURE OF CHARACTER

African American spokespersons laced nearly all of their public statements with the language of uplift—of "elevating" or "rising" along "the scale of being." These words invoked a set of ideas that framed much of northern black protest thought. The premises implicit in such phrases—here labeled uplift and elevation—comprised a loose network of values, beliefs, and rhetorical tropes that, in toto, constituted a key conceptual paradigm through which northern black elites understood their world. In turn, a great many of their responses to the problem of white supremacy drew upon the logic of uplift. African Americans' use of the language of uplift and elevation seemed to mirror that used by white moralists and commentators in the antebellum North. In sharing with white northerners concepts of social status, however, African Americans did not simply mimic uplift and elevation, they co-created them. Because of this, black responses to white supremacy relied upon a set of values held deeply and for their own merit, quite apart from any strategic utility they might have possessed. Few discussed explicitly the prevalence of elevation as the basis of black social and political thought, and fewer still self-consciously developed theories intended to explore the nature of uplift and elevation. Rather, because notions of elevation constituted the conceptual framework that underlay the ways in which African American spokespersons understood and expressed their concerns, it was difficult, if not impossible, for black elites—or, for that matter, any Americans—to grasp their significance. Uplift and elevation were less tropes to be manipulated than they were elements of a conceptual landscape that could not be imagined without them. Such is the nature of these paradigms. Elevation offered a common, though hardly fixed, vocabulary, a conceptual lingua franca through which Americans in the antebellum North of both races expressed their values and concerns. Precisely because it was vague, diffuse, and flexible, the language of elevation provided a loose network of words and understandings through which a wide array of ideas could be comprehended, manipulated, and expressed. At the same time, because it was shared, it expressed a very general and latent consensus, held by most Americans, not about specific issues or platforms, but about the broadest elements in the northern worldview—many of which Americans took so much for granted that they would have been hard pressed to even elucidate them. In this way—by marking the bounds of public speech—the ideology of elevation and uplift served to constrain the range of possible ideological options while it simultaneously permitted the expression of ideas by providing a comprehensible vocabulary that could frame them for an ever-broadening public sphere.

A key element of this consensus was a belief that the world was ordered along hierarchies, upon which individuals and social groups could rise and fall. Concepts of elevation derived from notions deep in the roots of Anglo-

American social thought. In the European tradition, the hierarchies that the concept envisioned most clearly recalled the early modern notion of the Great Chain of Being, which organized the universe in rigid hierarchies of beasts, men, and angels. However, it would be easy but inaccurate to suggest too direct a line of descent between ideas of the Great Chain and notions of social rising. As one scholar has stated, in a rapidly changing society, "the Chain of Being was only one (unusually specific) projection of a profound sense of and yearning for hierarchical arrangement." Eighteenth-century contemporaries viewed the Great Chain as a series of static natural hierarchies, which would have been rather alien to Americans just half a century later. By the nineteenth century, the hierarchies envisioned by the Great Chain had changed greatly. Romanticism, with its concern for the process of self-creation and self-fulfillment, had individualized the notion of hierarchy, making it as much a matter of interior introspection as outward observation. At the same time, it had brought hierarchy into the realm of human societies, applying its scales of development onto newly forming notions of ethnic groups and national peoples. By the time the market revolution struck the United States in the 1820s, the Great Chain had diversified into an array of separate scales and had become considerably more fluid, to adapt to the dynamic social structures of industrializing society.[14]

Among African American elites, elevation encompassed a broad set of notions, held together by the promise that people might move "upward" on a variety of "scales" or hierarchies. Most often, these were stated as moral or mental, though by the 1850s more radical black activists had begun calling for a "physical" elevation through economic or political gains. Notions of improvement, development, and progress peppered sentences dedicated to the themes of rising and uplift. In literally thousands of utterances, black leaders referred casually and incidentally to elevation: David Walker spoke of factors that kept blacks "from rising to the scale of reasonable and thinking beings"; Frederick Douglass hoped African Americans might "ascend to the elevated station in the scale of being for which we were evidently designed by a beneficent Creator." Some began newspapers dedicated to "the general improvement of Society," while others wanted to restore blacks to the "former elevation in the scale of being" they had occupied in ancient Africa. Still others wanted to "raise" black Americans to a level of equality with whites.[15] These diverse statements all shared important conceptual starting points: all imagined a series of historical contestations between social groups; these contestations took place over hierarchies of character traits on which humans and societies might rise or fall. Most Americans in the early nineteenth century, black and white, accepted this premise without question or even consideration. It was simply a given feature of their intellectual landscape.

Most of the protest thought of antebellum black elites relied on an implicit conception of human character premised on notions of elevation and comprised of three parts. These were the physical body, mental or intellectual capacities (often denoted "mind"), and personal morality and the realm of the soul. This tripartite model of distinct, complementary, and yet unequal components of human character undergirded nearly every analysis of African Americans' plight. It was a common substratum undergirding the thought of white Americans as well. For example, Albert Brisbane, the American Fourierist, began an association dedicated to "THE ELEVATION OF MAN" and "his complete and universal DEVELOPMENT—Moral, Intellectual, and Physical."[16] The evidence for such beliefs among black elites typically appeared less in the form of comprehensive essays dedicated to the topic than as premises of other arguments more overtly concerned with racial politics. For instance, one commentator, William J. Wilson, argued that Phillis Wheatley's genius had been encumbered, there being no opportunities "for her to make physical, moral, or mental progress."[17] Other statements were just as incidental; over time, they entered the realm of cliché, regularly invoked in institutional pronouncements and public speeches: "Let us cultivate our moral and mental faculties," urged the leader of a society of African American women activists, while a black minister argued for blacks' "moral and intelligent fitness for a just position in the scale of Christian civilization."[18]

Occasionally, black thinkers took the time to develop their arguments more explicitly. A black convention in 1847 declared, "Man is neither animal existence, nor a spiritual being, nor yet an intellectual creature alone. But man is a compound being, a being of mind, soul and body." It went on to urge African Americans to develop these three components of human character in harmony.[19] Charles L. Reason, the principal of New York City's Institute for Colored Youth, offered one of the few clear acknowledgments of the model. Man, he lectured a Philadelphia literary society, was of a "triple nature": "physical, intellectual, and moral." The task or "destiny" of man was to develop this three-fold character to the fullest. Applying the ever-present notion of fluid hierarchies of character, he described this process as a movement upward, from the domination of the bodily component over man to the hegemony of the mental. "From the first glimmering of thought in the ignorant—from the groveling desires and appetites of the sensual man," he lectured, "human character slopes upward, till on the mountain peak stands the intellectual good man."[20]

Others concurred with the popular idea that man ascends from the lowly depths of the material to the divine heights of the mental. Another black speaker argued that cultivation of the intellect would avert man from the base "gratification of his appetites and passions."[21] Black conventioneers in 1855 agreed with Charles Reason's hierarchy of character and its sequence of development, writing that "that which God once made in his own image [mind] is among the last in the order of creation." Only at the end of an untiring process of self-development would humans fulfill this destiny: "into that which is formed as a result of first beginnings"—the physical body—eventually "shall be breathed the light of superior intelligence."[22]

Black elites and their allies gave great credence to the innate value and perfectability of intellect. "Every one has the immaterial substance denominated mind," wrote one African American author, "in which the Almighty has, more or less, deposited intellectual matter that is capable of being drawn out."[23] Others confidently concluded that minds, even the African ones so commonly thought to be inferior, "are capable of high cultivation."[24] A. A. Guthrie, an Ohio clergyman and teacher of black youth, remarked, "Thought, reflection, reasoning, is the business of the mind, and forms the foundation of all progress."[25] To "intellectual cultivation" an important black newspaper ascribed the benefits of "equality of influence and standing,"[26] while a black woman's benevolent society considered "the cultivation of the intellectual powers" the highest of endeavor to have "engaged the attention of mankind."[27] Elevated intellect not only contributed to progress but served as an important resource in the competitive social order of antebellum America. Amos G. Beman, a Connecticut clergyman, echoed the common idea that intellect was necessary in a competitive social order. "More and more," he wrote, "the world is to be governed by the force of mind—cultivated mind—superior intelligence will secure itself the 'lion's share of the spoil.'"[28] Wrote another, "Ascendancy naturally and properly belongs to intellectual superiority."[29]

Black elites thought that while the advance of intellect represented the highest fulfillment of man's personal destiny, it was insufficient without a corresponding development of his "moral sense." "Intellectual and moral improvement should go hand in hand," wrote Robert Lewis, a seminal black racial theorist.[30] "It will not be enough to attend to the mere development and discipline of the intellectual powers," intoned William J. Watkins before a Philadelphia audience. "The moral and religious feelings of the heart must be cultivated, as of paramount interest," he said, citing as proof that often "the most splendid abilities are associated with the most dissolute morals."[31] Others similarly spoke of moral and mental uplift in the same breath. Sarah

Mapps Douglass, who taught black children in Philadelphia, voiced her hopes this way: "religion and education would raise us to an equality with the fairest in our land."[32] Similarly, New York educator Robert Gordon wrote of the need for "discipline of the heart, as well as of the head," warning that intellect without moral guidance constituted a "dangerous weapon," such as that wielded by the "atheistical and diabolical" Jacobins of Revolutionary France. Straying too close to intellect without regard for morals could easily lead to infamy. "Society frames its existence on moral worth," he believed; those lacking a developed moral sense could not "perform their duty to society."[33] Personal morality was more, of course, than merely a buttress for mental power; it had inherent value of its own. William Hamilton, a newspaper editor from New York, stated the value of morality succinctly before a black convention in 1834: "the highest state of morality is the highest state of happiness."[34]

In the words of black authors, mind, morals, and the capacity to develop character merged in a vision of uplift that pervaded their thought. From cultural elites to writers in the expanding popular press, contemporary white thinkers issued remarkably similar statements. Ralph Waldo Emerson, for example, stated that the "laws of the world" were "intellectual and moral" and thus required "intellectual and moral obedience." In man's personal "political economy," Emerson advocated investments in the "higher place" of "spiritual creation" instead of in "augmenting animal existence"; man, he cautioned, was not enriched by gratifying "animal sensation."[35] According to the *Southern Literary Messenger*, "[It is] the duty and province of knowledge to refine and expand the faculties, and to give us right conceptions of the works of the physical and moral worlds." This author revealed both the tripartite conception of character and its dictate to elevate, as well as the connections between mental and moral uplift, explaining "ignorance is the cause; and it has ever been the handmaid of vice" and, echoing the words of William Hamilton, "virtue and correct morals are the essentials of human happiness."[36]

It is not difficult to find the roots of black and white writers' regard for personal moral virtue in Anglo-American thought. In rejecting the ritual and doctrine of Anglicanism and Catholicism, the Puritan tradition had stressed a personal relationship with God in which inner moral purity glorified the deity; as evidence of membership among God's "elect," this purity also was manifest through success in the material world. Quaker practice in the middle colonies, through its focus on individual conscience, had emphasized to an even greater degree the centrality of personal virtue in fulfilling God's vision.[37] Such traditions persisted throughout the North in the eighteenth century: the First Great Awakening stripped American Protestant-ism of much of its predestinarian exclusivity, thus carrying it to a national audience. In the latter half of the century, political exigencies melded religious notions of moral virtue into secular conceptions of civic virtue. Religion and politics fused in the rhetoric of the Revolution, which identified English tyranny as a force opposing the divinely sanctioned search for civil freedom.[38] Following the founding of the nation, the industrial revolution had demanded a new conformity to moral values appropriate to the emerging market economy. As many scholars have suggested, Max Weber's classic formulation of the relationship between capitalism and the Puritan work ethic bore fruit fully only in the early nineteenth century, as the social order that emerged out of the market revolution increasingly prized the balance of wealth and morality that Congregationalism had celebrated.[39] One managed this difficult feat through individual efforts of self-cultivation in an increasingly public world of work.

"CHARACTER IS EVERYTHING": RESPECTABILITY AND THE SELF-HELP ETHIC

If one word encapsulated the rewards of self-improvement efforts and the benefits of living under the guidance of its resulting virtues, it was "respectable." That term, uttered countless times in the antebellum press, served as a master value, encompassing a host of traits—not all of them compatible—that came to define an ideal for human character in an expanding market society. Like whites, African American writers employed the term incessantly, most often in latent or unconscious ways. They sought "to reach a position of respectability and character" or to elevate themselves "to a rank of respectable standing with the community."[40]

Though respectability clearly had to do with a particular form of public regard for individual attainments, no simple or single definition can properly accommodate its many uses in antebellum rhetoric; it was invoked far too frequently and in ways far too diverse for that. The very fact that white and black writers alike employed it without ever seeing the need to clearly define it suggests that it was considered an ideal in itself, the value of which required neither argumentation nor explanation. This means not that it had no definition, merely that attempts to ascribe to it a narrow and static one misrepresent its role in antebellum northern thought. To attribute a concrete definition to a word used in such a variety of ways would miss its primary function, which was to serve as a discursive arena for debating the desired qualities of ideal men and women. The most important job of the word "respectable" was to implant the imprimatur of consensual value to whatever it modified: that which was respectable could be regarded as universally valued. To contest its meaning was to contest ideas of what ought to be valued in the context of an expanding market society. It was to participate in the construction and continual reconstruction of an important public sphere discourse, and commanding meaning in that discourse constituted an expression of considerable ideological power. Respectability thus served as a master value, its meaning and content contested precisely because it was universally seen to have inherent value.[41]

Respectability tended to connote a set of values closely linked with the qualities required for material and moral success in an expanding market economy. Success in achieving these qualities was premised on the absolute centrality of individual character. The character-based social theory of the expanding nineteenth-century capitalist order left little room for analyzing anonymous and impersonal structures of domination. These analyses would develop only slowly, over the century, and primarily through the efforts of a handful of radicals and working-class labor theorists (many of them European) for whom the promises of capitalism's benefits seemed so remote as to be unattainable. Most black leaders followed white moralists in subscribing to some version of the belief that individuals, through their successes or failures, primarily determined their own mental and moral status. Antebellum sermons and advice literature directed to the white middle class consistently lauded the possibility of social mobility and the virtues of the self-made man. "Real men—men of force of character—men who command respect—men who do good in the world—are self-made men," intoned one such volume.[42] Likewise, Unitarian minister William Ellery Channing celebrated America's unique capacity to permit man "the unfolding and perfecting of his nature": "In this country the mass of the people are distinguished by possessing means of improvement, of self-culture, possessed nowhere else." In a land absent hereditary titles and one in which an expanding market economy apparently offered unparalleled opportunities for acquiring wealth, social mobility became a key source of public regard. Channing said, "to have intercourse with respectable people, we must speak their language."[43] His statement must have struck a chord in the hopeful ears of many who endorsed qualifications for social rising that were attainable with apparent ease. Respectability largely meant that one had, through dint of individual industry and perseverance, cultivated one's inner character sufficiently to harvest the rewards of material success. Most importantly, this potential was available to all.[44]

Black elites argued for the value of the self-made man, who was judged on his accomplishments rather than any inherited or immutable status.

"Without the separating barriers of castes," Frederick Douglass editorialized, "the avenues to wealth and honor are here open to all who choose to enter them."[45] As a consequence, a black Californian wrote to one newspaper, "We live in an age of progress, where the relative qualities of individuals are computed in accordance with the resources they command."[46] "In this country, where money is the great sympathetic nerve which ramifies society," lectured Boston physician John S. Rock, "a man is respected in proportion to his success in business."[47] Austin Steward, a prominent black educator, similarly advocated the getting of wealth as an avenue to the coveted label: "money . . . is power," he told newly emancipated New York African Americans. Through it, he promised, they might "continually rise in respectability, in rank and standing."[48] Concomitant to sheer wealth, respectability for black leaders entailed economic independence. Those whose livelihoods depended on the charity or goodwill of others had no claim to respectability. Stating a belief that few antebellum Americans would have challenged, the national black convention of 1848 declared, "Independence is an essential condition of respectability. To be dependent, is to be degraded."[49] Austin Steward warned that "abject poverty is and ought to be regarded as the greatest, most terrible of all possible evils."[50]

Yet black thinkers were careful to temper the economic component of respectability with concern for the soul. Because material success was considered a manifestation rather than cause of social merit and divine favor, only the confidence man, the fraud, or the charlatan devoted himself wholly to the pursuit of gain. The omnipresent regard for money threatened to undermine important values. "I admit that gold is a great power," wrote one black northerner, "but I also contend, that knowledge is a greater."[51] Speaking of what he saw as white men's propensity to strive for success at all costs, Thomas Hamilton, the publisher of the *Anglo-African Magazine* and the *Weekly Anglo-African*, wondered if African Americans ought to "bow down and worship the golden image along with them?" He longed for the day when "wealth will cease to be the God of the American heart," and advocated a "nobler idolatry," which was "to be true men, and useful citizens."[52] Others lamented the advance of gold's "corrupting enchantments" over "the American heart." As a consequence, they claimed, "the acquirement of Knowledge and the culture of Morality and Virtue" had suffered.[53] Entrusted with the moral care of their families, black women in particular often championed the moral position in the debate over the primacy of wealth or soul. Some parodied those who espoused the belief that money would yield respect, warning African Americans against copying "the vices and follies of others" who were assumed to hold "superior stations."[54] Among the most outspoken critics of the unbridled pursuit of wealth was Frances Ellen Watkins, author and poet. "The respect that is only bought by gold is not worth much," she chided her readers. "We want more soul, a higher cultivation of all our spiritual faculties."[55]

Respectability thus did not mean that value derived solely or ultimately from the regard of others. Men and women may have judged others on the basis of their worldly success, but true value issued from strict adherence to the will of a higher power. The national black convention of 1834 considered one of its objects to be "promoting sound morality" through the inculcation of "all those virtues that alone can render man acceptable in the eyes of God."[56] This focus on individual character and inner morality comported easily with ideas—present since the days of Puritanism—that success in one's worldly vocation did not cause salvation or divine election so much as manifest a propensity toward it. The point of virtue and self-elevation was not to make money, but to embody God's ideal for humanity. Worldly success would likely flow as a natural result. "Occupation is not the end but the means," lectured Charles L. Reason, urging his listeners to view "accidents of occupation, position and name" as "what tools are to the workman."[57] Editor Thomas Hamilton agreed with this view of the vocations: "these are things, means, which will become part and parcel of every honest effort to advance."[58]

In offering the material world as a place where humans might alter their station on whatever "scale of being" was being considered at the moment, uplift and respectability promised a novel degree of individual autonomy in the formation of character, and thus in achieving salvation, whether defined on terms secular or sacred. Faith in personal action in the service of elevation constituted the promise as well as the burden of uplift ideology. For if success in the material world denoted elevated character, public regard, and godly election, then failure might easily be deemed—judiciously or not—evidence of inherent degradation or vice. Yet while it seemed to prioritize success in the world, such thinking also solaced those who faced difficulty in achieving it. Since material success manifested rather than caused divine favor, its absence did not necessarily negate the possibility of grace. The important component was not so much a favorable result in the race for worldly success—for appearances could always deceive fallible man—so much as a true and honest effort toward that end.

Above worldly success, black moralists prized individual action toward self-elevation. This was a duty one owed to God and was absolutely necessary for grace regardless of one's natural election or the outward appearances of success. One black Philadelphian stated it thus: "He who implanted the mind and endowed it with certain capabilities and faculties of development, hath also placed in our power the *means* thereof; and happy is he who makes the best use of them."[59] Black conventioneers put the point yet more strongly in a statement crafted in 1847: self-elevation was a "primeval duty"; the "very fact of being endowed with intellectual powers" evidenced God's intention of this. "Everything that lives, breathes and exists as a sentiment of spiritual existence, was made and designed for growth." Such thinking led to strong pressures to act in behalf of one's mental and moral well-being, sometimes in apparent violation of other fundamental values. "No man has a right to eschew any advantages afforded by nature or Providence" to improve, the convention concluded.[60]

The duty to take action in the world to become respectable muddled a distinction then becoming increasingly tenuous in the expanding market society: the distinction between natural rights, which guaranteed equality to all by virtue of inherent humanity, and the need to demonstrate to an anxious public the virtues required of those who might rule themselves. Elite black thinkers embraced Victorian America's penchant for great concern with personal virtue, wrestling with the implications of the divine mandate to self-elevate. As "a gift from God," all men shared equally a natural capacity to develop, editorialized one black newspaper. "But to maintain its inherent force," it continued, "every human being . . . must manifest their merits and claims to universal acknowledgment."[61]

Convinced of its utility as a fundamental value with intrinsic worth, African Americans elevated self-help beyond mere duty to the status of natural right. "There cannot be any conceivable right under any circumstance in life," charged the Reverend John Lewis, "for one to prevent another from improving his moral, mental, or physical condition by the exercise of the faculties which God his Maker has given him."[62] At a convention of Maryland blacks in 1852, the Reverend James A. Handy declared it "a high, an honorable, and a blessed privilege we enjoy, the right to improve ourselves and transmit to posterity happiness instead of misery." For Handy, self-improvement was not merely a benefit, but a sacred obligation. "It is," he said, "a duty to which mankind . . . owe to themselves and their Creator to embrace every opportunity for the accomplishment of this mental culture."[63] Others, like "Sydney," echoed the belief that the true source of elevation lay not in "external relations or peculiar circumstances," but in "inward rational sentiments" of individuals, which might "enable the soul to change circumstances to its own temper." The spirit that would earn one "respect" and "elevate him above his circumstances," he wrote, "must exist in the man."[64] Agricultural metaphors proved particularly useful to describe the process of uplift that black moral writers imagined. "Let us cultivate our moral and mental faculties," urged a group of black women activists,[65] while Robert Gordon asked his readers to think of their characters as they did of the fields they worked, lauding the man who "eradicates from it all noxious weeds, clears it, ploughs it, and sows his seed in the proper season." This "discipline of the heart," as Gordon called it, was the only reliable source of uplift in a competitive, often hostile social order.[66]

This underlying conception of man's duty to pursue self-elevation pervaded the public utterances of middle-class Americans both white and black, reflecting the overwhelming concern with personal character that resulted from the new mutability of social status. For Emerson, for example, success depended upon "intellectual and moral obedience."[67] African American elites clearly seem to have embraced the same language of character that was typical of white moral writers. Few failed at some point in their writings to endorse the importance of personal character as a social value with intrinsic worth. Junius Morrell, the prosperous African American trustee to a colony of black migrants to Canada, wrote to its director: "In all our recommendations to you, we shall endeavor to have an eye to character, knowing full well that by that alone you must *stand* or *fall*."[68] When one of the new parishioners of African Methodist Episcopal (AME) minister Daniel Payne refused him shelter, claiming that his humble appearance and meek demeanor had misled her as to his identity, he admonished her, "A title is nothing; character is every thing."[69]

"WORTHY OF THE PUBLIC CONFIDENCE": THE PROBLEM OF AUTHENTICITY

The rise of rampant individualism with the market economy did not proceed without crisis. The dynamic urban world of the North before the Civil War fostered anxieties that dominated the minds of bourgeois Americans and helped forge the texture of middle-class identity. These concerns fell into what one scholar has defined as three general but interrelated categories: social anxieties regarding the rise of the city and the decline of traditional sources of social deference, political anxieties triggered by the rise of mass parties and the nationalization of public opinion, and economic tensions surrounding the expansion of a speculative market economy and the new anonymous social relations attendant to it.[70] In short, the emergence of urban market society created a crisis in what may be termed social epistemology. Social identity—one's place in society—became unmoored from its traditional signifiers. Middle-class Americans and those aspiring to middle-class status reacted to the resulting sense of dislocation by seeking ways to "fix" or secure the public legitimacy of their class identities. They attempted to demonstrate their respectability through outward indicators like dress, behavior, and home furnishings. Victorian America's penchant for moralism, didacticism, and sentimentality, this school of thought argues, emerged from such transformations.[71]

At the center of the fears that attended the market revolution lay the tension between the requirement for individual efforts to uplift one's inner moral character and the practical utility of elevation, which lay in the acknowledgment of a largely anonymous public. The new climate put a premium on the appearance of success as well as suggesting new possibilities for achieving it. "So many advantages are associated with *position*, so captivating is the very idea of it, that every one is anxious to secure it," remarked a popular woman's magazine.[72] But along with the increasing importance of a public regard that affirmed one's value in society came the threat that some might seek the appearance of success without cultivating the character virtues that ought normally to produce it. Ralph Waldo Emerson expressed the concern in these words: "The popular notion of success stands in direct opposition in all points to the real and wholesome success. One adores public opinion, the other private opinion; one fame, the other desert; one feasts, the other humility; one lucre, the other love; one monopoly, and the other hospitality of mind."[73] The problem was that public opinion, reputation, and acknowledgment could now be earned by virtually anyone, or so it was thought. One might gain the good repute of an impersonal public that now more than ever lacked the means to discern the true nature of one's character. In an increasingly anonymous public sphere, who was to know if the outward signifiers of character reflected true qualities? More practically speaking, who was to know whether the man who offered the next opportunity for success was sincere or not? The need for public regard, often spoken of as "confidence," thus took on a new flavor. It became a force independent of and often inimical to personal moral integrity, and its abuse became a matter of widespread concern. "If anything marks the present age, it is the prevalence of imposture," one popular journal lectured. "Men too readily believe without evidence or examination," "judgements are often perverted by our affections and passions," and the mind was too prone "to believe that for which it most anxiously wishes." As a result, the author concluded, "there is scarcely a single province of human speculation or action which the disciple of charlatanism does not occupy, in which the meretricious is not put for that which is genuine, and in which falsehood does not ape the garb, the language, and the actions of truth."[74]

In a context pervaded by the myth of social elevation through individual effort, everyone—including the base, the lowborn, the ill-bred, and the vicious—had the capacity to at least appear to have achieved some level of social standing. The new premium on the facade of success threatened the very stability of the social order. By offering quick and easy roads to social standing, it undermined incentives to undertake the long and arduous work of self-improvement—the only true source of worth in a purportedly meritocratic society. Popular white moralizers dealt with this threat by stressing overwhelmingly the distinctions between internal realities and external appearances, lauding the former even at the expense of the latter. Argued one women's magazine, "The only *real* position is that which is derived from . . . uprightness of character." Character would confer a rank "which remains secure when houses, lands, and treasures are gone."[75] "If you would be truly valuable," declared another, "esteem not yourself according to your money and lands, but on the grace of your mind and person." At the same time moral counselors advised their women readers to consider first the cultivation of inner character, they also coached them on identifying it in others:

> No longer be won by faces with brainless heads to them; neither mistake a low bow for pure good manners; nor a well dressed head for quality; nor a fashionable coat for an estate; servile cringing for love; nor a smooth tongue for sense. Above all, do not mistake wit for wisdom; and cast a tender eye on him who has steady manly virtue and prudence in his conduct, and gives fair hopes of his minding at heart.[76]

If true character derived from inner qualities, the exterior befitting such virtue ought to accurately reflect its delicate balance of worldly success and personal integrity. "Be careful of your *personal appearance*," a writer for the *Ladies' Repository* advised his youthful readers. "As a man is responsible for all the influence he can acquire, he is bound to secure a decent apparel." At the same time, the author cautioned against an extravagance in dress, which might suggest a desire to reach beyond one's appropriate station. "I do not ask you to follow the fashions. . . . We hate foppishness—aping great men." Clothing should instead convey "modesty, intelligence, and sobriety."[77] The imperative to acquire dress that reflected one's character did, of course, contain seeming contradictions. Inner character was to be valued most highly, but if appearances could not be taken as reliable indicators of inner character, what did it matter what one wore or how one behaved? Did not excessive concern with behavior and dress merely encourage the problem: by teaching readers to identify integrity with dress, perhaps it made it all the easier for the confidence man to engage in the pretense of respectability. Most contemporaries would have responded that proper comportment and dress aided the struggle for virtue and inner character, and hence were worth pursuing for their own sake.

Such paradoxes suggested more than anything else the deep concern that attended the project of determining true social worth. That such determinations were beset with anxiety is perhaps most evident in the self-assuring tone of some writers' statements to the contrary. As one white writer argued, although a man may, by "mingling in polished society, acquire certain habits, and obtain certain rules, which will enable him to pass off as a gentleman," unless "a just regard for his fellow beings find a place in his heart, his politeness will be but disgusting hypocrisy." He went on to moralize hopefully: "Vain is the attempt to deceive the world. It has too sharp an eye, and too thoughtful a brain." [78] Would that it had been so simple.

Just as white moral theorists in the antebellum era wrestled incessantly with the paradox of an inner purity so apparently dependent on the affirmation of others, so too did African American spokespersons. Some African American commentators had faith that inner character could be reflected in personal exteriors: they claimed that the world had grown "too enlightened" to "estimate any man's character by his personal appearance," and that "the deportment of individuals is a characteristic of their breeding." [79] Others were not so sure. Of the imperative to succeed, which the new social order placed on people generally, one black author wrote, "Under such heavy pressures, they are strongly tempted to forego their own convictions of what is right, and seek for a reputation among their fellow men." They might "seek it at any price, instead of waiting to acquire it by diligence, patience and industry, which always awards merit, with honor, respectability and esteem." [80] Indeed, the world often seemed a place dominated by the battle between reality and facade, with the soul of the impressionable mind at stake. "The world is full of snares and temptations," a black woman activist lectured African American youths. "Vice will assume the semblance of virtue, and falsehood by a thousand seducing arts deceive the incautious heart to receive it as truth." [81] Consequently, many leaders spurned flamboyant attire: it too easily suggested pretense, falsity, an effort to rise above one's station while foregoing the necessary labors to uplift oneself. "When we say RESPECTABLE," Frederick Douglass wrote, "we mean intelligent, well-behaved persons, without reference to fantastic dress or pecuniary circumstances." [82] Editor Samuel Cornish also inveighed against adopting pretense as a means of social elevation: "Has any man yet been held in estimation on account of his fine dress?" he asked. [83]

African American spokespersons were completely conversant with the antebellum North's concerns with authenticity in the marketplace. The black press regularly debated the validity of novel medical treatments, frequently ran tales of rubes separated from their money and imposters unmasked, often informed readers of dangerous business deals unfolding, and universally declared as counterfeit religious movements like Mormonism.[84] Swindles that relied on the legal vulnerabilities of blacks aroused special attention. In an all-too-typical case in Cincinnati, an African American woman seeking help getting a fifty-dollar banknote cashed was approached by a local white man, who offered to complete the business for a fraction of what it would have cost her otherwise. When he refused to return the money she had given him, she turned in desperation to a local magistrate. She was left without recourse, though, for under Ohio law her testimony against the white man was inadmissible.[85] Such commonplace occurrences highlighted the disadvantages that made African Americans particularly vulnerable in the new market economy; they also suggested the efficacy of the black press in educating the community to swindles against which African Americans were uniquely defenseless.

The more dramatic case of Solomon Northup further suggests the close acquaintance with confidence tricksters that made African American spokespersons especially sensitive to the issue. Born free, the young Northup had spent his early manhood in upstate New York as a logger, working vigorously and eventually caring for a small family. In the hopes of better providing for them and of making something of himself in the world, he moved them to Saratoga Springs, the burgeoning spa town of New York City's cognoscenti, which was quickly growing as much in ill-repute as fame. But Northup's "flattering anticipations" of the town had not borne fruit. Saratoga instead had "seduced" him and his family away from the virtues of country life; it left them comfortable but not rising. "The society and associations at that world-renowned watering place," he euphemistically lamented, "were not calculated to preserve the simple habits of industry and economy to which I had been accustomed." Instead, it had replaced them with other traits, "tending to shiftlessness and extravagance." All of this he might have borne, had it not been for his one weakness: vanity. A proficient fiddler, he loved to play at local gatherings and receive the approbation of his fellows. Having established himself as a musician of some renown, he was easily misled. In town one day in 1841, he was approached by two men—both dressed "in the extreme of fashion," one with a manner "somewhat effeminate." The men had heard of his playing and offered him a chance to play professionally in a circus that traveled up and down the East Coast. "Such were the flattering representations they made, that I finally concluded to accept the offer," he recalled. Lured by the men away "from home and family, and liberty, for the sake of gold," he gave them his confidence "without reserve." In Washington, D.C., his mistake became clear. At dinner, having drunk alcohol spiked by his compatriots, he woke up in chains, headed for the auction block and the hell of southern slavery. Having willingly traveled south of the Mason-Dixon line, Northup found himself utterly bereft. His free papers declared fraudulent, he was sold into slavery in Louisiana, where he suffered the brutal work regime of a cotton plantation. He slaved for twelve years, until one of the letters he had managed to have smuggled North finally bore fruit; a Saratoga attorney took up the case, went down to Louisiana, and rescued the kidnapped freeman.[86]

Denuded of its references to slavery, Northup's narrative could have been the tale of any of a number of young men written of in the antebellum press. Stories of downfall through the weaknesses of those preyed upon by frauds and counterfeits were in fact often told in the nineteenth century, as warnings to ambitious young men who staked their futures in cities that might yield them fortune, but at the cost of their souls. Northup's tale contained a story familiar to antebellum readers: that of a young man seduced by possibilities of success in the cities through individual enterprise, hoodwinked by confidence men who play on his vanity, and finally betrayed by his vices into utter degradation. For antebellum northerners, it was genre, and very powerful genre at that.[87]

Some black spokespersons encountered confidence men in the midst of their very own flocks. Several celebrated cases and many lesser-known instances of fraud allegedly perpetrated by African American activists and white abolitionists indicated that the movement was hardly held in high regard by the larger public. If anything, the utter marginalization of most black northerners and the widespread contempt leveled at white abolitionists rendered both highly suspect in the public mind. More than a few African American activists contended with charges, sometimes brought by fellow activists, that they had participated in various fraudulent projects. Like their mainstream counterparts, black and abolitionist newspapers regularly carried notices warning the public of confidence games run by those claiming sympathy with black causes. "Every day brings to our knowledge fresh evidence of the utter unreliability of some itinerant colored 'brother' or other," one African American editor sadly remarked.[88] Those who authored popular and controversial slave narratives—such as Frederick Douglass, Henry Bibb, and Harriet Jacobs—faced challenges to their veracity by friend and foe alike. In the midst of the Bibb controversy, one abolitionist newspaper lamely admitted that it could not tell whether Bibb was "worthy of the public confidence or not."[89] In fact, a great majority of published slave narratives included lengthy appendices and authorizing apparatuses, usually featuring the endorsements of established activists or respected philanthropists, all intended to make their recitation of slavery's horrors believable to a suspicious audience.[90] In many ways, newly freed slaves with a story for the public must have appeared to be the quintessential "strangers" that antebellum northerners most feared. They were new to the public, often had no past against which their claims could be measured, and played heavily on the tender feelings of the warm-hearted. One black editor did not wonder "that imposters of color should rise and appear" among antislavery advocates. The "deep, wide, generous, inviting streams of human sympathy" present among the friends of the slave opened a wide gate for such imposters.[91] That fugitives were associated with a despised race only confirmed their illegitimacy.

The black press provided a particularly important forum for debating the veracity of various actors in the antislavery cause.[92] Editors sprinkled the black and abolitionist presses liberally with notices cautioning against those who might "impose upon the friends of humanity, and swindle them of their money."[93] Common ruses ran from falsely soliciting funds to purchase loved ones out of bondage to acting as agents for black benevolent institutions that had never endorsed them. A Julia Lewis was charged with collecting money "under the pretense of bringing on freedwomen as domestics," while one Castus Depp solicited subscriptions for the *Provincial Freeman* without ever forwarding the funds.[94]

It was important for black leaders to challenge, debate, and judge such cases in the press. At stake in policing fraud among themselves was nothing less than the health of the antislavery movement. The safeguarding of integrity constituted a sort of hygiene of respectability, intended to maintain the credibility of the movement. It was crucial that confidence tricksters be excised from the midst of true abolitionists for, as leaders said, "nothing is more common in men, than to associate *a cause*, with him who advocates it."[95] The consequences on the public mind of such frauds could be profound. Popular associations of black activists and white abolitionists with fraud frequently found their way into popular media, as in the case of Passmore Williamson, a Philadelphia Quaker and abolitionist. In 1855, Williamson encountered Jane Johnson, the slave of John H. Wheeler, U.S. minister to Nicaragua, on the docks of Philadelphia's port. Claiming that Pennsylvania law entitled her to freedom by virtue of setting foot on free soil, Williamson convinced Johnson to flee her master with her two children. Williamson left it to William Still, a black Philadelphian and central mover in the Underground Railroad there, and five black associates to secret them away. Still,

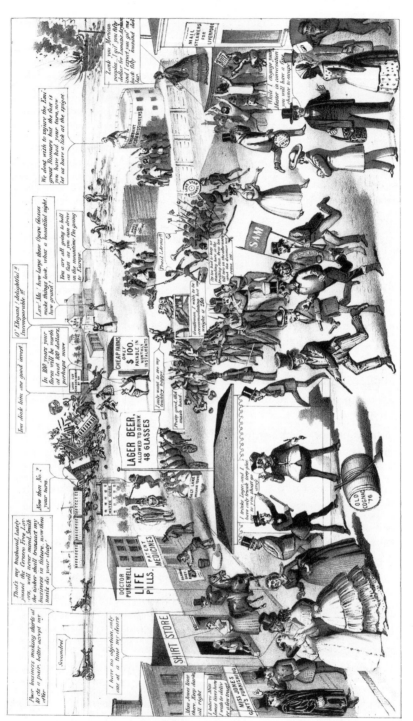

PLATE 3. "The Follies of the Age, Vive la Humbug!!" This popular Currier and Ives image mocked fads of the year 1855. Included are scenes of confidence schemes that took advantage of the credulity of the sincere. Lithograph by Currier and Ives (Philadelphia, 1855); courtesy of The Library Company of Philadelphia.

three of his fellows, and Williamson all went on trial for attempting to incite riot. While the African Americans were acquitted, Williamson received a four-month prison sentence which made him a cause célèbre among black activists and white abolitionists.[96] The views of the bulk of white northerners, however, were likely reflected in a Currier and Ives engraving depicting "the follies of the age," a visual catalogue of confidence games and humbugs (see Plate 3). Nestled prominently in the foreground is a scene depicting the Williamson-Johnson incident, wherein a white man suggests to an enslaved woman that she escape while he diverts the attention of her master (see Plate 4). In the antebellum North, which placed such a high premium on public regard and reputation, charges of fanaticism and anarchism were bad enough. Many activists could accept these, and even interpret them as signs of success. Abolitionists said of Wendell Phillips that "he and his friends were not the object of persecution because they were crazy, but because they were known not to be."[97] To be labeled false, however, threatened to toll the movement's death knell. Above all, abolitionists needed exposure and attention; a movement unworthy of the public's confidence would turn away even the most ardent potential converts.

In this climate of anonymity, mistrust, and temptation, education acquired a new and profound importance. In the Revolutionary generation, the Founding Fathers had stressed the need for a self-governing people to master first and foremost their own natural inclinations. Training would strengthen the mind's control over bodily passions and thus secure the future of a young republic threatened by the twin evils of anarchy and tyranny.[98] By the 1820s, the pitfalls and enticements of the market economy—particularly its frequent inability to discern true from false virtue, evident in its too common tendency to reward merely the pretense of integrity—multiplied the great significance of properly training those who sought respectability. The good news was that, because the human condition was mutable and improvable, it was subject to the influence of individual behavior: people *could* rise, provided the will to do so and the right conditions. "Training forms habit and character," the maxim of one educator of black youth, was a typical expression of this view.[99] The bad news was that the inner integrity required for true elevation of character required a discipline that did not come naturally to humans. The world was, in fact, a place that constantly confronted people with the challenge of discerning the difficult path of mental and moral discipline from the quick and easy one of mere empty appearance.

At the root of this understanding lay antebellum psychology. The notion of habit grew directly out of theories of epistemology such as those elu-

PLATE 4. *"The Follies of the Age" (detail). This scene refers to abolitionist Passmore Williams's aid of fugitive slave Jane Johnston in Philadelphia in 1855. Lithograph by Currier and Ives (Philadelphia, 1855); courtesy of The Library Company of Philadelphia.*

cidated by William J. Watkins, who set out the role of mind in education most comprehensively in a lecture before a moral reform society in Philadelphia. "Man, in the incipient stages of his being, receives an education, whether he will or not." Watkins argued that the young mind "is continually receiving impressions" from the world around it and is thus "perpetually forming habits." These habits could be healthy but could more easily be harmful; the inherent "depravity of the human heart" and "the contagious nature of vice" made it so. Though he believed vice was superable through proper training, Watkins lamented the facility with which the mind "imbibes false impressions, and with what difficulty they are corrected."[100] The men of Philadelphia's Banneker Institute went further, claiming that "the finer and more correct influence is materially weaker than united error." Since man was more readily inclined to suffer immorality within the comfort of the crowd than to boast morality alone, they argued, special pains for the mental and moral training of youth were necessary.[101] Such views were hardly atypical. Black newspapers argued constantly that the downtrodden needed to throw off the shackles of bad habit; as the *Colored American* put it, "The first thing to be done by our people in the elevation of their moral and civil condition is, to change long-standing habits, and throw off useless practices."[102]

These ideas found common currency in a world increasingly concerned with instilling, often through considerable repression of natural desires, the virtues that would ensure the collective health of the republic while leading to individual success in a competitive economy. Many white Americans deemed it necessary to inculcate the capacity to master natural inclinations. People, inherently depraved, could quickly descend into vice if left to their own devices. One white moralist wrote that man's "appetites and desires, though depraved, can be controlled." Unfortunately, though, he noted, too many had neglected to properly educate their young, with licentiousness— an overindulgence of natural passions—the result. "Where knowledge is slighted, vicious habits will be formed, to fill up the vacant hours that should have been devoted to useful and innocent thoughts." It was only through retraining, he argued, by "giving right direction to the mental energies," that proper morality could be restored.[103] Women's magazines regularly urged their readers to "give your children the habit of overcoming their besetting sins." Passion, greed, sulkiness, indolence, pride—all could be allayed through mastery of the art of "self-government."[104] An article entitled "It's So Hard to Quit It When You're Used to It," originally published in the *Philadelphia Observer* and reprinted in the black press, noted the sagacity of its title for those required "to relinquish an ugly habit." It also warned parents of yielding to their children's natural inclinations: "Let a young man indulge his sensual appetites in any way, and he will know how hard it is to leave off his sin when he has become used to indulgence."[105] Furthermore, the victory over vice could never be complete. As another author noted, "Let not a man trust his victory over his nature too far; for nature will lie buried a great time and yet revive upon the occasion of temptation."[106]

The implications of mastering the passions were significant. A self-governing people could look to no king, no centralized authority to maintain the virtue of the nation for them. Through the Revolution, Americans had minimized opportunities for prospective despots, but only at the risk of empowering masses whose capacity for self-governance was for many suspect, to say the least. The great expansion of the Jacksonian electorate had heightened these anxieties, particularly among traditional elites. But an expanding middle class also expressed considerable trepidation. Elements of that middle class, energized by the evangelicalism of the Second Great Awakening, sought through moral reform to counterbalance the effects of democratization with a healthy dose of internal repression. Charles G. Finney, the outstanding popular clerical figure of his day, argued that "moral depravity" consisted "in the committal of the will to the gratification or indulgence of self—in the will's following or submitting itself to be governed by impulses and desires of the sensibility instead of submitting itself to the law of the intelligence."[107] Education, and especially moral education, provided the logical solution to the problem. This belief made the careers of men like Horace Mann, Massachusetts's great promoter of public education, who lauded America's egalitarian republicanism but warned of the consequences of neglecting the responsibility to train a healthy generation of virtuous citizens. "If republican institutions do wake up unexampled energies in the whole mass of a people," he wrote, "then these same institutions ought also to confer upon that people unexampled wisdom and rectitude." He cautioned: "We must not add to the impulsive, without also adding to the regulating forces." The consequences of abdicating this responsibility could be dire; Mann envisioned "millions of men, each with appetites capacious of infinity, and raging to be satisfied." Education would serve to restrain the animal-like passions that republicanism inevitably unleashed. "What ravening, torturing, destroying, then, must ensue, if these hounds cannot be lashed back into their kennel! They must be governed; they cannot be destroyed."[108] Unitarian clergyman William Ellery Channing put it just as succinctly: "To raise the moral and intellectual nature, we must put down the animal. Sensuality is the abyss in which very many souls are lost. . . . Who would cultivate his soul must restrain his appetites."[109]

"WITH STEADY PURPOSE AND UNTIRING ZEAL": THE VIRTUES OF LABOR

For black and white northerners, the ultimate object of moral and mental training was to permit men to elevate their own characters so that they might function in the economy with both integrity and success, and thus deserve the coveted title of "respectable." Women would benefit by proxy, through the respectability that accrued to them from association with their husbands. Like white moralists in nineteenth-century America, in countless instances black elites lauded the values of thrift, industry, economy, sobriety, honesty, pluck, determination, independence, and a host of other virtues that made a person well suited to achieve success in a competitive market economy. Black newspapers regularly reprinted tales from the white press of young men who devoted themselves to business "with steady purpose and untiring zeal," obtained their credit through "plain and honest dealing," and made friends through "obliging deportment and accommodating disposition."[110]

Stripped of their titles, it would often have been difficult to tell the difference between the labor moralizing of the white and black presses. The pages of New York's *Colored American* were typical in frequently urging that readers "should cultivate honesty, punctuality, propriety of conduct, and modesty and dignity of deportment." To this already formidable list it added the need for "untiring habits of industry, the dint of perseverance," and "rigidness of economy."[111] In 1825, former slave and black educator Austin Steward counseled a group of black New Yorkers, freed in accordance with a gradual emancipation law, on the virtues required to succeed in a free labor economy. They were not to "think that industry or true happiness do not go hand in hand," for, as he put it, "to him who is engaged in some useful avocation, time flies delightfully and rapidly away." Steward urged his listeners to post on their doorways in letters of gold the words "industry, prudence, and economy," identifying them as "words of power to guide you to respectability." Steward continued with advice that would have pleased both Benjamin Franklin and the Puritan forebears from whom such values ultimately derived. He urged freedpeople to attain "a competency of the good things of this world," though he stated, "Immense wealth is not necessary for you, and would but diminish your real happiness." Advocating "sober, diligent, moderate labor," he promised them that "honest advancement of your worldly interest," would lead to a continual "rise in respectability, in rank and standing."[112]

The paragon of the secular moral virtues that antebellum Americans admired was Benjamin Franklin, whose *Autobiography* and aphorisms provided models of virtue for generations of Americans.[113] Northern African American spokespersons were not exceptional in their admiration of the great colonial. John Russwurm, the editor of *Freedom's Journal*, felt it incumbent upon his paper to "dwell occasionally upon the general principles and rules of economy," for, he wrote, "Though all men acknowledge the excellency of Franklin's maxims, yet comparatively few practice upon them."[114] William C. Nell, a black abolitionist from Boston, was fond of telling a story of his youth that demonstrated America's captivation with Franklin at the same time that it exposed the racial paternalism of Boston's white elite. As a youth in Boston's public schools in 1829, Nell's scholarship earned him and several white students a special award. While the white scholars were given medals and feted by the mayor at a Faneuil Hall dinner, Nell—because he was black—was merely given a copy of *The Life of Benjamin Franklin*. While incensed at the patronizing implication that he might be more needy of a book of moral maxims than a white student, Nell nonetheless retained his copy for decades after.[115]

Following Franklin, African American elites in the North embarked on a spate of institution-building efforts designed to effect personal elevation. Literary societies in particular became important means to elevate the mind and instill necessary virtues. Throughout the period, in conventions and newspaper editorials black public figures urged their people to form societies for their "improvement in moral and literary knowledge."[116] The mental exercise that such institutions promoted promised to instill proper habits into young men seeking respectability. Clearly the activities of such societies were better than the temptations of vice-ridden urban streets. Black New Yorkers desired a literary society for the "young men whose evenings are unemployed, and who now spend their leisure hours in the theatre or porter houses." A reading room, it was argued, would permit them to "establish for themselves a character"; in aiding black youth in "acquiring moral habits" and "erecting a reputation," the literary society had few parallels.[117]

The experience of former slaves who managed to find their ways north attested to the potency of Franklinesque labor virtues among antebellum African Americans. According to their published accounts, a great many authors of slave narratives seem to have been paragons of free labor virtue on their southern plantation: they worked hard to educate themselves, proved themselves the ablest hands (despite their principled hatred of the slave system), became trusted by masters and local whites alike, often rose to positions of leadership in the plantation economy, and sometimes bought themselves through their own hard work. By the time they reached Yankeedom, they were fitting models for those who read their tales. In his memoirs,

Josiah Henson, the former slave upon whom Harriet Beecher Stowe was reputed to have modeled Uncle Tom, admired the "energy, enterprise, and
self-reliance" he found upon arriving in the North and said he hoped to
instill precisely this "Yankee spirit" in other former slaves there.[118] Upon becoming free, John Jackson still worked nights as well as days, saving over
one hundred dollars in the course of a year. When asked how he could tol-
erate such work after having been a slave, he replied: "Because I felt I was
free, and that I worked because I wished." Jackson believed that this sense of
ownership over one's own labor was "more satisfactory than twenty theories,
as to the superiority of free labour over slave labour."[119] Undertheorized
though they may have been, such views endorsed conceptions of northern black abolitionists, who likewise believed that "every man and woman
are by right the owners of themselves" and that the greatest crime against
slaves was the denial of their "right of self-control."[120] Other former slaves
who had been converted to notions of Yankee thrift and industry displayed
their faith in new values by bestowing somewhat patronizing advice on their
brethren who remained in chains. William Hayden wrote of the respect he
received working in a rope-making operation, where he eventually rose to
the position of foreman and "was treated more as a white man than any
thing else." Offering his fidelity to his boss and master as an example, he
suggested to those still enslaved that with similar dutifulness they would be
"treated with kindness, and rendered still more happy in the bondage in
which Providence has seen fit to cast their lots."[121] Such sentiments were
not merely conventions of the slave narrative genre, intended to provide
evidence that freed African Americans would work. Surviving private correspondence also suggests that life in the North opened opportunities for
those raised in thralldom. Thomas Jones sent his wife and family north before he could escape his North Carolina plantation himself. Already pressured to hire himself out to earn the money necessary to flee himself, he
began receiving urgent letters from his wife asking for yet more money. "You
know you ought to send me some money to pay my board," she chastened
him, "you know I love to act independent."[122]

These "conversions" to northern values betray the great debt that abolitionism owed to the values of an expanding bourgeois economy.[123] Many
published accounts of African Americans' escape from bondage highlighted
the critical moment when the formerly enslaved came face to face with the
opportunities for elevation provided in the North, marveling in particular at
the availability of education. Under slavery, of course, most African Americans had been denied schooling; as Thomas Jones recalled, he had been
told scornfully, "that it was not for such as *me* to try to improve."[124] Similarly,

Frederick Douglass's owner had scolded his mistress for teaching Douglass to read, saying that "learning would *spoil* the best nigger in the world."[125] But upon reaching freedom, they often marveled at the sheer number of school-houses they saw. "It has been a matter of great wonder to me," remarked Lewis Clarke. "In Kentucky, if you should feed your horse only when you come to a school-house, he would starve to death."[126]

"EMPIRE OF THE HEART": WOMEN AND CHARACTER FORMATION

While accounts of former slaves stressed their successful internalization of the values required for success in a free labor society, northern African Americans meted out their greatest educational efforts to the young. "How important the moral and religious cultivation of their minds!" Nathaniel Paul noted of black youth.[127] Children's minds were considered especially malleable—to improvement in cases of proper training, and to degradation in cases of bad. The men of tomorrow, one educator lectured, "will be just such men as we choose to make them, so far at least as training forms habits and character."[128] In their high regard for children's education, black think-ers largely shared conceptions common with white reformers, so much so that they regularly reprinted articles from white newspapers, the language of which seemed identical to their own. The "moral habit" of children was "of infinitely more consequence" than any inconvenience parents might en-counter in their education, read one such piece. It was in childhood that "permanent impressions" were formed and the "natural propensity" of the child imprinted.[129] Pointing out that "it is more difficult to unlearn errors, and correct bad habits, than to acquire good habits at first," the *Colored American* took particular care to stress proper childhood training.[130]

This emphasis underlay the prescribed crucial role of women in the for-mation of character.[131] The bulk of opinion in the black media supported the popular view that women's natures suited them to domestic roles, the fore-most of which was to properly form their children. Women had little place in the public life of men, it was commonly asserted. The black press regu-larly reprinted articles from white newspapers modeling the proper com-portment of young ladies, the direction of which literally stripped women of their capacity for public speech. They were to have a "retiring delicacy which avoids the public eye." Their modesty would naturally dispose them "to be rather silent in company." This silence was not, young women were cautioned, to be considered a loss or disadvantage: "One may take a share in conversation without uttering a syllable."[132] Rather than achieving ful-fillment in public life, African American women, like their white counterparts, were expected to find compensation in the important familial tasks entrusted to them. "The great concerns of the active world are intended to be carried on by men," claimed one white newspaper, noting, "The nature of women . . . may be perfectly developed within the domestic circle alone. Her character is not incomplete because she has no voice in public affairs. . . . Enough is left to her, . . . even where political liberty is unknown, for the display of private excellence."[133]

Such views were not simply reprinted in the black press, they were produced there as well, and by African American women at that. In the leaves of the *Colored American,* "Ellen" argued that "the appropriate sphere for the female to use her influence over man, is the domestic fireside."[134] "Beatrice" wrote that, though woman lacked the physical strength, moral courage, and ambition of men, "yet she *may* have the wide field of the domestic circle to interest her."[135] So widespread were such beliefs that their champions claimed they constituted common knowledge: "The proper sphere of women is so strongly delineated by a Divine finger, that it must be apparent to every eye which is not willfully blind."[136] Of course, such statements created women's roles rather than reported divinely ordained ones. Their very claims to the contrary evidenced the tenuous, constructed character of gender definitions: arguments based on the authority of nature invoked a seemingly indisputable authority, yet they were necessary only because their hegemony was incomplete.

Relying on arguments about the organic nature of women, many considered the sex particularly suited to functions in the home. A great many men and women published in the black press simply considered women more naturally virtuous than men. According to one, "the female sex is greatly superior to the male in mildness, patience, benevolence, affection and attachment." Women's virtuous characters constituted "the solace, the cement, and the ornament of life."[137] This natural propensity to virtue suggested their primary task in the home. According to "Ellen," "female influence" could "mould the character of man, and direct his mind into what should be its proper channel." "The appropriate sphere for the female to use her influence over man," she concluded, "is the domestic fireside."[138] The responsibilities laid upon women were thus considerable; the very virtue of their families was thought to depend on them. Within their "sphere," women radiated influences that could be "pure, lovely, [and] holy," or "of the most debasing character."[139] It was in their homes that children were surrounded by "appendages and influences, all operating for good or evil."[140] Because character was formed early and "for eternity," one black newspaper suggested, "let infinite care attend all the means and measures of its conformation."[141] The actions and characters of parents at "the domestic altar" were all-important in creating the environment in which children's characters would form. "From their example and precepts," a women's magazine lectured, "the child derives his first idea of God, and of his own relation to Him as a dependent and accountable creature."[142] A national black convention confirmed this: "From the fire-side we must receive and teach the great lessons of self-confidence, self-dependence, perseverance, energy, and continuity."[143] Author Frances Ellen Watkins proved renowned at celebrating the virtues of domestic life for inculcating proper character in the young. In one of her first published stories, she wrote:

> Home should always be the best school for the affections, the birthplace of high resolves, and the altar upon which lofty aspirations are kindled, from whence the soul may go forth strengthened, to act its part aright in the great drama of life, with conscience enlightened, affections cultivated, and reason and judgement dominant.[144]

The weight of opinion in antebellum black public speech envisioned women serving both their children and their husbands. For their husbands, their first duty was to render the home a place of refuge for men seeking solace from the rigors of the competitive world of work. According to one black newspaper, the man who daily went forth into that world "cannot foresee what trial he may encounter." Yet if he could think of "the beaming and hopeful smile" and the "soothing attention" of home, his cross would be lightened.[145] According to one African American woman, the job of the mother, sister, or wife was to "throw a halo around the domestic hearth, and make HOME the delight of man, and the place he will seek with ardor after the toils of the day."[146] Others described woman as "the palace—the retreat from the strife and business of life; the abode of all the social virtues, and the home of the graces."[147] Few men could ask for more than the blessings of domestic security. The man who "returns home at night to meet the happy smiles and joyous greetings of his family" may retire "with a peaceful and contented mind. He enjoys his life more than the rich man surrounded with all the luxuries which wealth can procure."[148] Black spokespersons also urged women to succor and aid the husband as he sought advantage in the world of the public. Woman, according to a white newspaper article reprinted in the black press, "is formed to adorn and humanize mankind, to soothe his cares, and strew his path with flowers. In the hour of distress she is the rock on which he leans for support, and when fate calls him from existence, her tears bedew his grave."[149] The antebellum rhetoric of gender envisioned distinct yet complimentary roles for men and women. "Woman was created to be the 'help meet,' and not the idol nor slave of man."[150]

Even more important than aiding their husbands was women's duty to their children. Most commentators acknowledged that because raising children was a dual duty, shared by husband and wife alike, virtue was required of them both. Parents were to avoid "all vulgar expressions and blasphemous words," as well as "guard against excess in amusements, extravagance in dress, intemperance in drinking, and gluttony in eating."[151] Parents together bore great responsibilities, but it was left to woman "to impress on the heart, in living characters, the attribute to be prized above all others, virtue."[152] One lecturer commented that "females should, of the two sexes, be the most thoroughly educated in all the useful and practical branches of learning," for they had "the plastic power over the young minds under their care, to mould them in intelligence as well as virtue."[153] This "plastic power" constituted "the glory of the female character,"[154] and the key to their role as trainers of children. Through "precept and example," women could "train their minds to virtue, and instill into them true Moral and Religious principles."[155] An African American woman wrote to *The Liberator* that the "great responsibility" of woman to cultivate young minds called "for strict attention, on her part, to the benefits of good education."[156] African American men tended to approach women's roles with a combination of respect for the boundaries of the limited sphere into which black women had been placed and a condescension derived from their success at having placed women there. A convention of black men advocated imparting the value of the industrial education in "private residences" rather than public fora, for it was there that "we should get better access to the minds of our females." Having reached "their" females, "correct ideas" could "finally be inculcated in the sentiments of wives and mothers as to perform in moulding the future character of our youth."[157]

In her role as primary shaper of her children's character, it was imperative that woman herself embody the virtues she was to inculcate. In addition to the litany of virtues required of all respectable Americans, the women bore extra burdens. Among the virtues required of eldest daughters (who bore special responsibilities for raising younger children), one moralist listed generosity, gentleness, kindness, and forbearance. She "must be taught to think little of herself" and have "a sacred regard for the right of others."[158] This requirement for virtue among women extended to their limited participation in public life. According to one outspoken black editor, she "who would be thought respectable" should "give no countenance to men, who were so impudent as to halloo after them in the streets," for "a brazen faced, impudent woman is the most disgusting creature in the world."[159]

It was hoped that African American women would master two virtues in particular. The first of these was economy. This, according to *Freedom's Journal*, was "particularly becoming and useful in the female," for she commanded the household economy.[160] In what must have struck hard-pressed African American women as more of an imposition than a blessing, black wives were told that proper management of domestic resources was "so important a part of a woman's character, so necessary to her happiness and so essential to her performing properly the duties of a wife and of a mother, that it ought to have the precedence of all other accomplishments."[161] Along with economy, African American spokespersons prized in black women a quality best described as sincerity. In her work to provide her husband a refuge from the public world, she could offer that which often seemed utterly lacking in the marketplace: a security that the known would remain the known, an assurance that a man's perceptions had not been completely warped by the exigencies of an increasingly anonymous world of conniving strangers. As young husbands increasingly experienced the perfidy of the world, they would come to appreciate "the tongue that knows no guile" and "the thousand decencies which flow through domestic life, all unpretending as they are."[162] It was not, according to one African American woman, "gaudy show, nor the gilded trapping of pomp and pageantry which attracts the man of sense," it was "gentle, feminine affection."[163] The antislavery press lauded those "benevolent women" who prepared the bazaars that raised funds for the movement. Such women turned away from "fashionable pleasures, refusing to spend their leisure to serve their own interests."[164] "Fops, dandies and literary pretenders" may not have appreciated the virtues of such women, but those such as they built their lives around falsity anyway.[165]

The idealization of womanly virtue did not necessarily confine the African American woman to the home. Her better qualities did have a place in public, though in highly circumscribed roles. Black commentators both male and female lauded the application of "female influence" in public, where it could help the downtrodden and vicious "finally become good members of society." It could restore "those who may be walking the broad road to destruction" to "the paths of truth and virtue."[166] Once again, through their proxy roles in the home, they could still influence the public. "For instilling into the public mind, and diffusing through society those new opinions, in which all social changes must have their origin, women possess peculiar advantages. They have an access to the hearts of men, which no man has."[167]

Women's moral influence could also be expanded beyond the domestic sphere simply by bestowing their educational roles on a broader public. This was what the African Female Benevolent Society had in mind when it claimed "the cultivation of the youthful mind"—and not necessarily the minds of its members' own young ones—the greatest of its objects.[168] Similarly, African American women in Buffalo organized a literary society for "the improvement of those moral and intellectual faculties" of city children young enough to be "susceptible to every improvement."[169] While clearly subordinated to moral roles, the movement of African American women's influence into the public sphere was far from a trivial advance. It accorded to women a place in what would become black spokespersons' most crucial strategic task: the swaying of public opinion. It was with this sentiment at the forefront that the announcement for one of the multitudinous fundraising bazaars black women held argued for their proper role in public: "Let woman be free to carry forward the great work of regenerating public sentiment," it declared.[170] By embodying the domestic ideal and bringing that ideal before a hostile public, African American women engaged themselves in one of the most crucial elements of the discourse of respectability in antebellum America. Their roles in the household were clearly subordinated to men's, but that did not make them less significant. Indeed, because the ideology of separate spheres largely limited their roles to the home, public manifestations of black women's domestic virtues—rare or confined though they may have been—proved all the more potent.

CONCLUSION

In countless ways, the public and private statements of prominent African American figures in the antebellum North revealed the depths to which they shared the outlooks and values of their social, intellectual, and cultural milieus. Their notions regarding the structure of human character, its capacity for improvement and elevation, the value of respectability and the labor virtues it implied, and the deep need to train the young and themselves so that they might function suitably in an expanding market economy—all these echoed the language of white reformers, moralists, and etiquette writers and mirrored the concerns of a burgeoning white middle class. None of the concepts of character expressed in the statements of antebellum black elites were concocted in an ideological vacuum. African American thinkers operated in and contributed to a rich context of social thought, which in turn deeply informed their platforms.

The goal of this chapter has been to assess the degree to which black thought depended upon, and in fact helped create, the core precepts and premises that predicated northern society. The effort here has not been to place black thought into the intellectual camps of specific isms, such as transcendentalism, Fourierism, evangelicalism, or reformism. Nor has it been to delineate too specifically the genealogies of the ideas that found expression among black northerners. Many African American thinkers were quite conversant with the major philosophers of their day. Yet black protest thought as a whole drew its energy less from particular philosophical movements than from a far less formal pattern of discussion, carried out in newspaper debates, the pamphlet press, public speeches and sermons, and the pronouncements of institutions like black conventions. These were the mechanisms through which spokespersons continually forged and re-forged black public protest thought. No doubt a yet more informal layer of discussion characterized the daily lives of all black northerners: banter in barbershops and boardinghouses, thoughts exchanged in private correspondence, and exhortations heard on urban street corners. The popular thought crafted in these fora resisted doctrinalism and categorization in favor of a fluid ideological cosmopolitanism, which could borrow freely from the disparate ideological strands present. In drawing parallels between, say, Frederick Douglass and Theodore Parker, the point has not been to say that Douglass took from Parker. It is that they both molded their thought from similar clay, and it is understanding the nature of the clay that illuminates the congruities between black protest and a broader ideological context.

What remains to be seen is how black thinkers' apparently middle-class values might have been implicated in their assessment of the problems they faced and in the solutions they proffered. For no matter how much money or social status they possessed, African Americans throughout the North were denied the most basic acknowledgments of their equal and unfettered access to the benefits of citizenship. All blacks had to contend with a hostile society increasingly structuring itself at its deepest levels on the impossibility of black respectability, the immutability of black degradation, and the inevitability of black subservience (and perhaps extermination). As they well understood, no black northerner, regardless of wealth, was free from the problem of prejudice.

The public, therefore, among a democratic people, has a singular power, which aristocratic nations cannot conceive; for it does not persuade others to its beliefs, but it imposes them and makes them permeate the thinking of everyone by a sort of enormous pressure of the mind of all upon the individual intelligence.

Alexis de Tocqueville

CHAPTER 5

Slaves to a Wicked Public Sentiment

Black Respectability and the Response to Prejudice

On a wet April day in 1839, the African Clarkson Association of New York City, a somewhat typical black literary society and antislavery activist organization, met to hear its usual round of member-speakers. This particular meeting featured a talk by a rather obscure figure, Peter Paul Simons, a coal porter who appears almost nowhere else in the annals of antebellum black activism. Speaking over half a century after benevolent-minded whites had first established organizations in the city to uplift their newly emancipated black brethren, Simons delivered a rare critique and stunning rebuke of the entire thrust of black activism. His main purpose was to challenge what he saw as the utter dominance of moral uplift ideology among the black activist leadership. Decrying the incessant "trumpet sound" of "MORAL ELEVATION . . . OUR MORAL ELEVATION," Simons charged that black leaders presented this idea as "parent of all virtue, and he [who] would dare whisper in the faintest breath against it, is thought no less than the parent of all vice, crime, and degradation, that could possibly afflict humanity." Arguing with accuracy that the idea derived from white philanthropists' desire "to elevate Africans by morals," Simons claimed that a half-century's experience demonstrated that the strategy simply did not work and was no longer suited to serve as the centerpiece of black protest thought. Those whose parents had been "infatuated" with educating their children so that they might fill higher stations now found themselves "bitterly disappointed." Simons charged, "We see men of the highest standing among us filling very low stations." Freedom in the North, he claimed, "is nothing but a nickname for northern slavery."[1]

Worse than this, he argued, moral elevation served not as an agent of black liberation, but as a device to keep African Americans both subordinate and docile. "This long talk of moral elevation," he declared, "has made us a moral people, but no more," for moral elevation "has carried along with it blind submission." In the "great respect" and "soft manners" it demanded that blacks show to whites lay the "roots of degradation." This acquiescence, Simons charged, was no accident, but part of a conscious design "to hinder our people from acting collectively for themselves, . . . from acting in another way to obtain their rights." To Simons, the class divisions among blacks fostered by moral elevation exacerbated this process of disuniting a people who above all required solidarity. Black "men of education" had little to show for their efforts, he charged: "The cry of intellectual elevation has caused them to be proud, and they will be no man's servant. . . . They form classes of distinction, so as to be known from those who get an honest living by labor."[2]

Conditioned by several generations of protest thought rooted in black power ideologies, modern ears have difficulty disagreeing with Simons's assessment that the strategy of elevation was an ineffective model of protest. Antebellum black northerners' calls for racial uplift through self-improvement appear today to have been positively ineffectual, if not downright dysfunctional. How could effective protest have been built on such a basis? Did it not concede white superiority, if only transitorily, requiring that blacks approach whites as supplicants? Did it not compel blacks to request rights that whites enjoyed by simple virtue of their race, thus placing the bar of acceptable behavior much higher for blacks than whites? Were not the standards of behavior to which self-improvement aspired rooted in the culture of a white bourgeoisie rather than African American folk culture? Did not the strategy bypass democracy's basic premise that all people deserved rights by virtue of their simple humanity? How can we make sense of antebellum black leaders' apparently conciliatory statements? Is there any way to reconcile them with racial pride and effective protest?

Chapter 4 explored the ways in which African American elites shared the language of moral uplift with white Americans, even to the point of cofabricating those precepts. When African American spokespersons in the antebellum North celebrated the virtues of bourgeois morality, it argues, they had not fallen victim to a process whereby they had imbibed the values of an alien culture that operated against their interests as an oppressed people, but had instead laid claim to a potent tradition of moral rhetoric of which they were very much a part. What follows here is an intellectual history of the ways in which black elites in the antebellum North fashioned an argument for racial equality from the unlikely material of the middle-class discourse of respectability. Though implicated deeply in the construction of the discourse of civic morality, black thinkers forged it into a unique form, a potent weapon for changing the "public mind" on matters of race, eradicating prejudice, and eventually compelling whites to respect their demands for liberty and equality.

DARK, DEEP, AND HOPELESS: BLACK ELEVATION, WHITE ANXIETY

Black public protest thought formed in an ideological context that was undergoing profound transformations in the decades before the Civil War. Shifting social contexts for the process of racial formation produced important transformations in popular understandings of race after the turn of the nineteenth century. Key to this process was the erosion of the legal status of servitude as a legitimate basis for racial distinction. The steady demise of northern slavery from the 1770s on posed tremendous ideological challenges for a society that had since its founding equated the inferiority of African-descended people with their status as slaves. Coupled with the erosion throughout the urban North of traditional systems of deference politics in favor of a new, aggressive class politics, the end of slavery's legitimation of social hierarchies deeply undermined traditional notions of order. Bereft of the fact of enslavement as a rationale for black civic and social inferiority, northern whites wrestled with the implications of freed black people in a democratic republic. The story is well known and tragic: rather than adhere to the logic of natural rights and concede freed African Americans the full rights and privileges of citizens, too many northerners subtly recrafted notions of race to virtually write African-descended people out of the republic—to expunge them from the category of "all men" that the Declaration of Independence had declared inherently equal. Race in the North, once rooted primarily in Biblical explanation and relying heavily on the legal status of servitude, came to be marked by the standards of emerging bourgeois culture, the new "science" of race, and the blind hatred of the mob. For purposes ranging from the defense of working-class dignity to the cultivation of middle-class sentimentality, white northerners ascribed to freed blacks an identity as pariahs, inherently and irrevocably inferior, if sometimes secretly enviable in their ludicrous incapacity to adapt to modern life.

As expressed in behavior ranging from the small-scale and personal to the formation of public policies by the federal and northern state governments, the ideas of white northerners had a manifest impact on the ways African Americans lived their lives. Understanding this, black northerners did not insulate themselves from these forces but in fact engaged America in arguments over the nature and future of the race. A brief survey of popular racial imagery and ideology in the decades before the Civil War offers a convenient lens into the attitudes blacks found themselves forced to combat.

White Americans shared blacks' beliefs in a society fundamentally structured around hierarchies of character traits against which individuals and nations could be located. They premised their racism on the belief that African-descended people naturally and irrevocably occupied the lowest rungs of the social ladder. The case was made most cogently by the American Colonization Society (ACS), founded in 1816 by a collection of prominent national figures for the purposes of ridding America of its race problem by ridding it of its blacks. Leaders of the ACS refrained from a frontal assault on slavery, proposing instead that only freed blacks be sent to Africa. The Society considered these folk especially dangerous, contending that they were "as a body, more vicious and degraded than any other which our population embraces." They constituted, in its view, "a ragged set, . . . notoriously ignorant, degraded and miserable, [and] mentally diseased." Further, it argued, "[Their] freedom is *licentiousness*, and to many RESTRAINT would prove a blessing." Free blacks' unique position in American society—between bondage and complete citizenship—seemed particularly threatening. "Placed mid way between freedom and slavery," the Society claimed, "they feel neither the moral stimulants of the one, nor the restraint of the other." "Contaminated themselves, they extend their vices to all around them, to the slaves and to the whites." Their inherent viciousness rendered them "repugnant to our republican feelings, and dangerous to our republican institutions." An editorial in the official organ of the ACS put it succinctly: "The African in this country belongs by birth to the very lowest station in society; and from that station *he can never rise*, be his talents, his enterprise, his virtues what they may. . . . They constitute a class by themselves—a class out of which *no individual can be elevated*, and below which, none can be depressed."[3]

Fears that blacks themselves might not understand this to be the case pervaded the white North in the first half of the nineteenth century. A burgeoning popular press of cheap almanacs, etchings, broadsides, magazines, and other inexpensive print media sought to engrave the permanence of black degradation on the mind of an eagerly consuming public. Made possible through advances in printing technology and by an increasingly literate populace, the new media catered to a popular audience of working-class Americans, producing the earliest examples of inexpensive, mass-produced black stereotypes.[4]

Typical of the earliest efforts was the ostensibly humorous but racially vicious art of white artist Edward Clay. The etchings in Clay's *Life in Philadelphia* series, which appeared in 1828 and went through several editions, regularly presented the overdressed fops, ignorant Sambos, and fresh-speaking mammies that littered the popular press of the day. By far the most ubiquitous theme of such early images was that of blacks reaching beyond their allotted social grade. In one of Clay's cartoons, an overdressed black man greets a similarly overdressed woman on the street by asking, "How you find yourself did hot weeder Miss Chloe?" Her reply—"Pretty well I tank you Mr. Cesar only I aspire too much"—both mocks through malapropisms the impossible attempt of an inferior to "imitate" the speech of white people and betrays white fears of blacks who "aspired" to a social position higher than most whites thought they deserved (Plate 5).[5] The constant appearance in racist cartoons of "darky swells" clad beyond their means in imitation of white social elites signaled the frequent recurrence of this concern.

This image of "Zip Coon," as he was sometimes known, replaced a stock figure from eighteenth-century social satire, that of the dandy or fop. The dandy had served primarily to mock the social pretensions, and especially a weakness for fashion and susceptibility to fad, of those born below the stations they sought to occupy. In the United States, where notions of meritocracy and a fluid social hierarchy replaced the fixed social order of the Old World, race became the primary signifier of social and civic inclusion. The black dandy figure resulted.

In many respects he represented a cultural solution to the problem of the confidence man. Now in blackface, the early nineteenth-century dandy figure continued to express concerns over social pretension and false status, but it captured anew the struggles of a society increasingly committed to the myth of meritocracy and the boundaries of race. In America, "breeding" retained significance as a measure of social worth but in the newer, more vulgar, and more easily discerned sense permitted by a burgeoning science of human biology and race. In a society increasingly anxious about the authenticity of character in the expanding urban economy and concerned with defining its class identities in contradistinction to others, Zip Coon per-

"*How you find yourself dis hot weader Miss Chloe?*"
"*Pretty well I tank you M͞r Cesar only I aspire too much!*"

PLATE 5. *"How you find yourself?" Etchings such as this mocked the social pretensions of free black urbanites who "aspired" to social status above their stations. Lithograph by Edward Clay,* Life in Philadelphia, *plate 4 (Philadelphia: S. Hart, 1829); courtesy of The Library Company of Philadelphia.*

mitted white northerners to explore insecurities without challenging their root source—the expanding market economy itself. By displacing such fears onto the image of an irredeemably precapitalist African, white northerners cleared the space necessary to function in a competitive economic order without ever having to examine the inequities increasingly manifest in liberal capitalism.

The duplicity of Zip Coon in his role as respectable socialite could always be discerned; his attempts to rise above the lowly station his nature dictated could easily be countered. White northerners might concede that all white men had an equal chance in the race of life; Zip promised that no matter how unsuccessful one might be in that competition, someone would always be lower, and observably so. Racist images thus permitted antebellum whites to retain faith in the fundamental sanctity of the economic order even as that order may have eroded their social status, undermined their standard of living, and alienated them from their work. White northerners' concerns were evident in the many guises the black dandy figure took in antebellum press images. Cartoons variously mocked the middle-class pretensions of black masons, who in their pretensions erroneously assumed that they had something at stake in a political process closed to them; satirized those sporting classical names, which suggested a gravity absolutely beyond their stations (as with the names some masters mockingly imposed on their slaves); ridiculed those who assumed manners, often incorrectly, which suggested social status far beyond their means; and lampooned those whose defective notions of beauty led them to prize the purportedly grotesque physical features of blacks and shun the pleasing features of attractive whites.

As these images suggest, antebellum white supremacists argued first and foremost for the incapacity or inadvisability of black elevation. Prominent national figures endorsed this view. Ostensibly sympathetic to the African American plight, the ACS used such popular sentiment to nourish its claims that the prejudice that impeded black progress owed to an "*insurmountable* barrier of color," which would cause blacks to "remain *for ever* a distinct and inferior race." The "natural causes" of skin color had erected "invincible prejudices" that would forever deny blacks a place in the nation: "No talents however great, no piety however pure and devoted, no patriotism however ardent, can secure their admission." According to one Society auxiliary, "Nature has raised up barriers between the races, *which no man with a proper sense of the dignity of his species desires to see surmounted.*" [6] Prejudice ostensibly having been proven ineradicable, the Society went on to counter other alternatives to black migration to Africa, namely the uplifting of African Americans through acts of benevolence such as those of British precursors William Wilberforce and Thomas Clarkson. To this argument it contended that slavery had so degraded blacks as to render any attempt worthless. "No device of our philanthropy for elevating the wretched subjects of its debasement to the ordinary privileges of men, can descry one cheering glimpse of hope that our object can *ever* be accomplished," the Society argued. "Whatever may be attempted for the general improvement of society," it continued, "their wants are untouched.—Whatever may be effected for elevating the mass of the nation in the scale of happiness or of intellectual and moral character, their degradation is the same—dark, and deep, and *hopeless.*"[7]

Embodied in the Zip Coon stereotype, white fears of these unassimilable blacks grasping for inclusion into white society shifted easily into anxiety over black political activism. "Aspiring" through the political means of radical abolitionism provoked the strongest reactions among whites. The Zip Coon image presented to whites socially unincorporable blacks attempting to mimic white cultural styles and social norms. Black activists presented the fearful specter of these unassimilable people actively seeking to dismantle the legal and social mechanisms necessary to degrade black life and maintain the fiction of innate black inferiority. As such, the movement for abolition came under particular fire by white satirists, who lampooned black activism through the developing conventions of popular racist humor. In an exchange between an absurdly overdressed black couple depicted in one of Edward Clay's etchings, the racist implications of Zip Coon smoothly melded into scorn for black participation in the antislavery movement. Asked her opinion of the "new fashion shirt" a black man in one cartoon is wearing, his female companion responds: "I tink dey mighty elegum—I see you on New Year day when you carry de colour in de Abolition 'siety—You look just like Pluto de God of War!" (Plate 6).[8] The humor of such images relied on the absurd pretensions of blacks that were implied in them. Abolitionist activities, which presented opportunities for blacks to flaunt such pretensions, came under special fire.[9]

The possibility of black elevation roused the particular ire of white working classes, which even at this early period in the formation of their class identity predicated their opposition to capital as much on the terrain of whiteness as on the dignity of labor. A broadside entitled "The Results of Abolitionism," which appeared in Philadelphia in the mid-1830s, succinctly captured the fears of a group that saw blacks as a threat to its increasingly tenuous privileges (Plate 7). In the poster, a well-dressed black man supervises the construction of a building by white and black laborers. The two white laborers at the base of the building are mixing mortar and carrying bricks to the black workers, who are laying the bricks at the top of the building. The black supervisor admonishes a white worker: "White man Hurry up them bricks." Meanwhile, the two black workers coarsely direct the white laborers: "Bring up the mortar you white rascals," says one, while the other remarks, "You bog-trotters, come along with them bricks." The poster utterly embraces notions of social hierarchy as it documents white

PLATE 6. *"Mighty elegum."* The Zip Coon image of the black urban fop folded easily into
fears of blacks rising through antislavery efforts. Lithograph by Edward Clay,
Life in Philadelphia *(Philadelphia: S. Hart, 1829); courtesy of*
The Library Company of Philadelphia.

PLATE 7. *"The Results of Abolitionism!" This white labor broadside depicted the consequences of black freedom as a threatening elevation of blacks through the labor hierarchy, to the detriment of white labor. Wood engraving, artist unknown (Philadelphia, ca. 1835); courtesy of The Library Company of Philadelphia.*

laborers' fears of competition from blacks. Its iconography relies on popular understandings of labor and racial hierarchy, which it inverts to make its
point. The black workers are masons and skilled laborers, and consequently
occupy the upper reaches of the structure; meanwhile, the unskilled white
laborers appear below them, actually struggling to reach the top. The poster
must have aroused potent fears of the threats posed by the movement to
abolish slavery: emancipation would, it asserts, entail the inversion of racial
and labor hierarchies to the detriment of the white worker.[10]

"The Results of Abolitionism" argued not simply against the consequences of black activism on the status of white labor; it also explored the
mechanisms of class domination implicit in that degradation. In the image,
the vehicle for the elevation of middle-class black managers over white
laborers proves to be racially traitorous white capitalists who ally with blacks
to undermine the interests of white labor. The addition of the figure of the
fat white capitalist, who manipulates the social aspirations of middle-class
blacks for his own gain, signals the besieged state of mind of white laborers,
who easily conflated racial hatred with opposition to an increasingly repres-
sive regime of industrial work. The broadside thus constituted a call for
racial solidarity across class lines to defeat the larger menace of black competitors. In the broadside, the epitome of white workers' fears is the black
capitalist himself.

Such figures were not unknown. James Forten, for example, had made
a fortune as a Philadelphia sailmaker and employed both black and white
laborers. An Edward Clay etching reflected white worker's concern over
such black elites, channeling them into the political sphere. One *Life in Philadelphia* image satirizes blacks' alleged penchant for political unity and dependence on conservative white elites (Plate 8). In the image, an elderly
and well-to-do African American man — likely the client and perhaps former
slave of some wealthy white patron — grasps in one hand a switch, with which
he intends to scold the black youth he clutches in the other. On his head the
child wears a hat made of a copy of *The Mercury*, a Democrat newspaper, and
peddles copies of the *Democratic Press* at his feet. Referring to Democratic
populist Andrew Jackson, the older man angrily chides him: "What de de-
bil you hurrah for General Jackson for? — You black nigger! — I'll larn you
better — I'm a 'ministration man!!"[11] The humor here, such as it is, depends
upon the anger of an elderly man's excessive desire to police black political solidarity, which is contrasted with his manifest failure to corral even
the minimal challenge posed by a youthful renegade. The implication is
not simply that African American leaders lacked the capacity to unite their
people politically; it is also that the youth might actually prove wiser than

PLATE 8. *"I'm a 'ministration man!!"* Black leaders' failure to enforce the political solidarity
of their own constituents is lampooned in this cartoon, which also suggests the early-century
political affinity between black social elites and their Federalist patrons. Lithograph by
Edward Clay, Life in Philadelphia, *plate 7 (Philadelphia: S. Hart, 1829);
courtesy of The Library Company of Philadelphia.*

his stodgy comrade, who has become nothing but the puppet of the white
economic elites and political conservatives who championed the capitalist
class. For white working-class readers, the satisfaction derived from watch-
ing the erosion of this threatening cross-racial alliance of those assumed to
be class elites.

Coupled with white labor's fears of black elevation came the suggestion that if blacks could not rise, they could become, in a literal sense, more like whites through miscegenation. Never straying from its self-servingly cynical approach to human nature, the American Colonization Society argued that the same forces that rendered prejudice ineradicable also dictated that racial intermixture would never prove an effective solution. Citing "a principle of repulsion so strong as to forbid the idea of a communion of either interest or of feeling as utterly abhorrent," the Society reached its inevitable, melancholy conclusion that blacks' destiny lay in Africa. "Education and habit and prejudice" had so firmly riveted hatred of blacks in the American mind "that they have become as strong as nature itself—and to expect their removal, or even their slightest modification, would be as idle and preposterous as to expect that we could reach forth our hands, and remove the mountains from their foundations in the vallies." [12] If the rampant fears of interracial sexual union that appeared in the penny press were any indication, the ACS's idealized notion of racial repugnance could hardly be counted upon. Black abolitionists were only too fond of countering ACS claims with evidence of masters' attraction for their bondswomen. [13] As was the case with all of mixed racial ancestry, those such as Frederick Douglass and Henry Bibb had but to point to themselves.

Only an emerging white society insecure of its own hegemony and deeply concerned with policing its racial boundaries could have so casually fused fears of insurgent racial politics with those of sexual transgression. In one etching depicting a parlor scene, two mixed-race couples court (Plate 9). The black man, apparently exercising the innate skills ascribed to his race, entertains a white woman sitting on his lap with a song played on the lute. The white man, conspicuously modeled on abolitionist William Lloyd Garrison, kneels before a corpulent black woman in romantic subordination. Portraits of famous abolitionists hang on the walls in silent approbation. The implication lacks any trace of subtlety: efforts by whites to support black interests are tantamount to desiring the unthinkable consequence of social equality and intermarriage. The cartoon's title, "Practical Amalgamation," locates the dangers of any advance in black rights as leading inevitably and directly into the hallowed domestic sphere, where white masculinity would be degraded through the violation of white men's most treasured goods— the virtue of their women. [14] The white press echoed such crassly posed fears in words, suggesting, for example, that "the emancipation of the colored races of the South would not satisfy Frederick Douglass and his compatriots, without the same facility being obtained for blacks and whites to marry, and to be given in marriage together." [15]

Racial hierarchy and themes of black "rising" or "elevation" were not con-

PLATE 9. *"Practical Amalgamation." Nothing signaled whites' fears of black elevation more than the prospect of racial miscegenation. This image depicts a white man (modeled on William Lloyd Garrison) courting an overweight black woman, while a black man prepares to kiss a white woman. Pictures of abolitionist leaders look on the scene approvingly. Colored lithograph by Edward Clay (New York, ca. 1839); courtesy of The Library Company of Philadelphia.*

fined to a popular press intended for the working class. Magazines designed for more elite audiences also often evinced white concerns over black elevation. An image appearing in *Vanity Fair* in January 1861—just as several southern states seceded from the Union—was typical in evoking such fears. In "The Rising of the Afrite," three white men on a beach step away from a bottle that has just erupted into a cloud, which dominates the sky and contains at its zenith an African dressed as a genie. Text accompanying the image identifies him as the "tremendous evil Afrite" loosed by the fishermen of an *Arabian Nights* tale. According to the caption, this "devil of dissention and anarchy" had been released by southern politicians who had been fishing in the "troubled waters" of national politics. According to the text, the Afrite represented the "Awful Discord" that threatens "ruin-death!"; it urged the fishermen "to conjure the Afrite back into the bottle" (Plate 10).[16]

The rising Afrite clearly identified slavery and the oppression of blacks as a source of national tension. Yet the image easily accommodated several additional layers of meaning. For one, it disparaged blacks as "evil" and

PLATE 10. *"The Rising of the Afrite." This illustration graphically depicted black elevation as a threat to national harmony.* Vanity Fair 3, no. 56 (January 19, 1861), 31; *image courtesy of The Library Company of Philadelphia.*

"devils" just as casually as it castigated proslavery politicians. The image also exposed some fundamental social and racial presuppositions. Blacks were not only "released" onto the national scene as a spirit of discord, their freedom was presented as a spatial, and by implication social and political, rise. The logic of the cartoon as visual media allowed the clearest possible identification between the "freeing" of blacks and a movement upward, or elevation. The visual hierarchy of the image, which ordered degrees of freedom in terms of "higher" and "lower" space, assigned black freedom to elevated realms. In a society wherein new economic relations were undermining traditional social hierarchies, few Americans would have been insensitive to the implications of images such as "The Rising of the Afrite." Whether to urban working classes or white social elites, such cartoons spelled out in clear language the threats of black freedom to the stability of the national polity and the existing racial and social order.[17]

These images reveal the climate in which African Americans formulated their thinking on race and the nation. It was an atmosphere in which the North's transformation into an industrial society was eroding traditional social hierarchies, and in which new sources of social organization were being discovered in the burgeoning "science" of race, in developing theories of labor, and in evolving ideals of gender. Black Americans did not distance themselves from these arguments and, in fact, could not have. Rather, they built an ideological tradition founded on premises shared across wide segments of northern society, though the conclusions they drew differed markedly from those of white supremacists hostile to their interests.

Black leaders took great pains to respond to the images of blacks presented in the popular press and on the stage. A great many of them understood the cause of their inequality to lie largely in the way the race was presented to the public. The new media world, they noted, featured "ten thousand channels through which malign feelings find utterance and influence," including the pulpit, the press, and the lecture hall.[18] The theater—and in particular theaters housing the nation's newest popular entertainment craze, blackface minstrelsy—provoked the wrath of many black leaders. Samuel Cornish, the New York City clergyman and editor, excoriated theaters for, among other infidelities, presenting plays "which hold up to ridicule the foibles or peculiarities of an already too much oppressed people." Such venues, by presenting actors who represented blacks "in their most ridiculous light" fostered feelings of "disgust," permitting whites to imagine that the black character traits presented on stage "are the characteristics of the whole people." Cornish singled out T. D. Rice, alias "Jim Crow," for having "completely put down abolitionism in England."[19] Philadelphia's John H. Johnson also decried the "exaggerated exhibition of . . . slave manners and customs" presented on the minstrel stage. The great detriment of these exhibitions, Johnson argued, was that they suggested to white Americans that such Sambo-like practices constituted "the natural character of the blacks," when in fact slaves' admittedly "degraded and monkeyfied manners" was due to their treatment at the hands of masters rather than their inherent natures. By unfailingly portraying the "light-hearted and silly deportment" of the enslaved, the minstrel stage had "even pretended to raise a doubt respecting their real humanity."[20] After witnessing his first minstrel show, Frederick Douglass lauded the skill of the performers but could not endorse the enterprise wholesale. "They must cease to exaggerate the exaggerations of our enemies; and represent the colored man rather as he is, than as Ethiopian Minstrels usually represent him to be." Such presentations, Douglass charged, "cater to the lower elements of the baser sort."[21] Months later, Douglass's tone hardened considerably; he termed blackface minstrel groups "the filthy scum of white society, who have stolen from us a complexion denied to them by nature, in which to make money, and pander to the corrupt taste of their white fellow citizens."[22]

DISEASES OF THE WILL: THE PROBLEM OF PREJUDICE

Black elites responded to the plight of their people in terms deeply reminiscent of the social thought of their antebellum northern context. In addressing their peculiarly racial problems, they brought to bear concepts that were hardly specific to themselves. Had they not been confronted with the problems of prejudice and slavery, they would still have shared the concerns of many white Americans in the North. They would still have premised their worldview on elevation and a tripartite conception of human character (mind, morals, and the body), would still have expressed overriding concern with individual efforts to elevate oneself, and would still have sought respectability by attempting to assert not simply their success in the world but also their inner moral integrity.

But racial imperatives altered the language of elevation as it issued from black mouths. African American leaders and activists across a broad spectrum consistently applied metaphors of rising, uplift, and progress to their efforts to participate fully in national life. When black women founded the African Female Benevolent Society of Troy, New York, they declared their intention was "to raise ourselves to an equality" with whites.[23] John Russwurm, the coeditor of *Freedom's Journal*, denied the arguments of those who claimed that blacks "can never be materially advanced in the scale of being."[24] Samuel Cornish, his coeditor, argued for both "the general improvement of Society"[25] and for restoring blacks "to their former elevation in the scale of being."[26] Even militants like David Walker, whom many scholars consider exempt from the bourgeois class values of his day, spoke of blacks' position on "the scale of reasonable and thinking beings."[27] Throughout the period, in thousands of incidental references in statements addressing a wide variety of topics, black spokespersons envisioned their people rising along various scales until their elevation brought them to a state of equality with whites.[28] Culled from the antebellum intellectual milieu, these references to hierarchy and "scales of being" confronted blacks with a considerable problem: by a great many of these measures, blacks in general seemed to rank among the lowly.

Frequently, the protest thought that emerged from this strategy appeared to result in concessions of black inferiority. It is difficult to read the words of the northern African Americans who spearheaded the antebellum struggle for freedom without encountering such statements. For example, Thomas Hamilton claimed publicly, "In no direction can we be said to manifest force of character equal to the whites."[29] Such typical sentiments seemed to endorse Anglo-American standards against which blacks could only hope to fail. "The position which we now occupy . . . is a depressed one," lamented Connecticut minister Amos Beman; blacks, he said, could not match "the attainments of the most favored portions of the human family."[30] Others went further, claiming that blacks had been "groveling under" a humble state since their earliest existence.[31] What was worse, many seemed to lay the responsibility for this degradation as much at the feet of blacks themselves as at those of the whites who oppressed them. "It has been greatly owing to our own apathy that we are no further advanced than we are at present," declared a meeting of young African Americans in Cleveland, while a national convention reported that each barrier to black "elevation" was placed "as much by our own acquiescence, as by the dictate of public sentiment."[32] Another national convention of black leaders was willing to charge the nation with "all that guilt and wickedness" it had inflicted upon blacks, yet the group still asserted that "the many evils among ourselves" would prove ultimately more debilitating "than can all the *whites* put together."[33]

Such statements seem to constitute concessions of inferiority, remarkable in a tradition of protest thought. But these apparent admissions of black degradation need to be considered within their complex ideological context. Black protest relied on the premises of an intellectual milieu that African American elites shared and cofabricated with northern whites—in particular notions of social hierarchy and measures of "civilization" rooted in liberal capitalism and its bourgeois social order. In light of this context of thinking, antebellum black spokespersons confronted the task of explaining the admittedly degraded status of the race without relinquishing belief in its inherent ability to "rise." If, according to the American creed, all could rise, why had blacks not risen?

While hardly a militant challenge to white domination, black leaders' answers addressed charges that were unavoidable in the antebellum North by offering claims of their people's own degradation as testimony to the evils of the caste proscription that beset them. Such claims also served important community-building functions. When African American leaders told their followers that they lacked the capacity to compete with whites, they hoped to incite them to ever more strident efforts at self-elevation. These were jeremiads, directed against those apostates who had failed to embody blacks leaders' racial ideas. They were intended not to degrade self-image but to discipline listeners. Many African American leaders did share the middle-class outlooks of expanding urban America. Their protest rhetoric had helped build those outlooks, after all, infusing the American discourse of bourgeois morality with racial significance and emancipatory potential. As had the jeremiad tradition throughout seventeenth-century New England and the secular jeremiads of the Revolutionary era,[34] black jeremiads served to unite African Americans in the common cause of moral elevation, which was to say, in effective racial self-presentation. They set forth an imperative that corralled the non-elite into a community of the oppressed, defined by its struggle to find ways of compelling whites to grant the rights and liberty that they were due. After declaring to black New Yorkers, "There is none learned among us," William Hamilton, a prominent community leader from New York, retreated: "I am sorry to say it; but I speak with the intention to quicken you."[35]

Conspicuous examples of racial self-abnegation may be understood to have served positive functions, and they were less typical of black protest thought than some have asserted. More often than they highlighted blacks' own moral failings, African American leaders directed their ire at obstacles to black elevation imposed by whites. Even the puritanical *Colored American* left no doubt as to the cause of blacks' admitted degradation: they were "the involuntary subjects of a social and political despotism, . . . the guilt of which lies *wholly* at the white man's doors." Whites, the journal insisted, denied blacks "all the means of improvement, respectability and education."[36] Of course, slavery ranked first and foremost among these depredations. Answering charges that blacks' lack of progress in the arts owed to their inherently degraded natures, one commentator argued that it was no wonder that black artists like Phillis Wheatley had not achieved more. Stolen from Africa and kept in slavery, "what opportunity was there for her to make physical, moral, or mental progress?" he asked.[37] According to this line of thinking, slavery imposed circumstances that hindered blacks from developing their natural moral and mental faculties. "Never were any people more exposed to infidelity, than are the colored people of our country," charged newspaper editor Samuel Cornish.[38] Earlier, Cornish had responded to white charges of black inferiority by challenging slavery's apologists "to point us to the one *individual* who has enjoyed to the full extent all the privileges of his fairer brethren."[39]

While slavery constituted the greatest crime against black elevation, the limitations imposed on free black life also impeded the progress of the race. Alexander Crummell complained to a London audience that while slavery impeded the progress of the enslaved, "there are great difficulties in the way of the cultivation even of the *free* colored race in America."[40] In 1840, New York African Americans argued that, in depriving blacks of the vote, whites had removed "a stimulant to enterprise, a means of influence, and a source of respect" for free blacks.[41] The case for whites' degradation of free African Americans was, however, a bit more tenuous than that made for the enslaved. Freedom meant liberty from legal status as personless property. In an antebellum context, which prized above all an idealized vision of the liberal marketplace, it was a bit more difficult to make the case that the legally unenthralled still faced obstacles in the race of life. The solution to this problem lay in the concept of prejudice, which ran free even where slavery did not, and to which black leaders attributed elevation-inhibiting functions similar to those of slavery. Crummell argued that for free African Americans prejudice "prevents a full participation in the advantages of schools and colleges," while white abolitionist Gerrit Smith lamented with African American leaders that "cruel, heaven-defying prejudice" had closed for blacks "the avenues to riches and respectability—to happiness and usefulness."[42] In an optimistic moment, black educator Austin Steward stated his belief that, with the exception of prejudice, there was not "any other great impediment in the way to a higher state of improvement."[43]

For black elites in the antebellum North, the problem of prejudice was above all a problem of representation, reputation, and respectability. In particular, blacks faced hostile public opinion which, according to Henry Highland Garnet, "in this country is stronger than law."[44] "To what do the disabilities of the colored people and the slavery of this country owe their existence, more than to public opinion?" asked the black national convention of 1843. "What is a more fruitful source of evil than public opinion, when wrongly formed?"[45] Echoed the black national convention of 1853, "We battle against false and hurtful customs, and against the great errors and opinions which support such customs."[46] True, the enslaved bondspersons in the South lacked the right of self-ownership, deemed crucial to the healthy functioning of a free market economy, and true, slavery itself violated the deepest principles of democratic liberty and Christian charity. But the problems of African Americans in the nation did not stop in the slave states, for in black leaders' view the blight seeped northward, infiltrating the commercial republic and metastasizing under its veneer of liberal fair play. In the form of prejudice, this hostile public opinion was "stalking over the land, spreading in its course its pestilential breath, blighting and withering the fair and natural hopes of our happiness."[47] In the words of one black minister, through prejudice, slavery's "deadly poison is disseminated from the torrid regions of the South to the frigid North."[48] For another, prejudice was "the spirit of slavery"; it begat a "corrupt public sentiment," resulting in legal proscriptions against free blacks in the North.[49] This "wrong exercise of the sentiments and sympathies"—this "disease of the will"[50]—resulted in obstacles to black elevation that violated the values of the market, of democracy, and of God just as effectively as did slavery.

Prejudice was not simply the northern manifestation of slavery, however. It took on a life of its own, which then reinforced the institution that had originally bred it. Argued minister Hosea Easton, once "public sentiment" had "become so morally, civilly, and politically corrupted by the principles of slavery," it could become slavery's "auxiliary"—not simply a by-product of slavery but an agent of its perpetuation.[51] According to black emigrationist J. Theodore Holly, "the corrupt public sentiment of the North" wound up functioning as "the chief bulwark of American slavery."[52] For Samuel Cornish, "the real battleground between liberty and slavery is prejudice against color."[53]

In these theories of prejudice, black thinkers merged popular notions of Lockean and Humean epistemology with their own perceptions of an increasingly anonymous marketplace for public speech. Hosea Easton imagined public sentiment as a "current" of mental influences upon which the otherwise moribund mind is "borne along," until called upon by changing events "to a new exercise of thought."[54] According to Frances Ellen Watkins, these impressions worked for good or ill, depending on their content. "A thought is evolved and thrown out among the masses," she explained. "They receive it and it becomes interwoven with their mental and moral life—if the thought be good the receivers are benefitted, and helped onward to the truer life; if it is not, the reception of the idea is a detriment."[55]

The influence of the intangible words issued from speakers rarely seen and readers never known was considerable. This was especially so in the increasingly anonymous urban world, where reputation often proved central to success. According to J. Holland Townsend, who wrote for the *Anglo-African Magazine* in 1859, the resulting pressures of public opinion compelled people to take positions unthinkingly, even ones counter to their own interests, lest they suffer a "loss of influence and reputation." Under such pressures, he wrote, people "are strongly tempted to forego their own convictions of what is right, and seek for a reputation among their fellow men as the greatest good." They adopt others' views of right, he explained, for they are goaded by the pressure to be publicly accepted "at any price" instead of waiting to acquire the knowledge of right and wrong "by diligence, patience and industry, which always awards merit, with honor, respectability and esteem."[56] Frances Ellen Watkins similarly considered those thus hoodwinked to be the victims of unscrupulous men "who barter principles for expediency, the true and right for the available and convenient."[57] The new pressures of public opinion threatened to confront the republic with its greatest fear: a dependent, susceptible populace weak in character, which could be manipulated by conniving "interests" or "combinations" with a desire to undermine the democratic experiment for personal gain.

For black elites, the corruption of true sentiment by new and illegitimate media forces took the form of prejudice—ideological attacks against blacks' interest—rather than the disruption of traditional and local sources of political authority.[58] Proslavery apologists exhorted the ignorant masses to hate blacks to enhance their own security and status. Racial prejudice, which unthinkingly associated blackness with vice, entered the "public mind," festered, and influenced the behavior of white Americans. Thus black thinkers understood that racial slanders served to lower blacks "in the estimation of society" and rank them as inferiors.[59] They lamented the widespread idea—"perseveringly proclaimed in high places"—"that it is impossible for colored men to rise from ignorance and debasement, to intelligence and respectability." This notion, they worried, had "made a deep impression upon the public mind generally, and it is not without its effect upon us."[60]

Black leaders pointed to two mechanisms by which public sentiment was thus corrupted: influential men, such as those who led the American Colonization Society; and influential institutions, such as the penny press. The ACS represented "a strong combination against the people of color," composed of "master spirits of the day" who "turn public sentiment which ever way they please."[61] The Society was led by men the public listened to; "under the sanction of names so respectable, the common sense of the community was led astray," claimed the national black convention of 1833.[62] According to another, the Society had "distilled into the minds of the community a desire to see us removed."[63] More frightening yet were the operations of a hostile penny press: "[The press] takes hold of the public mind, and gets at the public heart; its influence reaches the spot to form and influence public opinion." [64] The *Colored American* lambasted the penny newspapers for corrupting the social and moral habits of their black readers,[65] while another black newspaper railed against the unprincipled man who edited such a sheet: this "destroyer of virtuous character" operated "on a multitude of minds, and poisons the moral atmosphere around him." He was "a destroyer of virtuous character"[66] who left his readers "*Slaves* to a wicked public sentiment."[67]

EVERY INDECOROUS ACT: RACIAL SYNECDOCHE AND THE PROBLEM OF REPRESENTATION

African American leaders considered the problem of prejudice their central concern. A "public mind" poisoned against blacks did not simply highlight the vices of black leaders' more downtrodden brethren; it fused all people of African descent into a single group united by an ascription of their vicious characters. Purveyors of public opinion slandered the entire group on the basis of individual acts, thus effacing the virtues of those who had successfully overcome their liabilities. The practice constituted what may be thought of as racial synecdoche, a reference to the figure of speech wherein a part is said to represent the whole. In the case of African Americans, the misdeeds of a few were said to represent the moral character of the entire race. In the antebellum North, this phenomenon tended to arise whenever individual blacks were thought to have affronted public morality or the racial order. Mourning the negative effects on blacks' public reputation caused by a fraudulent black minister, Austin Steward concluded: "It cannot be right to judge the character of a whole class or community by that of one person."[68] The mechanisms of the new media merely exacerbated a practice long under way. In an editorial in the *Colored American*, Samuel Cornish wrote: "If one of the baser sort of our people commit a crime, or is guilty of a misdemeanor, the cry is the niggers! the niggers!! Then the daily press with few honorable exceptions, fall in, magnify the evil, and throw the stigma and disgrace upon the whole body of colored people."[69] The implications of racial synecdoche for blacks' freedom struggle followed clearly. As racial theorist J. W. Lewis pronounced with exasperation, "Every indecorous act on their part is used as a weapon by the pro-slavery spirit of the age . . . to show that the colored people are not fit for freedom."[70]

Racial synecdoche constituted a perversely intense application of a principle of representation that was gaining ever wider practice in an expanding public sphere where social relations were becoming increasingly anonymous. As it became more and more infeasible to fix identity in such a con-

text—to personally know those encountered in the course of business—
weak surrogate means of identification arose. When Lewis Woodson wrote
to Samuel Cornish that "nothing is more common in men, than to associate
a cause, with him who advocates it,"[71] he may just as sagely have applied his
formulation to ethnic and national groups. Nothing was more common in
the antebellum North than to associate a nation with the individuals who
represented it. Joseph Willson noted the associative proclivity of antebellum northerners in calling for the scrupulous public comportment of black
Philadelphians: "the sight of one man . . . whatever may be his apparent condition . . . is the sight of a community; and the errors and crimes of one,
is adjudged as the criterion and character of the whole body."[72] In a world
in which it was impossible to know the characters of those with whom the
average urbanite interacted, ethnic, racial, and national signifiers—however
faulty as determinants of character—seemed to offer desperately needed
cues.[73]

Many African American spokespersons pointed out that as a result of this
problem of representation their people were held to higher standards of
conduct than were whites. Philadelphian John H. Johnson criticized this
practice, suggesting that the public formulate its opinions instead on a more
representative sampling of the black population. "To form a correct judgement upon the character of these people," he lectured, "a person should
take a view of those only who are known to have sober habits." Too often, he
complained, whites inflated the significance of an intemperate black man.
White Americans had their lowly elements, too, he said, yet "moral reporters
are not merely [nearly] so bitter in their language concerning them as they
are when reproaching the down-trodden and ignorant blacks."[74] According
to another commentator, "Popular prejudice will exaggerate the bad conduct of a colored man, while at the same time it closes all eyes to the claims
of the colored man of moral worth."[75]

The problem for blacks, of course, was that whites' opinions of their racial
or national character were grounded in notions of inherent and irrevocable
inferiority. Understanding the exact nature of these ideas—their sources
and means of sustenance—promised knowledge of how to end them. Did
the mere fact of African Americans' blackness cause prejudice, or did the
degraded conditions of black life cause it? This debate regarding whether
"color" or "condition" caused prejudice served as a constant subtext to black
activism. The American Colonization Society championed the argument
that the mere fact of blackness aroused the hatred of whites, and hence it opposed efforts to integrate blacks, saying that "improvement can never take
place except the race be amalgamated; and amalgamation is a day-dream."[76]

Some African Americans agreed, providing the Society with atypical yet prominent examples of African Americans who chose to leave the country of their birth and return to Africa, such as Lott Cary and Daniel Coker. Perhaps most notable among these was John Brown Russwurm, who cofounded and coedited *Freedom's Journal*, the nation's first black newspaper, in New York City in 1827. Russwurm argued that blacks in America were "considered a distinct people" whose status would never change. Even at the end of a thousand-year struggle, he predicted, "we should be exactly in our present situation: a proscribed race, however unjustly—a degraded people, deprived of all the rights of freemen in the eyes of the community." Blacks' situation being irredeemable in America, he concluded there was no other solution than to cast their eyes "upon some other portion of the globe where all these inconveniences are removed."[77] As a young man, the relatively conservative William Whipper concurred with this analysis of prejudice, though not with the solution, arguing instead that blackness itself, and whites' natural repugnance to it, must be the cause of their degradation. Echoing the ACS's logic, if not its sympathies, Whipper found prejudice an intractable component of human nature: "Its foundation is in man's selfish nature, pride and ambition, which rule and govern his worst passions. It grows spontaneous, inflates the instincts of the ignorant, and directs the minds of the learned. . . . It is older than kings or constitutions."[78]

Not surprisingly, many prominent African Americans disagreed. The Society and its defenders consistently ducked the issue of prejudice's causes, too often pleading that regardless of etiology blacks could never hope to escape its baneful maw.[79] Samuel Cornish attacked such logic as "deifying prejudice and paying homage at the shrine of one of the grossest sins that ever disgraced the human family."[80] It would have been far more just, in his mind, to simply purge prejudice from the public mind. Frequently citing examples from foreign regions where racial attitudes were reputed (often inaccurately) to be relatively benign—such as Europe, the Middle East, and Brazil[81]—black thinkers found that prejudice was "wholly acquired," like "other artificial states of being."[82] It was "habitual" and "unnatural."[83] One African American writer argued that blackness does not cause prejudice but merely "identifies degrading associations"—that is, it served as a symbol of blacks' material inferiority.[84] As another put it: "The color is of no account. It is only the index of slavery, and despised for that cause."[85] Frederick Douglass had a label for those who considered prejudice against color a law of nature: "numsculls."[86]

The question was important, for it signaled to black leaders the practicality, indeed the possibility, of eradicating prejudice, and hence directed their means. Should prejudice prove itself a deeply rooted function of whites' natural repugnance to blackness, as the American Colonization Society had argued since its inception, little hope could be held that blacks' liabilities would ever be removed, and colonization would become a likely expedient. But should prejudice result from specific conditions, such as slavery or the liabilities on black life imposed in the free states, the eradication of these would soon excise the beast. It was little wonder, then, that anticolonizationists hewed closely to an optimistic line of thought that could imagine the abolition of prejudice. As newspaper editor Mary Ann Shadd put it, "Some think it will vanish by a change of condition, and that we can, despite this prejudice, change that condition." [87] The earliest stage of black public protest founded itself on a rejection of colonization and so frequently imagined black and abolitionist enlightenment steadily corralling the hated monster of prejudice toward oblivion's cliffside. In 1818, for example, Prince Saunders celebrated the founding of a black literary society, the Pennsylvania Augustine Society, by preaching the value of classical and Christian education among African Americans. Through these auspices, he assured his listeners, benevolent feelings were spreading among whites, and their "unjust prejudices" were "beginning to subside." [88] Such statements not only proffered hope for the betterment of blacks' condition in America, they also fed the paternalistic desires of early white abolitionists, philanthropic patrons who had staked reputations and sometimes fortunes on the "elevatability" of the race. As the period wore on, blacks would have cause to moderate considerably their faith in this strategy; to those such as Peter Paul Simons, the clear persistence of prejudice in the face of decades of concerted efforts to rise suggested that its roots ran far deeper in the American psyche than they had assumed.

Regardless of causation, one thing was clear: prejudice, once in play, acted as a potent force. Whites, acting under this diseased sentiment, deemed blacks' alleged inferiority a just basis on which to exclude them from the full benefits of American life. In keeping blacks from liberty, the vote, public education, and equal and untrammeled access to the marketplace, whites had imposed barriers to black elevation. They had, in fact, degraded blacks, kept them from rising. The twisted logic of white supremacy then performed its consummate contortion: having successfully degraded blacks, whites then used the resulting fact of degradation to argue for blacks' inherent incapacity to participate in the civic community.

The problem, according to African American spokespersons, was that the public mind had became infected by racial prejudice. Individual whites, moved by these attitudes, supported the legislation that kept blacks enslaved or degraded, denied blacks admission into labor unions or public schools, and precipitated mob activity that targeted blacks and their abolitionist champions. Then, ludicrously enough, white commentators used the results of their prejudice, the actuality of black degradation, as "facts" that proved blacks' natural incapacity for equality. As early as 1793, Richard Allen and Absalom Jones exhibited frustration and weariness with white failures to accept evidence of black moral and mental equality. In an address to Philadelphia whites, they charged: "The judicious part of mankind will think it unreasonable, that a superior good conduct is looked for from our race, . . . yet you try what you can to prevent our rising from the state of barbarism you represent us as to be in."[89] Decades later, a black radical writing under the pseudonym "Sydney" claimed, "It is one of the most malignant features of slavery, that it leads the oppressor to stigmatize his victim with inferiority of nature, after he himself has . . . brutalized him."[90] One black Philadelphian described white supremacists thus: "After having taken all . . . pains to lower them in the estimation of the world these same men do speak of their low qualities in order to prove that they are a race that is naturally inferior."[91]

Black leaders thus envisioned a vicious cycle of three mutually reinforcing elements: slavery and racially proscriptive practices, the degradation they caused among African Americans, and the attitudes they fostered in white minds. The obstacles to elevation imposed by whites had the effect of debilitating black progress. The resulting conditions of black life, which nearly all contemporary black leaders admitted lagged behind whites, then suggested to whites not that they should remove the liabilities hampering black progress but that blacks were naturally and irredeemably inferior. As a consequence, whites felt the need to control blacks and restrain their participation in the life of the nation so as to protect the nation. And on and on the cycle went.

TO ACT AN IMPORTANT PART: SELF-ELEVATION AS A SOLUTION

Many black thinkers understood the challenge confronting them to be the interruption of this vicious cycle. The key, of course, was to eventually remove the barriers to elevation, for these not only impeded actual black elevation but indirectly fed the prejudice that kept those barriers in place. A black national convention put it best in its address to white America: "We do not solicit unusual favor, but will be content with rough-handed 'fair play.' . . . We do ask, in the name of all that is just and magnanimous among men, to be freed from all the unnatural burdens and impediments with which

American customs and American legislation have hindered our progress and improvement."[92] Affecting this kind of change directly proved almost impossible, however; asking was about as much as black public figures could do. To most, it seemed far more expedient to, in addition to appealing to white Americans' better natures, take steps themselves to change things. If blacks could not directly remove the obstacles confronting them, perhaps they could exert enough control over the public mind to begin to roll back the prejudice that buttressed institutional obstacles to elevation. Many identified a malleable public mind as the chief source of their oppression. The problem, wrote one black commentator, was that "rights and privileges belong to us, which the vitiated state of the public mind will not permit us to enjoy."[93] According to the call for a national black convention: "We battle against false and hurtful customs, and against the great errors and opinions which support such customs."[94] Declared the holders of an antislavery bazaar, "Our object is the abolition of slavery, through the renovation of public opinion."[95] Henry Highland Garnet also spoke of the need to change the public mind: "It is absolutely important that there should be *such* a presentation of wrongs as may reveal to the power-holding body the enormity of their oppression."[96] Declared others: "We must educate the people; we must, by a vigorous and united action, inform the public mind, and create an opinion in our favor."[97]

Many black leaders hoped to exert pressure over the public mind by controlling media, especially the traditional purveyor of racial stereotypes: the newspaper press. Declared a black national convention: "This engine had brought to the aid of prejudice a thousand stings." The press, it argued, "must be used in our behalf; aye! we must use it ourselves . . . to shame our opposers."[98] According to another, a press "so productive of mischief to us" in the proper hands "would be exerted . . . to counteract the influences against us." The press was "the vehicle of thought" and "a ruler of opinions."[99] It was a "mighty engine to pull down the strong holds of tyranny and oppression,"[100] and a "most potent reformer of public sentiment."[101]

Black elites worked indefatigably to counter hostile images in the white press. But beyond controlling media, which would always prove a difficult task for economically challenged communities, there had to be something more that African Americans could do to change the public mind. The possibilities were limited: they lacked access to formal politics and suffered under strenuous occupations that left scant time or energy for activism. Controlling little, they possessed few resources that permitted them to compete with the hostile forces arrayed against them. Yet there was an answer, for no matter how poor they were, African Americans could never be utterly destitute. They could, after all, always control themselves. Here was a key. Control over one's own behavior offered a means of affecting the racial balance, a means to which all had access. To black leaders, self-regulation thus offered a most potent means of breaking the cycle of oppression.

It was precisely in offering individual character as a space of uncontested authority and as a basis for changing white minds that the special resonance of emerging bourgeois values of respectability among black leaders consisted. They believed that through their own actions, behavior, and comportment, they could reform the prejudices which held them back. "We have to act an important part, and fill an important place . . . in the work of emancipation," intoned Samuel Cornish. "On *our* conduct and exertions much, very much depend. It is our part, by virtue, prudence, and industry, to uphold the hands of our devoted and sacrificing friends." [102] J. Holland Townsend urged African Americans to strive for elevation, reminding them of the "vast responsibilities" on blacks to "vindicate the character and experience of the race." [103] "I think," wrote Austin Steward to Samuel Cornish, "that our conduct as colored men will have a great bearing on the question that now agitates this land. . . . Let it be shown that we as a people are religious, industrious, sober, honest and intelligent, and my word for it, the accursed system of Slavery will fall, as did Satan from Heaven." [104] Even prejudice seemed conquerable given the benign influences of blacks' own agency. According to the black national convention of 1855, "All prejudice connected with the Yankee spirit is subject to moderation by the influences that might be brought to bear by a vigorous application of the trades within our reach." [105]

Relying on the same principle that premised their understanding of prejudice—that individual examples reflected on the whole—black leaders hoped to use their very liabilities to reverse the self-reinforcing process whereby prejudice begat obstacles to black elevation, and these obstacles in turn begat the conditions that rationalized prejudice. Perhaps blacks could exercise power in the one area where they all possessed it—themselves— to force a change in white attitudes. Instances of black elevation would offer material refutations of the premises underlying racial prejudice. The black-led American Moral Reform Society of Philadelphia stated the philosophy baldly: "If amidst all the difficulties with which we have been surrounded, and the privations which we have suffered, we presented an equal amount of intelligence with that class of Americans that have been so peculiarly favored, a *very grave and dangerous* question would present itself to the world, on the natural equality of man, and the best rule of logic would place those who have oppressed us, in the scale of inferiority." [106] Individuals had "risen above the mass," wrote one black leader in a typical statement, "and have shown that the man of color has the same immortal attributes" as all other men.[107] While it surely had collective significance, this effort could only be an individual one. Black leaders constantly sought group elevation (through, for instance, agitation to re-win the franchise), but self-elevation could by its nature be accomplished only through personal means; its value lay precisely in its applicability to every single African American, regardless of status or condition. "Each one for himself, must commence the improvement of his condition," wrote Samuel Cornish. "It is not in mass, but in individual effort and character, that we are to move onward to a higher elevation."[108] Boston's John Rock echoed this spirit of independent and enterprising self-reliance, telling an audience that "whenever the colored man is elevated, it will be by his own exertions."[109]

African Americans had then to literally enact the elevation they hoped to embody. The black national convention of 1848 declared, "The complete and entire extirpation of caste is dependent not alone upon the enunciation of principles, but likewise on the living representation of the facts of mental ability in our midst."[110] A frustrated Cornish excoriated his readers: "respectability and elevation" were no mere theories, but must become "a practical subject with us" were the strategy to succeed.[111] According to another black convention, African Americans would never see "the influence of prejudice decrease, and ourselves respected" until they possessed "those high intellectual enjoyments and acquirements, which . . . drowns in oblivion's cup their moral degradation."[112] Blacks in 1853 declared "the intelligent and upright free man of color" to be "an unanswerable argument in favor of liberty, and a killing condemnation of American slavery."[113] The idea was that individual examples of self-elevation would incrementally cause the forces of prejudice to relent, thus opening the door that much wider for other African Americans to uplift themselves. According to one black abolitionist, "The colored man who, by dint of perseverance and industry, educates himself and elevates himself, prepares the ways for others, gives character to the race, and hastens the day of general emancipation."[114] Another termed those African Americans who exemplified the self-help ethos "valiant pioneers effecting an opening through which their brethren may safely reach the goal of human prosperity."[115]

Far from instilling feelings of self-recrimination, such words might have empowered their readers with a sense of their personal agency in what Cornish called "the great cause of humanity and religion."[116] Far from imposing a burdensome set of moral obligations, self-elevation offered the solace that in a hostile, largely uncontrollable world, everyone—regardless of how poor or powerless—might take part in events with extraordinary historical and religious significance. "God," wrote the Reverend J. W. Lewis, "holds man responsible only for his moral conduct in the formation of his moral character, and on nothing more in his own existence has he control."[117] Even the most humble of northern blacks might take succor in thus understanding both the potential and limits of their own agency.

Still, the elevation strategy was a far from foolproof cure for blacks' ills, and it came with often unforeseen side effects. To begin to break the self-reinforcing cycle of prejudice required exercising a degree of self-control and manifesting a level of success unparalleled by all but the young lads in McGuffey's readers. One national convention of free blacks advised, "[We need] to be at least equal, if not superior as workmen, in order to overcome the prejudice existing against us."[118] The *Anglo-African Magazine* argued that children held a special place in opening the door to further elevation: "Let us teach them that they must aim to excel the whites—and nothing less," it intoned.[119]

Abolitionist allies were especially fond of admonishing blacks that good behavior was all the more necessary from those assumed to be vicious by nature. Some seemed to take almost a perverse pleasure in speaking of the nearly uncrossable distance between white and black moral status in the public mind, lecturing blacks interminably on the hypermorality required to traverse the gulf. According to one such benefactor, blacks were "an oppressed and vilified race, and . . . any impropriety of conduct on their part will be attended with ten-fold worse effects than on the part of the whites."[120] The inevitable call for blacks to exhibit a nearly superhuman virtue followed. Gerrit Smith, the wealthy New York landowner who gave parcels of land to black freedpeople, reportedly told the objects of his benevolence that they were "under the necessity of being better than the whites, because prejudice of color . . . is for them, and against you. . . . They may be idlers, and yet be respected. But, if your industry relax, you are denounced as lazy.—They may be spendthrifts, without greatly, or at all, harming their reputation. But yours is ruined, unless you are rigid economists."[121]

Under the weight of such pressures some black activists chafed. Sarah Parker Remond, wife of black abolitionist Charles Remond, wrote to a London newspaper: "We are expected to be not only equal to the dominant races, but to excel in all that goes toward forming a noble manhood or womanhood. We are expected to develop in the highest perfection a race which for eight generations in the United States has been laden with the curse of slavery. Even some of our friends seem to expect this, but our enemies demand it."[122] And a few, such as Peter Paul Simons, whose views introduced this chapter, sensed that moral elevation did little to address the double standard underlying white images of blacks: when whites acted viciously, they were seen has having fallen from fulfillable ideals; when blacks did, they were seen as merely exhibiting their true natures.

THE MANY EVILS AMONG OURSELVES

The moral admonitions that characterized the protest thought of antebellum black spokespersons derived largely from the imperative to alter the public mind on matters of race. Elite African Americans saw tremendous strategic significance in pursuing moral, intellectual, and material excellence. Their warnings and urgings to the black non-elite all directly or indirectly served this larger goal of presenting examples of black elevation that would refute the claims of white supremacy and force prejudice into retreat. In so many realms of life, the supposed fact of black degradation had become confused with blacks' very natures, at least in the all-important public mind. As their comments on the nature of prejudice indicated, many activists considered racial prejudice a failing of whites. Yet, consistent with the mythology of personal success—the view that individual morality rather than structural economic factors primarily determined worldly success— and commensurate with the deep sense of communal responsibility that still pervaded a society only then jettisoning its traditional pattern of paternalistic social relations, black leaders did not hesitate to consider their own responsibility in creating their situation. If not by considering their own agency, how else could blacks counter hostile white racial attitudes?

The logic was this: blacks' own failure to keep up with whites in important realms of competition had led whites to think that blacks were incapable of keeping up. Consequently, leaders resolved that the community had to do a better job of promoting its own elevation, despite the prejudice that interfered with those endeavors. African Americans had to use the limited agency at their disposal, to take responsibility for what they could and control what they could hope to control. As a consequence of this thinking, a veritable flood of advice issued from the mouths of black leaders, all directed to the black non-elite—virtues to cultivate and influences to shun, behaviors to avoid and habits to embrace. In general, such statements fell into four categories: education, occupations, the moral vices of the cities, and personal presentation. In each of these instances, black elites determined that, all unjust prejudice aside, African Americans themselves had hampered their own elevation through their own behavior. It was not simply that they had acted in ways that failed to embody moral elevation, but that in doing so they had supplied ammunition to blacks' enemies, and had thus helped poison the public mind against themselves.

Schooling was an especially significant site for racial redemption. Important to antebellum audiences generally for instilling the virtues required of the self-ruling republic and liberal marketplace, education served special roles for blacks. First off, it kept popular African America from descending into that vice that whites so commonly associated with blacks' natures. According to Baltimore educator William J. Watkins, "[The educated man] will not be so much inclined as others to seek happiness in the gratification of his appetites and passions. The attractions of the gambling table and the ale house are not, in his view, to be compared with those to be found in his own domicile." Proper schooling, he argued, could keep such a man away from "whirlpools of vice, . . . where too many of the youth of this present generation are reveling in licentiousness and gross sensuality." Educational efforts would thus not simply elevate individual blacks but would also benefit African Americans' collective reputation, for it would correct errors caused by prejudice. For example, establishing and participating in literary societies, he proposed, would "tend to clear us from the charge of indolence, or indifference, to our own welfare" as well as from "that foul aspersion, as to the inferiority of our intellectual capacities."[123] These societies would demonstrate that blacks were not "wholly given up to revelry and licentiousness, as we have been misrepresented," but would show "that the leisure hours of many are devoted to thought and literary advancement."[124] Finally, educational institutions could help train the people who could inform the public of these truths. Schools for young black men promised to "discipline and clothe properly the minds of those who lead in our public gatherings"; they would "qualify them for extensively promoting the improvement of the condition of the people of color in our country."[125]

No subject of education aroused more ire among black elites than the religious instruction offered by black ministers. Black spokespersons complained incessantly about black popular preachers, dismissing the worship style of those who "can get up a temporary excitement among a portion of their hearers" but who also indulged in "superstition" and "that wild, ranting fanaticism, which are the legitimate fruits of ignorance, and which can procure for them no other consideration than the pity of the intelligent, or the ridicule of the unthinking."[126] With journalistic hyperbole, Mary Ann Shadd went so far as to elevate a corrupt black clergy over prejudice as the primary source of blacks' troubles: "[To] our distinctive churches and the frightfully wretched instruction of our ministers—their gross ignorance and insolent bearing, together with the sanctimonious garb, and by virtue of their calling, a character for mystery they assume, is attributable more of the downright degradation of the free colored people of the north, than from the effect of a corrupt public opinion."[127] The preachings of Jarena Lee, a Philadelphia-based exhorter, provide a glimpse of the style to which Shadd objected. A series of visions early in life had moved Lee to become a minister for the African Methodist Episcopal Church, but conservative church leader Richard Allen steadfastly denied her a permanent appointment. An itinerant throughout her career, Lee traveled the Mid-Atlantic states during the time of the Second Great Awakening, stirring local people, black and white alike, to religious exuberance. At one meeting, Lee's journal reports, "conviction seizzed a woman, who fell to the floor crying for mercy"; at another there was "weeping in all direction."[128]

While Lee never attained a steady appointment, the far more conservative Daniel Payne, a minister in the African Methodist Episcopal Zion church, clashed throughout his career with parishioners who seemed to favor the style of those such as Lee. Payne remembered that the churchgoers at his new post in Washington, D.C., in 1848 complained about his style: "I had too fine a carpet on my floor, and was too proud." Most upsetting to his new parishioners was that he "would not let them sing their 'spiritual songs,'" which he considered mere "Corn-field Ditties." Later assigned to a church in Baltimore, Payne organized several literary and historical associations among the people, but these foundered for want of enthusiasm. He reported, "In the majority of cases these associations operated only as long as I presided over the Conferences" that organized them.[129] Payne's frustration at his failed attempts to impose respectable worship styles on his charges sounded a theme common to a great many black leaders in the antebellum North.

Ever concerned with the public presentation of the race, leaders like Payne called for an educated clergy who would put the lie to popular stereotypes of black preaching. They called for ministers trained in literature and the sciences, arguing that they and their brethren "have never had a competent clergy of our own, to supply our intellectual wants, to exalt our minds, liberalize our feelings, and prepare us for the performance of noble and virtuous deeds."[130] New York's *Colored American* characteristically offered one of the strongest voices in favor of an elite, educated clergy, expressly on the grounds that it would aid the race's public reputation. "No people need a thoroughly educated ministry more than we do," wrote editor Samuel Cornish. Such a clergy was indispensable in giving black Americans "a character and standing in the church," he wrote. "Until our white brethren learn to respect us more, and improve their social and christian intercourse with us, we cannot love each other as we ought."[131]

Along with secular and religious education, black elites evinced apprehension over the cultural styles and behavior of the non-elite in the realm of occupations and labor values. Editors, newspaper correspondents, and convention declarations railed against the dangers of city life, the greatest of which was the erosion of the work ethic. City living, through the many ills it fostered, was thought to undermine the quality of black residents' morals. Frederick Douglass's *North Star* endorsed the words of a white newspaper that declared, "One great cause, if not the great cause, of the degradation of the colored men at the North, is, no doubt, the way they crowd together in cities."[132] Douglass then complained that too many American blacks flocked to urban areas, where they soon became "engaged as waiters about hotels, barbers or boot-blacks, and the women washing white people's dirty clothes."[133] "Peter Paez," a pseudonymous correspondent to *Freedom's Journal*, feared the "contagion of the vices, and temptations to the luxuries of cities." Concomitantly, the degraded morals of black urbanites threatened, through the principle of racial synecdoche, to undermine the reputation of the race in general. The correspondent went on to warn of blacks "rushing into the already too populous towns, to indulge in idleness and dissipation; to lengthen the catalogue of vagrants, to fill the mouths of their enemies with arguments against them."[134] The cities, it was thought, gave blacks no opportunities to escape menial occupations, and hence brought discredit to the race. They were places where, according to one critic, "medium wealth and mediocre talents are completely thrown in the shade, where to attract the least general attention or command the slightest general respect requires a degree of wealth attainable by only a favored few."[135]

If the cities degraded not simply blacks' characters but their collective reputation as well, the same critic argued that the answer lay in retreating from such dens of vice to the virtuous country: "We must then turn our attention to the country and agricultural pursuits if we would gain a higher respectability for ourselves."[136] Fleeing the cities thus promised to rehabilitate the public reputation of the race. The writer Paez believed that "superior advantages derived to the agriculturists," especially in securing "respectability of character." Blacks who became farmers, he wrote, "will command a more respectable standing in society than the mass of their brethren."[137] Because blacks in Canada tended to live in the country rather than the city, wrote Douglass, "they are more respected in Canada than in the States, because they are engaged in more respectable occupations."[138] A statement from the black national convention of 1843 concurred: "The farmer alone, who is the owner of the soil he cultivates, can in reality be in . . . circumstances of independency." Four years later, the convention rhapsodized that the farmer was "an independent man," claiming, "The man of no other pursuit is so much so. . . . An agricultural life is productive of moral, mental and physical culture."[139]

If they could not flee the cities to practice the virtuous republican life of the independent yeoman farmer, non-elite African Americans were advised to at least find occupations higher on the hierarchy of labor than those they had been accustomed to occupy. Leaders were most fearful that the high concentration of African Americans among the ranks of the menially employed perpetuated the equation of blacks with servile work. Menial occupations, according to the national convention of 1848, "have been so long and universally filled by colored men, as to become a badge of degradation, in that it has established the conviction that colored men are only fit for such employments."[140] The solution, obviously, was to fill positions that presumably would result in greater respect from whites. Meeting at an 1855 national convention, a committee on employment urged, "[We must] destroy the opinion that we raise our children to that sweet stage of life which prepares them for business (16 years) with no other aspirations than to be a waiter."[141] The convention of 1848 counseled blacks to abandon menial occupations "as speedily as possible, and to seek what are called the more respectable employments."[142] Most importantly, blacks were to acquire skills in the trades: "Every colored mechanic is . . . an elevator of his race. Every house built by black men, is a strong tower against the allied hosts of prejudice. . . . Where a man may be thrown by misfortune, if he has in his hands a useful trade, he is useful to his fellow-man, and will be esteemed accordingly."[143] Martin Delany said that examples of competent black mechanics "will raise the colored class in this country, as by enchantment, from degradation to entire manhood and actual equality" with whites.[144]

Surely such advice was easier for the black rank and file to hear than to enact, and even hearing it likely raised the ire of those in economic straits too dire to hope for easy redemption. At times, elite leaders seemed to believe that African Americans took such jobs not out of necessity but as a conscious choice. For example, one black Californian wrote to the *Pacific Appeal*: "The man who forfeits his rank and sacrifices his position to menial labor, is unacquainted with the great wrongs he entails upon others. Members of a dominant race become imperious and cruel towards the subject race."[145] During the convention of 1848, a fierce debate between national leaders and lesser lights tempered the call for black men to flee menial occupation. "Though right in themselves," the convention's final statement conceded, menial employments were "degrading to us as a class."[146] Clearly, some black elites lacked sufficient connection to those they lectured to understand the exact nature of their plight. Others, however, consistently (if often only implicitly) acknowledged that working-class blacks had "been driven by public prejudice and the force of circumstances, into modes of living entirely inconsistent with the principles of human progression, viz: non-productive labor."[147]

Few leaders, however, doubted the value of economic enterprise in the project of racial elevation. The national convention of 1853 explained that blacks had become "the proscribed class of the community," a people "dependent and so little respected," because "the places filled in this community by our people have not involved responsibility and respect." Blacks, it advised, needed to participate more in business enterprises, "pursuits which tend to wealth, respectability and importance."[148] Many others agreed, proclaiming, "We want more financiers and not so many ministers," and arguing that black elevation required the cultivation "of a spirit of political and commercial enterprise."[149] For many, wealth seemed the avenue to elevation. Austin Steward lectured freedpeople that money was power; with it they could direct as they would the actions of their "pale, proud brethren." As African Americans became wealthier, he continued, they would "continually rise in respectability, in rank and standing." According to another advocate, wealth in a black man's hands could be "a powerful lever by which to lift his children to self-respect."[150] Leaders organized constantly to put their idea into practice, planning a wide range of manual labor schools and cooperative business enterprises. At various times black leaders advocated establishing among themselves "Trades Unions on a small scale," cooperative investment clubs ("copartnerships"), "building and accumulating fund associations," "protective union associations," "borrowing and loaning associations," and "mutual savings institutions."[151] Samuel Ringgold Ward and Frederick Douglass founded the short-lived American League of Colored Laborers in 1850, which they hoped would eventually act as a loan organization for black entrepreneurs.[152] Nearly all of these efforts failed in the long run, however, defeated by the wrath of hostile whites or the dearth of resources in black communities.

In addition to depressing possibilities for economic advancement, cities contained other ills against which African American spokespersons frequently railed. At a black state convention in New York, James McCune

Smith painted a typical picture of urban life's vice and license, and their significance for the freedom struggle. "The seduction of the City—policy gambling, porter houses, with their billiards and cards, create a gang of lazaroni of both sexes, women hastening through the streets, with their bonnets untied; men, shirtless and shoeless, hanging round the corners, or standing, walking, gutter-tumbling—signs which our foes call the type of our condition."[153] Lewis Woodson similarly railed against the sight of young black men who "haunt our church doors and the corners of our streets, offending the moral sense of all who go in and out or that pass by."[154] For these spokesmen, the problem was not simply that the lower orders acted viciously, it was that in acting viciously they brought down the ill regard of the public on blacks in general.

Once off the city streets, young urbanites encountered a tempting array of establishments all seemingly designed to reduce them to moral misery. The ready availability of liquor topped the list of the city's vices, consuming the reforming energies of scores of black activists. One black northerner wrote to the *Colored American,* declaring "grog shops and porter houses" to be "the most formidable barriers to the onward progress of the principles so ably advocated in your paper—the liberation of the enslaved, and the elevation and enfranchisement of the free."[155] For one thing, drink often took young men in the prime of their lives—a fate that an oppressed people could ill afford. According to Philadelphian Jacob White, "the *Respectable Groggeries* are ruining the very class of our people to whom we are to look as warriors who are to fight for our liberty, and our rights."[156] Beyond this, drinking degraded blacks' characters, thus supplying ammunition to their enemies. A group of African American ministers declared that the "monster sin" of intemperance "hardens prejudice against us."[157] Boston doctor John S. Rock put it clearly: "The negro who hangs around the corners of the streets, or lives in the grog-shops or by gambling, or who has no higher ambition than to serve, is by his vocation forging fetters for the slave, and is 'to all intents and purposes' a curse to his race."[158]

Black activists argued that other urban establishments contributed just as much to black degradation as did the porter houses. The theater, for example, was a "school of iniquity and scandal." Its "corrupting influence" lay "as a canker upon the young and thoughtless of our land, infusing, as it were, into their very natures, the seeds of misery and death."[159] A black newspaper reprinted and strongly endorsed a white reformer's condemnation of the theater. This pointed out that the "late hours which prevent all evening devotion, expose to strong temptations, and shroud in darkness 'deeds without a name,' seem intimately connected with the amusements of the stage."[160] Another echoed concerns familiar to antebellum urbanites black and white, concerned as they were with the ways of the confidence hustler: "[Theaters] dress up vice in so seductive a garb, as to hide its deformity, that we unconsciously fall into her embrace."[161]

The list of morally dangerous establishments went on and on. Regarding gambling dens, black editors warned their readers "to shun as they would a burning crater, these broad gates to moral, mental, and eternal death." They went on to admonish their brethren who permitted gambling in their establishments to end such practices, "as you love your country, hope for the emancipation of your brethren, and the elevation and enfranchisement of our whole people."[162] Maria Stewart, Boston's fiery orator, told her listeners to "flee from the gambling board and the dance-hall." Black Bostonians, she worried, partook of these "unbecoming" and "frivolous" amusements to such an extent "that it has become absolutely disgusting."[163] Black spokespersons warned that, worst of all, time spent in grogshops, theaters, dance halls, and gambling dens ultimately led young sinners to the brothel—"that house which is the way to Hell"—a place so reprobate that its name was literally unspeakable.

African American spokespersons also spent a remarkable amount of energy discussing the importance of personal presentation and display in public. Some, like Lewis Woodson, warned of the dangers of mean attire. Arguing against the practice of dressing black children in cast-off clothing, he wrote sarcastically: "If they are destined to the lowest stations in life, dress them in old clothes: this will inspire them with a proper sense of inferiority, and dependence on others."[164] More frequently, though, leaders expressed sensitivities to the social pretensions that whites feared in blacks, cautioning about the perils of overdressing. The New York *Weekly Anglo-African* urged black young men "to be content with a frieze coat and check shirt" rather than with "lace jackets" and "tinseled hats."[165] Women in particular were cautioned to conserve with respect to dress. "Agnes," a newspaper correspondent, believed "that thousands of the wretched females, who throng our streets, owe their degradation to a love of dress, and a desire to be fashionably arrayed." According to her, "many a vain woman has lost her virtue, not from the beauty of her person, but the allurement of her dress."[166] Theodore S. Wright, a New York City clergyman, thought that this general preference for extravagance reflected a more general inattentiveness to thrift among blacks. "The habit of living well and dressing expensively," he said, had produced in black New Yorkers "that negative, slip-shod economy, which consists in barely making the income eke out the expenditure. . . . We must abandon this careless mode of living, and substitute therefore a rigid economy of our time and of our means."[167] The national convention of 1848 begged the black rank and file, "Save your money—live economically—dispense with finery."[168]

Given antebellum society's preoccupation with authenticity, it was little wonder that black elites expressed so much concern over appearances. As the task of fixing identity—ensuring the good character of others—grew increasingly troublesome, dress and other signifiers of character played key roles in this process. On the one hand, dress and presentation were clearly seen as guides to what lay underneath. "In the United States much attention is paid to dress," wrote Lewis Woodson. "It is a custom . . . to determine the rank of persons by their dress, and treat them accordingly."[169] On the other hand, all knew that external appearance was only a guide—and often a misleading one at that—to the inner character. A preoccupation with *only* dress suggested a dangerous superficiality that could easily hide the character of a trickster or confidence man. "I know of nothing *more utterly contemptible*," wrote "Agnes," "than to value a man or woman for the clothes they wear."[170] There was actually no paradox here. Most northerners would have conceded that dress was a far from ideal determinant of character, but given a lack of better alternatives, they considered it a necessary fact of life. Whether or not one's dress actually reflected one's character, others would undoubtedly assume it did. It therefore became incumbent upon those who cared about their public reputations to police their attire scrupulously.

Woodson expressed exactly this sentiment in his essays on personal presentation. He certainly agreed that dress was a mere subordinate of inner character, writing that a respectable appearance "must be backed by good manners, and unimpeachable morals."[171] A vain concern with dress denoted "littleness and narrowness of mind." "Merit and not dress," he wrote, "constitutes real respectability."[172] Still, in his view, attention to dress was important. He noted, "As good dress adds much to the lustre of our virtues, it also brings more clearly to view, our ignorance, vulgarity, and vices. So that to be vain of good dress merely, without a corresponding amount of good breeding, is to show ourselves up conspicuously to the contempt of all good and intelligent people." The ideal—and it was one to which a wide variety of Americans would have acceded—was that "the inward and outer man should correspond."[173]

Imagine, then, how pernicious blacks' sartorial vices seemed to the spokespersons. Black elites shared with middle-class white northerners concerns regarding appearances and authenticity, but the burden of racial reclamation also lay heavily on their backs, for even the clothes that black people wore had an important role to play in the degradation or elevation of the race. Woodson feared that the "indignity and contempt" with which black people were treated arose from blacks' "want of proper attention to cleanliness and neatness of dress." When blacks dressed shabbily, he worried, they contributed to notions that they were unfit to participate in civilized society. "The want of a decent exterior is so repulsive, as to at once bar the affections, and entirely exclude us from the society, of all persons of taste and refinement," he wrote. "Every one must agree that the moral effect of mean dress is, to degrade us in our own eyes and in the eyes of all who behold us."[174] Woodson thus argued that "colored females should be extremely attentive to cleanliness and neatness of dress," for "they are well aware of the prejudices which exist against them in the community in which they live; and they should consider how imprudent it is, by neglecting their personal appearance, to heighten and aggravate that prejudice."[175] Woodson was far from alone. Mary Ann Shadd, who edited a newspaper in Canada, similarly subordinated the question of clothing to the interests of racial progress. "What profits a display of ourselves?" she asked. "Is it to be seen by another? How does that better our condition as a people?" Deftly uniting racial imperatives with underlying concerns regarding authenticity, she feared that whites would conclude of blacks: " 'They attend all to their exterior!' Negroes and Indians set more value on the outside of their heads than on what the inside needs."[176]

Such arguments may have fallen on deaf ears of non-elite African Americans who were accustomed to using dress to manifest personal pride, communal identity, and even racial resistance.[177] The black working class could only have taken offense at Martin Delany's claim that too many young black men thought only about "dress and pleasure," that these representatives of the race "do nothing but buggy-ride day after day, until their capital is exhausted, and probably before their business season returns; and thus they get into debt for boarding and washing, and out of credit with everybody."[178] The struggling black workers being ejected by white immigrants from all but the most menial jobs surely would have had choice words for Delany. So might those who earned the ire of black elites over the issue of display at funerals. Ultimately derived from West African cultural practice, emotive display at black funerals troubled those who clearly lacked an appreciation of this manifestation of a rich and ancient folk culture. "When we mourn for those who are taken from us, is it consistent that we should decorate our person with fine apparel, 'and study fashions to adorn the body?' " asked one black newspaper correspondent. "How absurd, how ridiculous it is, to see those whose hearts are laden with grief, who mourn with a sorrow that refuses comfort, giving directions about the cut of a garment, or the texture of the cloth. Instead of devoting ourselves to the solemn duty of committing the mortal part of the loved lost one to its parent earth, . . . we are considering how we shall look, and how well our 'mourning' will become us." The author concluded with a familiar refrain, worrying about the implications of such behavior on the image of blacks in the public mind.[179]

At root, the tensions apparent in black elites' thought regarding the public presentation of African American folk or working-class cultural styles were more about racial uplift strategy than about class tensions among African Americans. Elite whites could afford to see the white working classes as solely antagonists, and middle-class white reformers had the luxury to consider the unwitting targets of their zeal mere objects, defined as working-class precisely by their need for reformation. Black elites had no such advantage. Lumped together by prejudice in the public mind with the non-elite, they could ill afford to consider popular African America as distinct from themselves. As evidenced by elites' apparent frustration with non-elite behavior, this forced association grated considerably, especially when it failed to acknowledge leaders' success at achieving the markers of middle-class status. There was surely some self-interest at work, then, in controlling the behavior of the non-elite: it promised to deliver the deserved class recognition that black elites believed they had been denied.

Yet while their language concerning non-elite behavior often seemed to mirror that of white reformers in pursuing the self-interests of a middle class, it also served far different ends. Whereas among white reformers concerns with non-elite behavior in one way or another distanced them from their charges, elite blacks' regard for their working-class brethren reflected efforts to unite the community in a common purpose under a common identity. Black leaders first and foremost sought to use moral admonitions to the non-elite in the service of racial politics, to control black behavior so that hostile whites might be deprived of evidence to support their racist conclusions. Black leaders never considered the non-elite hopeless, if only because they could not afford to. Just as prejudice had to be eradicable, "degraded," non-elite blacks had to be elevatable. Otherwise, the arguments of the American Colonization Society would win the day, and blacks would all but concede the justice of keeping them oppressed. Such arguments could even justify removing them from the nation—a society deeply flawed by prejudice but nonetheless the place of their birth and (once they redeemed it) one boasting the most perfect form of government on earth. The search for cross-class racial unity often took the form of class tensions, not simply because class tensions existed, but because there were few other languages through which elite blacks could forge common cause with the non-elite. Rooted from its origins in the paternalistic social ethos of their early patrons, the black leadership only slowly found ways of incorporating the voices of working-class African Americans into its deliberations.

Clearly, black leaders found in moral admonitions a utility for racial politics. Examples of elevatable blacks promised to break the cycle of prejudice. Yet moral uplift ideology possessed another benefit that also determined its central place in black protest thought. For, even should the strategy of altering the public's perceptions of blacks fail, elevation would still benefit oppressed African Americans. It could not help but do so, for, in the minds of its advocates, uplift possessed inherent value as a social good in its own right. Steeped deeply in the language of moral reform, born in the Second Great Awakening and spread by an expanding middle class, and participating in its construction and perpetuation, African American activists and their white allies viewed self-regulation and elevation as a strategy through which they might change the public mind, but more fundamentally as a deeply held set of values with its own intrinsic merit.

Paternalistic white benefactors harped particularly on this line of thought, often offering it as a somewhat lame palliative to the failure of more deep-rooted structural changes. Philadelphia abolitionists argued the merits of self-elevation regardless of its impact on whites' perceptions: "Let the man of color cultivate the spirit of self-respect and independence, and without allowing his mind to be disturbed by prejudices which cannot be at once removed, pursue that course of quiet industry and unpretending virtue which will make him happy and respectable as an individual, and will contribute more than anything else to elevate the condition of his people."[180] Gerrit Smith, the wealthy abolitionist and Liberty Party presidential candidate, described African Americans burdened by the need to demonstrate a suspect virtue in these words: "Happy, thrice happy, the people, who are under peculiar obligations to be industrious, and frugal, and learned, and virtuous."[181] While the intrinsic rewards of self-elevation must have struck many African Americans as shallow compensation for their efforts, many black activists nonetheless embraced it. In a typical article entitled "Elevation," William C. Nell argued for the intrinsic merits of the uplift strategy. To him, the strategy had no drawbacks. "If others fail to appreciate the merit of the colored man, let us cherish the deserted shrine," he wrote.[182]

Blacks' faith in uplift despite the difficulties they faced putting it in play illustrates the depth with which they actually valued moral and mental uplift on their own terms. A distinction must be made between elevation as a strategy for pursuing racial politics versus elevation as a deeply held social value. Black activists embraced elevation not simply as a strategy for subverting prejudice but as a social good with inherent moral worth. Whether it worked or not to change the public mind, black leaders thought, moral and mental uplift would both fulfill the word of God and manifestly better the worldly lives of African Americans. As the black national convention of 1855 put it, elevation promised to render blacks "independent of the prejudices around them."[183]

SOMETHING "MANLIER" THAN SYMPATHIES: RESPECTABILITY AND THE FREEDOM STRUGGLE

Black leaders' concern with regulating the behavior of their non-elite charges may strike modern audiences as elitist, classist, and paternalistic — all well-founded charges by modern-day standards. Hardly the ideology of a mass movement, antebellum concern with moral uplift could never be confused with a radical political ideology. On the contrary, to many it seems to have embodied a capitulation to the cultural standards of oppressors and to have relied on appeals to their good graces rather than on militant demands made from positions of power. To these critics, the moral uplift components of black protest thought seem to have depended on conciliatory appeals to white generosity. Black leaders, according to this view, pursued a policy that implicitly conceded that they deserved fundamental rights only on sufferance or good behavior.

A brief review of the strategy behind racial uplift ideology suggests a different interpretation. African Americans understood the problem to be a self-reinforcing cycle of barriers to black "elevation," the consequent diminishing of black life (as measured by the standards of the black elite and blacks' white critics), and the resulting reinforcement of prejudicial attitudes that justified further proscription. African American spokespersons proposed to break this cycle by changing the "public mind" on matters of race, thus impelling whites to dismantle the obstacles to black elevation that not only degraded black life but perpetuated the conditions that fostered prejudice in the first place. None of this, it should be noted, required blacks to place any faith at all in the good graces of whites, for none of it *asked* anything of them. On the contrary, the moral uplift strategy sought to *compel*—to place white Americans in a position whereby they would be forced to change their practice and live up to their religious and political principles. Attending to respectability, a concept rarely considered in antebellum black thought, softens considerably the criticisms long leveled at elite black protest in the nineteenth century.

Black leaders frequently invoked respectability as a value. In part, this

reflected the rhetorical practice of an expanding urban bourgeoisie; ana-
logues in the writings of white contemporaries abound. Among many white
northerners, respectability frequently served as a codeword for middle-class
virtues. Contrasted with the "rough" laborer or the high-born social pre-
tender, the "respectable" man embodied the virtues of a new era of commercial enterprise. But to suggest that black notions of respectability thus
constituted a mere echo of white values minimizes the utterly pervasive role
of respectability in antebellum northern culture generally.

Respectability functioned among northern blacks and whites as what may
be termed a master value. That is, it was considered precious enough in its
own right to be sought not as a means to a greater good but as an end in
itself. In theory, the truly respectable man needed ask for nothing more.
Furthermore, the use of words like "respectable" required no overt explanation for antebellum audiences. Everyone knew the basics: respectability had
to do with achieving a state of inner integrity (most often virtues associated
with Christian morality and a new capitalist work ethic) and with cultivating
an exterior that accurately represented that inner character. Beyond this,
contemporaries could invoke respectability with the understanding that all
comprehended its inherent value, though they might not agree on the individual elements of character that comprised it. Antebellum northerners
rarely contested the value of respectability; secure in this, they contested
instead the qualities that made one respectable. Respectability's value in social contests depended precisely on this flexibility; it was a malleable notion,
manipulable by a variety of social groups for a similarly wide range of purposes. For example, working-class versions of respectability contended with
middle-class versions to sanction competing cultural styles.[184]

African Americans frequently attested to their faith in respectability as a
master value. The editors of the *Colored American* implicitly considered respectability the ultimate social reward when they railed against "the practice of admitting the licentious man within the pale of respectable society,
and awarding to him that confidence and respect which is due only to the
virtuous."[185] One of the newspaper's readers wrote in to similarly condemn
the vice-ridden in terms of respectability. "The debauchee and the roue
are not admitted into respectable society," he declared, and the young man
who drinks "is shunned by all having a claim to decency."[186] Others suggested using the master value of respectability to attack slavery. According to the black national convention of 1847, the slaveholder was considered "reputable and must be made disreputable." He was to be "outlawed"
from "social respectability," and "execrated by the community" until he re-
pented and freed his slaves.[187] Much of black leaders' rhetorical strategy

implicitly turned on the notion that public standing and reputation constituted men's and women's greatest assets, which they would imperil only under the gravest circumstances. If, then, African Americans could shape public opinion so as to make slavery and racial prejudice disreputable, they would gain a powerful lever with which they might remove the obstacles that impeded their self-elevation.

This was no small task, for respectability entailed notions of autonomy and independence that were utterly at odds with dominant images of blacks. Antebellum political theory, mired deeply in the tenets of republicanism, treasured the independent man, the man who owed his livelihood to no one else, and who shared a stake in society, which ensured his civic virtue. In the early republic, the precious right of self-governance could be entrusted only to such men—never to the apprentice, servant, or wife. Certainly it could not be entrusted to the slave. All such as these depended on another for their sustenance, and so could be swayed by the influence of their patron. Corrupted by such influence, the fragile experiment in self-rule might fail, falling to the tyranny of individuals who commanded their subordinates' allegiance or, worse yet, to the anarchy of the licentious masses. All this changed with the rise of the common man and the creation of the second party system in the 1820s and 1830s. Through a process few Americans fully understood, including African American elites, northern politics became sharply racialized. As the antebellum electorate expanded, licentiousness could no longer serve to demarcate the enfranchised from those unworthy of the vote. Making matters worse, slavery had largely been removed as a barrier between the vicious and the potentially virtuous. To many whites, and especially the newly enfranchised, blacks became vessels for the displaced licentiousness that had once deemed the propertyless white man unfit to wield the ballot. In a sense, blacks paid the price for the white working class's political participation. All blacks—regardless of class, wealth, or social status—assumed a common, often biologically determined inferiority. With slavery moribund, the foundations of racial prejudice shifted perceptibly, away from eroding legal definitions and toward evolving biological and moral essentialisms.

African Americans understood and shared the claims of antebellum political culture, though they failed to sense the deeper undercurrents of white supremacist thought that subverted those claims. Most importantly, they shared the belief that in a virtuous republic rights were yielded only to equals. Respectability signified all the qualities that made them the equals of America's finest citizens. According to one black spokesman: "Towards an equal, every action becomes just, kind, and very often noble. Self-respect induces all equals to respect those who belong to their order, interest impels them to cultivate good understanding with those whose assistance may at any moment be necessary to preserve life or property. Here lies the germ of that equality which the colored American has theoretically dreamed of, but which has been practically applied in too few cases."[188] Frederick Douglass delivered to his readers the melancholy news that "society is a hard-hearted affair. . . . The individual must keep society under obligation to him, or society will honor him only as a stranger and sojourner."[189] Others wrote that "true equality . . . can exist only among peers" and that "it is only by placing men in the same position in society, that all cast[e]s are lost sight of."[190] Putting the respectability strategy in play meant demonstrating publicly blacks' right to be respected as equals.

Deep economic ramifications pervaded the language of respectability. Respectability and its antecedent, the republican ideal of the yeoman farmer, both drew on common assumptions of social value and civic responsibility that featured economic independence as the watchword. The black national convention of 1847 paid particular attention to the infantilizing dependence of the servile, which could never render them equal. In one statement, the spirit of which blacks repeated throughout the period, it resolved: "Independence is an essential condition of respectability. To be dependent, is to be degraded. Men may indeed pity us, but they cannot respect us. . . . We must become equally independent with other members of the community."[191]

Here was a powerful tool that blacks hoped to exploit. African Americans claimed they lacked the respect of whites because they had not proven themselves their equals, as manifest in their economic subordination to whites. The opposite of this state of dependence, and the end they sought, was not so much independence as it was a greater degree of mutual *de*pendence, whereby whites would become as dependent upon blacks as blacks historically had been on whites. Black conventioneers in 1847 resolved, "We must make white persons as dependent upon us, as we are upon them."[192] Relying on notions of respectability, African Americans formulated an appeal that they considered far more powerful than benevolence or even faith in democratic ideals: an appeal to whites' rational calculation of their individual self-interest. The black national convention of 1855 saw this strategy as the answer to a nation overwhelmingly opposed to black elevation, despite its professed faith in natural rights philosophy. Acknowledging that blacks "must expect it to be a kind of domestic article purely native in its proclivities, to discourage us," delegates viewed an appeal to whites' self-interest as the one tool that might dislodge baneful prejudice. "Even this can be removed as circumstances shall show it to be their interest to do so," it continued.[193]

Socially, the strategy manifest itself in blacks' desires to render disreputable those who held slaves or harbored racial prejudice. Economically, the strategy entailed self-elevation sufficient to make whites begin to seek out blacks in economic matters. Martin Delany thus urged young black men to pursue lives of economic integrity and moral virtue, and thus become prosperous tradesmen, artisans, and mechanics. "Men of business, merchants and others, will seek an acquaintance of men of this description," he wrote, "because, according to business policy, and the laws of commercial economy, an interchange of trade being necessary for the sustenance of the system, it is their interest to so do."[194] According to this theory, a proper degree of racial interdependence would soon dispel the prejudice that hampered black elevation. "May we safely suppose," asked Lewis Woodson, "that a government which has shown such decided hostility towards us as individuals, would regard us with a more indulgent eye, when formed into communities, acquiring intelligence, wealth, and power?"[195] According to Samuel Cornish, should blacks become as wealthy as whites, "prejudice will hide her face." Once their wallets demanded that they respect blacks, the "fair sons and daughters of Columbia will forget the law of lights and shades."[196]

While respectability did embody upward economic mobility, then, it served as much more than a codeword for middle-class identity. It was a strategy for achieving a meaningful equality and entailed a stance toward whites that overtly rejected supplication, dependence, and help. The nationalistic Delany noted this in 1854 when he wrote: "Our submission does not gain for us an increase of friends nor respectability—as the white race will only respect those who oppose their usurpation, and acknowledge as equals those who will not submit to their rule."[197] Similarly, in 1847 black conventioneers declared that blacks must command "something manlier than sympathies"—the "respect and admiration" of those who sought to help themselves.[198] Respectability, the opposite of dependence and submission, offered a way of gaining the power that would compel whites to yield. Proper comportment was designed not to plead blacks' worthiness but to embody a way of living that would compel the respect of whites and hence begin to achieve blacks' equality. "Our object," declared the 1853 convention, "is not to excite pity for ourselves, but to command respect for our cause."[199]

Consequently, leaders incessantly sloughed off the well-meaning paternalism of white abolitionists, insisting on the absolute need to control their own movement. The *Colored American* appreciated the sentiments of white allies but considered that any effort to do more than "make the way level" would "do us *harm* rather than good,"concluding, "To improve and elevate our condition, emphatically, [is] the business of ourselves."[200] Frederick Douglass broke with his mentor, William Lloyd Garrison, on just this issue. Throughout his tenure as a newspaper editor, Douglass continued to argue the necessity of black independence from benevolent white abolitionists, arguing emphatically that "OUR ELEVATION AS A RACE, IS ALMOST WHOLLY DEPENDENT UPON OUR OWN EXERTIONS." From those who considered blacks targets of benevolence, Douglass could not expect "*a practical recognition of our equality.*" The black national convention of 1847 echoed this stance: "The first step which will mark our certain advancement as a people, will be our Declaration of Independence from all aid except from God and our own souls."[201] Entirely commensurate with the spirit of black protest, such statements highlight the sharp contrasts that existed between white and black uses of the language of moral elevation.

Though respectability distinguished black protest thought from its abolitionist forebears, it never deserted its roots in moral elevation. "If we wish to be respected," an early black national convention asserted, "we must build our moral character."[202] Such illustrations of the elevatability of African Americans, it was believed, would surely tip the scales against prejudice. In the words of the black national convention of 1848, "When capacity, undoubted capacity, is exhibited, then, and then alone, will the contempt and outrages, arising from actual or imagined inferiority, depart."[203] The national convention of 1832 put it well: through self-elevation, blacks could "acquire a moral and intellectual strength, that will unshaft the calumnious darts of our adversaries, and present to the world a general character, that they will feel bound to respect and admire."[204] The convention of 1835 thought that successful self-elevation would "remove many of the objections to immediate emancipation."[205]

This was not supplication. It was resistance, capitalizing on the oppressed's own agency and based on the premise that, if African Americans properly exercised their ability to control their own behavior, whites' own adherence to the logic of acquisitive capitalism would compel them to yield rights that blacks understood to be rightfully theirs. Black leaders did not offer whites their virtuous conduct as the price of admission into the civil community. Instead, they intended to use the one resource they knew they could all command—themselves—to put whites in a position whereby they would be forced by their own values to yield rights. African Americans asked for nothing from whites except that they adhere to their own professed principles. The great virtue of this strategy was that it required of whites only a small gesture—a short step toward the benign and familiar, rather than a giant leap into the revolutionary unknown. Its great failing lay in the weakness of its premise: that when challenged whites had much interest at all in choosing the logic of liberalism over the logic of white supremacy. Not yet exposed to decades of painful experience to the contrary and lacking alternatives more clearly fruitful, black leaders embraced respectability as a strategy to compel racial equality with all the desperation that their difficult condition demanded.

CONCLUSION: ANY MEANS NECESSARY VS. THE BEST MEANS AVAILABLE

This chapter began with Peter Paul Simons's sharp dissent from the dominant strategy of racial politics pursued by his colleagues. Simons charged that moral uplift did not work to elevate African Americans; that it misdirected blacks' energies, pointing them toward their inner characters and away from the economic and legal mechanisms of the unjust world around them; and that it sowed class division among Africans, thus disrupting blacks' fragile and crucial unity. Yet the respectability strategy that mobilized values of moral and mental elevation offered a rich seedbed of ideas from which a variety of critiques—including Simons's own—could be molded. It can in no way be reduced to a simple, timid, and unbridled desire for assimilation. The strategy of respectability did not entail blind submission, and overtly so. Neither did it rely on the good graces of whites who had proven themselves intransigent, nor did it seek integration into American society at the cost of self-respect or group rights. Black activists did not, as Simons claimed, lack courage and misapply their own agency. Instead, they searched doggedly for ways to use their agency to their best advantage.

Simons had missed, as have many who came after him, how deeply rooted in antebellum America were the premises that underlay the uplift and respectability strategy. These components of northern thought so deeply undergirded the political thought built upon them that few if any could even conceive of questioning them. First, the strategy implied faith in the neutral workings of the liberal marketplace—a faith that had yet to be destroyed by the fierce labor battles and sophisticated class critiques of the post–Civil War era. It depended on the laws of the marketplace permitting the possibility of blacks' own elevation, and on hostile whites valuing their own economic self-interest above their investment in racial prejudice. Second, it revealed a deep commitment to the public sphere as a realm of rational discourse, wherein it was assumed that words had power and arguments mattered. Again, this was a faith that it took oppressed Americans decades to realize was misplaced. Together, these two premises envisioned the public sphere as a marketplace of ideas, ideally ruled by laws that rendered it accessible to the salutary influence of blacks. Such hopefulness was manifest in the appeals that early black conventions addressed to the American people. One from 1835 read, "Prejudice, like slavery, cannot stand the omnipotence of Truth. It is as impossible for a bold, clear and discriminating mind that can calmly and dispassionately survey the structure upon which prejudice is founded, and the materials of which it is composed, to be chained within its grasp, as it is for the puny arm of rebellious man to control the operations of the universe."[206] As late as 1859, editors could optimistically encant that "no kind of energy, however evil in its direction, can continue to go wrong in this glorious republic of ours." The "checks and balances of public opinion," they believed, would prevent it.[207]

The uplift and respectability strategy also derived from a simple lack of better alternatives. Many black leaders conceived of it as a useful supplement to a variety of other, equally difficult measures. Only rarely did uplift seek to supersede other interventions into the self-reinforcing cycle of prejudice and caste degradation, such as direct political action or efforts to control the media levers that moved the public mind. Like these strategies, respectability expressly aimed to apply the limited agency that blacks did possess. It sought above all to enhance that agency by augmenting blacks' power—their ability to control public opinion and to define the terms of public debates. The strategy sought to place blacks in a position to coerce whites to yield rights owed to blacks, through the likely expedient of self-interest rather than fantasy solutions such as a national contest of arms. When the black national convention of 1835 declared itself "unable to conceive of any better method by which we can aid the cause of human liberty, than by improving our general character," it spoke for its own and following generations, which consistently found themselves bereft of options—ideological, political, and economic—that did not entail even harder struggles to uplift themselves.[208]

There can be little doubt that Simons was correct when he claimed that the strategy of uplift and respectability had failed to yield its promised results. By and large, moral virtue did not propel African Americans up the social ladder; in fact, the general trend among blacks in some contexts may have been downward.[209] And the relatively small proportion of African Americans who seemed to succeed on the terms of antebellum society were more likely to earn whites' popular wrath than their respect. Sites of black elevation, such as racially mixed schoolhouses, often fell quickly to the mob.

Moral uplift and respectability did little to directly address the economic, legal, and political structures that maintained white supremacy, opting instead to attack such problems through the circuitous route of individual character. Yet the fault here is hardly attributable to black leaders' shortcomings as thinkers. The conceptual resources simply did not exist to develop the potent critiques of capitalist society and race culture that characterized black protest in the twentieth century. Shut out by the prejudice of white labor's burgeoning awareness of such issues, antebellum black northerners turned to the handful of whites generous enough to espouse their cause. As potential counter-hegemons, their allies lacked much. Initially comprised of the wealthy and deeply paternalistic abolitionists of the revolutionary era and later by evangelical reformers who were often more invested in abolishing slavery than in elevating the freed, many of these white allies did little to foster the independence of black activists. Instead, they fed their charges a steady diet of placating rhetoric that drew little attention to the injustices of the bourgeois world they had created.

But the ultimate fate of the rhetoric of uplift and self-improvement lay far beyond the control of such white allies. Time and again black activists themselves shook off white abolitionists' cloying patronage—like Frederick Douglass, often asserting their own independence at the expense of important relationships. In similar fashion, their use of the rhetoric of uplift departed considerably from the intentions of white allies. Although the rhetoric of black activists and white abolitionists voiced similar themes, their listeners interpreted them quite differently. The pens of black activists could perform feats no white American could even attempt. They could use the language of self-improvement to create among American blacks a coherent sense of racial identity, a sense of themselves as a people sharing a common past and purpose and united in a single destiny. They could proffer ways in which even the humblest among them could participate in a climactic historical moment—a millennial struggle between freedom and slavery. They could, in short, build a black nation.

The American Negro must remake his past
in order to make his future.
Arthur A. Schomburg

CHAPTER 6

A Nation out of a Nation

Black Nationalism as Nationalism

In 1817, black Philadelphians convened at a meeting called by a member of
the city's African American elite, James Forten, a wealthy sailmaker. Forten
had been corresponding with another wealthy free black northerner, Paul
Cuffe, who owned whaling interests in Westport, Massachusetts. Forten had
agreed to a plan of Cuffe's for black Americans to colonize Africa. The
scheme had been endorsed by the American Colonization Society, which
had been established the year before by a group of national leaders to champion black emigration to Africa. Robert Finley, a white representative of
the Society, later remembered that Forten had warmed to the possibility of
black colonization of Africa: through settlement of that continent, Forten
had said, his people "would become a great nation."[1] Yet when Forten approached a mass meeting of black Philadelphians with the plan, his audience protested vigorously, fearing their forced removal from the land of
their birth. They deemed the Society's scheme a "cruel" effort to "banish or exile" them. Claiming their right "to participate in the blessings of
America," they declared the plan a violation of "the principles upon which
America is founded." Forten, though forced to "remain silent" to retain his
authority in the community, maintained his initial faith in the plan. After

the incident, he lamented the lost opportunity in a letter to Cuffe: black Americans, he wrote, "will never become a people until they com out from amongst the white people." [2]

The Philadelphia incident represents one of the earliest manifestations of black nationalism in America [3] and illustrates the three general elements most commonly associated with the ideology. The first is a group consciousness built on racial identity and pride. Forten and Cuffe envisioned through their colonization program the rise of blacks as a proud people united by a sense of racial identity. The second element may be considered a desire to develop social and political institutions autonomous from those of whites. Black nationalism often envisions the eventual formation of a black state to champion the rights of black people throughout the world—usually through the voluntary removal of African-descended people from their colonial polities. Forten believed that to become "a people" it was necessary for blacks to separate from—"com out from amongst"—white Americans. Finally, strains of black nationalism may also valorize a distinct black cultural heritage. By far the weakest element in nineteenth-century colonization efforts, this appeared in the Philadelphia example only implicitly, in the assumption by Forten, Cuffe, and the ACS that ethnic and cultural homogeneity were necessary components of a proper nation. Later black nationalists used a distinct black cultural heritage as a platform from which to critique the capitalist order that initially enslaved Africans and which continues to serve the interests of capital at the expense of people of color.

While the 1817 incident in Philadelphia is among the earliest examples of African Americans pursuing an organized plan to establish a separate black state, it is also among the most complex, for Forten's non-elite Philadelphia constituency rejected the plan.[4] It may strike many as ironic that the non-elite, the very ones most often associated with the popular black nationalism of later figures such as Marcus Garvey, spurned Forten's back-to-Africa movement. But it was no coincidence or aberration that the tables were turned in 1817, with elements of the black elite favoring migration and the great mass of the non-elite rejecting it. The tensions in nineteenth-century black nationalism that this incident reveals demand a reformulation of conceptions of the origins of black nationalism and of the ideology in general. In particular, Forten's meeting raises concerns regarding the relationship between those self-styled black "leaders" and the communities they served. Non-elite Philadelphians' rejection of the colonization plan signaled tensions within African American communities that are too often neglected in a literature frequently concerned with valorizing black solidarity and the agency of the non-elite. Who, then, originally and most profoundly

concocted black nationalism, and what does the answer imply for understanding the nature of antebellum black protest thought and free black communities?

The answers to these questions lie in a perspective on black nationalism
that is willing to understand it not primarily with the lens through which
it is most often analyzed—that of community or cultural studies[5]—but as
one nationalism in a world of rapidly multiplying nationalisms. What was
the relationship of black nationalism to other nationalisms that emerged
around the turn of the nineteenth century? Was it a "constructed" ideology,
"narrated" into an "invented tradition" or an "imagined community"?[6] If so,
what implications follow for understanding the nature and efficacy of black
protest thought? Was black nationalism of a piece with other nationalisms,
a mere reflection of the broader intellectual currents of Euro-American
political thought? Or did it constitute a political identity produced out of
an autonomous folk consciousness, one quite separate from the institutions
and perspectives of "white" America? How was the efficacy of black nationalism as a form of protest thought affected by its relationship to the over-
arching discourse of nation?

This chapter argues that black nationalism emerged from an ideological
context that lent ever-increasing currency to nationalisms founded upon
ethnic and racial essentialism. It was not originally the seemingly inevitable product of the popular expression of an organically linked community.
Rather, it was the conscious construction of an urban, bourgeois-looking
black intelligentsia, a black leadership that understood well its relationship to emerging public sphere discussions. To participate in those discussions, black activists sought to employ both the ideology of nationalism and
the new media technologies upon which it relied. Rather than presenting
itself as an ideologically unique expression of a separate culture, antebellum black nationalism claimed its place as a legitimate nationalism at a time
when only national status conferred the right of political self-determination
and when only certain types of "civilization" conferred national status.[7] How
Benedict Anderson describes "nation-ness"—as "the most universally legitimate value in the political life of our time"—was becoming true in the early
national and antebellum periods. A great many black thinkers consciously
embraced this potent ideological resource for achieving meaningful freedom and equality.[8] In the process, they forged a potent sense of *racial* identity—one that held greater promise than the class-encumbered values of
elevation and respectability for uniting African-descended people across
a wide spectrum of potential differences and compelling an intransigent
America to yield the liberty and equality it had so long denied blacks.

A quick methodological digression is necessary here, for only by reconceptualizing common approaches to black nationalism can we understand its nascence in the discourse of an urban northern intelligentsia rather than in the experience of the enslaved folk. The typical method for determining the origins of black nationalism involves, if often only implicitly, measuring past manifestations of potential black nationalism against a contemporary model, definition, or ideal. The scholarship thus tends to devolve into debates about whether a given ideology constituted a legitimate or mature nationalism. As only "true" nations are entitled to the benefits of self-determination for which nationalisms strive, this method quickly descends, as do nationalisms themselves, into a politics of authenticity.

Recent scholarship on nationalisms suggests an alternative approach, which sidesteps debates over black nationalism's legitimacy. Nationalisms, it says, are first and foremost discourses; that is, they are ideologies constructed through the process of public debate and contention. In this light, no coherent set of declared principles defines "true" nationalisms; the legitimacy of a nationalism can never be determined by mere recourse to the claims it makes.[9] To contest the legitimacy of a nationalism—to debate whether or not a specific manifestation of potentially nationalist speech ought to "count" as nationalism, or to claim national status for a people based on how they compare to an objective set of criteria, or even to posit an objective, measurable definition of "nation"—is to participate in the discourse of nation, endorse its premises, and leave unexamined its basic terms of debate.

Understanding the nature of black nationalism requires an examination of the *process of contention* rather than participation in those controversies.[10] In comprehending the nature of black (or any other) nationalism, it is more useful to ask "how does this speech relate to the discourse of nation?" than "should this speech count as nationalism?" A nationalism is worth considering a nationalism—or, more precisely, a subject of study by those interested in nationalism—by virtue of its participation in the discourse of nation. As one African American woman so eloquently said of contemporary African Americans, "we are a nation primarily because we think we are a nation."[11] The same is true of all nationalisms; as Anderson notes, nations are thought,[12] or—we should add—spoken and performed, into existence.[13]

The very "constructed" nature of black nationalism helps locate its origins among a black intelligentsia in the antebellum urban North. If nationalisms are defined primarily by their participation in the discourse of nation rather than by a set of objective criteria, then in order for a people to think itself into a nation, the concept of nationhood must be widely available and articulated. Access to and participation in the discourse of nation is a necessary prerequisite for expressing nationalism. In this view, the emergence of black nationalism first and foremost among the enslaved seems unlikely. It has been argued that "slave culture" constituted the earliest, albeit inchoately articulated, manifestation of black nationalism.[14] It is true that enslaved African Americans heard, understood, and acted on articulations of nationalism. The timing and rhetoric of Gabriel Prosser's rebellion in 1800, for example, suggests as much, as does recent work that has highlighted the role of black sailors in spreading the ideology of the bourgeois-democratic revolution.[15] Many former slaves, such as Henry Highland Garnet, seemed particularly attracted to nationalist discourse once free in the North. These African Americans in bondage clearly had a claim to a nascent black nationalism. Yet the social circumstances of free black elites in the urban North rendered them far more likely to conceive, sustain, and nurture a discourse of nation, informed though it surely was by the slave experience.[16]

While the enslaved had limited though highly qualified access to the discourse of nation, a black intelligentsia drawn from the elites of the urban North had far readier access. As in the case of the European nationalisms of the late eighteenth and early nineteenth centuries, this proved to be a core of relatively well-off, self-appointed representatives of the marginalized.[17] In the antebellum North, they looked like black clerics, educators, editors, and merchants. These were people highly restricted in public life by law and mob rule yet technically free to organize and march; ones who were permitted educations though were almost always segregated once in school; those sufficiently literate to form a community of writers, publishers, and readers who could sustain a flow of nationalist ideas in print; and ones marginally though inextricably linked to an urban economy and its values—in short, men and women who were enough *of* the bourgeois social order to be steeped in its ethos and armed with its resources yet who were sufficiently alienated from it to resent its exclusion and to have crafted (by both necessity and choice) an identity distinct from it.

POTENT REFORMERS OF PUBLIC SENTIMENT

African American spokespersons in the North took the step of building black unity through the discourse of nation as soon as they gained freedom, and hence access to the public sphere, during and after the American Revolution. As the numbers of free African Americans living north of the Mason-Dixon line grew, the communities they built served increasingly as vehicles for the expression of a unified black identity. The independent black church served as a training ground for black public leaders and as a forum for black clerics to set forth a vision of racial unity through public speech. Through parades and public celebrations, the streets themselves also became vehicles for the expression of a sense of blackness.

Newspapers proved the most important agents for propounding a nascent black nationalism. Nothing revealed black leaders' understanding of their qualified role on the margins of public sphere discourse more than their use of the press. Made possible by the introduction of cheaper newsprint and inexpensive new printing technologies, the penny press permitted any public speech to become regional, and often truly national. Between 1830 and 1850, the number of daily newspapers in the United States increased from 65 to 254,[18] and African American spokespersons quickly learned the dangers of this important tool to sway the "public mind." The problem, of course, was that the forces arrayed against them had long employed the fora of the public sphere, especially the press, in the service of white supremacy. The rise of a new class of newspapers, inexpensive to produce and purchase, gave voice to the increasingly vitriolic racism percolating through the white urban working classes.[19]

Black spokespersons were all too aware of the hostility of the penny press. In 1851, one black activist wrote to an associate, counting "a licentious venal press" and "a Jesuitical, wine-bibbing priesthood" among "the Northern cringing lickspittles" who defended slavery.[20] Similarly, the *Weekly Anglo-African* listed a "servile press" among the South's "menials among us here in the North." Later, its editors would refer to the "newspaper lying" of a "satanic press" that engaged in "historical perversion" to "show the brutality of the blacks" in moments of crisis.[21] According to African American critics, the press did not simply reflect a widespread hatred of blacks, it also fostered that hatred through its disproportionately powerful effect on public sentiment. "From the press and the pulpit we have suffered much by being incorrectly represented," wrote the editors of one black newspaper. The power of this hostile press had led even some of blacks' abolitionist "friends" astray; susceptible to its veiled influence, they found themselves unwittingly and "imperceptibly floating on the stream—actually living in the practice of prejudice."[22] The black national convention of 1853 highlighted the press, along with "the pulpit" and "the platform," as the most important of the "ten thousand channels through which malign feelings" toward blacks "find utterance and influence." These institutions, the conventioneers reported, "point their deadly missiles of ridicule, scorn and contempt at us; and bid us, on pain of being pierced through and through, to remain in our degradation." [23] The result was the baneful defamation of anyone of African descent. A bloody race riot in Philadelphia in 1842 convinced a melancholy Robert Purvis of "our utter and complete nothingness in public estimation." [24]

The press was certainly a rival; perhaps it could be an ally as well. At the very least, countermeasures were demanded, if only to retard the progress of blacks' degradation in the public repute. "We struggle against opinions," the black national convention of 1847 declared. "Our warfare lies in the field of thought." It concluded that blacks needed a newspaper "because a printing press is the vehicle of thought, is a ruler of opinions." [25] In the face of hostile public sentiment, the black national convention of 1835 declared that it was "only through the instrumentality of that most potent reformer of public sentiment[,] the public press, that any certain, speedy and radical change will be effected in the moral and political relation which we, as a people, hold in this country." [26] Seven years earlier, two black New Yorkers—Samuel Cornish and John Brown Russwurm—had arrived at similar conclusions. Limited though their paper's circulation was, the appearance of *Freedom's Journal* on northern streets heralded a new era in black protest. When their communities could sustain newspapers, black spokespersons found themselves no longer dependent on word of mouth, single-run pamphlet publications, or the efforts of well-meaning but often misguided white advocates to maintain a stream of arguments designed to defend the race from proscription. Through counter-speech, "a simple representation of facts," the editors hoped to "arrest the progress of prejudice, and to shield ourselves against the consequent evils." Their plan was to "vindicate our brethren, when oppressed," by laying their case "before the publick." [27]

Their efforts did not go unnoticed. Presses, like the streets, became literal battlegrounds over which blacks and abolitionists contended with white supremacists for the prize of public sentiment. The *New York Herald*, a typical penny daily of the white working class, launched racist harangues at papers "owned and controlled by a set of woolly-headed and thick-lipped Negroes" and found it useful to insult the rival *Sun*, another white-owned newspaper, by labeling it a "dirty, sneaking drivelling contemporary nigger paper." [28] Antiabolition forces targeted the black press alongside other sources of community activism, such as the church and prominent black-owned businesses. In October 1853, the Detroit offices of *The Voice of the Fugitive* succumbed to fire, which editor Henry Bibb, a former slave, suspected was set by an "incendiary." White-owned abolitionist newspapers were dealt similar malice. *Liberator* editor William Lloyd Garrison fell victim to a Boston mob, which tarred and feathered him, then paraded him through the streets at the end of a rope. In Illinois, a mob destroyed the printing establishment of abolitionist editor Elijah Lovejoy, killing him in the process.[29]

While the mob viewed a new and vociferous black press as a challenge to white northerners' mounting demands that racial boundaries be hardened and policed, African American newspapers did more than simply counter hostile speech with redeeming utterances. More than any other means, the black press linked African Americans throughout the country in an otherwise impossible national community. The 1837 prospectus for the *Colored American* described the journal's aim of uniting African Americans in the free states, readers "scattered in handfuls over nearly 5000 towns" who "can only be reached by the Press."[30] The editors of *Freedom's Journal* intended their newspaper to serve as "a medium of intercourse between our brethren in the different states," a medium that might eventually unite African Americans around the struggle for equality. The newspaper would also champion the interests of those "still in the iron fetters of bondage" and carry news of "everything that relates to Africa."[31] Black newspapers thus served as the great mechanism for constructing a unified, even pan-African black identity, one that could protest the interests of the free and slave, African and African American. Those otherwise divided — by free or slave status, regional cultural style, or a host of other factors — were at least rhetorically united by this sense of blackness. As the history of African-descended societies in other parts of the diaspora suggests, nothing about this process was inevitable, natural, or organic. Editors thoughtfully and self-consciously theorized a unified black identity under whose rubric all of African descent might fall, and they promoted this identity over the broadest region possible. African American spokespersons thus used newspapers to create what one scholar has termed "that remarkable confidence of community in anonymity which is the hallmark of modern nations."[32]

ALIENS AND ILLEGITIMATES

The press did far more than simply allow African Americans to defend themselves from public slanders. It permitted scattered, anonymous blacks to imagine themselves linked together in a nation that might promote their collective interests. Through public media like newspapers, African American elites gained access to the discourse of nation; by constructing those media themselves, they found the capacity to appropriate and reformulate ideas of nation in their own defense. Through public rituals such as parades, through sermons and public thanksgivings and memorial observances, and

through the protopolitical black convention movement, a black intelligentsia crafted a notion of black identity that drew heavily on the language of
nationalism surrounding them. They sought to counter the claims of those
such as Pennsylvania congressman Charles Brown, who argued that racial
equality would require an "amalgamation" of the races that would lead to
the "degeneration" of Americans, leaving them vulnerable "before some invading, superior, and purer northern nation."[33]

One way of doing this was to argue ever more strenuously against white
nationalism's fundamental terms of debate. The language of uplift and respectability did precisely this, primarily through the vehicle of environmentalism, that is, the idea that nurture rather than nature—condition rather
than color—had determined blacks' admittedly backward status. Through
a complex dialectic, white supremacy thus unwittingly reinforced the use of
self-help ideology in black protest rhetoric, investing it with a significance
that none but the marginalized could fully understand. Yet another path
was possible. If the language of racial nationalism could be used to oppress
blacks, perhaps it contained within it the seeds of something useful. Quietly
setting aside a strict reading of Enlightenment universalism, African Americans began to premise their plans for black elevation on this nationalist particularism.

Black thinkers' very definition of nation was rooted in a defensive reaction
to hostile racist nationalism. Alexander Crummell, a black Episcopal clergyman, told a Liberian audience in 1855 that "a nation is a collection of men,"
or "a section of the great commonwealth of humanity." Those who comprised the nation were "men of the same make, and nature, and appetencies,
and destiny, as ourselves, and the men of all other nations."[34] Such assertions contained an implicit claim to equality among men. (The conspicuous
exclusion of women never bothered those such as Crummell.) Slavery and
the prejudicial practices of the North were predicated on the assumption
that blacks were collectively and fundamentally inferior; Crummell's claim
to nationhood, in contrast, implied qualities for African-descended people
that by definition rendered them equally capable of communing with the
established nations of the world. National status thus promised very real
benefits for a people in crisis. A youthful Samuel M. Still, the son of Philadelphia Underground Railroad conductor William Still, wrote, "For want
[of] union we are sufering great inconveniance and loss even of nashinal
[national] character." He urged his people to come together "as soon as possible into an organized compact for our benefit and security." Through such
efforts, he argued, black people could eventually "come up as a nation out
of a nation."[35] "The nineteenth century wants a Black Nationality," wrote

Thomas Hamilton, editor of the *Weekly Anglo-African*, "because it is an instrumentality that cannot be dispensed with in the rehabilitation of the black race."[36]

The language of racial antagonism suffused antebellum black nationalism. Out of frustration with the pace of change, one young black man left the United States to teach Africans in Liberia. Citing "a spirit of antagonism" between the two races in America "which must ultimately terminate in the entire extirpation of the weaker race," he favored the development of a strong black nation in Africa to avert "the disastrous fate" that otherwise awaited American blacks.[37] Martin R. Delany, often considered the premier antebellum black nationalist, similarly followed white nationalists in imagining a world rife with racial conflict, though of course he differed mightily on the preferred outcome: "the great issue, sooner or later, upon which must be disputed the world's destiny, will be a question of black and white; and every individual will be called upon for his identity with one or the other."[38]

These thinkers responded to a core tenet of the nationalism emerging in antebellum America. As seemed evident in history, raw power ruled interactions between nations. While black spokesmen frequently employed the moral authority of their oppressed condition, they also understood and had to contend with this amoral language of national competition. J. Theodore Holly, an ardent advocate of immigration to Haiti, argued that "the antichristian sentiment upon which the modern nations of the world are still administered, is, that 'might makes right,' and that the weakest must go to the wall." This principle of brute force explained why Africa, "being powerless in consequence of the night-mare of ignorance and superstition that has so long brooded over her benighted shores," remained subject to the depredations of stronger nations.[39]

The world of nations envisioned by antebellum Americans black and white was an environment of competition, in which moral force served only to complement brute power. In such a climate, the nation-state offered defense and protection otherwise unavailable; in the words of Holly, "A commanding national influence is all-powerful in shielding and protecting each individual of the race." But Holly noted that there was "no powerful and enlightened negro nationality anywhere existing to espouse the cause and avenge the wrongs of their race." He believed the development of a strong nationality would permit black people to compete in the international game on equitable footing. "Let such a nationality be at once developed," Holly believed, and the African slave trade and slavery itself would be speedily abolished, for "such a nation would have the power and prestige of making itself heard, felt and respected on this question in the councils of the world."[40] Nationalism rationalized the exploitation of "weak" peoples—subordinated nations and the colonized—through appeal to amoral historical laws. Black nationalists transformed such hostile notions into a force for racial uplift by making black people a member of the community of nations.

In the terms of antebellum nationalism, the problem of race was a problem of statelessness. According to black clergyman Hosea Easton, because they lacked a state, African-descended people lacked a force that could champion their rights in an arena of fierce international competition. "Identified as belonging to no country," to "no people, race, or nation," he wrote, they had been "accounted as aliens and outcasts." They had thus been "denied their citizenship, and the benefits derivable therefore." Statelessness entailed more, though, than the lack of a political champion. The romantic nationalism of the antebellum era imagined the political authority of the state resting on the cultural form of the nation. Historical, organic links among members of the nation were manifest in a common culture. This logic was evident among black nationalists as well. Easton argued that blacks had been "stolen from their native country, and detained for centuries, in a strange land." In America, "their blood, habits, minds, and bodies, have undergone such a change, as to cause them to lose all legal or natural relations to their mother country." They were thus made nationless—"aliens and illegitimates."[41] The answer, of course, was to reformulate the African-descended into people accorded the rights and protections of a state—that is, members of a proper nation. In 1854, a convention of emigration-minded blacks accused white antislavery advocates of "erroneously urging us to lose our identity as a distinct race" while at the same time "propagating the doctrine in favor of a *universal Anglo-Saxon predominance.*" The task was to develop black identity so that it could support a black state. The convention argued that, just as "the English, French, Irish, German, Italian, Turk, Persion, Greek, Jew, and all other races, have their native or inherent peculiarities," so black people had "inherent traits, attributes . . . and native characteristics."[42] According to one black leader, only when black people had developed this sense of national identity would they "command respect, instead of courting sympathy from the class that abuse and proscribe [them]."[43]

These invocations of respectability were far from incidental, for the master value of respectability occupied a central place in antebellum black nationalism. African American thinkers had long appropriated bourgeois notions of respectability, which stressed the virtues required of an expanding liberal economic order, only to refashion them into a means of compelling whites to yield equality. Now they fused the language of respectability with that of nation, likewise using the idea to circumvent accommodationist impulses in favor of ones stressing black agency. Just as black protests' use of individual respectability promised to place whites in a position whereby their very interests compelled them to yield liberty and equality, so too national respectability offered a means through which black nationalists might wrest (rather than request) their long-denied freedoms from whites. Nationalism, because it envisioned an essentially amoral world of international competition, offered a particularly auspicious place to apply this more forceful course of protest. Because "all nations . . . are respected according to their ability to control," wrote one black nationalist, blacks could never hope for equality until they could "command and enforce respect."[44] Others spoke of the press as a means of obtaining "a respectable standing and place among the nations of the earth."[45] National respectability offered a means through which African American thinkers could employ the language of raw power, forgo the difficult dictates of personal morality, and command rather than plead for their rights.

Black spokespersons' synthesis of nationalism and respectability suggests the dangers of too easily assigning complex public discourses to sweeping categories of accommodation and resistance, integration and separation, assimilation and nationalism. Uplift and respectability, commonly associated with an assimilated elite's strategies of accommodation and integration, could and did embrace supposedly separatist qualities: the amoral language of power and strategies of compulsion. To the extent that any of the traditional polarities make sense, nationalism—commonly associated with separatism and a rejection of accommodation and integration—constituted a supreme instance of "assimilation," for it manifested a very close relationship with the language and culture of a broader America.

A PLACE AMONG THE MOST ENLIGHTENED: GLORIOUS NATIONAL EXAMPLES

Because of their close reliance on the discourses of the American public sphere, many black nationalists directed their arguments at demonstrating that African-descended people shared the traits, evident in their historical development, necessary to comprise a valid and respectable nation. Black thinkers' discussions of Africa and Haiti evinced a deep debt to contemporary romantic nationalism, though it diverged from that language as it manipulated nationalist tropes in the service of its own protest rhetoric. At nearly every point, African American leaders invoked the principles of nationalism to challenge the ideological means of their domination, only to endorse the fundamental premises upon which their domination had been predicated.

In the parlance of nineteenth-century nationalisms, "civilization" constituted the primary characteristic that qualified a people for national status.
Except for "progress," no word more clearly or more concisely conjured
the qualities befitting the admirable nation. Civilization entailed the mental
capacities of a people, as manifest in an array of achievements technological,
literary, and political. African American thinkers endorsed this conception.
"The world has made rapid advances in civilization," wrote William Wells
Brown, the black abolitionist, of his world. Hearkening to the expansion of
human liberty during the Age of Revolution, Brown sanguinely claimed that
"not only the civilized, but the semi-civilized are acting under the guidance
of the clearer light of the nineteenth century."[46] Such statements, which
ring ethnocentric to late-twentieth-century ears, were commonplace among
black public figures in the decades before the Civil War.

As proof of the capacity of black people to build an advanced civilization, African American spokespersons pointed to the ancient civilizations
of Africa. A great many black thinkers harkened back to the glories of the
black nations of antiquity. Peter Randolph, as an aside in his *Sketches of Slave
Life*, argued that "it must be acknowledged by every historian, that Ethiopia
was once the most civilized nation upon the earth."[47] R. B. Lewis similarly
took pride in the civilization of ancient Africans. "The celebrated Egyptians
or Africans of Egypt," he wrote, "were, at a very early age, a people who
took an elevated stand in the civilized world, and were familiar with all the
varieties of knowledge which flourished in those days."[48] The glories of ancient African civilizations like Egypt provided evidence that once Africans
had constructed a nation that could be considered great by all the standards of modern nation-builders. David Nickens advised a black audience
to "look through the dark vista of past ages, and read in the history of Han-
nibal and others, who were Africans." Such figures, he said, demonstrated
the "strength of intellect, and soundness of judgement, the military skill,
which existed in ancient Africa."[49]

African American leaders posited not merely that ancient African civilizations had been great, but that they had provided the source of civilization for Europe as well. Hosea Easton conceived of a lineage of civilization
founded in ancient Africa. "It is from the Egyptians, that many of the arts,
both of elegance and ability, have been handed down in an uninterrupted
chain, to modern nations of Europe," he wrote. "The Egyptians communi-
cated their arts to the Greeks; the Greeks taught the Romans many improve-
ments, both in the arts of peace and war; and to the Romans, the present
inhabitants of Europe are indebted for the[ir] civility and refinement." In
addition, he pointed out, Athens had been founded by the African Cecrops,

who had brought an Egyptian colony there in 1585 B.C. "The institutions he established among the Athenians gave rise to the spread of the morals, arts and sciences in Greece, and which since shed their lustre upon Rome, Europe, and America."[50] Among the most vociferous of those who claimed a noble black past was R. B. Lewis, whose *Light and Truth* presented an impressive, though indiscriminate, collection of authorities documenting the contributions of Africa to modern civilization. According to Lewis, ancient Africans first developed the alphabet, commerce, wine making, forged metals, music, the Homeric epic, fire, the ship, the pump, the library, and modern academic disciplines.[51] Historical examples of black people who had built great civilizations provided far more than pride. They demonstrated that nothing in the inherent capacities of the race denied its ability to rise in the present, and constituted proof that, if given the opportunity, black people could once again build a civilization that could rival any. In 1832, one black leader told a group of African Americans that "those who accuse us of inferiority" could see in the African past examples of the heights to which black people were capable of ascending.[52] Newspaper editor Samuel Cornish argued that the character traits that had built the great African civilizations still resided in African Americans. Black people, he argued, "have all the natural requisites to make them, in science and renown, what ancient Egypt once was."[53]

Rather than constituting a distinct strain of African American thought, antebellum black nationalism comported easily with other strains of antebellum black protest, including those often considered to be more conservative. The glorious past of ancient African civilizations melded easily with a linchpin of antebellum black protest—the notion of environmentalism. This was the argument that the admittedly benighted state of African-descended people owed to condition rather than color, nurture rather than nature. That African people had once accomplished admirable feats implied that something besides the inherent liabilities alleged of their descendants explained slavery and degradation. Whatever this something proved to be, environmentalism implied, would be found in historical circumstance rather than in black people themselves. While William Wells Brown mourned for his race's descent from its noble past, he remained convinced that "the negro has that intellectual genius which God has planted in the mind of man, that distinguishes him from the rest of creation."[54] Combined with this environmentalism, black Americans' laudable past suggested that once again they could elevate themselves to an exalted state among the nations of the planet. Peter Randolph used African history to demonstrate that, once the impediments to the development of a black civilization were removed, the race would ascend to the previous heights it had achieved in, for example, Ethiopia. "The enlightened nations of the present day are indebted to her [Ethiopia] for many of the arts of civilization," he noted. "Let it not be said, [t]hen, that the negro cannot be educated. *Free the slaves*, give them equal opportunities with the whites, and I warrant you, they will not fall short in comparison."[55]

While Africa presented black thinkers with a history rife with both splendor and sorrow, another historical model offered a different past upon which African Americans could draw national inspiration. The Caribbean island nation of Haiti tendered the clearest example of an existing nation that might represent the interests of black people throughout the world. In 1788, the calling of the French Estates General in response to the crown's fiscal crisis set the opening scenes of the French Revolution. In the colony of St. Domingue, whose high sugar production made it the jewel of the French colonial empire, political tensions on the continent soon inflamed long-smoldering political rifts between rival factions of white colonists and between whites and long-repressed free people of color. Revolutionary rhetoric spread quickly to the island, greatly heightening the stakes of the conflict and threatening to engulf it in a violent slave uprising. Despite the efforts of fragile coalitions of European powers to subvert the specter of a black republic, the Haitians continually frustrated France's efforts to regain control, culminating in the total defeat of Napoleon's forces in the first decade of the nineteenth century. Through opportunistic manipulation of tensions between European powers and island elites and through the efforts of a series of heroic military figures culled from the ranks of former slaves and free people of color, the black people of Haiti by 1804 had wrested their complete freedom from both slavery and European rule.[56]

Black northerners in the antebellum era drew considerable inspiration from this singular history. The taking of black freedom in Haiti seemed to be without precedent in both black and world history. A convention of New England black men lauded the Haitians as "the only people who achieved their independence by the sword, unaided by other nations."[57] J. Theodore Holly, the foremost advocate of emigration to Haiti in the antebellum North, wrote that "the ancient glory of Ethiopia, Egypt, and Greece, grows pale in comparison with the splendor of this Haytian achievement."[58] The Haitians' ability to bring to fruition the interests of the race rendered the island nation a source of intense pride for oppressed African Americans: one editor remarked that the history of Haiti was one "of extraordinary interest, abounding in incidents that none of us can read without a glow of pride of race."[59]

First and foremost, Haiti symbolized black peoples' ability to take for themselves their own freedom. It provided an example of militance that complied with the spirit of individual initiative and manly independence that northern Americans championed. According to Holly, the black revolution in the Caribbean vindicated the capacity of the race to act for itself. The Haitians had prevailed "not only without any aid whatever from white men, but in spite of his combined opposition to keep down in brutal degradation these self emancipated freemen." In a climate wherein dependency was viewed as licentious, feminine, and childlike and where many argued that these faults characterized blacks as a people, the ability to argue for African American initiative had considerable import. "White Americans have taken great pains to try to prove that we are cowards," Boston doctor John S. Rock told a black audience in 1858. "If the white man will take the trouble to fight the black man in Africa or in Hayti," he predicted, the black man would easily win, provided the fight was fair.[60]

The Haitian Revolution lent support to such claims, for it proffered a pantheon of martial heroes, all of whom were black. Holly considered Jean-Jacques Dessalines the "heroic avenger of his race," and Henri Christophe the "Frederick the Great" of Haiti.[61] George B. Vashon, an outspoken educator from Pittsburgh, wrote a poem commemorating the Haitian revolutionaries Toussaint-Louverture and Vincent Oje.[62] William J. Wilson, an educator who corresponded regularly with Frederick Douglass, remarked with regret that in a popular museum in New York City he failed to spy the portraits of Haitian revolutionaries Toussaint-Louverture, Jean-Pierre Boyer, or Faustin-Élie Soulouque. He took their absence as evidence of African Americans' need to develop a distinct and positive sense of black history.[63] The figure of Toussaint-Louverture especially appealed to black northerners. Henry Highland Garnet listed him as a "martyr to freedom" along with Lafayette and George Washington.[64] Referring to French plots to bribe and blackmail Toussaint-Louverture into betraying his country during the revolution, J. W. Lewis wrote: "One of the most beautiful exhibitions of honor, associated with national patriotism, is the conduct of Tousaint Laoverture, the African chieftain, and Washington of Hayti."[65] Even the moderate Frederick Douglass was to write that, because "no part of his greatness can be ascribed to blood relationship with the white race," Toussaint-Louverture demonstrated "beyond cavil or doubt the possibilities of the Negro race."[66]

The overriding virtues of these heroes were their martial spirit and unwillingness to compromise with slaveholders. As founders of a black nation, they were individual examples of the ability of the race as a whole to compete with other nations on equal terms. When applied to Haiti, this ability to compete and win in the international arena contributed much to the nation's sway over the imaginations of black activists. The Haitian Revolution had been directed against European powers, the agents of the oppression of black people, and had actually succeeded. George Lawrence Jr., who edited Thomas Hamilton's *Weekly Anglo-African* when the Civil War broke out, noted that Haiti was yet "the only land in which we have conquered our liberty by the sword against the bravest white warriors of the world." [67] J. Theodore Holly proclaimed proudly that, despite "contending against the armies of France, England, and Spain," the Haitians "shook off from their limbs the shackles and badges of their degradation, and successfully claimed a place among the most enlightened and heroic sovereignties of the world." [68] The Haitian victory demonstrated the race's ability to compete in an environment of international competition.

For many northern black activists, Haiti promised the best opportunity to unite with a strong black nation, and hence the possibility of national victories in the future. In part, some considered Haiti the most desirable site for a black nation by default; alternative black nations seemed few. One black editor remarked that Haiti "is the only nationality of our race in the Western Continent." [69] While Africa lay in the discord and political chaos caused by European colonialism, Haiti existed as a state built squarely upon the European model of a nation. "We can make of Hayti," wrote one black northerner, "the nucleus of a power that shall be to the black, what England has been to the white races." Such a nation would be "the hope of progress and the guarantee of permanent civilization." [70] J. Theodore Holly agreed that Haiti's history qualified it as the best candidate for the establishment of a black nationality. The history of that nation best manifested the "self-reliance and internal progress" he deemed necessary for a strong black nation. "The Haytian Revolution, and the subsequent history of that people, when compared with that of any other portion of the negro race, will substantiate this assertion beyond the power of successful contradiction." [71]

In framing arguments for black equality, the Haitian example offered considerable benefits. It provided a historically unique example of black achievement on which nationalist-minded black spokesmen rarely failed to linger. J. Theodore Holly noted repeatedly that the history of Haiti "presents us with the most irrefragable proof of the equality of the negro race, that can be found anywhere, whether in ancient or modern times." [72] Black understandings of Haitian history adhered to the logic of black nationalism, which often extended the logic of individual elevation. In effect, Haiti had accomplished for antebellum blacks what all who endorsed national elevation sought. Having engaged other nations in an essentially amoral contest of power and won, she would now prove a bastion, protecting the interests of the race and thus assuring conditions that would permit the "progress," or elevation over time, of black "civilization"—the group "mind." As an argument relying on the premises of elevation, black northerners' use of Haiti employed the environmental argument so central to discussions of black character. The Haitian Revolution proved that nothing inherent to the African character dictated that blacks should be inferior, for Haiti offered an example of black people who had shown the ability to create their own nation. That they did so despite unfavorable circumstances merely strengthened the claim. Holly stated that the Haitians had affected their own liberation "without the elevating influence of civilization among them; without a favorable position for development."[73] If anything did, the Haitian Revolution proved to the world that black people possessed all the character qualities necessary to make themselves a nation.[74]

This vision of Haiti suffered grave inaccuracies. Haiti was not, after all, a strong black nation, but a marginal one, holding onto its sovereign status quite perilously. As a former slave colony that had secured its independence through bloody revolt, Haiti was treated by other nations as an outcast, rather than as a legitimate member of the fraternity of states. Its plantation complex battered by years of turmoil, it received none of the outside aid needed to recover lost ground. Furthermore, its history hardly offered an unqualified lesson in democratic government. Although Toussaint-Louverture was widely regarded as an exemplary democratic figure, his successors—Jean-Jacques Dessalines, Henri Christophe, Alexandre Sabès Pétion, Jean-Pierre Boyer, and Faustin-Élie Sou,louque—could hardly boast as much. Autocracy, rather than democracy, proved the watchword of Haitian politics.

Though African American spokespersons did their best to spin this straw into gold, their efforts could not have been an unqualified success. The gulf between Haitian realities and black nationalism's image of Haiti merely suggests the degree to which the Euro-American discourse of nation dominated even the most radical invocations of a distinctly black past. From their conceptions of nations as fundamentally equal political entities locked in historic struggle to the values of "civilization" that underlay those conceptions, black northerners' versions of nationalism never sought to break out of the ideological parameters of the discourse. Indeed, they could not have, for their own thought (like that of their contemporaries) remained bounded by those parameters, such that alternatives were literally unthinkable. The rhetorical resistance that antebellum black nationalism offered sought to stretch or manipulate nationalist tropes rather than discard them.

WITH THEIR LIPS TO THE DUST: EUROPEAN NATIONAL HISTORIES

African American spokespersons' narration of African and Haitian histories clearly partook of a discourse of nation dominated by the ideas, tropes,
and values of the Euro-American nationalisms that preceded it. Not even
when they directly addressed the successes and failings of other nations did
they reveal more distanced understandings of nationalism as a discourse.
In that case especially the African American rhetorical strategy was one of
lampoon and subterfuge rather than direct frontal assault. Where African
Americans might have rejected nationalism and all of its trappings, many
instead revealed an ever-increasing reliance on the essentialist premises of
nationalist discourse.

While they spent much time lauding their own historical forebears, African American spokespersons also sprinkled their newspapers, convention
proceedings, and public speeches with liberal references to other national
peoples, both historic and contemporary. Black ideas of rival nations served
an underlying argument: that, as their own nation, black people were fundamentally equal to the peoples of Europe and hence fit to enjoy the rights
and privileges due to everyone represented by a nation. Black thinkers
posed this point in several ways. In speaking about the current status of the
peoples of European nations, they inevitably turned to the national histories
that had produced those Europeans. Here again they constructed upon the
premises of romantic nationalism critiques of white attitudes toward black
people. European nations and the United States justified their domination
over colored peoples of the world on the basis of their allegedly advanced
civilization. Citing histories rife with progress in the sciences and arts, these
nations justified their enslavement or iniquitous treatment of blacks on the
basis of Africans' alleged barbarism. Black nationalist theorists in the antebellum North challenged this claim. By manipulating contemporary motifs
of nationalism, they could both look to others' national histories for models
to emulate and lampoon European nations for their failure to embody the
qualities that their people defined as national virtues. Such forms of rhetorical play backed an agenda that was deadly serious. By either altering
the definition of nation or exposing its hypocrisies, blacks became agents in
contesting, and thus creating, nationalism itself.

Great Britain, of foreign nations, proved most readily available for favorable comparison with a potential black nation. America had entered the
nation game late, as the result of a long history of the expansion of the English or Anglo-Saxon nation. The history of that country offered examples

of national virtue as well as vice, even in its deepest origins. Many black leaders looked to the growth of America's ancient predecessor over time as a marvel. In a speech commemorating the opening of free schools in Ohio, clergyman A. A. Guthrie gushed over the achievements of the Anglo-Saxon nation. "No country has ever produced finer specimens of individual men or nobler developments of humanity," he said, commending England as a "splendid illustration" of the triumph of "mind over matter" and "the moral over the physical."[75] Few glorified the history of the Anglo-Saxon nation as much as Alexander Crummell, the Episcopal minister who had trained in Britain. The history of England demonstrated for Crummell the potential of a black nation. Just as it had taken years of "unwearied and plodding industry" for England to rise to the "front rank of nations," he said, so "the same process must be . . . carried out in the negro race." If successful, blacks too could "rise gradually into a state of higher and nobler civilization and improvement."[76] English history also provided examples of expansion and of the commercial enterprise that Crummell claimed was so essential to a healthy nation. Those "Scandinavian and Norman races" who helped found England had "streamed out from their crowded homes or hives in the far north, and formed . . . great and mighty nations." Since then, the British had continued to expand, "planting their restless energy" throughout the globe.[77] For Crummell, Anglo-Saxons provided a model of nation-building from which black people might profit. England's current status as a leader in the struggle against the international slave trade and slavery in general led David Walker, author of one of the most militant pamphlets to appear in the North, to laud the nation. "The blacks cannot but respect the English as a nation," he wrote, for "the English are the best friends the coloured people have upon earth."[78]

If selectively invoked Anglo-Saxon history provided models of national behavior, the English who settled America served as even nobler objects of emulation. Along with "the plough" and "the anvil," James McCune Smith commented, Anglo-Saxons brought to America "the Protestant religion, and that proclivity to organization, in which deTocqueville easily detected the necessary foundation of a successful republican super-structure."[79] Maria Stewart invoked this impressive Anglo-Saxon history in spurring black men to action. According to Stewart, black people, and black men in particular, too often failed to energetically defend the interests of the race: "Did the pilgrims, when they first landed on these shores, quietly compose themselves, and say: 'The Britons have all the money and all the power and we must continue their servants forever?' Did they sluggishly sigh and say: 'Our lot is hard; the Indians own the soil, and we cannot cultivate it?' No, they first made powerful efforts to raise themselves." Black men, she continued, had not exerted themselves to the same degree in supporting the race.[80]

Many black writers extended their admiration beyond the English to other European nations. Henry Bibb, a fugitive slave and newspaper editor, did not limit his admiration of European expansion to the English. Bibb defended black settlements in Canada by comparing them to Dutch, French, and Irish settlements in the New World. All, he argued, were attempts to improve otherwise uninhabitable land through settlement.[81] In addition to his praise of the English, Alexander Crummell applauded the Irish when commending their support of abolitionism: "The spirit of that beautiful isle hath ever been on the side of human freedom. Her children have always prized it beyond all price, and evinced their sincerity in the same by a zealous anxiety for the liberties of others."[82]

Most black spokespersons relied upon popular stereotypes of national characteristics in upholding Europeans as models from which black people might profit. Dutch and German people embodied the commerce, thrift, and industry valued in the new entrepreneurial age. While Thomas Hamilton remarked on "the Caucasian bent to trade" of the Dutch,[83] James McCune Smith upheld German people as the epitome of thrift and industry. The German immigrants to the United States, McCune insisted, "bring with them not only physical force and endurance, but also the highest skill, and the necessary means to enter at once as competitors" in the nation. Germans could compete in America with the peoples of other nations, for they embodied a litany of commercial virtues, including "a persistent vitality, strong nationality, intelligence and a capacity for organized effort." For Smith, the thrifty example of the Germans served "very much as a set-off to our [blacks'] extravagant habits and rapid living."[84]

Some black leaders also upheld Jewish people as role models, further evincing their reliance on national, ethnic, and racial stereotypes. Samuel Cornish, the editor of several newspapers, consistently advised his readership that through thrift and industry one could "make the very oppression intended for your injury, the means of your wealth and improvement." This was possible, he continued, for such "has been the case with the Jews in some part of Europe, [for] they have been oppressed until the wealth of whole towns and cities have been pressed into their hands."[85] Throughout his career as an editor, Cornish upheld what he took to be the Jewish model of self-elevation in urging his fellows to virtue. Black Americans, he wrote, should, "like the oppressed Jews in Europe, be prodigies of unceasing effort and of undying enterprise."[86] Another writer commented that Jews in Europe had been "steadily rising from a condition as unenviable as that of the free people of color in the United States" through their control of wealth. He urged the black man to strive for riches "for the benefit of his children and the best interest of his race."[87]

If black leaders elevated some groups, they lambasted others. Just as the ancient past provided models for a black nationality, so too it proffered a storehouse of counterexamples, which defined the inverse of the ideal black nation. Like many contemporary white thinkers, Hosea Easton, a black clergyman and racial theorist from New York, understood the history of races and nations in Biblical terms. The Greeks, in Easton's scheme, descended from one of the sons of Noah, who scattered with his people after the flood. Unlike most whites, though, Easton declared these early Greeks to have been "a savage race of men, traversing the woods and wilds, inhabiting the rocks and caverns, a wretched prey to wild beasts and to one another." In contrast, Easton explained, the descendants of Noah's son Ham, who founded the African civilization of Egypt, "were enjoying all the real benefits of civilized life" at this time.[88] According to Easton, Europe exhibited this heathen nature again after the fall of Rome swept away the last vestiges of civilization from the continent and yielded to the Teutonic and Celtic descendants of modern European nations.

Easton reveled in remarking upon the barbarism of this period, which was popularly understood as a "dark age" by American and European scholars. Far from the genteel civility in which modern Western European nations clothed themselves, he wrote, Europe during this period "exhibited a picture of the most Gothic barbarity."

> Literature, science, taste, were words scarce in use from this period to the sixteenth century. The Goths and Vandals, and other fierce tribes, who were scattered over the vast counties of the North of Europe . . . , were drawn from their homes by a thirst for blood and plunder. Great bodies of armed men . . . issued forth like regular colonies in quest of new settlements. . . . Wherever the barbarians marched, their route was marked with blood. They ravaged or destroyed all around them.[89]

In contrast to the Egyptians, who "at no age, cultivated the art of war to any great extent," the violent Europeans expanded, causing "almost an entire extinction of all civil and religious governments, and of the liberal arts and sciences."[90]

Whereas Europeans and European-descended people in America devalued Africans on the basis of their "heathen" and "barbaric" natures, Easton sought to demonstrate how Europeans themselves developed from the very characteristics they denigrated. Indeed, Europeans continued to embrace the barbaric violence that characterized their past. "It is not a little remarkable, that in the nineteenth century a remnant of this same barbarous people should boast of their national superiority," he remarked.[91] The proof of this assertion lay in Europeans' retention of a practice of slavery that was itself a manifestation of the barbarism that their nations so avidly denounced. In the opinion of several black thinkers, Europeans invented slavery, in the form of feudalism. Leaders of European peasants "reduced the great body of them to actual servitude," Easton wrote. "They were slaves fixed to the soil, and with it transferred from one proprietor to another, by sale, or by conveyance."[92] Alexander Crummell shared this idea, noting that "the whole western part of Europe was once in a state of abject vassalage." He, too, understood slavery as the product of a "system of Feudalism . . . hardly yet entirely extirpated from some of its foremost nations" and pointed to Russian serfs who continued to suffer under "irresponsible power and unrestrained tyranny."[93]

European nations often came under attack for adhering to religious and political systems understood to be antithetical to those of America. Roman Catholicism, according to A. A. Guthrie, had placed many of the French "into a semi-infidelity." The French Revolution, which Guthrie contended "scarce deserves the name," had done little to inculcate republican principles. Writing shortly after Louis Napoléon's overthrow of the Second Republic, Guthrie expected France to take rank among the progressive nations only "when she shall learn that the stability of a free government depends on the virtue and intelligence of the people, and not on the bayonets of her soldiery."[94]

Spain's descent over recent centuries from the heights of world power also offered valuable lessons on nationalism to African American thinkers. Guthrie censured the Spanish for an even greater adherence to the reactionary forces of Catholicism and monarchism than the French. Labeling the Iberian nation "among the most hopeless of European countries," the clergyman argued that Spain had been ruined by "Aristocracy, Monarchy and Priestcraft." He concluded by generously extending his criticisms to Portugal and all of Latin America as well.[95] J. Holland Townsend, a frequent writer for the *Anglo-African Magazine,* contended that the history of Spain demonstrated that "an ignorant people must always be a poor people," for Spain had once led the world in wealth, "yet at the present day that nation who has less wealth than Spain, must be poor indeed."[96]

While Germans and Jews served as model minorities for antebellum black Americans, black leaders offset the virtues of even these groups with the negative qualities implied in their stereotypes. M. H. Freeman's image of the typical Jew as "a Baron Rothschilds, to whose money bags kings and princes are compelled to pay assiduous court" reveals how difficult it proved for black thinkers to avoid imbibing the widespread anti-Semitism of the day.[97] The Germans, James McCune Smith noted, balanced the virtues of their thriftiness with several vices. Their proclivity to sell alcohol, the temperance-minded doctor noted, was among the worst of these, for it was through just such a strategy that white men had conquered the Indians.[98]

Black leaders tempered their admiration of even the most laudable nations, like Britain, by pointing out national vices from which African Americans should also learn. The English monarchy's antirepublican imperfections deeply qualified black appreciation. Like other Americans, black people in the North maintained a strong faith in the democratic tradition of the American Revolution. The wounds of wars against England were too fresh, and the metaphorical identification of the British as tyrannical enslavers of American colonials too recent, for black northerners to ignore. David Walker tempered his praise of England, for when he wrote in 1829 it still had slave-holding colonies in the West Indies, which, he noted, "oppress us sorely."[99] Alexander Crummell noted that adherence to Christianity barely compensated for the "semi-barbarism" and "brutal love of fight" of the British.[100] And A. A. Guthrie derided England, despite its progress, as having an "anti-republican government" which was "heartless, and unscrupulous in the means used for the attainment of its ambitious ends."[101] Yet despite the despotic tendencies of England, these black leaders admired the strength of the nation and the "energy" with which it had gained its position of preeminence, and they urged similar expenditures of energy on the part of black people. Maria Stewart urged black men to make a "powerful effort" toward achieving their own freedom,[102] while Thomas Hamilton chided black Americans for manifesting "feebleness of character" instead of "force of character."[103]

England also withstood sarcastic attacks on white nationalists' claim that it was the source of a superior Anglo-Saxon civilization. African Americans found this claim far too haughty, and though their history often fudged the details, they delighted in dwelling on the nation's barbaric origins. Several black authors remarked that, when found by the invading Romans, the people of England were hardly the epitome of civilization. Robert Gordon claimed that when Caesar found Britain "she was characterized by the stern despotism of Druidism, and uncivilization and gross idolatry obtained there as in other places of the heathen world," including "the horrible practice of sacrificing human victims,"[104] while William Craft claimed that "when

Julius Caesar came to this country [Britain], he said of the natives that they were such stupid people that they were not fit to make slaves of in Rome."[105] Others stated that when the Romans carted off the Britons to the slave markets of Rome, the Britons "were sold very cheap on account of their inaptitude to learn."[106] Britain's inglorious history continued even after Rome vacated her shores. According to one black writer, "the Angles and Saxons" who replaced Rome as the dominant power on the island "were both barbaric German tribes, who stole the country of the Britons, and appropriated it to their own uses."[107] The very foundations of English civilization, then, lay in a history of brutal expansion and barbaric tyranny.

African American writers did not fail to note that the popular mythology of English history claimed that Anglo-Saxons themselves eventually fell from the lofty heights of conquerors to become the lowly conquered. The idea that these exemplars of modern nationalism had been enslaved fired the satiric imaginations of several black spokesmen. Under the trope of the "Norman yoke," this idea had been a staple of English radical and liberal thought for centuries. This interpretation of history argued that the English penchant for liberty had been born in the Anglo-Saxon experience of democracy in the Teutonic forest and nurtured by their consequent enthralldom at the hands of the Norman conquerors of England in 1066. In achieving their freedom from Norman tyranny, the historical myth went, Anglo-Saxons had developed the principles of freedom that underlay the progressive civilizations of England and the United States. Taking up the idea of the Norman yoke, Alexander Crummell noted, "England herself, grand and mighty empire as she is, can easily trace back the historic footprints to the time, when even she was under the yoke. And the blood which beats high in her children's veins . . . was still, in its ancestral sources, the blood of slaves!"[108] John H. Johnson, a figure often seen in Philadelphia's black literary societies, dissented from the traditional conception of the Norman yoke to argue that slavery had found Anglo-Saxons pliant. He argued that under the feudal system in England, the Norman elite oppressed the commoners sorely. "These were of the great Saxon or Germanic race, who are said to be to [too] high spirited for slavery," he contended. "And yet it appears that their high spirits became reconciled to that condition as much as these blacks who are said to be naturally inferior."[109] A writer for the *Anglo-African Magazine* suggested the significance of this shared history: "what is to prevent our taking rank with them, seeing that we have a common history in misfortune?"[110]

Depictions of an Anglo-Saxon history rife with slavery and tyranny countered the very notions that white supremacy employed to justify the oppression of people of color. Far from carrying the blood of an ancient people who had epitomized freedom and progressive civilization, black writers argued, Anglo-Saxons originated in barbarism and despotism. By parodying the language of romantic nationalism, black thinkers' jibes challenged sentiments that relegated black people to the status of an inferior or even nonexistent nation. A writer for the *Anglo-African Magazine* identified only as "S.S.N." skewered the myth of a noble Anglo-Saxon past. While "Noah and Mrs. Noah may be ancestry enough for some folks," he joked, whites claimed that Horsa and Hengist, the two mythic Anglo-Saxons who first invaded England, "are father and mother to the great Anglo-Saxon race." Soon, he suggested, white people would be claiming that "the ancient Egyptians themselves were Anglo-Saxons." He continued to assert that, far from imbuing them with a love of freedom, the only claim Anglo-Saxon heritage could make on the character of present-day Americans was "that it runs in the blood to steal."[111]

African American thinkers often employed such satirical arguments as direct responses to claims that black people had no heritage or civilization to speak of, and hence no claim to equality. William Wells Brown responded to President Lincoln's concession that black people were inferior by virtue of their lack of civilization by deriding Lincoln's own Anglo-Saxon heritage. Brown sought to demonstrate that whites could claim a past no more glorious than blacks' own. "I am sorry that Mr. Lincoln came from such a low origin," the abolitionist stated with mock pity, "but he is not to blame." He concluded by admonishing his audience: "Ancestry is something which the white American should not speak of unless with his lips to the dust."[112]

CONCLUSION

Black nationalism as an articulated political ideology flourished first and foremost in the North. A free black intelligentsia there began to articulate it in the decades during and after the American Revolution, deepening it immeasurably in the years after the emergence of the black press and convention movement in the late 1820s and 1830s. Black nationalism thus emerged from an ideological context deeply conversant with a transatlantic public dialogue over the nature of peoples, races, and nations.

By the means through which nationalisms are best identified and measured, the black elites of the urban antebellum North proved far more likely progenitors of a tradition of black nationalism than did the black non-elite. How do we know that black nationalism derived from an urban intelligentsia rather than from the enslaved folk? How do we resolve the conflict between these two possible sources of black nationalism? Once again we must have recourse to recent scholarship on nationalism, which has stressed the constructed nature of nationalisms as ideologies. It has also stressed the futility of attempts to define legitimate nationalisms through objective means. On the basis of this scholarship, it seems best to measure nationalisms by criteria that do not themselves derive from the discourse of nation. By these criteria, nationalisms may be measured only by their relationship to the discourse of nation. This means that an ideology "counts" as a nationalism not because it conforms to objective criteria but because it purports to participate in the discourse of nation. A nationalism must, then, know that it is a nationalism.

By this measure, the enslaved folk seem unlikely progenitors of black nationalism. Nationalisms require first and foremost access to the discourse of nation—that is, knowledge of the ideas and tropes of nationalist rhetoric. Black elites, through their deep engagement with the "public mind" and the world of print media that reflected it, had this access. They lampooned, satirized, appropriated, and reconstructed a wide variety of nationalistic tropes and idioms in the service of emancipation and equality. Their speeches and writings, far more than the folk expressions of the enslaved, self-consciously operated within a discourse of nation.

To argue that black nationalism originated among free black urban elites rather than among enslaved African Americans is in no way to argue that the black non-elite lacked a sense of group identity built on a rich tradition of shared community culture. Nor is it to claim that black folk culture did not constitute a valid source of resistance. If nationalism is to have any discrete or useful analytical meaning, however, it must be possible to distinguish between a nonnational group identity and a national one. "National" identities appeared in a specific time and place and have histories distinct from the histories of cultures, intertwined though the two often are. What made African American spokespersons' sense of collective identity a national one, in contrast to that derived from a shared African American folk culture, was its participation in a historically specific discourse that self-consciously sought to engage that tradition in the quest for group rights.

Further evidence that antebellum black nationalism originated among an urban intelligentsia may be gleaned from its approach to the culture of the non-elite. Modern cultural nationalisms often claim that their people belong to the nation because of their shared cultural affinities. Nations, they contend, are the political manifestations of a people united by common histories and traditions. They thus muster claims of popular or folk culture to legitimate their political demands for self-determination.

While modern nationalisms often invoke claims of cultural unity to bolster their legitimacy, black leaders in the antebellum era did not use claims of a distinct culture to fashion their nationalism. The modern concept of culture, not to mention the value of claiming a distinct cultural style in resisting oppression, had not developed nearly enough for early black nationalists to invoke it.[113] "We must begin to . . . acknowledge and love our own peculiarities *if we have any*," claimed William J. Wilson, his qualification underscoring the protean nature of understandings of black culture in the antebellum period.[114] As black public figures' discussions of "respectable" behavior indicated, many eschewed any specter of a distinct black cultural style. That they did so in no way lessened the fervor of their nationalism. The most ardent nationalists, such as Philadelphia's John H. Johnson, considered "slave manners" to be "degraded" and "monkeyfied."[115] Their black nationalism did not seek to celebrate the culture of the non-elite. Instead, it sought to place the black cultural "genius" squarely within the pale of contemporary values of "civilization."

Their reliance on values of civilization that were shared with a broader intellectual milieu emphasizes that black thinkers' dialogue with a racist America proved key to the formation of black nationalism. Black nationalists built their ideology largely in response to the hostile tenets of America's racial nationalism, appropriating and refashioning elements of it, finding in that unlikely source a potent weapon for their defense. Despite the close affinities between the ideas of nationalism espoused by black and white Americans, blacks in no way merely mimicked the nationalism of their age. As we shall see in the next chapter, black thinkers inflected nationalistic ideas through the dual lenses of racial crisis and the rhetorical exigencies of participating in public discussion. No black person could craft a nationalism from the perspective of an American insider, privileged with the benefits of a complete and unfettered citizenship. Many, such as Canadian colonizationists like Henry Bibb, could not even speak from a position of technical freedom. In their exclusion from the benefits of American nationality black spokespersons found the need to argue for their political distinctiveness. That is what nationalisms often supply, after all: the ideological weaponry necessary for those excluded from the protections of the state to struggle for recognition and rights in the court of public opinion.

Of all the vulgar modes of escaping from the
consideration of the effect of social and moral
influences upon the human mind, the most vulgar is
that of attributing the diversities of conduct and
character to inherent natural differences.
John Stuart Mill

Why, indeed, was the black man created, if not to
fulfill his destiny *as a negro,* to the glory of God?
Austin Steward, black abolitionist and educator

CHAPTER 7

This Temple of Liberty

Black Racialism and American Identity

In April 1855, Uriah Boston, a prominent figure in the black community of
Poughkeepsie, New York, wrote a letter to *Frederick Douglass' Paper.* He expressed concern over the increasingly separatist tone of prominent black
abolitionists like William J. Wilson and James McCune Smith. Responding
to pieces they had written in the black press, Boston criticized the two for
"urging the colored people to preserve their identity with the African race."
He feared that any claim of distinct national identity on the part of black
people might lend credence to "the propriety and necessity of African colonization"—the dreaded scheme of the American Colonization Society. For
Boston, blacks could never constitute a nation within the nation. "You cannot mix nationalities," he wrote. "No man is a proper citizen of one certain
country while he claims at the same time to be a citizen of any other country." And blacks had no chance of contending with whites; in a contest of
raw power they could not hope to win. Boston imagined the outcome of "3
millions Africans charging 24 millions Americans on the ground selected
by the Americans themselves": "One such charge would result in the annihi-
lation of the African brigade, with no prospect of recruits." No, rather than
accentuate the differences between white and black, Boston believed that

blacks' "true policy" ought to be "to lessen the distinction between whites and colored citizens of the United States." They were, after all, Americans by birth, culture, and contribution to the nation.[1]

Boston's comments encapsulated a prominent strand in black activist thinking, typically labeled integrationism. As many contemporary critics of integrationism noted, however, blacks were not "proper citizens," for virtually nowhere in America did they exercise the full rights of citizens, untrammeled by slavery or racial prejudice. Set against Boston's views were those of thinkers typically considered more nationalistic, including Wilson, Smith, and particularly Martin R. Delany. The latter, a doctor by training and frequently Frederick Douglass's coeditor, spearheaded efforts in the 1850s to found a separate black state. His written justifications of such an exodus are often considered quintessential statements of antebellum black nationalism, and thus, by most measures, his position could not have been more removed from Boston's. Declaring hopes for racial equality in America dead, Delany rejected the universalistic underpinnings of integration, which asserted the natural rights of all peoples regardless of race or nation. He wrote: "our friends in this and other countries, anxious for our elevation, have for years been erroneously urging us to lose our identity as a distinct race, declaring that we were the same as other people; while at the very same time propagating the doctrine in favor of a *universal Anglo-Saxon predominance*." Agreeing with Boston that blacks in America could never hope to force the issue on whites, he arrived at a quite different conclusion: emigration, or the founding of a separate black state where African Americans could rule themselves. "No people can be free who themselves do not constitute an essential part of the *ruling element* of the country in which they live," he wrote. "The liberty of no man is secure, who controls not his own political destiny."[2]

The tension between the positions of Boston and Delany is often framed as one between nationalism and integration—as an endorsement of political self-determination or a rejection of those principles. Yet while they took opposing stands, both statements relied equally on the tenets of romantic ethnic nationalism. Boston had not rejected nationalism as an ideology; indeed, the language of nationalism pervades his writing. He merely rejected *black* nationalism as a particular form of it. In every other respect he endorsed tenets of nationalism—a conception of human politics as divided into distinct nations that contended largely through amoral contests of power. While Boston did not favor black political autonomy, he was still a committed nationalist—just an American one. Antebellum black thought was characterized not by a tension between nationalism and its opposite, but between different manifestations of nationalism. Somehow, by the 1850s, even rejections of black separatism stood captive to the principles of nationalism. It had become increasingly difficult to discuss any issue without becoming subsumed by the discourse of nationalism.

While deeply engaged with the contemporary discourse of nationalism, black thinkers could not have merely replicated it. Two factors dictated the degree to which their take on American nationalism would diverge from that of whites: the degree to which African Americans had access to the public discourse of nationalism and the degree to which they were excluded from the public life of the nation. Highly acclimated to an ever-broadening public sphere yet universally scorned as unfit for freedom, let alone equality with whites, black elites developed nationalistic ideas that tended to evolve down unique lines. Although African American northerners well understood their nationalizing context, they were not permitted to participate in it. They could never have championed the virtues of a nation predicated on the premise of Anglo-Saxon superiority, for they were never permitted to partake of its benefits. Their sense of nationalism borrowed from the premises of American ideology but owed everything to its dialogues with white and black Americans over obtaining blacks' rightful inheritance of the Founding Fathers' legacy. As much as they relied on American nationalism's premises and shared in its continual construction and reconstruction, early nineteenth-century black nationalists crafted an ideology that departed from its American original in important ways. More than any other facet of antebellum African American thought, black takes on American nationalism constructed the African-descended as a people, united in purpose and destiny.

The bedrock of American values and tropes upon which black thinkers constructed black nationalism was quickly metamorphosing from its own European origins. In the United States, romantic nationalism was built on the fact of ethnic diversity and the conspicuous presence of nonwhite races. The nation lacked the possibility of ethnic and especially racial homogeneity, which served as the telos of the romantic national project elsewhere. European nationalists defined ethnic groups as proto-nations, awaiting only the establishment of a state to become full-fledged members of the international community. American nationalists lacked the luxury of racial homogeneity, though an influx of non-English immigrants beginning in the 1820s caused them to wrestle with the ethnic composition of their nation. The rise of nativism, especially in the form of the American Party, spoke to the desires of many native-born Americans to craft an ethnic nationalism based on ethnic homogeneity. But the two-party political system worked to mobilize the new immigrant voters, the Democratic Party in particular attracting the attention of the working-class urbanites. Whigs and their Republican successors soon found themselves competing for the votes of new Americans. In framing their appeal to the newly enfranchised non-elite whites, they jettisoned paternalistic ties to free African Americans, which their political ancestors had exercised in the days of the Federalists. As nativism gave way to white supremacy as the primary definer of the civic community, it became clear that the United States would need to build ethnic diversity into its national narrative. The myth of Anglo-Saxonism vied with competing claims of Celts and Germans just enough to ensure that the nation's self-proclaimed core identity would be "white" first and "Anglo-Saxon" second.

In addition, the founding myth of the nation coalesced not primarily around shared ancient histories and organic cultural links but instead around a recent history of commitment to abstract principles of universal human liberty and the promises of economic liberalism. These commitments often stood directly at odds with the particularism implied in all romantic nationalisms. Rather than being rooted in the deep mythological histories of peoples assumed to be united by organic ties, this element of the American founding myth appealed to timeless and universal verities. All nations proclaimed that their citizen-members shared basic fundamental rights, but the United States had been predicated on a radical commitment to *universal* human equality. Whereas many in European nations understood citizenship to extend to all within the nation, American principles promised to extend the blessings of liberty to all of humanity. Most white Americans evaded the full implications of this, but they could do so only through exercises of tortured logic that left them exposed to charges of hypocrisy and vulnerable to challenges in constitution and law. Antebellum America effectively denied full citizenship to people of African descent, yet its promises were not utterly meaningless: they had, in fact, led to widespread emancipation and limited freedom in the North and had permitted an antislavery movement to develop within the borders of the nation. This movement, in instances ranging from the *Amistad* captives to fugitive slave rescues, had raised credible challenges to the slave regime.

America compensated for the poor quality of its nationalistic soil not simply with its unique brand of racial nationalism. It also embraced a founding myth rooted in Puritan forebears' understanding of themselves as a people chosen by God to redeem the world. The eighteenth century, and especially the American Revolution, secularized this mythology, endowing a national civil religion with divine mission. Underlying all was a millennial sense of destiny, built originally on Reformation foundations but which has survived into the present day. In the first half of the nineteenth century, two components supplemented this ideology: theodicy and the jeremiad. Theodicy sought to reconcile the infinite goodness and omnipotence of God with the existence of evil. It explained suffering: everything from the seventeenth-century persecution of Calvinist Protestants in Europe at the hands of the Anglican establishment in England to defeats in individual battles during the American Civil War. The jeremiad threatened lapsed believers with the consequences of apostasy. In colonial New England, Puritan ministers had invoked it to reinforce the tenuous faith of the godly community in the generations after the founders. Very frequently, when the jeremiad explained misfortune in terms of lapsed faith, it functioned as theodicy, interpreting calamity as the consequence of straying from the will of God. Its primary service, however, was to build community by offering believers a shared history endowed with divine meaning. It did this by maintaining the narrative thread of the godly community, resuscitating it when confronted by flagging credibility (as when a predicted millennium failed to appear) or by declension (the waning of an original sense of purpose in succeeding generations). These religious factors had long woven their way into American political discourse. In the early nineteenth century, they fused with the discourse of nationalism, which posited nationality as the sole legitimate means of representing the interest of the individual in the court of national and international politics, to serve as the conceptual framework through which a great many Americans understood their world and the events unfolding in it.

African Americans steered their manipulation of these elements of American nationalism down two general paths. One, which is considered in the second half of this chapter, invoked religious imagery to create a community of the oppressed imbued with a sense of mission. The first, to which we turn now, responded directly to the emerging paradox of racial science in a universalistic society. Relying on the principles of the American Revolution and the logic of uplift and elevation, African American thinkers answered claims of their innate depravity, claiming instead an important national destiny.

OF ONE BLOOD: NATIONAL ELEVATION AND RACIAL ENVIRONMENTALISM

Whether alleged by pioneers of racial science such as Samuel Morton or posited as a premise of popular entertainments such as blackface minstrelsy, the idea of blacks' irremediable inferiority presented African Americans their greatest challenge. Such claims served as the ideological linchpin uniting all rationalizations for denying blacks freedom and equal rights. It would have been one thing had African-descended people been only temporarily degraded: in such a case universal emancipation would have made sense. But, particularly in the North, where the status of servitude itself could no longer serve as a justification for the denial of rights, white supremacy increasingly depended on claims of innate and immutable inferiority. As black racial theorist J. W. Lewis put it: "It is extremely humiliating to American pride and arrogance, to be obliged to acknowledge the African race as a part of the human family." Lewis understood that the logic of American political ideology demanded that, were black people considered a part of "humanity," Americans would be "obliged by the obligation of universal brotherhood, to sustain fraternity with them as sentient beings."[3] Even in the only nominally free society of the North, rare but dangerous evidence of black elevation steadily mounted, for despite concerted efforts to keep them in a state of degradation, African Americans did become educated, participate in public debate, produce art and literature, and generally exhibit all the markers of what antebellum Americans considered civilization. Few could remain ignorant of the exploits of a Frederick Douglass, and local elites ignored at their pocketbooks' peril the elevated status of wealthy African Americans such as James Forten of Philadelphia or George DeBaptiste of Detroit. Hence it became all the more important to argue for the inherent inferiority of blacks.

Black thinkers generally responded as might be expected, labeling the claims of emerging racial science a function (and fiction) of white supremacy. Black people, wrote J. W. Lewis, had been "stigmatized for the last three or four centuries, by cruel proscriptive spirit, that has instilled into the mind of the present generation, an idea that they are the worst part of the human family."[4] Black thinkers noted the perverse logic through which prejudice reinforced the measures that degraded blacks, thus creating the "evidence" that reinforced prejudicial beliefs. The denigration of blacks, Hosea Easton noted, came in "rather bad grace" from the race that had imposed the liabilities under which African Americans labored.[5] John H. Johnson railed against those who degraded blacks through slavery and then "pretended to raise a doubt respecting their real humanity," while David Walker excoriated those who spoke of blacks "as descending originally from the tribes of *Monkeys* or *Orang-Outangs*."[6] Frederick Douglass, typically, issued the most graceful exposé of this self-reinforcing process: "Ignorance and depravity, and the inability to rise from degradation to civilization and respectability, are the most usual allegations against the oppressed. The evils most fostered by slavery and oppression, are precisely those which slaveholders and oppressors would transfer from their system to the inherent character of their victims. Thus the very crimes of slavery become slavery's best defense."[7]

Many black leaders flatly denied the existence of distinct races. William Well Brown lectured his listeners that there was nothing in "race or blood, in color or features, that imparts susceptibility of improvement to one race over another." Environment—nurture rather than nature, condition rather than color—determined the characters of black people.[8] Others attacked the popular idea "that there are physical and mental distinctions between the negro and the white man—distinctions which must ever prevent them from an equal and harmonious participation in the blessings of democratic freedom."[9] The majority of these assertions took the form of declarations that the human family was united as one. The New York *Anglo-African* declared in no uncertain terms that the black man was a "UNIT WITH THE GREAT HUMAN RACE."[10] A physician by training, James McCune Smith wrote frequently on matters of race, concluding that "the black comprises no special variety of the human race, no distinctive species of mankind." Black people were instead "part and parcel of the great original stock of humanity."[11]

Other statements attacked specific components of white racialism. Many attacked scientific racism at its weakest point. Contemporary racial theorists such as Louis Agassiz, Samuel Morton, Josiah Nott, and George Gliddon all claimed that different races of men constituted biologically distinct species. The obvious capacity for races to interbreed, however, clearly put the lie to such claims. John H. Johnson lambasted these "Solomons" and "greater pretenders to physical science," flatly denying "that there is as much difference in the instinct and susceptibility of the races of men, as there is in the races of the lower animals."[12] A group of New York African Americans issued a statement to the state's white citizens, proclaiming, "A difference of color is not a difference of species. Our structure and organization are the same, and not distinct from other men."[13] And Austin Steward, once a slave, noted that the manifest ability of the races to intermingle argued for the biological equality of Africans. If God had "designed their blood to commingle until that of the African is absorbed in that of the European," he wrote, "then it is right, and amalgamation of all the different races should be universally practiced and approved."[14]

Others attacked the geographic determinism of scientific racism. The *Anglo-African* rejected the notion "that because the negro is *found* indigenous in low marshy coasts within the tropics . . . he is *therefore* adapted by nature" to labor there. "While he can *endure* a tropical climate," the paper said, "he can endure labor best, and thrive most in that climate which being temperate, is fitted to him as a MAN."[15] Concluding an extended discussion of racial differences, J. W. Lewis conceded "the probability that geographical location and difference of climate, must have had the effect to cause the diversity of the human appearance, as to color and feature, for even on the African continent there is a great difference." But from this he determined that the differences existing among people of different races were insufficient to argue that the races were fundamentally distinct. "The great principles of physical law," he concluded, "are alike in all human beings, in natural or original character, irrespective of color."[16] Of all the antebellum black thinkers who spoke on the issue of racial science, physician James McCune Smith did so most comprehensively. Smith objected to the scientific practices of racial theorists, who, he claimed, compared normative human skulls with aberrant black ones to arrive at the conclusion that black people were more like apes than men. Smith also rejected the notions that facial angles could measure brain capacity, that brain capacity determined intelligence, and that the leg bones of blacks were always more bent than those of whites.[17]

Refuting the claims of racial science and asserting the unity of the human family were not sufficient, however, for these did little to explain the apparent differences in social development among the world's peoples, let alone obvious somatic variation. Writer Robert Gordon posed the question leveled by many white contemporaries: if the New Testament stated that "God hath made of one blood all nations of men to dwell on all the face of the earth,"[18] how did it come to pass that "some nations arrived at almost the very acme of power, glory, and intelligence, whilst others are ignorant, and degraded, with no power, no glory, no intelligence?"[19] Responding to this question was not easy. The answer obviously could not entail any claim of inherent and immutable characteristics, lest African Americans reinforce the idea that blacks' degraded status signaled their fitness for servitude. Rather, an answer had to claim that whatever inferiority blacks labored under was transient and changeable.

Black leaders began by recalling understandings of individual human character, claiming that external conditions rather than blacks' natures had led to their admittedly lowly state. Both the need to respond to the hostile tenets of American nationalism and the rhetorical benefits conferred by the discourse of nationalism led them to quickly meld ideas of elevation with those of nation and race. Moving from the individual to the collective, they applied their theories of character to nations, examining history for clues as to the mutability even of national genius. They started from a position that could not have been more inimical to the racial determinism brewing out of the antebellum milieu: environmentalism. So rampant were notions of black inferiority that merely arguing for blacks' elevatability defied popular opinion and learned discourse. In instance after instance African American spokespersons argued that "color is but matter—that mind makes the man" and that "it is not the color of the skin that makes the man or the woman, but the principle formed in the soul." Racial differences, such statements argued, might not be denied, but they had little to do with the capacity to rise. The value of all this lay in identifying a mutable site of reformation: the world. Black elevation required only the removal of the external liabilities that suppressed it: enslavement in the South and the practices resulting from prejudice in the North. A Pittsburgh education society argued that the "moral depravity" it conceded many blacks suffered under "arises not from any thing in the constituent principles of their nature, but wholly from their raising."[20] All that was required to demonstrate the veracity of black equality was to relieve the race of its unnatural burdens. J. Holland Townsend demanded that America "take down the dams and bring the current upon a dead level, and not continually keep us stemming the tide, with winds and currents against us."[21] Time and time again, black writers argued that whites raised in precisely the same manner would exhibit precisely the same defects.

The argument was not new. As early as 1794, black leaders had responded to the concerns of those in the new republic who feared that the inherent licentiousness of black people unfitted them for citizenship. Such was the charge to which Absalom Jones and Richard Allen, two Methodist ministers from Philadelphia, responded in the wake of an outbreak of cholera in the city in 1793. After the crisis, several leading whites had claimed that during the epidemic the city's blacks had manifested their vicious natures, taking advantage of the situation by charging exorbitant fees to tend the stricken and bury the dead. Some, it was charged, had even begun robbing the sick. In defending their flock, Allen and Jones argued that, even if some had stepped beyond the bounds of propriety, the cause was not their internal natures. "We believe if you would try the experiment of taking a few black children, and cultivate their minds with the same care . . . as you would wish for your own children, you would find them upon the trial, they were not inferior in mental endowments."[22] To Allen and Jones, all were subject to vice because all shared a fundamental humanity, regardless of race.

Later thinkers made the same claim. In 1810, Daniel Coker, a minister for the African Methodist Episcopal Church in Baltimore, argued against charges that blacks were inherently vice-ridden. In his *Dialogue Between a Virginian and an African Minister*, which presented his fictionalized discussions on race with a white slaveholder, Coker's southerner feared emancipating his slaves because of their base nature: "Many," the slaveowner said, "have been so accustomed to the meaner vices, habituated to lying, pilfering, and stealing, so that when pinched with want, they would commit these crimes, become pests to society, or end their days on the gallows." Coker responded by claiming that the Virginian had "very justly observed, that holding these men in slavery is the cause of their plunging into such vicious habits," and urged his adversary to "remove the cause, that the effects may cease."[23] By 1833, such ideas had lost none of their power. In a public speech in Boston, Maria Stewart challenged white America: "Give the man of color an equal opportunity with the white from the cradle to manhood, and from manhood to the grave, and you would discover the dignified statesman, the man of conscience, and the philosopher."[24]

The period from the late 1830s to the Civil War, as environmentalism was giving way to a more essentialized view of human character, found black activists clinging tenaciously to the principle of environmentalism. While the idea was hardly moribund in the antebellum years, in an age increasingly enamored with racial and nationalistic rhetoric it gradually became the province of reformers, abolitionists, and black activists. Consider, for example, a typical statement from the day—one not directly addressed to the issue of race—on the subject of "constitutional" differences among men. Writing in the *Ladies' Repository* in 1844, H. Dwight championed the great significance of education and early childhood training in the formation of character. Yet he argued against those who "in their zeal to show the paramount importance of cultivation" had "gone so far as to attribute all difference to education and the circumstances of life." He rejected a more extreme environmentalism, which he said was "opposed to all ideas of genius, which is a gift of nature." Dwight's moderate environmentalism more closely typified the prevailing spirit of the antebellum North than did the radical variety espoused by black leaders. As environmentalist thinking in antebellum culture waned, black versions—which had remained remarkably constant—became increasingly radical, merely by virtue of their stasis.[25]

African American spokespersons melded these ideas of elevation and environmentalism with the discourse of nationalism to subvert the claims of their critics. In a public discourse increasingly predicated on the principles of romantic ethnic nationalism, they argued not simply for the elevatability of the minds and morals of individuals, but for those of the entire race. An atmosphere of nationalistic ideas exacerbated the phenomenon of racial synecdoche, which understood the failings of individual African Americans as indicative of their qualities as a race. If blacks shared so much natural common ground, it behooved them to demonstrate that the race as a whole could rise to the standards of those with seats at the table of nations. Given the growth of nationalism among white Americans, it became imperative.

For answers, black thinkers applied the principle of environmentalism to the history of nations. There was no reason why environmentalist arguments could not be applied to groups. A nation was, after all, a conglomeration of individuals, and national character the group manifestation of individual character. Mind and morals, the two elements of individual character, were reflected in nations in the form of civilization. The task thus became arguing not just for the mutability of individual character but for the mutability of national genius—for the possibility of creating a noble and progressive black civilization. For one Philadelphian, the history of nations offered proof "of how low any race may be brought, and how high they may be raised." [26] Racial theorist J. W. Lewis stated that "art and civilization" had given "Russia power over the rude Circassian," while "the intelligence of England" gave that nation "power over the poor China-man." In the "history of the human race," he wrote, "the superiority of one class over an inferior one, is only the result of improved opportunity in becoming intelligent, in the progress of civilization." [27]

According to black thinkers history demonstrated that all nations were fundamentally equal, though each was subject to historical circumstances that may temporarily benefit one over the others. The development of an advanced civilization was not a product of the inherent natures of a people but a result of historical circumstances that had favored some nations over others. Echoing arguments for individual elevation, Hosea Easton argued that "whatever differences there are in the power of the intellect of nations, they are owing to the differences existing in the causal laws by which they are influenced," rather than in the inherent natures of national peoples themselves. [28] Likewise, Henry Bibb editorialized that "by the operation of favorable causes, . . . nations may be elevated to the highest possible standard of excellence." [29] J. W. Lewis typified the uplifting impulse behind antebellum black nationalism: "Individuals in different nations, at different periods of the world's history," had through "dint of talent and self-exertion risen to honor and distinction." [30] Alexander Crummell considered that the rise of a black nation would cause black people in general to "rise gradually into a state of higher and nobler civilization and improvement" which would be "to the glory of God." [31]

Foremost among black proponents of historical environmentalism was John H. Johnson, a Philadelphian with an outspoken though decidedly elitist outlook. A product of the city's black intelligentsia, Johnson conceded the lowly state of the southern slaves, but attributed their degradation not to their African origins but to the lessons taught by slavery. In Africa, he argued, where the "natural manners of mankind" could be found, black people manifested no servility. In fact, he claimed, "the African is servile to none but his sovereign." Consequently, he argued that the slaves had been "degraded by tyrannical oppression"—that "the degraded and monkeyfied manners of such blacks . . . have been formed by training them to it."[32] The lesson? That "man is controlled by circumstances." The behavior of other nations proved this: Hindus, Siamese, and Russian serfs were "cringing and worshipful to the upper classes." Placed in like circumstances, "the offspring of the noblest minds of any country could be formed into characters equally as degraded and ridiculous in conduct" as enslaved blacks.[33] This was a popular argument among black leaders. Wrote J. W. Lewis: "Bar every door to mental and physical improvement to the Englishman or American, set in motion the whole machinery of despotism on them, turn the scoff and obloquy of the whole civilized world against them, and thus embitter their condition for four centuries, by turning against them the entire military, political and civil power of the world, and the degraded condition of their ancestors, the ancient Gauls, would be far above them. They would be as low as the most degraded African in this country."[34] Robert Gordon flipped Lewis's analogy on its head, suggesting that, were the infant child of Africa "snatched from the debasing influences which surrounded it, and made the subject of sound mental and moral discipline, its pursuits, habits, feelings, and desires would necessarily become totally different from what they would otherwise be."[35]

Of all the conditions imposed upon African Americans that inhibited their development, slavery and the slave trade were of course the worst offenders. Few articulated the effects of slavery as clearly as J. W. C. Pennington, a black abolitionist and author of the first textbook on black history. Slavery had degraded slaves, Pennington wrote, and made whites think that black people were "endowed with inferior capacities to the rest of mankind."[36] He was willing to concede that slaves were "vicious," but he ascribed this vice to the conditions imposed by slavery. For one, they had had "the corrupting influence of the masters' bad example before their eyes." In addition, "by incessant labor, the continual application of the lash, and the most inhuman treatment that imagination can devise, their genius is overwhelmed and hindered from breaking forth." Pennington concluded by pointing out that, when properly educated, "they do not discover any want of ingenuity."[37]

Once slavery and other such barriers to elevation were removed, black spokesmen contended, black civilization inevitably would progress, thus justifying emancipation. But no one could expect miracles. These authors noted that it had taken England ages to develop into the "august pinnacle of civilization" that she had become;[38] likewise, it would take time and the appropriate conditions for a black nation to rise. William Craft used his argument about British inferiority to demonstrate that "it had taken a long time to make the English men what they now were, and, therefore, it was not wonderful [to be wondered at] if the negroes made slow progress in intellectual development."[39] William Wells Brown stated that, just as few Romans would have imagined the ascent of the ancient Germans, "the blacks on this continent . . . are fast rising in the scale of intellectual development, and proving their equality with the brotherhood of man."[40]

A NATION, NOT A RACE

Environmentalism applied to national histories offered the great benefit of responding to hostile whites in terms they might value. With the tenets of romantic ethnic nationalism seeping into the American psyche, black leaders found it imperative to respond to hostile arguments through values that enjoyed widespread ideological currency. But arguing on terrain chosen by their enemies exacted a price. As they increasingly contested the ground of romantic nationalism, there was increasingly some creep toward its essentialist premises: that there were distinct categories of mankind, hereditarily determined, and that each was endowed with a set of inherent and immutable characteristics. This was never a central strain in black thought, but it was an important one, if not for the foundations it laid for later black cultural nationalism, then for what it said of the consequences of engaging the discourse of the public sphere.

Some black thinkers fell into essentialist traps despite their reliance upon the logic of environmentalism. It was entirely possible for environmentalism to find common ground with essentialism: Revolutionary-era doctor and abolitionist Benjamin Rush did so in his treatises on the causes of blackness. Arguing that Africans' skin color resulted from a disease akin to leprosy—originally contracted through Africa's "greater heat, more savage manners, and bilious fevers"—Rush contended that environmentally derived characteristics could become hereditary. While he used his conclusions to argue that Africans thus deserved "a double portion of our humanity" rather than enslavement, he also argued that their malady could be cured through extensive bloodletting and the inducement of "artificial diarrhoea."[41]

At times some black leaders strayed toward positing that environment could impart hereditary characteristics. Writing in 1836, Hosea Easton was among the first African American writers to elaborate this possibility. Easton argued that context played a large part in influencing individual nature. "A proper degree of exercise is essential to the growth of the corporeal system," he theorized, concluding "that the form and size depends on the extent and amount of exercise." Where law and social custom fostered exercise, as in the American Indian, the body responded by developing. The key was, he said, that "no constitutional difference exists in the children of men, which can be said to be established by hereditary laws"; whatever differences did exist were "causal or accidental." Easton's environmentalism was at times mild, stating nothing more than that the diet and exercise of mothers bore effects on their unborn babies.[42] At other times, however, he clearly argued that differences caused by environment could become hereditary. Regarding claims of blacks' physical characteristics—"sloped foreheads; prominent eye-balls; projecting under-jaw; certain distended muscles about the mouth, or lower parts of the face; thick lips and flat noses; hips and rump projecting; crooked shins; flat feet, with large projecting heels"—Easton was "perfectly willing to admit the truth of these remarks," for he was "aware that no language . . . is sufficiently descriptive to set forth in its true character the effect of that cursed thing, slavery." In another instance, Easton applied his logic to himself in ways that seemed to threaten his own humanity. "I wonder that I am a man," Easton wrote after considering how the foul institution had subverted the intent of nature, "for though of the third generation from slave parents, yet in body and mind nature has never been permitted to half finish her work."[43]

While few echoed Easton's ambivalence to such a degree, others occasionally slipped into racial environmentalism as an alternative to the hereditary imputation of racial difference. J. W. C. Pennington, one of the first African American historians, argued that just as nature "tempered the bodies of the different species of men in a different degree, to enable them to endure the respective climates of their habitation, so she gave them a variety of colour and appearance with a like benevolent design."[44] Henry Bibb accused white racial theorists of the "great error" of speaking of the "different branches of the human family" without reference to their histories. Yet, as an example of the influence of unfavorable causes, he cited the increasing degradation of agricultural laborers in England and the lower classes in Ireland, predicting that examination would reveal that their foreheads had become "low and retiring."[45] While denying that blackness itself conferred degradation, Bibb conceded that degradation could become a biologically inherent, hereditary trait. When black spokesmen ascribed racial traits to

African-descended people, they often and curiously remarked upon its intrinsic peacefulness and ability to endure oppression. According to James McCune Smith, black people had contributed to America "neither arts nor arms, nor institutions, nor physical beauty," but "endurance and love."[46] Thomas Hamilton believed black people held this power to endure in common with "the feline race"—likely a reference to effeminacy. Martin Delany thought blacks "civil, peaceable and religious to a fault"; in his view, these were the "native characteristics" and "inherent traits, attributes" that were "peculiar" to blacks.[47] Others said that blacks possessed "a natural timidity, a great lack of physical courage." It was not, said others, the "genius of the race" to make war.[48]

While clearly subordinated to the overwhelming need to respond to hostile arguments, black racialism nonetheless conceded much to the contemporary terms of debate. At other times, spokespersons invoked claims of blacks' inherent traits for purposes that offset these dangers by enhancing black unity. When newspaper editor Thomas Hamilton remarked on the innate capacities of the black "race" he likely had in mind not an internalized sense of racial inferiority, but a jeremiad designed to effect black uplift through collective identity. "In vitality, . . . we are, if different, superior to the whites," he wrote. "But this vitality, if a necessary, is not a very noble quality," for it represented "the power to endure" rather than "the power to effect" or "the power to do." Citing black peoples' inability to match whites "in making money, and building ships and palaces," he criticized African Americans for their failure to cohere, like whites, in the face of oppression: "We do not coalesce, agglutinate, organize on this principle, nor on any other."[49] To the degree that they were conceded to exist, then, inherent differences could be employed to spur black people to action.

At other times, black spokespersons used racial inherence to satire white supremacy, challenging the standards that whites used to claim their own superiority. Shortly after asserting the "civil" and "peaceable" nature of the race, the emigration convention of 1854 raised the ugly specter of race war by pointing out that the "coloured races," which outnumbered Caucasians two to one, would not "passively submit to the universal domination" of a minority of whites.[50] A writer in the *Anglo-African* modestly proposed that the English had enslaved Africans with the express purpose of infusing "the new blood of the undying African" into "the veins of their children."[51] In response to whites' claims that black people bore the mark of Cain through their skin complexion, J. W. Lewis wondered if whites' "ugly, unnatural disposition" and propensity for killing their brothers did not indicate that Europeans actually bore the mark.[52] Continuing in the historical vein, black historian J. W. C. Pennington pointed out that, as Noah's skin was "dark olive," whites should assert their primacy cautiously, for "the purest white is as far removed from the primitive colour as the deepest black."[53] John S. Rock similarly rejected white standards and celebrated the inherent qualities of the race when he admired "the fine tough muscular system, the beautiful, rich color, the full broad features, and the gracefully frizzled hair of the Negro." These he contrasted with the physical features of white people, concluding that "when the white man was created, nature was pretty well exhausted," but "did the best she could under the circumstances."[54]

What explains the troubling presence of racial essentialism among these black leaders? Despite the fact that leaders employed much of it in the service of emancipatory speech, it still constituted the infiltration of white supremacy's basic premises into black thought. That it would enter black speech unwittingly does little to mitigate the dangers involved; in fact, it exacerbated the problem enormously. Was black protest thought so vulnerable to hostile public speech that it could incorporate notions apparently inimical to its interests? Did not the presence of such ideas in black protest thought indicate an acceptance, even if unwitting, of hostile terms of debate? What sense can be made of an antiracist movement that embraced the premises of racism? Once again, rhetorical exigencies may not negate the negative implications, but it may help mitigate them. As we have seen, black leaders' use of racialist rhetoric hardly counted as an unqualified endorsement of white supremacy's conclusions. African Americans' appropriation and reconfiguration of racial essentialism on their own behalf may in fact have constituted an expression of considerable power, albeit rhetorical.

But even beyond this, moments in which black spokespersons evinced faith in inherent race traits partook not so much of the discourse of race as of the discourse of nation. Confusion over the issue—among both antebellum contemporaries and modern scholars—is not surprising. Racial science itself existed in only an inchoate form in the antebellum North, and this allowed for considerable latitude around its boundaries, especially in the popular mind. Ideas of nation flowed easily into ideas of race. In the early nineteenth century, few Americans clearly distinguished between the concepts. The twentieth century's familiar distinction between the hereditary features of a race and the political features of a nation had not developed by the end of the antebellum period. Biological science had yet to define race as primarily a matter of heredity; nationalism, with its talk of organic links between ancient peoples, often considered that people had shared inherent, hereditary traits. Just as white people often failed to distinguish between races and nations, so did black thinkers.

As romantic nationalism and racial theory intertwined increasingly in the nineteenth century, the words melded together to a considerable degree, so much so that even African American authors fell victim to their vagaries.[55] J. Theodore Holly seemed to make little distinction between the two concepts in his writings on black nationalism. Speaking of the United States, he wrote, "The european nationality of this country, can, and is doing, as much to give prestige to the character of the white race throughout the world as any nationality in Europe."[56] Neither did Alexander Crummell seem to distinguish between races and nations when he used the example of the Anglo-Saxon "nation" to demonstrate the potential of the "negro race."[57] J. W. Lewis, in his essay on the nature of the "African race," employed ideas of race and nation nearly interchangeably, labeling skin color a "peculiar diversity in national existence." And though race itself was not mentioned, an article in the New York *Anglo-African* evidenced the profusion of terms describing modes of human organization that was common in antebellum America. The author held that humanity was "but one life," though "made up of millions upon millions of molecular lives" organized into "nationalities and empires and peoples and tribes."[58]

As inconsistent as the application of these words was, each did possess distinct connotations. "Race" (or, in early versions, "rase") found its way into common English usage in the second half of the sixteenth century, emerging roughly with Europe's renewed interest in the observation of nature. It matured in the eighteenth, as the Enlightenment's mania for classification waxed. From its earliest incarnations, "race" had carried connotations of reproduction and biology—of breeds, stocks, lineages, and genealogies. As applicable to plants and animals as to humans, the word has always envisioned humans operating in the natural world. "Nation," a medieval word, preceded "race" in common English usage by at least two centuries, well before the "discovery" of uncivilized peoples and the rebirth of interest in the natural world that marked the Early Modern period. Like "race," "nation" referred to groupings of humans. In contrast to "race," however, its connotations lay in the political rather than the natural world. Of course, the word came to take on organic, hereditary components, but these never completely eclipsed its purely political usages (such as speaking of "the nation" as "the public").[59] The important thing was that a nation was something more than a race; it was a race sufficiently refined and elevated to have developed "civilization." While nations existed in a natural world that included races, not all races were or could become nations.

Retention of the political connotations of "nation" could always serve to distinguish it from "race" in important ways. Even when they confused the two words, African American authors suggested important differences in the concepts that underlay them. Even when they did not use the actual word "nation," they posited the black race as having all the qualities of a legitimate one, particularly a right to the respect of other nations. Whereas the human race described a biological category to which blacks might not even belong, nations described advanced social organizations, developed from ethnic groups, that shared basic rights to be acknowledged in the court of international affairs. Antebellum black nationalists did not claim they were owed treatment exactly equal to that of other nations; most understood the international arena to be one where might often made right. But they did demand what all legitimate nations deserved—the right of self-determination. The status of nationhood constituted what black northerners considered a national form of respectability. All people, including primitives and barbarians, belonged to a race. But such folk could never comprise a fully developed nation. Nationhood, then, promised to confer on blacks a claim not simply to humanity, but to rights and privileges becoming rare in an increasingly particularistic age.

Antebellum black nationalists took advantage of the fluid boundary between the discourses of nation and race to gain a measure of political legitimacy. According to popular ideas of antebellum Americans, different races were characterized by inequality, but nations seemed to share a fundamental equality. Functioning as a nation in the amoral international order, as black nationalists envisioned their race doing, implied a measure of respect that was absent in popular discussions of races, especially discussions of the black race. Suffused with religious ideas like the curse of Ham or by nascent conceptions of biological difference, popular racial ideas never spoke of races as equal. In contrast, understandings of the ways nations interacted implied some measure of equality; competition between nations, like competition between individuals in the liberal marketplace, took place on a playing field assumed to be neutral, even if individual talents or national geniuses were not. In return for associating black people with an equal and legitimate nation, they occasionally conceded differences between national peoples that bordered on the inherent, if not hereditary. These unintended incursions of essentialist rhetoric into their speech were the price black leaders paid for what they hoped might prove a powerful lever to move the public mind. In every instance black nationalists sought to twist the inherent differences of black people into arguments for racial uplift. They sought to demonstrate through individual and collective action their capacity to develop the "civilization" required to elevate the race to a nation.

ATION'S OTHERWISE PURE DRAPERY

While th̶ ̶m̶o̶v̶e̶ ̶f̶r̶o̶m̶ ̶r̶a̶c̶i̶a̶l̶ ̶t̶o̶ ̶n̶a̶t̶i̶o̶n̶tion constituted a defensive gesture designed to ̶p̶r̶o̶t̶e̶c̶t̶ ̶A̶f̶r̶i̶c̶a̶n̶ ̶A̶m̶e̶r̶i̶c̶a̶ns from charges of racial inferiority, black national̶i̶s̶t̶s̶ ̶a̶l̶s̶o̶ ̶a̶c̶c̶o̶m̶p̶l̶i̶s̶h̶e̶d̶ ̶a̶n̶ ̶a̶g̶gressive manipulation of the central tropes of American nationalism. In particular, the country's founding in a revolutionary struggle to achieve universal human liberty offered powerful symbols to innumerable black writers and speakers. Regardless of their position on the political spectrum and their degree of cynicism regarding America, African American spokespersons universally invoked the Founding Fathers' professed commitment to the equality of mankind. In the Declaration of Independence and the Constitution those such as Alexander Crummell found guarantees of "individual freedom, without let or hindrances." These founding documents provided for a government that would be impartial to all citizens—"indifferent to all arbitrary and conventional considerations."[60] Such ideas had manifest efficacy in justifying blacks' claims to equality. Black activists in Ohio predicated a petition to the state's whites for relief of their burdens on "the desire of universal man for liberty" and "your own acts when oppressed by Great Britain."[61] Time and again leaders celebrated the efforts of national founders who had "exhausted their blood and treasure" in "an arduous war, which achieved our independence and laid the foundation of the only reasonable republic on earth."[62]

If America's Revolutionary tradition offered a means through which African Americans might gain access to the benefits of American life, it also contained one glaring liability for black leaders. America had been founded on a belief that all deserved liberty without respect to race, but these very Founders had left slavery intact in the Constitution. How could a reverence for the spirit of the Revolutionary generation be reconciled with the Founders' all-too-obvious shortcomings? Did their willful neglect of slavery in the letter of the Constitution (and hence their tacit complicity with slavery) mean they believed slavery to be consistent with the democratic principles of the nation? In short, did the Revolutionary tradition buttress or undermine slavery and racial prejudice?

The overwhelming majority of African American leaders argued that regardless of the constitutional results the spirit that activated the American Revolutionaries was in every way inimical to the institution of slavery and the practices of racial prejudice. Many sought to strengthen the power of their appeal to founding principles by arguing that most of the Founding Fathers had intended to eliminate slavery. "It cannot be that the authors of our Constitution intended to exclude us from its benefits," wrote James Forten. Those Americans, sensitive to depredations which they themselves had just escaped, "felt that they had no more authority to enslave us, than England had to tyrannize over them." [63] Theodore Wright of New York argued that the Founders had "supposed that the great principles of liberty would work the destruction of slavery throughout this land." [64] According to black leaders, the national founding mythology (or at least its proper spirit) included black people under its broad aegis—that "the natural and indestructible principles of man" secured "the purest liberty God ever conferred" upon mankind.[65]

But the Revolution had been incomplete. The new nation "proclaimed freedom to all mankind" and "offered her soil as a refuge to the enslaved of all nations," wrote Philadelphia leaders. But they pointed to "one dark spot" that "still dimmed its lustre": "Domestic slavery existed among a people who had themselves disdained to submit to a master." [66] Most presented slavery as inconsistent with founding myths and national principles by pointing out that the country became "contaminated with slavery" under rule by tyrannical colonial overlords rather than by freedom-loving Americans. Only under the British did "the human species first became an article of merchandize," argued Nathaniel Paul.[67] A radical few, such as Illinois's H. Ford Douglas, refused to exonerate colonials from complicity, condemning the self-justifying claims of those like Thomas Jefferson as mere rationalizations. The Framers debated slavery openly and still left it intact, according to Douglas, thus "engrafting into the Constitution a clause legalizing and protecting one of the vilest systems of wrong ever invented by the cupidity and avarice of man." [68] Militants like Henry Highland Garnet echoed these claims, lecturing enslaved African Americans that the colonials had revolted in the name of universal human liberty only to deny that freedom to others. Once in power, he asked, "Did they emancipate the slaves? No; they rather added new links to our chains." They "blew but one blast of the trumpet of freedom and then laid it aside." [69] Choosing profit over principles, expedience over ethics, the slaveholders of the Revolutionary generation had used the threat of disunion to blackmail the nascent United States into complicity with the greatest possible violation of liberty.

The lessons of the incomplete Revolution served as one of the most solid cornerstones of black protest thought. Exposing the "gross inconsistency of a people who had themselves 'farried o'er the wave' for freedom's sake" also provided black speakers some of their most eloquent and rhetorically satisfying moments.[70] Mulling over the existence of slavery in the nation's capital, editor Philip Bell remarked that he who studies America "will hear the words of freedom, and he will see the practice of slavery." His indictment of Americans' hypocrisy continued: "Men who sell their fellow creatures will discourse to him of indefensible rights; he will be taught the affinity between the democrat and the tyrant; he will look for charters, and find ———; expect liberty, and be met by bigotry and prejudice."[71] Such a nation, concluded an Ohio black convention, "forfeits her claim to be called Christian or Republican."[72] Continuing in this vein, one black newspaper correspondent asked in the wake of the Compromise of 1850, "Would not the Devil do well to *rent out hell* and move to the United States?"[73] Samuel Ringgold Ward issued dire warnings to the republic of the consequences of its hypocrisy: "If Republican Institutions are to be despised, if Profession and Principle are to be, in America, two *distinct*, not only, but *antagonistic* entities; if hypocrisy is always to be written in legible characters, upon the figurehead of American Democracy; if complete, unchecked, eternal supremacy is to be given to the Despotism now controlling this question, then, *not* upon the Blacks, will descend the indignant scorn of an on-looking world."[74]

If such statements excoriated the nation for its unfulfilled promises, they also suggested the depth of black leaders' commitment to its underlying principles. Hearkening back to Revolutionary principle was far more than a powerful rhetorical strategy; it lay at the basis of black leaders' self-conception. J. W. Lewis declared his natural rights to be "a gift of my Maker," and insisted, "No power on earth, acting under any legal authority, can trample down my right, without stepping over the boundaries of God's dominion."[75] In short, black leaders believed and proclaimed that the Declaration of Independence extended to all. Conspicuously bracketing the question of women's rights, Michigan blacks resolved in convention that "the definition of 'the people,' is all men."[76] Wrote James Forten, "This idea embraces the Indian and the European, the savage and the Saint, the Peruvian and the Laplander, the white man and the African."[77] Ohio leaders cared not "how degraded the man" or "where he may dwell"; all, they vowed, possessed an innate love of liberty.[78] Human rights were "not to be graduated by the shades of color that tinge the cheeks of men," nor were they to be denied to any, "however low in the scale of civilization."[79]

In their minds, black thinkers' fundamental commitment to natural rights philosophy clearly put them at odds with the nation, but not against its best principles. In the words of Austin Steward, slavery was the "foul stain" cast upon the nation's "otherwise pure drapery."[80] Even ardent black nationalists such as Martin Delany referred to the United States as a "wrecked but not entirely shattered system."[81] Many black leaders drew a distinction between the nation and its principles, remarking that "mere devotion to preservation of the Republic is not devotion to freedom."[82] And black thinkers consistently stressed the limited nature of their demands, stressing that they desired not to overturn the revolution, merely to fulfill it. "We profess to be republicans, not jacobins nor agrarians," proclaimed the black and white trustees of Noyes Academy, a school opened to black and white alike in 1834.[83] This strategy possessed the great virtue of demanding little of the nation—simply that it adhere to its own principles. "We do not ask you to countenance any change destructive to your form of government," Ohio conventioneers petitioned the state legislature, explaining that the changes for which they asked would constitute "but the legitimate result of a proper appreciation of the Declaration of Independence and our Bill of Rights."[84] Declared others, "We do not war with those principles."[85] By resisting America on the grounds that it failed to live up to its own ideals, African Americans proclaimed themselves not revolutionaries, but American Revolutionaries—upholders of the true spirit of the American republic. They claimed the tradition of the Revolution for themselves, even if it required jettisoning the empty husk of democracy that was the United States. "We love our country," resolved the black national convention of 1843, "but *we love liberty more.*"[86]

Few were capable of expressing the resultant feelings toward the nation as eloquently as Frederick Douglass. His famous Fifth of July address, delivered before an audience in Rochester, New York, in 1852, is well remembered as a masterpiece of oratory. The key to the speech's power consisted in metonymy: Independence Day served as a metaphor for citizenship and national inclusion, the event itself celebrating not just the signing of the Declaration of Independence but the principles of universal human liberty contained in it. Those enjoying the full benefits of American liberty and citizenship could partake of the celebration; those denied liberty and citizenship could not. Douglass had been invited to speak at the event as a gesture of inclusion, an expression of liberality on the part of the town's white citizens. Yet just as blacks' mere presence in the nation hardly constituted their enjoyment of national promises, so too Douglass's presence at the celebration could not stand in for equal participation. To ask Douglass to speak was "to drag a man in fetters into the grand illuminated temple of liberty, and call upon him to join in joyous anthems," it was an act of "inhuman mockery and sacrilegious irony."[87]

Douglass's questioning of his own ability to address the audience as a participant in the civic community served as the speech's central figure for blacks' liminality. "Why am I called upon to speak here today?" he asked.

"What have I or those I represent to do with your national independence? Are the great principles of political freedom and of natural justice, embodied in that Declaration of Independence, extended to us?" Any attempt to speak as an American, Douglass claimed, would be hollow. It was not that Douglass chose not to speak, it was that whatever speech he could muster would be meaningless, moot, without liberty and equal rights. On this remarkable day, when even "the dumb might eloquently speak" to express their gratitude to the nation that had secured their freedoms, the ever loquacious Douglass could not even begin to. To do so required the speaker to be included in the national project, and, said Douglass, he was "not that man." To have spoken without such qualification, Douglass feared, would have been to participate in the fiction of American freedom, to have become an accomplice in the fantasy that arguments remained to be marshaled, or that opportunities for persuasion persisted. The time for speech was over, Douglass declared. "It is not light that is needed, but fire; it is not the gentle shower, but thunder."[88]

Yet of course Douglass had been speaking, if only as an outsider, and he continued to, even as he argued against his capacity to do so. And it was in the questioning of his own presence—both at the podium and in the nation—that he launched his most potent attacks on the slaveholding republic:

> Am I to argue that it is wrong to make men brutes, to rob them of their liberty, to work them without wages, to keep them ignorant of their relations to their fellow men, to beat them with sticks, to flay their flesh with the last, to load their limbs with irons, to hunt them with dogs, to sell them at auction, to sunder their families, to knock out their teeth, to burn their flesh, to starve them into obedience and submission to their masters? Must I argue that a system thus marked with blood and stained with pollution is wrong? No; I will not.

The speech thus constituted a supreme instance of *praeteritio*, wherein the denial of his capacity to speak actually permitted Douglass to speak volumes. To the slave, Douglass told his audience,

> your celebration is a sham; your boasted liberty an unholy license; your national greatness, swelling vanity; your sounds of rejoicing are empty and heartless; your denunciation of tyrants, brass-fronted impudence; your shouts of liberty and equality, hollow mockery; your prayers and hymns, your sermons and thanksgivings, with all your religious parade and solem-

nity, are to him mere bombast, fraud, deception, impiety, and hypocrisy—a thin veil to cover up crimes which would disgrace a nation of savages.

This language, with its heavy emphasis on possessive pronouns, placed Douglass and his enslaved brethren exactly on the margin, perched between citizenship and utter alienation—*in* the country but not *of* it, at the celebration but mute. "This Fourth of July is *yours*," he intoned to his white audience, "not *mine. You* may rejoice, *I* must mourn." [89]

Such sentiments, fueled by mounting frustration, often led to outright denials of loyalty to America. In 1856, California African Americans met in convention, where a heated floor debate erupted over a resolution declaring blacks' loyalties to the nation. The conflict began when a William H. Newby spoke against a resolution declaring that California's African Americans "hail with delight" the "onward progress" of the nation and would "freely cast [their] lot in the fortunes of battle, to protect her against foreign invasion." Such statements had become common moments in black petitions and resolutions, designed to argue for black rights on the ideological terrain of oppressors rather than risk charges of sedition. But now Newby argued that a blind allegiance to a country that oppressed them acknowledged "a degree of servility, that would make us undeserving of the sympathy and respect of just men." Newby echoed the principles Douglass had set forth, contending that those who may not partake fully of American liberty had no place declaring their patriotism. "In a white man," he stated, patriotism "may be worthily indulged. . . . But to the colored people . . . patriotism may be a vice." In a nation wherein "the same institutions that bless the white man, are made to curse the colored man," he could not in good conscience attest to his loyalty. "I would hail the advent of a foreign army upon our shores," he continued, "if that army provided liberty to me and my people in bondage." Newby's argument carried the day, and the resolution went down in defeat. Once again, African Americans had pledged their ultimate loyalty to the principles underlying the republic, not to the nation that had violated them. [90]

When events conspired against black interests, as seemed the case increasingly as the 1850s wore on, denunciations of American identity could become extreme indeed. For example, in the wake of the Dred Scott decision in 1857 many northern blacks surpassed mere rhetoric in renouncing the country of their birth. Ohio conventioneers declared that "colored men are absolved from all allegiance to a government which withdraws all protections." [91] Robert Purvis, a prominent black Philadelphian, declared the nation "one of the basest, meanest, most atrocious despotisms that ever saw the face of the sun." He rejoiced in the prospect of "this atrocious government being overthrown, and a better one built up in its place."[92]

Britain in particular offered a nation to which blacks imagined owing alternative allegiances. The Canadian provinces, long a haven for liberty-seeking slaves from America, had been free since Great Britain abolished slavery in her empire in 1832. Despite a monarchical form of government that warred with the democratic principles upon which the United States had been founded, Canada offered many blacks a viable alternative to the slaveholding republic. Many black leaders asserted that, in the event of renewed warfare between Britain and the United States (the War of 1812 was well within living memory), those African Americans seeking refuge in Canada had little incentive to fight for their native country. "What inducement," asked Austin Steward, "have colored men to defend with their lives the United States?"[93] Such queries were not mere rhetoric. In 1841, when Great Britain commandeered the U.S. slave trader *Creole* and released its captives, talk of war challenged African Americans to assess their allegiances. Many echoed the black editor who asked, "If war be declared, shall we fight with the chains on our limbs? . . . Shall we make our bodies a rampart in defence of American slavery?"[94] When in 1838 a few hundred New Yorkers skirmished over Canadian land in an incident known as the Patriot War, fugitive slaves in Canada faced a similar dilemma. J. W. Loguen, the African Methodist Episcopal Zion minister who frequently lectured to the fugitives, insisted that in the event of war between the two nations "the blacks of Canada will be found over-leaping national boundaries," ready to "imprint upon the soil of slavery as bloody a lesson as was ever written."[95] In the 1850s, black emigrationists also considered Canada a site where blacks might join together to become "terrible in any conflict which might ensue" with America.[96]

AT FREEDOM'S SHRINE

Despite the deep frustrations they manifested, statements rejecting the United States did not drown out professions of national loyalty. Time and again black leaders asserted their claims to American identity, often in statements simultaneously attacking the nation's racial injustice. Rejections of America never opposed the principles underlying its founding, merely the nation that had failed to ensure those principles for all it encompassed. Nonetheless, counterbalancing blacks' faith in America were clear rhetorical imperatives that demanded they assert their loyalty—notably, the charge laid against them that they constituted a threatening alien presence in the nation. Blacks' critics had labeled them "a distinct and inferior race, repugnant to our republican feelings, and dangerous to our republican institutions."[97] African Americans therefore first needed to demonstrate their very fitness for inclusion in the civic community.

In the face of such charges African Americans often contended that despite being black they were above all American. "We are native born Americans," claimed Cincinnati blacks. "We owe no allegiance to any other country on earth."[98] According to Austin Steward, blacks were "allied to this country by birth."[99] Former slave Henry Bibb claimed America as his native country; he rejected American colonizationists, saying, "If they carry me to the shores of Africa they carry my lifeless body."[100] As Bibb's remarks indicated, statements of American identity were often directed against efforts to remove blacks to Liberia. "We can never give countenance," resolved one black convention, "to any scheme based upon the assumption that colored Americans have not as good [a] right to life, liberty and the pursuits of happiness as white and red Americans."[101] In the wake of calls to emigrate blacks, African Americans in Wilmington, Delaware, resolved that they were "natives of the United States." Africa, they insisted, was "neither our nation nor home." Blacks in Rochester, New York, concurred, stating, "We do not consider Africa to be our home, any more than the present whites do England, Scotland, or Ireland."[102] The movement to remove blacks from the nation constituted a rhetorical imperative to which African Americans responded through simple negation: the American Colonization Society claimed blacks should go to Africa because they did not belong in America; most black leaders responded by claiming that they should not, because they did.

By virtue of their American nativity, black leaders claimed, they were American by culture and civic education. "Our language, habits, manners, morals and religion are all different from those of Africans," declared Wilmington blacks.[103] Blacks were American, argued others, "by birth, genius, habits, language, &c."[104] Black New Yorkers professed to be both "American and republican," infused since youth with faith in the "operations of our government."[105] The black national convention of 1853 similarly premised its argument for inclusion on this basis of shared culture: "We ask that, speaking the same language and being of the same religion, worshipping the same God, owing our redemption to the same Savior, and learning our duties from the same Bible, we shall not be treated as barbarians."[106]

Black leaders claimed status as Americans not simply by culture but also by contribution. The statement of a convention of New York African Americans in 1840 pointed out, "[Since the founding of the nation], our fathers, and we ourselves, have lent our best strength in cultivating the soil, in developing its vast resources, and contributing to its wealth and importance."[107] In 1832 at a black protest of July the Fourth, Peter Osbourne, a leader from New Haven, Connecticut, asked: "Our forefathers fought, bled and died to achieve the independence of the United States. Why should we forebear contending for the prize?"[108] Military service in particular seemed to justify blacks' claims to liberty. "In times when patient toil and hardy industry were demanded, . . . we have ever been present and active," a New York black convention pointed out. "*In times of peril has our aid been called for, and our services promptly given.*" It went on to rehearse a long history of black participation in the United States' struggles for liberty.[109] "The facts of history," claimed the national convention of 1853, demonstrated the "courage and fidelity" displayed by blacks' ancestors "in defending the liberties and in achieving the independence of our land."[110] Others—notably historians J. W. C. Pennington, William Wells Brown, and William Howard Day—fleshed out black contributions to the nation's founding, effectively establishing the study of black history through a recounting of African Americans' manifest willingness to support the nation in times of crisis.[111] Enlarging upon the exploits of men like Crispus Attucks, a fugitive slave whom African Americans claimed to be the first to fall during the Boston Massacre in 1765; Peter Salem, a black soldier who reputedly shot the British Major Pitcairn at Bunker Hill; and blacks who participated in the War of 1812, the encyclopedic nature of the information their books offered was central to their point. William C. Nell called such recitations "facts piled Olympus high in proof that the colored American has ever proved loyal, and ready to die, if need be, at Freedom's shrine."[112]

Yet it was at *freedom's* shrine, and not America's, that African American leaders paid obeisance. Even in their most ardent expressions of patriotism, spokespersons let it be known that blacks owed their primary loyalty to liberty rather than to the nation. Leaders professed American identity almost always in the service of arguments for inclusion in the benefits of national life. Antebellum black history threw down a gauntlet before blacks' critics. As Charles L. Remond put it, "If colored people have . . . shrunk from dangers or responsibility, let it be made to appear." Remond believed, as did so many others, that "the history of the country must ever testify on their behalf." He therefore claimed for blacks "every advantage set forth in the Constitution" on "the naked principle of merit."[113]

Laying claim to the spirit of the Revolution offered blacks a way of expressing loyalty to the nation without conceding their own inferiority and a way of resisting their oppression without the risk of further alienating a potentially helpful public through claims of sedition. But the tightrope that Revolutionary rhetoric permitted them to walk never left the specter of violence too far from their minds. The Founders, after all, had staked their own and their nation's fates on the right of a people to change their government when it became destructive of their inalienable rights. True, "prudence" dictated that such upheavals should not be undertaken for "light and transient causes," yet African Americans pointed out that surely the oppressions under which the American revolutionaries had suffered paled in comparison to their own. David Walker asked white Americans if their sufferings under their British overlords had been "one hundredth part as cruel and tyrannical as you have rendered ours under you?"[114] "If the American revolutionists had excuse for shedding but one drop of blood," claimed fugitive slaves in New York, "then have the American slaves excuse for making blood flow 'even unto the horsebridles.'"[115] As early as 1808 Boston blacks were asking: if white Americans thought freedom a "privilege truly desirable to be enjoyed, when her mother nation was about to invade her land," why should it not be the same "to any or all nations of the earth," blacks included?[116] "Flora," a Philadelphian, compared the oppressions that blacks suffered to those that led English Protestants to behead a Catholic king.[117] Many thus concluded that oppressed blacks surely had the right to secure their natural rights, through violence if necessary. The militant H. Ford Douglas declared that a government that "fails to protect the rights of man . . . ought to be eraced from the category of nations, and be numbered with the sleeping despotisms that have long sunk beneath the proud and majestic march of advancing civilization."[118]

The threat of violence in defense of black rights hung undeniably over all invocations of the Revolutionary tradition. Black thinkers frequently claimed themselves in the midst of "a second revolutionary struggle" against the forces of tyranny.[119] They predicted a "great and coming conflict with their haughty oppressors," a "sharp contest between the friends of Freedom and the southern oligarchy."[120] These were to be the direct results of a policy of denying blacks their God-given rights, leaders warned. Stephen Myers, editor of a black newspaper in Albany, New York, warned that unless the slave regime ceased its oppressive practices—such as "the cruel separation of families"—"revolution will but the sooner break out."[121] Others provoked dire visions of "Spartacus and his servile band" or "the horrors of the revolutionary scenes of St. Domingo," as the logical consequences of oppression.[122] When a black newspaper reprinted the *Confessions of Nat Turner* in late 1859, the moral was that "humanity will out," even in the midst of slavery, to "engender from its bosom forces that will contend against oppression."[123]

Spokespersons designed such arguments to appeal as much to the self-interests of oppressors as to their better natures. Blacks had little access to effective peaceful mechanisms for securing their rights. Almost utterly deprived of the means to defend themselves through the political system, they were left only with options that lay outside of formal politics. Ohio blacks complained that they were, "by the organic law of the State, . . . prevented from defending those precious rights by any other than violent means." The "natural consequences" of such a policy would follow: the state, they warned, "will contain within her limits a discontented population—dissatisfied, estranged—ready to welcome any revolution or invasion as a relief, for they can lose nothing and gain much."[124] Thomas Hamilton of the *Weekly Anglo-African* noted that "oppressed men resolving to liberate themselves make use, and are justified in that use, of the best means in their power to that end." Deprived of access to the political system or even of noble warfare, the tools of the resistant slave—"the tinder-box, the match, and the torch"—were "the only weapons of warfare left him." To those whites who criticized such methods of resistance as barbaric, Hamilton charged that those who had enslaved and debased Africans were "rather bad judges of what niceties their victims should use in their endeavors to release themselves from such a hellish thraldom."[125]

Arguments such as this hoped to elicit change by presenting it as an alternative to even more nightmarish outcomes. Indeed, many argued that the very forces that proslavery apologists found so reprehensible had served to maintain their fragile regime far beyond its years. Thomas Hamilton declared that the northern movement to abolish slavery was far from "inimical to the institution of slavery." Rather, he argued, it served "as its greatest safety valve; the escape pipe through which the dangerous element incident to slavery found vent."[126] Elsewhere, Hamilton termed the Underground Railroad and Christianity "the two great safety-valves" that released or subdued "the restless and energetic among the slaves."[127] The *Colored American* concurred, claiming that only the South's close ties with the North had prevented it from exposure to "HEAVEN'S CURSE" and the "REVENGE OF BLOOD GUILTINESS." Leave the South to itself, it continued, "and her *patriotic slave system* would soon work out its own redemption through *rivers of blood*."[128]

Apart from its rhetorical efficacy in confronting an intransigent nation, the threat of black-initiated revolutionary change also held great promise as the force through which the nation would be redeemed. In black thinkers'

Revolution folded effortlessly into notions of national
... any of their white contemporaries, they understood
... ite upon which God would fulfill his plan of creating
... t of man. Unlike their white contemporaries, they
... the creation of a racial paradise. Wrote William J.
Wilson:

> This we fully believe to be the ultimate design of God. On this continent,
> which for so many centuries lay buried from sight of civilization, God in-
> tends, in his providence, ultimately to bring men of every clime, and hue,
> and tongue, in one great harmony, to perfect the greater system of man's
> highest earthly government. Then shall be the reign of perfect peace.[129]

While they clearly shared elements of national destiny with other Americans, black thinkers could not endorse the others' faith in its progress.
America was indeed a place destined by God as the most free and perfect form of government on earth, but that promise had yet to be fulfilled. National redemption remained to be worked out, perhaps through
the words and bodies of African Americans themselves. One black Penn-
sylvanian lauded blacks' efforts to elevate themselves, trusting that "God
may use them to save this nation from that abyss of ruin towards which its
brutal pride and folly are driving it headlong."[130] America represented to
blacks not an achieved millennium but one yet to happen. The National
Convention of 1835 put the issue succinctly: "If America is to be instrumen-
tal through the providence of Almighty God in blessing other portions of
the peopled earth" through its example, "how necessary is it that she should
first purify her own dominions." Purification clearly entailed the extension
of political liberties to blacks, so that, in the words of the convention, "the
laws of our country may cease to conflict with the spirit of that sacred in-
strument, the Declaration of Independence."[131] Only then would America
be "the great example of all nations aspiring to become free."[132]

THE ULTIMATE DESIGN OF GOD

In addition to appealing to the principles of the American Revolution and
the logic of elevation, African American nationalism in the antebellum
North drew upon religious language and imagery. Relying on their own theodicy and jeremiads and melding these with important principles of nationalism, African American leaders addressed white America and black. To the
former they issued dire warnings of the consequences of betraying divine
favor through the practice of enslavement and discrimination. In the latter

they sought to imbue a sense of destiny similar to that which white Americans enjoyed. Religious black nationalism told African American northerners they were part of a special community with a divine mission. It told them *how* to be in that community, and why.[133]

Black thinkers embraced American nationalism's premise of chosenness, though they took their assumptions down radically different pathways. Many agreed that America had been destined to fulfill a special role in world history and God's plan. Edward Blyden considered America "the place which seems to have been designed for the rejuvenescence of eastern senility, for the untrammeled exercise and healthful growth of the principles of political and ecclesiastical liberty."[134] This view often presented the institution of slavery as not inherently or necessarily evil. Recounting the ancient history of slavery, seminal black historian J. W. C. Pennington suggested that many slaves in the ancient world had held favored status and were blessed by humane treatment. Those in ancient Athens, he contended, enjoyed rights to free speech and to the fruits of their own labor. These nominal slaves, he claimed, suffered little of the "caprice and passion" imposed on those in southern bondage.[135] In some interpretations, the slave trade actually figured as an agent of beneficence. According to African colonizationist Edward Blyden, the slave trade accompanied two great advances in "the history of human improvement": the invention of the printing press and the "discovery" of America. Originally a boon for Blyden's benighted people, the trade "dragged Africa, rather tardy in the march of nations," into an age of civilization and improvement. At this point, Blyden claimed, Europeans' "glorious design of civilizing poor benighted Africa" offset the forced deportation of Africans from their homeland. As in the ancient form of slavery that Pennington lauded, Europeans in the trade's early days regarded the care of their slaves as a solemn oath; in Blyden's words, they "felt bound to instruct them, and, in every way, to ameliorate their condition." The relation between European and African at this stage of the trade resembled that of "guardian and protégé" rather than master and slave.[136]

Like so many previous chosen people, however, Europeans and white Americans lost God's favor through a fatal betrayal of divine law. Some, like New York minister Nathaniel Paul, described slavery itself as contrary to the "sacred mandate of heaven."[137] David Walker believed that Jesus had "handed a dispensation," or special favor, to Europeans; but Europeans had, he lamented, "made *merchandise* of us," and thus violated their covenant.[138] Others suggested that it was the peculiar form of American slavery that violated the will of God. According to Blyden, "the virulent features of the trade were not developed until the enormous gains which were found to result

from the toil of the African." At that point, he explained, the profit mo-
tive began to displace the civilizing imperative, and "unutterable cruelties"
resulted.[139] What had originally been a salutary institution that benefited
Africans by bringing them into the pale of western civilization degenerated
into an inhuman exercise in tyranny, opposed to the will of God. Nathaniel
Paul's views echoed Thomas Jefferson's argument in the draft of the Declaration of Independence. Had European nations not habituated Americans
to "the absurd luxuries of life," Paul argued, "the spirit of pure republicanism" that existed in the breasts of the patriots of the American Revolution
would have ensured that slavery never would have gained a foothold in the
nation.[140] In thus displacing responsibility for American slavery by foisting it
onto the backs of the European colonizers who introduced the slave trade,
Paul (and Jefferson) salvaged a core of America that might be set right.

   In these conceptions, the story of modern American slavery echoed a tradition of Christian millennialism, which had its roots in the Old Testament
narrative of God's covenant with the children of Abraham, their descent
into Egyptian bondage, and their subsequent deliverance by God. The tri-
umphalist elements of this narrative never strayed far from the cautionary
tales it contained. Black thinkers found inspiration not simply in their frequent references to the Exodus from Egypt but in the New Testament's description of the relationship between God and the Israelites, a description
that frequently bordered on anti-Semitic. Typical of this approach was the
interpretation of Episcopal clergyman William Douglass, who preached that
the Israelites had been under God's "special guidance, government and protection," had been "favored above all other nations with the means of religious instruction, temporal security and prosperity." When they "groaned
under the Egyptian yoke, God delivered them with a high hand and with
an out-stretched arm." Yet throughout their history they remained a "rebellious and stiff-necked people." When at last the Jews strayed from divine
will by putting Jesus to death, God's justice "was signally executed upon
the Jewish nation"—Jerusalem fell brutally to the Romans during the Jewish
War of the first century A.D.[141] J. W. Loguen offered a similar interpretation.
Israel had been God's chosen nation, but the pharisee Caiaphas "gave up
his church and country to be murdered when he gave up Jesus to be murdered." God passed on his grace to the newly formed Christian church. The
lesson: "When a church ceases to honor its Lord by a life devoted to his
uses—when it is a covering for selfish and worldly aims, it has like the Jewish
Church . . . lost its life." The implications were clear: just as God passed on
his grace to Christendom in the wake of Jewish apostasy, so too He would

abandon the Christian church and the American nation for betraying His divine will by enslaving Africans.[142]

The story of enslavement in America, then, replicated the original fall from God's grace. As a type of this archetypal Eden tale, enslavement posed a problem that had confronted Judeo-Christian theology since its inception. Christianity posited a supremely powerful deity who was also supremely benevolent. How could such a god permit evil and suffering to exist? It is not difficult to understand the poignancy of such questions among African-descended people, who had been subjected to far more than their fair share of misfortune. As racial theorist J. W. Lewis wrote: "It is a question in the mind of many, why an infinite God can allow such a violation of human rights, and so much physical suffering, and so much blood-stained soil." The stakes here were terribly high; nothing less than their faith in Christianity lay on the line. As Lewis put it, if he could believe that God could "by an act of arbitrary power despise his own work," it would obliterate in his mind "all love and reverence to that God as a good being."[143] The solution was to believe that God was all powerful yet chose not to exercise his power completely; that men were permitted to perpetrate evil but God worked more subtly to redeem the world. Nathaniel Paul put these words in the mouth of God: "It is my sovereign prerogative to bring good out of evil, and cause the wrath of man to praise me." Consequently, Paul concluded, "what was in itself evil and vicious, was permitted to carry along with it some circumstance of palliation."[144] In this case, palliation appeared in the guises of Christianity and civilization. According to another black leader, when God "suffered the first swarthy man to be inveighed, entrapped, and stolen from Africa," he "overruled the evil intentions of men for the benefit of mankind," by placing blacks "in the midst of the path of progress."[145] Although "Almighty God has not permitted us to remain in the land of our forefathers," wrote former slave Austin Steward, he allowed Africans "to behold those best and noblest of his gifts to man"—namely, religious and civil liberty. African Americans owed their enjoyment of American life, limited though it was, "to that curse, the bitter scourge of Africa." "Slavery," he told his compatriots, "has been your curse, but it shall become your rejoicing."[146]

Yet a question remained: why had God waited so long for the hour of their deliverance? The answers drew upon the notion of free will in much the way Puritan theodicy did. Human virtue—the capacity to honor God—lay in free will; obedience without moral choice was meaningless. God had the power to enforce his law, yet chose not to interfere with humans' exercise of free will so that they might honor God by choosing virtue. According to Loguen, the Christian nation "was free to obey God according to its own mind."[147] According to William Douglass, God forbore punishment of sinners as a sign of his infinite mercy, granting them time that they "may be suitably affected, and so be led to repentance and salvation."[148] Blacks' misfortune, then, did not at all signify their abandonment by God. To the contrary, it served as the means of their redemption. Edward Blyden theorized that before the coming of the millennium "one of the most ancient and powerful states must pass through a series of unprecedented calamities." From the ashes of this thus-purified people "must spring forth the germ of the chosen people," whose regeneration would herald "the redemption and delivery of Africa."[149] Poet Frances Ellen Watkins explained black suffering with similar logic: "Adversity, to the race, has been a training school."[150]

But training for what? Of the forthcoming destruction of slavery few African American northerners had much doubt. Speaking at an anniversary celebration of the ending of the slave trade to America, George Lawrence cautioned that "the time is fast approaching when the iron hand of oppression must cease to tyrannize over injured innocence."[151] "The day of exact reckoning is approaching," warned another, "a day when, whether men will or no, the just measure shall be meted out to all, . . . and this our portion of it will not surely be forgotten."[152] Their faith secure that the final days were nigh, blacks launched continual jeremiads directed to white Americans, illustrating the dangers of their recalcitrant stance toward slavery's abolition. Through these, they hoped to "touch the heart of the American nation" and warn those loyal to the slaveholding country "of their follies and the fate of the great empires of antiquity."[153] Pointing out that in the past God had "destroyed kings and princes, for their oppression of the poor slaves,"[154] they charged white America: "You are verily guilty. . . . God will hold you responsible."[155] According to William Douglass, a merciful God long "holds back the bolt," but "nothing but timely repentance can avert a national punishment."[156] God had not "forgotten how to use His right hand for the deliverance of the poor and oppressed," wrote historian J. W. C. Pennington, and warned, "If tyrants have forgotten the history of the doings of that right hand in olden times, He is able to write a new one for their especial benefit."[157] The means for delivering this judgment might be the slaves themselves, cautioned H. Ford Douglas: "You must either free the slaves, or the slaves will free themselves. All history confirms the fact."[158] David Walker launched the most strident attacks of all, warning white Americans, "Unless you speedily alter your course, *you* and your *Country are gone*!!!!!! For God Almighty will tear up the very face of the earth!!! . . . Oh Americans!

Americans!! I warn you in the name of the Lord, (whether you will hear, or forbear,) to repent and reform, or you are ruined!!!" [159]

Where exactly African Americans stood in relation to the coming millennium was a matter of some debate, but most black spokespersons assigned them a primary role. "The Providences of God have placed the Negro Race, before Europe and America, in the most commanding position," lectured Alexander Crummell. "From the sight of us, no nation, no statesmen, no ecclesiastics, and no ecclesiastical institution, can escape." [160] Long dormant, long benighted, God had ordained the present as the time when the people of Africa would awaken from their national slumbers. The result would be the reemergence of a black nation onto the world stage. "Long years of darkness, imbecility and slavery, have been our portion," a black national convention told its constituents, "but God hath appointed us unto restoration. For princes shall come out of Egypt, and Ethiopia shall soon stretch forth her hands unto God." [161] David Walker believed "that God has something in reserve for us which . . . will repay us for all our suffering and miseries"; blacks would soon "take a stand among the nations of the earth." [162] The coming millennium promised an end to blacks' persecutions. George Lawrence wrote that it would disperse "the dark clouds of ignorance and superstition"; "reason, virtue, kindness and liberty" would "rise in glory and triumph," while "prejudice and slavery be cast down to the lowest depths of oblivion." [163] In his *Duty of a Rising Christian State,* Alexander Crummell predicted that the world would soon behold "a manly, noble, and complete African nationality!" which would "falsify all the lying utterances of the speculative ethnographies and the pseudo-philosophies which have spawned from the press of modern days against us." [164]

If these views of a divine history endowed with special meaning for blacks seemed tinged with the millennial, they were. Antebellum black nationalists postulated a history driven by the struggle between tyranny and liberty, slavery and freedom, God and Mammon. According to black abolitionist H. Ford Douglas, "the struggle of the oppressed against the oppressor" was one that "every where marks the pages of ancient History," from the days of Babylon to America's own revolutionary struggle against Britain.[165] "On earth's broad arena—through Time's revolving cycles," avowed a black woman abolitionist, "this warfare has been continuous." [166] This view of history comported easily with dominant political languages. When William Seward spoke of an "irrepressible conflict" between freedom and slavery, African American thinkers easily picked up the refrain, infusing the statesman's secular millennialism with overt religious significance.[167]

DIVINE INSTRUMENTALITIES FOR DIVINE ENDS

Over the course of the period from the Revolution to the Civil War, the consensus on the actual agent of black redemption changed in important ways. Of course redemption ultimately stemmed from God, but man's role in the process was less clear. What exactly did God want of oppressed African Americans? Where did His will stop and theirs begin? Early in the century, many black religious thinkers admonished blacks to patiently await God's coming. By the Civil War, however, a growing segment of activists, frustrated at the pace and direction of change, began suggesting that blacks become active and even violent instruments of His will.

The early view drew inspiration from Revolutionary-era African Americans like Jupiter Hammond, whose *Address to the Negroes in the State of New York* (1787) masters frequently read to their bondspersons. Drawing from the epistles of St. Paul, Hammond found what he called "a plain command of God for us to obey our masters." He further urged, "We ought to do it cheerfully, and freely."[168] Typical of black messianic interpretations of this perspective were the words of Robert Roberts, who authored a manual for African American domestic servants some forty years after Hammond's sermon was first published. "It is much better to be the oppressed than to stand in the place of the oppressor," Roberts instructed his readers, "for patience is very acceptable in the sight of God, and in due time will be rewarded, because God hath promised that it shall be so."[169] Others tempered such difficult advice by at least clarifying the terms of salvation. Two years later, Robert Alexander Young, an obscure black New Yorker who was likely a popular preacher among the working class, penned a sermon prophesying the coming of a messiah, who would be a mulatto—to all appearances white—and who would be "ordained of God, to call together the black people as a nation in themselves." Young advised his fellows to bear their burdens patiently while waiting for this leader.[170]

In contrast to these working-class manifestations of black messianism, middle-class leaders deeply implicated in black political struggles envisioned African Americans themselves playing increasingly significant roles.[171] As the crisis of the antebellum era deepened, and as a cadre of middle-class black leaders matured, black protest shifted its focus from God's agency to their own. In 1858, Peter H. Clark, a black activist from Cincinnati, declared that blacks had erred in thinking "that a political millennium was coming." Frustrated by decades of seemingly futile protest and discouraged by the Republican Party's racist form of antislavery, Clark determined "never to petition for a right again." Instead, if he could "seize" his rights, he would do so.[172] If African Americans could not wait on God to deliver them from without, they would have to work out their own redemption from within. This view was typified in the thought of Henry Highland Garnet, the New York minister, editor, and lecturer who issued a call to slave rebellion in 1843. Like Robert Roberts, Garnet believed that slaves were "duty bound to reverence and obey" God's commandments, but he differed radically from the Pauline approach of those like Hammond and Roberts. For Garnet, God required the enslaved "to love him supremely." Though slavery opposed the will of God and "hurls defiance in the face of Jehovah," the obligation to obey God remained. The enslaved had a "SOLEMN DUTY" to throw off their oppressors using "EVERY MEANS, . . . MORAL, INTELLECTUAL, AND PHYSICAL THAT PROMISES SUCCESS."[173] Garnet turned the tables on the Pauline theology that masters sought to instill in the enslaved. According to him, God commanded slaves not to "obey in everything those who are your earthly masters"[174] but instead to seek their freedom. Garnet thus helped revolutionize understandings of black agency, at least rhetorically. He transformed the problem from one of justifying resistance in the face of a Christian commandment to obey to one that posed a tension between obedience to God and obedience to masters. Now, by heeding the words of English radicals who insisted that "rebellion to tyrants is obedience to God," the oppressed had a duty to resist, openly and actively.

Increasingly, African American spokespersons believed they were to play conspicuous and active roles in the impending Apocalyptic contest. James McCune Smith told his readers, "We live in the heroic age of our country, and the negro is the hero."[175] Frances Ellen Watkins likewise believed that blacks in America were to play "a conspicuous part in the great struggle of the latter day of the world's history."[176] In these final days, many considered blacks "Divine instrumentalities for Divine ends."[177] It was here that black millennialism began its work of creating a political entity out of a diverse people. In essence, African Americans became the elect. As J. W. Loguen argued (once again bringing to bear a healthy dose of anti-Judaism), "The Christian Church to-day is in the state the Jewish Church was when it excommunicated its Lord. It is a dead carcass, dissolving as its essence is turned to uses." Just as the "Jewish church" had fallen from divine favor through disobedience, Loguen argued, so had the Christians by sustaining slavery; just as God had passed his covenant from Jews to Christians, and then from the English to English settlers of America and their descendants, so he would pass it from white Americans to African Americans.[178] True to this view, Alexander Crummell placed blacks within a version of John Winthrop's "City of a Hill" speech that was well suited for the age of romantic nationalism: "There is *one* MORAL good we can do the world," he told a Liberian audience. "The world *needs* a higher type of true nationality than it now has: why should not we furnish it?" Why not, he asked, "make OURSELVES a precedent?"[179]

This narrative of a unified people responding properly to their oppression by adhering to God's will promised a great reward for its suffering: a central place in history. For one, it placed great significance on a people otherwise bereft of agency. As James McCune Smith wrote of "the negro": "the progress of mankind is intrusted to his keeping."[180] Properly obedient to the will of God, African Americans could become, in the words of Loguen, "lights of the age, and saviors of the country—monarchs of progress, in politics, in morals, and religion."[181] The sense of meaning and purpose thus imparted was not to be scoffed at. Educator and former slave Austin Steward had once wondered "whether the black man would become extinct and his race die out"—"whether they would wither in the presence of the enterprising Anglo-Saxon as have the natives of this country." But his faith had given him new hope: "Now I have no such wondering inquiring to make; being persuaded that the colored man has yet a prominent part to act in this highly-favored Republic."[182]

African American northerners' growing trust in their divine mission led to a fundamental reordering of their narrative. Paradoxically, as they embraced the sense of peoplehood proffered by Exodus, they departed from it in important ways. The Israelites had been delivered not by themselves, after all, but by the hand of God, working through the individual figure of Moses. This messianic component placed a supernatural intermediary between the oppressed and their deliverance and thus undermined their agency. Increasingly, blacks abandoned this style of messianism. They began to favor more direct intervention in their own salvation. This marked an emerging awareness of their own political agency and the steady growth of a desire to fashion their own responses to oppression. In the 1820s, it was hoped that God would "elevate" blacks to the status of nation and thus redeem them; by the eve of the Civil War, blacks argued that their own self-elevation would redeem the nation, Africa, and indeed the world.

Spurred by the patronage of the American Colonization Society, which was founded in 1816 to offer a solution to America's post-Revolutionary "race problem," black leaders first exhibited this redemptionist impulse toward Africa. The Society pioneered a moderate line on race, perhaps liberal in its day, that intended to deal with the presence of slavery in a republican democracy. Their consciences pricked by the universalist logic of the Revolution, many whites (especially in the Upper South and Mid-Atlantic states) were troubled by slavery but unwilling to risk the social consequences of widespread emancipation. Slave or free, they reasoned, blacks simply lacked the virtues necessary to function in a self-governing republic. By offering to fund the removal of blacks to Africa once they had been freed, the Society hoped to circumvent this problem. This plan mollified all but the most fire-breathing southern slaveholders by offering a plan of emancipation that was gradual, compensated, and voluntary. The Society sold its program to the objects of its suspect beneficence by promising them a special place in history: it implanted the idea that black Americans might redeem Africa by bringing it the benefits of civilization and Christianity. Beyond suggesting once again the common ideological roots that black nationalism shared with America, it is symbolic of the depths of black despair that this shallow attempt to rationalize the removal of black people from the continent appealed to a vocal minority of African Americans. Echoing important themes from the theodicy, Maryland blacks argued that God, in his providence, placed the benighted children of Africa in America, where they had been "elevated and blessed" in preparation for their final purpose, which was the redemption of Africa.[183] "Ours is a great destiny," exulted emigrationist and missionary Alexander Crummell. Through the agency of blacks, he predicted, "the shades of ignorance and Superstition, that have so long settled upon the mind of Africa, shall be dispelled."[184]

By the Civil War several thousand African Americans, a minuscule proportion of the four million in the nation, had relocated to Liberia under the auspices of the ACS. Yet while most blacks quickly intuited the Society's false concern for the plight of oppressed blacks, the encounter with colonization served a vital function. Blacks in general rejected colonization and its rationale wholesale, but the ACS had supplied them with a logic they could use to argue for their inclusion in the American project. Their rejections to their removal took myriad forms, the most powerful of which was that their purpose was to redeem not Africa, but America. Instead of intending for them a primary role in redeeming Africa, said one, "God may use them to save this nation from that abyss of ruin towards which its brutal pride and folly are driving it headlong."[185] If, as the ACS argued, blacks possessed a special redemptive potential, why not expend it on America? Argued Ohio blacks, "The amount of labor and self-sacrifice required to establish a home in a foreign land, would if exercised here, redeem our native land from the grasp of slavery."[186] Instead of leaving for Africa, Samuel Cornish wrote, blacks should "stay and seek the purification of the whole lump."[187] "Our work here," editorialized another, "is to purify the State, and purify Christianity from the foul blot which here rests upon them."[188] It was, after all,

America that God had intended as the site of the millennium. "On this continent," wrote one black commentator, "God intends . . . ultimately to bring men of every clime, and hue, and tongue, in one great harmony, to perfect the greater system of man's highest earthly government. Then shall be the reign of perfect peace."[189]

Those who sought to colonize Africa and those who argued for the purification of the United States shared far more than is often acknowledged. The debate between colonizationists and their opponents did not speak to fundamental cleavages in values. The culture of those favoring a return to Africa was no more "African" than was that of their challengers. Patterns of procolonization sentiment were guided overwhelmingly by the rhetorical exigencies of participating in public sphere debates rather than by cultural identity. Freed African Americans in the North developed their sense of national destiny in the decades following the Revolution by appropriating emerging languages of nationalisms and applying them to their own status as an oppressed people. As we have seen, their public rhetoric early in the nineteenth century embraced Africa as a symbol of a national affiliation, which lent them credibility in a world rapidly organizing itself around such allegiances. Their general abstention from African colonization from the late 1820s through the 1840s responded not to an altered cultural stance toward Africa, but to the threat posed by a powerful national organization dedicated to exiling blacks from the land of their birth. Just as a desire to leave the United States for Africa did not signal a distinct cultural identity, a desire to stay did not signify deeply "assimilated" mind-sets. Frustration proved a far more likely determinant of colonizationist sentiment than the presence or lack of African cultural retentions. Lacking the nefarious rhetoric of the Society, blacks likely would have woven a return to Africa far more thoroughly into their public speech. As it was, it took several decades of disappointments to drive some, like Henry Highland Garnet and Martin R. Delany, back into the colonizationist fold, and even then the truce between white and black colonizationists remained tenuous. More significant than the actual site of redemption, a shared vision of their divinely ordained mission united African Americans in a historical community of the oppressed.

In testimony to their chosenness, African Americans compared themselves incessantly with ancient Israelites, endowing their daily trials with Biblical significance. Just as "the sacrifice of Jewish blood prepared the way for Hebrew freedom," so too "the Negroes in America would [not] achieve their freedom without sacrifice."[190] And just as the ancient Israelites had done, so too enslaved African Americans prayed "the great Jehovah to soften the hard hearts of the many Pharaohs, that they may let the people go free!"[191] The American Colonization Society was "actuated by the same motives which influenced the mind of Pharaoh"; its troublesome advocacy of black migration led potential black colonizationists to groan that the ACS made it impossible for blacks, "like the children of Israel, to make a grand exodus from the land of bondage." "The Pharaohs, they complained, "are on both sides of the blood-red waters!"[192] Some chose another route, fleeing instead to Canada: "Like the overpassed Israelites, 'they went out with their wives and their little ones.'"[193]

Such references aided the most important function of this Ethiopianism, which was to build among African Americans a sense of their unity as a historical and political force. This was something that could be assumed by no one in the antebellum era; it had to be grown and nurtured before it could flower among the masses. Religious black nationalism told its adherents not simply that they belonged to a nation, but *how* they could belong to it. Maintaining unity required the subordination of individual wills to the greater project of group elevation. It meant thinking always of the interests of the race before the interests of the self. David Walker, for one, excoriated disloyal blacks for "telling news and lies to our *natural enemies*, against each other." Perhaps he had in mind those African Americans who helped foil the slave revolutions contemplated by Denmark Vesey and Gabriel Prosser; maybe he thought of those who pursued their own profit at the expense of any person of African descent. "Respectable men" would never behave thus. His famous *Appeal* first and foremost reminded his readers that their very survival depended on inculcating national loyalty, "that unless you are united, keeping your tongues within your teeth, you will be afraid to trust your secrets to each other, and thus perpetuate our miseries."[194]

Such discipline might in the end matter terribly. Anticipating truly Apocalyptic racial struggle, William J. Wilson wrote: "When the final day does come, as come it must, and should it be a hand-to-hand struggle, it may then be with the Anglo-African a question of numbers." Blacks' national strength may then mean "not merely the question of his liberty, but entire indemnity for the past, full security for the future, and the most perfect and fullest equality for all time to come." While waiting for that day, he continued, "it behooves every one to be on the alert; to be on the watch-tower on in the drill, or measuring strength."[195] Other leaders contributed to the objective of imparting a great urgency to the time between the present and the end. "Stand boldly up in your own national characteristics," Austin Steward urged. "Band together in one indissoluble bond of brotherhood, to stand shoulder to shoulder in the coming conflict."[196] As a people, wrote another, blacks needed to develop "undivided energy, determination or patriotism," for "where these traits are not found in individuals, they cannot be found in the community in which they live—and where they cannot be found in the community, it is in vain they will be sought in the nation."[197]

The black national project also required a steadfast commitment to the divine being who ordained a special role for blacks in history. According to J. W. C. Pennington, "the highest obligation of an oppressed people, is fidelity to god and firm trust in Him as the God of the oppressed."[198] In the same breath that he urged blacks to rally around their own national standard, Austin Steward also told them to "show by your perseverance and industry, your honor and purity, that you are men, colored men, but of no inferior quality."[199] Here could be invoked the entire edifice of moral uplift and respectability. National destiny lent that project a great imperative—a faith that proper comportment and moral discipline were owed not simply to temporal authority, but to the god who had promised such a remarkable salvation. Given the great responsibilities accompanying their role, asked Theodore Wright, "Shall we not be true to this high position, this glorious trust?"[200]

The subtle almost indefinable feeling of repulsion
toward the Negro, which is common to most
Americans—cannot be stormed and taken by assault;
the garrison will not capitulate, so their position
must be mined, and we will find ourselves in
their midst before they think it.
Charles W. Chestnutt

Black Protest and the Continuing Revolution

Black communities in the North in the period between the Revolution and
the Civil War bore and nurtured a public tradition of African American
protest. Nearly every tenet of twentieth-century black protest thought—
from Martin Luther King Jr.'s concern with the "content of our characters"
to Stokely Carmichael's call for "Black Power"—can trace its roots to the
body of ideas developed by black spokespersons in the antebellum North.
In the process of creating a protest tradition, black spokespersons also produced something rarely attributed to them—a notion of what it meant to be
of African descent in both America and the world. The construction of black
protest and black identity in the antebellum North occurred not through
the recognition of an essential affinity among all African-descended people
on the basis of shared culture but from a conscious and public process of
dialogue and contestation with a hostile white America.

This America understood itself as fundamentally committed to the principles of the American Revolution. According to Sacvan Bercovitch, the
American Revolution served as the archetypal event that defined Americans' conception of their nation, its history, and its destiny. The Revolu-

tion served as a reservoir of shared values upon which rested a widespread consensus about the principles of American society. These included beliefs (sometimes contradictory) in universal rights, the rights of property and value of entrepreneurship, representative democracy as the most perfect form of government, the need for civic virtue, and the providential mission of the nation to extend that form of government over the continent. To invoke the Revolution as an historical paradigm through which other events could be interpreted and understood was thus to appeal to a set of core principles practically beyond dispute.[1]

Different social groups thus used the Revolution in their rhetoric to confer an otherwise unattainable authority in the realm of public discourse. In the hands of popular historians like George Bancroft, the Revolution functioned as an archetype for the mission of America, which was to "progress" by spreading the principles of the Revolution over time (into the future) and space (into the West). Through the value of progress, Bancroft elevated change itself, rather than a specific goal, to the rank of national telos.[2] The value of progress served as the continuing revolution's central hegemonic force. By positing change as a goal, but by directing that change toward the maintenance and expansion of the bourgeois order established by the Revolution, the continuing revolution effectively subverted radicalism. That which sought to subvert order did itself preserve order, because order was defined as subversion and change. According to Bercovitch, finding a true radicalism in such a hegemonic discourse proved nearly impossible. To Bercovitch, potentially "radical" writers like Emerson and Melville lacked not "courage of radical commitment"; instead, "they had invested radicalism itself in a vision dedicated to the containment of revolution."[3] The trope of the continuing revolution thus channeled the potentially radical into a "consensual" framework, one that upheld rather than undermined a petit bourgeois social order.

One might soundly conclude that the hegemonic influence of the paradigm of the continuing revolution was manifest in a failure to examine key tenets of American democracy. True radicalism, we suspect, would have required a praxis that would have exposed the mythologies underlying cherished beliefs and challenged unquestioned assumptions about the social order. Like so many other Americans, African American thinkers in the antebellum North rarely, if ever, engaged in such a praxis. Instead, they operated within the paradigm of the continuing revolution. They in fact relied on it so much that they became unparalleled champions of its principles.[4]

Bercovitch's focus on the Revolution is too narrow. Through ideas of up-lift and respectability, as well as those of nation, black protest thought drew upon the values and fundamental social presuppositions of the northern culture in which African American elites lived and participated. Yet they did so in ways that rendered black thought a distinct element of the American intellectual tradition. Utterly marginalized by the quasi-freedom that fol-lowed the northern emancipations after the American Revolution, African Americans found themselves forced to seek redress through participation in a hegemonic public culture that limited the range of ideological options available to black leaders. In addition, they occupied a place in the African diaspora that rendered them particularly likely to rely on borrowed cultural elements, rather than those "retained" from previous generations. The elite African Americans who considered themselves leaders crafted challenges to racial inequality that appealed to cherished American values rather than stepped outside the bounds of the American ideological landscape. Con-strained like all contemporary Americans by existing language and systems of explanation, black elites found themselves challenged to develop rhetori-cal strategies rooted in the American tradition. They sought not to revolu-tionize existing discourse, but to appeal to its core values in changing the "public mind" on racial matters.

The crafters of the black protest tradition operated within the bounds of an ideological landscape composed of the loose configuration of ideas, cultural symbols, and figures of speech that every American employed to interpret and discuss her or his world. This ideological landscape both per-mitted and constrained the formation of ideas by providing the languages through which they were expressed. The discourse was flexible—it could be challenged and stretched to varying degrees, depending upon circum-stances. Historians have suggested, for example, that the public discourse of America during the Constitutional debate was particularly open to chal-lenge and possibility.[5] By the antebellum era, ideological possibilities had contracted somewhat, yet there remained considerable room for debate. The national debate over slavery grew into a deeply conflicted ideological discourse that could be resolved only through civil war.

Northern blacks in the antebellum era operated within such a realm of consensual discourse. They agreed on very few of the specifics of protest strategy and tactics, yet most of their disagreements occurred within a larger framework of fundamental congruity. The power and strength of black lead-ers' thought lay not in frontal assaults against the basic premise of America, but in constant sniping, in guerrilla warfare directed at its edges. Rather than suggest an ideologically revolutionary overturning of national tenets,[6] black activists mocked, parodied, and subverted the nation into a recognition of its own hypocrisy. They drew upon America's own logics and languages in attempting to force it to live up to its promises. Their failure to develop a truly radical alternative to American ideology, one that viewed America from without, was not an indictment of their lack of intellectual resourcefulness or of their will to resist their oppression.

Black thinkers readily understood this to be the case. Nothing emblematized this more than their consistent claim that they had contributed significantly to the nation and hence deserved to enjoy its benefits. Such arguments often appear today to have been ineffective and accommodationist impulses that failed to identify (let alone critique) important instruments of racial control. But a well-founded concern with questions of political economy, structural racism, and cultural nationalism threatens to obscure the significance of African Americans' complicity in the fabrication of American culture. When New York blacks declared, "We have helped contribute, to a considerable extent, not only to the means of the State, but likewise to its character and respectability," they did far more than make an "integrationist" claim to national inclusion.[7] They laid claim, and with justification, to American identity in a way too often missed by modern audiences. Americanness was not something black cultural others "assimilated," it was something African Americans cofabricated with other Americans by simple virtue of their presence, despite—indeed, because of—their incapacity to participate fully in national life. Hostile whites could long deny blacks a place at the national table, but having brought African Americans' ancestors to American shores they could not obviate their presence altogether. Blacks' public relationship with whites in the North mirrored slaves' domestic relationships with their masters in the South in at least one sense: just as the culture of slaves infiltrated the lives of their owners in covert ways and despite gross power imbalances, so too did the marginalized African Americans in the free states participate in fabrication of the culture of the North.

The point of arguing for antebellum black elites' claim to American public culture is not to reenliven what was once termed contributionist Negro history. This tradition tended to laud black leaders for their acceptance of American ideology rather than critique them for accepting hostile terms of racial debate. As we have seen, however, this acceptance could act against their very interests in several ways. It could, for example, neglect an awareness of class oppression by funneling it into the larger rubric of race. Or it could participate in a rhetoric of civilization that reinforced ethnocentrism. Or it might bolster stifling gender norms that promised racial emancipation only at the expense of black women's subjugation. It is imperative that the pitfalls of black elites' cofabrication of American culture be acknowledged. Yet it is also crucial that the false boundaries between black and American culture be eroded, for these cannot help but obscure the relationship between African Americans and the national culture, steering our understandings instead into the parochial terms of cultural nationalism. The cultural nationalism approach invariably presents black elites as almost pathologically stuck between cultures and tacitly threatens to present American culture (and the benefits of participating in it) as the proper domain of someone other than blacks. Properly understanding the role of African American thinkers in their own oppression—and, in more general terms, the ways in which the discourses of their societies contribute to the marginalization of the oppressed—is exactly why it is important to investigate the sources and functions of elite black thought. African American spokespersons laid claim to a powerful tradition of public speech, in a way that modern historiography has trouble labeling as anything other than integrationist, assimilationist, and therefore accommodationist. Not one of these claims, let alone the chain of logic that connects the one to the next, is justified by a close reading of the sources.

The African American ministers, editors, and activists who formulated the black public protest tradition did not see their dearly held cultural values as belonging to their oppressors. They claimed those values—uplift, respectability, civilization, natural rights philosophy, republicanism, liberalism—as their own. Indeed, they championed them. In doing so, they did no violence to their own cultural heritage, and could not have, for such values *were* their own cultural heritage. Their sermons, lectures, and editorials had helped build those values, just as their labor had helped to build the North's cities.

There were serious limitations to black spokespersons' manipulation of the values and public discourse of the America they helped fabricate. Eating from the ideological table of their oppressors, they became so reliant on its menu that they may have imbibed some of its more distasteful offerings. Clearly, the struggle for black freedom often conflicted with efforts to liberate women from oppressive gender ideals. The strategy of attempting to change white minds dictated that African Americans conform to certain basic values in American society, among which middle-class standards of male and female behavior ranked highly. The resulting efforts to demonstrate blacks' gender normativity often mandated that black spokespersons argue all the more vociferously that African Americans could and did live up to ideals of masculinity and femininity that did little to raise black women to equality with black men. The frequent equation of rights with manhood, for example, suggested that black protest's gender stance reinforced rather than questioned existing norms.

African American thinkers also evinced troubling concessions to the racialism of their day. Modern students note with alarm instances in which black thinkers manifested the very racial and ethnic stereotyping that had contributed so much to their own misfortune. Black newspapers regularly reprinted tales of exotic Asian foreigners and seemed more than willing to cite white authorities who supported the potential of black intellect at the expense of that of Native Americans.[8] Black northerners' references to Chinese people as "grotesque," with "filthy" habits and "features totally devoid of expression," seem to contradict the racial tolerance expected of victims of racial intolerance.[9] Some black thinkers endorsed central tenets of emerging racial science, speaking of races as biologically distinct entities existing along hierarchies of civilization and even placing black people, if only transitorily, near the bottom. Deeply steeped in the values of Western civilization, the ethnocentrism of many elite black northerners even found voice against the black non-elite, whom many of the elite viewed as unrefined and barbaric, if nonetheless salvageable. Given the pervasive racialism of their day, it is perhaps surprising that black thinkers did not falter more often than they did. Sensing the inherent dangers of racialism, black protest by and large preferred to champion a radical environmentalism that was rapidly becoming obsolete in an age of romantic nationalism and racial science.

Perhaps most fundamentally, though, black protest failed to understand, let alone critique, the nature of the economic order to which it owed its problems. The unique and paradoxical exigencies of northern black life—the fact that general emancipation had happened there at all, the persistence of an economy dependent on the produce of slavery, the character virtues believed to be necessary to succeed in such an economy, and even an underlying commitment to white privilege, which seemed to controvert national principles—all owed their existence to the bourgeois capitalism of America in the age of the market revolution. An incapacity to identify these realities surely hamstrung the freedom struggle. Although, as I have argued, black strategies for uplift through respectability were neither as accommodationist nor as integrationist as some scholars have deemed, they did rely on values that were gaining currency through the expansion of a bourgeois social order that celebrated the liberal marketplace's twin mythologies of meritocracy and the neutrality of the state. Black elites, merely by employing such valued notions in the freedom struggle, could not help but lend them a sense of legitimacy. Even the greatest of their achievements, the building of a public black racial identity, was qualified by this failure to critique the economic structures of oppression. In many ways, the price of building a unified, pan-African black identity was the jettisoning of the critical apparatus for critiquing their economic order and the society bred by it. Antebellum black nationalism, by championing unities alleged to transcend class differences, did little to further an understanding of the deep structural forces underlying their oppression. The net effect of black elites' fabrication of black protest from the ideological material of the antebellum North was a tragic misdirection of critical capacity, which many would say is being corrected only now.

In addition to the threat of accepting hostile terms of debate, the strategy of appealing to the values of oppressor culture raised serious questions of efficacy. Black leaders operated within a cultural and intellectual milieu shared with their oppressors. Largely shut out of the political and institutional life of the nation, they yet remained steeped in its values. Embracing, sharing, and cofabricating the values of their milieu, they trusted that their enemies would hold to those values with the same fervor and sincerity. Hence, nearly every argument they made sought to appeal to that which America seemed most to cherish: democracy, republicanism, liberalism, Christianity, respectability, elevation, nationalism, manhood. They trusted that these, when put on the scale against whatever benefit might accrue from slavery and prejudice, could not help but prove more precious.

Such was not the case. Some white Americans lacked a sincere belief in the principles they claimed to value; others adhered to rival versions of them, versions that rationalized the enslavement of their brothers and sisters and the marginalization of those legally but not fully free. This was of course crippling to the black freedom struggle. Whites could afford a shallow faith in national principles; blacks could not. Whites had the privilege and luxury of championing democracy despite withholding it from women and people of color. Blacks, though, had no room for error. They staked all on the possibility of changing white attitudes and lost—if not the battle, then the war. Despite even the millennial victory represented by the Civil War and widespread emancipation, racial prejudice proved too stubborn a weed to root out. What followed the end of Reconstruction was a period that has been called the Nadir—segregation, disfranchisement, mob violence, lynching campaigns, and the utter derogation of America's founding principles and promises.

It was not that African Americans had misplaced their faith in American values so much as that they had mistakenly trusted in *whites'* faith in those principles: they assumed wrongly that white Americans were at root willing to overcome their prejudice if the right appeal could be made. The national convention of 1847 thus quoted the aphorism, "Give me the song-making of a people and I will rule that people." [10] By hearkening back to the core traditions of American society—the universalism of the Revolution, the morals of bourgeois society, and the cultural genius of romantic ethnic nationalism—they believed they possessed the capacity to change the public mind on matters of race. Like Jürgen Habermas a century later, they believed in the essential rationality of the public sphere and its capacity to justly distribute rights and resources. [11] Through the inexorable logic of their rhetoric, they hoped to position white America so that it had only two ways to move: it could accede to reasonable demands rooted in America's cherished precepts, and thus strengthen and honor the national mission; or it could continue to deny blacks' freedom and equality, and thus risk hypocrisy and the betrayal of its founding principles.

What black elites grossly underestimated were the overwhelming advantages of white racial privilege. While black activism helped drive the nation to the civil war that abolished slavery, its rhetoric was not powerful enough to excise the attitudes that fostered the tragic failure of Reconstruction and its bloody aftermath. White supremacy's racial fantasies served psychic needs that were too strong to allow yielding of the concessions necessary to bring America's promises to fruition. Its contradictions to liberalism ultimately proved to be not a weakness, easily exploited by the exposure of hypocrisy in its adherents, but its greatest strength. White supremacy's capacity to cloak inequity under a veneer of liberal fair play has ever served both itself and the interests of capital.

Since the antebellum period, the idea that public argument *could* yield racial equality regained favor periodically, but it has withered since the latter half of the 1960s. This disillusionment seems justified. The pervasive intransigence of post–civil rights America—its failure to continue the important work that the movement only began, to continue to make the necessary material sacrifices required to achieve our centuries-long promises of social equality—has all too amply demonstrated the justice of many African Americans' deep cynicism with strategies of persuasion. In the quest for social justice, recent history seems to suggest that change will always require more than simply the power of "breathing thoughts, and burning words," as one black writer put it in 1859. [12] It requires also the ally of raw power: the power of the purse, the power of a committed federal government, or the power of international confederates.

Antebellum black thinkers forged their protest thought in the midst of the hegemonic culture of a racist America. The inevitable liabilities in such a course did not, however, bankrupt black protest thought. African American spokespersons did a remarkable job of anatomizing American society for potent ideological resources and useful rhetorical elements. They parlayed their marginal status in an affluent society into a protest tradition powerful enough to begin the inexorable process of polarizing the nation and bringing about the war that ended slavery. In the process, they made themselves a test of America. "By us and our cause," sermonized Alexander Crummell, "the character and the greatness of individuals and of nations . . . are to be decided. . . . This is the age of BROTHERHOOD AND HUMANITY; and the Negro Race is its most distinguished test and criterion."[13]

American civilization should not be credited for creating the possibility of black liberation, for the racial loophole provided by the Declaration of Independence was hardly intentional. It would be the most specious form of national self-aggrandizement to celebrate a political system that first denied liberty to blacks, then created the slim possibility that they might through decades of struggle and blood sacrifice acquire what had been stolen from them—something originally theirs by right. Yet it is true that Revolutionary ideology unwittingly proffered African Americans an ideological lever for wresting their rights, that bourgeois morality offered them a language for forging alliances with white reformers, and that nationalism offered them a potent basis for building group solidarity. However, it was African Americans' own agency, their willingness and ability to exploit cracks in the surface of white supremacy, and not the inherent nobility of national promises never fulfilled that constituted the sine qua non of whatever freedoms African Americans have wrested from the nation.

Also counterbalancing the shortcomings of antebellum black protest was the success of African American leaders' dialogue with America in forging black identity. Challenged to uphold a united front before a hostile society, spokespersons wrangled incessantly with the problem of presenting the race to an expanding and increasingly anonymous public. Moral admonitions to the black non-elite, for example, revealed both black leaders' positive self-identification with the non-elite as well as their fear that such associations might threaten the prospect of gaining respect, and hence equality and abolition, from whites. To the limited extent that scholars have explored the sometimes troubling implications of these elements of black protest, some have contended that such exigencies drove black elites into a class collaboration with bourgeois whites at the expense of their identity with non-elite blacks. While this phenomenon has been documented in other times and places in the African diaspora, and while class and other tensions among Africans Americans inhibited the formation of a monolithic black society, it has been easy to overplay such divisions and their effects on the formation of black protest thought.

In fact, black elites in the North forged from the crucible of antebellum race relations a rare degree of racial unity. They theorized about it constantly and postulated it before their communities and the world. While many prominent leaders did hold little in common with the black rank and file, many others came from or constantly identified with the communities that had conferred their leadership status. Elite leaders did encounter challenges to their status from the non-elite over differences in class and cultural style. Yet such tensions should not obscure the fact that African Americans, perhaps more than any other group of Americans at the time, successfully crafted alliances and affinities among themselves across lines of class and culture. In fact, the tensions between self-proclaimed black leaders and their purported constituents were the by-product of the conjoining of social groups that in other realms of American society never even attempted to unify. Tension thus often appeared as a by-product of success rather than as a herald of failure.

As fragile as it may have been, the forging of a black identity that envisioned all people of African descent as one people did not, as is often assumed, occur by default, but as the result of black Americans' conscious creation. Because of their unique position in the diaspora, African American elites were able to construct a vision of black identity that elided distinctions that in other parts of the New World fettered the emergence of a single identity for people of color. Black elites' notion of group identity also encompassed all people of African descent, regardless of class, skin color, relationship to slavery, or regional cultural style. This was not, course, the only source of African American identity available, for non-elite blacks had long been forging a rich folk culture that provided a source of both solace and resistance. The form of identity set forth by elite leaders differed from this folk basis of black identity in several important ways. For one, it was largely rhetorical, crafted through words uttered in public and printed in popular media. While less tangible than its folk counterpart, black elites' notion of identity had the advantage of speaking in terms acknowledged and valued by blacks' oppressors. The notion of identity propagated by African

American elites functioned self-consciously and intentionally in a national community's discourse of politics.

Black public identity, as we might call it, had an influence greatly disproportionate to the number who crafted it. White Americans tended to cull what they considered the representative men and women of the race from the ranks of these leaders. To the extent that white people willingly listened to any words uttered by black people, they listened to the words of these elites. Uniquely positioned between the black rank and file and a largely white public, the forgers of the black public protest tradition both carried the burden of speaking for the non-elite and enjoyed the limited privileges accorded their elite status.

In this book I have strayed considerably from the common (and crucial) practice of seeking to write the history of African Americans from the bottom up. I have instead tried to reclaim what may be considered the traditional sources of African American intellectual history as worthy subjects of study. My goal has been to redeem the authors of those texts from the charge that their elitism—whether based on social class, masculinity, or any other measure—rendered them unfit and insignificant spokespersons for the race. My aim has emphatically been not to champion a revitalization of integrationist strategies or a return to the days when the nation turned to patriarchal elites when it sought black spokespersons. Nor is it to argue the virtues of a body of protest thought built on bourgeois values. I concede without hesitation the elite biases of most of my sources.

I am, however, suggesting that we reconsider the realm of public speech as a potent force in its own right rather than as a mere subordinate to the larger claims of cultural nationalism and culturally based identity politics. The lesson in the story I have told may be that the freedom struggle often requires engagement with the culture of oppressors, despite the liabilities inevitable in that engagement. It is with some hubris that modern-day advocates for liberation suggest that viable critiques of postindustrial society must emerge from outside that society's frame of ideological reference. As the experience of antebellum black activists attests, it is not so easy for historical actors to determine when they are operating with the cultural baggage of their oppressors; it is even more difficult to determine which elements of oppressor culture *ought* to be jettisoned.

It may be as important to understand the dangers of struggling to achieve such an outside perspective on cultural discourse as it is to understand the dangers of failing to. All may acknowledge the consequences of falling victim to ideological hegemony—that is, to internalizing tenets of an oppressor culture and society that undermine the project of liberation. However, it may be just as troublesome to believe that one has escaped the ideological stranglehold of one's oppressors while yet remaining an unwitting captive to their terms of debate. Who is to say that, like antebellum black intellectuals, today's generation of cultural critics and liberation theorists are not similarly bound to crucial tenets of oppressor culture from which they are simply incapable of standing apart and analyzing from an outside perspective? Perhaps future generations of liberation-minded scholars will find the late twentieth century's generation as culturally bound as ours finds its antebellum progenitors. Given the improbability of ever successfully critiquing every element of subordination, it seems useful to withhold judgment when in doubt rather than predicate strategy upon a false sense of veracity. To do anything else leads to a restriction of ideological options that seems at best uncalled for and at worst counterproductive.

Epilogue

The Civil War, and especially the Reconstruction, offered the possibility, unparalleled throughout the rest of the African diaspora, that the United States would reforge itself into a biracial democracy.[1] Once the transition had been made from a war to preserve the union to a war to abolish slavery, Union victory promised blacks a long-sought millennium. After the pyrrhic episode of Andrew Johnson's presidency, Reconstruction's Radical phase promised that the race's destiny was at hand. With black men now enfranchised, the redemption and purification of America could proceed; meaning could be found in black suffering. Liberalism's promises of racial neutrality would now become realities: color would no longer matter for anything important. Having gained access to formal politics, African Americans could protect themselves from the depredations of their enemies. Having been granted a level playing field, their energies would be rewarded with economic success.

In fact, Union victory in the Civil War and universal emancipation posed the ideology of black protest its greatest challenge, in terms of both its core assumptions and its strategies. Before the war, black spokespersons had unfailingly demanded that white America simply give them a chance to demonstrate the truths underlying their analyses of a prejudiced American society. Through the Civil War and Reconstruction, whites grudgingly conceded that chance. How would blacks fare? When given the opportunity, would their program yield the results black leaders had long claimed were possible? Everything was at stake in vindicating antebellum black protest thought: spokespersons' positions as black leaders, the destiny of the race and of America, even the nature of their relationship with a mysterious and mercurial God. Had antebellum black northerners been correct to employ the universalism of the American Revolution as a lever with which they might call the nation back to its first principles? Had they been right to stress self-help, moral uplift, and elevation as the keys to rising in a liberal economic order and thus compelling whites to yield rights? Had they been justified in their growing sense that the conversation with white America mattered little when compared to the power of national entities to fight for their own interests? Never before had black activists faced the hope and challenge of so practical a test of their ideas.

The experiment was doomed from the start by forces that ensured it would never be granted a fair chance of success. Even the earliest attempts to institute systems of free labor during the war had demonstrated the shallowness of America's faith in free labor ideology when put to the test. Blacks had long been told and had long preached that their national inclusion awaited only a demonstration of their ability to function in a neutral and competitive economic environment. In the post-emancipation South, however, the connivance of self-interested reformers, the limits of permissible state intervention, and above all the intransigence of slaves' former masters scuttled the experiment in free labor before it even began. As early as Port Royal it became clear that a true experiment would not even be attempted—that, despite the tremendous difficulties it faced, it would never be granted the level playing field considered so necessary to success in a free market economy. Whites, even those who had claimed the greatest sympathy with blacks' cause, cared less for their free labor ideology than for the need for racial control. Much had been lost in the war, and faith in the experiment had never been high or widespread. When early experimentation in free labor failed to deliver a class of thrifty and virtuous independent yeomen farmers, even many of those who had been sympathetic reasoned that the task was too hard, and blacks naturally unfitted for it.[2]

Others more hostile to the notion of racial progress could simply conclude that they had been right all along, that black people were naturally and irrevocably fitted for nothing more than servitude. In defeat, white supremacy proved itself a far more potent foe than ever it had on the battlefield. In ten thousand daily interactions, white southerners demonstrated their willingness to sell their democratic principles for the benefits of racial privilege, raising the political and constitutional costs of Radical Reconstruction and steadily galvanizing a weary North against the experiment in biracial democracy. Ignoring the blatant violation of liberalism's basic tenets, most white Americans abandoned the freedpeople to their former masters, then absolved themselves of all responsibility for the consequences. Thomas H. Huxley, the British scientific philosopher who described himself as "Darwin's bulldog," wrote shortly after the Civil War to endorse the new approach: "Whatever the position of stable equilibrium into which the laws of social gravitation may bring the negro, all responsibility for the result will henceforward lie between nature and him. The white man may wash his hands of it, and the Caucasian conscience be void of reproach evermore."[3]

The legacy of America's bloodiest conflict and its political aftermath was not the reformation of American society along racially just lines, but the worst half-century of race relations in the nation's history. Anyone needing evidence that the story of America is not a story of steady, inevitable progress toward positive goals need only glimpse the horrors of Jim Crow race relations; a more depressing example of modern barbarism does not exist.

What had once seemed a possible millennium became yet another hell. Of America's various Chosen Peoples, Confederates saw themselves as forced by defeat out of Canaan and into the desert. Yet there they found an oasis, a concession, in the form of a Promised Land of white racial domination. Blacks had also crossed a wilderness in flight from bondage, but they had traversed the opposite path—from the desert into what they hoped would be a Canaan. Instead, they found themselves wandering through yet another Sinai.

This story has been told, but rarely in ways that fully acknowledge the significance of the protest thought forged in the North in the decades before the Civil War. During and after the Civil War, antebellum black spokespersons' analyses retained tremendous significance. Important established black leaders as well as newly emerging ones steeped in the ethos of northern black protest became key figures in black Reconstruction. A considerable number of those active in the antebellum North went south during or shortly after the war, through the auspices of the Union Army, church and benevolent organizations, or their own entrepreneurial enterprise. The names of these men and women are writ large in the story of Reconstruction: H. Ford Douglas, Martin R. Delany, Charlotte Forten, Susie King Taylor, James T. Rapier, Richard H. Cain, and others. They brought with them a protest ideology that had been developing for decades in the North, implanting it in the places they occupied: state legislatures and judiciaries, the halls of Congress, Freedmen's Bureau schools, revitalized black churches, missionary associations, and local communities.

There was some cause to imagine that the northerners' protest ideology might have served the Reconstruction South well. In the aftermath of slavery, the South faced a situation remarkably similar to that of the post-Revolutionary North: a white America, already predicated on the principles of white supremacy, confronting the novel "problem" of widespread black freedom. Both regions dealt with the end of legalized enslavement and the free labor it had guaranteed with a spate of informal, quasi-legal measures that denied the highly touted promises of liberalism that had accompanied the abolitionist transformations. Both featured an industrializing economy and an expanding market society that largely relegated blacks to preindustrial pursuits designed to deprive them of the benefits of modernization by preserving privileged economic niches for whites. Both, as a function of the expanding market economy, witnessed the steady incorporation of representations of these oppressed "others" into forms of popular entertainment that permitted whites to sublimate their fears and project their fantasies onto black bodies. In both, freedom was attended by a "hardening" of racial lines, as whites, now lacking the status of slavery itself as a marker of inferiority, struggled for new methods of securing their privilege by policing the racial boundaries. And both, in their periods of general emancipation, pioneered new ways of using the authority of science to enshrine that racial privilege in the workings of nature.

There the similarities ended. In the antebellum North a small handful of elites claimed to represent in public sphere debates a relatively modest number of non-elite northern brethren with whom they shared a common social and cultural milieu. In the Reconstruction South the situation became much more complex. Northern black elites in the South formed only a component of a large and shifting black leadership class composed not simply of black "carpetbaggers" but also of antebellum free blacks and those who had risen from the ranks of the formerly enslaved. This new leadership purported to lead not 250,000 free African Americans but 4,000,000, most of whom until recently had been enslaved. In addition, all male black leaders faced the novel luxury, after 1866, of voting for and holding elective office. This gave them access to the resources of the state yet also pulled them into a vortex of complex party politics from which they had long or ever been excluded. Finally, formal politics in the Reconstruction South hardly operated in its normal consensual mode, which frequently sublimated fundamental ideological strife. As Lawrence Powell has stated, Democrats and Republicans during Reconstruction contested not simply victory in the game of politics, but the very rules by which the game was to be played.[4]

These factors confronted black carpetbaggers' protest ideology with challenges it had never before confronted. The moral uplift, elevation, and respectability components of black thought were sustained in the Reconstruction, and in remarkably static form. Black teachers in freedmen's schools, churches, the Freedmen's Bureau, and local politics—many of them born and educated in the North—generally continued to preach the mantra of elevation, incorporating it into the class rhetoric of black society and the emerging institutional life of the postwar black South.[5] Self-help and the economic virtues of antebellum society premised the manual training school movement, which provided the basis of black education throughout the region for decades and served as the ground upon which Booker T. Washington's leadership was later predicated.[6]

It is far from clear that these ideas could have responded appropriately to the economic and political gerrymandering that inhibited black elevation after the war. The experience of the Civil War and Reconstruction suggested that black leaders' analysis of prejudice had simply been wrong. For one, it had depended too heavily on an analysis of slavery as the source of blacks' ills. Too often spokespersons in the antebellum era had chanted stock phrases illustrating this, such as "Remove slavery, and the prejudice will speedily wear away."[7] At particularly frustrating moments some leaders had intuited the depths of racial prejudice. In 1846, James McCune Smith, frustrated by the failure of an equal rights bill in New York, confided to a friend, "There is in that majority a hate deeper than I imagined." Whites, Smith found, seemed willing to concede both their political and pecuniary self-interest to retain the privilege of racial caste.[8]

During the war some black northerners, like Philadelphian William Parham, remained skeptical of the future, reserving hope until slavery's offspring, prejudice, had been eradicated as well. Prejudice would live on after slavery, he predicted. "True the North is growing anti slavery, but at the same time, it grows more strongly anti negro. . . . Without equality we are slaves still."[9] Far more common, however, were hopeful proclamations that a new day had dawned, that the long-sought millennium was at hand. Those such as J. T. Shuften, the editor of a black newspaper in Reconstruction Georgia, optimistically proclaimed that with slavery gone the days of racial prejudice were over. The Negro, he wrote, "is now a free man, and as a free man he has the right to acquire wealth as the product of his honest labor, and with that wealth he has the inalienable right to dispose of it as he may think proper." This new power of the purse promised a degree of influence that would banish forever the hated monster, prejudice. Shuften predicted, "Our cry in the future shall be, 'Millions to our friends, but not one cent to our foes.'"[10] Such words had been uttered for decades before the war, but the aftermath of slavery lent them a new promise—one that was to remain utterly unfulfilled.[11]

The fault for black thinkers' failure to properly analyze prejudice can hardly be laid at their feet. Slavery was after all a large and persistent evil, and it did have manifest effects on racial attitudes in the North. As their complex analysis of prejudice attests, black intellectuals did not by and large echo the errors of white abolitionists, who all too often neglected the problems of the free in favor of the cause of the slave. Yet African American leaders themselves would understand the true depth of racial prejudice only long after slavery's demise. Their ideology likely precluded them from critiquing the problems confronting them as forcefully as they might have otherwise. While African American leaders continually decried the nation's failure to provide a level playing field for black enterprise, their society's deep reliance on the values of self-help made it all too easy—especially after the demise of slavery, the institution that many perceived as the source of prejudice—to turn a blind eye to these continual depredations and instead blame the victims of discrimination themselves. Before the war, black leaders had predicated their claims on their ability to succeed in a race-neutral environment. "Remove all obstacles, and give the black man an equal chance," they said, "and then should he not succeed, he will not ask you or anyone else to mourn over his failure."[12] Too many whites, blind to the obstacles that still remained, held them to their word. Black thought, also steeped in self-help, had too much faith in the promise of the race-neutral society to consider more pessimistic outcomes as anything other than aberrations.

In addition to failing to respond to the nation's endemic need to purchase white privilege at the cost of racial equality, the expression of antebellum protest ideology in the postwar South heightened internal tensions within African American society. In the antebellum North the bourgeois-seeming values of the elite had generated considerable conflict when urged upon a non-elite who were steeped in black folk and popular culture. When the ethos of that same elite encountered four million African Americans with lives rooted in a radically dissimilar culture, tensions were bound to flare even more. It was not so much that the freedpeople did not want to partake of the benefits of the market economy; it was that they had no interest in making sacrifices for an economy that seemed bent on recommitting them to labor that would promise them nothing and which they rightfully despised. The uplift ideology of bourgeois northerners clashed with the pre-industrial ethos of the formerly enslaved. Many of the latter rejected the northerners' concern with participating in a competitive capitalist economy that demanded virtues and values that were at odds with centuries of folk experience. The voices of white politicians calling for black elevation as a prerequisite for inclusion only amplified the cultural conflict. Such calls pressured black leaders, who might otherwise have been able to sugarcoat the bitter pill of free plantation labor, and deservedly raised the suspicions of freedpeople constantly subjected to the new "advice." Many black politicians found themselves frustrated, caught between a desire to champion their constituents' interests and the need to work within a political system that was bent on subjugating the freedpeople to the status of a rural proletariat.[13]

The few voices of black nationalism in the period, which might have offered a counterpoint to self-help and elevation, were drowned out in the promise of inclusion. Even Martin R. Delany, the staunchest of antebellum separatists, had joined the Union war effort. After the war, he worked for the Freedmen's Bureau, lecturing the former bondspersons on ways they might become prosperous yeomen, independent of their former masters. Still, even Delany succumbed to the promise of inclusion. Having served South Carolina's Republican regime, he became disenchanted with the slow-moving Radical platform and bolted to the Democratic Redeemers in 1876. He would later revive his plans for African colonization, but only after the bitter frustrations of Reconstruction had reduced his hopes that the race might one day make a home for itself within America's borders. For many other leaders as well, the novelty of political participation during Reconstruction submerged the frustrations of the 1850s. Throughout the 1860s and 1870s, thousands of everyday slights suffered by freedpeople in the South incubated those frustrations, nurturing the basis of a rural proletariat ready and willing to act on a sense of its corporate violations. The first hints of mass uprising against white supremacy arose in 1879, when tens of thousands of blacks fled the racial tyranny of the South in what became known as the Exoduster movement. The national black leadership responded badly to this popular, largely leaderless movement. Their unsympathetic calls for blacks to stay put exposed the degree to which the social gulf between leaders and constituents had opened in the years following the Civil War.[14]

Black elites' response to the Exoduster movement demonstrated that the thin social glue that had marginally united elite and popular African America in the antebellum North could not bind together those separated by the stronger class and status differences of the postwar South. Increasingly, scholars have begun to emphasize these social distinctions among African Americans in the Jim Crow era,[15] such that it has become an article of faith that these distinctions were born in experiences similar to those of the antebellum North. Yet it is well to remember that although leadership patterns in these two eras were tied by ideological continuities that extended from antebellum to postbellum times, they were also conditioned by social contexts that differed greatly. The postwar South could never hope to achieve whatever thin sense of consensus had been achieved above the Mason-Dixon line. In the antebellum North, the range of social experience of the quarter million free blacks who lived there differed markedly from that which reigned in the postwar South. In the South, a much more highly variegated social structure had long meant that the mass of African Americans differed greatly from the small ranks of exceptional elites. Before the war, free or enslaved status, as well as important distinctions among the free, had served to structure a steep black social pyramid. Emancipation, by failing to appreciably uplift the black masses economically, did little to mute these distinctions. The antebellum free blacks of Deep South cities like Charleston, Savannah, Mobile, and New Orleans had often played conspicuous roles in the black political leadership in their states during Reconstruction, though they frequently fell under attack from the formerly enslaved, who charged them with self-aggrandizement and neglect of the interests of the mass. Some may have avoided Republican politics altogether, viewing it as an enterprise fit only for their social inferiors.[16]

With the failure of Reconstruction, some of these elites retreated to their old patterns, relying once again on the patronage of wealthy whites rather than on a risky alliance with the disfranchised folk. Others, however, would not. Southerners such as T. Thomas Fortune, Ida B. Wells, Henry McNeal Turner, and Mary Church Terrell emerged from a tradition of activism pioneered in the antebellum North. They could look to mentors from this tradition, such as Frances Ellen Watkins Harper and James Mercer Langston, who had lived through the war to inspire a new generation. Others, such as W. E. B. Du Bois, would themselves come from the North. For the first time a truly national cadre of committed public activists, perched between black folk experience and a public sphere dominated by whites, could emerge to fill the ranks of the "race men" and women who carried the struggle forward into the twentieth century.

Notes

ABBREVIATIONS

BAP   *The Black Abolitionist Papers*, 5 vols., edited by C. Peter Ripley [...] y E.
         Finkenbine, Michael F. Hembree, and Donald Yacavone.

BAPC   *The Black Abolitionist Papers, 1830–1865* (microfilm collection), edited
         by George E. Carter, C. Peter Ripley, and Jeffrey Rossbach.

BIP   Banneker Institute Papers, Gardiner Collection, Historical Society of
         Pennsylvania, Philadelphia

DA   *A Dictionary of Americanisms, On Historical Principles*, edited by Mit-
         ford M. Mathews (Chicago: University of Chicago Press, 1951).

DARE   *Dictionary of American Regional English*, edited by Frederic G. Cassidy
         (Cambridge, Mass.: Belknap, 1996).

HSP   Historical Society of Pennsylvania, Philadelphia

LCP   Library Company of Philadelphia, Philadelphia

NC30   *Constitution of the American Society of Free Persons of Colour, for Improv-
         ing Their Condition in the United States; for Purchasing Lands; and for
         the Establishment of a Settlement in Upper Canada, Also the Proceedings
         of the Convention, with Their Address to the Free Persons of Colour in the
         United States* (Philadelphia: J. W. Allen, 1831), i.e., proceedings of
         first national convention, held in 1830.

NC31   *Minutes and Proceedings of the First Annual Convention of the People of
         Colour, Held by Adjournments in the City of Philadelphia, from the Sixth
         to the Eleventh of June, Inclusive, 1831* (Philadelphia: By Order of the
         Committee of Arrangements, 1831).

NC32   *Minutes and Proceedings of the Second Annual Convention, for the Improve-
         ment of the Free People of Color in These United States, Held by Adjournments
         in the City of Philadelphia, from the 4th to the 13 of June Inclusive, 1832*
         (Philadelphia: By Order of the Convention, 1832).

NC33   *Minutes and Proceedings of the Third Annual Convention, for the Improvement
         of the Free People of Colour in These United States, Held by Adjournments
         in the City of Philadelphia, from the 3d to the 13th of June Inclusive, 1833*
         (New York: By Order of the Convention, 1833).

NC34   *Minutes of the Fourth Annual Convention, for the Improvement of the Free
         People of Colour, in the United States, Held by Adjournments in the Asbury
         Church, New York, from the 2d to the 12th of June Inclusive, 1834* (New
         York: By Order of the Convention, 1834).

NC35   *Minutes of the Fifth Annual Convention for the Improvement of the Free People
         of Colour in the United States, Held by Adjournment, in the Wesley Church,
         Philadelphia, from the First to the Fifth of June, Inclusive, 1835* (Philadel-
         phia: William P. Gibbons, 1835).

NC43   *Minutes of the National Convention of Colored Citizens: Held at Buffalo, on the*
                15th, 16th, 17th, 18th and 19th of August, 1843. For the Purpose of Con-
                sidering Their Moral and Political Condition as American Citizens (New
                York: Piercy and Reed, 1843).

NC47   *Proceedings of the National Convention of Colored People, and Their Friends,*
                Held in Troy, N.Y., on the 6th, 7th, 8th and 9th October, 1847 (Troy, N.Y.:
                J. C. Kneeland and Co., 1847).

NC48   *Report of the Proceedings of the Colored National Convention, Held at Cleve-*
                land, Ohio, on Wednesday, September 6, 1848 (Rochester: John Dick,
                1848).

NC53   *Proceedings of the Colored National Convention, Held in Rochester, July 6th,*
                7th and 8th, 1853 (Rochester: Office of Frederick Douglass' Paper,
                1853).

NC55   *Proceedings of the Colored National Convention, Held in Franklin Hall,*
                Sixth Street, below Arch, Philadelphia, October 16th, 17th and 18th, 1855
                (Salem, N.J.: National Standard Office, 1856).

OED   *Oxford English Dictionary,* 2d ed., 20 vols., edited by J. A. Simpson and
                E. S. C. Weiner (Oxford: Clarendon, 1989).

RHHDAS   *Random House Historical Dictionary of American Slang,* 2 vols., edited by
                J. E. Lighter (New York: Random House, 1997).

Note: Minutes of the black national conventions denoted by the abbreviation "*NC*"
are reproduced in H. H. Bell, *Minutes of the Proceedings of the National Negro Conven-*
tions, 1830–1864.

INTRODUCTION

1. *BAP,* 1:540. The tale has appeared at least once before the abolitionist movement in the Western literary tradition in, of all places, Chaucer, to make the point
that control of knowledge and language has implications for social power relations.
In the prologue to "The Wife of Bath's Tale," the Wife counters the arguments of
a tradition of misogynistic writers by asking, "Who painted the leon, tel me who?"
(698), thus charging men with constructing "auctoritee" in their gender interests.
Norton Anthology of English Literature, 1:150.

2. The original reads: "Hereditary bondsmen! know ye not, / Who would be free,
themselves must strike the blow?" Lord Byron, *Childe Harold's Pilgrimage,* canto ii,
stanza 76.

3. This conception of the problem evolved in a context of sociological and historical thinking highly predisposed toward the model pioneered by Chicago-school
sociologists such as Robert Park. The classic texts here are Myrdal, *An American Di-*
lemma; Cox, *Caste, Class, and Race;* E. F. Frazier, *The Negro Family in the United States*
and *The Negro Church in America;* and Gordon, *Assimilation in American Life.* Classic
historical treatments include Handlin, *Boston's Immigrants, The Uprooted,* and *Race and*
Nationality in American Life; Glazer and Moynihan, *Beyond the Melting Pot.* For recent

approaches that still rely on some conception of the assimilation-separation paradigm, see Barkan, "Race, Religion, and Nationality in American Society"; Landrine and Klonoff, *African American Acculturation*; Salins, *Assimilation, American Style*. For an overview of the issue, see Kazal, "Revisiting Assimilation: The Rise, Fall, and Reappraisal of a Concept in American Ethnic History."

4. Huggins, *Black Odyssey*.

5. Patricia Nelson Limerick expresses similar concerns in "Has 'Minority' History Transformed the Historical Discourse?"

6. For a comprehensive overview but rather polemical critique of the community studies/culturalist paradigm, see C. E. Walker, *Deromanticizing Black History*. Also valuable is Peter Kolchin's more moderate take in "Re-evaluating the Antebellum Slave Community."

7. Studies that discuss black separatism or black nationalism in the antebellum North include H. H. Bell, "The Negro Emigration Movement, 1849–1854"; Essien-Udom, *Black Nationalism*; Lynch, "Pan-Negro Nationalism in the New World, Before 1862"; McAdoo, *Pre–Civil War Black Nationalism*; Draper, *Rediscovery of Black Nationalism*; Stuckey, *Ideological Origins of Black Nationalism*, 1–29, and *Slave Culture: Nationalist Theory and the Foundations of Black America*; Carlisle, *Roots of Black Nationalism*; F. J. Miller, *Search for a Black Nationality*; Pinkney, *Red, Black, and Green*; J. E. Turner, "Historical Dialectics of Black Nationalist Movements in America"; R. L. Hall, *Black Separatism in the United States*; Levesque, "Interpreting Early Black Ideology"; V. P. Franklin, *Black Self-Determination*; Kinshasa, *Emigration vs. Assimilation*; Tate, "Black Nationalism: An Angle of Vision" and "Black Nationalism and Spiritual Redemption"; Herod and Herod, "Core Values, Myths, and Myth Systems in Afro-American National Consciousness"; McCartney, *Black Power Ideologies*; Adeleke, *UnAfrican Americans*.

CHAPTER ONE

1. *Frederick Douglass' Paper*, May 12, 1854.

2. Ibid.

3. Ibid.

4. Jordan, "American Chiaroscuro."

5. William Whipper, *An Address Delivered in Wesley Church on the Evening of June 12, Before the Colored Reading Society of Philadelphia, for Mental Improvement* (Philadelphia: John B. Roberts, 1828), in Porter, *Early Negro Writing*, 115–16.

6. Berlin, *Many Thousands Gone*. Berlin's chronological typology differs from that used here. The best single overview of the history of free people of color throughout the Atlantic world remains Cohen and Greene, *Neither Slave Nor Free*, esp. 1–19.

7. Cohen and Greene, *Neither Slave Nor Free*, 13–16; *Frederick Douglass' Paper*, May 12, 1854.

8. Curtin, *Rise and Fall of the Plantation Complex*, 91–92; Graham, "Slavery and Economic Development: Brazil and the United States South in the Nineteenth Cen-

tury"; Temperly, "Capitalism, Slavery and Ideology"; Toplin, *Abolition of Slavery in Brazil*; E. Foner, *Nothing but Freedom*.

9. Cohen and Greene, *Neither Slave Nor Free*, 1–18; Berlin, *Many Thousands Gone*, 8.

10. Berlin, "Time, Space, and the Evolution of Afro-American Society in British Mainland North America"; Berlin, *Slaves Without Masters*, chaps. 8, 6; Berlin, "Structure of the Free Negro Caste in the Antebellum United States."

11. For more on the black North, see Berlin, *Many Thousands Gone*, 47–63, 177–94; Horton and Horton, *In Hope of Liberty*; S. White, *Somewhat More Independent*; Piersen, *Black Yankees*; Nash, *Forging Freedom*; McManus, *Black Bondage in the North*; L. J. Greene, *The Negro in Colonial New England*.

12. Berlin, "Revolution in Black Life"; Zilversmit, *First Emancipation*.

13. For comparative perspectives on emancipation in the United States, see Drescher, "Brazilian Abolition in Comparative Perspective"; E. Foner, *Nothing but Freedom*; Mullin, "British Caribbean and North American Slaves in an Era of War and Revolution"; D. B. Davis, *Problem of Slavery in the Age of Revolution*.

14. Curry, *The Free Black in Urban America*, 266.

15. Reprinted in *Anglo-African Magazine* 1, no. 8 (August 1859): 255.

16. Willson, *Sketches of the Higher Classes of Colored Society*, 23–24.

17. Ibid.

18. *Colored American*, September 30, 1837.

19. Charles L. Remond, "Address to a Legislative Committee in the Massachusetts House of Representatives, 1842," *Liberator*, February 25, 1842.

20. For the classic statement on this theme, see Morgan, *American Slavery, American Freedom*.

21. *Colored American*, September 26, 1840.

22. E. Foner, *Nothing but Freedom*; Oakes, "Political Significance of Slave Resistance."

23. Peter Humphries Clark, "A Few Thoughts for the Consideration of the Emigrationists," *Provincial Freeman*, March 24, 1855, in *BAPC*, 9:905–6.

24. *NC48*, 18. See also Henry Highland Garnet's call for slave rebellion: "While you have been oppressed," he wrote his brethren in bonds, "we have been partakers with you; nor can we be free while you are enslaved. We, therefore, write to you as being bound with you." Stuckey, *Ideological Origins of Black Nationalism*, 165.

25. The sample was developed from the federal manuscript census returns from Boston, Buffalo, Chicago, Cincinnati, and Detroit for 1850 and 1860. It includes data on every African American identified in the census. I am indebted to Dr. James O. Horton and the Afro-American Communities Project at the Smithsonian Institution National Museum of American History for access to these data.

26. *Liberator*, July 27, 1855; "Report of the Committee on Mechanical Branches Among the Colored People of the Free States," *NC55*, 16.

27. *Provincial Freeman*, August 22, 1855, in *BAPC*, 9:788.

28. *Liberator*, September 9, 1864.

29. *Anti-Slavery Bugle*, November 27, 1858, in *BAPC*, 11:423–24.

30. Ibid.

31. *Voice of the Fugitive*, August 27, 1851, in *BAPC*, 7:68.

32. *NC53*; *Voice of the Fugitive*, November 5, 1851, in *BAPC*, 7:166.

33. *Frederick Douglass' Paper*, May 20, 1853.

34. *NC30*, iii–iv.

35. *NC34*, 32–33.

36. Ibid.

37. Ibid., 10, 13, 14; *NC35*, 11.

38. *NC33*, 8.

39. *Colored American*, December 30, 1837. Similarly, a committee report from the 1855 national convention limited its authors' aspirations for the education of black northerners because, it explained, "the masses cannot be deeply learned, in fact only partially developed." *NC55*, 15.

40. Henry McKinney to the Convention, July 4, 1853, *NC53*, 43.

41. *NC43*, 6.

42. *NC35*, 6; *NC47*, 4; *NC48*, 3; *NC53*, 6.

43. *Liberator*, May 11, 1833.

44. *National Enquirer*, June 3, 1837, in *BAPC*, 2:68.

45. *NC53*, 4–5.

46. *Colored American*, December 30, 1837.

47. *NC33*, 5, 9.

48. *Frederick Douglass' Paper*, May 20, 1853.

49. *Liberator*, May 11, 1833.

50. *Provincial Freeman*, March 25, 1854, in *BAPC*, 8:701. See also *Provincial Freeman*, June 28, 1856, in *BAPC*, 10:191.

51. *NC34*, 10, 13, 14.

52. *NC48*, 5.

53. *NC48*, 13.

54. Ibid., 6.

55. *NC48*, 19.

56. *NC53*, 25.

57. Ibid., 39.

58. *Colored American*, January 27, 1838.

59. *Anglo-African Magazine* 1, no. 5 (May 1859): 160.

60. *Colored American*, May 16, 1840.

61. Sidney's reply to "William Whipper's Letters, No. 11," *Colored American*, March 6, 1841.

62. U.S. federal census data from 1850 and 1860, provided by the Afro-American Communities Project, National Museum of American History, Smithsonian Institution, Washington, D.C. Convention participants in the sample group were verified through at least one outside source, such as city directories or secondary sources. For leaders found in both the 1850 and the 1860 census, census information for the year closest to the participant's dates of service were used; if that was inconclusive,

the 1860 sample was used. In profiling "economic elite" and "five-cities" groups, the data for 1850 and 1860 were aggregated; in every case differences in factors between the two census years was less than 4 percent. Only adult males (age 18+) were used.

63. It should be noted that the category of "mulatto" reflected not a biological reality so much as a social convention. It cannot be employed uncritically, as when the assumption is made that whatever constituted a "mulatto" was the same in the eyes of different people or even in the eyes of the same person over time. Perceptions of "mulatto" status were not—and could not—be rooted in specious notions of biology or often unknowable personal racial genealogies. Skin complexion being a marker of class distinction throughout the diaspora, ascriptions of one's color often became determined partially by that status. In effect, social definitions of race often confused etiologies: historically, light skin complexion often denoted class status, but socially class status might suggest skin complexion. Attaining a measure of class and social status might "lighten" one in the eyes of others. The federal census left the matter of determining the "color" of African Americans to the census taker. Instructions read: "In all cases where the person is white, leave the space blank; in all cases where the person is black, insert the letter B; if mulatto, insert M. It is very desirable that these particulars be carefully regarded." "1850 Census: Instructions to Marshals and Assistant Marshals," in Ruggles, Sobek, et al., *Integrated Public Use Series*, http://www.ipums.umn.edu (accessed April 7, 2000). See also Horton, "Shades of Color: The Mulatto in Three Antebellum Northern Communities." More generally on the social meaning of light skin complexion, see Jordan, "American Chiaroscuro"; Williamson, *New People*; Degler, *Neither Black Nor White*.

64. See Carol V. R. George, "Widening the Circle: The Black Church and the Abolitionist Crusade, 1830–1860," in Perry and Fellman, *Antislavery Reconsidered*, 75–95.

65. *North Star*, June 22, 1849.

66. *Freedom's Journal*, March 16, 1827.

67. Newman, "Transformation of American Abolition," Ph.D. diss., chaps. 4–5.

68. Takaki, *Iron Cages*, 28–35.

69. Joseph Sydney, *An Oration, Commemorative of the Abolition of the Slave Trade in the United States; Delivered Before the Wilberforce Philanthropic Association, in the City of New York, on the Second of January, 1809* (New York: J. Seymour, 1809), reprinted in Porter, *Early Negro Writing*, 361.

70. Nash, *Forging Freedom*, 100–133; Litwack, "Emancipation of the Negro Abolitionist."

71. William Hamilton, *An Oration, on the Abolition of the Slave Trade, Delivered in the Episcopal Asbury African Church, in Elizabeth St. New York, January 2, 1815* (New York: N.Y. African Society, 1815), in Porter, *Early Negro Writing*, 391, 395, 396; *BAP*, 3:358.

72. William Hamilton, *An Oration Delivered in the African Zion Church, on the Fourth of July, 1827, in Commemoration of the Abolition of Domestic Slavery in this State* (New York: Gray and Bunce, 1827), in Porter, *Early Negro Writing*, 101–2.

73. *NC47*, 18–19.

74. Tocqueville, *Democracy in America*, 1:374.

75. My understandings of what constitutes the "truly political" here are informed by, but do not stem from, the problem Eugene Genovese sets forth in *From Rebellion to Revolution*. For an early statement of this position, see his "The Legacy of Black Nationalism and Roots of Black Nationalism." See also Frederickson and Lasch, "Resistance to Slavery." This is not to say, however, that "pre-political" resistance could not have political *implications*. I am persuaded by the argument James Oakes makes in "The Political Significance of Slave Resistance."

76. "Pragmatic" here does not signify the philosophy of John Dewey. For an analysis formally informed by that perspective, see Glaude, *Exodus!*

77. Wm. [William] Watkins to Friend [John P.] Burr, August 13, 1838, *Pennsylvania Freeman*, September 6, 1838, in *BAP*, 3:281.

78. Ibid.

79. *Colored American*, March 29, 1838.

80. Ibid., March 6, 1841.

81. Wm. [William] Watkins to Friend [John P.] Burr, August 13, 1838, *Pennsylvania Freeman*, September 6, 1838, in *BAP*, 3:280.

82. *Colored American*, March 6, 1841.

83. *NC48*, 19.

84. *NC53*, 22–23, 30.

85. Martin R. Delany, "Great Continental and West Indian Convention," May 29, 1856, *Provincial Freeman*, May 31, 1856, in *BAPC*, 10:172.

86. *Colored American*, February 13, 1841.

87. *Frederick Douglass' Paper*, May 12, 1854, in *BAP*, 4:222.

88. See Hutchinson, *Harlem Renaissance in Black and White.*

89. In this respect, the Civil War and promises of Reconstruction actually delayed black activists' eventual disillusionment with the system. That took the nadir of Jim Crow. See the Epilogue.

90. Wicks, *Address*, 6.

CHAPTER TWO

1. The poem appeared in the *Lynn Mirror*, May 28, 1831, and is quoted in Faler, *Mechanics and Manufacturers*, 128–29. Faler identifies the author only as a "Lynn historian."

2. Blackfacing took place not merely on the stage. As blacks came to be excluded from militia and artillery Election Days in New England or from Independence Day festivities in Philadelphia, whites in blackface appeared at those gatherings. Roediger, *Wages of Whiteness*, 105. See also the problem Eric Lott sets up in *Love and Theft*, chap. 1.

3. Williams-Meyers, "Pinkster Carnival: Africanisms in the Hudson River Valley," 15. Restrictions on Pinkster and Election Day were imposed gradually, in some places lagging considerably behind the end of slavery. In Massachusetts, for instance, where slavery ended in 1783, it was not until 1831 that Election Days were switched to

colder months to inhibit revelry. Roediger, *Wages of Whiteness*, 101. For the legislated end of slave celebrations, see also S. White, "'It Was a Proud Day'"; S. White, "Pinkster: Afro-Dutch Syncretization in New York City and the Hudson Valley." White's "'It Was a Proud Day'" offers the best treatment of the transition from slave festivals to post-emancipation celebrations. For important treatments of black public celebrations following the northern emancipations, see Wiggins, "'Lift Every Voice'"; Sweet, "The Fourth of July and Black Americans in the Nineteenth Century"; McKivigan and Silverman, "Monarchial Liberty and Republic Slavery: West Indies Emancipation Celebrations in Upstate New York and Canada West"; Wiggins, *O Freedom!*; Geneviève Fabre, "African-American Commemorative Celebrations in the Nineteenth Century," in Fabre and O'Meally, *History and Memory in African-American Culture*.

4. Antislavery celebrations did not begin after the last mass northern emancipation in New York in 1827. Among the first public celebrations organized by free African American leaders were several commemorating the abolition of the slave trade. The distinction to be made here is between "folk" celebrations, carried out primarily by slaves with the complicity of masters, and those put on by a free, ostensibly middle-class African American leadership. While the latter predated the end of the former, it was the elimination of the slave celebrations that provided an opportunity for African American leaders to employ their observances to incorporate non-elite African Americans into an activist culture, which stressed seemingly bourgeois values. See Gravely, "Dialectic of Double Consciousness in Black American Freedom Celebrations, 1808–1863"; S. White, "'It Was a Proud Day,'" 34–35. For older antislavery celebrations, see A. Jones, *A Thanksgiving Sermon*; William Hamilton, *An Address to the New York African Society, for Mutual Relief* (New York, 1809), in Porter, *Early Negro Writing*, 33–41; Carman, *An Oration Delivered at the Fourth Anniversary of the Abolition of the Slave Trade*; Parrott, *An Oration on the Abolition of the Slave Trade*; Sidney, *An Oration, Commemorative of the Abolition of the Slave Trade in the United States*.

5. For more on training days, see Piersen, *Black Yankees*, 122, 136–39. For a look at white training days, see Mook, "Training Day in New England."

6. For more discussions of public slave festivities in the antebellum North, see S. White, "'It Was a Proud Day'"; Roediger, *Wages of Whiteness*, 100–104; S. White, *Somewhat More Independent*, 95–106; S. White, "Pinkster"; Piersen, *Black Yankees*, 117–40; Williams-Meyers, "Pinkster Carnival"; Cohen, "In Search of Carolus Africanus Rex"; M. Wade, "'Shining in Borrowed Plumage'"; Reidy, "'Negro Election Day' and Black Community Life in New England." For the concept of social inversion at public festivities, see Bakhtin, *Rabelais and His World*; Stallybrass and White, *Politics and Poetics of Transgression*; V. W. Turner, *Ritual Process*, 176–77.

7. See Genovese, *Roll, Jordan, Roll*, 87–96.

8. James Fenimore Cooper, *Satanstoe* (1845; reprint, New York, n.d.), 66–67; quoted in S. White, "'It Was a Proud Day,'" 24, 23, 27; quoted in M. Wade, "'Shining in Borrowed Plumage,'" 215. Accounts from the South echoed the sentiments of northern observers. In 1843, for example, William Cullen Bryant witnessed South

Carolina slaves dancing "a sort of burlesque of our militia trainings, in which the words of command and the evolutions were extremely ludicrous." Quoted in L. W. Levine, *Black Culture and Black Consciousness*, 17.

9. Frederick Douglass, "What Are the Colored People Doing for Themselves," July 14, 1848, in Brotz, *African-American Social and Political Thought*, 204–5. See also "The First of August Fair at Buffalo," in *North Star*, June 29, 1849.

10. *North Star*, August 4, 1848.

11. Ibid., July 28, 1848.

12. *NC32*, 27; *NC34*, 14. See also *NC31*, 11.

13. *North Star*, July 28, 1848.

14. Douglass, "What Are the Colored People Doing for Themselves?" in Brotz, *African-American Social and Political Thought*, 205.

15. *North Star*, February 9, 1849.

16. "A Statistical Inquiry into the Condition of the People of Color of the City and Districts of Philadelphia," in ibid., February 2, 1849.

17. Quoted in S. White, "'It Was a Proud Day,'" 40. It should be noted that Cornish also understood black celebrations in terms of their strategic implications, asking, "Have they not rather a tendency to injure us, by exciting prejudice, and making the public believe we care for nothing so much as show?" and voicing his fear that public festivals "will injure our reputation and our interest as a people." *Freedom's Journal*, June 29, 1827.

18. *Colored American*, April 29, 1837.

19. Ibid., August 15, 1840.

20. James McCune Smith, "The German Invasion," *Anglo-African Magazine* 1, no. 3 (March 1859), 85.

21. *North Star*, January 28, 1848.

22. Ibid., July 14, 1848.

23. Quoted in Gravely, "Dialectic of Double Consciousness," 306.

24. *Liberator*, September 1, 1848.

25. *North Star*, April 20, 1849.

26. *Colored American*, April 29, 1837.

27. Ibid., August 25, 1838.

28. *Emancipator*, August 17, 1843, in *BAPC*, 4:652.

29. *Western Herald*, August 11, 1842, in *BAPC*, 4:461.

30. *Liberator*, September 1, 1848.

31. Ibid.

32. *Liberator*, August 13, 1858.

33. *Colored American*, April 29, 1837.

34. *Liberator*, August 7, 1846.

35. *North Star*, August 10, 1849.

36. *Colored American*, August 25, 1838.

37. *Western Herald*, August 11, 1842, in *BAPC*, 4:461.

38. *Liberator*, September 1, 1848.

39. Ibid., August 11, 1832.

40. *Colored American*, August 5, 1837.

41. *Philanthropist*, August 18, 1841, in *BAPC*, 4:162.

42. *Emancipator*, August 17, 1843, in *BAPC*, 4:652.

43. *Liberator*, July 7, 1848.

44. Ibid., August 13, 1858.

45. *Signal of Liberty*, August 11, 1848, in *BAPC*, 5:747.

46. *National Enquirer*, August 31, 1836, in *BAPC*, 1:699.

47. *Colored American*, August 5, 1837. If the numbers reported for this gathering were correct, it would have been one of the largest Emancipation Day celebrations recorded in the antebellum North. Though his memory may have inflated the numbers, Austin Steward recalled a meeting of 10,000 having gathered at a Canandaigua, New York, Emancipation Day celebration in 1847. Steward, *Twenty-Two Years a Slave*, 309–12. On other large celebrations, see Quarles, *Black Abolitionists*, 117–29; Gravely, "Dialectic of Double Consciousness," 304, 314 n. 23.

48. *Colored American*, August 25, 1838.

49. *Signal of Liberty*, August 11, 1848, in *BAPC*, 5:747.

50. *Liberator*, September 1, 1848.

51. *Colored American*, April 29, 1837.

52. *Freedom's Journal*, July 6, 1827.

53. Ibid., April 27, 1827.

54. *Colored American*, August 25, 1838.

55. *National Enquirer*, August 31, 1836, in *BAPC*, 1:699.

56. *Colored American*, August 25, 1838.

57. *North Star*, August 4, 1848.

58. Ibid., August 11, 1848.

59. *National Enquirer*, August 31, 1836, in *BAPC*, 1:699.

60. *Colored American*, August 25, 1838; August 17, 1839. That two cities so far removed from New York City took pains to collect funds for the *Colored American* indicates the wide influence such newspapers had. They were read far beyond their immediate communities and carried news from even farther.

61. *Liberator*, August 7, 1846.

62. Ibid., August 13, 1858.

63. Davis D. Turner et al. to the Banneker Institute, November 5, 1857, BIP, box 5G, folder 3; Parker T. Smith to the Banneker Institute, October 29, 1857, BIP, box 5G, folder 6; Parker T. Smith, Davis D. Turner, and A. M. Campbell to the Banneker Institute, April 1, 1858, BIP, box 5G, folder 8.

64. *Liberator*, July 26, 1839.

65. *Colored American*, August 31, 1839. The cost of tickets for the temperance meal was not specified.

66. G. [George] T. Burrell and O. [Octavius] V. Catto to the Banneker Institute, May 25, 1859, BIP, box 5G, folder 3.

67. Minutes of the Banneker Institute, July 1855, BIP, box 5G, folder 3.

68. *Liberator,* September 1, 1848.

69. *Douglass' Monthly* 2 (1859): 113, quoted in Gravely, "Dialectic of Double Consciousness," 305.

70. *National Enquirer,* August 31, 1836, in *BAPC,* 1:699.

71. *Liberator,* July 26, 1839.

72. Ibid.

73. *Philanthropist,* August 18, 1841, in *BAPC,* 4:162.

74. *National Enquirer,* August 17, 1836, in *BAPC,* 1:691.

75. *Colored American,* August 25, 1838.

76. *Western Herald,* August 11, 1842, in *BAPC,* 4:461.

77. *Colored American,* August 25, 1838.

78. In 1838, Cincinnati's Emancipation Day dinner was billed as a "total abstinence dinner." *Colored American,* August 25, 1838.

79. Ibid., August 15, 1840.

80. For more on the distinction made between distilled and brewed alcoholic beverages, see Yacovone, "Transformation of the Black Temperance Movement."

81. *Liberator,* August 13, 1858.

82. Such was the case with Buffalo's celebration in 1858. There, on the day of the celebration, planners met to organize a convention for black leaders throughout the region, to be held the following month. *Frederick Douglass' Paper,* September 17, 1858. For another example, see *Anti-Slavery Bugle,* July 20, 1850, in *BAPC,* 6:546.

83. *Philanthropist,* August 18, 1841, in *BAPC,* 4:162; *Colored American,* August 25, 1838.

84. Buffalo organizer George Weir Jr. sent notice to Frederick Douglass of an August 1 celebration as early as April. *North Star,* April 20, 1849.

85. *Liberator,* September 1, 1848.

86. *North Star,* August 10, 1849. See also ibid., September 14, August 24, 1849.

87. "Report of Committee Appointed to Celebrate the Anniversary of the Emancipation of the Slaves in the British West India Islands," August 1858, BIP, box 5G, folder 9.

88. *Colored American,* July 27, 1839.

89. Quoted in Piersen, *Black Yankees,* 120; quoted in S. White, "'It Was a Proud Day,'" 22.

90. Neither Goury's name nor Leach's appeared on the records of the state and national black conventions they might have attended, nor on the records of local meetings held in their respective cities. Hardenburg marshaled in several New York City parades and attended the national black conventions of 1834 and 1835. See S. White, "'It Was a Proud Day,'" 44; H. H. Bell, *Minutes of the Proceedings of the National Negro Conventions.* Marshals had been consistent elements of the slave festivals; their positions were distinct from that of king or governor.

91. See Shane White's critique of Ira Berlin's argument that Negro Election Day provided the basis for later black politics. S. White, "'It Was a Proud Day,'" 49; Berlin, "Time, Space, and the Evolution of Afro-American Society in British Main-

land North America," 54. For positions similar to Berlin's, see Piersen, *Black Yankees*, chap. 11; Reidy, "'Negro Election Day.'"

92. "Grand Bobalition, or 'GREAT ANNIBERSARY FUSSIBLE,'" Broadside Collection, portfolio 53, no. 11, Rare Book and Special Collections Division, Library of Congress, Washington, D.C. See also Phillip Lapsansky, "Graphic Discord: Abolitionist and Antiabolitionist Images," in Yellin and Van Horne, *Abolitionist Sisterhood*, esp. 218–21.

93. S. White, "'It Was a Proud Day,'" 20–21. Of public parades, Mary Ryan has written that "these processions—what we might today call demonstrations—were quite properly seen in the 1830s, 1840s and 1850s as insurgent public actions," designed as militant gestures of democratic faith at a time "when such popular democratic action was still suspect." Ryan, "The American Parade," in L. Hunt, *New Cultural History*, 137. For more on parades and public processions, see Sean Wilentz, "Artisan Republican Festivals and the Rise of Class Conflict in New York City, 1788–1837," in Frisch and Walkowitz, *Working-Class America*; S. G. Davis, *Parades and Power*; Marston, "Public Rituals and Community Power"; Scobey, "Anatomy of the Promenade."

94. Otter, *History of My Own Time*, 114–17.

95. Sol Smith, *Theatrical Management in the West and South* (New York, 1968), 12, quoted in Roediger, *Wages of Whiteness*, 101, and in S. White, "'It Was a Proud Day,'" 17.

96. Gilje, *Road to Mobocracy*, 32, 228; Wilentz, *Chants Democratic*, 169.

97. See Gilje, *Road to Mobocracy*, esp. 287; Roediger, *Wages of Whiteness*, 100–111; L. L. Richards, *"Gentlemen of Property and Standing."*

98. Roediger, *Wages of Whiteness*, 107–8; Lapsansky, "'Since They Got Those Separate Churches,'" 64. David Roediger counted at least ten race riots between 1829 and 1841; Leon Litwack counted five alone in Philadelphia between 1832 and 1849. Roediger, *Wages of Whiteness*, 103; Litwack, *North of Slavery*, 100. For more on riots in the antebellum North, see Grimsted, *American Mobbing*; Gilje, *Road to Mobocracy*; Werner, *Reaping the Bloody Harvest*; S. G. Davis, "'Making the Night Hideous'"; Runcie, "'Hunting the Nigs' in Philadelphia"; Grimsted, "Rioting in Its Jacksonian Setting."

99. *Hazard's Register*, September 27, 1834, 200–204, in Foner and Lewis, *The Black Worker*, 1:170.

100. Quoted in Litwack, *North of Slavery*, 101. See also Du Bois, *Philadelphia Negro*, 27–29; Nash, *Forging Freedom*, 274.

101. Foner and Lewis, *The Black Worker*, 1:175–76. The committee suggested that white townspeople refuse to buy the produce of "any one who employs Negroes to do that species of labor white men have been accustomed to perform." It also planned to negotiate with black freeholders for the sale of their land in an attempt to remove them from the town entirely.

102. Winch, *Philadelphia's Black Elite*, 149–50; Litwack, *North of Slavery*, 102.

103. *Freedom's Journal*, July 13, 1827.

104. *Weekly Anglo-African,* December 29, 1860, in *BAPC,* 13:72.

105. *Liberator,* September 1, 1848.

106. Berlin, *Many Thousands Gone,* 192; Berlin, "Time, Space, and the Evolution of Afro-American Society"; Reidy, "Negro Election Day"; Wiggins, *O Freedom!*; Piersen, *Black Legacy.*

107. Geneviève Fabre, "African-American Commemorative Celebrations in the Nineteenth Century," in Fabre and O'Meally, *History and Memory in African-American Culture,* 72–91.

108. Report of Committee Appointed to Celebrate the Anniversary of the Emancipation of the Slaves in the British West India Islands, August 1858, BIP, box 5G, folder 9.

109. J[eremiah] Sanderson to W[illia]m C. Nell, July 20, 1842, in *BAPC,* 4:444.

110. *Colored American,* July 28, 1838.

111. *Weekly Anglo-African,* December 29, 1860, in *BAPC,* 13:72.

112. *National Anti-Slavery Standard,* October 16, 1845, in *BAPC,* 5:82.

113. *Weekly Anglo-African,* July 23, 1859.

114. Frederick Douglass, "What to the Slave is the Fourth of July," delivered July 4, 1852, in Aptheker, *Documentary History,* 1:331.

115. *Liberator,* June 16, 1854.

116. Quoted in Gravely, "Dialectic of Double Consciousness," 307.

117. In much the same way, Democrats and Whigs educated a broad segment of Americans, bringing them into the first truly mass political parties. See J. A. Baker, *Affairs of Party.* For more extensive discussion of addresses given at antislavery celebrations, see Chapters 4–7.

118. This demand for a new racial identity constituted an early expression of the "New Negro" figure in the black protest tradition. For later manifestations, see Gates, "The Trope of a New Negro and the Reconstruction of the Image of the Black."

119. See Carol V. R. George, "Widening the Circle: The Black Church and the Abolitionist Crusade, 1830–1860," in Perry and Fellman, *Antislavery Reconsidered,* 75–95.

CHAPTER THREE

1. "The Name 'Negro,'" *The Crisis* 34 (March 1928), reprinted in Sundquist, *Oxford W. E. B. Du Bois Reader,* 70–72.

2. To this list, many other names could be added, such as the African Clarkson Association, a New York mutual aid society begun in 1825, or the African Female Benevolent Society of Troy, New York, which published its constitution in 1834. Philadelphia and Albany also had churches with the word "African" in their names. Capsule histories of most of these institutions may be found in *BAP,* vol. 3.

3. Berlin, "Time, Space, and the Evolution of Afro-American Society in British Mainland North America." For other treatments that endorse the culturalist interpretation, see Draper, *Rediscovery of Black Nationalism,* 19–20; Pease and Pease, *They*

Who Would Be Free, 101–3; Pinkney, *Red, Black, and Green,* 22–23; Moses, *Golden Age of Black Nationalism,* 32; Berry and Blassingame, *Long Memory,* 388–97; Stuckey, *Slave Culture,* chap. 4; Horton, *Free People of Color,* 153–60; Smitherman, "'What Is Africa to Me?'"; Collier-Thomas and Turner, "Race, Class and Color," 5–31. Consult also Moore, *The Name "Negro"*; Fairchild, "Black, Negro, or Afro-American?"; T. W. Smith, "Changing Racial Labels." The discussion that follows is concerned only with the issue of names as it has been applied to African Americans as a whole. For practices associated with the naming of individuals, see Genovese, *Roll, Jordan, Roll,* 443–50; Berlin, "Time, Space, and the Evolution of Afro-American Society"; Robert L. Hall, "African Religious Retentions in Florida," in Holloway, *Africanisms in American Culture,* 101–3.

4. This is the argument Sterling Stuckey makes in *Slave Culture,* chap. 1.

5. Horton, *Free People of Color,* 154; *Constitution of the African Marine Fund* (New York, 1810), in Porter, *Early Negro Writing,* 43.

6. *Freedom's Journal,* March 16, 1827, in Aptheker, *Documentary History,* 1:84. For examples of the argument made in this paragraph, see Stuckey, *Slave Culture,* chap. 4; Horton, *Free People of Color,* chap. 7.

7. Rawley, *Transatlantic Slave Trade,* chaps. 14–16; Berlin, "Time, Space, and the Evolution of Afro-American Society," 51–52.

8. Berlin, *Many Thousands Gone,* 374; McManus, *Black Bondage in the North,* 210.

9. See, for example, Jordan, *White over Black,* 305–8; Nederveen Pieterse, *White on Black.*

10. Berlin, *Many Thousands Gone,* 254–55.

11. Greenbaum, "Comparison of African American and Euro-American Mutual Aid Societies in 19th Century America," 111; Handlin, *Boston's Immigrants,* chap. 6.

12. Staudenraus, *African Colonization Movement.*

13. Brewer, "John B. Russwurm."

14. Sterling Stuckey makes this argument in *Slave Culture,* 202. See also Mehlinger, "Attitude of the Free Negro Toward Colonization."

15. *Liberator,* February 22, 1834.

16. Quoted in Horton, *Free People of Color,* 159.

17. *RHHDAS,* 2:657; *OED,* 10:304.

18. *RHHDAS,* 2:657.

19. "How graceless Ham *leughed* at his Dad, / Which made *Canaan* a niger." Ibid.

20. It is not difficult to find English instances of "nigger." Most notoriously, the peoples of colonized India were subjected to the epithet, and at the very time the word was coming to be described as an American particularism.

21. *OED,* 10:402.

22. *DARE,* 3:788. See also the account of English actor Charles Mathews's trip to New York, where he encountered the African Grove Theater, which he found "called the Niggers' (or Negroes') theatre." Mathews, *The London Mathews,* 11. See also Mary Duncan's account of her visit to New York City in 1852: "It is the humour of some [whites] to indulge and spoil them [blacks], allowing in them familiarity which they

would not permit in a white, while others trample on them, reproach them for being 'niggers,' &c. In either case they are not treated fairly." Duncan, *America as I Found It*, 218.

23. *RHHDAS*, 2:657.

24. *DARE*, 3:788.

25. *OED*, 10:403.

26. Ibid., 10:404.

27. Slotkin, *Fatal Environment*.

28. Runcie, "'Hunting the Nigs' in Philadelphia," 190.

29. *RHHDAS*, 2:656.

30. Ibid., 657; *DARE*, 2:788.

31. More work needs to be done on the history of the word "nigger" in the twentieth century, and especially the emergence of its dual connotations: among whites as the worst possible epithet to employ against a black person, and among blacks as a term of endearment marking in-group status. This latter use of "nigger" among blacks emerged during the early twentieth century, probably as a result of Harlem Renaissance authors' concern with celebrating black folk culture, including popular speech. Black southerners had long used the term in just this way. Perhaps their employment of it in slavery and after functioned as one of the myriad ways blacks masked meanings from whites, in the process inverting or subverting caste hierarchy. Their intentions often proved indecipherable to whites, who generally heard to their satisfaction evidence of properly subordinated slave personalities. Blacks, of course, relying on subtle and impenetrable cues, knew better. Hence, white reporters' incessant confusion over whether or when "nigger" served as an insult among blacks.

32. *DA*, 2:1117.

33. Ibid., 2:1121. See also Bryson, *Made in America*, 75.

34. *DARE*, 3:789, 790; *OED*, 10:402, 404.

35. *RHHDAS*, 2:657; *OED*, 10:402, 403; *DA*, 2:1120.

36. *DA*, 2:1120.

37. *DARE*, 3:791.

38. *OED*, 10:404.

39. On Charles Brown (Artemis Ward), see Sala, *Yankee Drolleries*, and "Artemus Ward in the South," *Vanity Fair* 3 (1861), 251–52; on David Ross Locke (Petroleum V. Nasby), Locke, *Nasby Papers*; on George William Bagby (Mozis Addums), [George William Bagby], "The Letters of Mozis Addums to Billy Ivins, Part I," *Southern Literary Magazine* 26, no. 2 (1858): 121–25. For an example of African American spokespersons using the term "nigger" in this manner, see "Colorphobia.—A Discovery," *North Star*, April 28, 1849.

40. See, for example, C. [Edward Williams Clay], "Set-to Between the Champion Old Tip & the Swell Dutchman of Kinderhook—1836" (New York: H. R. Robinson, 1836), in Still Photographs and Prints Division, Library of Congress, Washington, D.C.

41. *DARE*, 3:788.

42. *RHHDAS*, 2:657.

43. Ibid., 2:658, 656. Over a century after the "N-word" complex began bifurcating in the North, scholar John Dollard documented the ways white southern practice continued to straddle the divide between what northerners defined as respectful and disparaging pronunciations of the words. "Evidently southern white men say 'nigger' as standard practice, 'nigruh,' a slightly more respectful form, when talking to a northerner (from whom they expect criticism on the score of treatment of Negroes), but never Negro; that is the hallmark of a northerner and a caste-enemy." Dollard, *Caste and Class in a Southern Town*, 47.

44. L. W. Levine, *Highbrow/Lowbrow*. With particular respect to language, see Cmiel, "'Broad Fluid Language of Democracy,'" 917, 928. Important studies of middle-class culture in this period include Halttunen, *Confidence Men and Painted Women*; Kasson, *Rudeness and Civility*; Bushman, *Refinement of America*.

45. Bryson, *Made in America*, 75.

46. For an insightful examination of the emergence of conflicting class cultures, see Nissenbaum, *Battle for Christmas*, esp. chap. 3.

47. *RHHDAS*, 2:661; *OED*, 10:404.

48. *RHHDAS*, 2:658.

49. *Century Magazine*, 30:786.

50. *RHHDAS*, 2:658.

51. *DA*, 2:1121.

52. *OED*, 10:404.

53. *DA*, 2:1120.

54. *RHHDAS*, 2:659.

55. *DA*, 2:1120.

56. D. Walker, *Appeal*, 55n.

57. *RHHDAS*, 2:658.

58. See Litwack, *North of Slavery*, 225–26.

59. My thanks to Peter Hinks for bringing this fact to my attention.

60. *Freedom's Journal*, August 8, 1828.

61. H. Easton, *Treatise*, 40.

62. *RHHDAS*, 2:658.

63. *Liberator*, June 4, 1831.

64. R. B. Lewis, *Light and Truth*, 342. The term "black" was also used in this period. In petitions delivered by Massachusetts slaves to the colonial government in 1774 and 1777, petitioners referred to themselves as "Blackes." See also petitions submitted to the Massachusetts legislature in 1787 and 1788, in Aptheker, *Documentary History*, 1:8, 9, 6, 10.

65. *Colored American*, October 6, 1838.

66. Frederick Douglass, who uniformly favored "colored" as the appropriate term for the race, lapsed into the N-word complex only when addressing the charges of racial science, as in his essay *The Claims of the Negro Ethnologically Considered*.

67. *RHHDAS*, 2:656.

68. *DARE*, 3:788.

69. *NC30*.

70. Cohen and Greene, *Neither Slave Nor Free*, 11–16. For French origins of the term, see Gwendolyn Midlo Hall, "Saint Domingue," in ibid., 174; Léo Elisabeth, "The French Antilles," in ibid., 135. For Brazil, see Degler, *Neither Black Nor White*; Skidmore, *Black into White*; Graham, *Idea of Race in Latin America*.

71. Johnson and Roarke, *Black Masters*; Berlin, *Slaves Without Masters*.

72. Berlin, *Slaves Without Masters*, 35–36, 58.

73. In 1791 free blacks in South Carolina referred to themselves as "Free-Men of Colour" in a petition to the state legislature. Memorial to the Honorable New Members of the Senate of the State of South Carolina, 1791, in Aptheker, *Documentary History*, 1:26. The phrase had existed in colonial law but had been long displaced by the more inclusive "negroes, mulattoes, and musteez." By the early nineteenth century, its reappearance was surprising enough to occasion considerable legal confusion. *Negro Law of South Carolina, Collected and Digested by John Belton O'Neall, One of the Judges of the Courts of Law and Errors of the Said State* . . . (Columbia, S.C.: John G. Bowman, 1848), in *Statutes on Slavery*, ser. 7, vol. 2, pp. 14–15.

74. Aptheker, *Documentary History*, 1:30–31.

75. *Negro Law of South Carolina, Collected and Digested by John Belton O'Neall, One of the Judges of the Courts of Law and Errors of the Said State* . . . (Columbia, S.C.: John G. Bowman, 1848), in *Statutes on Slavery*, ser. 7, vol. 2, pp. 14–15.

76. "Petition of Burke to the Honorable the Legislature of Virginia [*sic*], 1815," in Aptheker, *Documentary History*, 1:67; Petition of Moses to the Legislature of Virginia, 1822, in ibid., 1:77. See also the petition of Lewis Bolah to the Senate and House of Delegates of the Commonwealth of Virginia, 1824, in ibid., 1:79.

77. Quoted in Fredrickson, *Black Image in the White Mind*, 4.

78. Garrison, *Thoughts on African Colonization*, 2:63; "Meeting of the people of color of Philadelphia, January 1817," in ibid., 2:9; Saunders, *Address*. In their attack on slanders against Philadelphia blacks, published in 1794, Richard Allen and Absalom Jones used the phrase "people of colour" but more frequently referred to their people as "Africans" or "black people." *A Narrative of the Proceedings of the Black People, during the late awful calamity in Philadelphia* (Philadelphia, 1794), in Aptheker, *Documentary History*, 1:32–38.

79. See New York statutes from 1806, 1808, and 1817; the Illinois statute of 1819; and federal statutes from 1807, 1808, and 1820. "An Act Relative to Slaves and Servants," in *Laws Relative to Slaves and Servants, Passed by the Legislature of New-York, March 31st, 1817. Together with Extracts from the Laws of the United States Respecting Slaves* (New York: Samuel Wood and Sons, 1817), 3, in *Statutes on Slavery*, ser. 7, vol. 1, pp. 85–124; *Laws Relative to Slaves and the Slave-Trade* (New York: Samuel Stansbury, 1806), reprinted in ibid., 1:55–84; *Selections from the Revised Statutes of the State of New York: Containing All the Laws of the State Relative to Slaves, and the Law Relative to the Offence of Kidnapping* (New York: Vanderpool and Cole, 1830), reprinted in ibid., 2:1–46; *Slave Code of the State of Illinois, Being an Abstract of Those Laws Now in Force in This State,*

Which Affect the Rights of Colored People, as Such, Both Bond and Free (n.p.: Will Co. Anti-Slavery Society, 1840), in ibid., 2:81–92; *Illinois Slavery. The Laws Now in Force, Which Oppress and Hold in Bondage the Colored People* (n.p., n.d.), in ibid., 2:97–100.

80. *Slave Code of the State of Illinois, Being an Abstract of Those Laws Now in Force in This State, Which Affect the Rights of Colored People, as Such, Both Bond and Free* (n.p.: Will Co. Anti-Slavery Society, 1840), in *Statutes on Slavery*, ser. 7, vol. 2, p. 4.

81. *Selections from the Revised Statutes of the State of New York: Containing All the Laws of the State Relative to Slaves, and the Law Relative to the Offence of Kidnapping* (New York: Vanderpool and Cole, 1830), in *Statutes on Slavery*, ser. 7, vol. 2, pp. 5, 7.

82. *Freedom's Journal*, March 16, 1827, in Aptheker, *Documentary History*, 1:85; D. Walker, *Appeal.*

83. Records of the 1830–31 meetings appear in Garrison, *Thoughts on African Colonization*, 2:9–51.

84. The proceedings of nearly every black convention held in the antebellum North used the phrases "colored people" or "colored citizens." Foner and Walker, *Proceedings of the Black State Conventions.*

85. Figures derived from R. J. Young, "Political Culture of Northern African-American Activists," Ph.D. diss., 279–80. See also Stuckey, *Slave Culture*, 203.

86. L. Foner, "Free People of Color in Louisiana and St. Domingue"; Everett, "Free Persons of Color in Colonial Louisiana."

87. Aptheker, *Documentary History*, 1:31.

88. Garrison, *Thoughts on African Colonization*, 2:46.

89. D. Walker, *Appeal*; Garnet, *Past and Present Condition.*

90. *NC35*, 14–15.

91. *National Reformer*, October 1838, quoted in Stuckey, *Slave Culture*, 206.

92. *Colored American*, September 16, 1837. See also Whipper's letter to Douglass in 1848, challenging the editor for terming the *North Star* a "colored newspaper." Instead of destroying prejudice, Whipper claimed, endorsing complexional denominations would "advocate its perpetuity"; he argued that it was for blacks to place themselves "under that ban of proscription which you have framed for others." *North Star*, February 4, 1848.

93. *Frederick Douglass' Paper*, April 20, 1855.

94. S.S.N., "Anglo-Saxons, and Anglo-Africans," *Anglo-African Magazine* 1, no. 8 (August 1859): 251.

95. *Liberator*, July 16, 1831; *Anti-Slavery Bugle*, February 16, 1856, in *BAPC*, reel 10, frames 59–60.

96. *Colored American*, March 4, 1837.

97. Ibid., March 15, 1838.

98. Ibid., May 29, 1841.

99. Ibid., March 4, 1837.

100. Ibid., September 2, 1837.

101. *National Reformer*, October 1838, quoted in Stuckey, *Slave Culture*, 207. Wat-

kins's understanding of words echoed Lockean notions current at the time. See Cmiel, "'Broad Fluid Language of Democracy,'" 915.

102. Moses, *Golden Age of Black Nationalism*, 32.

103. "Meeting of the people of color of New Haven, Conn., August 8, 1831," in Garrison, *Thoughts on African Colonization*, 2:30–31; "Meeting of the people of color of Columbia, Pa., August 5, 1831," in ibid., 2:31–32.

104. One of his own writers, "S.S.N.," rebuked Hamilton for his newspaper's name, as well as for the racial essentialism he believed references to African identity implied. S.S.N., "Anglo-Saxons, and Anglo-Africans," *Anglo-African Magazine* 1, no. 8 (August 1859): 249–51.

105. Augustus William Hanson, "Address Delivered September 3rd, 1838, Before the New York Association for the Political Elevation and Improvement of the People of Color," *Colored American*, September 15, 1838.

106. *Pennsylvania Freeman*, September 6, 1838, in *BAP*, 3:279–80.

107. *Colored American*, March 13, 1841.

108. Ibid., March 4, 1837.

109. "Proceedings of the National Emigration Convention of Colored People," in Aptheker, *Documentary History*, 1:366.

110. James M'Cune Smith, "On the Fourteenth Query of Thomas Jefferson's Notes on Virginia," *Anglo-African Magazine* 1, no. 8 (August 1859): 236–37.

CHAPTER FOUR

1. Ellison, *Invisible Man*, 498–99.

2. Lawrence Levine addresses blacks' disillusionment with the American success ethos in "Marcus Garvey and the Politics of Revitalization," in Franklin and Meier, *Black Leaders of the Twentieth Century*, 112.

3. Quoted in Werner, *Reaping the Bloody Harvest*, 58, 56.

4. *Cincinnati Gazette*, August 17, 1829, quoted in Litwack, *North of Slavery*, 73.

5. *Liberator*, March 8, 1834.

6. Ibid., February 23, 1833.

7. Ibid., April 13, 1833.

8. *Colored American*, July 13, 1839.

9. *Liberator*, February 23, 1833; Austin Steward to Messrs [William Lloyd] Garrison and [Isaac] Knapp, March 12, 1833, in Woodson, *Mind of the Negro*, 187.

10. *Colored American*, July 13, 1839.

11. A. [Austin] Steward to the Rev. J. Budd, June 1833, in Steward, *Twenty-Two Years a Slave*, 351; *Liberator*, July 16, 1836.

12. A. [Austin] Steward to the Rev. J. Budd, June 1833, in Steward, *Twenty-Two Years a Slave*, 351–52.

13. *Liberator*, February 23, 1833; Lyman A. Spalding to Austin Steward & Benj. [Benjamin] Paul, February 4, 1832, in Steward, *Twenty-Two Years a Slave*, 355; Austin

Steward to Messrs [William Lloyd] Garrison and [Isaac] Knapp, March 12, 1833, in Woodson, *Mind of the Negro*, 186; *Liberator*, April 13, 1833.

14. Jordan, *White Over Black*, 510; see also 217–28, 482–511. For antecedents, see Lovejoy, *Great Chain of Being*; Tillyard, *Elizabethan World Picture*.

15. David Walker, "Address Delivered Before the General Colored Association at Boston," *Freedom's Journal*, December 19, 1828; *North Star*, January 19, 1849; *The Rights of All*, May 29, 1829; *Colored American*, April 22, 1837; "Constitution of the African Female Benevolent Society of Troy," in Wicks, *Address Delivered Before the African Female Benevolent Society of Troy*, 13.

16. Albert Brisbane, *Association; or a Concise Exposition of the Practical Part of Fourier's Social Science*, in Grob and Beck, *American Ideas*, 403.

17. Ethiop, "Afric-American Picture Gallery," *Anglo-African Magazine* 1, no. 7 (July 1859): 218.

18. Sara G. Staley, "Address of the Lady's Anti-Slavery Society of Delaware, Ohio, 1856," in *Proceedings of the State Convention of Colored Men, Held in the City of Columbus, Ohio, January 16th, 17th, and 18th* (n.p., 1856), 382; Amos Gerry Beman, "The Education of the Colored People," *Anglo-African Magazine* 1, no. 11 (November 1859): 338.

19. *North Star*, January 21, 1848.

20. *Pennsylvania Freeman*, April 7, 1853, in *BAPC*, 8:199–202.

21. William J. Watkins, *An Address Delivered Before the Moral Reform Society in Philadelphia* (Philadelphia: Merrihew and Gunn, 1836), 12–13, in *BAPC*, 1:684–90. Such appetites and passions were the same body-bound qualities that Founding Fathers like Thomas Jefferson and John Adams had feared might undermine America's fragile experiment in self-rule. See Takaki, *Iron Cages*, chaps. 1–3; Bailyn, *Ideological Origins of the American Revolution*, chap. 1.

22. "Report of the Committee on Mechanical Trades," *NC55*, 14.

23. Robert Gordon, "Intellectual Culture," *Anglo-African Magazine* 1, no. 6 (June 1859): 187.

24. Robert Benjamin Lewis, *Light and Truth: Collected from the Bible and Ancient and Modern History* (Boston: A Committee of Colored Gentlemen, 1844), 334. For nearly identical language, see H. Easton, *Treatise*, 7.

25. Guthrie, *Address on Education and Human Progress*, 7.

26. *Colored American*, May 6, 1837.

27. "Constitution of the African Female Benevolent Society of Troy," in Wicks, *Address Delivered Before the African Female Benevolent Society of Troy*, 13.

28. Amos Gerry Beman, "The Education of the Colored People," *Anglo-African Magazine* 1, no. 11 (November 1859): 338, 339.

29. Sara G. Staley, "Address of the Ladies' Anti-Slavery Society of Delaware, Ohio, 1856," *Proceedings of the State Convention of Colored Men, Held in the City of Columbus, Ohio, . . . 1856*, in Aptheker, *Documentary History*, 1:382.

30. R. B. Lewis, *Light and Truth*, 334.

31. William J. Watkins, *An Address Before the Moral Reform Society in Philadelphia* (Philadelphia: Merrihew and Gunn, 1836), 5, 7, in *BAPC*, 1:684–90.

32. *Liberator*, September 8, 1832.

33. Robert Gordon, "Intellectual Culture," *Anglo-African Magazine* 1, no. 6 (June 1859): 189, 188.

34. William Hamilton, "Address to the Fourth Annual Convention of the People of Color of the United States," *NC34*, 7.

35. Emerson quoted in Rischin, *American Gospel of Success*, 40, 43.

36. "Benefits of Knowledge on Morals," *Southern Literary Messenger* 4, no. 12 (1838): 772, 773–74.

37. For surveys of religious thought in this period, see McLoughlin, *Revivals, Awakenings, and Reform*, 24–97; Mead, *Lively Experiment*, 16–71.

38. Nathan O. Hatch, "The Origins of Civil Millennialism in America: New England Clergymen, War with France, and the Revolution," in Katz and Murrin, *Colonial America*, 497–518. See also Bloch, *Visionary Republic*; Hatch, *Democratization of American Christianity*.

39. Weber, *The Protestant Ethic and the Spirit of Capitalism*. The literature examining the transition to a market economy is immense. The most comprehensive synthesis is Sellers, *The Market Revolution*. For the impact of modernization on the mores of nineteenth-century Americans, see Kasson's *Rudeness and Civility*. For an example of the ways in which traditional work values conflicted with those called for by the emerging market-oriented economy, see M. R. Smith, *Harper's Ferry and the New Armoury*. The process involved boils down to one of class formation. Generally following E. P. Thompson in *The Making of the English Working Class*, much scholarship over the last two decades has documented the emergence of class society in the United States following the turn of the nineteenth century. For a review of classic works, see Jentz, "Industrialization and Class Formation in Antebellum America." For works covering working-class formation, see Gutman, *Work, Culture, and Society in Industrializing America*, 3–78; Rosenzweig, *Eight Hours for What We Will*; Wilentz, *Chants Democratic*; Denning, *Mechanic Accents*; Sean Wilentz, "The Rise of the American Working Class, 1776–1877," in Moody and Kessler-Harris, *Perspectives on American Labor History*, 83–151; Gish, "The Children's Strikes"; M. Kaplan, "New York City Tavern Violence and the Creation of a Working-Class Male Identity." For studies concerned with middle-class formation, see P. E. Johnson, *Shopkeeper's Millennium*; Boyer, *Urban Masses and Moral Order in America*; Ryan, *Cradle of the Middle Class*; Blumin, "Hypothesis of Middle-Class Formation in Nineteenth-Century America"; Blumin, *Emergence of the Middle Class*; Rubin, *Making of Middlebrow Culture*. For works that address the role of religion in the process of class formation, see Cross, *Burned-Over District*; Johnson, *Shopkeeper's Millennium*; Kloppenberg, "Virtues of Liberalism"; Hanley, "The New Infidelity"; Howe, "Evangelical Movement and Political Culture in the North during the Second Party System"; Schantz, "Religious Tracts, Evangelical Reform, and the Market Revolution in Antebellum America."

40. Paul, *Address*, 18–19.

41. My understanding of respectability and class formation are derived from Halttunen, *Confidence Men and Painted Women*; Kasson, *Rudeness and Civility*; Szuberla, "Ladies, Gentlemen, Flirts, Mashers, Snoozers, and the Breaking of Etiquette's Code"; Bushman, *Refinement of America*; and Scobey, "Anatomy of the Promenade." The presence of "respectability" among non-middling classes—such as African Americans, with their pariah status, or working-class whites—raises important questions. The language of respectability among the non–middle class might suggest a non-middle-class source of such values—the implication being that black elites could have espoused respectability while remaining ideologically autonomous. Yet the etiology is not yet clear: the language of respectability among those other than a white middle class might just as easily offer evidence of successful bourgeois hegemony. Broder's essay "Informing the 'Cruelty'" attempts, I think nobly but inconclusively, to posit a form of working-class respectability that is independent of middle-class values. Some have begun to explore the issue of respectability among African Americans: Silcox, "The Black 'Better Class' Political Dilemma"; Higginbotham, *Righteous Discontent*; Gatewood, *Aristocrats of Color*; Gaines, *Uplifting the Race*; Harvey, "'These Untutored Masses'"; Wolcott, "Culture of the Informal Economy." The antebellum roots of the issue remain largely unexplored, with the exception of J. B. Stewart, "Emergence of Racial Modernity and the Rise of the White North."

42. Quoted in Halttunen, *Confidence Men and Painted Women*, 28.

43. "Self Culture: An Address Introductory to the Franklin Lectures, Delivered at Boston, Sept. 1838," in Channing, *Works*, 19.

44. For more, see Cawelti, *Apostles of the Self-Made Man*; Wyllie, *The Self-Made Man in America*; Rischin, *American Gospel of Success*.

45. *North Star*, July 7, 1848.

46. *Pacific Appeal*, July 12, 1862.

47. *Liberator*, March 12, 1858.

48. Steward, *Twenty-Two Years a Slave*, 160–61.

49. "An Address to the Colored People of the United States," in *NC48*, 19.

50. Steward, *Twenty-Two Years a Slave*, 159.

51. D.A.P., "Fragments of Thought—No. 2," *Anglo-African Magazine* 1, no. 4 (April 1859): 120.

52. "A Word to Our People," *Anglo-African Magazine* 1, no. 9 (September 1859): 295, 297, 298.

53. *Pacific Appeal*, July 12, 1862, in *BAPC*, 14:392–93.

54. Jane Rustic, "Chit Chat, or Fancy Sketches," *Anglo-African Magazine* 1, no. 11 (November 1859): 340, 342.

55. Frances Ellen Watkins, "Our Greatest Want," *Anglo-African Magazine* 1, no. 5 (May 1859): 160.

56. James M'Cune Smith, "Civilization. Its Dependence on Physical Circumstances," *Anglo-African Magazine* 1, no. 1 (January 1859), 14; *NC34*, 31.

57. *Pennsylvania Freeman*, April 7, 1853, in *BAPC*, 8:199–202.

58. "A Word to Our People," *Anglo-African Magazine* 1, no. 9 (September 1859): 297. See also Frances Ellen Watkins's statement that "every gift, whether gold or talent, [must] subserve the cause of crushed humanity and carry out the greatest idea of the present age, the glorious idea of human brotherhood." Watkins, "Our Greatest Want," *Anglo-African Magazine* 1, no. 5 (May 1859): 160.

59. Willson, *Sketches of the Higher Class of Colored Society in Philadelphia*, 94.

60. *North Star*, January 21, 1848.

61. *Pacific Appeal*, July 12, 1862, in *BAPC*, 14:392.

62. John W. Lewis, "Essay on the Character and Condition of the African Race," in J. W. Lewis, *Life, Labors, and Travels of Elder Charles Bowles*, 228.

63. "The Free Colored People's Convention," *Baltimore Sun*, July 29, 1852, in Foner and Walker, *Proceedings of the Black State Conventions*, 2:45.

64. Sidney's reply to "William Whipper's Letters, No. 11," *Colored American*, March 6, 1841, in *BAP*, 3:357. Such sentiments were commonplace. The editors of the *Colored American* warned that blacks' "theories of respectability and elevation" would be in vain if "each one for himself" did not "commence the improvement of his condition." It was not in the mass, they urged, but in "individual effort and character, that we are to move onward to a higher elevation." April 22, 1837. See also Nathaniel Paul's admonition to freed African Americans in 1827, in which he charged that "individuals have been blest of the Almighty in proportion to the manner in which they have appreciated the mercies conferred upon them." In short, God offered all people the potential for elevation, but it was man's place to exploit it. Paul, *Address*, 18.

65. Sara G. Staley, "Address of the Ladies' Anti-Slavery Society of Delaware, Ohio, 1856," *Proceedings of the State Convention of Colored Men, . . . 1856*, in Aptheker, *Documentary History*, 1:382.

66. Robert Gordon, "Intellectual Culture," *Anglo-African Magazine* 1, no. 6 (June 1859): 189.

67. Emerson quoted in Rischin, *American Gospel of Success*, 40.

68. Junius C. Morrell to Mr. Austin Steward, [1831], in Steward, *Twenty-Two Years a Slave*, 345.

69. Payne, *Recollections of Seventy Years*, 112.

70. Halttunen, *Confidence Men and Painted Women*, 20.

71. Ibid. These issues of authenticity and class formation are also explored in Blumin, "Explaining the New Metropolis"; Watts, "Masks, Morals, and the Market"; O'Malley, "Specie and Species."

72. "Advantage of Position," *Ladies' Repository* 18, no. 3 (1858): 174.

73. Ralph Waldo Emerson, "Success," in Grob and Beck, *American Ideas*, 1:367.

74. Dr. D. McCauley, "Humbugiana," *DeBow's Review* 1, no. 5 (May 1846): 444–46.

75. "Advantage of Position," *Ladies' Repository* 18, no. 3 (1858): 174.

76. "Advice to the Ladies," *Ladies' Repository* 3, no. 9 (1843): 276.

77. The Editor [Rev. E. Thompson], "Hints to Youthful Readers," *Ladies Repository* 4, no. 9 (September 1844): 266.

78. Ibid., 266–67.

79. *Freedom's Journal,* March 16, 1827; *North Star,* March 30, 1849.

80. J. Holland Townsend, "Our Duty in the Conflict," *Anglo-African Magazine* 1, no. 9 (September 1859): 292.

81. Wicks, *Address Delivered Before the African Female Benevolent Society of Troy,* 7.

82. *North Star,* January 26, 1849.

83. *Freedom's Journal,* July 18, 1828.

84. On medical treatments, see *North Star,* March 17, 1848, and June 8, 1849. On rubes and impostors, see *Freedom's Journal,* October 3, 31, December 26, 1828, and January 16, 1829. On real estate deals, see *Colored American,* August 5, 1837. On Mormonism, see *Colored American,* September 29, 1838, and May 18, 1839.

85. *Colored American,* March 22, 1838.

86. Northup, *Twelve Years a Slave,* 19, 29, 32–34, 36–39.

87. The genre character of Northup's narrative is suggested by the recurrence of the relationship between slavery and counterfeit in popular thought. Consider, for instance, evangelist Henry Ward Beecher, who likened the confidence man—the urban trickster who cloaked nefarious designs under the guise of respectable appearance—to the slave trader. Illustrating the tragedy of the rural youth's declension into the grip of the urban confidence man, he recalled the agony of the youth's journey from moral purity to vice in terms of the African's capture and enslavement: "the midnight massacre, the phrenzy of the ship's dungeon, the living death of the middle passage, the wails of separation, and the dismal torpor of hopeless servitude." Those who traded not in the bodies of Africans but the morals of youth "are all among us!" he recognized in astonishment, ready to chain the future of the republic to "that most inexorable of all taskmasters—sensual habit." Henry Ward Beecher, *Seven Lectures to Young Men, on Various Important Subjects* (Indianapolis, 1844), 100–101, quoted in Halttunen, *Confidence Men and Painted Women,* 6.

88. *Provincial Freeman,* February 17, 1855, in *BAPC* 9:451. For a typical example, see the notice in the *Liberator,* August 19, 1864, in *BAPC* 15:506, cautioning the public against a woman fraudulently collecting money to place freedwomen in domestic service.

89. *National Anti-Slavery Standard,* January 3, 1850, in *BAPC,* 6:333. For more on Henry Bibb, see *National Anti-Slavery Standard,* January 3, 1850, in *BAPC,* 6:332; Henry Bibb to Esteem Friend [James G. Birney], February 25, 1845, in *BAP,* 3:460–61.

90. Selections from the dispute over Douglass's narrative were reprinted in the *North Star,* October 13, 1848. Jean Fagan Yellin's remarkable reconstruction of the facts surrounding Harriet Jacobs's narrative can be found in her edited edition of Jacobs's memoir, *Incidents in the Life of a Slave Girl,* xiii–xxiv, 227–51. Henry Bibb's troubles—primarily with white abolitionist James G. Birney—may be found in Henry Bibb to James G. Birney, February 25, 1845, in *BAPC,* 4:990. The newspaper quote appears in *National Anti-Slavery Standard,* January 3, 1850, in *BAPC,* 6:332. For a strong treatment of this subject, see Robert Burns Stepto, "I Rose and Found My

Voice: Narrative, Authentication, and Authorial Control in Four Slave Narratives," in Davis and Gates, *The Slave's Narrative*. See also F. S. Foster, *Witnessing Slavery*, 54–55. Curiously, the actual role white benefactors played in the production of slave narratives—as opposed to questions over the authenticity of the experiences recounted—has yet to be treated comprehensively.

91. *Friend of Man*, July 24, 1839, in *BAPC*, 3:149.

92. See, for example, *North Star*, October 27 and January 19, 1848.

93. *Liberator*, August 8, 1845, in *BAPC*, 5:68.

94. On Lewis, see *Liberator*, August 19, 1854; on Depp, see *Provincial Freeman*, February 17, 1855, in *BAPC*, 9:451.

95. *Colored American*, July 22, 1837, in *BAPC*, 2:120.

96. The incident is related by William Still in Blockson, *Underground Railroad*, 76–82.

97. Thomas Wentworth Higginson, "The Eccentricities of Reformers" in Curti, *American Issues*, 440.

98. Takaki, *Iron Cages*, chaps. 1–3.

99. Guthrie, *Address on Education and Human Progress*, 19.

100. William J. Watkins, *An Address Delivered Before the Moral Reform Society in Philadelphia* (Philadelphia: Merrihew and Gunn, 1836), 4, in *BAPC*, 1:684–90.

101. George R. Taylor and William G. Minton (The Committee Appointed to Examine the Causes of the Literary Apathy of the Institute) to the Banneker Institute, 1860, BIP, box 5G, folder 19.

102. *Colored American*, May 6, 1837.

103. "Benefits of Knowledge on Morals," *Southern Literary Messenger* 4, no. 12 (1838): 772–73.

104. "Advice to Mothers," *Ladies' Repository* 15, no. 9 (1855): 538.

105. *Colored American*, July 14, 1838.

106. "Acquiring New Habits," *Ladies' Repository* 22, no. 10 (1862): 581.

107. Charles G. Finney, *Lectures on Systematic Theology*, in Grob and Beck, *American Ideas*, 1:330.

108. Horace Mann, "The Necessity of Education in a Republican Government," in Grob and Beck, *American Ideas*, 1:378–79.

109. "Self Culture: An Address Introductory to the Franklin Lectures, Delivered at Boston, Sept. 1838," in Channing, *Works*, 22.

110. *Colored American*, June 16, 1838.

111. Ibid., May 6, 1837.

112. Steward, *Twenty-Two Years a Slave*, 159, 158, 161. Theodore Wright, a New York pastor, similarly lectured the black recipients of forty-acre parcels of land donated by abolitionist philanthropist Gerrit Smith. He urged his listeners to promote "self-reliance" and "economy." T. S. Wright, *Address to the Three Thousand Colored Citizens of New-York*, 15, 13.

113. B. Franklin, *Autobiography*.

114. *Freedom's Journal*, March 16, 1827.

115. *Liberator*, December 28, 1855.

116. *NC35*, 9.

117. *Colored American*, October 5, 1839. See also "Philomethen Lectures," ibid., January 13, 1838; "Phoenixonian Literary Society," ibid., July 8, 1837; "Our Literary Societies," ibid., March 11, 1837. For analyses, see Lapsansky, "'Discipline of the Mind'"; for the role of literary societies more generally in antebellum northern culture, see Wach, "'Expansive Intellect and Moral Agency.'"

118. Henson, *Truth Stranger Than Fiction*, 140.

119. J. A. Jackson, *Experience of a Slave in South Carolina*, 28.

120. *NC55*, 25; *Frederick Douglass' Paper*, November 3, 1854.

121. Hayden, *Narrative*, 38.

122. T. H. Jones, *Experience of Thomas Jones*, 42.

123. The relationship between abolitionism and the expansion of capitalism has been the subject of untold discussion. Two penetrating introductions may be found in Temperly, "Capitalism, Slavery, and Ideology"; and Bender, *Antislavery Debate*.

124. T. H. Jones, *Experience of Thomas Jones*, 15–16.

125. F. Douglass, *Narrative of the Life of Frederick Douglass*, 57.

126. Clarke, *Narratives of the Sufferings of Lewis and Milton Clarke*, 62–63.

127. Paul, *Address*, 21.

128. Guthrie, *Address on Education and Human Progress*, 19.

129. "Parental Lies," reprinted in *Freedom's Journal*, January 29, 1829.

130. *Colored American*, October 6, 1838. See also the newspaper's statement in another context that it was "hard to change confirmed habits, however injurious and sinful." Ibid., September 30, 1837.

131. The concern with defining appropriate gender roles has been a prominent feature of most of the recent work in women's history in nineteenth-century America. As the last two decades have witnessed a veritable revolution in the study of gender in American history, any attempt to survey the literature here would be futile. For important studies that diversely examine the relationship between gender, class, and public culture, see Smith-Rosenberg, "Beauty, the Beast and the Militant Woman"; Cott, *Bonds of Womanhood*; Kerber, *Women of the Republic*; Smith-Rosenberg, "Sex as Symbol in Victorian America"; Ryan, *Cradle of the Middle Class*; Ryan, *Empire of the Mother*; Lebsock, *Free Women of Petersburg*; P. Baker, "The Domestication of Politics"; Smith-Rosenberg, *Disorderly Conduct*; Matthews, "Race, Sex, and the Dimensions of Liberty in Antebellum America"; Ginzberg, "'Moral Suasion is Moral Balderdash'"; Stansell, *City of Women*; Ryan, *Women in Public*; Hansen, *A Very Social Time*. For general works on African-American women and activism in the antebellum North, see Rosalyn Terborg-Penn, "Discrimination Against Afro-American Women in the Woman's Movement, 1830–1920," and Linda Perkins, "Black Women and Racial 'Uplift' Prior to Emancipation," both in Steady, *The Black Woman Cross-Culturally*; Lapsansky, "Friends, Wives, and Strivings" and "Feminism, Freedom, and Community"; Yee, *Black Women Abolitionists*; Tate, "Political Consciousness and Resistance among Black Antebellum Women"; Yellin and Van Horne, *Abolitionist Sister-*

hood. The gender attitudes of antebellum black spokespersons have yet to be compre-hensively studied. Two important contributions are Sealander, "Antebellum Black Press Images of Women"; and James Oliver Horton, "Freedom's Yoke: Gender Con-ventions among Free Blacks," in Horton, *Free People of Color*, 98–121.

132. "From Gregory's Legacy to his Daughters, Hints to Young Ladies," reprinted in *Colored American*, September 15, 1838.

133. "A Fragment," reprinted in ibid., August 17, 1839.

134. Ibid., September 30, 1837.

135. "Beatrice" [pen name], "Female Education," *Liberator*, July 7, 1832.

136. "Domestic Character," *Colored American*, December 22, 1838.

137. "Varieties," *Freedom's Journal*, April 11, 1828.

138. *Colored American*, September 30, 1837.

139. "Woman," from the *Washington County Journal*, in *North Star*, May 26, 1848.

140. *Frederick Douglass' Paper*, July 29, 1853.

141. *Colored American*, September 30, 1837.

142. L.B.L., "Family Worship," *Colored American*, January 26, 1839.

143. *Frederick Douglass' Paper*, July 29, 1853.

144. Frances Ellen Watkins, "The Two Offers," *Anglo-African Magazine* 1, no. 10 (October 1859): 311.

145. "Temper," *Colored American*, May 6, 1837.

146. Ibid., September 30, 1837.

147. Rev. Edmund S. James, "Lectures on 'Female Character and Influence,'" ibid., November 23, 1839.

148. "Blanche" [pen name], "Riches and Poverty," *The Oracle* (Philadelphia) 1, no. 2 (March 1860), manuscript literary journal, Gardiner Collection, HSP, box 2G, folder 14.

149. "Varieties," *Freedom's Journal*, April 13, 1827.

150. "Colored Females," *Colored American*, November 17, 1838. Similarly, James McCune Smith admired German immigrants for what he perceived as their healthy domestic partnerships. The German man could rely on his wife to help "in laying out his plans of life and in executing the same." Indeed, "his *vrow* is in old Scripture language, 'a help meet' for the German man." James McCune Smith, "The German Invasion," *Anglo-African Magazine* 1, no. 3 (March 1859): 84.

151. *Colored American*, September 30, 1837.

152. "Woman," from the *Washington County Journal*, in *North Star*, May 26, 1848.

153. *Colored American*, November 25, 1837.

154. "From the *African Observer*, The Shelter for Coloured Orphans," *Freedom's Jour-nal*, March 14, 1828.

155. *Colored American*, September 30, 1837.

156. "Beatrice" [pen name], "Female Education," *Liberator*, July 7, 1832.

157. "Report of The Committee on Mechanical Branches among the Colored People of the Free States," in *NC*55, 18.

158. "The Eldest Daughter," *Colored American*, October 6, 1838.

159. "Original Communication, for the Freedom's Journal, Hints to the Ladies," *Freedom's Journal*, July 18, 1828.

160. "Economy," *Freedom's Journal*, December 26, 1828.

161. "Economy necessary to the female character," *Colored American*, November 11, 1837.

162. "Selected. Domestic Character," *Colored American*, December 22, 1838.

163. *Colored American*, September 30, 1837.

164. "Rochester Anti-Slavery Fair," *North Star*, December 15, 1848.

165. *North Star*, January 5, 1849.

166. "An Address, Delivered before the Female Branch Society of Zion, by Wm. Thompson, at Zion's Church," *Colored American*, June 3, 1837.

167. Richard Hildreth, "What Can a Woman Do?" *North Star*, March 24, 1848.

168. "Address, delivered at Buffalo, by one of our young brethren, at an Exhibition of the Young Ladies' Literary Society, December 27, 1837," *Colored American*, February 3, 1838.

169. Eliza A. T. Dungy, "An Eulogy on the Death of Mrs. Jane Lansing, with an Address," in Wicks, *Address Delivered Before the African Female Benevolent Society of Troy*, 10.

170. "The Anti-Slavery Bazaar at Minerva Hall," *North Star*, January 7, 1848.

CHAPTER FIVE

1. *Colored American*, June 1, 1839.

2. Ibid.

3. Garrison, *Thoughts on African Colonization*, 1:125, 128, 127, 135, 136. See also D. A. Egerton, "Its Origin Is Not a Little Curious.'"

4. Zboray, "Antebellum Reading and the Ironies of Technological Innovation," 95–108.

5. Clay, *Life in Philadelphia*, plate 4, courtesy Prints Division, LCP.

6. Garrison, *Thoughts on African Colonization*, 1:135, 136, 139.

7. Ibid., 1:135, 136.

8. Clay, *Life in Philadelphia*, courtesy Prints Division, LCP.

9. See the now copious literature exploring a series of "Bobalition" broadsides that circulated throughout the North from the 1810s through the 1840s, including Melish, *Disowning Slavery*; Waldstreicher, *In the Midst of Perpetual Fetes*; Phillip Lapsansky, "Graphic Discord: Abolitionist and Antiabolitionist Images," in Yellin and Van Horne, *Abolitionist Sisterhood*, 201–30; S. White, "'It Was a Proud Day'"; and Gates, *Signifying Monkey*.

10. "The Results of Abolitionism!" (n.p., ca. 1835), courtesy Prints Division, LCP.

11. Clay, *Life in Philadelphia*, courtesy Prints Division, LCP.

12. Garrison, *Thoughts on African Colonization*, 1:137.

13. See, for example, David Ruggles, *The Extinguisher Extinguished!* (1834), in Aptheker, *Documentary History*, 1:151.

14. "Practical Amalgamation," colored lithograph by Edward W. Clay (New York: John Childs, 1839), courtesy Print Division, LCP.

15. *New York Herald*, quoted in *North Star*, November 10, 1848.

16. *Vanity Fair* 3, no. 56 (January 19, 1861): 31, 30.

17. Ibid., 30.

18. "Address of the Colored National Convention, to the People of the United States," in *NC53*, 16–17.

19. *Colored American*, December 9, 1837.

20. John H. Johnson, untitled lecture to the Banneker Institute, BIP, box 5Ga, folder 1, pp. 6, 7.

21. *North Star*, June 29, 1849.

22. Ibid., October 27, 1848.

23. "Constitution of the African Female Benevolent Society of Troy," in Wicks, *Address Delivered Before the African Female Benevolent Society of Troy*, 13.

24. *Freedom's Journal*, October 5, 1827.

25. *Rights of All*, May 29, 1829, in Dann, *Black Press*, 40.

26. *Colored American*, April 22, 1837.

27. David Walker, "Address Delivered Before the General Colored Association at Boston," *Freedom's Journal*, December 19, 1828.

28. Statements such as this were far too commonplace to allow for more than a sampling of such language here. Samuel Cornish declared the function of the newspaper he began editing in 1829 to be "the general improvement of Society" but of special interest to blacks (*Rights of All*, May 29, 1829). Addressing a state meeting of black men in New York in the same year, William Hamilton declared the function of the convention to be to consider "the best means to promote their [black Northerners'] elevation" (*NC34*, 4). In 1837, the *Colored American*, a black newspaper published in New York City, hoped that God soon would restore the children of Africa "to their former elevation in the scale of being" (*Colored American*, April 22, 1837).

29. "A Word to Our People," *Anglo-African Magazine* 1, no. 9 (September 1859): 295.

30. Amos Gerry Beman, "The Education of the Colored People," *Anglo-African Magazine* 1, no. 11 (November 1859): 338.

31. Wicks, *Address Before the African Female Benevolent Society of Troy*, 4.

32. *Colored American*, March 2, 1839.

33. "Report of the Committee on Mechanical Branches," in *NC55*, 16.

34. Bercovitch, *American Jeremiad*; Bercovitch, *Rites of Assent*; Howard-Pitney, *Afro-American Jeremiad*.

35. W. Hamilton, *Oration Delivered in the African Zion Church*, in Porter, *Early Negro Writing*, 103.

36. *Colored American*, July 8, 1837.

37. Ethiop, "Afric-American Picture Gallery," *Anglo-African Magazine* 1, no. 7 (July 1859): 218.

38. *Colored American*, March 18, 1837.

39. *Freedom's Journal*, June 1, 1827.

40. *BAP*, 1:277–78.

41. *Minutes of the State Convention of Colored Citizens, held at Albany, on the 18th, 19th and 20th of August, 1840, for the purpose of considering their political condition* (New York, 1840), in Aptheker, *Documentary History*, 1:200.

42. *BAP*, 1:277–78; Gerrit Smith to T. S. Wright, Charles L. Reason, and James McCune Smith, August 1, 1846, in T. S. Wright, *Address to the Three Thousand Colored Citizens of New-York*, 3.

43. Steward, *Twenty-Two Years a Slave*, 319.

44. *Weekly Anglo-African* 1, no. 9 (September 19, 1859), in Stuckey, *Ideological Origins of Black Nationalism*, 167.

45. *NC43*, 28.

46. *Frederick Douglass' Paper*, May 20, 1853.

47. *NC33*, 32–33.

48. Speech by Andrew Harris, New York City, May 7, 1839, *Emancipator*, May 16, 1839, in *BAP*, 3:295.

49. Speech of Theodore S. Wright, Utica, New York, October 20, 1836, *Friend of Man*, October 27, 1836, in *BAP*, 3:184.

50. *Colored American*, March 13, 1841.

51. H. Easton, *Treatise*, 39. According to Frederick Douglass, blacks subjected to whites operating under prejudice were "victims of a deplorable habit, which has to them become confounded with their very natures." *North Star*, July 7, 1848.

52. J. Theodore Holly, "Thoughts on Hayti. Number VI," *Anglo-African Magazine* 1, no. 11 (November 1859): 363.

53. *Colored American*, June 9, 1838.

54. H. Easton, *Treatise*, 7.

55. Frances Ellen Watkins, "Our Greatest Want," *Anglo-African Magazine* 1 (1859): 160.

56. J. Holland Townsend, "Our Duty in the Conflict," *Anglo-African Magazine* 1, no. 9 (September 1859): 292.

57. Frances Ellen Watkins, "Our Greatest Want," *Anglo-African Magazine* 1 (1859): 160.

58. Nissenbaum, *Battle for Christmas*, chap. 2; Halttunen, *Confidence Men and Painted Women*, 15–16; L. L. Richards, *"Gentlemen of Property and Standing*,*"* 52–62.

59. J. W. Lewis, "Essay on the Character and Condition of the African Race," in J. W. Lewis, *Life, Labors, and Travels of Elder Charles Bowles*, 252.

60. "An Address to the Colored People of the United States," National Convention of Colored Freemen (Cleveland), *Liberator*, October 27, 1848, in *BAPC*, 5:812–14.

61. *NC34*, 4–5.

62. *NC33*, 35.

63. *NC34*, 5.

64. *NC43*, 28.

65. *Colored American*, August 8, 1840.

66. *Freedom's Journal*, February 28, 1829.

67. *Colored American*, March 18, 1837.

68. Steward, *Twenty-Two Years a Slave*, 189. "Is it right," asked Buffalo leaders, "that the whole colored community should be implicated for the opinions or misconduct of some of their people?" "An Appeal to the Citizens of Buffalo, January 4, 1838," *Colored American*, January 27, 1838.

69. *Colored American*, April 29, 1837.

70. J. W. Lewis, "Essay on the Character and Condition of the African Race," 252.

71. Lewis Woodson to Samuel Cornish, *Colored American*, July 22, 1837.

72. Willson, *Sketches of the Higher Classes of Colored Society*, 13.

73. My ideas on the problem of fixing identity derive from Kasson, *Rudeness and Civility*; and Halttunen, *Confidence Men and Painted Women*.

74. Johnson, untitled lecture to the Banneker Institute, 18–19.

75. J. W. Lewis, "Essay on the Character and Condition of the African Race," 252–53.

76. Garrison, *Thoughts on African Colonization*, 1:140.

77. *Freedom's Journal*, March 14, 1829.

78. *Frederick Douglass' Paper*, November 3, 1854.

79. See, for example, John Brown Russwurm's remarks in *Freedom's Journal*, March 28, 1829: "It is not our province here to enquire why prejudices should be in the pathway of the man of colour, all we know is that they are there, and are ever likely to remain."

80. *Freedom's Journal*, October 5, 1827.

81. Garrison, *Thoughts on African Colonization*, 1:145–46; R. B. Lewis, *Light and Truth*, 305; *Colored American*, March 11, 1837.

82. *Colored American*, March 11, 1837. See also David Ruggles, *The Extinguisher Extinguished!* (1834), in Aptheker, *Documentary History*, 1:151.

83. *Colored American*, September 26, 1840.

84. William Henry Hall to Philip A. Bell, *Pacific Appeal*, July 12, 1862, in *BAPC*, 14:392.

85. *Frederick Douglass' Paper*, November 3, 1854, in *BAP*, 4:243. See also William Henry Hall to Philip A. Bell, ed., *Pacific Appeal*, July 12, 1862, in *BAPC*, 14:392.

86. *North Star*, May 5, 1848.

87. Mary Ann Shadd to Frederick Douglass, January 25, 1849, *North Star*, March 23, 1849.

88. Saunders, *Address*, 6.

89. Absalom Jones and Richard Allen, "An Address to the those who keep Slaves, and approve the Practice," *A Narrative of the Proceedings of the Black People, during the late awful calamity in Philadelphia*, in Porter, *Negro Protest Pamphlets*, 9.

90. Sydney's reply to "William Whipper's Letters, No. 11," *Colored American*, March 6, 1841, in *BAP*, 3:357.

91. Johnson, untitled lecture to the Banneker Institute, 4.

92. "Address of the Colored National Convention, to the People of the United States," *NC53*, 8.

93. J. Holland Townsend, "The Policy That We Should Pursue," *Anglo-African Magazine* 1, no. 10 (October 1859): 325.

94. *Frederick Douglass' Paper*, May 20, 1853.

95. *North Star*, December 3, 1847.

96. *Colored American*, March 6, 1841.

97. "Address of Executive Committee of Colored Citizens of San Francisco," *Elevator*, May 26, 1865, in *BAPC*, 15:903.

98. *NC48*, in *Liberator*, October 27, 1848.

99. *NC47*, 27–28, 18.

100. *Colored American*, June 2, 1838.

101. *NC35*, 6.

102. *Colored American*, March 4, 1837.

103. J. Holland Townsend, "Our Duty in the Conflict," *Anglo-African Magazine* 1, no. 9 (September 1859): 292.

104. *Colored American*, June 2, 1838.

105. *NC55*, 17.

106. *National Enquirer*, January 28, 1837, in *BAPC*, 1:921–22.

107. *Colored American*, May 16, 1840.

108. Ibid., April 22, 1837.

109. John S. Rock, March 5, 1858, in *Liberator*, March 12, 1858.

110. "Report of the Committee on Education," *NC48*, in *North Star*, January 21, 1848.

111. *Colored American*, April 22, 1837.

112. *NC32*, 34.

113. *NC53*, 17.

114. John S. Rock, March 5, 1858, in *Liberator*, March 12, 1858.

115. William Cooper Nell, in *North Star*, May 4, 1849.

116. *Colored American*, March 4, 1837.

117. J. W. Lewis, "Essay on the Character and Condition of the African Race," 228.

118. "Report of Committee on Manual Labor," *NC55*, 12.

119. "A World to Our People," *Anglo-African Magazine* 1, no. 9 (September 1859): 298.

120. *Colored American*, June 22, 1839.

121. *North Star*, August 4, 1848.

122. Sarah P. Remond to Editor, *London Daily News*, November 7, 1865, in *BAP*, 1:568–69.

123. Watkins, *Address Before the Moral Reform Society*, 12–13.

124. "Amicus" [pen name], "Our Literary Societies," *Colored American*, March 11, 1837.

125. *Pennsylvania Freeman*, April 7, 1853, in *BAPC*, 8:199–202; *Liberator*, September 29, 1832.

126. *Colored American,* June 8, 1837; Watkins, *Address Before the Moral Reform Society,* 14.

127. Mary Ann Shadd to Frederick Douglass, January 25, 1849, *North Star,* March 23, 1849.

128. Lee, *Religious Experience and Journal of Mrs. Jarena Lee,* 24, 45.

129. D. A. Payne, *Recollections of Seventy Years,* 93–94, 137.

130. "Report of Committee on Education," *Proceedings of the Convention of the Colored Freemen of Ohio,* Cincinnati, January 14–19, 1852, in *BAPC,* 7:337–39; Lewis Woodson in *Colored American,* July 22, 1837.

131. *Colored American,* August 12, 1837.

132. From *Boston Bee,* reprinted in *North Star,* December 1, 1848.

133. *North Star,* February 23, 1849.

134. "Peter Paez" [pen name], *Freedom's Journal,* August 31, 1827.

135. M. H. Freeman, "The Educational Wants of the Free Colored People," *Anglo-African Magazine* 1, no. 4 (April 1859): 117–18.

136. Ibid.

137. "Peter Paez," *Freedom's Journal,* August 31, 1827.

138. *North Star,* February 23, 1849.

139. *NC43,* 30; *NC47,* 27.

140. "An Address to the Colored People of the United States," *NC48,* 55.

141. "Report of the Committee on Mechanical Branches among the Colored People of the Free States," *NC55,* 18.

142. *NC48,* 55.

143. Ibid., 55, 56.

144. *North Star,* June 16, 1848.

145. *Pacific Appeal,* July 12, 1862, in *BAPC,* 14:392.

146. *NC48,* 55.

147. *NC55,* 15.

148. *NC53,* 27–28.

149. Prospectus for *The Champion of Equal Rights,* from *Colored American,* November 10, 1838; *Voice of the Fugitive,* February 26, 1852, in *BAP,* 4:108.

150. Steward, *Twenty-Two Years a Slave,* 160–61; M. H. Freeman, "The Educational Wants of the Free Colored People," *Anglo-African Magazine* 1, no. 4 (April 1859): 118.

151. "Convention of Colored People for the State of Ohio," *Anti-Slavery Bugle,* December 4, 1858, in *BAPC,* 11:431; *NC55,* 19; *Voice of the Fugitive,* February 26, 1852, in *BAP,* 4:109; *New York Daily Tribune,* March 20, 1851, in Foner and Lewis, *The Black Worker,* 1:246–47.

152. *New York Tribune,* July 3, 1850, in Foner and Lewis, *The Black Worker,* 1:245. See also *North Star,* June 13, 1850.

153. *New York Daily Tribune,* March 20, 1851, in Foner and Lewis, *The Black Worker,* 1:246–47.

154. "Augustine" [Lewis Woodson], *Colored American,* February 16, 1839.

155. *Colored American*, November 3, 1838.

156. Jacob C. White Jr., "What Rum is Doing for the Colored People" (manuscript), March 24, 1854, BIP, Box 5Ga.

157. *Weekly Advocate*, February 18, 1837, in *BAPC*, 1:947–48.

158. John S. Rock, March 5, 1858, in *Liberator*, March 12, 1858.

159. *North Star*, 25 May 1849.

160. "Rev. Robert Turnbull, of Boston," reprinted in *Colored American*, March 14, 1840.

161. "Examiner" [pen name], *Colored American*, April 25, 1840.

162. *Colored American*, November 11, 1837.

163. Sterling, *We Are Your Sisters*, 157–58.

164. *Colored American*, September 9, 1837.

165. T. S. Wright, *Address to the Three Thousand Colored Citizens of New-York*, 13.

166. "Agnes" [correspondent], in *Colored American*, August 26, 1837.

167. T. S. Wright, *Address to the Three Thousand Colored Citizens of New-York*, 13.

168. *Liberator*, October 27, 1848.

169. *Colored American*, August 12, September 8, 1837.

170. "Agnes," in ibid., August 26, 1837.

171. "Augustine" [Lewis Woodson], *Colored American*, August 12, 1837.

172. Ibid., September 9, 1837.

173. Ibid.

174. Ibid., August 12, 1837.

175. Ibid.

176. Mary Ann Shadd, "Hints to the Colored People of the North," quoted in *North Star*, June 8, 1849.

177. See White and White, *Stylin'*.

178. Martin R. Delany, in *North Star*, June 16, 1848.

179. "H" on "Mourning Apparel," in *Colored American*, July 31, 1841.

180. *A Statistical Inquiry into the Condition of the People of Color of the City and Districts of Philadelphia*, quoted in *North Star*, February 2, 1849.

181. *North Star*, August 4, 1848.

182. Ibid., May 4, 1849.

183. *NC55*, 17.

184. Broder, "Informing the 'Cruelty.'"

185. "Examiner" [correspondent], *Colored American*, April 25, 1840.

186. *Colored American*, August 4, 1838.

187. "Report of the Committee on Abolition," *NC47*, 32.

188. *Pacific Appeal*, July 12, 1862, in *BAPC*, 14:392.

189. *Frederick Douglass' Paper*, March 4, 1853, in Foner and Lewis, *The Black Worker*, 1:255.

190. John S. Rock, March 5, 1858, in *Liberator*, March 12, 1858; *NC43*, 32.

191. *Liberator*, October 27, 1848.

192. Ibid.

193. *NC55*, 17.

194. Martin R. Delany, *North Star*, June 16, 1848.

195. "Augustine" [Lewis Woodson], in *Colored American*, February 7, 1837.

196. *Rights of All*, September 8, 1829, in Dann, *Black Press*, 301–2.

197. Martin R. Delany, "The Political Destiny of the Colored Race, on the American Continent," *Proceedings of the National Emigration Convention of Colored People* (Pittsburgh, 1854), in Bracey, Meier, and Rudwick, *Black Nationalism in America*, 97.

198. *NC47*, in *BAP*, 4:9.

199. *NC53*, 8.

200. *Colored American*, September 1, 1838.

201. *NC47*, 8.

202. *NC32*, 35.

203. "Report of the Committee on Education," *NC48*, in *North Star*, January 21, 1848.

204. *NC32*, in *BAP*, 3:111.

205. *NC35*, 29.

206. Ibid.

207. "A Word to Our People," *Anglo-African Magazine* 1, no. 9 (September 1859): 297.

208. *NC35*, 29.

209. Hershberg, "Free Blacks in Antebellum Philadelphia."

CHAPTER SIX

1. Isaac Van Arsdale Brown, *Memoirs of the Rev. Robert Finley* (New Brunswick, 1819), in Sterling, *Speak Out in Thunder Tones*, 25.

2. For Philadelphians' reactions, see Aptheker, *Documentary History*, 1:7; James Forten to Paul Cuffe, January 25, 1817, in Bracey, Meier, and Rudwick, *Black Nationalism in America*, 46. See also L. D. Thomas, *Rise to Be a People*, 97–98; Quarles, *Black Abolitionists*, 3–5; Nash, *Forging Freedom*, 237.

3. Scholars frequently cite Paul Cuffe as an early pan-Africanist and black nationalist. Esedebe, *Pan Africanism*, 9–10; J. E. Turner, "Historical Dialectics of Black Nationalist Movements in America"; Geiss, *Pan-African Movement*, 79, 3–4; Lynch, "Pan-Negro Nationalism in the New World," 2:153.

4. The Hortons mention the 1817 Philadelphia incident in *In Hope of Liberty*. Two other sources that describe the incident briefly but fail to explore its significance are Turner, "Historical Dialectics of Black Nationalist Movements in America," 167; F. J. Miller, *Search for a Black Nationality*, 49–51. Blacks' popular dissent to the colonization plan is conspicuously elided in Lamont Thomas's biography of Paul Cuffe, *Rise to Be a People*. Forten's contemporaries apparently never knew of, or at least refrained from disclosing, his initial endorsement of the Colonization Society. At a speech before the New York State Anti-Slavery Society convention in September 1837, prominent black minister Theodore S. Wright recalled the history of the struggle against colo-

nization thus: "In 1817, the people of color in Philadelphia, with James Forten at their head . . . resolved that they never would leave the land." *Colored American*, October 4, 1837; speech of Theodore S. Wright at New York State Anti-Slavery Society Convention, September 20, 1837, in Aptheker, *Documentary History*, 1:170. The standard works on black colonization and the American Colonization Society are F. J. Miller, *Search for a Black Nationality*; and Staudenraus, *African Colonization Movement*.

5. Timothy Brennan has written that "in cultural studies, the 'nation' has often lurked behind terms like 'tradition,' 'folklore,' or 'community,' obscuring their origins." Brennan, "The National Longing for Form," in Bhabha, *Nation and Narration*, 48.

6. Bhabha, *Nation and Narration*; Hobsbawm and Ranger, *Invention of Tradition*, esp. 13–14; B. Anderson, *Imagined Communities*.

7. I agree with David Waldstreicher that the nationalism of blacks in this period "drew less on recognized and preserved Africanisms than on the nationalist popular political culture that pervaded American public life at this time." Waldstreicher, *In the Midst of Perpetual Fetes*, 317.

8. B. Anderson, *Imagined Communities*, 12.

9. "There is no 'scientific' means of establishing what all nations have in common." Timothy Brennan, "The National Longing for Form," in Ashcroft, Griffiths, and Tiffin, *Post-Colonial Studies Reader*, 170.

10. Perhaps scholars working in this field should heed Eric Hobsbawm's dictum that "no serious historian of nations and nationalism can be a committed political nationalist." Hobsbawm, *Nations and Nationalism*, 12.

11. Gwaltney, *Drylongso*, 5. My understanding of nationalisms generally derives primarily from the following sources: Eley and Suny, *Becoming National*; Ashcroft, Griffiths, and Tiffin, *Post-Colonial Studies Reader*; Connor, *Ethnonationalism*; Chatterjee, *The Nation and Its Fragments*; Greenfield, *Nationalism: Five Roads to Modernity*; Brass, *Ethnicity and Nationalism*; Hobsbawm, *Nations and Nationalism*; Bhabha, *Nation and Narration*; B. Anderson, *Imagined Communities*; Gellner, *Nations and Nationalism*; Armstrong, *Nations before Nationalism*. For an excellent overview of the historiography and state of the field, see the introduction to Eley and Suny, *Becoming National*, 3–38. On the nature of nationalist discourse, Eley and Suny state that "the most important point to emerge from the more recent literature" is our new understanding of the nation's "manufactured or invented character, as opposed to its deep historical rootedness"; they point out that we "constitute nations discursively, through the process of imaginative ideological labor." *Becoming National*, 8. See also Hobsbawm, *Nations and Nationalism*, 5–8; McPherson, *Is Blood Thicker than Water?*, 31.

12. B. Anderson, *Imagined Communities*, 28.

13. To acknowledge black nationalism as a "constructed" discourse is not to evade the task of describing it. Far from making the task of understanding black nationalism easier, it opens the door to the daunting endeavor of mapping black manifestations of nationalism within a larger discourse of nationalism.

14. Stuckey, *Slave Culture*.

15. Genovese, *From Rebellion to Revolution*, epilogue; Bolster, *Black Jacks*; Gilroy, *Black Atlantic*. See also Waldstreicher, *In the Midst of Perpetual Fetes*, 315 n. 32.

16. Several scholars have suggested an important difference between resistance predicated on communal consciousness and political resistance designed to overturn the slave system. Enslaved African Americans surely resisted, the argument runs, yet all resistance was not necessarily political insofar as it did not serve to end slavery. Political resistance thus required the ability to imagine the destruction of the slave system and a praxis to put that vision into place. Kolchin, *American Slavery*, 163–64; L. W. Levine, *Black Culture and Black Consciousness*, 54–55; Genovese, *Roll, Jordan, Roll*, 148–49; Genovese, "The Legacy of Slavery and the Roots of Black Nationalism." See also Parish, *Slavery*, 73. We may consider nationalism a discourse of political resistance, insofar as it posited the destruction of the institution of slavery and the transformation of millions of enslaved people of African descent into free citizens of a black nation. None of this is to suggest that resistance not predicated on such a political basis could not have political (indeed, revolutionary) effects. See Oakes, "Political Significance of Slave Resistance."

17. Citing a slew of recent writers on the history of nationalism, Eley and Suny argue that "nationalist doctrine materializes as the product of tiny intellectual elites." *Becoming National*, 14.

18. Saxton, *Rise and Fall of the White Republic*, 95–96.

19. Studies of African Americans' employment of antebellum print culture in the construction of their protest thought and nationalism promise one of the most exciting growth fields in the history of African Americans and the early republic. Recent interesting studies of the antebellum press generally include Zboray, "Antebellum Reading and the Ironies of Technological Innovation"; Saxton, *Rise and Fall of the White Republic*, 77–108. Surprisingly little has appeared on the early black press, despite historians' long usage of these sources. Frankie Hutton's *The Early Black Press in America* is an unsatisfactory starting place. For the origins of the nineteenth-century newspaper press more generally, see Schudson, *Discovering the News*; Schiller, *Objectivity and the News*.

20. William P. Powell to Sydney Howard Gay, March 23, 1851, *BAP*, 1:252–54.

21. *Weekly Anglo-African*, November 5, 1859, and January 21, 1860, in Dann, *Black Press*, 77, 85.

22. *Freedom's Journal*, March 16, 1827.

23. *NC53*, 16–17.

24. Robert Purvis to Henry Clarke Wright, August 22, 1842, in *BAP*, 3:389.

25. *NC47*, in *BAP*, 4:7–10.

26. *NC35*, 6.

27. *Freedom's Journal*, March 16, 1827.

28. Quoted in Saxton, *Rise and Fall of the White Republic*, 104.

29. *Liberator*, October 28, 1853; Feldberg, *Turbulent Era*, 91; Dillon, *Abolitionists*, 93.

30. *Colored American*, March 4, 1837.

31. *Freedom's Journal*, March 16, 1827.

32. B. Anderson, *Imagined Communities*, 40.

33. Quoted in Horsman, *Race and Manifest Destiny*, 274. I generally agree with David Waldstreicher that nationalism was not originally a weapon of white supremacy but instead one of antislavery activism, and that only later, through the rhetoric of the ACS, did nationalism become racialized. The point is well taken, especially as it implies the central role that African Americans played in the creation of American nationalism and opposes a view of them "borrowing" notions originally assumed to be "white." Yet, as white supremacists quickly did their own appropriating, it seems more appropriate to focus on the dialogic quality of both white and black constructions of nation and race. The important elements of each body of thought cannot be understood without reference to long and shifting debates in the public sphere. Waldstreicher, *In the Midst of Perpetual Fetes*, 310.

34. Crummell, *Duty of a Rising Christian State*, 6.

35. Address of Samuel M. Still, n.d., Gardiner Collection, HSP, box 10G, folder 19. That this speech appears to be the exercise of a high-school-aged youth suggests how pervasive notions of nationalism had become by the 1850s; the call for a black nation had, in fact, evolved into a standard, practicable in a student essay.

36. *Weekly Anglo-African*, May 11, 1861, in Dann, *Black Press*, 267.

37. Benjamin S. Bebee to Rev. McClain, July 30, 1852, in Woodson, *Mind of the Negro*, 130–31.

38. Martin R. Delany, "The Political Destiny of the Colored Race, on the American Continent," *Proceedings of the National Emigration Convention of Colored People* (Pittsburgh, 1854), in Bracey, Meier, and Rudwick, *Black Nationalism in America*, 96, 98.

39. J. Theodore Holly, "Thoughts on Hayti. Number VI," *Anglo-African Magazine* 1, no. 11 (November 1859): 364.

40. Ibid., 364–65.

41. H. Easton, *Treatise*, 36–37. See also Orlando Patterson's theory of "natal alienation" in *Slavery and Social Death* and Hannah Arendt's thoughts on "stateless" peoples in *The Origins of Totalitarianism*, chap. 9.

42. Delany, "Political Destiny of the Colored Race," in Bracey, Meier, and Rudwick, *Black Nationalism in America*, 94–95.

43. J. Holland Townsend, "The Policy that We Should Pursue," *Anglo-African Magazine* 1, no. 10 (October 1859): 326.

44. "Movement Among the Colored People of Cincinnati," *African Repository* 26 (July 1850): 219, reprinted in Bracey, Meier, and Rudwick, *Black Nationalism in America*, 85–86.

45. Junius C. Morel to Samuel Cornish, *Colored American*, May 3, 1838.

46. *Liberator*, December 14, 1849.

47. Randolph, *Sketches of Slave Life*, 78.

48. R. B. Lewis, *Light and Truth*, 287.

49. David Nickens, "Address to the People of Color in Chillicothe," July 20, 1832, *Liberator*, August 11, 1832.

50. H. Easton, *Treatise*, 9–10.

51. R. B. Lewis, *Light and Truth*, 280–312. Martin R. Delany, the outspoken black nationalist, had little positive to say about Lewis's book. Claiming that the book was "nothing more than a compilation" of existing authorities, hardly creditable itself, Delany believed it had but one redeeming feature. While George R. Gliddon, the popular nineteenth-century race theorist, claimed Anglo-Saxon roots for civilization and so "makes all ancient black men, white," Lewis "makes all ancient great white men, black." See Delany, *Condition, Elevation, Emigration and Destiny of the Colored People of the United States*, 128–29. Delany's resistance likely was an offhand response to a potential rival, for he was not himself beyond the use of hyperbole in the service of race pride. In his "Political Destiny of the Colored Race," for example, Delany claimed that the Europeans who had "discovered" the New World found Africans—a remnant of an expedition of Carthaginians—among the population. Thus, he argued, it was Africans who discovered America. Delany, "Political Destiny of the Colored Race," in Bracey, Meier, and Rudwick, *Black Nationalism in America*, 99.

52. David Nickens, "Address to the People of Color in Chillicothe," in Bracey, Meier, and Rudwick, *Black Nationalism in America*, 36.

53. *Colored American*, May 6, 1837. J. W. C. Pennington similarly recounted tales of Aesop and Terence to demonstrate the literary capacity of ancient—and thus contemporary—African peoples. See J. W. C. Pennington, "A Review of Slavery and the Slave Trade," *Anglo-African Magazine* 1, no. 4 (April 1859): 124.

54. W. W. Brown, *The Black Man*, 35.

55. Randolph, *Sketches of Slave Life*, 78–79.

56. The standard work on the Haitian Revolution is C. L. R. James, *Black Jacobins*. See also A. N. Hunt, *Haiti's Influence on Antebellum America*.

57. *Liberator*, August 19, 26, 1859.

58. J. Theodore Holly, "Thoughts on Hayti," *Anglo-African Magazine* 1, no. 6 (June 1859): 185.

59. *Weekly Anglo-African*, March 16, 1861, in Dann, *Black Press*, 265.

60. *Liberator*, March 12, 1858.

61. J. Theodore Holly, "Thoughts on Hayti. Number II," *Anglo-African Magazine* 1, no. 7 (July 1859): 220.

62. Quoted in James T. Holly, *A Vindication of the Capacity of the Negro Race for Self-Government and Civilized Progress*, in Brotz, *African-American Social and Political Thought*, 152–53. The significant portion of the poem reads:

> Thy coming fame, Oje! is sure;
> Thy name with that of L'Ouverture,
> And the noble souls that stood
> With both of you, in times of blood,
> Will live to be the tyrant's fear—
> Will live, the sinking soul to cheer!

63. William J. Wilson to Frederick Douglass, March 5, 1853, in *BAP*, 4:142.

64. Speech by Henry Highland Garnet, August 16, 1843, in *BAP*, 4:409. The speech is known as Garnet's "Address to the Slaves of the United States of America."

65. J. W. Lewis, "Essay on the Character and Condition of the African Race," in J. W. Lewis, *Life, Labors, and Travels of Elder Charles Bowles*, 253.

66. Quoted in W. E. Martin, *Mind of Frederick Douglass*, 271.

67. *Weekly Anglo-African*, March 16, 1861, in Dann, *Black Press*, 265.

68. J. Theodore Holly, "Thoughts on Hayti," *Anglo-African Magazine* 1, no. 6 (June 1859): 185. Holly employed considerable hyperbole in portraying Haiti as a stable and prosperous democracy. Between the establishment of Haitian independence in 1804 and 1859, six Haitian heads of state were deposed. The international ostracism imposed by colonial powers leery of a black nation early relegated Haiti to a history of poverty and neglect. That despite these problems black northerners continually celebrated the black nation in the Caribbean was testimony to its great appeal as a symbol of black freedom. Holly, in fact, turned the Haitian history of despotism into a virtue, commenting that "the jealous spirit of liberty maintained among the Haytian people" had guaranteed that even the messiahs who had delivered the nation into freedom only to betray its principles later had not escaped "the tyrant's doom." In this, a convention of New England black men concurred, calling the constant changes of government that followed the founding of Haiti "progressive steps towards Republicanism." It should also be noted that Holly qualified his assessment of Haiti, in the process manifesting his own prejudices. Because Haiti "sprang into being from the lowest depths of degradation of slavery," he contended, she remained riddled with "ignorance and barbarism," and her religion was blighted by the "corruptest forms of that corrupt Church" of Rome. For Holly, Haiti's lack of civilization provided an argument for the emigration of enlightened African Americans, who would elevate the nation to a position of international respect. J. Theodore Holly, "Thoughts on Hayti. Number II," *Anglo-African Magazine* 1, no. 7 (July 1859): 220; *Liberator*, August 19, 26, 1859, in Aptheker, *Documentary History*, 1:434.

69. *Weekly Anglo-African*, March 16, 1861, in Dann, *Black Press*, 265.

70. "Volunteer" to Editor, *Weekly Anglo-African*, April 13, 1861, in Dann, *Black Press*, 266.

71. J. Theodore Holly, "Thoughts on Hayti. Number VI," *Anglo-African Magazine* 1, no. 11 (November 1859): 366.

72. J. Theodore Holly, "Thoughts on Hayti," *Anglo-African Magazine* 1, no. 6 (June 1859): 185.

73. Ibid.

74. Bruce Dain writes that black leaders tempered their invocations of Haiti so as "to avoid further provoking the slaveholders" and thus inhibiting emancipation. My evidence regarding Egypt and Haiti suggests that Dain seriously underplays the militant language and radical potential of Haiti in black protest thought. It seems to me far more likely that talk of Haiti would recede relative to visions of Egypt not due to a desire to avoid provoking slaveholders but rather because, as Dain admits,

the former was more "vulnerable to white derision." Dain, "Haiti and Egypt in Early Black Racial Discourse in the United States," 140, 155. See also A. N. Hunt, *Haiti's Influence on Antebellum America.*

75. Guthrie, *Address on Education and Human Progress,* 13.

76. Speech by Alexander Crummell, delivered at Freemason's Hall, London, England, May 19, 1851, in *BAP,* 1:278.

77. Crummell, *Duty of a Rising Christian State,* 7.

78. D. Walker, *Appeal,* 41.

79. James M'Cune Smith, "The German Invasion," *Anglo-African Magazine* 1, no. 2 (February 1859): 47.

80. Sterling, *We Are Your Sisters,* 156.

81. *Voice of the Fugitive,* February 26, 1851, in *BAPC,* 6:837.

82. Crummell, *The Man; The Hero; The Christian,* 52.

83. "A Word to Our People," *Anglo-African Magazine* 1, no. 9 (September 1859): 298.

84. James McCune Smith, "The German Invasion," *Anglo-African Magazine* 1, no. 2 (February 1859): 51; James M'Cune Smith, "The German Invasion," *Anglo-African Magazine* 1, no. 3 (March 1859): 84, 85. Smith authored two different articles under the same name; they appeared in successive months of the *Anglo-African Magazine.*

85. *Rights of All,* September 8, 1829, in Dann, *Black Press,* 302.

86. *Colored American,* May 6, 1837.

87. M. H. Freeman, "The Educational Wants of the Free Colored People," *Anglo-African Magazine* 1, no. 4 (April 1859): 118.

88. H. Easton, *Treatise,* 10.

89. Ibid., 10–11.

90. Ibid., 18–19.

91. Ibid., 12.

92. Ibid., 11–12.

93. Crummell, *The Man; The Hero; The Christian,* 33.

94. Guthrie, *Address on Education and Human Progress,* 12.

95. Ibid., 11–12.

96. J. Holland Townsend, "American Caste, and Common Schools," *Anglo-African Magazine* 1, no. 3 (March 1859): 80.

97. M. H. Freeman, "Educational Wants of the Free Colored People," 118.

98. J. M. Smith, "The German Invasion," *Anglo-African Magazine* 1, no. 3 (March 1859): 85–86.

99. D. Walker, *Appeal,* 41.

100. Crummell, *Duty of a Rising Christian State,* 7.

101. Guthrie, *Address on Education and Human Progress,* 13.

102. Sterling, *We Are Your Sisters,* 156.

103. "A Word to Our People," 296.

104. Robert Gordon, "Intellectual Culture," *Anglo-African Magazine* 1, no. 6 (June 1859): 190.

105. Exchange between William Craft and Dr. James Hunt, August 27, 1863, in *BAP*, 1:541.

106. W. W. Brown, *The Black Man*, 33.

107. S.S.N., "Anglo-Saxons, and Anglo-Africans," *Anglo-African Magazine* 1, no. 8 (August 1859): 247.

108. Crummell, *The Man, The Hero, The Christian*, 33.

109. John H. Johnson, untitled lecture to the Banneker Institute, BIP, box 5Ga, folder 1, p. 15.

110. S.S.N., "Anglo-Saxons, and Anglo-Africans," 248.

111. Ibid., 247–49.

112. W. W. Brown, *The Black Man*, 34.

113. On the emergence of this sense of cultural style, see Hutchinson, *Harlem Renaissance in Black and White*, 29–124.

114. William J. Wilson to Frederick Douglass, March 5, 1853, in *BAP*, 4:142 (emphasis added).

115. Johnson, untitled lecture to the Banneker Institute, 14.

CHAPTER SEVEN

1. *Frederick Douglass' Paper*, April 20, 1855.

2. Martin R. Delany, "The Political Destiny of the Colored Race, on the American Continent," *Proceedings of the National Emigration Convention of Colored People* (Pittsburgh, 1854), in Bracey, Meier, and Rudwick, *Black Nationalism in America*, 94–95, 89.

3. J. W. Lewis, "Essay on the Character and Condition of the African Race," in J. W. Lewis, *Life, Labors, and Travels of Elder Charles Bowles*, 233. There was a decidedly republican tinge to Lewis's idea: "Because aristocracy cannot live without distinction," he wrote, the idea that there is no fundamental distinction between races, nations, or social classes "is absurd in the mind of modern despotism" (238).

4. Ibid., 246.

5. H. Easton, *Treatise*, 23.

6. John H. Johnson, untitled lecture to the Banneker Institute, BIP, Box 5Ga, folder 1, p. 7; D. Walker, *Appeal*, 10.

7. Frederick Douglass, "The Claims of the Negro Ethnologically Considered," in Brotz, *African-American Social and Political Thought*, 232.

8. Henry Bibb, in *Pennsylvania Freeman*, January 13, 1848, in *BAPC*, 5:551; Maria Stewart in Sterling, *We Are Your Sisters*, 158; W. W. Brown, *The Black Man*, 35. See also J. W. Lewis, "Essay on the Character and Condition of the African Race," 231.

9. James M'Cune Smith, "On the Fourteenth Query of Thomas Jefferson's Notes on Virginia," *Anglo-African Magazine* 1, no. 8 (August 1859): 226.

10. "A Statistical View of the Colored Population of the United States—From 1790 to 1850," *Anglo-African Magazine* 1, no. 4 (April 1859): 100.

11. J. M. Smith, "On the Fourteenth Query of Thomas Jefferson's Notes on Virginia," 234.

12. Johnson, untitled lecture to the Banneker Institute, 17.

13. *Liberator,* February 12, 1831.

14. Steward, *Twenty-Two Years a Slave,* 331.

15. "Statistical View of the Colored Population of the United States," 97.

16. J. W. Lewis, "Essay on the Character and Condition of the African Race," 236. See also William Wells Brown's statement: "[T]here is nothing in race or blood, in color or features, that imparts susceptibility of improvement to one race over another. The mind left to itself from infancy, without culture, remains a blank. Knowledge is not innate. Development makes the man." W. W. Brown, *The Black Man,* 35–36.

17. J. M. Smith, "On the Fourteenth Query of Thomas Jefferson's Notes on Virginia," 226–27.

18. Acts 17:26.

19. Robert Gordon, "Intellectual Culture," *Anglo-African Magazine* 1, no. 6 (June 1859): 189–90.

20. Board of Managers of the Africa Education Society of Pittsburgh, "To the Citizens of Pittsburgh and the Public Generally," *Liberator,* January 22, 1833.

21. J. Holland Townsend, "The Policy That We Should Pursue," *Anglo-African Magazine* 1, no. 10 (October 1859): 326.

22. Absalom Jones and Richard Allen, *A Narrative of the Proceedings of the Black People, during the late awful calamity in Philadelphia, in the year 1793* (Philadelphia, 1794), in Aptheker, *Documentary History,* 1:36.

23. Daniel Coker, *A Dialogue Between a Virginian and an African Minister* (Baltimore, 1810), in Porter, *Negro Protest Pamphlets,* 26–27.

24. Sterling, *We Are Your Sisters,* 157.

25. Rev. H. Dwight, "Diversity of Character," *Ladies Repository* 4, no. 9 (September 1844): 270.

26. Johnson, untitled lecture to the Banneker Institute, 15.

27. J. W. Lewis, "Essay on the Character and Condition of the African Race," 238–39.

28. H. Easton, *Treatise,* 8.

29. *Voice of the Fugitive,* February 26, 1851.

30. J. W. Lewis, "Essay on the Character and Condition of the African Race," 338.

31. Speech by Alexander Crummell, May 19, 1851, in *BAP,* 1:278.

32. Johnson, untitled lecture to the Banneker Institute, 6–7.

33. Ibid., 9–11.

34. J. W. Lewis, "Essay on the Character and Condition of the African Race," 249.

35. Gordon, "Intellectual Culture," 189–90.

36. J. W. C. Pennington, "A Review of Slavery and the Slave Trade," *Anglo-African Magazine* 1, no. 4 (April 1859): 124.

37. Ibid., 157–58.

38. Gordon, "Intellectual Culture," 190.

39. *BAP,* 1:541. In contending that it was "the cultivation both of the human mind

and the religious affections of the heart that have produced" present English civilization, Robert Gordon concurred with the notion that it took time to elevate nations.
"Intellectual Culture," 190.

40. W. W. Brown, *The Black Man*, 36.

41. Quoted in Jordan, *White Over Black*, 518–19; Takaki, *Iron Cages*, 33.

42. H. Easton, *Treatise*, 5, 21, 22.

43. Ibid., 23, 26.

44. Pennington, "Review of Slavery and the Slave Trade," 158. Note Pennington's
use of the word "species" to denote what would today be termed a "race." This usage
was not random; he used it also to frame the question: "Must we conclude that one
species is inferior to another, and that the inferiority depends upon their *colour*, or
their *features*, or their *form?*" (158). Pennington's usage reflected the variability of the
words used to talk about differences among human groups during that period.

45. *Voice of the Fugitive*, February 26, 1851, in *BAPC*, 6:379.

46. James McCune Smith, "The German Invasion," *Anglo-African Magazine* 1, no. 2
(February 1859): 48. J. W. Loguen also believed love and endurance to be the
race's natural genius, claiming, "[T]he African is the most loving of all the tribes of
humanity. . . . He sympathizes more than others with human suffering and enjoyment, and is therefore a more perfect receptacle for the influx of Divine affections."
Loguen, *As a Slave and as a Freeman*, 319–20.

47. Delany, "Political Destiny of the Colored Race," in Bracey, Meier, and Rudwick, *Black Nationalism in America*, 94, 95.

48. Peter Paul Simons, speech before the African Clarkson Association, New York
City, April 23, 1839, *Colored American*, June 1, 1839; H. Easton, *Treatise*, 20.

49. "A Word to Our People," *Anglo-African Magazine* 1, no. 9 (September 1859):
294–95.

50. Delany, "Political Destiny of the Colored Race," *Anglo-African Magazine* 1:11
(November 1859): 366.

57. Speech by Alexander Crummell, delivered at Freemason's Hall, London, England, May 19, 1851, in *BAP*, 1:278.

58. J. W. Lewis, "Essay on the Character and Condition of the African Race," 236;
Aptheker, *Documentary History*, 1:99. See also J. W. C. Pennington's use of the word
"species" to describe what today would be called "races." Pennington, "Review of
Slavery and the Slave Trade," 158.

59. *OED*, s.v. "nation," "race."

60. *Minutes of the State Convention of Colored Citizens, held at Albany, on the 18th, 19th
and 20th of August, 1840, for the purpose of considering their political condition* (New York,
1840), in Aptheker, *Documentary History*, 1:203.

61. *State Convention of the Colored Citizens of Ohio, convened at Columbus, January 10–
13, 1849* (Oberlin, 1849), in Aptheker, *Documentary History*, 1:278.

62. James Forten, *A Series of Letters by a Man of Color* (Philadelphia, 1813), in
Aptheker, *Documentary History*, 1:61.

63. Ibid., 1:61–62.

64. *Colored American,* October 4, 1837.

65. *Minutes of the State Convention of Colored Citizens, held at Albany, . . . 1840,* in Aptheker, *Documentary History,* 1:203.

66. *Liberator,* April 14, 1832.

67. Paul, *Address,* 12.

68. *Minutes of the State Convention, of the Colored Citizens of Ohio, convened at Columbus, January 15–18, 1851* (Columbus, 1851), in Aptheker, *Documentary History,* 1:317.

69. Henry Highland Garnet, *A Memorial Discourse; by Rev. Henry Highland Garnet* (Philadelphia, 1865), in Aptheker, *Documentary History,* 1:228, 232.

70. Ibid., 1:228.

71. *Weekly Advocate,* January 14, 1837, in Dann, *Black Press,* 181.

72. *Proceedings of a Convention of the Colored Men of Ohio* (Cincinnati, 1858), in Aptheker, *Documentary History,* 1:413.

73. William P. Newman to Frederick Douglass, *North Star,* October 24, 1850.

74. *Aliened American,* April 9, 1853, in Dann, *Black Press,* 54.

75. J. W. Lewis, "Essay on the Character and Condition of the African Race," 229.

76. State Convention of Michigan, "An Address to the Citizens of the State of Michigan," in *BAPC,* 4:692–94.

77. Forten, *Series of Letters by a Man of Color,* in Aptheker, *Documentary History,* 1:60.

78. *Minutes of the State Convention, of Colored Citizens of Ohio,* in Aptheker, *Documentary History,* 1:317.

79. State Convention of Colored Men, "Address to the Senate and House of Representatives of the State of Ohio," *Anti-Slavery Bugle,* February 16, 1856, in *BAPC,* 10:59–60.

80. Steward, *Twenty-Two Years a Slave,* 323.

81. Delany, "Political Destiny of the Colored Race," in Bracey, Meier, and Rudwick, *Black Nationalism in America,* 92.

82. *Aliened American,* April 9, 1853.

83. *Liberator,* October 25, 1834.

84. State Convention of Colored Men, "Address to the Senate and House of Representatives of the State of Ohio," *Anti-Slavery Bugle,* February 16, 1856, in *BAPC,* 10:59–60.

85. "Address to the Citizens of Ohio," n.d., in *BAPC,* 4:712–13.

86. *NC43,* 5.

87. Dunbar, *Masterpieces of Negro Eloquence,* 42–47.

88. Ibid.

89. Ibid.

90. *Proceedings of the Second Annual Convention of the Colored Citizens of the State of California* (San Francisco, 1856), in *BAP,* 4:356–57.

91. "Convention of Colored People for the State of Ohio," *Anti-Slavery Bugle,* December 4, 1858, in *BAPC,* 11:431.

92. *National Anti-Slavery Standard,* May 23, 1857, in *BAP,* 4:364.

93. Steward, *Twenty-Two Years a Slave,* 322.

94. *Liberator*, April 1, 1842.

95. Loguen, *As a Slave and as a Freeman*, 344.

96. Delany, "Political Destiny of the Colored Race," in Bracey, Meier, and Rudwick, *Black Nationalism in America*, 109.

97. *African Repository*, 3:25, quoted in Garrison, *Thoughts on African Colonization*, 1:135.

98. *Frederick Douglass' Paper*, October 20, 1854, in *BAPC*, 9:160.

99. Steward, *Twenty-Two Years a Slave*, 327.

100. *National Anti-Slavery Standard*, May 3, 1849, in *BAPC*, 5:1079.

101. *Palladium of Liberty*, August 21, 1844, in *BAPC*, 4:900.

102. Garrison, *Thoughts on African Colonization*, 2:37, 43.

103. Ibid., 2:37.

104. H. Easton, *Treatise*, 21.

105. *Minutes of the State Convention of Colored Citizens, at Albany, . . . 1840*, in Aptheker, *Documentary History*, 1:201.

106. *NC53*, 9.

107. *Minutes of the State Convention of Colored Citizens, at Albany, . . . 1840*, in Aptheker, *Documentary History*, 1:200.

108. *Liberator*, December 1, 1832. A New York anticolonization meeting resolved: "[T]his is our home, and this our country. Beneath its sod lie the bones of our fathers: for it some of them fought, bled, and died." "An Address to the Citizens of New-York," January 1831, in Garrison, *Thoughts on African Colonization*, 2:17. According to a contemporaneous meeting of Brooklyn African Americans, "Our fathers were among the first that peopled this country; their sweat and their tears have been the means, in a measure, of raising our country to its present standing. Many of them fought, and bled, and died for the gaining of her liberties." "Address to the Colored Citizens of Brooklyn, (N.Y.) and to its Vicinity," June 3, 1831, in Garrison, *Thoughts on African Colonization*, 2:27.

109. *Minutes of the State Convention of Colored Citizens, at Albany, . . . 1840*, in Aptheker, *Documentary History*, 1:201 (emphasis in original).

110. *NC53*, 11.

111. Nell, *Services of Colored Americans*; Nell, *Colored Patriots*; Day, *Loyalty and Devotion of Colored Americans*; W. W. Brown, *The Negro in the American Rebellion*.

112. Wm. C. Nell, "Colored American Patriots," *Anglo-African Magazine* 1, no. 2 (February 1859): 31.

113. Charles L. Remond, "Address to a Legislative Committee in the Massachusetts House of Representatives, 1842," *Liberator*, February 25, 1842.

114. D. Walker, *Appeal*, 75.

115. *Anti-Slavery Bugle*, September 28, 1850, in Aptheker, *Documentary History*, 1:301–2.

116. *The Sons of Africa: An Essay on Freedom. With Observations on the Origin of Slavery* (Boston, 1808), in Aptheker, *Documentary History*, 1:52.

117. Flora, "Is a Nation justified in rising against its Rulers?" *Oracle* (Philadelphia) 1, no. 2 (March 1860), manuscript black literary magazine, Gardiner Collection, HSP, Box 2G, folder 14.

118. *Anti-Slavery Bugle*, August 31, 1850, in *BAPC*, 6:560.

119. *Free Soil Republican*, May 10, 1849, in *BAPC*, 5:1018.

120. Steward, *Twenty-Two Years a Slave*, 330.

121. *Northern Star and Freeman's Advocate*, March 17, 1842, in Dann, *Black Press*, 72.

122. *Freedom's Journal*, October 17, 1828.

123. *Weekly Anglo-African*, December 31, 1859, in Dann, *Black Press*, 83.

124. State Convention of Colored Men, "Address to the Senate and House of Representatives of the State of Ohio," *Anti-Slavery Bugle*, February 16, 1856, in *BAPC*, 10:59–60.

125. *Weekly Anglo-African*, January 21, 1860, in Dann, *Black Press*, 85. See also Henry Bibb's speech to Michigan blacks, in which he warned, "All protection that is left you is that which nature has bestowed; therefore, as you have no other means, you must protect yourselves by whatever means you possess." *Liberator*, March 9, 1849.

126. *Weekly Anglo-African*, November 5, 1859, in Dann, *Black Press*, 77.

127. *Anglo-African Magazine*, 1, no. 1 (January 1859), in Aptheker, *Documentary History*, 1:415.

128. *Colored American*, September 2, 1837 (emphasis in original).

129. Ethiop, "The Anglo-African and the African Slave Trade," *Anglo-African Magazine* 1, no. 9 (September 1859): 286.

130. *NC53*, 41.

131. *NC35*, 27, 28.

132. Uriah Boston to Frederick Douglass, *Frederick Douglass' Paper*, August 31, 1855.

133. For valuable discussions of religion among antebellum black activists, see Glaude, *Exodus*; Albert J. Raboteau, "'Ethiopia Shall Soon Stretch Forth Her Hands': Black Destiny in Nineteenth-Century America," in *Fire in the Bones*, 37–56; Hodges, *Black Itinerants of the Gospel*, 1–49; Moses, *Wings of Ethiopia*, 164; Howard-Pitney, *Afro-American Jeremiad*; Charles P. Henry, "Jeremiads and the Ideological Functions of Black Religion," in *Culture and African-American Politics*; Will B. Gravely, "The Rise of African Churches in America (1786–1822): Reexamining the Contexts," in Wilmore, *African American Religious Studies*; Moses, *Black Messiahs and Uncle Toms*, 30–48, 67–85; Sweet, *Black Images of America*; Fordham, *Major Themes in Northern Black Religious Thought*; George, *Segregated Sabbaths*. For critiques of the crusading impulse in the religious nationalism of antebellum black activists, see Adeleke, *UnAfrican Americans*, 26; Fredrickson, *Black Liberation*, 69; C. E. Walker, *Deromanticizing Black History*, 91. Several studies follow the progress of religious ideas from the antebellum North into the postwar South: J. T. Campbell, *Songs of Zion*; W. E. Montgomery, *Under Their Own Vine and Fig Tree*; Wheeler, *Uplifting the Race*; C. E. Walker, *Rock in a Weary Land*.

134. Edward W. Blyden, "A Chapter in the History of the African Slave Trade," *Anglo-African Magazine* 1, no. 6 (June 1859): 179.

135. J. W. C. Pennington, "A Review of Slavery and the Slave Trade," *Anglo-African Magazine* 1, no. 5 (March 1859): 94–96.

136. Blyden, "Chapter in the History of the African Slave Trade," 179.

137. Paul, *Address*, 6–7.

138. D. Walker, *Appeal*, 35 (emphasis in original).

139. Blyden, "Chapter in the History of the African Slave Trade," 179.

140. Paul, *Address*, 7, 12.

141. William Douglass, "The Forbearance and Retributive Justice of God," in *Sermons Preached in the African Protestant Episcopal Church of St. Thomas', Philadelphia*, 130.

142. Loguen, *As a Slave and as a Freeman*, 57.

143. J. W. Lewis, "Essay on the Character and Condition of the African Race," 246, 230.

144. Paul, *Address*, 11, 8.

145. T. S. Wright, *Address to the Three Thousand Colored Citizens of New-York* (New York, 1846), 18.

146. Steward, *Twenty-Two Years a Slave*, 154, 156. See also James McCune Smith's statement that "the negro variety of mankind is placed within the pale of civilization, with the chances of becoming part and parcel thereof." James McCune Smith, "Civilization. Its Dependence on Physical Circumstances," *Anglo-African Magazine* 1, no. 1 (January 1859): 17.

147. Loguen, *As a Slave and as a Freeman*, 59.

148. W. Douglass, "Forbearance and Retributive Justice of God," 131.

149. Blyden, "Chapter in the History of the African Slave Trade," 178.

150. Frances Ellen Watkins, "The Self-Redeeming Power of the Colored Races of the World," *Anglo-African Magazine* 1, no. 10 (October 1859): 314.

151. George Lawrence, *An Oration on the Abolition of the Slave Trade* (New York, 1813), in Aptheker, *Documentary History*, 59.

152. Ethiop, "The Anglo-Saxon and the African Slave Trade," *Anglo-African Magazine* 1, no. 9 (September 1859): 285–86.

153. J. Holland Townsend, "Our Duty in the Conflict," *Anglo-African Magazine* 1, no. 9 (September 1859): 292.

154. Jones and Allen, *Narrative of the Proceedings*, in Aptheker, *Documentary History*, 1:20.

155. *Colored American*, March 18, 1837.

156. W. Douglass, "Forbearance and Retributive Justice of God," 126, 127.

157. J. W. C. Pennington, "The Great Conflict Requires Great Faith," *Anglo-African Magazine* 1, no. 11 (November 1859): 344.

158. "Speech of Hezekiah F. Douglass, at the Sixteenth Anniversary of West Indian Emancipation, at Cleveland, August 1, 1850," *Anti-Slavery Bugle*, August 31, 1850, in *BAPC*, 6:560.

159. D. Walker, *Appeal*, 39–40 (emphasis in original).

160. Crummell, *The Man; the Hero; the Christian*, 73.

161. NC47, 22.

Jeremiah

162. David Walker, "Address Delivered Before the General Colored Association at Boston," *Freedom's Journal*, December 19, 1828.

163. Lawrence, *Oration on the Abolition of the Slave Trade*, in Aptheker, *Documentary History*, 1:59; *NC34*, 6.

164. Crummell, *Duty of a Rising Christian State*, 19.

165. "Speech of Hezekiah F. Douglass, at the Sixteenth Anniversary of West Indian Emancipation."

166. Sara G. Staley, "Address of the Ladies' Anti-Slavery Society of Delaware, Ohio, 1856," *Proceedings of the State Convention of Colored Men, Held in the City of Columbus, Ohio*, in Aptheker, *Documentary History*, 1:381.

167. See, for example, Townsend, "Our Duty in the Conflict," 291–92.

168. Jupiter Hammond, *An Address to the Negroes in the State of New York* (New York: Carroll and Patterson, 1787), in Porter, *Early Negro Writing*, 316–17.

169. R. Roberts, *House Servant's Directory*, xi.

170. Robert Alexander Young, *The Ethiopian Manifesto, Issued in Defense of the Black Man's Rights in the Scale of Universal Human Freedom* (New York: For the Author, 1829), in Stuckey, *Ideological Origins of Black Nationalism*, 37–38.

171. The Reverend Nathaniel Paul of New York City functioned as an intermediary between these two modes of millennialism. Paul believed that among the slaves would be found one "who shall take his brethren by the hand, and lead them forth from worse than Egyptian bondage, to the happy Canaan of civil and religious liberty." Such a man would also help Africa "take her place among the other nations of the earth" and usher in a time when "justice and equality shall be the governing principles that shall regulate the conduct of men of every nation." Paul, *Address*, 22–23.

172. *Anti-Slavery Bugle*, December 4, 1858, in *BAPC*, 11:431–32.

173. Henry Highland Garnet, "An Address to the Slaves of the United States of America" (1843), in T. R. Frazier, *Afro-American History*, 106.

174. Colossians 3:22.

175. James McCune Smith, "The German Invasion," *Anglo-African Magazine* 1, no. 2 (February 1859): 48. See also Austin Steward: "The colored man has yet a prominent part to act in this highly-favored Republic." Steward, *Twenty-Two Years a Slave*, 239.

176. Watkins, "Self-Redeeming Power of the Colored Races of the World," 315.

177. Loguen, *As a Slave and as a Freeman*, viii.

178. Ibid., 348–49.

179. Crummell, *Duty of a Rising Christian State*, 24–25.

180. James McCune Smith, "Civilization. Its Dependence on Physical Circumstances," *Anglo African Magazine* 1, no. 1 (January 1859), 17. See also Theodore S. Wright: "The cause of our common race [whites and blacks], is, in a manner, entrusted to our hands." T. S. Wright, *Address to the Three Thousand Colored Citizens of New-York*, 18.

181. Loguen, *As a Slave and as a Freeman*, ix–x.

182. Steward, *Twenty-Two Years a Slave*, 239.

183. "The Free Colored People's Convention," *Baltimore Sun*, July 29, 1852, in Foner and Walker, *Proceedings of the Black State Conventions*, 2:45–46.

184. Crummell, *The Man; the Hero; the Christian*, 75.

185. *NC53*, 41.

186. "Convention of Colored People for the State of Ohio," *Anti-Slavery Bugle*, December 4, 1858, in *BAPC*, 11:431.

187. *Colored American*, September 30, 1837.

188. "Apology," *Anglo-African Magazine* 1, no. 1 (January 1859): 4.

189. Ethiop, "The Anglo-African and the African Slave Trade," 286.

190. *Liberator*, November 3, 1865.

191. Randolph, *Sketches of Slave Life*, 79.

192. Garrison, *Thoughts on African Colonization*, 2:28; Garnet, "Address to the Slaves of the United States," in Aptheker, *Documentary History*, 1:231.

193. Steward, *Twenty-Two Years a Slave*, 178.

194. D. Walker, *Appeal*, 11.

195. Ethiop, "The Anglo-African and the African Slave Trade," 286.

196. Steward, *Twenty-Two Years a Slave*, 332.

197. J.N.S. [John N. Still] to Henry Bibb, February 3, 1852, *Voice of the Fugitive*, February 26, 1852, in *BAPC*, 4:108–9.

198. Pennington, "The Great Conflict Requires Great Faith," 344.

199. Steward, *Twenty-Two Years a Slave*, 332.

200. T. S. Wright, *Address to the Three Thousand Colored Citizens of New-York*, 18–19.

CONCLUSION

1. Bercovitch, *Rites of Assent*, chap. 6.

2. For other useful discussions related to the theme of national destiny and progress, see Nisbet, *History of the Idea of Progress*, 193–206; Callcott, *History in the United States*, esp. 160–66. For a view of the notion of progress that stresses the millennial elements in antebellum American historical mythology, see D. B. Davis, *Slavery and Human Progress*, pt. 3, chap. 2.

3. Bercovitch, *Rites of Assent*, 189.

4. Leonard I. Sweet, in *Black Images of America*, has explored most thoroughly the ways in which African American thinkers approached Bancroft's national mythology. I disagree with Sweet's depiction of black thinkers' unqualified "assimilation" into American culture (76). With great self-consciousness, African Americans qualified their endorsement of the national tenets set forth by Bancroft. William J. Wilson, a New York City school teacher who frequently contributed to Frederick Douglass's newspaper under the pseudonym "Ethiop," argued that Bancroft's dictum, "Our country is bound to allure the world to Liberty by the beauty of its example," should be modified. "In order that it may speak the truth," Wilson wrote, "it

should read, 'Our country is bound to allure the world to *Slavery!*'" *Frederick Douglass' Paper*, December 22, 1854.

5. I draw here upon those studies that fall within the "republican synthesis." Classic examples include Pocock, *Virtue, Commerce, and History* and *Machiavellian Moment*. For a review of this literature, see Rogers, "Republicanism: The Career of a Concept." I prefer the approaches to republicanism that stress a multiplicity of political "tongues" rather than one monolithic mode of discourse. See Kramnick, "The 'Great National Discussion.'"

6. Sterling Stuckey is the foremost proponent of the view that antebellum black people threatened America with a truly revolutionary alternative to its reigning ideology. Stuckey believes that the folk culture of slaves provided the source of such an alternative, but that black leaders in the antebellum North generally failed to embrace it. See Stuckey, *Slave Culture: Nationalist Theory and the Foundations of Black America.*

7. *Minutes of the State Convention of Colored Citizens, held at Albany, . . . 1840*, in Aptheker, *Documentary History*, 1:200.

8. A typical example appeared in *Freedom's Journal* in 1827. The newspaper reprinted a piece from an abolitionist newspaper that hoped to demonstrate the possibility of civilization among blacks through examples of high cultural achievement. A footnote in the piece compared the capacities of Africans with those of Indians: "'The African,' says Sir James Yeo, who has for a considerable time been stationed upon the coast of Africa, 'is very superior in intellect and capacity to the generality of Indians in North America. They are more sociable and friendly to strangers, and except in the vicinity of European settlements, are a fine and noble race of men.'" *Freedom's Journal*, May 18, 1827.

9. *Frederick Douglass' Paper*, September 22, 1854.

10. *NC*47, 19.

11. Habermas, *Structural Transformation of the Public Sphere.*

12. J. Holland Townsend, "Our Duty in the Conflict," *Anglo-African Magazine* 1, no. 9 (September 1859): 292.

13. Crummell, *The Man, The Hero, the Christian*, 73.

EPILOGUE

1. E. Foner, *Nothing but Freedom*, chap. 2.

2. W. L. Rose, *Rehearsal for Reconstruction*; Berlin et al., *Slaves No More*; E. Foner, *Reconstruction.*

3. Huxley, "Emancipation—Black and White," 67.

4. Powell, "Correcting for Fraud," 633–34.

5. J. Jones, *Soldiers of Light and Love*; Richardson, *Christian Reconstruction*; C. E. Walker, *Rock in a Weary Land.*

6. Meier, *Negro Thought in America*, chap. 6.

7. *National Era*, March 18, 1847.

8. James McCune Smith to Gerrit Smith Esq., December 28, 1846, in *BAP*, 3:479. Clarence Walker reaches conclusions similar to mine in *A Rock in a Weary Land*, 141.

9. William H. Parham to Jacob C. White, Jr., October 6, 1862, Gardiner Collection, HSP, Box 6G, folder 17a.

10. *Augusta (Ga.) Colored American*, 6 January 1866.

11. Ransom and Sutch, *One Kind of Freedom*; Litwack, *Been in the Storm So Long*; E. Foner, *Reconstruction*.

12. *Douglass' Monthly*, September 1859, quoted in E. Foner, *Free Soil, Free Labor, Free Men*, 299.

13. For a discussion of some of these tensions, see Holt, *Black over White*.

14. Painter, *Exodusters*, 26–29.

15. See, e.g., Gaines, *Uplifting the Race*; Higginbotham, *Righteous Discontent*; Gatewood, *Aristocrats of Color*.

16. Holt, *Black over White*; Hine, "Black Politicians in Reconstruction Charleston, South Carolina"; August Meier, "Afterword: New Perspectives on the Nature of Black Political Leadership during Reconstruction," in Rabinowitz, *Southern Black Leaders of the Reconstruction Era*, 404–5.

Bibliography

PRIMARY SOURCES

Manuscript Collection

Gardiner Collection, Historical Society of Pennsylvania, Philadelphia
  Banneker Institute Papers

Periodicals

African Repository and Colonial Journal. Washington, D.C., 1825–65
Aliened American. Cleveland, 1852–56
AME Christian Recorder. Philadelphia, 1852–60
American and Foreign Anti-Slavery Reporter. New York, 1840–46
American Anti-Slavery Reporter. New York, 1833–34
Anglo-African Magazine. New York, 1859–60
Anti-Slavery Bugle. Salem, Ohio, 1851–61
Colored American. Augusta, Ga., 1865–66
Colored American. New York, 1837–41
The Complete Fortune Teller, &C. N.p., ca. 1815
DeBow's Review. New Orleans, La., 1846–69
Douglass' Monthly. Rochester, N.Y., 1859–63
Frederick Douglass' Paper. Rochester, N.Y., 1851–59
Freedom's Journal. New York, 1827–29
Genius of Freedom. New York, 1845–47
Genius of Universal Emancipation. Baltimore, 1821–38
Impartial Citizen. Syracuse, N.Y., 1849–50
The Ladies' Respository. Cincinnati, Ohio, 1841–76
Liberator. Boston, 1831–65
Mirror of Liberty. New York, 1838–40
Mystery. Pittsburgh, 1843–47
National Anti-Slavery Standard. New York, 1840–65
The National Era. Washington, D.C., 1847–60
National Reformer. Philadelphia, 1838–39
New Pantheon, or the Age of Black. New York, 1860
North Star. Rochester, N.Y., 1847–51
Northern Star and Freeman's Advocate. Albany, N.Y., 1842–43
Provincial Freeman. Windsor, Toronto, Chatham, 1854–57
Rams' Horn. New York, 1846–48
The Rights of All. New York, 1829
Southern Literary Messenger. Richmond, Va., 1835–64

Vanity Fair. New York, 1860–62
Voice of the Fugitive. Windsor, Mass., 1850–52
Weekly Advocate. New York, 1837
Weekly Anglo-African. New York, 1859–63

Other Primary Sources

Abbott, Edith. *Historical Aspects of the Immigration Problem: Select Documents.* Chicago, 1926.

Abbott, John S. C. *South and North; Or, Impressions Received During a Trip to Cuba and the South.* New York, 1860.

Abdy, Edward Strutt. *American Whites and Blacks, in Reply to a German Orthodermist.* London, 1842.

———. *Journal of a Residence and Tour in the United States of North America, from April, 1833, to October, 1834.* London, 1835.

African Civilization Society. *Constitution of the African Civilization Society.* New Haven, Conn. 1861.

African Methodist Episcopal Church. *Articles of Association of the African Methodist Episcopal Church of the City of Philadelphia.* Philadelphia, 1799.

Allen, William Francis, Charles Pickard Ware, and Lucy McKim Garrison, comps. *Slave Songs of the United States: The Complete Original Collection.* New York, 1867.

Allen, William. *The American Prejudice Against Color. An Authentic Narrative Showing How Easily the Nation Got into an Uproar.* London, 1853.

American Convention for Promoting the Abolition of Slavery and Improving the Condition of the African Race. *Address of the American Convention for Promoting the Abolition of Slavery and Improving the Condition of the African Race.* Philadelphia, 1804.

———. *An Address to the Free People of Colour and Descendants of the African Race.* Philadelphia, 1819.

American Moral Reform Society. *Minutes and Proceedings of the First Annual Meeting of the American Moral Reform Society.* Philadelphia, 1837.

Anderson, Osborne. *A Voice from Harper's Ferry.* Boston, 1861.

Andrews, William L., ed. *Sisters of the Spirit: Three Black Women's Autobiographies of the Nineteenth Century.* Bloomington: Indiana University Press, 1986.

———. *Three Classic African-American Novels.* New York: New American Library, 1990.

Aptheker, Herbert, ed. *A Documentary History of the Negro People in the United States from Colonial Times Through the Civil War.* 7 vols. New York: Citadel, 1968.

Arese, Francesco. *A Trip to the Prairies and in the Interior of North America, 1837–1838.* New York, 1934.

Asher, Jeremiah. *An Autobiography, with Details of a Visit to England, . . . by Rev. Jeremiah Asher.* Philadelphia, 1862.

———. *Incidents in the Life of the Rev. J. Asher.* London, 1850.

Ashworth, Henry. *A Tour in the United States, Cuba, and Canada.* London, 1861.

Aunt Sally; Or, the Cross the Way of Freedom. Cincinnati, Ohio, 1858.

Baer, Warren. *Champagne Charlie! or, The "Sports" of New-York: Exhibiting in Lively Colors all the ins and outs, and ups and downs, of every class of fast Gothamites.* . . . New York: R. M. DeWitt, 1868.

Ball, Charles. *Fifty Years in Chains; Or, the Life of an American Slave.* New York, 1858.

———. *Slavery in the United States: A Narrative of the Life and Adventures of Charles Ball, a Black Man.* New York, 1837.

Bayley, Solomon. *Incidents in the Life of Solomon Bayley.* Philadelphia, 1859.

Bearse, Austin. *Reminiscences of Fugitive-Slave Law Days in Boston.* Boston, 1880.

Bell, Andrew, of Southampton. *Men and Things in America; Being the Experience of a Year's Residence in the United States, in a Series of Letters to a Friend.* London, 1838.

Bell, Howard Holman, ed. *Minutes of the Proceedings of the National Negro Conventions, 1830–1864.* New York: Arno, 1969.

———. *Search for a Place: Black Separatism and Africa, 1860.* Ann Arbor: University of Michigan Press, 1969.

Bibb, Henry. *Narrative of the Life and Adventures of Henry Bibb, an American Slave.* New York, 1849.

Black, Leonard. *The Life and Sufferings of Leonard Black, a Fugitive from Slavery.* Providence, R.I., 1847.

The Black Swan at Home and Abroad; or, a Biographical Sketch of Miss Elizabeth Taylor Greenfield, the American Vocalist. Philadelphia, 1855.

Blair, Frank Preston. *The Destiny of the Races of This Continent.* Washington, D.C., 1859.

Blyden, Edward Wilmot. *The Negro in Ancient History.* Washington, D.C., 1869.

Bobo, William M. *Glimpses of New York City.* Charleston, S.C., 1852.

Bontemps, Arna, ed. *Five Black Lives: The Autobiographies of Ventura Smith, James Mars, William Grimes, the Rev. G. W. Offley, and James L. Smith.* Middletown, Conn.: Wesleyan University Press, 1971.

Bonynge, Francis. *The Future Wealth of America: Being a Glance at the Resources of the United States.* New York, 1852.

Bormann, Ernest G., comp. *Forerunners of Black Power: The Rhetoric of Abolition.* Englewood Cliffs, N.J.: Prentice-Hall, 1971.

Bracey, John H., Jr., August Meier, and Elliott Rudwick, eds. *Black Nationalism in America.* Indianapolis: Bobbs-Merrill, 1970.

Branagan, Thomas. *Serious Remonstrances.* Philadelphia, 1805.

Brent, Linda [Harriet Jacobs]. *Incidents in the Life of a Slave Girl.* Edited by Lydia Marie Child. 1861. Reprint, New York: AMS Press, 1973.

Brothers, Thomas. *The United States of North America as They Are; Not as They Are Generally Described: Being a Cure for Radicalism.* London, 1840.

Brotz, Howard, ed. *African-American Social and Political Thought, 1850–1920.* New Brunswick, N.J.: Transaction, 1992.

Brown, Henry "Box." *Narrative of Henry Box Brown, Who Escaped from Slavery in a Box 3 Feet Long and 2 Wide.* Boston, 1849.

Brown, John. *Slave Life in Georgia.* London, 1855.

Brown, Josephine. *Biography of an American Bondman.* Boston, 1856.

Brown, Paola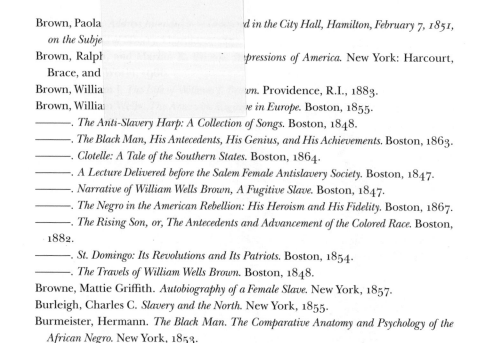 d in the City Hall, Hamilton, February 7, 1851, on the Subje

Brown, Ralph pressions of America. New York: Harcourt, Brace, and

Brown, Willia vn. Providence, R.I., 1883.

Brown, Willia e in Europe. Boston, 1855.

———. The Anti-Slavery Harp: A Collection of Songs. Boston, 1848.

———. The Black Man, His Antecedents, His Genius, and His Achievements. Boston, 1863.

———. Clotelle: A Tale of the Southern States. Boston, 1864.

———. A Lecture Delivered before the Salem Female Antislavery Society. Boston, 1847.

———. Narrative of William Wells Brown, A Fugitive Slave. Boston, 1847.

———. The Negro in the American Rebellion: His Heroism and His Fidelity. Boston, 1867.

———. The Rising Son, or, The Antecedents and Advancement of the Colored Race. Boston, 1882.

———. St. Domingo: Its Revolutions and Its Patriots. Boston, 1854.

———. The Travels of William Wells Brown. Boston, 1848.

Browne, Mattie Griffith. Autobiography of a Female Slave. New York, 1857.

Burleigh, Charles C. Slavery and the North. New York, 1855.

Burmeister, Hermann. The Black Man. The Comparative Anatomy and Psychology of the African Negro. New York, 1853.

Calloway-Thomas, Carolyn, ed. "William G. Allen on 'Orators and Oratory.'" Journal of Black Studies 18, no. 3 (March 1988): 313–36.

Campbell, John. Negro-Mania: Being an Examination of the Assumed Equality of the Various Races of Men. Philadelphia, 1851.

Campbell, Robert. A Pilgrimage to My Motherland. An Account of a Journey Among the Egbas and Yorubas of Central Africa, in 1859–60. New York, 1861.

Carman, Adam. Oration Delivered at the Fourth Anniversary of the Abolition of the Slave Trade. New York, 1811.

 Carter, George E., C. Peter Ripley, and Jeffrey Rossbach, eds. The Black Abolitionist Papers, 1830–1865 (microfilm collection). Sanford, N.C.: Microfilming Corporation of America, 1981.

Catto, William T. A Semi-Centenary Discourse Delivered in the First African Presbyterian Church in Philadelphia. Philadelphia, 1857.

Chambers, William. American Slavery and Colour. London, 1857.

———. Things as They Are in America. Philadelphia, 1854.

Channing, William E. The Works of William E. Channing. Boston: American Unitarian Association, 1882.

Cherry, Conrad, ed. God's New Israel: Religious Interpretation of American Destiny. Englewood Cliffs, N.J.: Prentice-Hall, 1971.

Chester, T. Morris. Negro Self-Respect and Pride of Race; Speech of T. Morris Chester, Esp., of Liberia. Philadelphia, 1862.

Child, Lydia Maria. The Liberty Bell. Boston, 1839.

Clamorgan, Cyprian. The Colored Aristocracy of St. Louis. St. Louis, 1858.

Clarke, Lewis. *Narratives of the Sufferings of Lewis and Milton Clarke.* Boston, 1846.

Clay, Edward W. *Life in Philadelphia* (collection of lithographs). Philadelphia: S. Hart, 1829.

Colfax, Richard H. *Evidence Against the Views of the Abolitionists.* New York, 1833.

Colored Citizens of Philadelphia. *A Memorial to the Honorable Senate and House of Representatives of the Commonwealth of Pennsylvania.* Philadelphia, 1854.

Colored People of Providence. *Will the General Assembly Put Down Caste Schools?* Providence, 1857.

Condition of the American Colored Population, and of the Colony at Liberia. Boston, 1833.

Constitution of the American Society of Free Persons of Colour, for Improving Their Condition in the United States; for Purchasing Lands; and for the Establishment of a Settlement in Upper Canada, Also the Proceedings of the Convention, with Their Address to the Free Persons of Colour in the United States. Philadelphia: J. W. Allen, 1831.

Convention of Radical Political Abolitionists. *Proceedings of the Convention of Radical Political Abolitionists Held at Syracuse, New York.* New York, 1855.

Cooper, James Fenimore. *Notions of the Americans: Picked Up by a Traveling Bachelor.* New York, 1850.

Cornish, Samuel, and Theodore S. Wright. *The Colonization Scheme Considered.* Newark, 1840.

Cox, Francis A., and James Hoby. *The Baptists in America; A Narrative of the Deputation from the Baptist Union in England to the United States and Canada.* London, 1836.

Craft, William. *Running a Thousand Miles for Freedom.* London, 1860.

Creecy, James R. *Scenes in the South, and Other Miscellaneous Pieces.* Philadelphia, 1860.

Croly, David Goodman. *Miscegenation: The Theory of the Blending of the Races, Applied to the American White Man and Negro.* New York, 1864.

Crowther, Samuel. *Journal of an Expedition up the Niger and Tshadda Rivers, Undertaken by MacGregor Laird, Esq. in Connection with the British Government, in 1854.* London, 1855.

Crummell, Alexander. *Africa and America: Addresses and Discourses.* Springfield, Mass.: Willey & Co., 1891.

———. *The Condition of the Black and Colored Population of the United States.* London, 1848.

———. *Destiny and Race: Selected Writings, 1840–1898.* Edited by Wilson Jeremiah Moses. Amherst: University of Massachusetts Press, 1992.

———. *The Duty of a Rising Christian State to Contribute to the World's Well-Being and Civilization, and the Means by Which It May Perform the Same.* London, 1856.

———. *Emigration, an Aid to the Evangelization of Africa.* Boston, 1865.

———. *The Future of Africa.* New York, 1862.

———. *The Man; the Hero; the Christian!: A Eulogy on the Life and Character of Thomas Clarkson.* New York, 1847.

———. *Marriage and Divorce.* Monrovia, 1864.

———. *The Relations and Duties of Free Colored Men in America to Africa. A Letter to Charles B. Dunbar.* Hartford, 1861.

Cudjo. *A Negro Sermon, Delivered in Alabama.* N.p., 1847.

Cuffe, Paul. *Brief Account of the Settlement and Present Situation of the Colony of Sierra Leone in Africa.* New York, 1812.

——. *Narrative of the Life and Adventures of Paul Cuffe, a Pequot Indian.* Vernon, 1839.

Curti, Merle, ed. *American Issues: The Social Record.* 4th ed. Philadelphia: J. B. Lippincott, 1960.

Dann, Martin E., ed. *The Black Press, 1827–1890: The Quest for National Identity.* New York: Capricorn, 1971.

Day, William Howard. *The Loyalty and Devotion of Colored Americans in the Revolution and War of 1812.* Boston, 1861.

Delany, Martin R. *Blake or the Huts of America.* 1859. Reprint, Boston: Beacon, 1970.

——. *The Condition, Elevation, Emigration and Destiny of the Colored People in the United States.* Philadelphia, 1852.

——. *The Origin and Objects of Ancient Freemasonry.* Xenia, Ohio, 1904.

Dewees, Jacob. *The Great Future of America and Africa.* Philadelphia, 1854.

Dixon, James. *Transatlantic Rambles . . . in the United States, Cuba, and the Brazils.* London, 1851.

Dorr, David F. *A Colored Man Round the World. By a Quadroon.* N.p., 1858.

Douglass, Frederick. *The Anti-Slavery Movement. A Lecture . . . Before the Rochester Ladies' Anti-Slavery Society.* Rochester, N.Y., 1855.

——. *The Claims of the Negro Ethnologically Considered.* Rochester, N.Y.: Lee, Mann and Co., 1854.

——. *Lectures on American Slavery.* Buffalo, N.Y., 1851.

——. *Life and Times of Frederick Douglass.* 1892. Reprint, New York: Collier, 1962.

——. *The Life and Writings of Frederick Douglass.* Edited by Phillip S. Foner. 4 vols. New York: International Publishers, 1950–55.

——. *My Bondage and My Freedom.* New York, 1855.

——. *Narrative of the Life of Frederick Douglass, an American Slave, Written by Himself.* Boston, 1845.

Douglass, William. *Annals of the First African Church in the United States of America.* Philadelphia, 1862.

——. *Sermons Preached in the African Protestant Episcopal Church of St. Thomas', Philadelphia.* Philadelphia, 1854.

Downs, Robert B. *Images of America: Travelers from Abroad in the New World.* Urbana: University of Illinois Press, 1987.

Drew, Benjamin, ed. *A North-Side View of Slavery. The Refugee: Or the Narratives of Fugitive Slaves in Canada.* Boston, 1856.

Dunbar, Alice Moore, ed. *Masterpieces of Negro Eloquence: The Best Speeches Delivered by the Negro from the Days of Slavery to the Present Time.* New York: Bookery Publishing Co., 1914.

Duncan, Mary. *America as I Found It.* London, 1852.

Easton, Clement, ed. *The Leaven of Democracy: The Growth of the Democratic Spirit in the Time of Jackson.* New York: George Braziller, 1963.

Easton, Hosea. *A Treatise on the Intellectual Character and Civil and Political Condition of the Colored People of the United States.* Boston, 1837.

Eldridge, Elleanor. *Elleanor's Second Book.* Providence, 1842.

———. *Memoirs of Elleanor Eldridge.* Providence, 1840.

Everest, Robert. *A Journey Through the United States and Part of Canada.* London, 1855.

Ferguson, William F. L. *America by River and Rail; or, Notes by the Way on the New World and Its People.* London, 1856.

Finkelman, Paul, ed. *Fugitive Slaves.* New York: Garland, 1989.

Fishel, Leslie H., and Benjamin Quarles, eds. *The Black American: A Documentary History.* 3d ed. Glenview, Ill.: William Morrow, 1976.

Flournoy, John Jacobus. *An Essay on the Origin, Habits, &c. of the African Race.* New York, 1835.

Foner, Philip S., ed. "John Brown Russwurm, A Document." *Journal of Negro History* 54 (October 1969): 393–97.

Foner, Philip S., and Ronald L. Lewis, eds. *The Black Worker: A Documentary History from Colonial Times to the Present.* 4 vols. Philadelphia: Temple University Press, 1978.

Foner, Philip S., and Herbert Shapiro, eds. *Northern Labor and Antislavery: A Documentary History.* Westport, Conn.: Greenwood, 1994.

Foner, Philip S., and George E. Walker, eds. *Proceedings of the Black National and State Conventions, 1865–1900.* Philadelphia: Temple University Press, 1986.

———. *Proceedings of the Black State Conventions, 1840–1865.* 2 vols. Philadelphia: Temple University Press, 1978.

Forster, William. *Memoirs of William Forster.* Edited by Benjamin Seebohm. 2 vols. London: Alfred W. Bennett, 1865.

Forten, Charlotte. *The Journals of Charlotte Forten.* Edited by Brenda Stevenson. New York: Oxford University Press, 1988.

Forten, James, Jr. *Address Before the American Moral Reform Society.* Philadelphia, 1837.

———. *Address to Ladies' Antislavery Society of Philadelphia.* Philadelphia, 1836.

Foster, George C. *New York by Gaslight, and Other Urban Sketches.* Edited by Stuart M. Blumin. 1850. Reprint, Berkeley: University of California Press, 1990.

Franklin, Benjamin. *The Autobiography of Benjamin Franklin.* Edited by R. Jackson Wilson. New York: Modern Library, 1981.

Frazier, Thomas R., ed. *Afro-American History: Primary Sources.* 2d ed. Chicago: University of Chicago Press, 1988.

Garnet, Henry Highland. *An Address to the Slaves of the United States of America.* New York, 1848.

———. *A Memorial Discourse by Rev. Henry Highland Garnet.* Philadelphia, 1865.

———. *The Past and Present Condition and the Destiny of the Colored Race.* New York, 1848.

———, ed. *Walker's Appeal in Four Articles and An Address to the Slaves of the United States of America.* New York, 1849.

Garrison, William Lloyd. *Thoughts on African Colonization.* 2 vols. Boston: Garrison and Knapp, 1832.

————. *William Lloyd Garrison and the Fight Against Slavery: Selections from "The Liberator."* Edited by William E. Cain. Boston: Bedford, 1995.

Gates, Henry Louis, Jr., ed. *Three Classic African-American Novels.* New York: Vintage, 1990.

Gates, Henry Louis, Jr., and William L. Andrews, eds. *Pioneers of the Black Atlantic: Five Slave Narratives from the Enlightenment, 1772–1815.* Washington, D.C.: Civitas, 1998.

Gausted, Edwin S., ed. *A Documentary History of Religion in America, to the Civil War.* Grand Rapids, Mich.: William B. Eerdman's, 1982.

Godley, John Robert. *Letters from America.* London, 1844.

Hodges, Graham Russell, ed. *Black Itinerants of the Gospel: The Narratives of John Jea and George White.* Madison, Wisc.: Madison House, 1993.

Grant, Joanne, ed. *Black Protest: History, Documents, and Analyses, 1619 to the Present.* New York: Fawcett World Library, 1968.

Grattan, Thomas Colley. *Civilized America.* 2 vols. London, 1859.

Greeley, Horace. *An Overland Journey from New York to San Francisco in the Summer of 1859.* 1860. Reprint, New York: Knopf, 1964.

Green, Alfred M. *Letters and Discussion on the Formation of Colored Regiments and the Duty of the Colored People.* Philadelphia, 1862.

Grimsted, David, ed. *Notions of the Americans.* New York: G. Braziller, 1970.

Grob, Gerald N., and Robert N. Beck, eds. *American Ideas: Source Readings in the Intellectual History of the United States.* 2 vols. New York: Free Press, 1963.

Grund, Francis Joseph. *The Americans in Their Moral, Social, and Political Relations.* London, 1837.

————. *Aristocracy in America.* London, 1839.

Guthrie, A. A. *Address on Education and Human Progress.* Putnam, Ohio, 1851.

Hamilton, Thomas. *Men and Manners in America.* Edinburgh, 1834.

Hamilton, William. *An Oration Delivered in the African Zion Church, on the Fourth of July, 1827, in Commemoration of the Abolition of Domestic Slavery in this State.* New York: Gray and Bunce, 1827.

Harper, Frances Ellen Watkins. *A Brighter Coming Day: A Frances Ellen Watkins Harper Reader.* Edited by Frances Smith Foster. New York: Feminist Press at the City University of New York, 1990.

————. *Poems on Miscellaneous Subjects.* Boston, 1854.

Hayden, William. *Narrative of William Hayden. Containing a Faithful Account of His Travels for a Number of Years, Whilst a Slave, in the South.* Cincinnati, Ohio, 1846.

Helper, Hinton Rowan. *The Negroes in Negroland; the Negroes in America; and Negroes Generally.* New York, 1868.

Henson, Josiah. *An Autobiography of the Rev. Josiah Henson.* Boston, 1879.

————. *Truth Stranger Than Fiction: Father Henson's Story of His Own Life.* Boston, 1858.

Hollinger, David A., and Charles Capper, eds. *The American Intellectual Tradition: A Sourcebook.* 2 vols. New York: Oxford University Press, 1989.

Holly, James Theodore. *A Vindication of the Capacity of the Negro Race as Demonstrated by Historical Events of the Haitian Revolution.* New Haven, Conn., 1857.

Holsey, Lucius Henry. *Autobiography, Sermons, Addresses, and Essays of Bishop L. H. Holsey.* Atlanta, 1898.

Houchins, Sue E., ed. *Spiritual Narratives.* New York: Oxford University Press, 1988.

Houstoun, Matilda Charlotte Fraser. *Hesperos.* London, 1850.

Howard H. Bell, ed. *Black Separatism and the Caribbean, 1860.* Ann Arbor: University of Michigan Press, 1970.

Hughes, Benjamin F. *Eulogium on the Life and Character of William Wilberforce, Esq.* New York, 1833.

Huxley, Thomas H. "Emancipation—Black and White." In *Collected Essays,* Vol. 3, *Science and Education.* New York: D. Appleton, 1897.

Jackson, John Andrew. *The Experience of a Slave in South Carolina.* London, 1862.

Jackson, Margaret Y., ed. *The Struggle for Freedom, Phase I: As Revealed in Slave Narratives of the Pre–Civil War Period, 1840–1860.* Chicago: Adams, 1976.

Jackson, Rebecca. *Gifts of Power: The Writings of Rebecca Jackson, Black Visionary, Shaker Eldress.* Edited by Jean McMahon Humez. Amherst: University of Massachusetts Press, 1981.

Jacobs, Harriet. *Incidents in the Life of a Slave Girl: Written by Herself.* Originally edited by L. Maria Child; edited and with an introduction by Jean Fagan Yellin. Cambridge, Mass.: Harvard University Press, 1987.

Johnson, R. M. *"Multum in Parvo!" Liberia as It Is.* Philadelphia, 1853.

Johnston, James [Finlay Weir]. *Notes on North America: Agricultural, Economic, and Social.* 2 vols. Boston, 1851.

Jones, Absalom. *A Thanksgiving Sermon, . . . On Account of the Abolition of the Slave Trade.* Philadelphia: Fry and Krammerer Press, 1808.

Jones, Thomas H. *The Experience of Thomas Jones, Who Was a Slave for Forty-Three Years.* Boston, 1850.

Katz, William Loren, ed. *Flight from the Devil: Six Slave Narratives.* Trenton, N.J.: Africa World Press, 1996.

Keckley, Elizabeth. *Behind the Scenes, or, Thirty Years a Slave, and Four Years in the White House.* New York, 1868.

Knox, Robert. *Races of Man: A Fragment.* 2d ed. London, 1862.

Kurtz, Paul, ed. *American Thought Before 1900: A Sourcebook from Puritanism to Darwinism.* New York: Macmillan, 1966.

Lane, Lunsford. *The Narrative of Lunsford Lane, Formerly of Raleigh, N.C.* 2d ed. Boston, 1842.

Langston, John Mercer. *Freedom and Citizenship.* Cleveland, 1858.

———. *From the Virginia Plantation to the National Capitol.* Hartford, Conn., 1894.

———. *A Speech on "Equality before the Law."* St. Louis, 1866.

Latrobe, John H. B. *African Colonization.* Washington, D.C., 1862.

Lee, Jarena. *Religious Experience and Journal of Mrs. Jarena Lee, Giving an Account of Her Call to Preach the Gospel.* Philadelphia, 1849.

Leeds Anti-Slavery Society. *Fugitive Slaves: Douglass, Pennington, Wells Brown, Garnett, Bibb and Others*. London, n.d.

Leggett, William. *Democratick Editorials: Essays in Jacksonian Political Economy by William Leggett*. Compiled and edited by Lawrence H. White. Indianapolis: Liberty, 1984.

Lerner, Gerda, ed. *Black Women in White America: A Documentary History*. New York: Pantheon, 1973.

Lewis, John W. *The Life, Labors, and Travels of Elder Charles Bowles, of the Free Will Baptist Denomination*. Watertown, Conn.: Ingalls and Stowell's Steam Press, 1852.

Lewis, R. B. [Robert Benjamin]. *Light and Truth; Collected from the Bible and Ancient and Modern History, Containing the Universal History of the Colored and Indian Race, from the Creation of the World to the Present Time*. Boston, 1844.

Lieber, Francis. *Letters to a Gentleman in Germany, Written After a Trip from Philadelphia to Niagara*. Philadelphia, 1834.

———. *The Stranger in America: Comprising Sketches of the Manners . . . of the United States*. London, 1835.

Locke, David Ross. *The Nasby Papers. Letters and Sermons Containing the Views on the Topics of the Day, of Petroleum V. Nasby*. Indianapolis, 1864.

Loewenberg, Bert James, and Ruth Bogin, eds. *Black Women in Nineteenth-Century American Life: Their Words, Their Thoughts, Their Feelings*. University Park: Pennsylvania State University Press, 1976.

Loguen, Jermain Wesley. *The Rev. J. W. Loguen, as a Slave and as a Freeman. A Narrative of Real Life*. Syracuse, N.Y., 1859.

Lowell, James Russell. *The Biglow Papers: A Critical Edition*. Edited by Thomas Wortham. DeKalb: Northern Illinois University Press, 1977.

MacKay, Charles. *Life and Liberty in America: Or, Sketches of a Tour in the United States and Canada, in 1857–8*. London, 1859.

McPherson, James M., ed. *The Negro's Civil War: How American Negroes Felt and Acted During the War for the Union*. New York: Knopf, 1965.

Marryat, Frederick. *A Diary in America, With Remarks on Its Institutions*. London, 1839.

———. *Second Series of a Diary in America with Remarks on Its Institutions . . .* Philadelphia, 1840.

Martin, J. Sella. *The Hero and the Slave. Founded on Fact*. Boston, 1863.

Mason, George C. *Reminiscences of Newport*. Newport, R.I., 1884.

Mathews, Charles. *The London Mathews; Containing an Account of This Celebrated Comedian's Trip to America*. Philadelphia, 1824.

———. *Mathews in America; or, the Theatrical Wanderer: A Cargo of New Characters, Original Songs*. 1824.

Mathews, Richard. *Sketches of Mr. Mathews's Trip to America: Comprising a Full Account of His Admirable Lecture on Peculiarities, Characters, and Manners*. London, 1824.

May, S. J. *Proceedings of the American Anti-Slavery Society at Its Third Decade*. New York, 1864.

Meachum, John B. *An Address to All the Colored Citizens of the United States*. Philadelphia, 1846.

Merrill, Walter M., ed. *The Letters of William Lloyd Garrison.* Cambridge, Mass.: Harvard University Press, 1971.

Minutes and Proceedings of the First Annual Convention of the People of Colour, Held by Adjournments in the City of Philadelphia, from the Sixth to the Eleventh of June, Inclusive, 1831. Philadelphia, 1831.

Minutes and Proceedings of the Second Annual Convention, for the Improvement of the Free People of Color in These United States, Held by Adjournments in the City of Philadelphia, from the 4th to the 13 of June Inclusive, 1832. Philadelphia, 1832.

Minutes and Proceedings of the Third Annual Convention, for the Improvement of the Free People of Colour in These United States, Held by Adjournments in the City of Philadelphia, from the 3d to the 13th of June Inclusive, 1833. New York, 1833.

Minutes of the Fifth Annual Convention for the Improvement of the Free People of Colour in the United States, Held by Adjournment, in the Wesley Church, Philadelphia, from the First to the Fifth of June, Inclusive, 1835. Philadelphia, 1835.

Minutes of the Fourth Annual Convention, for the Improvement of the Free People of Colour, in the United States, Held by Adjournments in the Asbury Church, New York, from the 2d to the 12th of June Inclusive, 1834. New York, 1834.

Minutes of the National Convention of Colored Citizens: Held at Buffalo, on the 15th, 16th, 17th, 18th and 19th of August, 1843. For the Purpose of Considering Their Moral and Political Condition as American Citizens. New York, 1843.

Mitchell, David W. *Ten Years in the United States; Being an Englishman's View of the Men and Things in the North and South.* London, 1862.

Mitchell, William. *The Underground Railroad.* London, 1860.

Morton, Samuel G. *Crania Aegyptica; or Observations on Egyptian Ethnography, Derived from Anatomy, History and the Monuments.* Philadelphia, 1844.

————. *Crania Americana: or, A Comparative View of the Skulls of Various Aboriginal Nations of North and South America.* Philadelphia, 1839.

Moses, Wilson Jeremiah, ed. *Classical Black Nationalism: From the American Revolution to Marcus Garvey.* New York: New York University Press, 1996.

Mullane, Dierdre. *Crossing the Danger Water: Three Hundred Years of African-American Writing.* New York: Doubleday, 1993.

Murray, Henry Anthony. *Lands of the Slave and the Free.* London, 1855.

Myers, J. C. *Sketches on a Tour Through the Northern and Eastern States, the Canadas and Nova Scotia.* Harrisonburg, Va., 1849.

Nell, William C. *The Colored Patriots of the American Revolution.* Boston, 1855. Reprint, New York, 1968.

————. *Services of Colored Americans, in the Wars of 1776 and 1812.* Boston, 1851.

————, comp. *Property Qualification or No Property Qualification.* New York, 1860.

Nesbit, William. *Four Months in Liberia: Or African Colonization Exposed.* Pittsburgh, 1855.

New York Committee of Vigilance. *The First Annual Report of the New York Committee of Vigilance, for the Year 1837.* New York, 1837.

Niger Valley Exploring Party. *Official Report of the Niger Valley Exploring Party, by M. R. Delany*. Leeds, England, 1861. Reprint, Philadelphia: Rhistoric, 1969.

Nisbet, Richard. *The Capacity of Negroes for Religious and Moral Improvement Considered*. London, 1789.

Noel, Baptist Wriothesley. *Freedom and Slavery in the United States of America*. London, 1863.

Northup, Solomon. *Twelve Years a Slave. Narrative of Solomon Northus, a Citizen of New York, Kidnapped in Washington City in 1841 and Rescued in 1853*. Auburn, N.Y., 1853.

Norton Anthology of English Literature. 4th ed. Edited by M. H. Abrams. New York: Norton, 1979.

Nott, Josiah C. *Instincts of Races*. New Orleans, 1866.

———. "The Mulatto a Hybrid—Probable Extermination of the Two Races if the White and Blacks Are Allowed to Intermarry." *American Journal of the Medical Sciences* 6 (1843): 252–56.

———. *Two Lectures on the Natural History of the Caucasian and Negro Races*. Mobile, Ala., 1844.

Nott, Josiah C., and George R. Gliddon. *Types of Mankind*. New York, 1844.

Oldmixon, John W. *Transatlantic Wanderings*. London and New York, 1855.

Osofsky, Gilbert, ed. *The Burden of Race: A Documentary of Negro-White Relations in America*. New York: Harper and Row, 1967.

———. *Puttin' on Ole Massa: The Slave Narratives of Henry Bibb, William Wells Brown, and Solomon Northup*. New York: Harper Torchbooks, 1969.

Otter, William. *History of My Own Time*. Edited by Richard Stott. Emmitsburg, Md., 1835. Reprint ed., Ithaca: Cornell University Press, 1994.

Pairpoint, Alfred J. *Uncle Sam and His Country*. London, 1857.

Parrish, Lydia Austin, comp. *Slave Songs of the Georgia Sea Islands*. 1942. Reprint, Hatboro, Pa., 1965.

Parrott, Russell. *An Oration on the Abolition of the Slave Trade; Delivered on the First of January, 1814. At the African Church of St. Thomas*. Philadelphia: Printed for the Different Societies, by Thomas T. Stiles, 1814.

Patterson, Paul. *The Playfair Papers, or Brother Jonathan, the Smartest Nation in All Creation*. 3 vols. London, 1841.

Paul, Nathaniel. *An Address, Delivered on the Celebration of the Abolition of Slavery, in the State of New York, July 5, 1827, by Nathaniel Paul, Pastor of the First African Baptist Society in the City of Albany*. Albany, N.Y.: Printed by John B. Van Steenbergh, 1827.

Payne, Buckner H. *The Negro: What is His Ethnological Status?* Cincinnati, Ohio, 1867.

Payne, Daniel A. *Recollections of Seventy Years*. Nashville, Tenn., 1888.

[Pease, Elizabeth]. *Society of Friends in the United States: Their Views of the Anti-Slavery Question, and Treatment of the People of Colour*. Darlington, England, 1840.

Pennington, James W. C. *Covenants Involving Moral Wrong are not Obligatory upon Man: A Sermon Delivered in the Fifth Congregational Church*. Hartford, Conn., 1842.

———. *The Fugitive Blacksmith; or, Events in the History of James W. C. Pennington*. 3d ed. London, 1850.

———. *A Text Book of the Origin and History, &c. &c. of the Colored People.* Hartford, Conn., 1841.

Pennsylvania Antislavery Convention. *Proceedings of the Pennsylvania Antislavery Convention.* Harrisburg, 1837.

[Philanthropist]. "Vital Statistics of Negroes and Mulattoes." *Boston Medical and Surgical Journal* 17 (1842): 168–70.

Porter, Dorothy. "The Organized Education Activities of Literary Societies." *Journal of Negro Education* 5 (1936): 557.

———, ed. *Early Negro Writing, 1760–1837.* Boston, 1971. Reprint, Baltimore: Black Classic Press, 1995.

———. "Early Manuscript Letters Written by Negroes." *Journal of Negro History* 24 (April 1939): 199–210.

———. *Negro Protest Pamphlets: A Compendium.* New York: Arno, 1969.

Price, George R., and James Brewer Stewart, eds. *To Heal the Scourge of Prejudice: The Life and Writings of Hosea Easton.* Amherst: University of Massachusetts Press, 1999.

Prichard, James C. *The Natural History of Mankind.* 2 vols. London, 1855.

Proceedings of the Celebration for the Integration of Boston Public Schools. Boston, 1856.

Proceedings of the Colored National Convention, Held in Franklin Hall, Sixth Street, below Arch, Philadelphia, October 16th, 17th and 18th, 1855. Salem, N.J.: National Standard Office, 1856.

Proceedings of the Colored National Convention, Held in Rochester, July 6th, 7th and 8th, 1853. Rochester, N.Y.: Office of Frederick Douglass' Paper, 1853.

Proceedings of the National Convention of Colored People, and Their Friends, Held in Troy, N.Y., on the 6th, 7th, 8th and 9th October, 1847. Troy, N.Y.: J. C. Kneeland and Co., 1847.

Provisional Constitution and Ordinances for the People of the United States. N.p., 1856.

[Purvis, Robert]. *Appeal of Forty Thousand Citizens, Threatened with Disfranchisement, to the People of Pennsylvania.* Philadelphia, 1838.

———. *A Tribute to the Memory of Thomas Shipley, the Philanthropist.* 1836. Reprint, Philadelphia, 1969.

Quarles, Benjamin, ed. *Blacks on John Brown.* Urbana: University of Illinois Press, 1972.

———. "Letters from Negro Leaders to Gerrit Smith." *Journal of Negro History* (1942): 450–51.

Randolph, Peter. *Sketches of Slave Life: Or, Illustrations of the "Peculiar Institution."* 2d ed. Boston, 1855.

Ratner, Lorman, ed. *Pre–Civil War Reform: The Variety of Principles and Programs.* Englewood Cliffs, N.J.: Prentice-Hall, 1967.

Remond, Charles Lenox. *Speech Before the Rhode Island Antislavery Society.* Boston, 1837.

Report of the Proceedings of the Colored National Convention, Held at Cleveland, Ohio, on Wednesday, September 6, 1848. Rochester: John Dick, 1848.

Ripley, C. Peter, Roy E. Finkenbine, Michael F. Hembree, and Donald Yacavone, eds.

The Black Abolitionist Papers. 5 vols. Chapel Hill: University of North Carolina Press, 1985–92.

––––––. *Witness for Freedom: African American Voices on Race, Slavery, and Emancipation.* Chapel Hill: University of North Carolina Press, 1993.

Rischin, Moses, ed. *The American Gospel of Success: Individualism and Beyond.* Chicago: Quadrangle, 1965.

––––––. *Immigration and the American Tradition.* Indianapolis: Bobb-Merrill, 1976.

Roberts, Robert. *House Servant's Directory: Comprising Hints on the Arrangement and Performance of Servants' Work.* Boston, 1827. Reprint ed., edited by Graham Russell Hodges, Armonk, N.Y.: M. E. Sharpe, 1997.

Roper, Moses. *A Narrative of the Adventures and Escape of Moses Roper, from American Slavery.* Philadelphia, 1838.

Ruchames, Louis, ed. *Racial Thought in America: A Documentary History.* Vol. 1, *From the Puritans to Abraham Lincoln.* Amherst: University of Massachusetts Press, 1969.

Ruggles, David. *The Abrogation of the Seventh Commandment by the American Churches.* New York, 1835.

––––––. *An Antidote for a Poisonous Combination.* New York, 1838.

––––––. *The Extinguisher Extinguished! or, David M. Reese, M.D. "Used Up."* New York, 1830.

Ruggles, Steven, Matthew Sobek, et al., eds. *Integrated Public Use Microdata Series: Version 2.0.* Minneapolis: Historical Census Projects, University of Minnesota, 1997. Available online at http://www.ipums.umn.edu.

Russel, Chloe. *The Complete Fortune Teller, and Dream Book.* Exeter, N.H., 1824.

Sala, George Augustus. *Yankee Drolleries. The Most Celebrated Works of the Best American Humorists.* London, 1866.

Salvatore, Nick. *We All Got History: The Memory Books of Amos Webber.* New York: Times Books, 1996.

Saunder, Frederick. *A Voice to America; or, The Model Republic.* New York, 1855.

Saunders, Prince. *An Address, Delivered at Bethel Church, Philadelphia; on the 30th of September, 1818, before the Pennsylvania Augustine Society, for the Education of People of Colour.* Philadelphia: Joseph Rakestraw, 1818.

Sidney, Joseph. *An Oration, Commemorative of the Abolition of the Slave Trade in the United States.* New York, 1809.

Smith, James McCune. *A Lecture on the Haitian Revolution; with a Sketch of the Character of Toussaint L'Ouverture.* New York, 1841.

Spring, Lindley. *The Negro at Home: An Inquiry after His Capacity for Self-Government.* New York, 1868.

St. Thomas's Church Friendly Society. *Constitution and Rules to Be Observed and kept by the Friendly Society of St. Thomas's African Church of Philadelphia.* 1797. Reprint, Philadelphia: Rhistoric, 1969.

Stampp, Kenneth, ed. *The Causes of the Civil War.* 3d ed. New York: Touchstone, 1991.

State Convention of the Colored Citizens of Pennsylvania. *Minutes of the State Convention of the Colored Citizens of Pennsylvania.* Philadelphia, 1848.

Sterling, Dorothy, ed. *Speak Out in Thunder Tones: Letters and Other Writings by Black Northerners, 1787–1865*. Garden City, N.Y.: Doubleday, 1973.

———. *We Are Your Sisters: Black Women in the Nineteenth Century*. New York: Norton, 1984.

Steward, Austin. *Twenty-Two Years a Slave, and Forty Years a Free Man; Embracing a Correspondence of Several Years*. 1856. Reprint, New York: Negro Universities Press, 1969.

Stewart, Maria W. *America's First Black Woman Political Writer: Essays and Speeches*. Edited by Marilyn Richardson. Bloomington: Indiana University Press, 1987.

———. *Meditations from the Pen of Mrs. Maria Stewart*. Washington, D.C., 1879.

———. *Religion and the Principles of Morality*. Boston, 1831.

Still, William. *A Brief Narrative of the Struggle for the Rights of the Colored People of Philadelphia in the City Railway Cars*. Philadelphia, 1867.

———. *The Underground Rail-Road*. Philadelphia, 1872.

Storing, Herbert S., comp. *What Country Have I? Political Writings by Black Americans*. New York: St. Martin's, 1970.

Stuckey, Sterling, ed. *The Ideological Origins of Black Nationalism*. Boston: Beacon, 1972.

Sullivan, Edward Robert. *Rambles and Scrambles in North and South America*. London, 1852.

Sundquist, Eric J., ed. *The Oxford W. E. B. Du Bois Reader*. New York: Oxford University Press, 1996.

Takaki, Ronald T., ed. *Violence in the Black Imagination: Essays and Documents*. New York: Oxford University Press, 1972.

Thompson, John. *The Life of John Thompson, a Fugitive Slave; Containing His History of 25 Years in Bondage, and His Providential Escape*. Worcester, Mass., 1856.

Thompson, William Tappan. *Major Jones's Sketches of Travel*. Philadelphia, 1848.

Tocqueville, Alexis de. *Democracy in America*. Edited by Phillips Bradley. 2 vols. 1840. Reprint, New York: Vintage, 1945.

Trollope, Anthony. *North America*. Edited by Robert Mason. 1862. Reprint, London: Penguin, 1992.

Trotter, James Monroe. *Music and Some Highly Musical People*. Boston, 1878.

Truth, Sojourner. *The Narrative of Sojourner Truth*. 1850. Reprint, edited by Margaret Washington, New York: Vintage, 1993.

Virey, Julien-Joseph. *Natural History of the Negro Race*. Charleston, S.C., 1837.

Walker, David. *David Walker's Appeal to the Coloured Citizens of the World*. Boston, 1829.

Ward, Samuel Ringgold. *Autobiography of a Fugitive Negro*. London, 1855.

Watkins, William J. *An Address Before the Moral Reform Society in Philadelphia*. Philadelphia: Merrihew and Gunn, 1836.

Watson, Henry. *Narrative of Henry Watson, A Fugitive Slave*. Boston, 1850.

Weld, Theodore Dwight, Angelina Grimke Weld, and Sarah Grimke. *Letters of Theodore Dwight Weld, Angelina Grimke Weld, and Sarah Grimke, 1822–1844*. New York and London, 1934.

Whipper, William. *Eulogy on William Wilberforce, Esq.* 1833. Reprint, Philadelphia: Rhistoric, 1969.

Whitfield, James M. *America and Other Poems.* Buffalo, N.Y., 1853.

Wicks, Elizabeth. *Address Delivered Before the African Female Benevolent Society of Troy, on Wednesday, February 12, 1834.* Troy, N.Y., 1834.

Wilkerson, James. *Wilkerson's History of His Travels and Labors, in the United States, as a Missionary.* Columbus, Ohio, 1861.

Wiley, Bell I., ed. *Slaves No More: Letters from Liberia, 1833–1869.* Lexington: University Press of Kentucky, 1980.

Williams, George Washington. *The American Negro, from 1776 to 1876.* Cincinnati, Ohio, 1876.

Williams, James. *Life and Adventures of James Williams, a Fugitive Slave, with a Full Description of the Underground Railroad.* San Francisco, 1874.

———. *Narrative of James Williams, an American Slave, Who Was for Several Years a Driver on a Cotton Plantation in Alabama.* Boston, 1838.

Williams, Samuel. *Four Years in Liberia.* Philadelphia, 1857.

[Willson, Joseph]. *Sketches of the Higher Classes of Colored Society in Philadelphia. By a Southerner.* Philadelphia, 1841.

[Wilson, Armistead]. *Calumny Refuted, by Facts from Liberia.* New York, 1848.

———. *A Tribute for the Negro: Being a Vindication of the Moral, Intellectual, and Religious Capabilities.* Manchester, N.H., 1848.

[Wilson, Harriet E.] "Our Nig." In *Our Nig; or, Sketches from the Life of a Free Black,* 2d ed., edited by Henry Louis Gates Jr. New York: Random House, 1983.

Woodson, Carter G., ed. *The Mind of the Negro as Reflected in Letters Written During the Crisis, 1800–1860.* 1926. Reprint, New York: Russell and Russell, 1969.

———. *Negro Orators and Their Orations.* 1925. Reprint, New York: Russell and Russell, 1969.

Wright, Frances. *Course of Popular Lectures, As Delivered by Frances Wright.* New York, 1830.

Wright, Theodore S. *An Address to the Three Thousand Colored Citizens of New-York: Who Are the Owners of One Hundred and Twenty Thousand Acres of Land in the State of New-York, Given to Them by Gerrit Smith, Esq. of Peterboro, September 1, 1846.* New York, 1846.

Young, Robert Anderson. *The Negro: A Reply to Ariel.* Nashville, Tenn., 1867.

SECONDARY SOURCES

Books

Abelson, Elaine. *When Ladies Go A-Thieving: Middle-Class Shoplifters in the Victorian Department Store.* New York: Oxford University Press, 1989.

Abrahams, Roger D. *Singing the Master: The Emergence of African-American Culture in the Plantation South.* New York: Penguin, 1992.

Abzug, Robert H. *Cosmos Crumbling: American Reform and the Religious Imagination.* New York: Oxford University Press, 1994.

Adeleke, Tunde. *UnAfrican Americans: Nineteenth-Century Black Nationalists and the Civilizing Mission.* Lexington: University of Kentucky Press, 1998.

Agnew, Jean-Christophe. *Worlds Apart: The Market and the Theater in Anglo-American Thought.* Cambridge: Cambridge University Press, 1986.

Allen, Thomas W. *The Invention of the White Race: The Origin of Racial Oppression in Anglo-America.* New York: Verso, 1997.

Alter, Peter. *Nationalism.* Translated by Stuart McKinnon-Evans. London: Edward Arnold, 1989.

Anderson, Benedict. *Imagined Communities: Reflections on the Origin and Spread of Nationalism.* London: Verso, 1983.

Andrews, William L. *To Tell a Free Story: The First Century of Afro-American Autobiography.* Chicago: University of Chicago Press, 1986.

Aptheker, Herbert. *Abolitionism: A Revolutionary Movement.* Boston: Twayne, 1989.

———. *Anti-Racism in U.S. History: The First Two-Hundred Years.* New York: Greenwood, 1992.

———, ed. *One Continual Cry: David Walker's Appeal to the Colored Citizens of the World, 1829–1830.* New York: Published for A.I.M.S. by Humanities Press, 1965.

Arendt, Hannah. *The Origins of Totalitarianism.* 1951. Reprint, San Diego, Calif.: Harcourt Brace Jovanovich, 1985.

Armstrong, John A. *Nations before Nationalism.* Chapel Hill: University of North Carolina Press, 1982.

Ashcroft, Bill, Gareth Griffiths, and Helen Tiffin, eds. *The Post-Colonial Studies Reader.* London: Routledge, 1995.

Ashworth, John. *"Agrarians" and "Aristocrats": Party Political Ideology in the United States, 1837–1846.* London: Royal Historical Society, 1983.

Bailyn, Bernard. *Ideological Origins of the American Revolution.* Cambridge, Mass.: Harvard University Press, 1967.

Baker, Houston A., Jr. *Long Black Song: Essays in Black American Literature and Culture Theory.* New York: Methuen, 1984.

———. *Modernism and the Harlem Renaissance.* Chicago: University of Chicago Press, 1987.

Baker, Jean A. *Affairs of Party: The Political Culture of Northern Democrats in the Mid-Nineteenth Century.* Ithaca: Cornell University Press, 1983.

Bakhtin, Mikhail M. *Rabelais and His World.* Translated by Helene Iswolsky. Cambridge, Mass.: Harvard University Press, 1968.

Balibar, Etienne, and Immanuel Wallerstein. *Race, Nation, Class: Ambiguous Identities.* London: Verso, 1988.

Bann, Stephen. *Romanticism and the Rise of History.* New York: Twayne, 1995.

Barkin, Michael. *Crucible of the Millennium: The Burned-Over District of New York in the 1840s.* Syracuse: Syracuse University Press, 1986.

Baron, Ava, ed. *Work Engendered: Toward a New History of American Labor*. Ithaca: Cornell University Press, 1991.

Bauman, Zygmunt. *Modernity and the Holocaust*. Ithaca: Cornell University Press, 1989.

Bay, Mia. *The White Image in the Black Mind: African-American Ideas about White People, 1830–1925*. New York: Oxford University Press, 2000.

Beard, Charles A., and Mary R. Beard. *The American Spirit: A Study of the Idea of Civilization in the United States*. New York: Macmillan, 1942.

Bederman, Gail. *Manliness and Civilization: A Cultural History of Gender and Race in the United States, 1880–1917*. Chicago: University of Chicago Press, 1995.

Bell, Howard Holman. *A Survey of the Negro Convention Movement, 1830–1861*. New York: Arno, 1969.

Bender, Thomas, ed. *The Antislavery Debate: Capitalism and Abolitionism as a Problem in Historical Interpretation*. Berkeley: University of California Press, 1992.

Benjamin, Lois. *The Black Elite: Facing the Color Line in the Twilight of the Twentieth Century*. Chicago: Nelson-Hall, 1991.

Bennett, Lerone. *The Shaping of Black America*. Chicago: Johnson, 1975.

Bercovitch, Sacvan. *The American Jeremiad*. Madison: University of Wisconsin Press, 1978.

———. *The Rites of Assent: Transformation in the Symbolic Construction of America*. New York: Routledge, 1993.

Berger, Peter L., and Thomas Luckmann. *The Social Construction of Reality: A Treatise on the Sociology of Knowledge*. Garden City, N.Y.: Anchor, 1967.

Berkhofer, Robert F., Jr. *The White Man's Indian: Images of the American Indian from Columbus to the Present*. New York: Vintage, 1978.

Berlin, Ira. *Many Thousands Gone: The First Two Centuries of Slavery in North America*. Cambridge, Mass.: Harvard University Press, 1998.

———. *Slaves Without Masters: The Free Negro in the Antebellum South*. New York: Pantheon, 1974.

Berlin, Ira, Barbara J. Fields, Steven J. Miller, Joseph P. Reidy, and Leslie S. Rowland, eds. *Slaves No More: Three Essays on Emancipation and the Civil War*. New York: Cambridge University Press, 1992.

Berlin, Ira, and Ronald Hoffman, eds. *Slavery and Freedom in the Age of the American Revolution*. Charlottesville: University Press of Virginia, 1983.

Bernal, Martin. *Black Athena: The Afroasiatic Roots of Classical Civilization*. Vol. 1, *The Fabrication of Ancient Greece, 1785–1985*. New Brunswick, N.J.: Rutgers University Press, 1987.

Bernstein, Iver. *The New York City Draft Riots: Their Significance for American Society and Politics in the Age of the Civil War*. New York: Oxford University Press, 1990.

Berry, Mary Frances, and John W. Blassingame. *Long Memory: The Black Experience in America*. New York: Oxford University Press, 1982.

Bethel, Elizabeth Rauh. *The Roots of African-American Identity: Memory and History in Free Antebellum Communities*. New York: St. Martin's, 1997.

Bhabha, Homi K. *The Location of Culture.* London: Routledge, 1994.

———, ed. *Nation and Narration.* London: Routledge, 1990.

Birney, William. *James G. Birney and His Times.* Appleton: D. Appleton and Company, 1890.

Black Public Sphere Collective, ed. *The Black Public Sphere.* Chicago: University of Chicago Press, 1995.

Blackett, R. J. M. *Beating Against the Barriers: The Lives of Six Nineteenth-Century Afro-Americans.* Ithaca: Cornell University Press, 1986.

———. *Building an Antislavery Wall: Black Americans in the Atlantic Abolitionist Movement, 1830–1860.* Ithaca: Cornell University Press, 1989.

Blassingame, John W. *The Slave Community: Plantation Life in the Antebellum South.* New York: Oxford University Press, 1972.

Blight, David W. *Frederick Douglass's Civil War: Keeping Faith in Jubilee.* Baton Rouge: Louisiana State University Press, 1989.

Bloch, Ruth H. *Visionary Republic: Millennial Themes in American Thought, 1756–1800.* Cambridge: Cambridge University Press, 1985.

Blockson, Charles L. *The Underground Railroad: First-Person Narratives of Escapes to Freedom in the North.* New York: Prentice-Hall, 1987.

Blumin, Stuart M. *The Emergence of the Middle Class: Social Experience in the American City, 1760–1900.* Cambridge: Cambridge University Press, 1989.

Boime, Albert. *The Art of Exclusion: Representing Blacks in the Nineteenth Century.* London: Thames and Hudson, 1990.

Bolster, W. Jeffrey. *Black Jacks: African-American Seamen in the Age of Sail.* Cambridge, Mass.: Harvard University Press, 1997.

Booth, Newell S., Jr., ed. *African Religions: A Symposium.* New York: NOK, 1977.

Borchert, James. *Alley Life in Washington: Family, Community, Religion, and Folklife in the City, 1850–1970.* Urbana: University of Illinois Press, 1980.

Boskin, Joseph. *Sambo: The Rise and Demise of an American Jester.* New York: Oxford University Press, 1986.

Boyer, Paul S. *Urban Masses and Moral Order in America, 1820–1920.* Cambridge, Mass.: Harvard University Press, 1978.

Bracey, John H., Jr., August Meier, and Elliott Rudwick, eds. *Blacks in the Abolitionist Movement.* Belmont, Calif.: Wadsworth, 1970.

Brass, Paul R. *Ethnicity and Nationalism: Theory and Comparison.* New Delhi: Sage, 1991.

Brinton, Crane. *Ideas and Men: The Story of Western Thought.* New York: Prentice-Hall, 1950.

Bronner, Simon, ed. *Consuming Visions: Accumulation and Display of Goods in America, 1880–1920.* New York: W. W. Norton, 1989.

Bryan, Carter R. *Negro Journalism in America Before Emancipation.* Journalism Monographs, no. 12. Lexington, Ky.: Association for Education in Journalism, 1969. 33 pp.

Bryson, Bill. *Made in America: An Informal History of the English Language in the United States.* New York: W. Morrow, 1994.

Bullock, Penelope L. *The Afro-American Periodical Press, 1838–1909.* Baton Rouge: Louisiana State University Press, 1981.

Burman, Stephan. *The Black Progress Question: Explaining the African-American Predicament.* Thousand Oaks, Calif.: Sage, 1995.

Bushman, Richard L. *The Refinement of America: Persons, Houses, Cities.* New York: Vintage, 1980.

Cable, Mary. *American Manners and Morals: A Picture History of How We Behaved and Misbehaved.* New York: American Heritage, 1969.

Callcott, George H. *History in the United States, 1800–1860: Its Practice and Purpose.* Baltimore: Johns Hopkins University Press, 1970.

Campbell, James T. *Songs of Zion: The African Methodist Episcopal Church in the United States and South Africa.* New York: Oxford University Press, 1995.

Carby, Hazel V. *Multicultural Fictions.* Birmingham, U.K.: University of Birmingham Press, 1979.

———. *Reconstructing Womanhood: The Emergence of the Afro-American Woman Novelist.* New York: Oxford University Press, 1987.

Carlisle, Rodney P. *The Roots of Black Nationalism.* Port Washington, N.Y.: Kennikat, 1975.

Carnes, Mark C., and Clyde Griffen, eds. *Meanings for Manhood: Constructions of Masculinity in Victorian America.* Chicago: University of Chicago Press, 1990.

Cawelti, John G. *Apostles of the Self-Made Man.* Chicago: University of Chicago Press, 1965.

Chatterjee, Partha. *The Nation and Its Fragments: Colonial and Post-Colonial Histories.* Princeton: Princeton University Press, 1993.

Chestnutt, Helen M. *Charles Waddell Chestnutt: Pioneer of the Color Line.* Chapel Hill: University of North Carolina Press, 1952.

Cmiel, Kenneth. *Democratic Eloquence: The Fight Over Popular Speech in Nineteenth-Century America.* New York: W. Morrow, 1990.

Cohen, David W., and Jack P. Greene, eds. *Neither Slave Nor Free: The Freedman of African Descent in the Slave Societies of the New World.* Baltimore: Johns Hopkins University Press, 1972.

Coleman, William. *Biology in the Nineteenth Century: Problems of Form, Function, and Transformation.* Cambridge: Cambridge University Press, 1977.

Collison, Gary. *Shadrach Minkins: From Fugitive Slave to Citizen.* Cambridge, Mass.: Harvard University Press, 1997.

Commager, Henry Steele. *The Era of Reform, 1830–1860.* 1960. Reprint, Malabar, Fla.: R. E. Krieger, 1982.

Condit, Celeste Michelle, and John Louis Lucaites. *Crafting Equality: America's Anglo-African World.* Chicago: University of Chicago Press, 1993.

Connor, Walker. *Ethnonationalism: The Quest for Understanding.* Princeton: Princeton University Press, 1994.

Cott, Nancy F. *The Bonds of Womanhood: "Woman's Sphere" in New England, 1780–1835.* New Haven: Yale University Press, 1977.

Courlander, Harold. *Negro Folk Music, U.S.A.* New York: Columbia University Press, 1963.

Cox, Oliver C. *Caste, Class, and Race: A Study in Social Dynamics.* New York: Monthly Review Press, 1970.

———. *Race Relations: Elements and Social Dynamics.* Detroit: Wayne State University Press, 1976.

Cross, Whitney R. *The Burned-Over District: The Social and Intellectual History of Enthusiastic Religion in Western New York, 1800–1850.* Ithaca: Cornell University Press, 1950.

Crow, Jeffrey J., and Larry E. Tise, eds. *The Southern Experience in the American Revolution.* Chapel Hill: University of North Carolina Press, 1978.

Cruse, Harold. *The Crisis of the Negro Intellectual.* New York: William Morrow, 1967.

Curry, Leonard P. *The Free Black in Urban America, 1800–1850: The Shadow of the Dream.* Chicago: University of Chicago Press, 1981.

Curtin, Philip D. *The Rise and Fall of the Plantation Complex: Essays in Atlantic History.* Cambridge: Cambridge University Press, 1990.

Daniel, Walter C. *Black Journals of the United States.* Westport, Conn.: Greenwood, 1982.

Daniels, John. *In Freedom's Birthplace: A Study of Boston Negroes.* Boston: Houghton Mifflin, 1914.

Davidson, Cathy N., ed. *Reading in America: Literature and Social History.* Baltimore: Johns Hopkins University Press, 1989.

Davis, Charles T., and Henry Louis Gates Jr. *The Slave's Narrative.* Oxford: Oxford University Press, 1985.

Davis, David Brion. *The Problem of Slavery in the Age of Revolution, 1770–1823.* Ithaca: Cornell University Press, 1975.

———. *The Problem of Slavery in Western Culture.* Ithaca: Cornell University Press, 1966.

———. *Slavery and Human Progress.* New York: Oxford University Press, 1984.

———, ed. *Ante-Bellum Reform.* New York: Harper and Row, 1967.

Davis, Susan G. *Parades and Power: Street Theater in Nineteenth-Century Philadelphia.* Philadelphia: Temple University Press, 1986.

Deacon, Desley. *Managing Gender: The State, the New Middle Class and Women Workers, 1830–1930.* Melbourne: Oxford University Press, 1989.

Degler, Carl N. *Neither Black Nor White: Slavery and Race Relations in Brazil and the United States.* New York: Macmillan, 1971.

Denning, Michael. *Mechanic Accents: Dime Novels and Working-Class Culture in America.* Rev. ed. London: Verso, 1998.

Dennison, Sam. *Scandalize My Name: Black Imagery in American Popular Music.* New York: Garland, 1982.

Dent, Gina, ed. *Black Popular Culture.* Seattle: Bay, 1992.

Dick, Robert C. *Black Protest: Issues and Tactics.* Westport, Conn.: Greenwood, 1974.

Dillon, Merton. *The Abolitionists: The Growth of a Dissenting Minority.* New York: W. W. Norton, 1974.

Diop, Cheikh Anta. *The African Origin of Civilization: Myth or Reality.* Edited and translated by Mercer Cook. Chicago: Lawrence Hill, 1974.

Diop, Cheikh Anta, and David M. Reimers. *Ethnic Americans: A History of Immigration and Assimilation.* New York: Dodd, Mead, 1973.

Dollard, John. *Caste and Class in a Southern Town.* New Haven: Yale University Press, 1937.

Draper, Theodore. *The Rediscovery of Black Nationalism.* New York: Viking, 1970.

Drimmer, Melvin. *Issues in Black History: Reflections and Commentaries on the Black Historical Experience.* Dubuque, Iowa: Kendall/Hunt, 1987.

Duberman, Martin, ed. *The Antislavery Vanguard: New Essays on the Abolitionists.* Princeton: Princeton University Press, 1965.

Du Bois, W. E. B. *The Philadelphia Negro: A Social Study.* 1899. Reprint, New York: Schocken, 1967.

———. *The Souls of Black Folk.* Chicago: A. C. McClurg, 1903. Reprint, New York: Norton, 1999.

Duffy, John H., and H. Nicholas Muller. *An Anxious Democracy: Aspects of the 1830s.* New York: Greenwood, 1982.

Early, Gerald. *Lure and Loathing: Essays on Race, Identity, and the Ambivalence of Assimilation.* New York: Penguin, 1993.

Egerton, Douglas R. *Gabriel's Rebellion: The Virginia Slave Conspiracies of 1800 and 1802.* Chapel Hill: University of North Carolina Press, 1993.

Ekirch, Arthur A. *The Idea of Progress in America, 1815–1860.* New York: Columbia University Press, 1944.

Eley, Geoff, and Ronald Grigor Suny, eds. *Becoming National: A Reader.* Oxford: Oxford University Press, 1996.

Elkins, Stanley. *Slavery: A Problem in American Institutional and Intellectual Life.* Chicago: University of Chicago Press, 1959.

Ellison, Ralph. *Invisible Man.* New York: Random House, 1947.

———. *Shadow and Act.* New York: Random House, 1964.

Epstein, Dena J. Polacheck. *Sinful Tunes and Spirituals: Black Folk Music to the Civil War.* Urbana: University of Illinois Press, 1977.

Erenberg, Lew. *Steppin' Out: New York Nightlife and the Transformation of American Culture, 1890–1930.* Westport, Conn.: Greenwood, 1981.

Esedebe, P. Olisanwuche. *Pan Africanism: The Idea and the Movement, 1776–1963.* Washington, D.C.: Howard University Press, 1982.

Essien-Udom, E. U. *Black Nationalism: A Search for Identity in America.* New York: Dell, 1962.

Etzioni-Halevy, Eva. *Classes and Elites in Democracy and Democratization: A Collection of Critical Essays.* New York: Garland, 1997.

Fabre, Geneviève, and Robert O'Meally, eds. *History and Memory in African-American Culture.* New York: Oxford University Press, 1994.

Faler, Paul G. *Mechanics and Manufacturers in the Early Industrial Revolution: Lynn, Massachusetts, 1780–1860.* Albany: State University of New York Press, 1981.

Fanon, Frantz. *Black Skin, White Masks.* Translated by Charles Lam Markmann. New York: Grove, 1967.

Farrison, William E. *William Wells Brown: Author and Reformer.* Chicago: University of Chicago Press, 1969.

Fauset, Arthur H. *Sojourner Truth, God's Faithful Pilgrim.* Chapel Hill: University of North Carolina Press, 1938.

Feagin, Joe R. *Racial and Ethnic Relations.* Englewood Cliffs, N.J.: Prentice-Hall, 1984.

Feldberg, Michael. *The Turbulent Era: Riot and Disorder in Jacksonian America.* New York: Oxford University Press, 1980.

Finkelman, Paul, ed. *His Soul Goes Marching On: Responses to John Brown and the Harper's Ferry Raid.* Charlottesville: University Press of Virginia, 1995.

Fisher, Philip, ed. *The New American Studies: Essays from Representations.* Berkeley: University of California Press, 1991.

Foner, Eric. *Free Soil, Free Labor, Free Men: The Ideology of the Republican Party Before the Civil War.* Oxford: Oxford University Press, 1970.

———. *Nothing but Freedom: Emancipation and Its Legacy.* Baton Rouge: Louisiana State University Press, 1983.

———. *Politics and Ideology in the Age of the Civil War.* New York: Oxford, 1980.

———. *Reconstruction: America's Unfinished Revolution, 1863–1877.* New York: Harper and Row, 1988.

Fordham, Monroe. *Major Themes in Northern Black Religious Thought, 1800–1860.* Hicksville, N.Y.: 1975.

Foster, Frances Smith. *Witnessing Slavery: The Development of Ante-Bellum Slave Narratives.* Westport, Conn.: Greenwood, 1979.

Fox, Early Lee. *The American Colonization Society, 1817–1840.* Baltimore: Johns Hopkins University Press, 1919.

Franklin, John Hope, and August Meier, eds. *Black Leaders of the Twentieth Century.* Urbana: University of Illinois Press, 1982.

Franklin, John Hope, and Alfred A. Moss Jr. *From Slavery to Freedom: A History of Negro Americans.* 6th ed. New York: Knopf, 1988.

Franklin, V. P. *Black Self-Determination: A Cultural History of African-American Resistance.* 2d ed. New York: Lawrence Hill, 1992.

Frazier, E. Franklin. *Black Bourgeoisie.* New York: Free Press, 1957; Free Press Paperbacks, 1997.

———. *The Negro Church in America.* New York: Schocken, 1963.

———. *The Negro Family in the United States.* New York: Citadel, 1948.

Fredrickson, George M. *The Black Image in the White Mind: The Debate on Afro-American Character and Destiny, 1817–1914.* New York: Harper and Row, 1971.

———. *Black Liberation: A Comparative History of Black Ideologies in the United States and South America.* New York: Oxford University Press, 1995.

———. *White Supremacy: A Comparative Study of American and South African History.* New York: Oxford University Press, 1981.

Friedman, Lawrence J. *Gregarious Saints: Self and Community in American Abolitionism, 1830–1870.* Cambridge: Cambridge University Press, 1982.

———. *The White Savage: Racial Fantasies in the Postbellum South.* Englewood Cliffs, N.J.: Prentice-Hall, 1970.

Frisch, Michael H., and Daniel J. Walkowitz, eds. *Working-Class America: Essays on Labor, Community, and American Society.* Urbana: University of Illinois Press, 1983.

Fry, Gladys-Marie. *Night Riders in Black Folk History.* Knoxville: University of Tennessee Press, 1975.

Fullinwider, S. P. *The Mind and Mood of Black America: 20th Century Thought.* Homewood, Ill.: Dorsey, 1969.

Gabriel, Ralph Henry. *The Course of American Democratic Thought.* New York: Ronald Press, 1940.

Gaines, Kevin K. *Uplifting the Race: Black Leadership, Politics, and Culture in the Twentieth Century.* Chapel Hill: University of North Carolina Press, 1996.

Gates, Henry Louis, Jr. *Figures in Black: Words, Signs, and the "Racial" Self.* New York: Oxford University Press, 1987.

———. *The Signifying Monkey: A Theory of Afro-American Literary Criticism.* New York: Oxford University Press, 1988.

———, ed. *Black Literature and Literary Theory.* New York: Methuen, 1984.

———, *"Race," Writing, and Difference.* Chicago: University of Chicago Press, 1986.

———, *Reading Black, Reading Feminist.* New York: Meridian Books, 1990.

Gatewood, Willard B. *Aristocrats of Color: The Black Elite, 1880–1920.* Bloomington: Indiana University Press, 1990.

Geiss, Imanuel. *The Pan-African Movement: A History of Pan-Africanism in America, Europe, and Africa.* Translated by Ann Keep. New York: Africana, 1974.

Gellner, Ernest. *Nations and Nationalism.* Ithaca: Cornell University Press, 1983.

Genovese, Eugene. *From Rebellion to Revolution: Afro-American Slave Revolts in the Making of the Modern World.* Baton Rouge: Louisiana State University Press, 1979.

———. *Roll, Jordan, Roll: The World the Slaves Made.* New York: Random House, 1974.

George, Carol V. R. *Segregated Sabbaths: Richard Allen and the Rise of Independent Black Churches, 1760–1840.* New York: Oxford University Press, 1973.

Gerteis, Louis S. *Morality and Utility in American Antislavery Reform.* Chapel Hill: University of North Carolina Press, 1987.

Gilfoyle, Timothy J. *City of Eros: New York City, Prostitution, and the Commercialization of Sex, 1790–1920.* New York: Norton, 1992.

Gilje, Paul A. *The Road to Mobocracy: Popular Disorder in New York City, 1763–1834.* Chapel Hill: University of North Carolina Press, 1987.

Gilroy, Paul. *The Black Atlantic: Modernity and Double Consciousness.* Cambridge, Mass.: Harvard University Press, 1993.

Glaude, Eddie S., Jr. *Exodus! Religion, Race, and Nation in Early Nineteenth-Century Black America.* Chicago: University of Chicago Press, 2000.

Glazer, Nathan, and Daniel Patrick Moynihan. *Beyond the Melting Pot: The Negroes,*

Puerto Ricans, Jews, Italians, and Irish of New York City. Cambridge, Mass.: Harvard University Press, 1963.

Glickstein, Jonathan A. *Concepts of Free Labor in Antebellum America*. New Haven: Yale University Press, 1991.

Goings, Kenneth W., and Raymond A. Mohl, eds. *The New African-American Urban History*. Thousand Oaks, Calif.: Sage, 1996.

Goldberg, David Theo. *Racist Culture: Philosophy and the Politics of Meaning*. Cambridge: Cambridge University Press, 1993.

Golden, James L., and Richard D. Rieke. *The Rhetoric of Black Americans*. Columbus, Ohio:, 1971.

Gordon, Milton. *Assimilation in American Life: The Role of Race, Religion, and National Origins*. New York: Oxford University Press, 1964.

Gossett, Thomas F. *Race: The History of an Idea in America*. New York: Schocken, 1963.

Gould, Stephen Jay. *The Mismeasure of Man*. New York: Norton, 1981.

———. *Ever Since Darwin: Reflections in Natural History*. 1973. Reprint, New York: Norton, 1992.

Graham, Richard, ed. *The Idea of Race in Latin America, 1870–1940*. Austin: University of Texas Press, 1990.

Greene, Lorenzo Johnston. *The Negro in Colonial New England, 1620–1776*. New York: Columbia University Press, 1942.

Greenfield, Liah. *Nationalism: Five Roads to Modernity*. Cambridge, Mass.: Harvard University Press, 1992.

Griffin, C. S. *The Ferment of Reform, 1830–1860*. Arlington Heights, Ill.: Harlan Davison, 1967.

Griffith, Cyril E. *The African Dream: Martin R. Delany and the Emergence of Pan-African Thought*. University Park: University of Pennsylvania Press, 1975.

Grimsted, David. *American Mobbing, 1828–1861: Toward Civil War*. New York: Oxford University Press, 1998.

———. *Melodrama Unveiled: American Theater and Culture, 1800–1850*. Chicago: University of Chicago Press, 1968.

Grissom, Mary Allen. *The Negro Sings a New Heaven*. Chapel Hill: University of North Carolina Press, 1930.

Gronowicz, Anthony. *Race and Class Politics in New York City Before the Civil War*. Boston: Northeastern University Press, 1998.

Gross, Bella. *Clarion Call: The History and Development of the Negro People's Convention Movement in the United States from 1817–1840*. New York: n.p., 1947.

Grossberg, Lawrence, ed. *Cultural Studies*. New York: Routledge, 1992.

Gutman, Herbert G. *The Black Family in Slavery and Freedom, 1750–1925*. New York: Pantheon, 1976.

———. *Work, Culture, and Society in Industrializing America*. New York: Alfred A. Knopf, 1976.

Gwaltney, John Langston. *Drylongso: A Self-Portrait of Black America*. New York: Random House, 1980.

Habermas, Jürgen. *The Structural Transformation of the Public Sphere: An Inquiry into a Category of Bourgeois Society.* Translated by Thomas Burger. Cambridge, Mass.: MIT Press, 1989.

Hall, David D. *Cultures of Print: Essays in the History of the Book.* Amherst: University of Massachusetts Press, 1996.

Hall, Raymond L. *Black Separatism in the United States.* Hanover, N.H.: University Press of New England, 1978.

Hall, Stuart, and Tony Jefferson, eds. *Resistance Through Rituals: Youth Subcultures in Post-War Britain.* London: Hutchinson, 1989.

Haller, John S., Jr. *Outcasts from Evolution: Scientific Attitudes of Racial Inferiority, 1859–1900.* Urbana: University of Illinois Press, 1971.

Halttunen, Karen. *Confidence Men and Painted Women: A Study of Middle-Class Culture in America, 1830–1870.* New Haven: Yale University Press, 1982.

Hamilton, Charles V. *The Black Preacher in America.* New York: Morrow, 1972.

Handlin, Oscar. *Boston's Immigrants, 1790–1880: A Study in Acculturation.* Cambridge, Mass.: Harvard University Press, 1941; reprint, 1979.

———. *Race and Nationality in American Life.* Boston: Little, Brown, 1957.

———. *The Uprooted: The Epic Story of the Great Migrations That Made the American People.* Boston: Little, Brown, 1951.

Hansen, Karen V. *A Very Social Time: Crafting Community in Antebellum New England.* Berkeley: University of California Press, 1994.

Harding, Vincent. *There Is a River: The Black Struggle for Freedom in America.* New York: Vintage, 1983.

Hare, Nathan. *The Black Anglo-Saxons.* 2d ed. Chicago: Third World, 1991.

Harley, Sharon, and Rosalyn Terborg-Penn, eds. *The Afro-American Woman: Struggles and Images.* Port Washington, N.Y.: Kennikat, 1978.

Harris, Marvin. *The Rise of Anthropological Theory: A History of Theories of Culture.* New York: Crowell, 1968.

Harris, Neil. *Cultural Excursions: Marketing Appetites and Cultural Tastes in Modern America.* Chicago: University of Chicago Press, 1990.

Hartman, Saidiya V. *Scenes of Subjection: Terror, Slavery, and Self-Making in Nineteenth-Century America.* New York: Oxford University Press, 1997.

Hatch, Nathan O. *The Democratization of American Christianity.* New Haven: Yale University Press, 1989.

Haynes, Robert V. *Blacks in White America Before 1865.* New York: D. McKay, 1972.

Heermance, J. Noel. *William Wells Brown and Clotelle: A Portrait of the Artist in the First Negro Novel.* Hamden, Conn.: Archon, 1969.

Helms, Janet E., ed. *Black and White Racial Identity: Theory, Research, and Practice.* Westport, Conn.: Greenwood, 1990.

Henry, Charles P. *Culture and African-American Politics.* Bloomington: Indiana University Press, 1990.

Herbers, John. *The Black Dilemma.* New York: John Day, 1973.

Hershberg, Theodore, ed. *Philadelphia: Work, Space, Family, and Group Experience in the Nineteenth Century.* New York: Oxford University Press, 1980.

Herskovits, Melville J. *The Myth of the Negro Past.* New York: Harper and Brothers, 1941.

Higginbotham, Evelyn Brooks. *Righteous Discontent: The Women's Movement in the Black Baptist Church, 1880–1920.* Cambridge, Mass.: Harvard University Press, 1993.

Higham, John. *Strangers in the Land: Patterns of American Nativism, 1860–1925.* New Brunswick, N.J.: Rutgers University Press, 1955.

———, ed. *Ethnic Leadership in America.* Baltimore: Johns Hopkins University Press, 1978.

Hine, Darlene Clark, ed. *The State of Afro-American History: Past, Present, and Future.* Baton Rouge: Louisiana State University Press, 1986.

Hinks, Peter P. *To Awaken My Afflicted Brethren: David Walker and the Problem of Antebellum Slave Resistance.* University Park: Pennsylvania State University Press, 1997.

Hobsbawm, Eric. *Nations and Nationalism Since 1780: Programme, Myth, Reality.* 2d ed. New York: Cambridge University Press, 1991.

Hobsbawm, Eric, and Terence Ranger, eds. *The Invention of Tradition.* Cambridge: Cambridge University Press, 1983.

Hodge, Francis. *Yankee Theater: The Image of America on the Stage, 1825–1850.* Austin: University of Texas Press, 1964.

Hodges, Graham Russell. *Root and Branch: African Americans in New York and East Jersey, 1613–1863.* Chapel Hill: University of North Carolina Press, 1999.

Hofstadter, Richard. *Social Darwinism in American Thought.* 1944. Reprint, Boston: Beacon, 1992.

Holloway, Joseph E., ed. *Africanisms in American Culture.* Bloomington: Indiana University Press, 1990.

Holt, Thomas. *Black over White: Negro Political Leadership in South Carolina during Reconstruction.* Urbana: University of Illinois Press, 1977.

Hoover, Dwight W., ed. *Understanding Negro History.* Chicago: University of Chicago Press, 1969.

Hord, Fred L. *Reconstructing Memory: Black Literary Criticism.* Chicago: Third World, 1991.

Horsman, Reginald. *Race and Manifest Destiny: The Origins of American Racial Anglo-Saxonism.* Cambridge, Mass.: Harvard University Press, 1981.

Horsmanden, Daniel. *The New York Conspiracy.* Boston: Beacon, 1971.

Horton, James O. *Free People of Color: Inside the African-American Community.* Washington, D.C.: Smithsonian Institution Press, 1993.

Horton, James O., and Lois E. Horton. *Black Bostonians: Family Life and Community Struggle in the Antebellum North.* New York: Holmes and Meier, 1979.

———. *In Hope of Liberty: Culture, Community, and Protest Among Northern Free Blacks, 1700–1860.* New York: Oxford University Press, 1997.

Howard, Victor B. *Conscience and Slavery: The Evangelistic Calvinist Domestic Missions, 1837–1861.* Kent, Ohio: Kent State University Press, 1990.

Howard-Pitney, David. *The Afro-American Jeremiad: Appeals for Justice in America.* Philadelphia: Temple University Press, 1990.

Hroch, Miroslav. *Social Preconditions of National Revival in Europe: A Comparative Analysis of the Social Composition of Patriotic Groups Among the Smaller European Nations.* Cambridge: Cambridge University Press, 1985.

Huggins, Nathan Irvin. *Black Odyssey: The African-American Ordeal in Slavery.* New York: Pantheon, 1977. Reprint, New York: Vintage, 1990.

———. *Harlem Renaissance.* New York: Oxford University Press, 1971.

Huggins, Nathan Irvin, Martin Kilson, and Daniel Fox, eds. *Key Issues in the Afro-American Experience.* New York: Harcourt, Brace, Jovanovich, 1971.

Hunt, Alfred N. *Haiti's Influence on Antebellum America: Slumbering Volcano in the Caribbean.* Baton Rouge: Louisiana State University Press, 1987.

Hunt, Lynn, ed. *The New Cultural History.* Berkeley: University of California Press, 1989.

Hunter, Carol M. *To Set the Captives Free: Reverend Jermain Wesley Loguen and the Struggle for Freedom in Central New York, 1835–1872.* New York: Garland, 1993.

Hutchinson, George. *The Harlem Renaissance in Black and White.* Cambridge, Mass.: Belknap Press of Harvard University Press, 1995.

Hutton, Frankie. *The Early Black Press in America, 1827–1860.* Westport, Conn.: Greenwood, 1993.

Ignatiev, Noel. *How the Irish Became White.* New York: Routledge, 1995.

Ione, Carole. *Pride of Family: Four Generations of American Women of Color.* New York: Summit, 1991.

Jackson, Blyden, Jr. *A History of Afro-American Literature.* Baton Rouge: Louisiana State University Press, 1989.

Jacobs, Donald M., ed. *Courage and Conscience: Black and White Abolitionists in Boston.* Bloomington: Indiana University Press, 1993.

James, C. L. R. *The Black Jacobins: Toussaint L'Ouverture and the San Domingo Revolution.* 1938. 2d ed., New York: Vintage, 1963.

Jaynes, Gerald David, and Robin M. Williams Jr., eds. *A Common Destiny: Blacks and American Society.* Washington, D.C.: National Academy Press, 1989.

Johnson, Homer Uri. *From Dixie to Canada: Romance and Realities of the Underground Railroad.* 1896. Reprint, Westport, Conn.: Greenwood, 1970.

Johnson, James Weldon. *Black Manhattan.* New York: Knopf, 1930.

Johnson, Michael P., and James L. Roarke. *Black Masters: A Free Family of Color in the Old South.* New York: Norton, 1984.

Johnson, Paul E. *A Shopkeeper's Millennium: Society and Revivals in Rochester, New York, 1815–1837.* New York: Hill and Wang, 1978.

Jones, Arthur. *Wade in the Water: The Wisdom of the Spirituals.* Maryknoll, N.Y.: Orbis, 1993.

Jones, Jacqueline. *Labor of Love, Labor of Sorrow: Black Women, Work, and the Family, From Slavery to the Present.* New York: Vintage, 1985.

————. *Soldiers of Light and Love: Northern Teachers and Georgia Blacks, 1865–1873.* Chapel Hill: University of North Carolina Press, 1980.

Jordan, Winthrop D. *White Over Black: American Attitudes Toward the Negro, 1550–1812.* New York: W. W. Norton, 1968. Reprint, New York: Oxford University Press, 1977.

Joyner, Charles. *Down by the Riverside: A South Carolina Slave Community.* Urbana: University of Illinois Press, 1984.

Kammen, Michael. *Mystic Chords of Memory: The Transformation of Tradition in American Culture.* New York: Alfred A. Knopf, 1991.

Kaplan, Sidney, and Emma Nogrady Kaplan. *The Black Experience in the American Revolution.* Amherst: University of Massachusetts Press, 1989.

Kasson, John F. *Amusing the Millions: Coney Island at the Turn of the Century.* New York: Hill and Wang, 1978.

————. *Rudeness and Civility: Manners in Nineteenth-Century Urban America.* New York: Hill and Wang, 1990.

Katz, Stanley N., and John M. Murrin, eds. *Colonial America: Essays in Politics and Social Development.* New York: Knopf, 1983.

Katzman, David M. *Before the Ghetto: Black Detroit in the Nineteenth Century.* Urbana: University of Illinois Press, 1973.

Keil, Charles. *Urban Blues.* Chicago: University of Chicago Press, 1991.

Kellas, James G. *The Politics of Nationalism and Ethnicity.* New York: St. Martin's, 1991.

Kerber, Linda K. *Women of the Republic: Intellect and Ideology in Revolutionary America.* New York: W. W. Norton, 1980.

Kinshasa, Kwando Mbiassi. *Emigration vs. Assimilation: The Debate in the African-American Press, 1827–1861.* Jefferson, N.C.: Macfarland, 1988.

Kliger, Samuel. *The Goths in England: A Study in Seventeenth- and Eighteenth-Century Thought.* Cambridge: Cambridge University Press, 1952.

Kohn, Hans. *American Nationalism: An Interpretive Essay.* New York: Collier, 1957.

————. *The Idea of Nationalism: A Study in Its Origins and Background.* New York: Macmillan, 1944.

————. *Nationalism: Its Meaning and History.* Princeton: D. Van Nostrand, 1965.

Kolchin, Peter. *American Slavery, 1619–1877.* New York: Hill and Wang, 1993.

Kousser, J. Morgan, and James M. McPherson, eds. *Region, Race, and Reconstruction: Essays in Honor of C. Vann Woodward.* New York: Oxford University Press, 1982.

Krehbiel, Henry Edward. *Afro-American Folksongs: A Study in Racial and National Music.* New York: G. Schirmer, 1962.

Kusmer, Kenneth L., ed. *Black Communities and Urban Development in America, 1720–1990.* 10 vols. New York: Garland, 1991.

La Capra, Dominick, ed. *The Bounds of Race: Perspectives on Hegemony and Distance.* Ithaca: Cornell University Press, 1991.

Landrine, Hope, and Elizabeth A. Klonoff. *African-American Acculturation: Deconstructing Race and Reviving Culture.* Thousand Oaks, Calif.: Sage, 1996.

Lane, Roger. *William Dorsey's Philadelphia and Ours: On the Past and Future of the Black City in Philadelphia.* New York: Oxford University Press, 1991.

Laurie, Bruce. *Working People of Philadelphia, 1800–1850*. Philadelphia: Temple University Press, 1980.

Leach, William. *Land of Desire: Merchants, Power, and the Rise of a New American Culture*. New York: Pantheon, 1993.

Lebsock, Suzanne. *The Free Women of Petersburg: Status and Culture in a Southern Town, 1784–1860*. New York: W. W. Norton, 1984.

Lenz, Gunter, ed. *History and Tradition in Afro-American Culture*. Frankfurt: Campus, 1984.

Lenz, Gunter, Hartmut Keil, and Sabine Brock-Sallah, eds. *The New American Studies: Essays from Representations*. Berkeley: University of California Press, 1991.

———. *Reconstructing American Literary and Historical Studies*. New York: St. Martin's, 1990.

Leverenz, David. *Manhood and the American Renaissance*. Ithaca: Cornell University Press, 1989.

Levine, Lawrence W. *Black Culture and Black Consciousness: Afro-American Folk Thought from Slavery to Freedom*. Oxford: Oxford University Press, 1977.

———. *Highbrow/Lowbrow: The Emergence of Cultural Hierarchy in America*. Cambridge, Mass.: Harvard University Press, 1988.

———. *The Opening of the American Mind: Canons, Culture, and History*. Boston: Beacon, 1996.

Levine, Robert S. *Martin Delany, Frederick Douglass, and the Politics of Representative Identity*. Chapel Hill: University of North Carolina Press, 1997.

Lindberg, Gary. *The Confidence Man in American Literature*. New York: Oxford University Press, 1982.

Litwack, Leon F. *Been in the Storm So Long: The Aftermath of Slavery*. New York: Knopf, 1979.

———. *North of Slavery: The Negro in the Free States, 1790–1860*. Chicago: University of Chicago Press, 1961.

Litwack, Leon F., and August Meier, eds. *Black Leaders of the Nineteenth Century*. Urbana: University of Illinois Press, 1988.

Locke, Alain LeRoy. *The Negro and His Music, Negro Art: Past and Present*. 1936. Reprint, New York: Arno, 1969.

Loggins, Vernon. *The Negro Author, His Development in America to 1900*. Port Washington, N.Y.: Kennikat, 1959.

Loney, Glenn, ed. *Musical Theater in America: Papers and Proceedings of the Conference on Musical Theater in America*. Westport, Conn.: Greenwood, 1984.

Lott, Eric. *Love and Theft: Blackface Minstrelsy and the American Working Class*. New York: Oxford, 1993.

Lovejoy, Arthur O. *The Great Chain of Being: A Study of the History of an Idea*. Cambridge, Mass.: Harvard University Press, 1936.

Lovell, John. *Black Song: The Forge and the Fame: The Story of How the Afro-American Spiritual Was Hammered Out*. New York: Macmillan, 1972.

Lynch, Hollis R. *Edward Wilmot Blyden: Pan-Negro Patriot, 1832–1912.* London: Oxford University Press, 1967.

———. *James Theodore Holly: Ante-Bellum Black Nationalist and Emigrationist.* Los Angeles: Center for Afro-American Studies, University of California, 1977.

McAdoo, Bill. *Pre–Civil War Black Nationalism.* New York: D. Walker, 1983.

McCartney, John T. *Black Power Ideologies: An Essay in African-American Political Thought.* Philadelphia: Temple University Press, 1992.

McFeely, William S. *Frederick Douglass.* New York: Norton, 1991.

McKelvey, Charles. *The African-American Movement: From Pan-Africanism to the Rainbow Coalition.* Dix Hills, N.Y.: General Hall, 1994.

MacLeod, Duncan J. *Slavery, Race, and the American Revolution.* London: Cambridge University Press, 1974.

McLoughlin, William G. *Revivals, Awakenings, and Reform.* Chicago: University of Chicago Press, 1978.

McManus, Edgar J. *Black Bondage in the North.* Syracuse: Syracuse University Press, 1973.

McPherson, James M. *Is Blood Thicker Than Water? Crises of Nationalism in the Modern World.* Toronto: Vintage Canada, 1998.

———. *Marching Towards Freedom: The Negro in the Civil War, 1861–1865.* New York: Knopf, 1968.

———. *The Struggle for Equality: Abolitionists and the Negro in the Civil War and Reconstruction.* Princeton: Princeton University Press, 1964.

Magubane, Bernard Makhosezwe. *The Ties That Bind: African-American Consciousness of Africa.* Trenton, N.J.: Africa World Press, 1987.

Mangan, J. A., and James Walvin, eds. *Manliness and Morality: Middle-Class Masculinity in Britain and America, 1800–1940.* New York: St. Martin's, 1987.

Martin, Waldo E., Jr. *The Mind of Frederick Douglass.* Chapel Hill: University of North Carolina Press, 1984.

Mates, Julian. *America's Musical Stage: Two Hundred Years of Musical Theater.* Westport, Conn.: Greenwood, 1985.

Maultsby, Portia K. *Afro-American Religious Music: A Study in Musical Diversity.* Springfield, Ohio: Wittenberg University, 1981.

Mbiti, John S. *African Religions and Philosophy.* London: Heinemann, 1969.

———. *Introduction to African Religion.* New York: Praeger, 1975.

Mead, Sidney E. *The Lively Experiment: The Shaping of Christianity in America.* New York: Harper and Row, 1963.

Meier, August. *Negro Thought in America, 1880–1915.* Ann Arbor: University of Michigan Press, 1969.

Meier, August, and Elliott Rudwick, eds. *Black History and the Historical Profession, 1915–1980.* Urbana: University of Illinois Press, 1986.

Melish, Joanne Pope. *Disowning Slavery: Gradual Emancipation and "Race" in New England, 1780–1860.* Ithaca: Cornell University Press, 1998.

Memmi, Albert. *The Colonizer and the Colonized.* Translated by Howard Greenfeld. New York: Orion, 1965.

Merck, Frederick. *Manifest Destiny and Mission in American History: A Reinterpretation.* 1963. Reprint, Cambridge, Mass.: Harvard University Press, 1995.

Meyer, Donald B. *The Positive Thinkers: A Study of the American Quest for Health, Wealth, and Personal Power.* Garden City, N.Y.: Doubleday, 1965.

Miller, Floyd J. *The Search for a Black Nationality: Black Emigration and Colonization, 1787–1863.* Urbana: University of Illinois Press, 1975.

Miller, Perry. *The New England Mind: The Seventeenth Century.* 1939. Reprint, Cambridge, Mass.: Harvard University Press, 1982.

Mintz, Sidney W., and Richard Price. *The Birth of African-American Culture: An Anthropological Perspective.* 1976. Reprint, Boston: Beacon, 1992.

Montgomery, David. *Beyond Equality: Labor and the Radical Republicans, 1862–1872.* New York: Knopf, 1967.

Montgomery, William E. *Under Their Own Vine and Fig Tree: The African-American Church in the South, 1865–1900.* Baton Rouge: Louisiana State University Press, 1993.

Moody, J. Carroll, and Alice Kessler-Harris, eds. *Perspectives on American Labor History: The Problem of Synthesis.* DeKalb: Northern Illinois University Press, 1990.

Moore, Richard B. *The Name "Negro": Its Origin and Evil Use.* 1960. Reprint, Baltimore: Black Classic, 1992.

Morgan, Edmund S. *American Slavery, American Freedom: The Ordeal of Colonial Virginia.* New York: Norton, 1975.

Morse, Jonathan. *Word by Word: The Language of Memory.* Ithaca: Cornell University Press, 1990.

Moses, Wilson Jeremiah. *Black Messiahs and Uncle Toms: Social and Literary Manipulations of a Religious Myth.* University Park: University of Pennsylvania Press, 1982.

———. *The Golden Age of Black Nationalism, 1850–1925.* New York: Oxford University Press, 1978.

———, ed. *The Wings of Ethiopia: Studies in African-American Life and Letters.* Ames: Iowa State University Press, 1990.

Mullin, Michael. *Africa in America: Slave Acculturation and Resistance in the American South and the British Caribbean, 1736–1831.* Urbana: University of Illinois Press, 1992.

Myrdal, Gunnar. *An American Dilemma: The Negro Problem and Modern Democracy.* New York: Harper and Brothers, 1944.

Nagel, Paul C. *This Sacred Trust: American Nationality, 1798–1898.* New York: Oxford University Press, 1971.

Nash, Gary B. *Forging Freedom: The Formation of Philadelphia's Black Community, 1720–1840.* Cambridge, Mass.: Harvard University Press, 1988.

Nash, Gary B., and Jean R. Soderlund. *Freedom by Degrees: Emancipation in Pennsylvania and Its Aftermath.* New York: Oxford, 1991.

Neale, R. S. *Class and Ideology in the Nineteenth Century.* London: Routledge, 1972.

Nederveen Pieterse, Jan. *White on Black: Images of Africa and Blacks in Western Popular Culture*. New Haven: Yale University Press, 1992.

Newman, Richard, and Marcia Sawyer. *Everybody Say Freedom: Everything You Need to Know About African-American History*. New York: Penguin, 1996.

Nisbet, Robert. *History of the Idea of Progress*. New York: Basic, 1980.

Nissenbaum, Stephen. *The Battle for Christmas: A Cultural History of America's Most Cherished Holiday*. New York: Vintage, 1996.

Novick, Peter. *That Noble Dream: The "Objectivity Question" and the American Historical Profession*. New York: Cambridge University Press, 1989.

Odum, Howard Washington. *The Negro and His Songs: A Study of Typical Negro Songs in the South*. 1925. Reprint, New York: Negro Universities Press, 1968.

Ofari, Earl. *Let Your Motto Be Resistance: The Life and Thought of Henry Highland Garnet*. Boston: Beacon, 1972.

Okoye, Felix N. *The American Image of Africa: Myth and Reality*. Buffalo, N.Y.: Black Academy, 1971.

Oliver, Paul. *Songsters and Saints: Vocal Traditions on Race Records*. New York: Cambridge University Press, 1984.

Omi, Michael, and Howard Winant. *Racial Formation in the United States*. New York: Routledge, 1986.

Painter, Nell. *Exodusters: Black Migration to Kansas after Reconstruction*. Lawrence: University Press of Kansas, 1976.

———. *Sojourner Truth: A Life, A Symbol*. New York: W. W. Norton, 1996.

Palmié, Stephan, ed. *Slave Cultures and the Cultures of Slavery*. Knoxville: University of Tennessee Press, 1995.

Parish, Peter J. *Slavery: History and Historians*. New York: Harper and Row, 1989.

Parsons, Talcott, and Kenneth B. Clark, eds. *The Negro American*. Boston: Beacon, 1967.

Patterson, Orlando. *Slavery and Social Death: A Comparative Study*. Cambridge, Mass.: Harvard University Press, 1982.

Pauli, Hertha. *Her Name Was Sojourner Truth*. New York: Avon, 1962.

Pease, William H., and Jane H. Pease. *Black Utopia: Negro Communal Experiments in America*. Madison: University of Wisconsin Press, 1963.

———. *Bound with Them in Chains: A Biographical History of the Antislavery Movement*. Westport, Conn.: Greenwood, 1972.

———. *They Who Would Be Free: Blacks' Search for Freedom, 1830–1861*. New York: Atheneum, 1974.

Peiss, Kathy. *Cheap Amusements: Working Women and Leisure in Turn-of-the-Century New York*. Philadelphia: Temple University Press, 1986.

Perry, Lewis. *Radical Abolitionism: Anarchy and the Government of God in Anti-Slavery Thought*. Ithaca: Cornell University Press, 1973.

Perry, Lewis, and Michael Fellman, eds. *Antislavery Reconsidered: New Perspectives on the Abolitionists*. Baton Rouge: Louisiana State University Press, 1979.

Pessen, Edward. *Jacksonian America: Society, Personality, and Politics.* Homewood, Ill.: Dorsey, 1978.

Peterson, Thomas V. *Ham and Japheth: The Mythic World of Whites in the Antebellum South.* Metuchen, N.J.: Scarecrow, 1978.

Pfaff, William. *The Wrath of Nations: Civilization and the Furies of Nationalism.* New York: Simon and Schuster, 1993.

Phillips, Ulrich Bonnell. *Life and Labor in the Old South.* Boston: Little, Brown, 1929.

Piersen, William D. *Black Legacy: America's Hidden Heritage.* Amherst: University of Massachusetts Press, 1993.

―――. *Black Yankees: The Development of an Afro-American Subculture in Eighteenth-Century New England.* Amherst: University of Massachusetts Press, 1988.

Pierson, George Wilson. *Tocqueville and Beaumont in America.* New York: Oxford University Press, 1938.

Pinkney, Alphonso. *Red, Black, and Green: Black Nationalism in the United States.* Cambridge: Cambridge University Press, 1976.

Pocock, J. G. A. *Machiavellian Moment: Florentine Political Thought and the Atlantic Republican Tradition.* Princeton: Princeton University Press, 1975.

―――. *Virtue, Commerce, and History: Essays on Political Thought and History, Chiefly in the Eighteenth Century.* Cambridge: Cambridge University Press, 1985.

Poliakov, Leon. *The Aryan Myth: A History of Racist and Nationalist Ideas in Europe.* Translated by Edmund Howard. New York: Barnes and Noble, 1996.

Potter, David. *The South and the Sectional Crisis.* Baton Rouge: Louisiana State University Press, 1968.

Pugh, David G. *Sons of Liberty: The Masculine Mind in Nineteenth-Century America.* Westport, Conn.: Greenwood, 1983.

Putney, Martha S. *Black Sailors: Afro-American Merchant Seamen and Whalemen Prior to the Civil War.* Contributions in Afro-American and African Studies No. 103. New York: Greenwood, 1987.

Quarles, Benjamin. *Allies for Freedom: Blacks and John Brown.* New York: Oxford University Press, 1974.

―――. *Black Abolitionists.* New York: Oxford University Press, 1969.

―――. *Black Mosaic: Essays in Afro-American History and Historiography.* Amherst: University of Massachusetts Press, 1988.

―――. *Frederick Douglass.* 1948. Reprint, New York: Atheneum, 1968.

Rabinowitz, Howard N. *Race Relations in the Urban South, 1865–1890.* Urbana: University of Illinois Press, 1978.

―――, ed. *Southern Black Leaders of the Reconstruction Era.* Urbana: University of Illinois Press, 1982.

Raboteau, Albert J. *A Fire in the Bones: Reflections on African-American Religious History.* Boston: Beacon, 1995.

―――. *Slave Religion: The "Invisible Institution" in the Antebellum South.* New York: Oxford University Press, 1978.

Radway, Janice A. *Reading the Romance: Women, Patriarchy, and Popular Literature.* Chapel Hill: University of North Carolina Press, 1984.

Ransom, Roger L., and Richard Sutch. *One Kind of Freedom: The Economic Consequences of Emancipation.* New York: Cambridge University Press, 1977.

Rawick, George P. *From Sundown to Sunup: The Making of the Black Community.* Westport, Conn.: Greenwood, 1972.

Rawley, James A. *The Transatlantic Slave Trade: A History.* New York: Norton, 1981.

Redkey, Edwin S. *Black Exodus: Black Nationalist and Back-to-Africa Movements, 1890–1910.* New Haven: Yale University Press, 1969.

Reed, Harry. *Platform for Change: The Foundations of the Northern Free Black Community, 1775–1865.* East Lansing: Michigan State University Press, 1994.

Reed, Ishmael. *Mumbo Jumbo.* 1972. Reprint, New York: Scribner, 1996.

Rhodes, Jane. *Mary Ann Shadd Cary: The Black Press and Protest in the Nineteenth Century.* Bloomington: Indiana University Press, 1998.

Richards, Leonard L. *"Gentlemen of Property and Standing": Anti-Abolition Mobs in Jacksonian America.* London: Oxford University Press, 1970.

Richardson, Joe Martin. *Christian Reconstruction: The American Missionary Association and Southern Blacks, 1861–1890.* Athens: University of Georgia Press, 1986.

Richey, Russell E., and Donald G. Jones, eds. *American Civil Religion.* New York: Harper and Row, 1974.

Rigsby, Gregory U. *Alexander Crummell: Pioneer in Nineteenth-Century Pan-African Thought.* Contributions in Afro-American and African Studies No. 101. New York: Greenwood, 1987.

Robinson, Cedric. *Black Marxism: The Making of the Black Radical Tradition.* London: Zed, 1983.

Roediger, David R. *The Wages of Whiteness: Race and the Making of the American Working Class.* London: Verso, 1991.

Rollin, Frank A. *Life and Public Services of Martin R. Delany.* Boston: Lee and Shepard, 1883.

Rose, Ann C. *Victorian America and the Civil War.* Cambridge: Cambridge University Press, 1992.

Rose, Willie Lee. *Rehearsal for Reconstruction.* Indianapolis: Bobbs-Merrill, 1964.

Rosenzweig, Roy. *Eight Hours for What We Will: Workers and Leisure in an Industrial City, 1870–1920.* Cambridge, Mass.: Harvard University Press, 1983.

Rotundo, E. Anthony. *American Manhood: Transformations in Masculinity from the Revolution to the Modern Era.* New York: Basic, 1993.

Rubin, Joan Shelley. *The Making of Middlebrow Culture.* Chapel Hill: University of North Carolina Press, 1992.

Rudwick, Bracey Meier, August Meier, and Elliott Rudwick, eds. *Blacks in the Abolitionist Movement.* Belmont, Calif.: Wadsworth, 1971.

Russell, Sandi. *Render Me My Song: African-American Women Writers from Slavery to the Present.* London: Pandora, 1990.

Russell, Tony. *Blacks, Whites, and Blues.* New York: Stein and Day, 1970.

Ryan, Mary. *The Cradle of the Middle Class: The Family in Oneida, New York, 1790–1865.* New York: Cambridge University Press, 1981.

————. *The Empire of the Mother: American Writing About Domesticity, 1830 to 1860.* New York: Haworth, 1982.

————. *Women in Public: Between Banners and Ballots, 1825–1880.* Baltimore: Johns Hopkins University Press, 1990.

Salins, Peter D. *Assimilation, American Style.* New York: Basic, 1977.

Samuels, Shirley, ed. *The Culture of Sentiment: Race, Gender, and Sentimentality in Nineteenth-Century America.* New York: Oxford University Press, 1992.

Saxton, Alexander. *The Rise and Fall of the White Republic: Class Politics and Mass Culture in Nineteenth-Century America.* London: Verso, 1990.

Scarborough, Dorothy. *On the Trail of Negro Folk-Songs.* Cambridge, Mass.: Harvard University Press, 1925.

Schiller, Dan. *Objectivity and the News: The Public and the Rise of Commercial Journalism.* Philadelphia: University of Pennsylvania Press, 1981.

Schor, Joel. *Henry Highland Garnet: A Voice of Black Radicalism in the Nineteenth Century.* Westport, Conn.: Greenwood, 1977.

Schudson, Michael. *Discovering the News: A Social History of American Newspapers.* New York: Basic, 1978.

Sellers, Charles. *The Market Revolution: Jacksonian America, 1815–1846.* New York: Oxford University Press, 1991.

Semmes, Clovis E. *Cultural Hegemony and African-American Development.* Westport, Conn.: Praeger, 1992.

Shafer, Boyd C. *Faces of Nationalism: New Realities and Old Myths.* New York: Harcourt Brace Jovanovich, 1972.

Shaw, Arnold. *Black Popular Music in America: From the Spirituals, Minstrels, and Ragtime to Soul, Disco, and Hip-Hop.* New York: Schirmer, 1986.

Shell, Marc. *Children of the Earth: Literature, Politics, and Nationhood.* New York: Oxford University Press, 1993.

Shepard, Leslie. *The History of Street Literature: The Story of Broadside Ballads, Chapbooks, Proclamations, News-Sheets, Election Bills, Tracts, Pamphlets, Cocks, Catchpennies, and Other Ephemera.* Detroit: Singing Tree, 1973.

Sidbury, James. *Ploughshares into Swords: Race, Rebellion, and Identity in Gabriel's Virginia, 1730–1810.* New York: Cambridge University Press, 1997.

Silverman, Jason H. *Unwelcome Guests: Canada West's Response to American Fugitive Slaves, 1800–1865.* Millwood, N.Y.: Associated Faculty Press, 1985.

Simpson, George Eaton. *Black Religions in the New World.* New York: Columbia University Press, 1978.

Skidmore, Thomas E. *Black into White: Race and Nationality in Brazilian Thought.* New York: Oxford University Press, 1974.

Slaughter, Thomas P. *Bloody Dawn: The Christiana Riot and Racial Violence in the Antebellum North.* Oxford: Oxford University Press, 1991.

Slotkin, Richard. *The Fatal Environment: The Myth of the Frontier in the Age of Industrialization, 1800–1890.* New York: Atheneum, 1985.

Smith, Anthony D. *The Ethnic Origins of Nations.* New York: Basil Blackwell, 1986.

Smith, Edward D. *Climbing Jacob's Ladder: The Rise of Black Churches in Eastern American Cities, 1740–1877.* Washington, D.C.: Smithsonian Institution Press, 1988.

Smith, Merrit Roe. *Harper's Ferry and the New Armoury: The Challenge of Change.* Ithaca: Cornell University Press, 1977.

Smith, Theophus H. *Conjuring Culture: Biblical Formations of Black America.* New York: Oxford University Press, 1994.

Smith-Rosenberg, Carroll. *Disorderly Conduct: Visions of Gender in Victorian America.* New York: Alfred A. Knopf, 1985.

Snyder, Louis L. *The Idea of Racialism.* Princeton, N.J.: D. Van Nostrand, 1962.

Snyder, Robert. *Voice of the City: Vaudeville and Popular Culture in New York.* New York: Oxford University Press, 1989.

Sobel, Mechal. *The World They Made Together: Black and White Values in Eighteenth-Century Virginia.* Princeton: Princeton University Press, 1987.

Stallybrass, Peter, and Allon White. *The Politics and Poetics of Transgression.* Ithaca: Cornell University Press, 1986.

Stansell, Christine. *City of Women: Sex and Class in New York, 1789–1860.* Urbana: University of Illinois Press, 1987.

Stanton, William. *The Leopard's Spots: Scientific Attitudes Toward Race in America, 1815–59.* Chicago: University of Chicago Press, 1960.

Stapp, Carol Buchalter. *Afro-Americans in Antebellum Boston: An Analysis of Probate Records.* New York: Garland, 1993.

Starling, Marion Wilson. *The Slave Narrative: Its Place in American History.* Washington, D.C.: Howard University Press, 1988.

Staudenraus, Philip J. *The African Colonization Movement, 1816–1865.* New York: Columbia University Press, 1961.

Steady, Filomina Chioma, ed. *The Black Woman Cross-Culturally.* Cambridge, Mass.: Schenkman, 1981.

Stepto, Robert. *From Behind the Veil: A Study of Afro-American Narrative.* Urbana: University of Illinois Press, 1991.

Sterling, Dorothy. *The Making of an Afro-American: Martin Robinson Delany, 1812–1885.* Garden City, N.Y.: Doubleday, 1971.

Stuckey, Sterling. *Going Through the Storm: The Influence of African-American Art on History.* New York: Oxford University Press, 1996.

———. *Slave Culture: Nationalist Theory and the Foundations of Black America.* New York: Oxford University Press, 1987.

Sundquist, Eric J. *To Wake the Nations: Race in the Making of American Literature.* Cambridge, Mass.: Harvard University Press, 1993.

———, ed. *Frederick Douglass: New Literary and Historical Essays.* Cambridge: Cambridge University Press, 1990.

Sweet, Leonard I. *Black Images of America, 1784–1870.* New York: Norton, 1976.

Taeuber, Karl, and Alma Taeuber. *Negroes in Cities: Residential Segregation and Neighborhood Change.* Chicago: Aldine, 1965.

Takaki, Ronald. *Iron Cages: Race and Culture in Nineteenth-Century America.* New York: Knopf, 1979. Reprint, New York: Oxford, 1991.

————, ed. *Violence in the Black Imagination: Essays and Documents.* Expanded ed. New York: Oxford University Press, 1993.

Tanner, Jo A. *Dusky Maidens: The Odyssey of the Early Black Dramatic Actress.* Westport, Conn.: Greenwood, 1992.

Taylor, William R. *In Pursuit of Gotham: Commerce and Culture in New York.* New York: Oxford University Press, 1992.

————, ed. *Inventing Times Square: Commerce and Culture at the Crossroads of the World.* New York: Russell Sage Foundation, 1991.

Thomas, Lamont D. *Paule Cuffe: Black Entrepreneur and Pan-Africanist.* Urbana: University of Illinois Press, 1988.

————. *Rise to Be a People: A Biography of Paul Cuffe.* Urbana: University of Illinois Press, 1986.

Thompson, E. P. *The Making of the English Working Class.* New York: Vintage, 1963.

Thompson, Robert F. *The Flash of the Spirit: African and Afro-American Art and Philosophy.* New York: Vintage, 1984.

Thornton, John. *Africa and Africans in the Making of the Atlantic World, 1400–1680.* Cambridge: Cambridge University Press, 1992.

Thorpe, Earl E. *Black Historians: A Critique.* New York: William and Morrow, 1971.

————. *The Central Theme of Black History.* Durham: North Carolina State University Press, 1969.

————. *The Mind of the Negro: An Intellectual History of Afro-Americans.* Baton Rouge: Louisiana State University Press, 1961.

————. *Negro Historians in the United States.* Baton Rouge: Louisiana State University Press, 1958.

Tillyard, E. M. W. *The Elizabethan World Picture.* London: Chatto and Windus, 1943.

Toll, Robert C. *Blacking Up: The Minstrel Show in Nineteenth-Century America.* New York: Oxford University Press, 1974.

Toll, William. *The Resurgence of Race: Black Social Theory from Reconstruction to the Pan-African Conferences.* Philadelphia: Temple University Press, 1979.

Toplin, Robert Brent. *The Abolition of Slavery in Brazil.* New York: Atheneum, 1972.

Turner, Victor W. *The Ritual Process: Structure and Anti-Structure.* Chicago: Aldine, 1969.

Ullman, Victor. *Martin R. Delany: The Beginnings of Black Nationalism.* Boston: Beacon, 1971.

VanDeburg, William L. *Slavery and Race in American Popular Culture.* Madison: University of Wisconsin Press, 1984.

Van Willigenburg, Theo, Robert Heeger, and Wibren van der Burg, eds. *Nation, State, and the Coexistence of Different Communities.* Kampen, Netherlands: Kok Pharos House, 1995.

Vickerman, Milton. *Crosscurrents: West Indian Immigrants and Race.* New York: Oxford University Press, 1999.

Vlach, John Michael. *By the Work of Their Hands: Studies in Afro-American Folklife.* Ann Arbor: University of Michigan Press, 1991.

Voegeli, V. Jacque. *Free but Not Equal: The Midwest and the Negro During the Civil War.* Chicago: University of Chicago Press, 1967.

Waldstreicher, David. *In the Midst of Perpetual Fetes: The Making of American Nationalism, 1776–1820.* Chapel Hill: University of North Carolina Press, 1997.

Walker, Clarence E. *Deromanticizing Black History: Critical Essays and Reappraisals.* Knoxville: University of Tennessee Press, 1991.

———. *A Rock in a Weary Land: The African Methodist Episcopal Church During the Civil War and Reconstruction.* Baton Rouge: Louisiana State University Press, 1982.

Walker, George E. *The Afro-American in New York City, 1827–1860.* 1975. Reprint, New York: Garland, 1993.

Walker, Peter F. *Moral Choices: Memory, Desire, and Imagination in Nineteenth-Century American Abolition.* Baton Rouge: Louisiana State University Press, 1978.

Walker, Robert H. *Reform in America: The Continuing Frontier.* Lexington: University Press of Kentucky, 1985.

Walters, Ronald. *American Reformers, 1815–1860.* New York: Hill and Wang, 1978.

Walzer, Michael. *Exodus and Revolution.* New York: Basic, 1985.

Warner, Lucille Schulberg. *From Slave to Abolitionist: The Life of William Wells Brown.* New York: Dial, 1976.

Warner, Michael. *The Letters of the Republic: Publication and the Public Sphere in Eighteenth-Century America.* Cambridge, Mass.: Harvard University Press, 1990.

Washington, Joseph R., Jr. *Black Religion: The Negro and Christianity in the United States.* Boston: Beacon, 1964.

Weber, Max. *The Protestant Ethic and the Spirit of Capitalism.* Translated by Talcott Parsons. London: Routledge, 1992.

Weiss, Richard. *The American Myth of Success: From Horatio Alger to Norman Vincent Peale.* New York: Basic, 1969.

Werner, John M. *Reaping the Bloody Harvest: Race Riots in the United States during the Age of Jackson, 1824–1849.* New York: Garland, 1986.

Wheeler, Edward L. *Uplifting the Race: The Black Minister in the New South, 1865–1902.* Lanham, Md.: University Press of America, 1986.

White, Deborah Gray. *Ar'n't I a Woman? Female Slaves in the Plantation South.* New York: Norton, 1985.

White, Hayden V. *Metahistory: The Historical Imagination in Nineteenth-Century Europe.* Baltimore: Johns Hopkins University Press, 1973.

White, Shane. *Somewhat More Independent: The End of Slavery in New York City, 1770–1810.* Athens: University of Georgia Press, 1977.

White, Shane, and Graham White. *Stylin': African American Expressive Culture from Its Beginnings to the Zoot Suit.* Ithaca: Cornell University Press, 1998.

Wiggins, William H. *O Freedom!: Afro-American Emancipation Day Celebrations.* Knoxville: University of Tennessee Press, 1987.

Wilentz, Sean. *Chants Democratic: New York City and the Rise of the American Working Class, 1788–1850.* New York: Oxford University Press, 1984.

Williams, John A., and Charles F. Harris, eds. *Amistad 1: Writings on Black History and Culture.* New York: Vintage, 1970.

———. *Amistad 2: Writings on Black History and Culture.* New York: Vintage, 1972.

Williams, Lorraine A., ed. *Africa and the Afro-American Experience: Eight Essays.* Washington, D.C.: Howard University Press, 1977.

Williams, Raymond. *Keywords: A Vocabulary of Culture and Society.* New York: Oxford University Press, 1985.

Williamson, Joel. *New People: Miscegenation and Mulattoes in the United States.* New York: Free Press, 1980.

Willis, David, and Richard Newman, eds. *Black Apostles at Home and Abroad.* Boston: G. K. Hall, 1982.

Wilmore, Gayraud S., ed. *African American Religious Studies.* Durham: Duke University Press, 1989.

———. *Black Religion and Black Radicalism.* Garden City, N.Y.: Doubleday, 1972.

Winch, Julie. *Philadelphia's Black Elite: Activism, Accommodation, and the Struggle for Autonomy, 1787–1848.* Philadelphia: Temple University Press, 1988.

Winks, Robin. *The Blacks in Canada.* New Haven: Yale University Press, 1971.

Withington, Ann Fairfax. *Toward a More Perfect Union: Virtue and the Formation of American Republics.* New York: Oxford University Press, 1991.

Wolseley, Ronald E. *The Black Press, U.S.A.* Ames: University of Iowa Press, 1990.

Wright, Donald R. *African Americans in the Early Republic, 1789–1831.* Arlington Heights, Ill.: Harlan Davidson, 1993.

Wyllie, Irvin G. *The Self-Made Man in America: The Myth of Rags to Riches.* New Brunswick, N.J.: Rutgers University Press, 1954.

Yee, Shirley J. *Black Women Abolitionists: A Study in Activism, 1828–1860.* Knoxville: University of Tennessee Press, 1992.

Yellin, Jean Fagan. *The Intricate Knot: Black Figures in American Literature.* New York: New York University Press, 1972.

———. *Women and Sisters: The Antislavery Feminists in American Culture.* New Haven: Yale University Press, 1989.

Yellin, Jean Fagan, and John C. Van Horne, eds. *The Abolitionist Sisterhood: Women's Political Culture in Antebellum America.* Ithaca: Cornell University Press, 1994.

Young, Robert J. *Antebellum Black Activists: Race, Gender, and Self.* New York: Garland, 1996.

Zboray, Ronald. *A Fictive People: Antebellum Economic Development and the American Reading Public.* New York: Oxford University Press, 1993.

Zilversmit, Arthur. *The First Emancipation: The Abolition of Slavery in the North.* Chicago: University of Chicago Press, 1967.

386/391

Clar

Articles

Adeleke, Tunde. "Black Biography in the Service of a Revolution: Martin R. Delany in Afro-American Historiography." *Biography* 17 (Summer 1994): 248–67.

Allen, Ernest, Jr. "Afro-American Identity: Reflections on the Pre–Civil War Era." *Contributions in Black Studies* 7 (1985–86): 45–93.

Allen, Norm R., Jr. "Reactionary Black Nationalism: Authoritarianism in the Name of Freedom." *Free Inquiry* 15, no. 4 (1995): 10–11.

Allison, Robert J. "'From the Covenant of Peace, A Simile of Sorrow': James Madison's American Allegory." *Virginia Magazine of History and Biography* 99, no. 3 (1991): 327–50.

Amin, Samir. "The Nation: An Enlightened or Fog-Shrouded Concept?" *Research in African Literatures* 28, no. 4 (1997): 8–18.

Andrews, William L. "Frederick Douglass, Preacher." *American Literature* 54, no. 4 (1982): 592–97.

Appleby, Joyce. "Introduction: Republicanism and Ideology." *American Quarterly* 37, no. 4 (Fall 1985): 461–73.

Aptheker, Herbert. "Afro-American Superiority: A Neglected Theme in Literature." *Phylon* 31 (Winter 1970): 336–42.

Arnesen, Eric. "'Like Banquo's Ghost It Will Not Down': The Race Question and the American Railroad Brotherhoods, 1880–1920." *American Historical Review* 99, no. 5 (December 1994): 1601–33.

Bacon, Margaret Hope. "'One Great Bundle of Humanity': Frances Ellen Watkins Harper (1825–1911)." *Pennsylvania Magazine of History and Biography* 113, no. 1 (January 1989): 21–43.

Baker, Paula. "The Domestication of Politics: Women and American Political Society, 1780–1920." *American Historical Review* 89 (June 1984): 620–64.

Barkan, Elliot R. "Race, Religion, and Nationality in American Society: A Model of Ethnicity—From Contact to Assimilation." *Journal of American Ethnic History* 14, no. 2 (Winter 1995): 38–75.

Barker, Anthony J. "Review Article: Frederick Douglass and Black Abolitionism." *Slavery and Abolition* 14, no. 2 (August 1993): 117–27.

Bell, Howard Holman. "National Negro Conventions of the Middle 1840s: Moral Suasion vs. Political Action." *Journal of Negro History* 42, no. 4 (October 1957): 247–60.

———. "The Negro Emigration Movement, 1849–1854: A Phase of Negro Nationalism." *Phylon* 20 (Summer 1959): 132–42.

———. "Negro Nationalism: A Factor in Emigration Projects, 1858–1861." *Journal of Negro History* 47 (January 1962): 42–53.

Berlin, Ira. "The Revolution in Black Life." In *The American Revolution: Explorations in the History of American Radicalism*, edited by Alfred F. Young, 349–82. DeKalb: Northern Illinois University Press, 1976.

(Chy

————. "The Slave Trade and the Development of Afro-American Society on British Mainland North America, 1619–1775." *Southern Studies* 20, no. 2 (1981): 122–36.

————. "The Structure of the Free Negro Caste in the Antebellum United States." *Journal of Social History* 9, no. 3 (Spring 1976): 297–318.

————. "Time, Space, and the Evolution of Afro-American Society in British Mainland North America." *American Historical Review* 85, no. 1 (February 1980): 44–78.

Billington, Ray Allen. "James Forten: Forgotten Abolitionist." *Negro History Bulletin* 13 (November 1949): 31–36, 45.

Blair, Walter. "Charles Matthews and His 'A Trip to America.'" *Prospects* 2 (1976): 1–23.

Blight, David A. "In Search of Learning, Liberty, and Self-Definition: James McCune Smith and the Ordeal of the Antebellum Black Intellectual." *Afro-Americans in New York Life and History* 9, no. 2 (July 1985): 7–26.

Blumin, Stuart M. "Explaining the New Metropolis: Perception, Deception, and Analysis in Mid-Nineteenth-Century New York." *Journal of Urban History* 11, no. 1 (November 1984): 9–38.

————. "The Hypothesis of Middle-Class Formation in Nineteenth-Century America: A Critique and Some Proposals." *American Historical Review* 90, no. 2 (April 1985): 299–338.

Bogin, Ruth. "Sarah Parker Redmond: Black Abolitionist from Salem." *Essex Institute Historical Collections* 110, no. 2 (April 1974): 120–50.

Breen, T. H. "Ideology and Nationalism on the Eve of the American Revolution. Revisions Once More in Need of Revising." *Journal of American History* (1997): 13–39.

Brewer, William. "Henry Highland Garnet." *Journal of Negro History* 13 (January 1928): 36–52.

————. "John B. Russwurm." *Journal of Negro History* 13 (October 1928): 413–22.

Broder, Sherri. "Informing the 'Cruelty': The Monitoring of Respectability in Philadelphia's Working-Class Neighborhoods in the Late Nineteenth Century." *Radical America* 21, no. 4 (1987): 34–47.

Brown, Delindus R. "Free Blacks' Rhetorical Impact on African Colonization: The Emergence of Rhetorical Exigence." *Journal of Black Studies* 9, no. 3 (March 1979): 251–65.

Brown, Elsa Barkley. "Negotiating and Transforming the Public Sphere: African-American Political Life in the Transition from Slavery to Freedom." *Public Culture* 7 (1994): 107–46.

Browning, James B. "The Beginnings of Insurance Enterprise Among Negroes." *Journal of Negro History* 22, no. 4 (October 1937): 417–32.

Bunzel, John H., and Anita Susan Grossman. "Black Studies Revisited." *Public Interest* no. 127 (1997): 71–80.

Burnham, Dorothy. "The Life of the Afro-American Woman in Slavery." *International Journal of Woman's Studies* 1, no. 4 (1978): 363–77.

Calloway-Thomas, Carolyn. "William G. Allen: On 'Orators and Oratory.'" *Journal of Black Studies* 18, no. 3 (1988): 313–36.

Catronovo, Russ. "Radical Configurations of History in the Era of American Slavery." *American Literature* 65, no. 3 (September 1993): 523–48.

Cheek, William F. "John Mercer Langston: Black Protest Leader and Abolitionist." *Civil War History* 16 (June 1970): 101–20.

Chideya, Farai. "All Eyez on Us: It's Time for the Hip-Hop Generation to Get Real." *Time* no. 24 (March 1997): 47.

Christensen, Lawrence O. "Peter Humphries Clark." *Missouri Historical Review* 88 (January 1994): 145–56.

Cmiel, Kenneth. "'A Broad Fluid Language of Democracy': Discovering the American Idiom." *Journal of American History* 79, no. 3 (December 1992): 913–36.

Cohen, David Steven. "In Search of Carolus Africanus Rex: Afro-Dutch Folklore in New York and New Jersey." *Journal of the Afro-American Historical and Genealogical Society* 5 (Fall–Winter 1984): 147–68.

Collier-Thomas, Bettye, and James Turner. "Race, Class and Color: The African American Discourse on Identity." *Journal of American Ethnic History* (Fall 1994): 5–31.

Collison, Gary L. "Alexander Burton and Salem's 'Fugitive Slave Riot' of 1851." *Essex Institute Historical Collections* 128 (January 1992): 17–26.

Cooper, Frederick. "Elevating the Race: The Social Thought of Black Leaders, 1827–1850." *American Quarterly* 24, no. 5 (December 1972): 604–25.

Crapol, Edward P. "John Tyler and the Pursuit of National Destiny." *Journal of the Early Republic* 17 (1997): 467–91.

Crew, Spencer. "Black New Jersey before the Civil War: Two Case Studies." *New Jersey History* 99 (1981): 67–86.

Dain, Bruce. "Haiti and Egypt in Early Black Racial Discourse in the United States." *Slavery and Abolition* 14, no. 3 (December 1993): 139–61.

Davidson, Phebe. "Jarena Lee (1783–18??)." *Legacy: A Journal of American Women Writers* 10, no. 2 (1993): 135–41.

Davis, Susan G. "'Making the Night Hideous': Christmas Revelry and Public Disorder in Nineteenth-Century Philadelphia." *American Quarterly* 34 (Summer 1982): 185–99.

Davis, Thomas J. "Modern Black Nationalism: From Marcus Garvey to Louis Farrakhan." *Library Journal* 121, no. 18 (1996): 90.

Desrochers, Robert E., Jr. "'Not Fade Away': The Narrative of Venture Smith, an African American in the Early Republic." *Journal of American History* (June 1997): 40–66.

Dixon, Chris. "An Ambivalent Black Nationalism: Haiti, Africa, and Antebellum African-American Emigrationism." *Australian Journal of American Studies* 10, no. 2 (December 1991): 10–25.

Doak, Kevin M. "What Is a Nation and Who Belongs? National Narratives and the Ethnic Imagination in Twentieth-Century Japan." *American Historical Review* 102, no. 2 (April 1997): 283–309.

Doriani, Beth Maclay. "Black Womanhood in Nineteenth-Century America: Subversion and Self-Construction in Two Women's Autobiographies." *American Quarterly* 43, no. 2 (1991): 199–222.

Drake, St. Clair. "The American Negro's Relation to Africa." *Africa Today* 14, no. 6 (December 1967): 12–15.

Drescher, Seymour. "Brazilian Abolition in Comparative Perspective." *Hispanic American Historical Review* 68, no. 3 (August 1988): 429–60.

Dyson, Michael Eric. "Malcolm X and the Revival of Black Nationalism." *Tikkun* 8, no. 2 (1993): 45–48.

Early, Gerald. "Understanding Afrocentrism: Why Blacks Dream of a World Without Whites." *Civilization* 2, no. 4 (1995): 31–39.

Egerton, Douglass A. "'Its Origin is Not a Little Curious': A New Look at the American Colonization Society." *Journal of the Early American Republic* 5 (1985): 463–80.

Ernst, Robert. "Negro Concepts of Americanism." *Journal of American History* 39 (July 1954): 206–19.

Everett, Donald E. "Free Persons of Color in Colonial Louisiana." *Louisiana History* 7, no. 1 (1966): 21–50.

Fairchild, Halford H. "Black, Negro, or Afro-American? The Differences Are Crucial!" *Journal of Black Studies* 16, no. 1 (September 1985): 47–55.

Farley, Reynolds. "The Urbanization of Negroes in the United States." *Journal of Social History* 2 (1968): 241–58.

Fields, Barbara Jeanne. "Slavery, Race, and Ideology in the United States of America." *New Left Review* 181 (May–June 1990): 95–118.

Fisher, Mike M. "Lott Cary, the Colonizing Missionary." *Journal of Negro History* 7 (October 1922): 380–418.

Foner, Laura. "The Free People of Color in Louisiana and St. Domingue: A Comparative Portrait of Two Three-Caste Slave Societies." *Journal of Social History* 3 (1970): 406–30.

Fordham, Monroe. "Nineteenth-Century Black Thought in the United States: Some Influences of the Santo Domingo Revolution." *Journal of Black Studies* 6, no. 2 (December 1975): 115–26.

Foster, Frances Smith. "Between the Sides: Afro-American Women Writers as Mediators." *Nineteenth Century Studies* 3 (1989): 53–64.

Fox, Robert Elliot. "Afrocentrism and the X-Factor." *Transition* 57 (1992): 17–25.

Franklin, John Hope. "George Washington Williams and the Beginnings of Afro-American Historiography." *Critical Inquiry* 4 (1978): 658–59.

Fredrickson, George M., and Christopher Lasch. "Resistance to Slavery." *Civil War History* 13 (1967): 315–29.

Gaines, Kevin. "Assimilationist Minstrelsy as Racial Uplift Ideology: James D. Corrothers's Literary Quest for Black Leadership." *American Quarterly* 45, no. 3 (September 1993): 341–69.

Gardner, Eric. "'This Attempt of Their Sister': Harriet Wilson's *Our Nig* from Printer to Reader." *New England Quarterly* 66 (June 1993): 226–46.

Gates, Henry Louis, Jr. "The Trope of a New Negro and the Reconstruction of the Image of the Black." *Representations* 24 (Fall 1988): 129–55.

Genovese, Eugene D. "The Legacy of Slavery and the Roots of Black Nationalism." *Studies on the Left* 6, no. 6 (November–December 1966): 3–26.

Ginzberg, Lori D. "'Moral Suasion is Moral Balderdash': Women, Politics, and Social Activism in the 1850s." *Journal of American History* 73, no. 3 (December 1986): 601–22.

Gish, Clay. "The Children's Strikes: Socialization and Class Formation in Paterson, 1824–1836." *New Jersey History* 110, nos. 3–4 (1992): 20–38.

Goldberg, David. "Raking the Field of the Discourse of Racism." *Journal of Black Studies* 18, no. 1 (September 1987): 58–71.

Goldman, Anita Haya. "Negotiating Claims of Race and Rights: Du Bois, Emerson, and the Critique of Liberal Nationalism." *Massachusetts Review* 35, no. 2 (1994): 169–201.

Goodheart, Lawrence B. "The Chronicles of Kidnapping in New York: Resistance to the Fugitive Slave Law, 1834–1835." *Afro-Americans in New York Life and History* 8, no. 1 (January 1984): 7–15.

Goodman, Paul. "The Manual Labor Movement and the Origins of Abolitionism." *Journal of the Early Republic* 13 (Fall 1993): 355–402.

Graham, Richard. "Slavery and Economic Development: Brazil and the United States South in the Nineteenth Century." *Comparative Studies in Society and History* 23 (1981): 620–55.

Grant, Susan-Mary. "When is a Nation Not a Nation? The Crisis of American Nationality in the Mid-Nineteenth Century." *Nations and Nationalism* 2, no. 1 (1996): 105–29.

Gravely, William B. "Dialectic of Double Consciousness in Black American Freedom Celebrations, 1808–1863." *Journal of Negro History* 67, no. 4 (Winter 1982): 302–17.

Greenbaum, Susan D. "A Comparison of African American and Euro-American Mutual Aid Societies in 19th Century America." *Journal of Ethnic Studies* 19, no. 3 (Fall 1991): 95–120.

Greene, Veryl. "The Allen A.M.E. Church, Jamaica, NY, 1834–1900: The Role of the Black Church in a Developing 19th-Century Community." *Afro-Americans in New York Life and History* 16 (January 1992): 31–39.

Grimsted, David. "Rioting in Its Jacksonian Setting." *American Historical Review* 77, no. 2 (April 1971): 361–97.

Gross, Bella. "The First National Negro Convention." *Journal of Negro History* 31 (October 1946): 435–43.

———. "*Freedom's Journal* and the *Rights of All*." *Journal of Negro History* 17 (July 1932): 241–86.

Harper, Philip Brian. "Eloquence and Epitaph: Black Nationalism and the Homophobic Impulse in Responses to the Death of Mac Robinson." *Social Text*, no. 28 (1991): 68–86.

Harris, Robert L. "Early Black Benevolent Societies, 1780–1830." *Massachusetts Review* 20, no. 3 (Autumn 1979): 603–25.

Harvey, Paul. "'These Untutored Masses': The Campaign for Respectability among White and Black Evangelicals in the American South, 1870–1930." *Journal of Religious History* 21, no. 3 (1997): 302–17.

Hanley, Mark Y. "The New Infidelity: Northern Protestant Clergymen and the Critique of Progress, 1840–1855." *Religion and American Culture* 1, no. 2 (Summer 1991): 203–26.

Hearn, Jeffrey. "Poststructuralism and the Study of the Past: An Introduction in Spite of Itself." *Maryland Historian* 24, no. 1 (Spring–Summer 1993): 1–7.

Hedlin, Raymond. "Muffled Voices: The American Slave Narrative." *Clio* 10, no. 2 (1981): 129–42.

Hellwig, David J. "Strangers in Their Own Land: Patterns of Black Nativism, 1830–1930." *American Studies* 23, no. 1 (1982): 85–98.

Hemphill, Essex. "If Freud Had Been a Neurotic Colored Woman: Reading Dr. Frances Cress Welsing." *Outlook*, no. 13 (1991): 50–55.

Henderson, Errol A. "Black Nationalism and Rap Music." *Journal of Black Studies* 26, no. 3 (1996): 308–39.

Henle, Ellen, and Marlene Merril. "Antebellum Black Coeds at Oberlin College." *Oberlin Alumna Magazine* (January–February 1980): 18–21.

Henricksen, Thomas H. "African Intellectual Influences on Black Americans: The Role of Edward W. Blyden." *Phylon* 36, no. 3 (1975): 279–90.

Herod, Charles C. "Afro-American Nationalism." *Canadian Review of Studies in Nationalism* 14 (1987): 37–47.

Herod, Charles C., and Augustina B. Herod. "Core Values, Myths, and Myth Systems in Afro-American National Consciousness." *Canadian Review of Studies in Nationalism* 17, nos. 1–2 (1990): 193–204.

Hershberg, Theodore. "Free Blacks in Antebellum Philadelphia: A Study of Ex-Slaves, Freeborn, and Socio-Economic Decline." *Journal of Social History* 5 (1972): 183–209.

Hill, Errol. "Remarks on Black Theater History." *Massachusetts Review* 28, no. 4 (1987): 609–14.

Hine, William C. "Black Politicians in Reconstruction Charleston, South Carolina: A Collective Study." *Journal of Southern History* 49 (1983): 555–84.

Hinks, Peter P. "Free Blacks and Kidnapping in Antebellum Boston." *Historical Journal of Massachusetts* 50 (Winter 1992): 352–73.

Hirsch, Leo H. "The Negro in New York." *Journal of Negro History* 16 (1931): 382–473.

Hoganson, Kristin. "Garrisonian Abolitionists and the Rhetoric of Gender, 1850–1860." *American Quarterly* 45, no. 4 (December 1993): 556–95.

Hoopes, J. "Semiotic and American History." *Semiotica* 83, nos. 3–4 (1991): 251–82.

Horne, Gerald. "The Thomas Hearings and the Nexus of Race, Gender and Nationalism." *Black Scholar* 22, nos. 1–2 (1991): 45–47.

Horton, James O. "Freedom's Yoke: Gender Conventions Among Antebellum Free Blacks." *Feminist Studies* 12 (Spring 1986): 51–76.

———. "Shades of Color: The Mulatto in Three Antebellum Northern Communities." *Afro-Americans in New York Life and History* 8 (July 1984): 32–59.

Houseley, Kathleen. "'Yours for the Oppressed': The Life of Jehiel C. Beman." *Journal of Negro History* 77, no. 1 (1992): 17–29.

Howard-Pitney, David. "The Jeremiads of Frederick Douglass, Booker T. Washington, and W. E. B. Du Bois and Changing Patterns of Black Messianic Rhetoric, 1841–1920." *Journal of American Ethnic History* 6, no. 1 (Fall 1986): 47–61.

Howe, Daniel Walker. "The Evangelical Movement and Political Culture in the North During the Second Party System." *Journal of American History* 78 (March 1991): 1216–39.

Hutton, Frankie. "Social Mobility in the Antebellum Black Press." *Journal of Popular Culture* 26, no. 2 (Fall 1992): 71–84.

Ignatiev, Noel. "The Revolution as an African-American Exuberance." *Eighteenth-Century Studies* 27 (Summer 1994): 605–13.

Jacoby, Tamar. "Garvey's Ghosts: When David Dinkins Confronted the Boycotters, He Ran Up Against a Long History of Black Nationalism." *New Republic* (July 1990): 18–19.

James, Darius H. "Panther." *Grand Street* 13, no. 3 (1995): 178–91.

Jentz, John B. "Industrialization and Class Formation in Antebellum America: A Review of Recent Case Studies." *American Studies* 30, no. 3 (1985): 303–25.

Johnson, Jerah. "New Orleans's Congo Square: An Urban Setting for Early Afro-American Culture Formation." *Louisiana History* 32, no. 2 (1991): 117–57.

Johnson, Paul E. "Democracy, Patriarchy, and American Revivals, 1780–1830." *Journal of Social History* 24, no. 4 (1991): 843–50.

Jones, Rhett S. "In the Absence of Ideology: Blacks in Colonial America and the Modern Black Experience." *Western Journal of Black Studies* 12, no. 1 (1988): 30–39.

Jordan, Winthrop D. "American Chiaroscuro: The Status and Definition of Mulattoes in the British Colonies." *William and Mary Quarterly*, 3d ser., 19 (1962): 183–200.

Joshi, Manoj K. "Frederick Douglass and the Emigrationist Movement." *Western Journal of Black Studies* 9, no. 3 (1985): 135–43.

Kaplan, Michael. "New York City Tavern Violence and the Creation of a Working-Class Male Identity." *Journal of the Early Republic* 15 (Winter 1995): 591–617.

Kass, Amalie M. "Dr. Thomas Hodgkin, Dr. Martin Delany, and the 'Return to Africa.'" *Medical History* 27, no. 4 (1983): 373–93.

Kazal, Russell A. "Revisiting Assimilation: The Rise, Fall, and Reappraisal of a Concept in American Ethnic History." *American Historical Review* 100, no. 2 (April 1995): 437–71.

Kerber, Linda K. "Abolitionists and Amalgamators: The New York City Race Riots of 1834." *New York History* 48 (January 1967): 28–39.

Kirk-Greene, A. H. M. "America in the Niger Valley: A Colonization Centenary." *Phylon* 22 (Autumn 1962): 225–39.

Kloppenberg, James T. "The Virtues of Liberalism: Christianity, Republicanism, and Ethics in Early American Political Discourse." *Journal of American History* 74, no. 1 (June 1987): 9–33.

Kolchin, Peter. "Re-evaluating the Antebellum Slave Community: A Comparative Perspective." *Journal of American History* 70, no. 3 (December 1983): 569–601.

Korenman, Joan S. "African-American Women Writers, Black Nationalism, and the Matrilineal Heritage." *CLA [College Language Association] Journal* 38, no. 2 (1994): 143–61.

Kramnick, Isaac. "The 'Great National Discussion': The Discourse of Politics in 1787." *William and Mary Quarterly*, 3d ser., 45, no. 1 (January 1988): 3–32.

Lapsansky, Emma Jones. "'Discipline of the Mind': Philadelphia's Banneker Institute, 1854–1872." *Pennsylvania Magazine of History and Biography* 117, no. 1–2 (January–April 1993): 83–102.

——. "Feminism, Freedom and Community: Charlotte Forten and Women Activists in Nineteenth-Century Philadelphia." *Pennsylvania Magazine of History and Biography* 113, no. 1 (January 1989): 3–19.

——. "Friends, Wives, and Strivings: Networks and Community Values Among Nineteenth-Century Philadelphia Afro-American Elites." *Pennsylvania Magazine of History and Biography* 108, no. 1 (1984): 3–24.

——. "'Since They Got Those Separate Churches': Afro-Americans and Racism in Jacksonian Philadelphia." *American Quarterly* 32, no. 1 (Spring 1980): 54–78.

Larson, Fred. "Henry Bibb, A Colonizer." *Journal of Negro History* 5, no. 4 (October 1920): 437–47.

Lasch-Quinn, Elizabeth. "Radical Chic and Race." *Salmagundi* 112 (Fall 1996): 8–25.

Lawson, Ellen N. "Sarah Woodson Early: 19th Century Black Nationalist 'Sister.'" *Umoja* 5, no. 2 (Summer 1981): 15–26.

Lears, T. J. Jackson. "The Concept of Cultural Hegemony: Problems and Possibilities." *American Historical Review* 90, no. 3 (June 1985): 567–93.

Lemann, Nicholas. "Black Nationalism on Campus." *Atlantic Monthly* 271, no. 1 (1993): 31–47.

Levesque, George A. "Before Integration: The Forgotten Years of Jim Crow Education in Boston." *Journal of Negro Education* 48, no. 2 (1979): 113–25.

——. "Boston's Black Brahmin: Dr. John S. Rock." *Civil War History* 26 (December 1980): 326–46.

——. "Interpreting Early Black Ideology: A Reappraisal of Historical Consensus." *Journal of the Early Republic* 1 (Fall 1981): 269–87.

Lewis, David Levering. "Parallels and Divergences: Assimilationist Strategies of Afro-America and Jewish Elite from 1910 to the Early 1930s." *Journal of American History* 71, no. 3 (December 1984): 543–64.

Lewis, Earl. "To Turn as On a Pivot: Writing African Americans into a History of Overlapping Diasporas." *American Historical Review* 100, no. 3 (June 1995): 765–87.

Limerick, Patricia Nelson. "Has 'Minority' History Transformed the Historical Discourse?" *Perspectives* 35, no. 8 (November 1997): 34–35.

Litwack, Leon F. "The Emancipation of the Negro Abolitionist." In *The Antislavery Vanguard: New Essays on the Abolitionists*, edited by Martin Duberman, 137–55. Princeton: Princeton University Press, 1965.

Lynch, Hollis R. "Pan-Negro Nationalism in the New World, before 1862." In *Boston University Papers on Africa*, edited by Jeffrey Butler, 2:149–79. Boston: Boston University Press, 1966.

McElroy, Frederick L. "Booker T. Washington as Literary Trickster." *Southern Folklore* 49, no. 2 (1992): 89–108.

McKivigan, John R., and Jason H. Silverman. "Monarchial Liberty and Republic Slavery: West Indies Emancipation Celebrations in Upstate New York and Canada West." *Afro-Americans in New York Life and History* 10, no. 1 (January 1986): 7–18.

Mangan, J. A. "Men, Masculinity, and Sexuality: Some Recent Literature." *Journal of the History of Sexuality* 3, no. 2 (1992): 303–13.

Marable, Manning. "Black Fundamentalism: Farrakhan and Conservative Black Nationalism." *Race and Class* 39, no. 4 (April–June 1998): 1–22.

———. "Black Fundamentalism: Louis Farrakhan and the Politics of Conservative Black Nationalism." *Dissent* 45, no. 2 (1998): 69–76.

———. "History and Black Consciousness: The Political Culture of Black America." *Monthly Review* 47, no. 3 (July–August 1995): 71–88.

Marston, Sallie A. "Public Rituals and Community Power: St. Patrick's Day Parades in Lowell, Massachusetts, 1841–1874." *Political Geography Quarterly* 8, no. 3 (July 1989): 255–69.

Matijasic, Thomas D. "The Foundations of Colonization: The Peculiar Nature of Race Relations in Ohio During the Early Ante-Bellum Period." *Queen City Heritage* 49, no. 4 (Winter 1991): 23–30.

Matthews, Jean. "Race, Sex, and the Dimensions of Liberty in Antebellum America." *Journal of the Early Republic* 6 (Fall 1986): 275–91.

Maynard, Steven. "Rough Work and Rugged Men: The Social Construction of Masculinity in Working-Class History." *Labour* 23 (1989): 159–69.

Mehlinger, Louis A. "The Attitude of the Free Negro Toward Colonization." *Journal of Negro History* 1 (July 1916): 276–301.

Meier, August. "The Emergence of Negro Nationalism: A Study in Ideologies, Part I." *Midwest Journal* 4 (Winter 1951–52): 96–104.

———. "The Emergence of Negro Nationalism: A Study in Ideologies, Part II." *Midwest Journal* 4 (Summer 1952): 95–111.

Melman, Billie. "Claiming the Nation's Past: The Invention of an Anglo-Saxon Tradition." *Journal of Contemporary History* 26 (1991): 575–95.

Milbauer, John A. "Folk Monuments of Afro-Americans: A Perspective on Black Culture." *Mid-America Folklore* 19 (Fall 1991): 99–109.

Miller, Floyd J. "The Father of Black Nationalism: Another Contender." *Civil War History* 17, no. 4 (December 1971): 310–19.

Monroe, Sylvester. "The Risky Association." *Time* (27 June 1994): 39.

Mook, H. Telfer. "Training Day in New England." *New England Quarterly* 11, no. 4 (December 1938): 675–97.

Morrison, Samuel E. "A Poem on Election Day." *Proceedings of the Colonial Society of Massachusetts* 18 (February 1915): 54–61.

Moses, Wilson J. "Civil Religion, Civil Activism, and Afro-American Identity: Antebellum Black Leaders and the Art of Biography." *Reviews in American History* 18, no. 1 (1990): 55–63.

Mullin, Michael. "British Caribbean and North American Slaves in an Era of War and Revolution, 1775–1807." In *The Southern Experience in the American Revolution*, edited by Jeffrey J. Crow and Larry E. Tise, 235–67. Chapel Hill: University of North Carolina Press, 1978.

Muwakkil, Salim. "Divided Loyalties." *In These Times* (17 February 1997): 24–26.

———. "A Separate Peace?" *In These Times* (13 November 1995): 24–5.

Nadell, James. "Boyz in the Hood: A Colonial Analysis." *Journal of Black Studies* 25, no. 4 (1995): 447–64.

Nantambu, Kwame. "Pan-Africanism versus Pan-African Nationalism: An Afrocentric Analysis." *Journal of Black Studies* 28, no. 5 (1998): 561–74.

Oakes, James. "The Political Significance of Slave Resistance." *History Workshop* 22 (1986): 89–107.

O'Connell, Maurice R. "O'Connell, Young Ireland, and Negro Slavery: An Exercise in Romantic Nationalism." *Thought* 64, no. 253 (1989): 130–36.

Oden, Gloria C. "*The Journal of Charlotte L. Forten*: The Salem-Philadelphia Years (1854–1862) Reexamined." *Essex Institute Historical Collection* 119, no. 2 (April 1983): 119–36.

Ogunleye, Tolagbe. "The Self-Emancipated Africans of Florida: Pan-African Nationalists in the 'New World.'" *Journal of Black Studies* 27, no. 1 (1996): 24–38.

Olson, Edwin. "Social Aspects of Slave Life in New York." *Journal of Negro History* 26, no. 1 (1941): 66–73.

O'Malley, Michael. "Specie and Species: Race and the Money Question in Nineteenth-Century America." *American Historical Review* 99, no. 2 (April 1994): 369–95.

Ongiri, Amy Abugo. "We Are Family: Black Nationalism, Black Masculinity, and the Black Gay Cultural Imagination." *College Literature* 24, no. 1 (1997): 280–94.

Over, William. "New York's African Theatre." *Afro-Americans in New York History and Life* 3 (1979): 8–9.

Patterson, Orlando. "Going Separate Ways: The History of an Old Idea." *Newsweek* (30 October 1995): 43.

Pease, William H., and Jane H. Pease. "Antislavery Ambivalence: Immediatism, Expedience, Race." *American Quarterly* 17, no. 4 (Winter 1965): 682–95.

———. "Black Power—The Debate in 1840." *Phylon* 29 (Spring 1968): 19–26.

———. "Boston Garrisonians and the Problem of Frederick Douglass." *Canadian Journal of History* 2, no. 2 (September 1967): 29–48.

————. "Organized Negro Communities: A North American Experiment." *Journal of Negro History* 47 (January 1962): 19–34.

Peterson, Dale E. "Response and Call: The African-American Dialogue with Bakhtin." *American Literature* 65, no. 4 (December 1993): 761–75.

Porter, Dorothy B. "David M. Ruggles, an Apostle of Human Rights." *Journal of Negro History* 28 (January 1943): 23–50.

————. "The Organized Education Activities of Literary Societies." *Journal of Negro Education* 5 (1936): 555–76.

————. "Sarah Parker Redmond, Abolitionist and Physician." *Journal of Negro History* 20, no. 1 (January 1935): 287–93.

Powell, Lawrence. "Correcting for Fraud: A Quantitative Reassessment of the Mississippi Ratification Election of 1868." *Journal of Southern History* 55, no. 4 (November 1989): 633–58.

Prakash, Gyan. "Subaltern Studies as Postcolonial Criticism." *American Historical Review* 99, no. 5 (December 1994): 1475–90.

Pride, Armistead S. "*Rights of All*: Second Step in the Development of Black Journalism." *Journalism History* 4, no. 4 (1977): 129–31.

Quarles, Benjamin. "Antebellum Free Blacks and the 'Spirit of '76.'" *Journal of Negro History* 61 (July 1976): 229–42.

————. "The Breach Between Douglass and Garrison." *Journal of Negro History* 23 (April 1938): 144–54.

Quinn, Edythe Ann. "'The Hills' in the Mid-Nineteenth Century: The History of a Rural Afro-American Community in Westchester County, New York." *Afro-Americans in New York Life and History* 14, no. 2 (1990): 35–50.

Rahman, Ahmad A. "The Million Man March: A Black Woodstock?" *Black Scholar* 26, no. 1 (1996): 41–44.

Rawick, George. "The Historical Roots of Black Liberation." *Radical America* 2 (July 1968): 1–13.

Reed, Harry A. "Henry Highland Garnet's Address to the Slaves of the United States of America Reconsidered." *Western Journal of Black Studies* 6, no. 4 (1982): 186–92.

————. "Not by Protest Alone: Afro-American Activists and the Pythian Baseball Club of Philadelphia, 1867–1869." *Western Journal of Black Studies* 9, no. 3 (1985): 144–51.

Reidy, Joseph P. "'Negro Election Day' and Black Community Life in New England, 1750–1860." *Marxist Perspectives* 1 (Fall 1978): 272–87.

Richards, Phillip M. "Phillis Wheatley and Literary Americanization." *American Quarterly* 44, no. 2 (June 1992): 163–91.

Riss, Arthur. "Racial Essentialism and Family Values in *Uncle Tom's Cabin*." *American Quarterly* 46, no. 4 (December 1994): 513–44.

Rogers, Daniel T. "Republicanism: The Career of a Concept." *Journal of American History* 79, no. 1 (June 1992): 11–38.

Runcie, John. "'Hunting the Nigs' in Philadelphia: The Race Riot of August 1834." *Pennsylvania History* 39, no. 2 (1972): 187–218.

Saillant, John. "Lemuel Haynes' Black Republicanism and the American Republican Tradition, 1775–1820." *Journal of the Early Republic* 14 (Fall 1994): 293–324.

Saxton, Alexander. "Problems of Class and Race in the Origins of Mass Circulation Press." *American Quarterly* 36, no. 2 (Summer 1984): 211–34.

Schantz, Mark S. "Religious Tracts, Evangelical Reform, and the Market Revolution in Antebellum America." *Journal of the Early Republic* 17 (Fall 1997): 425–66.

Schwartz, Regina M. "Nations and Nationalism: Adultery in the House of David." *Critical Inquiry* 19 (1992): 131–50.

Scobey, David. "Anatomy of the Promenade: The Politics of Bourgeois Sociability in Nineteenth-Century New York." *Social History* 17, no. 2 (May 1992): 203–27.

———. "Commercial Culture, Urban Modernism, and the Intellectual Flaneur." *American Quarterly* 47, no. 2 (June 1995): 330–42.

Sealander, Judith. "Antebellum Black Press Images of Women." *Western Journal of Black Studies* 6, no. 3 (1982): 159–65.

Shalhope, Robert E. "In Search of the Elusive Republic." *Reviews in American History* 19, no. 4 (December 1991): 468–73.

———. "Republicanism and Early American History." *William and Mary Quarterly*, 3d ser., 39 (1982): 334–56.

Shankman, Arnold. "Black on Green: Afro-American Editors on Irish Independence, 1840–1921." *Phylon* 41, no. 3 (1980): 284–99.

Sherman, Joan R. "James Monroe Whitfield, Poet and Emigrationist: A Voice of Protest and Despair." *Journal of Negro History* 57 (April 1972): 165–76.

Sherwood, H. N. "Paul Cuffee." *Journal of Negro History* 47 (January 1962): 42–53.

Silcox, Harry C. "The Black 'Better Class' Political Dilemma: Philadelphia Prototype Isaiah C. Wears." *Pennsylvania Magazine of History and Biography* 113, no. 1 (January 1989): 45–66.

Silverman, Jason H., and Donna J. Gillie. "'The Pursuit of Knowledge Under Difficulties': Education and the Fugitive Slave in Canada." *Ontario History* 74, no. 2 (1982): 95–112.

Simon, John. "Malcolm X." *National Review* 44, no. 25 (1992): 45–47.

Smith, Eleanor. "Frederick Douglass: A Reevaluation." *Western Journal of Black Studies* 1, no. 2 (June 1977): 123–30.

Smith, Robert P. "William Cooper Nell: Crusading Black Abolitionist." *Journal of Negro History* 55, no. 3 (July 1970): 182–99.

Smith, Tom W. "Changing Racial Labels: From 'Colored' to 'Negro' to 'Black' to 'African American.'" *Public Opinion Quarterly* 56, no. 4 (Winter 1992): 496–514.

Smitherman, Geneva. "'What Is Africa to Me?': Language, Ideology, and *African American*." *Word: A Black Culture Journal* 2, no. 1 (Winter 1993): 1–28.

Smith-Rosenberg, Carroll. "Beauty, the Beast and the Militant Woman: A Case Study in Sex Roles and Social Stress in Jacksonian America." *American Quarterly* 23, no. 4 (October 1971): 562–84.

———. "Captured Subjects/Savage Others: Violently Engendering the New American." *Gender and History* 5 (1993): 177–95.

———. "Dis-Covering the Subject of the 'Great Constitutional Discussion,' 1786–1789." *Journal of American History* 74 (1992–93): 841–73.

———. "Sex as Symbol in Victorian America." *Prospects* 5 (1980): 51–70.

———. "Subject Female: Authorizing American Identity." *American Literary History* 5 (1993): 481–511.

Snorgrass, J. William. "The Black Press in the San Francisco Bay Area, 1856–1900." *California History* 60, no. 4 (1981–82): 306–17.

Southern, Eileen. "Black Musicians and Early Ethiopian Minstrelsy." *Black Perspective in Music* 3, no. 1 (1975): 77–83.

Starobin, Robert S., and Dale Tomich. "Black Liberation Historiography." *Radical America* 2 (September–October 1968): 24–28.

Stewart, James Brewer. "The Emergence of Radical Modernity and the Rise of the White North, 1790–1840." *Journal of the Early Republic* 18, no. 2 (Summer 1998): 181–217.

Streitmatter, Rodger. "Maria W. Stewart: The First Female African-American Journalist." *Historical Journal of Massachusetts* 21 (Summer 1993): 44–59.

Stuckey, Sterling. "Through the Prism of Folklore: The Black Ethos in Slavery." *Massachusetts Review* 9 (1968): 417–37.

Sumler-Lewis, Janice. "The Forten-Purvis Women of Philadelphia and the American Anti-Slavery Crusade." *Journal of Negro History* 66, no. 4 (Winter 1981–82): 281–88.

Sweet, Leonard. "The Fourth of July and Black Americans in the Nineteenth Century: Northern Leadership Opinion Within the Context of the Black Experience." *Journal of Negro History* 61 (July 1976): 256–75.

Szuberla, Guy. "Ladies, Gentlemen, Flirts, Mashers, Snoozers, and the Breaking of Etiquette's Code." *Prospects* 15 (1990): 169–96.

Szwed, John F. "Race and the Embodiment of Culture." *Ethnicity* 2, no. 1 (1975): 19–33.

Tate, Gayle T. "Black Nationalism: An Angle of Vision." *Western Journal of Black Studies* 12, no. 1 (1988): 40–48.

———. "Black Nationalism and Spiritual Redemption." *Western Journal of Black Studies* 15, no. 4 (1991): 213–22.

———. "Political Consciousness and Resistance among Black Antebellum Women." *Women and Politics* 13, no. 1 (Winter 1993): 67–89.

Teed, Paul. "Racial Nationalism and Its Challengers: Theodore Parker, John Rock, and the Antislavery Movement." *Civil War History* 61, no. 2 (1995): 142–60.

Temperly, Howard. "Capitalism, Slavery, and Ideology." *Past and Present* 75 (1977): 94–118.

Terry, Esther. "Sojourner Truth: The Person Behind the Libyan Sibyl." *Massachusetts Review* 26, nos. 2–3 (1985): 425–44.

Thomas, John L. "Romantic Reform in America, 1815–1865." *American Quarterly* 17, no. 4 (Winter 1965): 656–81.

Thompson, Vincent Bakpetu. "Leadership in the African Diaspora in the Americas Prior to 1860." *Journal of Black Studies* 24 (September 1993): 42–76.

Topor, Wolor. "The Concept of God in the African Philosophy." *Journal of African Religion and Philosophy* 1, no. 2 (1990): 1–6.

Turner, James E. "Historical Dialectics of Black Nationalist Movements in America." *Western Journal of Black Studies* 1, no. 3 (September 1977): 164–83.

Wach, Howard M. "'Expansive Intellect and Moral Agency': Public Culture in Antebellum Boston." *Proceedings of the Massachusetts Historical Society* 107 (1995): 30–56.

Wade, Melvin. "'Shining in Borrowed Plumage': Affirmation of Community in the Black Coronation Festivals of New England, ca. 1750–1850." *Western Folklore* 40, no. 3 (July 1981): 211–31.

Wade, Richard. "The Negro in Cincinnati, 1800–1830." *Journal of Negro History* 29 (1954): 43–57.

Wahle, Kathleen O'Mara. "Alexander Crummell: Black Evangelist and Pan-Negro Nationalist." *Phylon* 29 (Winter 1968): 388–95.

Waldstreicher, David. "Rites of Rebellion, Rites of Assent: Celebrations, Print Culture, and the Origins of American Nationalism." *Journal of American History* (June 1995): 37–61.

Walker, Clarence E. "The American Negro as Historical Outsider, 1836–1935." *Canadian Review of American Studies* 17, no. 2 (1986): 137–52.

Warner, Robert A. "Amos Gerry Beman—1812–1874, a Memoir on a Forgotten Leader." *Journal of Negro History* 22, no. 2 (April 1937): 200–221.

Watson, Charles H. "Portrayals of the Black and the Idea of Progress: Simms and Douglass." *Southern Studies* 20, no. 4 (Winter 1981): 339–50.

Watts, Steven. "Masks, Morals, and the Market: American Literature and Early Capitalist Culture, 1790–1820." *Journal of the Early Republic* 6 (Summer 1986): 127–49.

Wesley, Charles. "The Negro in the Organization of Abolition." *Phylon* 2 (1941): 223–35.

———. "The Negroes of New York in the Emancipation Movement." *Journal of Negro History* 24 (January 1939): 65–103.

———. "The Participation of Negroes in Anti-Slavery Political Parties." *Journal of Negro History* 29 (January 1944): 32–74.

———. "Racial Historical Societies and the American Heritage." *Journal of Negro History* 37 (January 1952): 11–35.

"What's In a Name?" *Economist* (7 January 1989): 28.

White, Shane. "Impious Prayers: Elite and Popular Attitudes Toward Blacks and Slavery in the Middle-Atlantic States, 1783–1810." *New York History* 67, no. 3 (1986): 260–83.

———. "'It Was a Proud Day': African Americans, Festivals, and Parades in the North, 1741–1834." *Journal of American History* 81, no. 1 (June 1994): 13–31.

———. "Pinkster: Afro-Dutch Syncretization in New York City and the Hudson Valley." *Journal of American Folklore* 102, no. 403 (January–March 1989): 68–75.

———. "A Question of Style: Blacks in and Around New York City in the Late 18th Century." *Journal of American Folklore* 102, no. 403 (1989): 23–44.

————. "'We Dwell in Safety and Pursue Our Honest Callings': Free Blacks in New York City, 1783–1810." *Journal of American History* 75, no. 2 (1988): 445–70.

Wiggins, William H. "'Lift Every Voice': A Study of Afro-American Emancipation Celebrations." In *Discovering Afro-America*, edited by Roger D. Abrahams and John F. Szwed, 46–57. Leiden, the Netherlands: Brill, 1975.

Wilentz, Sean. "Backward March: Echoes of Marcus Garvey." *New Republic* (6 November 1995): 16–18.

————. "On Class and Politics in Jacksonian America." *Reviews in American History* 10 (1982): 45–64.

Wilkinson, Doris Y. "The 1850 Harvard Medical School Dispute and the Admission of African-American Students." *Harvard Library Bulletin* 3 (Fall 1992): 13–27.

Williams-Meyers, A. J. "Pinkster Carnival: Africanisms in the Hudson River Valley." *Afro-Americans in New York Life and History* 9, no. 1 (January 1985): 7–18.

Wolcott, Victoria W. "The Culture of the Informal Economy: Number Runners in Inter-War Black Detroit." *Radical History Review* 69 (1997): 47–75.

Woodward, C. Vann. "History from Slave Sources." *American Historical Review* 79 (April 1974): 470–81.

Woolf, Stuart. "The Construction of a European World-View in the Revolutionary-Napoleonic Years." *Past and Present*, no. 137 (1992): 72–101.

Work, Monroe N. "The Life of Charles B. Ray." *Journal of Negro History* 4 (October 1919): 361–71.

Yacovone, Donald. "The Transformation of the Black Temperance Movement, 1827–1854: An Interpretation." *Journal of the Early Republic* 8 (Fall 1988): 285.

Young, Robert J. "The Political Economy of Black Abolitionists." *Afro-Americans in New York Life and History* 18, no. 1 (January 1994): 47–71.

Zboray, Ronald. "Antebellum Reading and the Ironies of Technological Innovation." *American Quarterly* 40, no. 1 (March 1988): 65–82.

Zelinsky, Wilbur. "The Population Geography of the Free Negro in Antebellum America." *Population Studies* 3 (1949–50): 386–401.

Dissertations

Alessandra, Lorini. "Public Rituals, Race Ideology and the Transformation of Urban Culture: The Making of the New York African-American Community, 1825–1918 (New York City)." Ph.D. diss., Columbia University, 1991.

Bartholomaus, Craig W. "'Of One Blood': The Nineteenth Century African-American Literary Response to Racial Stereotyping." Ph.D. diss., University of Colorado, 1991.

Bay, Mia Elisabeth. "The White Image in the Black Mind: African American Ideas about White People, 1830–1925." Ph.D. diss., Yale University, 1993.

Black, Daniel P. "The Black Male Concept of Manhood as Portrayed in Selected Slave and Free Narratives (1794–1983)." Ph.D. diss., Temple University, 1993.

Bowers, Detine Lee. "A Strange Speech of an Estranged People: Theory and Practice of Antebellum African-American Freedom Day Orations." Ph.D. diss., Purdue University, 1992.

Early, Gerald Lyn. "'A Servant of Servants Shall He Be . . .': Paternalism and Millennialism in American Slavery Literature, 1850–1859." Ph.D. diss., Cornell University, 1982.

Foster, Herbert James. "The Urban Experience of Blacks in Atlantic City, New Jersey: 1850–1915." Ph.D. diss., Rutgers University, 1981.

Luckett, Judith Ann Blodgett. "Protest, Advancement, and Identity: Organizational Strategies of Northern Free Blacks, 1830 to 1860." Ph.D. diss., Johns Hopkins University, 1993.

McRae, Norman. "Blacks in Detroit, 1736–1833: The Search for Freedom and Community and Its Implications for Educators." Ph.D. diss., University of Michigan, 1982.

Massey, Karen Gwynn. "Ritual Improvisation: A Challenge to Christian Education from the Nineteenth-Century African-American Slave Community." Ph.D. diss., Southern Baptist Theological Seminary, 1991.

Newman, Richard. "The Transformation of American Abolition: Tactics, Strategies, and the Changing Meaning of Activism, 1780–1830s." Ph.D. diss., State University of New York, Buffalo, 1998.

Oliver, Albert G. "The Protest and Attitudes of Blacks Towards the American Colonization Society and the Concepts of Emigration." Ph.D. diss., St. John's University, 1978.

Peck, Gary Richard. "Black Radical Consciousness and the Black Christian Experience: Toward a Critical Sociology of Afro-American Religion." Ph.D. diss., University of North Carolina at Chapel Hill, 1983.

Pride, Armstead S. "A Register and History of Negro Newspapers in the United States, 1827–1950." Ph.D. diss., Northwestern University, 1950.

Roberts, Rita Jean. "In Quest of Autonomy: Northern Black Activism Between the Revolution and the Civil War." Ph.D. diss., University of California, Berkeley, 1988.

Simmons, Adam Dewey. "Ideologies and Programs of the Negro Antislavery Movement, 1830–1861." Ph.D. diss., Northwestern University, 1983.

Stapp, Carol Buchalter. "Afro-Americans in Antebellum Boston: An Analysis of Probate Records." Ph.D. diss., George Washington University, 1990.

Sumner-Lewis, Janice. "The Fortens of Philadelphia: An Afro-American Family and Nineteenth Century Reform." Ph.D. diss., Georgetown University, 1976.

Tate, Gayle T. "Tangled Vines: Ideological Interpretations of Afro-Americans in the Nineteenth Century." Ph.D. diss., City University of New York, 1984.

Terborg-Penn, Rosalyn. "Afro-Americans in the Struggle for Woman's Suffrage." Ph.D. diss., Howard University, 1976.

Whelchel, Love Henry, Jr. "The Case for Abolition in the Writings of William Wells Brown." Ph.D. diss., Duke University, 1981.

Wilson, Carol. "Freedom at Risk: The Kidnapping of Free Blacks in America, 1780–1865." Ph.D. diss., West Virginia University, 1991.

Yizar, Terrye Barron. "Afro-American Music in North America before 1865: A Study of 'The First of August Celebration' in the United States." Ph.D. diss., University of California, 1984.

Young, Robert J. "The Political Culture of Northern African-American Activists, 1830–1859." Ph.D. diss., Syracuse University, 1992.

Index

Presbyterian

Philadelphia, Pa.: black elites in, 25;
black mechanics in, 28; black celebrations in, 63–68, 70, 78; black
institutions in, 84; 1834 race riot in,
94; slave rescue in, 141; rejection of
colonization by blacks in, 209–10

Phillips, Wendell, 143

Pinkster celebrations: 19, 57; black
leadership and, 43–44; black folk
culture at, 56, 80; white views of, 58,
73; kings of, 71, 92

Pittsburgh, Pa., 85

Plantation society, 15–18

Port Royal, S.C., 292

Potter, E. R., 71

Powell, Lawrence, 294

Prejudice: persistence after Civil War,
11; unites blacks in white minds, 25,
48; as obstacle to elevation, 176,
182–83, 296; and slavery, 176, 295;
blacks' analysis of, 176–80, 291;
debates over sources of, 180–82,
214–15; blacks challenge, 188–89,
198–200, 204, 206; drink and, 194;
and black protest, 285–86; during
Reconstruction, 291, 294–95. *See also*
Public mind

Press. *See* Newspapers, black

Property ownership among free blacks,
22–24, 29, 39, 43

Prosser, Gabriel, 55, 213, 277

Protestantism, 129–30, 240–41

Public mind, 83, 235; and racism,
112–13, 188, 254; black efforts to influence, 159, 184, 281, 285–86; black
elevation and, 159, 214–15. *See also*
Prejudice; Public opinion

Public opinion: and class formation,
136–37; and prejudice, 176–79; and
problem of representation, 179–
80; and nationalism, 236. *See also*
Prejudice; Public mind

Public sphere, 3, 47, 48, 298; black

participation in, 55–56, 83, 89–90,
220, 281, 283, 289; black women's
exclusion from, 151, 153; blacks' faith
in, 206–7; blacks in, after American Revolution, 213; presence of
blacks in, through newspapers, 214;
significance of, 249, 289

Puritans, 129–30, 240–41, 269

Purvis, Robert, 49, 215, 260–61

Quakerism, 129

Race: definitions of, in Atlantic world,
13; definitions of, in North, 79,
159, 202; origins and etymology of,
253; relationship to nationalism,
253

Race riots. *See* Mob violence

Racial caste systems: three-tiered, 13,
15, 17; in New Orleans, 42, 103; in
Caribbean, 103, 107. *See also* Free
colored populations

Racial labels, 82–117; and black identity, 83–84, 106–7; and African
culture, 85–89; "N-word" complex,
92, 94, 96; as signifiers of class, 94–
97; and racial conflict, 97–100; and
black respectability, 100–103; in
law, 103–4; and black convention
movement, 105; and debates over
race-specific activism, 107–15; and
black colonization, 144–15
—"Afric-American," 111
—"African," 87, 89–91, 104–5, 107,
109, 112, 116; "colored" replaces, 83–
85; blacks abandon as racial label,
91, 105–6
—"American," 82, 108–9
—"Black," 104, 109
—"Colored": advocated as racial label,
102, 105–6, 109–13; uses of, 105,
106; use as label for all blacks, 106–7;
debated as racial label, 110–12

1. environment argument
   (on black character)

   224

2. appropriation of Am Rev   255 — index 262-266

   (2a) FD "4th of July"   258-260 - 25th anniversary of NY
                                      emancipation day